Fodor's

AMSTERDAM &
THE NETHERLANDS

2nd Edition

Fodor's Travel Publications   New York, Toronto, London, Sydney, Auckland
www.fodors.com

Be a Fodor's Correspondent

Your opinion matters. It matters to us. It matters to your fellow Fodor's travelers, too. And we'd like to hear it. In fact, we need to hear it.

When you share your experiences and opinions, you become an active member of the Fodor's community. That means we'll not only use your feedback to make our books better, but we'll publish your names and comments whenever possible. Throughout our guides, look for "Word of Mouth," excerpts of your unvarnished feedback.

Here's how you can help improve Fodor's for all of us.

Tell us when we're right. We rely on local writers to give you an insider's perspective. But our writers and staff editors—who are the best in the business—depend on you. Your positive feedback is a vote to renew our recommendations for the next edition.

Tell us when we're wrong. We're proud that we update most of our guides every year. But we're not perfect. Things change. Hotels cut services. Museums change hours. Charming cafés lose charm. If our writer didn't quite capture the essence of a place, tell us how you'd do it differently. If any of our descriptions are inaccurate or inadequate, we'll incorporate your changes in the next edition and will correct factual errors at fodors.com immediately.

Tell us what to include. You probably have had fantastic travel experiences that aren't yet in Fodor's. Why not share them with a community of like-minded travelers? Maybe you chanced upon a beach or bistro or B&B that you don't want to keep to yourself. Tell us why we should include it. And share your discoveries and experiences with everyone directly at fodors.com. Your input may lead us to add a new listing or highlight a place we cover with a "Highly Recommended" star or with our highest rating, "Fodor's Choice."

Give us your opinion instantly at our feedback center at www.fodors.com/feedback. You may also e-mail editors@fodors.com with the subject line "Amsterdam and the Netherlands Editor." Or send your nominations, comments, and complaints by mail to Amsterdam and the Netherlands Editor, Fodor's, 1745 Broadway, New York, NY 10019.

You and travelers like you are the heart of the Fodor's community. Make our community richer by sharing your experiences. Be a Fodor's correspondent.

Goede reis!

Tim Jarrell, Publisher

FODOR'S AMSTERDAM & THE NETHERLANDS

Editors: Margaret Kelly, Carolyn Galgano

Writers: Niels Carels, Karina Hof, Ann Maher, Tim Skelton

Production Editor: Jennifer DePrima
Maps & Illustrations: Mark Stroud and David Lindroth, *cartographers;* Bob Blake, Rebecca Baer, *map editors;* William Wu, *information graphics*
Design: Fabrizio La Rocca, *creative director;* Guido Caroti, Siobhan O'Hare, *art directors;* Tina Malaney, Chie Ushio, Ann McBride, Jessica Walsh, Nora Rosansky, *designers;* Melanie Marin, *senior picture editor*
Cover Photo: (Lisse Kukenhof Gardens) Steve Bly/Alamy
Production Manager: Angela L. McLean

2nd Edition

ISBN 978–1–4000–0509–3

ISSN 1937–8599

SPECIAL SALES

This book is available at special discounts for bulk purchases for sales promotions or premiums. Special editions, including personalized covers, excerpts of existing books, and corporate imprints, can be created in large quantities for special needs. For more information, write to Special Markets/Premium Sales, 1745 Broadway, MD 6-2, New York, New York 10019, or e-mail specialmarkets@randomhouse.com.

AN IMPORTANT TIP & AN INVITATION

Although all prices, opening times, and other details in this book are based on information supplied to us at press time, changes occur all the time in the travel world, and Fodor's cannot accept responsibility for facts that become outdated or for inadvertent errors or omissions. So **always confirm information when it matters,** especially if you're making a detour to visit a specific place. Your experiences—positive and negative—matter to us. If we have missed or misstated something, **please write to us.** We follow up on all suggestions. Contact the Amsterdam & The Netherlands editor at editors@fodors.com or c/o Fodor's at 1745 Broadway, New York, NY 10019.

PRINTED IN COLOMBIA

10 9 8 7 6 5 4 3 2 1

CONTENTS

CONTENTS

ABOUT THIS BOOK

Our Ratings

Sometimes you find terrific travel experiences and sometimes they just find you. But usually the burden is on you to select the right combination of experiences. That's where our ratings come in.

As travelers we've all discovered a place so wonderful that its worthiness is obvious. And sometimes that place is so experiential that superlatives don't do it justice: you just have to be there to know. These sights, properties, and experiences get our highest rating, **Fodor's Choice**, indicated by orange stars throughout this book.

Black stars highlight sights and properties we deem **Highly Recommended,** places that our writers, editors, and readers praise again and again for consistency and excellence.

By default, there's another category: any place we include in this book is by definition worth your time, unless we say otherwise. And we will.

Disagree with any of our choices? Care to nominate a place or suggest that we rate one more highly? Visit our feedback center at www.fodors.com/feedback.

Budget Well

Hotel and restaurant price categories from ¢ to $$$$ are defined in the opening pages of each chapter. For attractions, we always give standard adult admission fees; reductions are usually available for children, students, and senior citizens. Want to pay with plastic? **AE, D, DC, MC, V** following restaurant and hotel listings indicate if American Express, Discover, Diners Club, MasterCard, and Visa are accepted.

Restaurants

Unless we state otherwise, restaurants are open for lunch and dinner daily. We mention dress only when there's a specific requirement and reservations only when they're essential or not accepted—it's always best to book ahead.

Hotels

Hotels have private bath, phone, TV, and air-conditioning and operate on the European Plan (aka EP, meaning without meals), unless we specify that they use the Continental Plan (CP, with a Continental breakfast), Breakfast Plan (BP, with a full breakfast), or Modified American Plan (MAP, with breakfast and dinner) or are all-inclusive (including all meals and most activities). We

always list facilities but not whether you'll be charged an extra fee to use them, so when pricing accommodations, find out what's included.

Listings

★	Fodor's Choice
★	Highly recommended
✉	Physical address
✛	Directions or Map coordinates
🕮	Mailing address
☎	Telephone
🖷	Fax
🌐	On the Web
✎	E-mail
🎫	Admission fee
⊙	Open/closed times
Ⓜ	Metro stations
▭	Credit cards

Hotels & Restaurants

🏨	Hotel
⤵	Number of rooms
♨	Facilities
ⵂⵂ	Meal plans
✕	Restaurant
🕮	Reservations
🎩	Dress code
⌇	Smoking
🍷	BYOB

Outdoors

🏌	Golf
⛺	Camping

Other

☾	Family-friendly
⇨	See also
✉	Branch address
☞	Take note

Experience Amsterdam and the Netherlands

WHAT'S WHERE

Numbers refer to chapter numbers.

2 Amsterdam. If only those 13th-century fishermen who decided to dam up the Amstel could see what became of their marsh. It's the capital and spiritual "downtown," of a nation, where Gothic monuments interface with neon billboards and Golden Age drinking holes neighbor techno-playing coffee shops. Wander just outside the city center and you'll find tree-lined canals, hidden courtyards, and brown cafés—it's a postcard-perfect image.

7 Day Trips. How could you visit Holland and not tiptoe through the tulip fields? Or take in some of the Netherlands' famous folkloric "costume towns"? This country is so manageably small, there's practically no excuse not to visit at least a few other towns and cities on day trips from Amsterdam.

8 **The Randstad: Rotterdam, The Hague, Haarlem and Delft.** Bombed to the ground in World War II, Rotterdam is today one of the world's busiest industrial ports, with a phenomenal skyline and a keepin'-it-real appreciation for the underground. By contrast, the historically well-preserved Haarlem and Delft are sweet dollhouselike cities. International tribunals, high courts, embassy rows, and diplomatic immunities make their home in The Hague, as do a burgeoning Chinatown, students of the prestigious music conservatory, and Vermeer's *Girl with a Pearl Earring*.

9 **Belgium: Brussels, Brugge and Gent.** The European Union's capital seat and the Continent's most underrated city will treat you to the earthly delights of Paris while encouraging you to feel as laid-back as you would in Amsterdam. A section or two of Brussels may be overrun by Babel-tongued Eurocrats in pointy shoes, but even they contribute to a unique posh-meets-pragmatic *joie de vivre*. Brugge and Gent are Flemish fairy-tale towns with long brewing traditions.

QUINTESSENTIAL AMSTERDAM AND THE NETHERLANDS

Canals

Amsterdam's canals are constant reminders that man—or the Dutch, anyway—can control nature and actually make a nice life off it. More than 60 mi of canals, 400 stone bridges, and 90 islands have been created since the 17th century. Today, the *Grachtengordel* is a UNESCO World Heritage Site, not to mention prime real estate. On days with even the slightest sun, cafés with canal-side seating are where it's at. In warmish weather, the waterways truly come to life, as locals hop in their boats, taking anyone and anything normally welcome in their living room for a riparian wine-and-cheese soiree. Once associated with 1970s antiestablishment types, houseboats are increasingly a more affordable option for domicile-desperate locals, as well as visitors seeking quaint lodging (and not minding mediocre plumbing).

Gezelligheid

If you listen carefully to local speech and detect what sounds like a mild throat clearing, no doubt you're hearing one of the most cherished words in Lowlands parlance—*gezellig*. The term is frequently translated to mean "cozy," though anyone who has had the chance to experience Dutch *gezelligheid* (coziness) will confirm that cozy doesn't quite cut it. From the word *gezel* meaning "mate," gezelligheid quite literally refers to the general conviviality of a place or a person. Even if you don't have the chance to snug up on an Amsterdammer's couch, you can still witness signs of the spirit in lingering café conversations, those unsolicited cookies alongside your coffee, little lights along the canals at night, and house cats meowing out the window.

According to 19th-century French writer Joris-Karl Huysmans, Amsterdam is "a dream, an orgy of houses and water," and it's no less true 100 years later.

Tolerance

"Tolerance" has long been a buzzword of the country's live-and-let-live approach to governance. The nation as a whole has historically been seen as liberal and left-leaning, though "tolerate" is a simplistic translation for the Dutch verb *gedogen*, which suggests something more like "turn a blind eye to." In everyday policy, this means doing damage control. Ethics that threaten consensus are zoned to their own neighborhoods (e.g. prostitutes) and potential problems are regulated (e.g. pot). One famous Amsterdammer notorious for refusing to sugarcoat anything he found intolerable was filmmaker Theo van Gogh. In 2003, he was brutally murdered by a fellow Dutchman associated with a homegrown Islamic terrorist group. To many, the event marked a cataclysmic shift in the tides of so-called tolerance.

Vices

Even though their heyday may be fading, cannabis, and call girls, are still plentiful, professionalized, and permitted by the government. Being virtuous about venality, however, even in this open society there's protocol. Rules apropos of both hookers and hash are as follows: buy only in controlled zones, use with caution, leave your camera at home. Taking stoned pictures in coffee shops and photographing living lingerie could result in your being kicked to the curb, literally. In general, vice visitors are advised to check for updates on the changing laws, particularly regarding the legal sale of soft drugs.

IF YOU LIKE

Quirky shops

Some would use the word "cheap," but selective spending is a better way to describe consumption in the Lowlands. It's no wonder Amsterdam has an array of quirky establishments commanding money for the most unexpected of everyday items. And we're not just talking about cheese shops.

De Condomerie. Said to be the world's first shop devoted to condoms, De Condomerie is ideally located, sharing the same block as the city's gay leather scene and just around the corner from the Red Light District. For both men and women, there's an impressive range of prophylactics in various sizes, designs, and novelties to suit your sexual humor. Joking aside, the staff and the online shop (⊕ *www.condomerie. com*) are ready to answer your most personal questions.

De Witte Tanden Winkel. Named "the white teeth shop," this cute store offers more types of toothbrushes, toothpaste, and related dental care products than you knew existed. And even if you're satisfied with your trusty Oral-B, the toothbrush Ferris wheel will provoke a smile.

Lambiek. To enter here is to enter another world and to have thousands more little worlds at your fingertips. Lambiek takes pride in being the oldest comic bookstore on the Continent. Founded in 1968, this is the brick-and-mortar version of the comiclopedia that shop owner and comic encyclopedia editor Kees Kousemaker devoted himself to until his death in 2010.

Diamonds

Though the Dutch are known for living modestly, their capital city is renowned for purveying the most immodest rock on earth. Diamonds first made their way to the Netherlands in 1568 when a polisher decided to call Amsterdam home, and his colleagues in the field soon followed. Jews, in particular, established successful businesses in cutting, polishing, and trading diamonds—this was one of the few industries whose inclusion was not dictated by trade guild membership, and therefore open to Jews.

Coster Diamonds. If you prefer to keep your diamond duty short and sweet, we suggest visiting this smaller homage to the stone, conveniently located on Museumplein. A replica of their most famous cut, the Koh-I-Noor diamond, is on show, and jewelers patiently await your flash of plastic.

Gassan Diamonds. This company is one of the few outlets still located in Amsterdam's original diamond district. Visitors can get a free behind-the-gleams tour of the cutting room, and groups can pre-arrange an excursion that ends with a champagne toast.

Once the bubbly has been drunk, an expert's magnifying glass will inspect the small shiny bits lying at the bottom of each glass. All the zirconias will be sifted through to find the one real deal (the value of the lucky imbiber's prize is determined by the group tour fee).

At the on-site store, select your favorite piece for goldsmiths to inlay, or stop by the Amsterdam Diamond Center near the Dam, which Gassan also owns.

Drinking from the Source

The Netherlands, Belgium, and Germany form a Bermuda Triangle of fresh brews and fine distillations known to shipwreck many a sober spirit. Enjoy the ride and fear not, deep-fried bar snacks and late-night *frites met mayonnaise* (french fries with gobs of mayo) will put you back on the radar.

Brouwerij 't IJ. What could be more Beneluxian than drinking a Trappist-inspired pilsner in the foot of a giant windmill? Each year this microbrewery produces 180,000 liters of its most beloved brews. Tours are offered from time to time.

Heineken Experience. It's the Jolly Green Giant of European beers and, unexotically universal though it may be, a Heine does taste better in Holland. A tour through the old brewery gives visitors a course in Brewing 101, some heady facts about the company's history, and samples!

Museum van de Gueuze, Brussels. It hardly seems right to call this a museum; since 1900, this brewery, also known as the Cantillon brewery, has produced Lambik and other specialty beers. Although Lambik is the quintessential Brussels beer, this is, sadly, the only brewery of its kind left in Brussels. Commercially brewed Lambiks bear scant resemblance to the real thing, so drink up while you can.

Wynard Fokking. Nestled in a tiny alleyway behind Dam Square, this bar has been pouring Dutch *jenever* (the forefather to Anglicized gin) since 1679. This is an only-in-Amsterdam experience. The distillery next door offers tours and sells jenever by the bottle.

Flowers

Nowhere else in the world will you be exposed to such a dazzling diversity of flowers. Whether you're horticulturally inclined and seek some interesting species to introduce to your garden back home, or simply feel like tripping out on some Technicolor tulips, Holland is *the* place.

Bloemenveiling, Aalsmeer. Bulbs are no longer the viable form of currency they were during the Tulip Mania that came over the Lowlands in the 1630s, but flowers remain an ever-blossoming boon to the Dutch economy. Within just microsecond intervals of time, no fewer than 19 million flowers and two million plants are sold every weekday in the world's largest auction house, which is also responsible for establishing the global going rate of flowers.

Bloemenmarkt, Amsterdam. Nary be there an infertile moment along the Singel canal on which the city's floating flower market is moored. Every day locals buy robust bouquets on their way to dinner parties, while travelers pick up bulbs, seeds, and green-thumbed souvenirs.

Should buds or bids be your thing, the 20-minute bus ride from Amsterdam is well worth it.

Keukenhof, Lisse. It's the largest flower garden on earth, with roots—in terms of legacy, not botany—that date back to the 15th century. And the parking lot is just big enough for the tour buses it must accommodate March through May. Over the years, the park has become increasingly kitschy, with its schizophrenic collection of outdoor sculptures and random landscape installations, but many will still marvel at the beds upon beds of tulips and, even more impressive, the florid fields you encounter on the drive there.

AMSTERDAM TOP ATTRACTIONS

Albert Cuypmarkt

(A) Check out the city's most popular market as much for its vibrant, varied products as for the multicultural, pan-capitalist production. Since 1905, Albert Cuypstraat has hosted the now 300+ cluster of stalls and stores behind them, selling everything from fresh-cut flowers and hot-off-the-griddle *stroopwafels* (honey-filled wafers) to Tupac T-shirts and Moroccan wedding dresses.

Amsterdams Historisch Museum

Though given relatively little marquee space, the AHM is one of the best museums to devote your time and attention, particularly if you're low on either. Amsterdam's history is engagingly displayed all under one roof, from medieval times until the Golden Age through the radical '60s until life after Y2K.

Anne Frankhuis

(B) Not only is this the home of the most widely read Dutch author, but the setting of her famous book. Thoughtful visitors will be too haunted by the story's abominable ending to relish a museum-going experience, but many appreciate the foundation's efforts to raise awareness about Europe's anti-Semitic past and discrimination everywhere.

Begijnhof

(C) The city's most famous *hofje* (hidden courtyard) was established in the 14th century for vow-taking religious women known as beguines. A community of spiritually devout women still inhabits the surrounding homes today, sharing their peaceful courtyard with two churches, the oldest house in town (No. 34), and tourists searching for a quadrant of quiet.

Heineken Experience

(D) The most obvious enthusiasts here are young gents traveling (or stumbling) in groups, but the Heineken Experience has been suitable for the entire family ever since the building stopped brewing in 1988. Learn the brand's history, observe beer being made, lose yourself in the 4-D film, and of course, taste-test.

Hermitage Amsterdam

(E) Since its grand reopening in 2009, the Hermitage Amsterdam has had lines out the door and acclaim audible almost all the way to St. Petersburg. This largest dependency of the famous Russian museum has two permanent presentations detailing its own historic premises, while also hosting a splendid rotation of art.

Rijksmuseum

(F) With renovation likely to go on until 2013, the state museum, as its name means, is showing only the most rock-star pieces of its collection in a consolidated wing. But make no mistake: Rembrandt's *The Night Watch* and *The Kitchen Maid* by Vermeer are certainly worth the entrance fee.

Tassenmuseum Hendrikje

This Golden Age canal house holds the largest assembly of bags and purses in the Western world. Experience 500 years of history through its 4,000-piece collection—from 17th-century goat-leather coin purses to today's waiting-listed must-haves—and the rotating exhibitions of contemporary designers.

Van Gogh Museum

Two hundred paintings, 500 drawings, and 750 letters by the post-Impressionist make the Van Gogh Museum an imperative stop for even the merely cocktail conversant among art appreciators. Though for *The Starry Night* you'll have to hit the MoMA in New Amsterdam, stellar masterpieces abound (as do their plastic souvenir spawn).

THE NETHERLANDS AND BELGIUM TOP ATTRACTIONS

Delfshaven

(A) What better way to appreciate Rotterdam's uniquely modern silhouette than by spending time in the one district spared from World War II bombing and the city's subsequent reconstruction? Situated along the River Maas, Delfshaven is a favorite neighborhood among locals and visitors for its easygoing, twinkling-lit entertainment.

Delft

(B) It doesn't get any Dutcher than Delft. This picturesque city, Vermeer's hometown nestled between The Hague and Rotterdam, is famous for its signature blue-and-white pottery. As the last remaining Delftware factory of 32 once in operation, De Koninklijke Porceleyne Fles **is still flourishing**, as it did when established in 1653.

Escher in Het Paleis Museum

(C) Superbly repurposed, this former queen's palace is now a museum devoted to the Dutch graphic artist M. C. Escher. In addition to the exhaustive collection of his paintings and prints, you'll be treated to thoughtfully curated biographical material and an interactive exhibition of various optical illusions starring none other than you.

Grand'Place

(D) Plazas, *pleinen*, squares—they're all over Europe, but none is quite so spectacular as Brussels's Grand'Place. In the shadow of the 15th-century Hôtel d'Ville's vaulted splendor, you'll find a kaleidoscopic assemblage of cafés, vendors, musicians, not to mention the positively Pixar-esque flower carpet in August and a life-size crèche at Christmas.

Kröller-Müller Museum
(E) Located in the Hoge Veluwe National Park in the province of Gelderland, the Kröller-Müller may have the most fantastic museum backyard on the Continent. Yet its contents is even more impressive; it has the world's second largest Van Gogh collection, which hangs alongside Picassos, Gauguins, Mondrians, and Seurats.

Manneken Pis
(F) "It's so little!" many a tourist will utter upon seeing this famed bronze fountain of a micturating boy. Small he may be, but this early 17th-century statue draws big crowds, curious to see which of his 800 fly-flapping costumes he'll be in.

Mauritshuis
(G) You won't want to miss this museum, though with 12 homey rooms in an understated mansion, blink and you might. These days, the Maurithuis beckons many a "Pearl girl"—*Girl with the Pearl Earring* tourists—but the other Vermeers, Rembrandts, and Rubens are equally cultworthy.

Musée des Instruments de Musique
(H) Seen too much art? Tasted too many pralines? Stimulate your ears at this museum with a collection of more than 7,000 instruments from around the world. Over a thousand instruments are on display in the four main galleries, each accompanied by descriptive texts and sound bites that you listen to via infrared headphone.

Waterland Neetlje Jans
Besides drugs and tulips, don't forget that the Dutch are also expert at dealing in and with water. This fascinating museum details the country's two millennia of taming the tides and pays due respect to daddy of all dikes: the Delta Works, which was built after the devastating North Sea flood of 1953.

AMSTERDAM WITH KIDS

For each racy adult attraction Amsterdam offers, a dozen deserve a PG—Pure Goodness the entire family can enjoy. It's not for nothing that UNICEF identified Dutch children as the most fortunate in the world. Alongside exceptional infant care and happy dairy cows, the peaceful, open-minded society produces chill parents who tend to raise remarkably well-adjusted little ones. Here are tips on what to do with your own. For monthly events, consult *Time Out Amsterdam's* Family listings.

Um, Museums? Yes!

Many of Amsterdam's museums have children's programs—the Van Gogh Museum and Rijksmuseum offer special audio tours, and the Tassenmuseum will host a kids' bag-decorating party. However, if high culture leaves them cold, go find NEMO. The Netherlands' biggest science center is sure to entertain and educate the entire family with five floors' worth of interactive exhibits, clever multimedia programs, and live demos. After you've learned all there is to know about soap bubbles, extraterrestrial life, and your brain, savor the panoramic view and an ice cream on the spectacular roof deck, where vitamin D–deprived locals sun in the summer.

Where the Wild Things Are

Compared to other metropolitan zoos, Artis is small. But you can forgive its Noah-like modesty—it's a 150-plus-year-old institution built on a sinking city in the first country to elect an animal-rights party to parliament. From apes to zebras, all the major species are present, plus there are regular sea lion shows, butterfly expos, and spectacular (read: slightly gruesome) feeding sessions. Your ticket will also grant you entrance next door to the planetarium and the not-to-be-missed aquarium. For those with shorter attention spans, various neighborhoods have free public petting zoos. At the local *kinderboerderij*, kids not only rub elbows with farm animals, but are often allowed to bottle-feed them. If your fellow travelers wish to find their own bottle, Kinderboerderij de Pijp (⊕ *www.kinderboerderijdepijp.nl*), open weekdays 11–5 and weekends 1–5, is a stone's throw from the champagne bar atop the Okura Hotel.

To Tucker Them Out

If little ones want to swim, public pools are open year-round and don't require a membership. The Zuiderbad (⊕ *www.oudzuid.amsterdam.nl*) on Museumplein is a local favorite, while the Brediusbad (⊕ *www.westerpark.nl*) in Westerpark has an outdoor pool in summer, and the Sportsplaza Mercator (⊕ *www.sportfondsen.nl*) in West has—for better or worse—an on-premise KFC. Rather stay dry? Tun Fun (⊕ *www.tunfun.nl*) is a giant indoor playground with megaslides, ball pools, inflatable bouncers, laser games, and a disco for anyone 12 and under. Meanwhile, the restaurant quiets adults with espresso and Wi-Fi. No mountains to speak of, but the Netherlands has some avid climbing clubs. Klimmuur Amsterdam (⊕ *www.deklimmuur.nl*), which caters to first-timers and boasts its own kids' climbing club, has a 21-meter-high indoor wall. Prefer to stay grounded? Monday trough Saturday before 5, kids are welcome to strike out at Knijn Bowling (⊕ *www.knijnbowling.nl*). Last but not least, soccer lovers won't want to miss a World of Ajax tour (⊕ *www.amsterdamarena.nl*) through the city's famous *futbol* stadium.

1

FREE OR ALMOST FREE

Regardless of the fluctuating dollar-to-euro exchange rate, the Netherlands is an expensive country to visit. Besides flowers, cheese, and wine, everything seems pricier in Amsterdam than in a major American city. Here, though, are some cost-free exceptions.

Music to the Ears

Give your ears a free tune-up at one of the many free lunchtime concerts scheduled during the culture season. Check venues' monthly calendars, but as a general guideline, classical performances take place at 12:30 on Tuesdays in the Muziktheater and the Muziekgebouw and on Wednesdays in the Concertgebouw. Arrive a half hour early to guarantee your seat. Less in demand, though a no less lovely way to pass 30 minutes, the Conservatorium van Amsterdam and various churches also hold recitals for the public.

Cultural Capital

Linger in the glassed-in corridor outside the Amsterdam Historical Museum (entrance at Kalverstraat 92), known as the Schuttersgalerij, where Amsterdam's wealthy civic guards, peers of those in Rembrandt's *The Night Watch*, gaze down at you from 15 huge Golden Age paintings.

Even if you're not searching for your Dutch ancestors in its 20 mi (35 km) worth of digital records, the Amsterdam City Archives merits a visit. A permanent exhibition of artifacts and ephemera documenting the city is displayed throughout the building; the former bank in itself is worth the tour.

There's no entrance fee for the Hollandsche Schouwburg, but this memorial to the 104,000 Dutch Jews who were killed in World War II may take a toll on you.

Once a popular theater, and later, a deportation center, a visit here is a somber experience, albeit a salient way to learn about an unforgettable chapter in Amsterdam's history. Besides the permanent exhibition on Jewish persecution, there are various multimedia presentations and a digital monument.

Free Spirit

Seeking a meditative moment? By day, any of Amsterdam's public parks is ideal for a stretch or a stroll. The centrally located Vondelpark is a visitor's favorite (outfitted with its own Picasso sculpture), though Saphartipark in the Pijp has an impressive jungle gym for adults who like to exercise al fresco. The city's man-made forest, the Amsterdamse Bos, is a haven for cyclists, Nordic walkers, kayakers, and even some urban tent-toters.

AMSTERDAM TODAY

"Amster-damaged." "Good girls go to heaven, bad girls to Amsterdam." Slogans on gift-store T-shirts are testament that, more than anything else, the city's decadent reputation is a self-perpetuated industry largely fueled by tourism. While your average Dutchman wouldn't balk at a joint, theirs is the last language you'll hear at a coffee shop. And though Amsterdam tweens may go on the pill before they learn to drive, Dutch couples are known for committed relationships that begin on the school playground.

Today's Amsterdam

. . . is less smoky. In July 2008, the Netherlands, like several other European countries, passed a smoking ban in all public establishments. This means that you'll have to smoke your cigarette on the curb, a terrace, or, in a handful of bars and concert venues, in a designated smoking room that feels like a human-size aquarium, minus any decorative algae. Although *blowen* (smoking pot) is still permitted in coffee shops, *roken* (smoking cigarettes) is not, so those who like to add tobacco to their joints are also asked to take it outside.

. . . is less smutty. Over the last five years, Amsterdam's infamous Red Light District has gone a tad soft. In 2007, the city did some major house flipping, closing down 51 windows, 18 of which were converted into studio space for artists in the Red Light Fashion Amsterdam project. While politicians—and the designers who enjoyed rent-free ateliers—claimed this move would reduce the trafficking of women and related crime, some sex industry spokespeople claim that the cutbacks have only caused the business to go underground and unchecked.

. . . is more ethnically diverse. A seaport with a five-runway airport, Amsterdam has always attracted newcomers. But in recent years it has made international headlines as the city with the most nationalities in the world, last estimated at 176.

. . . is more customer service–oriented. There was an era when your average Dutch waitress was either so aloof you could skip town before she'd notice you left without paying or so self-righteous you'd be scolded for mentioning the dead mouse at the bottom of your pea soup. Fortunately, the City of Amsterdam has since established the Welcome Academy, red-Windbreaker-wearing volunteers intent on making visitors feel at home. Although you'll occasionally find cranky employees, the hospitality industry, has improved over the years and been taken over by bright, young multilinguals who have watched enough American sitcoms to know that the customer is always right.

. . . is less open-minded when it comes to the many "-isms" it once championed.

Live and let live might have been an appropriate motto for this society historically cool with abortion, euthanasia, drugs, and sex. But, like much of Europe, the powers-that-be are becoming more conservative, and thus threatening Amsterdam's status as the most liberal city on earth. Besides sweeping the Red Light District clean, since 9/11 the Netherlands has become less hospitable than ever to immigrants, particularly those from non-Western nations, who face complicated and expensive restrictions on entrance and residence.

AMSTERDAM FAQS

What's the best way to pay for things?

The Netherlands is notoriously credit card–phobic, with locals using their European bank–issued debit cards to pay even for a cup of coffee. While larger establishments will accept your Visa (and sometimes other major credit cards), to avoid surcharges, cash is your safest bet. Either come with bills or use your bank card to take out a lump sum at a compatible ATM. Don't expect small shops or restaurants to accept your €100 or €500 bills (best to change them at a bank) and pocket at least a euro's worth in coins to pay your entrance into public restrooms.

How should I dress?

Anything goes in Amsterdam. OK, the most uppity of restaurants might cater to a sport coat and high-heeled clientele, and some of the more hair gel–prone dance clubs have a no-sneakers policy, but sartorial rules are nearly nil. After all, jeans are worn to the opera, drag to the grocery store, and butt cracks regularly peekaboo from bike seats. If you want to fit in, be yourself—individualism is far more fashionable than any monogram—and pack rain gear.

What's the difference between Holland and the Netherlands?

The Netherlands is the country's official name. Holland is its colloquial, albeit erroneous, appellation that metonymically refers to North Holland, the province in which Amsterdam is located.

Can I get around without a bike?

All major cities in the Netherlands have an efficient tram-and-bus network, and Amsterdam has an ever-expanding metro system. Taxis are pricey, but worth taking if you're walking-impaired, traveling in a group, or a state of mind too altered to read a map.

Can I have fun without being high?

If you like art, cycling, scenic water views, a lively café culture, paid sex, and/or beer, yes.

Will our children be exposed to sleaze left and right?

No. Amsterdam is far more Mother Goose than Kama sutra. If you need to shield impressionable eyes, however, it's best to avoid the Red Light District, where bikinied prostitutes are on display alongside graphically merchandised sex shops and live sex-show marquees. A warning, too, about late-night channel surfing: topless telephone sex operators are more prevalent than Leno or Letterman.

GREAT ITINERARIES

AMSTERDAM, ROTTERDAM, BRUGGE, AND BRUSSELS

Day 1: Welcome to Amsterdam

Begin your journey in the city's aorta, Dam Square, a perfect example of Amsterdam's warm-blooded capacity to hold old and new on one bit of earth. The Royal Palace and De Nieuwe Kerk, a 15th-century church where Dutch naval heroes rest, peacefully coexist with chain stores and Madame Tussauds. Across the square, Hotel Krasnapolsky provides a ritzy retreat from the crowds, with one of the best tea services in town. If you're in the mood for something stronger, sneak down the alley behind the hotel for a nip of jenever at Wynard Fokking. Drop in on the Begijnhof, just off the Spui, and spend the rest of your day exploring the Jordaan's *hofjes* (hidden courtyards).

Day 2: Culture and a Cruise

Amsterdam is home to three art behemoths—the Rijksmuseum, the Van Gogh Museum, and the recently renovated Hermitage Amsterdam. Depending on your patience (in both queues and galleries), cap it at two per day. Afterwards, get some fresh air in the Vondelpark. Rent in-line skates from café Vondeltuin; stroll the perimeters of the ponds; or people-, bike-, and dog-watch. When the sun sets, catch an avant-garde ensemble playing at Bimhuis, listen to improv at jazz bar Alto, or find a brown café for a warm brandy and a slice of *appeltaart*. From March through October, you can enjoy dinner aboard a candlelighted canal cruise.

Logistics: The I amsterdam Card, which can be purchased for one-, two-, and three-day validities, gives you free or discounted entrance into the city's major museums, free use of trams and buses, discounts at several restaurants, and a free canal cruise. See ⊕ *www.iamsterdamcard.com.*

Day 3: Ports and Skyscrapers in Rotterdam

As the country's second-most populated city and the largest European seaport, Rotterdam has a vast, high-vaulted vibe unlike any other Dutch town. Its appearance is anachronistically modern, thanks to the rebuilding that took place after German bombs blasted the city to smithereens in 1940. Tragedy though it was, the destruction produced unparalleled architecture and design, not to mention hospitality for infrastructure that more Baroque cities would consider profane (think skate parks and a B-list celebrity-star walk of fame). Visit the Netherlands Architecture Institute, and for visual reinforcement of what you've learned, sail along the River Maas, taking in the skyline and admiring the Old Harbor's facade. If the waters aren't too choppy, venture to the less cosmetically enhanced industrial coastline, where chartered tours will take you for a behind-the-scenes peek into the ports of various multinationals. With such a multiethnic population, Rotterdam is your best bet for indulging in non-Continental comestibles.

Logistics: Trains depart regularly from Amsterdam to Rotterdam. The new high-speed Fyra will deliver you in 36 minutes. To arrange a walk on Rotterdam's industrial side, contact: **Industrial Tourism** (☎ *010/218–9194* ⊕ *www. industrieeltoerisme.com*).

Day 4: The Abbeys and Beer of Brugge

This fairy-tale-like UNESCO World Heritage Site remains intact with Gothic churches, abbeys, and bell towers, along with museums displaying Flemish Primitive paintings. While self-indulgence is pooh-poohed by their Protestant neighbors to the north, Belgians are historically Catholic and accordingly less resistant to earthly indulgences. Lucky for the hungry and thirsty visitor. Pop into one of the cheerful bistros, cafés, or pubs offering delicious Flemish fare and a sinful selection of Belgian beers.

Logistics: With departures every half hour, Brugge is a two-hour train ride from Rotterdam.

Day 5: Art Deco and Bonbons in Brussels

Not as cozy as Amsterdam, nor as chic as Paris, Brussels is often overlooked by Euro trekkers. But this trilingual metropolis has much to offer, and in even one day can satiate like no other. A quadrant of stately Gothic buildings form the main square known as the Grote Markt (in Flemish) or Grand'Place (in French). Take it all in, perhaps from one of the grand cafés, but save room for plenty more consumption. The streets are paved with chocolatiers, their storybooklike windows beckoning you to delicately packaged bonbons or freshly churned hot chocolate. The smell of powdered sugar ricocheting off Nutella and cream-laden Belgian waffles lingers everywhere. Whet your second appetite by taking a self-guided walking tour of the city's famous Art Deco buildings, beginning at the Horta Museum where you can pick up a guide. On your way back into the center, make the customary pilgrimage

A FEW TIPS

■ Amsterdam is safer than most cities, but be wary. Safeguard your valuables and avoid walking alone at night. Use extra care when visiting the Red Light District.

■ Public transportation is excellent throughout the Netherlands, though nearly all cities are walkable.

■ For a view nonpareil, take a canal cruise in at least one of the cities that you visit.

to Manneken Piss, the bronze fountain of a wee boy taking a wee. Mussels and *frites* are the when-in-Rome approach to dinner in Brussels, but you could do no wrong by trying any of the seafood dishes on most menus, even in the restaurant district where maître d's practice sidewalk seduction. Brussels is the EU's headquarters, though quite conceivably should be recognized as the Continent's gastronomical governing body.

Logistics: Brussels is the regional train hub. Regular high-speed train service connects you to Paris in less than 1½ hours, London in 2 hours, or you can take the 2½-hour regular train back to Amsterdam.

GREAT ITINERARIES

AMSTERDAM, HAARLEM, DE HOGE VELUWE, DELTA WORKS, THE HAGUE, AND SCHEVENINGEN

Day 1: Canal-crawling in Amsterdam

Make your first acquaintance with Amsterdam in the garden-themed Jordaan, with its postcard-perfect canals, hidden courtyards, and politely moored houseboats. Begin your journey on the corner of Raadhuisstraat and Prinsengracht. If you don't mind a quick cardio workout, climb to the top of the 279-foot Westerkerk tower, which offers a sublime view of the city. Whether on foot or *fiets* (bicycle), continue your canal crawl northward, peeking into artists' galleries, antiques stores, and clothing boutiques. Work up your appetite for a satellite dish–size pancake at the Pancake Bakery. And when it's time to turn those bike lights on, make your way to the nonstop nightlife that is Leidseplein. For concerts and dancing to your favorite decade, head to Paradiso or Melkweg. Across the street is the Sugar Factory, should you be sweet on nu-jazz collectives, slam poetry, and cross-genre histrionics.

Day 2: Pedaling to Haarlem

With Amsterdam's Haarlemmerplein as your starting point, hop on the bike path and forge westward to the metropolis for which the square is named. The approximately 12-mi (19-km) ride to Haarlem is one super-Dutch sight after another: a medieval dike, a windmill, a steam-pumping station-turned-museum, an old sugar mill, sand dunes, and little towns in between. By the time you spot the tower of Haarlem's Town Hall, get ready to dismount—a stroll is in order. The city is

renowned for its elegant square, church organs played by Haydn and Mozart, and the nation's oldest museum. If *zadelpijn* (aka sore butt) has set in, you and your bike can always take the train back to Amsterdam.

Logistics: You can rent a bike from several companies in Amsterdam. **Yellow Bike** (✉ *Nieuwezijds Kolk 29*, ☎ *020/620–6940* ⊕ *www.yellowbike.nl*) has good tours.

Day 3: Cycling and Cubism in De Hoge Veluwe

Now that you've had a taste of Dutch urban life, get ready for a whiff of nature. Keep in mind, though, that most scenes of green in the Netherlands are the work of man. Years spent tweaking dams, dikes, and polders has made the Lowlands an inhabitable landscape today. De Hoge Veluwe, in the province of Gelderland, is the finest the country has to offer by way of a national park. Plus, it provides free bikes for navigating modest hills and dips through 13,590 acres of woodlands, plains, heather fields, and sand drifts. Besides the fellow polyglot species zooming by on shiny white two-wheelers, you might spot a wild boar or sheep. Once tuckered out, make your way to the Kröller-Müller Museum, which has a serious collection of Picassos, Mondriaans, and Seurats, as well as a superb sculpture garden to which Rodin is no stranger.

Logistics: Once within the park, the distance to the museum depends on your starting point: 1½ mi from the Otterlo entrance, 2½ mi from Hoenderloo, and a little more than 6 mi from Schaarsbergen.

Day 4: Cruising Along the Afsluitdijk

Trade in your bike for something motorized and take the scenic route southward to witness a sublime example of

technology trumping nature. The Delta Works is a massive dam and flood barrier—24-foot-high banks stretch 20 mi (32 km) along the A7 motorway. Give yourself at least a kilometer to get used to driving on the concrete tendril engulfed by blue. On your right, you'll see the North Sea's inlet, known as the Zuiderzee, while on your left, fishermen dot the freshwater banks of the Ijselmeer.

Logistics: Budget and Avis have convenient locations in Amsterdam and throughout the country. You can also join one of the many groups by visiting almost any tourist information center.

Day 5: Museum-hopping in The Hague

No one will try to convince you otherwise if your impression of The Hague is that of super sobriety, what with all the royalty, diplomats, international judges, and civil servants running around. But don't forget that the Count's Hedge, as the city's official Dutch name actually means, also does justice to arts and culture. The Mauritshuis is visited frequently for its pop star of a piece, *Girl with a Pearl Earring*, while the Gemeetemuseum holds the most Mondriaans under one roof, and the Escher Museum is, in a word, awesome. For when you get peckish, there's a veritable embassy row's worth of eateries, from grandma-friendly Dutch cafés to posh hotel dining rooms, and one of the most prominent Chinatowns in the country. The Hague's Indonesian restaurants are said to be hemisphere-altering.

Logistics: Check the lavish-as-it-gets Hotel Des Indes for special discount rates on Thursday through Sunday arrivals. ⊕ *www.hoteldesindesthehague.com*

Day 6: Sun and Fun in Scheveningen

Once you've had your fill of The Hague's manicured gardens and stately buildings, take a side trip to Scheveningen, the Netherlands' most popular esplanade. Restaurants, clubs, casinos, bungee jumps, ice cream stands, and trinket shops create an almost American ethos, though dip into the frigid waters of the North Sea and you'll be quickly reminded that the Jersey Shore is far away.

Logistics: For optimum safety and security, park your car in one of Scheveningen's three public garages or two open car parks.

BEATING THE EURO

To go Dutch is a native practice indeed, but don't think your host country will be footing half your vacation bills. The Netherlands is an expensive place to visit. Here, however, are ways to save.

Travel Off-Season
To save on airfare, book your trip in the fall or winter (except around Christmas) when neither tulips nor tourism are in bloom.

Lodge Like a Local
Dutch hotels are overpriced and underwhelming. If you're used to American luxury, be ready to recalibrate your star system by at least 1, meaning a 5-star Amsterdam hotel feels more like a New York City 4-star, and even fancy suites tend to be space challenged. Particularly if you're staying more than two nights, consider a more affordable, more personal short-term apartment rental. While you're at it, go for that canal-side home or houseboat you've always dreamed of.

Move Like a Local
If your hotel is away from the city center or you plan to cover lots of ground, rent a bike. For those less comfortable on two wheels, take public transportation. If you plan to ride frequently, buy a multiple-ride *strippenkaart*, which you can share with your cotravelers, or an OV-chipkaart.

Self-Hydrate
For a country that's spent centuries diking and damming, you'd think getting a drink of water would be no biggie. Think again. To prevent an extra €2 (or more) from being added to your restaurant tab, be sure to ask specifically for *glaasje kraanwater* (tap water). Some just-plain-mean establishments will refuse, but if you find a compassionate server, a small (sometimes nearly shot-size) glass of lukewarm

liquidity will appear. In any case, BYO H2O in your travel bag.

To Market, To Market
For discounted food, drink, clothing, cosmetics, and Amsterdam souvenirs, take advantage of the city's several dozen open-air markets, many of which operate Monday through Saturday. The vendors may not do gift wrap but you'll save some significant euros.

Cultural Cost-Cutting
The electronic I amsterdam Card provides free or discounted admissions to many of Amsterdam's top museums, a free canal cruise, free use of public transport, and 25% off various attractions and restaurants; savings can be more than €100. A one-day pass costs €38, a two-day costs €48, and a three-day costs €58. It can be purchased at the Centraal Station branches of the VVV (Netherlands Board of Tourism) and the GVB (City Transport Company), at some hotels and museums, and online (⊕ *www.iamsterdamcard.com*).

The Last Minute Ticket Shop offers tickets for comedy clubs, the ballet, opera, symphony, and theater at a 50% discount. Though you must make your purchase on performance day in person at the office (☉ *Mon.–Sat. 12–7:30 and Sun. 12–6*), preview the daily selection online (⊕ *www.lastminuteticketshop.nl*).

If you travel to the Netherlands frequently or plan on visiting several museums within a year's time, consider investing in a *Museumkaart* (museum card). This gives you 365 days of free entry to more than 440 museums nationwide. It can be purchased for €44.95 and, if you're under 25, for €22.45 at participating museums and online (⊕ *www.museumkaart.nl*).

Exploring Amsterdam

WORD OF MOUTH

"We sat at a table outside, in Amsterdam, next to a canal—how could it get any better?"

—T4TX

"It took me a day or so to gauge the rhythm of the place, but when you start to harmonize, it's a supremely well-balanced way of life."

—Fashionista

WELCOME TO EXPLORING AMSTERDAM

TOP REASONS TO GO

★ **Golden Age canals:** Hop aboard to glide past mansions shimmering on a summer's day or under bridges twinkling with fairy lights at night. Amsterdam from the water is astonishing.

★ **Two wheels good:** Experience the best cycling city in the world and zip about like a local. Everybody, but everybody, cycles everywhere.

★ **Secrets in the city:** Explore a cultural capital packed with surprises. The hidden courtyards of old almshouses, elegant gardens tucked behind 17th-century facades, a hidden church in an old merchant's house.

★ **Café culture:** There's a bar for every mood, every vintage of customer, for loud nights out or brandies after the opera. As you relax on a sunny terrace surrounded by relaxed locals doing the same thing, you'll marvel how this city has got the work/life balance just right.

1 **The Old City Center.** Heritage and hustle, where church towers soar above medieval defenses, and in the center, the infamous red light district.

2 **The Waterfront.** Across the IJ and along the water, a shiny, new Amsterdam is emerging.

3 **The Canal Ring.** The Golden Age city plan of beautiful waterways lined with 17th-century gabled mansions.

4 **Jordaan and the Leidseplein.** Eat, drink, and sing in neighborly Jordaan or party in nightlife HQ Leidseplein.

5 **Museum District.** Amsterdam's culture zone where high heels clack down the PC Hooftstraat for luxury retail relief.

6 **The Pijp.** An arty, bohemian, global village where you can taste a multitude of multicultural treats.

7 **East of the Amstel.** Wide boulevards and high-ceilinged cafés create the unique streetscape while, culturally speaking, markets, parks, and houses of worship lean to the East.

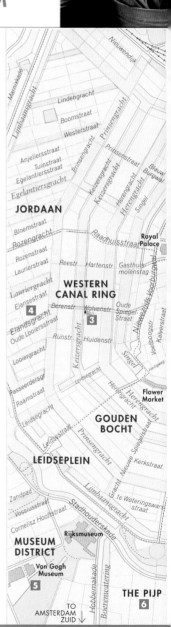

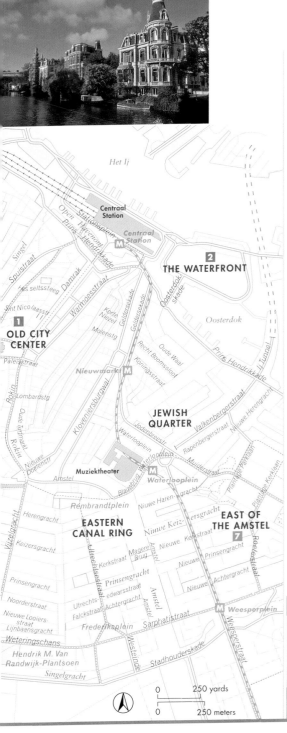

2

GETTING ORIENTED

There are no straight lines in central Amsterdam, but once understood, it's an easy city to navigate—or purposely get lost in. For starters it is teeny. Think of it as an onion with Centraal Station as the stem and the city folding out as layers, each on a somewhat circular path under the guidance of the Canal Ring. To stay oriented, just follow each onion layer around, which will lead you east-west, while the thoroughfare streets run north-south. To stay safe, always watch out for bikes and trams. Keep off the bike paths, which are well paved and often mistaken for sidewalks. Bikers have the right-of-way, so if you hear a bell, move quickly. Trams function similarly, and will also ring their bell (a much louder, clangy one) before they move. Just look both ways, and look both ways again before crossing streets.

Updated by
Ann Maher

"Amsterdam is a city, but it is also a country by itself, a small nation inside a larger one" wrote Geert Mak in his revered chronicle about the Dutch capital. For many visitors, Amsterdam will not only seem quite different from the rest of the Netherlands, but anywhere else in the world.

Set on 160 man-made canals that stretch for 75 km, traversed by 1,200 or so bridges, Amsterdam has the largest historical inner city in Europe. Its circle of waterways, the Grachtengordel, is a 17th-century urban expansion plan for the rich and gives central Amsterdam its distinctive shape. Unlike other major European cities, Amsterdam is not defined by its palaces or estates but by domestic architecture. It's not ancient (by European standards); the joy is in the detail. Elaborate gables and witty gable stones denoting the trade of a previous owner; floating houseboats and hidden hofjes. Even street names tell stories, whether of Golden Age painters in the Pijp or naval heroes farther west.

It's also a city built on a human scale, easy to walk around (even better by bike), but backed up by clanging trams for transport in dire weather (or with a flat tire).

With 750,000 friendly souls, 176 nationalities, and with almost everything a scant 10-minute bike ride away, it's a village packing the cultural punch of a metropolis. There are scores of concerts every day, numerous museums, summertime festivals, and a legendary party scene. It's vibrant, but not static (which is why the entry of the Grachtengordel into the UNESCO World Heritage Site list has not been greeted with universal joy). The city is making concerted efforts to appeal to culture-loving tourists rather than sex-drugs-and rock 'n' rollers with initiatives like Project 1012, which aims to diversify the economy of the Red Light District. Like construction in the rest of the city, it's a work in progress, but there is light at the end of the tunnel. The scaffolding is coming down around Museumplein, and new architectural landmarks such as film institute EYE across the IJ are going up.

Despite the disruptions, it's impossible to resist Amsterdam's charms. You won't be the first visitor to exclaim wistfully that you could really imagine living here: joining the shoals of cyclists flowing over bridges and alongside canals on their way to and from work or enjoying the evening sunshine with an aperitif in a canalside bar. It's an endlessly fascinating city.

PLANNING

2

WHEN TO GO

There's no bad time to visit Amsterdam, but there are two big seasons. Tulip time is mid-March to mid-May, when the global rush to the bulb fields is matched by a springtime surge in hotel bookings and the line for the Anne Frank House. It is also bustling in the summer months when there's an enormous variety of cultural events and festivals. Queens Day (April 30) and Museum Night (first week in November), are worth visits in their own right. Take advantage of Tulip Days (third weekend in April), Open Garden Days (third weekend in June), and Open Monument Day (second weekend in September) for seeing heritage properties and some extraordinary gardens rarely open to the public.

HOW'S THE WEATHER?

Amsterdam is only 7 feet above sea level, so the city is always a little damp. There is high humidity in the summer and a fair amount of rain, especially in the winter, but, moisture aside, Amsterdam's weather is ultimately comfortable. The temperatures are rarely extreme and there are lots of balmy days, especially in June, July, and August. November to April is overcast and windy with a bit of snow and ice around the New Year. Whatever the weather, it doesn't hang about for long, so plan for every eventuality. Wear layers to put on or take off, have sturdy shoes for walking on the cobblestones, and bring a good umbrella.

GETTING AROUND

The best way to see Amsterdam is by bike or on foot, but the city's public transport system, GVB, is extremely reliable. It operates the buses, trams, metro, and ferries with service 24 hours a day. The ticket system used is the OV-chipkaart, a credit-card-sized smart card that you use to check in and out of the transport network. There are GVB one-day or multiday versions, but if there's a sudden deluge you can leap on a tram or bus and pay on board—you'll receive a disposable ticket valid for an hour—but it's the least value-for-money option. For discounted travel (ages 4–11, 65+, student), you need to buy a personalized card with a photo that you load with credit. There's a one-off fee (about the same as a one-day pass to Amsterdam) for this card.

STOP/GO BUS

The blue and green Stop/Go bus (formerly the *Opstapper*, is a useful public transport option that trundles round the elegant Prinsengracht—heart of the historic canal sector—from Waterlooplein (outside the Stopera) to Centraal Station and Oosterdok (outside the library). You can hail it on the street or get on at one of the starting points mentioned above. There are no fixed stops—just tell the driver when you want to get off. It passes right in front of the Anne Frank House, in walking distance of the Leidseplein, and maybe by your hotel. The buses run every 12 minutes from 9:30 AM to 5:30 PM. There are eight seats, and there is room for an additional eight standing passengers.

A BIT OF HISTORY

Amsterdam's history as a commercial hub began in 1275, when Floris V, count of Holland, decreed that the fledgling settlement would be exempt from paying tolls. Consequently, the community, then called "Aemstelredamme," was soon taking in tons of beer from Hamburg, along with a lot of thirsty settlers. The beer profits opened up other fields of endeavor, and by the 17th century Amsterdam had become the richest and most powerful city in the world. It had also produced the world's first-ever multinational company: the East India Company (VOC), which shipped spices, among other goods, between Asia and Europe. Amsterdam was, in Voltaire's words, "the storage depot of the world." While the rest of Europe still felt it necessary to uphold the medieval tags of "honor" and "heroism," Amsterdam had the luxury of focusing just on money—and the consequent liberty it created.

WATER TAXIS

A bright yellow water taxi provides a novel, if expensive, means of getting about, but the price is per trip, not per person, so the cost can be split amongst a group (each boat carries up to eight people). The cost is €1.75 per minute within the center, with a pickup charge of €7.50. Centraal Station to the Anne Frank House, for example, takes 30 minutes; the Web site gives other timings. There are landing stages throughout the city where you might find one waiting, or you can book by telephone. **Contact Water Taxi** (☎ *020/535–6363* ⊕ *www.water-taxi.nl*).

HOURS OF OPERATION

Restaurants are usually open evenings 6–11, although some kitchens close as early as 10, and many are closed on Sunday and Monday.

Major sights, such as Amsterdam's Koninklijk Paleis (Royal Dam Palace) have summer opening hours; parks are open dawn to dusk; the scenic courtyard *hofjes* (almshouses) are usually open at the discretion of the inhabitants. Museum hours vary; to give some instances, the city's famous Van Gogh museum is open 10–6 (and on Friday, 10–10), and the Anne Frank House is open 9–9 mid-March–mid-September and until 10 in July and August, and 9–7 mid-September–mid-March.

Note that when this book refers to summer hours, it means approximately Easter (between March 22 and April 25) to October; winter hours run from November to Easter.

MONEY-SAVING TIPS

The **I amsterdam City Card** provides free and discount admissions to many of Amsterdam's top museums (but not the Anne Frank House), plus a free canal ride, free use of public transport, and a 25% discount on various attractions and restaurants; savings can be very substantial. A 24-hour pass costs €38, a 48-hour costs €48, and a 72-hour costs €58. The pass comes with a booklet in Dutch, English, French, German, Italian, and Spanish. It can be purchased at branches of the VVV, the GVB (both at Centraal Station), and through some hotels and museums.

Queensday (the Queen's birthday), Amsterdam's biggest street party, happens every year on April 30th.

If you are here for a few more days or intend to visit museums in other parts of the Netherlands, such as Haarlem, a *Museumkaart* (Museum Card) might offer better value. This gives you free entry to more than 440 museums throughout the country for a year, including the top draws in Amsterdam (except the Anne Frank House). It is available upon showing ID at VVV offices and participating museums for €44.95.

VISITOR INFORMATION

The VVV (Netherlands Board of Tourism) has several offices around Amsterdam. The office in Centraal Station is open daily 8–8; the one on Stationsplein, opposite Centraal Station, is open daily 9–5; on Leidseplein (ticket bureau), daily 9–5; and at Schiphol Airport, daily 7–10. Each VVV has information principally on its own region. Stop by any of the offices for tour recommendations, maps, and calendars of events. The helpful staff can speak many languages. For a small fee, they can book hotel rooms or other accommodation. The rates change daily, and VVV gets details from the hotels every morning. In the summer, there are also a few extra helpers outside Centraal Station and key tourist spots like the Westerkerk who can help with basic inquiries and directions. Look for people wearing bright red I amsterdam T-shirts.

Contact **VVV—Netherlands Board of Tourism** (⊕ www.iamsterdam. com✉ *Spoor 2b/Platform 2b, Centraal Station, Centrum* ✉ *Stationsplein 10, Centraal Station* ✉ *Leidseplein 26 terrace side, Leidseplein*✉ *Schiphol Airport (arrivals 2), Badhoevedorp).*

THE OLD CITY CENTER

Variety really is the spice of life when you're visiting Amsterdam. This city has enjoyed a rich and turbulent history, and so much of it can be seen in the old center where history, sex, education, and religion are all well represented.

Dam Square is a useful landmark bridging the older (east) and newer (west) sides of the center. From here you can head off to worship naval heroes in the Nieuwe Kerk or, for some retail therapy, pop into the De Bijenkorf (which lives up to its name—the beehive—during big sales). The core of the oldest part of the city is Amsterdam's most famous area, the Red Light District, known locally as *de Wallen*, with the Ouderkerk, its oldest church, bang in the middle. Business in the two main canals and narrow alleyways leading off them is conducted against an implausibly scenic backdrop (porn emporiums and coffee shops at ground level, gables on the top) with atmospheric views from the bridges. (Although this is relative; there's no comparison with the non-red-light-district leafy environs of the southern sections of these same canals below the Damstraat). Its eastern perimeter is Zeedijk, which leads from Centraal Station through Amsterdam's little Chinatown. There's a bit more in Gelderskade and Nieuwmarkt, where the street opens up into a vibrant square packed with cafés and dominated by the hulking presence of ex-weigh house and medieval gateway, De Waag.

Heading southwards along the Kloveniersburgwal is a rewarding wander with diversions on both sides of the water: Look for churches, chapels, attractive canals, and some notable historic buildings that today house departments of the University of Amsterdam. Farthest west, running parallel to Rokin, is theater district Nes; heading east is the Old Jewish Quarter, which includes the synagogue complex of the Joods Historisch Museum, Amsterdam's most famous flea market behind the Muziektheater/City Hall complex on Waterlooplein, and behind all that, the Rembrandthuis. But if you get lost, even the worst student of foreign languages can easily get help by asking for "The Dam."

TIMING

You can walk round the center of Amsterdam easily in a few hours if you want a brief immersion into these very different districts, but there are enough sites and museums to last several days. The joy of the city is in the detail, so factor in time for meandering.

Numbers in the margin correspond to points of interest on the Old City Center map.

WESTERN HALF OF THE CENTER

As you walk up the Damrak from Centraal Station, you're heading toward the commercial center of the city—and the place where most visitors organically converge—Dam Square, the heart of a city since a dam was built over the Amstel in the 12th century. Home to the Royal Palace, the Nieuwe Kerk, and the oddly phallic National Monument, it's actually rather dull in itself, but it fulfills the role of focal point for protests and celebrations. There's a lot of shopping of the chain-store variety in pedestrianised Nieuwendijk and Kalverstraat leading off Dam. On weekends, at the Muntplein end, football fans might be tempted by the enthusiastic Oranje Voetbal Museum while non-football fans have coffee with a view at the new café atop the Kalvertoren shopping mall nearby. The top cultural stops in this district are the Amsterdams Historisch Museum and the peaceful Begijnhof, the best known of the almshouses built round a central courtyard or hof. The entrance to this can be found off graceful Spui which is the literary headquarters of the city. It's a beautiful square with a clutch of great bookshops and it hosts famous book and art markets. The area around Spui has a reputation for being the intellectual heart of the city, since it was where, until recently, most of the newspapers were based.

TOP ATTRACTIONS

⑯ **Amsterdams Historisch Museum** *(Amsterdam Historical Museum).* Any
🅒 city that began in the 13th century as a boggy swamp to become the
Fodor'sChoice trading powerhouse of the world in the 17th century has a fascinat-
★ ing story to tell, and this museum does it superbly. It's housed in a rambling amalgamation of buildings, once a convent, which was used as Amsterdam's Civic Orphanage. If you approach it from Spui, walk past the entrance to the Begijnhof and straight ahead for the glassed **Schuttersgalerij** (Civil Guards Gallery) lined with huge portraits of city militias. Though not in the same league as the *The Night Watch*, you can see them for free. The David and Goliath statues that dominate one end of the hall used to be in the stylishly revamped museum café Mokum, which you can access from Kalverstraat through an impressive doorway. Surrounding the café terrace are rows of wooden lockers once used by the orphans but now adorned with photos and artwork depicting Amsterdam's cultural life.

Inside the museum, the satellite-imagery blast through Amsterdam's growth and development just off the entrance hall is brilliantly executed. You can follow a chronological route through the 24 galleries with period objects, film, and exhibits or skip about. On the art front, there are many fine portraits and cityscapes, but don't miss the 1538

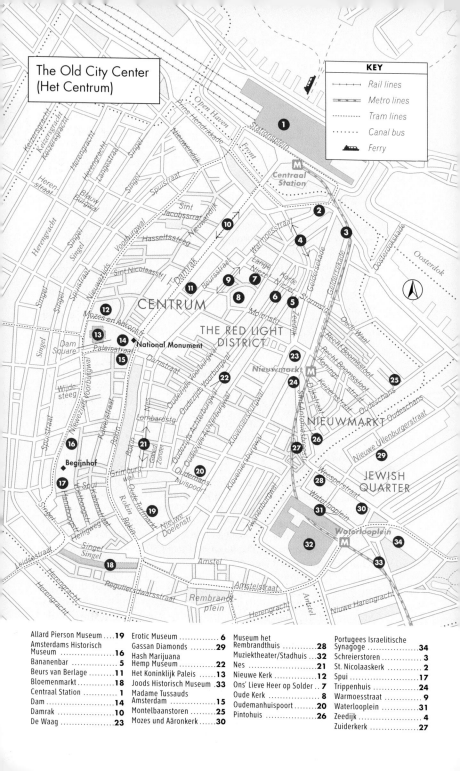

The Old City Center (Het Centrum)

KEY

Rail lines	
Metro lines	
Tram lines	
Canal bus	
Ferry	

Bird's Eye View of Amsterdam by Cornelis Anthonisz, the *Anatomy Lesson of Dr Deijman* (1656) by Rembrandt, or Hendrik Breitner's *Portrait of Dam Square* (1898). The Golden Age and VOC empire-building period is well covered, of course, but social and cultural history of the 20th century is just as good. It's a great museum for kids. You can winch a horse out of a canal using Sinck's contraption, or ride a bike through the 1920s. Luud Schimmelpennink was way ahead of his time when he proposed car-sharing schemes in the 1960s (and free white bikes, too), and here's an original to (virtually) steer round Amsterdam. Marvelous. ⊠ *Kalverstraat 92 and Nieuwezijds Voorburgwal 357, Centrum* ☏ *020/523–1822* ⊕ *www.ahm.nl* ✉ *€10 adults, €5 (ages 6–18)* ☉ *Weekdays 10–5, weekends 11–5.*

⑪ ★ **Beurs van Berlage** *(Berlage's Stock Exchange).* Down otherwise tacky Damrak is the old stock-exchange building that received a hostile reception when it was first built but is now revered as Amsterdam's first modern building and the country's most important piece of 20th-century architecture. Built between 1898 and 1903 by H.P. Berlage, the building became a template for the style of a new century. Gone were all the ornamentations of the 19th-century "Neo" styles. The new Beurs, with its simple lines and the influence it had on the Amsterdam School architects who followed Berlage, earned him the reputation of being the "Father of Modern Dutch Architecture."

The building is in fact a political manifesto that preaches the oneness of capital and labor. Built upon 4,880 wooden piles, each of the Beurs van Berlage's 9 million bricks is meant to represent an individual, who together form a strong and democratic whole. Berlage showed particular respect for the labor unions by exposing their works and accenting the important structural points with natural stone. Today, the Beurs serves as a true Palazzo Publico with concert halls (home to the Dutch Philharmonic Orchestra) and space for exhibitions of architecture and applied arts. The small museum has exhibits about the former stock exchange and its architect and offers access to the lofty clock tower and strong room, but these can be viewed only by taking part in an architecture tour organized by Artiflex (☏ *020/620–8112*). Stop in at the café to admire the stunning symbolist mosaics by Jan Toorop over a coffee (☉ *Mon.–Sat. 10–6, Sun. 11–6).* ⊠ *Damrak 277, Centrum* ☏ *020/530–4141* ⊕ *www.beursvanberlage.nl* ✉ *Varies based on exhibition* ☉ *Varies based on exhibition.*

⑱ **Bloemenmarkt** *(Flower Market).* This is the last of the city's floating markets. In days gone by, merchants would sail up the Amstel loaded down with blooms from the great tulip fields to delight patrons and housewives. Today, the flower sellers stay put, but their wares are still offered on stalls-cum-boats along with fridge magnets and other cheesy Amsterdamorabilia. ⊠ *Singel (between Muntplein and Koningsplein), Centrum* ☉ *Mon.–Sat. 9–5:30.*

❶ **Centraal Station** *(Central Station).* The main hub of transportation in the Netherlands, this building was designed as a major architectural statement by P.J.H. Cuypers. Although sporting many Gothic motifs (including a unique wind vane disguised as a clock in its left tower), it is

The Royal Palace (Het Koninklijk Paleis) was originally built as a city hall during the Dutch Golden Age, when the government could afford such luxuries.

now considered a landmark of Dutch Neo-Renaissance style. (Cuypers also designed the city's other main gateway, the Rijksmuseum, which lies like a mirrored rival on the other side of town.) The building of the station required the creation of three artificial islands and the ramming of 8,600 wooden piles to support it. Completed in 1885, it represented the psychological break with the city's seafaring past, as its erection slowly blocked the view to the IJ. Another controversy arose from its Gothic detailing, which was considered by uptight Protestants as a tad too Catholic—like Cuypers himself—and hence earned the building the nickname the "French Convent" (similarly, the Rijksmuseum became the "Bishop's Castle"). Currently sections of Centraal Station, both inside and outside the main entrance, are under construction with the new North/South metro line. If you are visiting the tourist office or restaurant on platform 2b, wander down to look at the magnificent golden gate of the Queen's waiting room (alas, you can't go in) and a modern take on Dutch Delft tiles, including one styled "2b or not 2b." ⊠ *Stationsplein, Centrum* ☎ *0900–9292 (public transport information).*

QUICK BITES

A particularly stylish place to wait for a train is 1e Klas (⊠ *Platform 2B, Centraal Station, Centrum* ☎ *020/625–0131*), whose original Art Nouveau brasserie interior, no longer restricted to first-class passengers, is perfect for lingering over coffee, a snack, or a full-blown meal accompanied by fine wine. Whatever the hour, it's a fine place to savor the sumptuousness of *fin de siècle* living. Don't miss the gilded portals of the Queen's waiting room a few doors down.

14 **Dam** *(Dam Square)*. Home to the Koninklijk Paleis (Royal Palace) and the Nieuwe Kerk, Dam Square (or just Dam), is Amsterdam's official center. It traces its roots to the 12th century and the dam built over the Amstel (hence the city's name). The waters (the Damrak) once reached right up to Dam, with ships and barges sailing to the weigh house. Folks came here to trade, talk, protest, and be executed. In the 17th century it was hemmed in by houses and packed with markets. Behind the Nieuwe Kerk there's an atmospheric warren of alleys with proeflokaal (tasting house) De Drie Fleschjes (the three small bottles) on Gravenstraat dating from 1650. In the 19th century the Damrak was filled in to form the street leading to Centraal Station, and King Louis, Napoléon's brother, demolished the weigh house in 1808 because it spoiled the view from his bedroom window in the Royal Palace. Today the Dam is a bustling meeting point with street performers and fairs on high days and holidays. The **National Monument** is the towering white obelisk opposite the Palace on the other side of Damrak. It was erected in 1956 as a memorial to the Dutch soldiers who died in World War II. Designed by architect J. J. P. Oud (who thought that De Stijl minimalism was in keeping with the monument's message), it's the focal point for Remembrance Day on May 4 that commemorates Dutch lives lost in wars and peace-keeping missions around the world. Every year, the Queen walks from the Koninklijk Paleis to the monument and lays flowers. The monument contains 12 urns: 11 are filled with earth from all the Dutch provinces, and the 12th contains earth from the former colonies (Indonesia, Surinam, and the Antilles). Oud designed the steps to be used as seating, and today it's still a favored rest spot and a great place to watch the world go by. ✉ *Follow Damrak south from Centraal Station. Raadhuisstraat leads from Dam behind the Palace to intersect main canals.*

> **BUILDING IN A SWAMP**
>
> In order to build the Royal Palace, architect Jacob van Campen had to dig deep in search of solid ground using the standard local technique of driving wooden piles down through layers of swamp and sand to anchor the foundation. What was less standard was the sheer number of piles—a figure that every Dutch child knows—13,659.

13 **Het Koninklijk Paleis** *(Royal Palace)*. From the outside, it is somewhat hard to believe that this gray-stained building was declaimed by poet and diplomat Constantijn Huygens as the "Eighth Wonder of the World." It was built between 1648 and 1665 as the largest secular building on the planet. From the inside, its magnificent interior inspires another brand of disbelief: this palace was actually built as a mere city hall. Golden Age artistic greats such as Ferdinand Bol, Govert Flinck (Rembrandt's sketches were rejected), and Jan Lievens were called in for the decorating. In the building's public entrance hall, the **Burgerzaal,** the world was placed quite literally at one's feet: two maps inlaid in the marble floor show Amsterdam as the center of the world, and as the center of the universe.

The building has remained the Royal Palace ever since Napoléon's brother squatted there in 1808, and it's one of three palaces at the

Fodor's Choice
★

CLOSE UP

Lieverdje's Radical Past

The innocent-looking statue of a woolen sock–clad boy in the middle of Spui Square, called Het *Lieverdje* (The Little Darling–local street slang for wild street boys), formed the focal point for the particularly wacky and inspired Amsterdam social coalition known as the Provo movement (precursors to the hippies). Taking their name from their ultimate goal, "to provoke"—this group first rose around Robert Jasper Grootveld, who hosted absurdist anticonsumerist "happenings" off Leidseplein. In 1964, he moved his shows to the Spui around the Lieverdje statue that had just been erected there. The crowds that gathered to see the happenings had repeated clashes with the police. During the student war protest of the 1960s, the Lieverdje statue was repeatedly and symbolically set on fire. Today pranksters occasionally dress him up in silly garb just because they can.

disposal of Queen Beatrix, who hosts official receptions and state visits here. Royal memories of Amsterdam are probably a bit mixed. Her wedding in 1966 was disrupted by a radical student group throwing smoke bombs at her carriage, and in 1980 her coronation was derailed by riots on the Dam. And at the 2010 Dodenherdenking (Remembrance of the Dead) ceremony by the National Monument, a man screamed during the two-minute silence prompting a panic and stampede among the crowd, who no doubt feared a rerun of the 2009 Queen's Day tragedy when a gunman drove through the route of the royal procession killing seven. Renovations and official occasions mean opening times can vary considerably. ☒ *Dam, Centrum* ☎ *020/620–4060* ⊕ *www. koninklijkhuis.nl* ☐ *€7.50* ☉ *July–Aug., daily 12–6. Check Web site for outside these months.*

⓬ **Nieuwe Kerk** *(New Church).* Begun in the 14th century, the Nieuwe
★ Kerk (it celebrated its 600th birthday in 2010) is a soaring Late Gothic structure whose tower was never completed because the authorities blew all their money on the building of the Palace. Whereas the Oude Kerk had the blessing of the Bishop of Utrecht, the Nieuwe Kerk was supported by the local well-to-do merchant class—the result was an endless competition between the two parochial factions. Don't miss the magnificently sculpted wooden pulpit by Albert Vinckenbrinck constructed after the Great Fire of 1645. It took him 19 years to complete, though there is now a bit missing: the scales from a lady of justice were an impulsively generous gift to the Canadians, who liberated Amsterdam. Other features include the unmarked grave of the poet Vondel (the "Dutch Shakespeare") and Rombout Verhulst's extravagantly sculpted eulogy to naval hero Adm. Michiel de Ruyter (you can peer through a glass to see his actual coffin in the crypt). De Ruyter daringly sailed his invading fleet up the river Medway in England in the 17th century, causing Sir William Batten, surveyor of the Queen's Navy, to explode to diarist Samuel Pepys, "By God, I think the devil shits Dutchmen!" The two organs are exceptional. At the royal marriage in

2002, there was a magical moment as the painted shutters of the Great Organ unfurled behind Prince Willem and Princess Maxima as they walked up the aisle. The Nieuwe Kerk has been the investiture church for Dutch monarchs since 1815, and has broadened its appeal by serving as a venue for organ concerts and special—invariably excellent and often cutting-edge—exhibitions that attract a half-million visitors a year. Outside the church, you can see the sundial from which all town clocks were calibrated up to 1880. ⊠ *Dam, Centrum* ☎ *020/638–6909* ⊕ *www.nieuwekerk.nl* 💶 *€5 Admission varies according to exhibition* ⊙ *Daily 10–6, Thur. 10–10. Exhibition times vary*.

⓱ Spui *(Spui Square)*. This beautiful and seemingly tranquil tree-lined square hides a lively and radical recent past. Journalists and bookworms have long favored its many cafés, and the Atheneum News Center (No. 14–16) and its adjoining bookstore are the city's best places to peruse an international array of literature, magazines, and newspapers. More cultural browsing can be enjoyed on the Spui's book market on Friday and its art market on Sunday. ⊠ *Bounded by Spuistraat and Kalverstraat, Centrum*.

QUICK
BITES
Several of the bar-cafés and eateries on Spui are good places to take a break. The ancient **Hoppe** (⊠ *Spui 18–20, Centrum* ☎ *020/420–4420*) has been serving drinks between woody walls and on sandy floors since 1670. Next door is elegant **Café Luxembourg** (⊠ *Spui 24, Centrum* ☎ *020/620–6264*). For a superdelicious breakfast, lunch or high tea, try **Gartine** ⊠ *Taksteeg 7, Centrum* ☎ *020-320/4132*. If you just want to eat and run, try Broodje van Kootje (⊠ *Spui 28, Centrum* ☎ *020/623–7451*) for a classic Amsterdam *broodje* (sandwich).

WORTH NOTING

⑩ Damrak *(Dam Port)*. This unavoidable and busy street leading up to Centraal Station, which is being smartened up as the "red carpet" to the city, is lined with a mostly tawdry assortment of shops, attractions, hotels, and greasy-food dispensers. It's a shame, because behind the neon signs are some beautiful examples of lovely Dutch architecture. Damrak, and its extension, Rokin, was once the Amstel River, bustling with activity, its piers loaded with fish and other cargo on their way to the weigh house at the Dam. Now the only open water that remains is a patch in front of the station that provides mooring for canal tour boats. ⊠ *Centrum*.

⑮ Madame Tussauds Amsterdam. This branch of the world-famous wax museum, above the Peek & Cloppenburg department store, depicts Holland's glitterati, including Golden Age celebrities—there's a life-size, 3-D rendering of a painting by Vermeer (alas, the lighting is dubious), and an understandably displaced-looking Piet Mondriaan. Of course, there is also a broad selection of international superstars, including Barack Obama, but bring your own ironic distance, or skip it altogether. People-watching in the Dam is much more entertaining than an hour and a half (their recommended tour time) wax-watching in Madame Tussauds. ⊠ *Dam 20, Centrum* ☎ *020/523–0623* ⊕ *www.madametussauds.nl* 💶 *€21* ⊙ *Sept.–June, daily 10–5:30; July and Aug., daily 10–8:30*.

THE RED LIGHT DISTRICT

Say "Amsterdam" and people's reflexive response is often "the Red Light District." Forming a rough triangle from Centraal Station bordered by Warmoesstraat, Damstraat, and Zeedijk, this famous district incorporates the two oldest canals in the city (the Oudezijds Voorburgwal and the Oudezijds Achterburgwal) and its oldest building (the Oudekerk). It has been an area for prostitution since the 14th century but it's changing fast. Through Project 1012 (the postal code for the district), the city is aiming to halve the numbers of coffee shops and windows for prostitution (around 200) to combat organized crime. Judging by the number of "to let" signs, they are well on the way. If you decide to take a stroll around the *de wallen* (as the Red Light District is called) don't let a little sleaze scare you away. This is also the most historic, and was at one point, the wealthiest part of town.

In the 16th century, the residents of the Oudezijds Voorburgwal were so rich that the area was nicknamed "the Velvet Canal." And even before the recent cleanup, it has always been a real district with families and tradespeople, students and professionals living alongside the sex shops, bars, churches, and brothels. The city goal is more economic diversity, with cutting-edge art and fashion for sale in the windows; the message is buy the dress, not the woman.

TOP ATTRACTIONS

⑤ Bananenbar *(Banana Bar)*. Since the 1970s, this supersleazy bar has featured naked barmaids doing "now you see it, now you don't" tricks that involve fruit, which hardly merits landmark status, although along with **Caso Rosso** across the canal, whose show is deemed to be slightly classier, it is a red-light institution. ⊠ *Oudezijds Achterburgwal 137, Centrum* ☎ No phone.

⑦ Ons' Lieve Heer op Solder *(Our Lord in the Attic Museum)*. With its
Fodor'sChoice   elegant gray-and-white facade and spout gable, this appears to be just
★   another lovely 17th-century canal house, and on the lower floors it is. But tucked away in the attic is a clandestine place of Catholic worship, a *schuilkerk* (hidden church), one of the very few to survive more or less in its original state. Catholic masses were officially forbidden from 1578, but the protestant authorities in Amsterdam turned a blind eye provided the churches were not recognizable as such from the outside. The Oude Kerk was decatholicized and stripped of its patron, St. Nicholas, so this little church, consecrated in 1663, was dedicated to him until the St Nicolaaskerk opened in 1887. The chapel itself is a triumph of Dutch classicist taste, with magnificent marble columns, gilded capitals, a colored-marble altar, and the *Baptism of Christ in the Jordan* (1716) painting by Jacob de Wit presiding over all. As well as the hidden chapel, the warren of other rooms in the house with their period furnishings provide an atmospheric glimpse into the life of a rich merchant. The museum is undergoing reconstruction until 2012 but staying open throughout. ⊠ *Oudezijds Voorburgwal 40, Centrum* ☎ 020/624–6604 ⊕ *www.opsolder.nl* 💶 €7 ⊗ *Mon.–Sat. 10–5, Sun. 1–5.*

Even if you have no plans to patronize, the Red Light District is like no other on earth. Don't miss this once-in-a-lifetime window-shopping experience.

8 Oude Kerk *(Old Church)*. Amsterdam's oldest church has evolved over
★ three centuries to look as it does today. What began as a wooden chapel in 1306 was built up to a hall church and then a cross basilica between 1366 and 1566 (and fully restored between 1955 and 1979). It was violently looted during the Reformation and stripped of its altars and images of saints—though the looters did leave the 14th-century paintings still visible on its wooden roof, as well as the Virgin Mary stained-glass windows that had been set in place in 1550. The famed Vater-Muller organ was installed in 1726. Don't miss the carved choir stalls that illustrate proverbs relating to cardinal sins, among other things. Within this open, atmospheric space, there's a gravestone for Rembrandt's wife Saskia van Uylenburgh and also for Kilaen van Rensselaer, one of the Dutch founders of what is now New York, and by the door, a bronzed hand cupping a naked breast. This is one of a series of sculptures placed throughout Amsterdam in1982 by an anonymous artist. The Oude Kerk is as much exhibition space as a place of worship, hosting the annual World Press Photography competition and top-notch modern-art shows. Its carillon is played every Saturday between 4 and 5. ⊠ *Oudekerksplein 23, Centrum* ☎ *020/625–8281* ⊕ *www.oudekerk. nl* ⊠ *€7.50* ☉ *Mon.–Sat. 10:30–5:30, Sun. 1–5:30.*

3 Schreierstoren. Amsterdam's distinctive defense tower began life in 1486
★ as the end point of the city wall. The term *schreiren* suggests the Dutch word for wailing. As lore would have it, this "Weeping Tower" was where women came to cry when their sailor husbands left for sea and to cry again when they did not return (there's a gable stone from 1569 of a woman and a boat on the Gelderskade side). The word *schreier* actually

comes from an Old Dutch word for a "sharp corner" and is a rather more accurate derivation for the tower's name. It's also famous as the point from which Henry Hudson set sail to America. A plaque on the building tells you that he sailed on behalf of the Dutch East India Company to find a shorter route to

> **A SECOND HOME**
>
> Prior to the reformation, the Oude Kerk was known as the "living room" because peddlers displayed their goods in the church and beggars slept there.

the East Indies. In his failure, he came across Canada's Hudson Bay and later—continuing his unlucky streak—New York harbor and the Hudson River. He eventually landed on Manhattan and named it New Amsterdam. The VOC café attached has a lovely view and serves gin and other delights. On the next floor up, there's a nautical shop for modern-day sailors. ✉ *Prins Hendrikkade 94–95, Centrum* ⊕ *www. schreierstoren.nl.*

❾ Warmoesstraat. This touristy strip of hostels, bars, and coffee shops began life as one of the original dikes along the Amstel before evolving into the city's richest shopping street. It's here that the famous 17th-century poet Vondel did business from his hosiery shop at No. 101, and where Mozart's dad tried to unload tickets for his son's concerts in the area's upscale bars. It entered a decline in the 17th century when the proprietors decamped for fancier digs on the Canal Ring; sailors (and the businesses that catered to them) started to fill in the gaps. In the 19th century, the street evolved, along with its extension **Nes,** into the city's primary debauchery zone. Karl Marx was known to set himself up regularly in a hotel here, not only to write in peace but to ask for the occasional loan from his cousin-in-law, Gerard Philips, founder of that capitalist machine Philips.

If you can squeeze past backpackers heading for the coffee shops and other tourist traps, there are hangouts such as the arty Hotel Winston (No. 123); restful oases serving stellar quiche such as De Bakkerswinkel (No. 69); specialty stores, such as Geels and Co. (No. 67), with its infinite selection of coffees and teas, and the spacious W139 (No. 139) gallery, dedicated to the very outer edges of conceptual art. ✉ *Between Dam and Nieuwe Brugsteeg, Centrum.*

QUICK BITES

Zeedijk offers five of the best quick snack–meal stops in town. The most revered is auspiciously placed across from the Buddhist Temple: **Nam Kee** (✉ *Zeedijk 111–113, Centrum* ☎ *020/624–3470*) where the steamed oysters are sublime. There's a restaurant in Gelderskade, and the newest outpost is in the Pijp on Marie Heineken Plein. Considered the best noodles in town, **Snackbar Bird** (✉ *Zeedijk 77, Centrum* ☎ *020/420–6289*) offers wok-fried-in-front-of-your-eyes dishes from Thailand; for a more lingering or less cramped meal, you might want to try its restaurant across the street. **A-Fusion** (✉ *Zeedijk 130, Centrum* ☎ *020/330-4068*) got a satisfied nod from feared foodie critic Johannes van Dam, which has made this a hotspot, with its Asian delicacies and Hong Kong's favorite bubble tea.

CLOSE UP

Leaning Houses

Ever wonder why all of Amsterdam's old houses lean like drunken sailors on a Saturday night? After the great fires of 1421 and 1452, which swept through and destroyed nearly three quarters of the city, building regulations became stricter and wooden structures were forbidden. Only two early timbered examples remain in Amsterdam, though others might be lurking behind more "modern" facades: the Houten Huis (Wooden House) at the Begijnhof built in the second half of the 15th century, and No. 1 Zeedijk, completed in 1550. Since brick is a substantially heavier material than wood (and the city is still sinking into the mud at a slow and steady pace), all structures were built on wooden pilings slammed deep into the sand. Without enough depth (and Jordaan construction was particularly suspect), or with fluctuating water table levels, the wooden pilings begin to crumble and the house tilts. Today, rotten wooden pilings can be replaced with cement ones, without tearing down the building.

The ultimate Dutch snack, raw herring, can be enjoyed at **De Amsterdam-sche Visch Handel** (✉ *Zeedijk 129, Centrum* ☎ *020/624–2070*), which also offers deliciously nutty whole-wheat buns. A Zeedijk and students' fave, **Latei** (✉ *Zeedijk 143, Centrum* ☎ *020/625–7485*) combines a dense interior of high-quality kitsch (all of it for sale) with the serving of coffee, open-face sandwiches, and healthy snacks.

❹ Zeedijk. Few streets have had a longer or more torrid history than Zeedijk, which has been around since Amsterdam began life as a boggy hamlet. In the 15th and 16th centuries, its businesses serviced the lonely, thirsty sailors disembarking from the ships of the East India Company. By the 1970s, the only traffic Zeedijk saw was drug traffic. Tourists were advised to avoid the neighborhood at night because of the junkies and high crime rates. A few years back, the city started cracking down, and it's now much easier to accept the stray, dubious-looking character as merely part of the scenery as opposed to its definition.

There are several interesting sights along the Zeedijk. The 17th-century **Sint Olofskapel** (St. Olaf Church), named after the patron saint of dikes, sports a life-affirming sculpture: grains growing out of a supine skeleton (this used to be a positive message). It's now a conference center for the NH Barbizon Palace Hotel. Across the street at No. 1 is one of only two houses with timbered facades left in the city. Dating from around 1550, **In't Aepjen** (In the Monkeys) provided bedding to destitute sailors if they promised to return from their next voyage with a monkey. Each floor juts out more than the one below so rainwater falls directly onto the street and goods can be hauled up easily. Café Maandje at No. 65 was the first openly gay bar run by legendary lesbian biker chick Bet van Beeren (1902–67). A model of its interior can be viewed at the Amsterdams Historisch Museum, complete with trophy ties she snipped off customers. The Chinese community dominates the end of the street, where street signs are in Dutch and Mandarin.

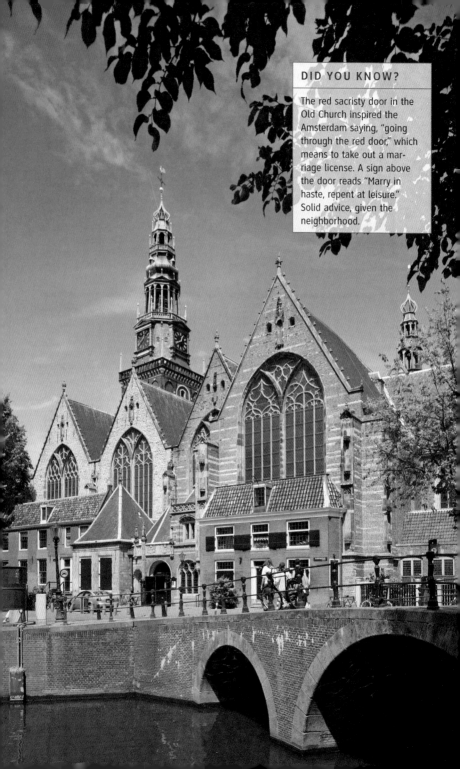

There are around 10,000 Chinese in Amsterdam, a 20th-century presence much younger than the Dutch in China (Taiwan was under Dutch control in 1624). The highlight is the Lotus Flower Buddhist Temple **Fo Guang Shan He Hua** (No. 118). Chinatown extends into Geldersekade and Nieuwmarket and every year there are small (but colorful) New Year celebrations. ⊠ *Oudezijde Kolk (near Centraal Station) to Nieuwmarkt, Centrum.*

WORTH NOTING

❻ Erotic Museum. "Five floors of highly suggestive trinkets and photos" is probably a better description than "museum." Beatles fans may like the original and satisfyingly suggestive sketch by John Lennon, perhaps rendered when he and Yoko did their weeklong bed-in for peace at the Hilton just down the road.

HARTJESDAGEN

The third weekend in August is the time for an annual Amsterdam tradition, the Hartjesdagen (heart days) on the Amsterdamse Zeedijk. An arts festival with cross-dressing overtones, you can drop your jaw at spectacular stiletto-heeled running races, swing to Latin American street bands, compete in a song festival for new talent, and enjoy opera performances and other acts. The highlight is on Sunday when a drag-queen parade traipses across a central podium. Intimate and relaxed, Hartjesdagen is unpretentious and welcoming and embodies that delightful Dutch shared coziness called *gezelligheid.*

There's a new cultural aspect on the third floor in La Gallery Provocatrice that encompasses a wide range of artistic genres. ⊠ *Oudezijds Achterburgwal 54, Centrum* ☎ *020/624–7303* 💳 *€7* ☉ *Sun.–Thurs. 11*AM*–1*AM*; Fri. and Sat. 11*AM*–2*AM.*

㉒ Hash Marijuana Hemp Museum. One would think that more effort could have gone into the name of this institution—lateral thinking being one of the positive effects of its subject. Regardless, here's your chance to suck back the 8,000-year history of hemp use. **Cannabis College**, at No. 124, covers similar territory and is free, though they ask for a donation if you want to tour the garden (⊕ *www.cannabiscollege.com*). ⊠ *Oudezijds Achterburgwal 148, Centrum* ☎ *020/624–8926* ⊕ *www. hashmuseum.com* 💳 *€9* ☉ *Daily 10* AM*–11* PM.

❷ St. Nicolaaskerk *(St. Nicholas Church).* The architect A. C. Bleys designed this church, built in 1887, with its dark and eerie interior as a replacement for all the clandestine Catholic churches that operated during the Reformation. After the Oude Kerk and "Our Lord in the Attic" chapel, this church became the third and (probably final) Sint Nicolaas church. The all-purpose patron saint of children, thieves, prostitutes, sailors, and the city of Amsterdam, transforms into Sinterklaas in mid-November when he arrives from "Spain" on a "steamboat" with his helper Zwarte Piet (Black Pete) and horse Amerigo. The eve of his birthday on December 6 is celebrated as a family feast when everyone exchanges presents and poems. Note that the church is open only when volunteer custodians are available. It hosts a Gregorian chant vesper service September to June on Sunday at 5. ⊠ *Prins Hendrikkade 76, Centrum* ☎ *020/330–78129* 💳 *Free* ☉ *Tue.–Fri. 11–4, Mon. and Sat. 12–3.*

NIEUWMARKT AND ENVIRONS

At the bottom of the Zeedijk and bordering the Red Light District lies Nieuwmarkt and the brooding Waag, ex-gatehouse to the city. It's been a marketplace since the 17th century, selling cheese, herbs, cloth, and fish, as well as spices brought back from the ships of the Dutch East Indies Company. Public executions and other gruesome punishments took place here as well, supplying cadavers to the Surgeon's Guild for dissection. This is where Rembrandt came to watch Professor Tulp in action before painting *The Anatomy Lesson*. During WWII, it was known for a flourishing black market and as a collection place where Jews were held before being shipped off to concentration camps. Today it's an upscale local gathering place, ringed by restaurants, cafés, jazz clubs, and a microbrewery. There's a farmers' market every Saturday and more occasional antiques and curiosities sales.

After the hustle (literally) of the Red Light District, the neighborhood provides a refreshing break. Due east are a cluster of less-touristed, quiet little canal-lined streets (the Rechtboomsloot is especially scenic). Directly south, straight up the Kloveniersburgwal, is the University of Amsterdam, housed in a myriad of lovely old buildings along and between the canals.

QUICK BITES

You may want to sniff out your own favorite among the many café-restaurants that line this square. There's **In De Waag** (⊠ *Nieuwmarkt 4, Centrum* ☎ *020/422-7772*), which highlights its epic medieval roots with candlelight. An arty and studenty option is **'t Loosje** (⊠ *Nieuwmarkt 32–34, Centrum* ☎ *020/627-2635*), which is graced with tile tableaux dating from 1912. **Café Stevens** (⊠ *Gelderskade 123, Centrum* ☎ *020/620-6970* is a snug corner bolt-hole overlooking the square with wooden tables and bowls of big fat chips. **Café Nagel** (⊠ *Kroomboomsslot 47, Centrum*) is an arty hangout open after 4 (and until 3 in the morning on weekends) in a beautiful canal close by.

TOP ATTRACTIONS

⑲ Allard Pierson Museum. Once the repository of the nation's gold supply, this former National Bank with its stern Neoclassical façade is now home to other treasures. Dynamite helped remove the safes and open up the space for the archaeological collection of the University of Amsterdam in 1934, and the museum traces the early development of Western civilization, from the Egyptians to the Romans, and of the Near Eastern cultures (Anatolia, Persia, Palestine) in a series of well-documented (if old-fashioned) displays. It links internally to the University of Amsterdam's Bizondere Collecties (special collections) showcase with interesting exhibitions and a stylish café. ⊠ *Oude Turfmarkt 127, Centrum* ☎ *020/525-2556* ⊕ *www.allardpiersonmuseum.nl* ☎*€6.50. Children under 16 half-price* ☉ *Tues.–Fri. 10–5, weekends 1–5.*

㉓ De Waag *(Weigh House).* Built in 1488, the Waag functioned as a city gate, Sint Antoniespoort, until 1617. It would be closed at exactly 9:30 PM to keep out not only bandits but also the poor and diseased who built shantytowns outside the city's walls. When Amsterdam expanded, it began a second life as a weighing house for incoming goods. The top floor of the building accommodated the municipal militia and several guilds, including the stonemasons who did the evocative decorations that grace each of the seven towers' entrances. One housed a teaching hospital for the Surgeons' Guild. The Theatrum Anatomicum (Anat-omy Theater), with its cupola tower covered in painted coats of arms, was the first place in the Netherlands to host public autopsies. For obvi-ous reasons, these took place only in the winter. Now the building is occupied by a café-restaurant and the Waag Society: the **Society for Old and New Media** (⊕ *www.waag.org*). ⊠ *Bounded by Kloveniersburgwal, Geldersekade, and Zeedijk, Centrum.*

> ## NARROW HOUSES
>
> There are a few other superskinny houses in Amsterdam besides the Little Trip House. The narrowest rear gable is at Singel No. 7 at only 1 meter wide. The building on Oude Hoogstraat 22 is only 2.02 meters (7 feet) wide and 6 meters (19 feet) deep.

㉔ ★ Trippenhuis (Trip House). As family home to the two Trip brothers, "Purveyors of Waepens, Artilleree, Shotte, and Amunition of Werre," who made their fortune during the 17th-century Golden Age, this noted house's buckshot-gray exterior and various armament motifs—including mortar-shape chimneys—designed by Justus Vingboons, are easily explained. But the Corinthian-columned facade actually covers two symmetrical buildings (the dividing wall is positioned behind the middle windows), one for each brother, making it the widest residence (at 22 meters) in Amsterdam. From 1815 to 1885 it housed the national museum or Rijksmuseum and is now the home of The Royal Nether-lands Academy of Arts and Sciences (though they weren't allowed to call it "Royal" under German occupation in the war). Be sure to look across the canal to No. 26, the door-wide white building topped with golden sphinxes and the date of 1696, which is known as the "Little Trip House" or "House of Mr. Trip's Coachman." The story goes that the coachman remarked that he would be happy with a house as wide as the Trippenhuis door. By way of response, Mr. Trip built just that with the leftover bricks. ⊠ *Kloveniersburgwal 29, Centrum* ☎ *No phone.*

WORTH NOTING

㉑ Nes. Nes is a refreshingly quiet corridor filled with theaters and restau-rants; in earlier days it was packed with monasteries and convents, until the Alteration (or Protestant changeover), which kick-started Amster-dam's march toward the Golden Age. The Frascati Theater (No. 59–65) began life as a coffeehouse in the 18th century, but it wasn't until the 1880s that the Nes really blossomed with cafés filled with dance, song, and operetta performances; stars often represented the less uptight seg-ment of the Jewish community. Adjacent to the southern end of the Nes is **Gebed Zonder End,** the "Prayer without End" alleyway, which got its name because it was said you could hear prayers from behind the walls of the convents that used to line this alley. ⊠ *Between Langebrugsteeg and Dam, Centrum.*

20 **Oudemanhuispoort** *(Old Man's House Gate).* Landmarked by its famous chiseled pair of spectacles set over the Oudezijds Achterburgwal pediment—a sweet reference to old age—this passage led to a pensioners' house, an "Oudemannenhuis," first built in 1754. Today, bikes, not canes, are in evidence, as this former almshouse is now part of the University of Amsterdam. One charming relic from its founding days is the covered walkway, which would have been lined with tiny shops whose rents helped subsidize the 18th-century elderly. Adorned with red shutters, the stalls now house an array of antiquarian booksellers. At the Kloveniersburgwal end stands a statue of Mother Amsterdam protecting two elders, sculpted by Anthonie Ziessenis in 1786. ⊠ *Between Oudezijds Achterburgwal, and Kloveniersburgwal, Centrum.*

> **A TASTE OF HOLLAND**
>
> Jacob Hooy & Co. (⊠ *Kloveniersburgwal 12, on the west side of Nieuwmarkt*) is Amsterdam's oldest (since 1743) medicinal herb and spice shop. Try the typical Dutch *drop* (licorice) candy that comes in sweet, salty, or extra salty flavors. It's an acquired (or addictive) taste.

QUICK BITES

As to be expected from a theatrical neighborhood, the Nes offers some prime eating and drinking holes. Fans of Belgian beer should certainly stop at the patio of **De Brakke Grond** (⊠ *Nes 43, Centrum* ☎ *020/422-2666* ⊕ *www.brakkegrond.nl*), part of the Flemish Cultural Center, to partake in one or two of the dozens of options. On the "Prayer Without End" alley, which runs parallel to Nes's south end, is **Kapitein Zeppos** (⊠ *Gebed Zonder End 5, Centrum* ☎ *020/624-2057*), which is named after a '60s Belgian TV star; this former cigar factory is soaked with jazzy old-world charm.

THE JEWISH QUARTER

From medieval times up to Nazi occupation, Amsterdam was considered a sort of second Jerusalem for immigrating Jews from all over Europe. The city came to be known as Mokum (the Hebrew word for "place"), as in *the* place for Jewish people.

Since the 15th century, the *Joodse Buurt* (Jewish Quarter) has traditionally been considered the district east of the Zwanenburgwal. The Quarter got its start thanks to the Inquisition, which drove Sephardic Jews from Spain after 1492. Holland's war with Spain inspired the 1597 Union of Utrecht—it was formulated to protect Protestants from the religious oppression that came with Spanish invasions, but essentially meant that all religions were tolerated. This provided a unique experience for Jewish people because, unlike elsewhere in Europe, they were not forced to wear badges and live in ghettos. These and other freedoms helped attract many Yiddish-speaking Ashkenazi Jews from Eastern Europe who were escaping pogroms. In the 17th century, only the Catholics remained barred from open worship. This explains the 17th-century synagogues in the city and the complete absence of Catholic churches from that period.

By 1938, 10% of Amsterdam's population was Jewish. They had hugely influenced the city's culture and language (the Yiddish word *mazel*, meaning "luck," is still used as a standard farewell). Today, what remains much more painfully ingrained in the city's psyche is what happened during the Nazi occupation, when the Jewish population was reduced to one-seventh of its size. There were many examples of bravery and the opening of homes to hide Jewish people, but there are many more—and less often told—stories of collaboration. Although the current Jewish population has risen to 20,000, the Jewish community itself exists largely beneath the surface of Amsterdam, and most place Dutch identity before Judaism.

> ### REBUILDING MOKUM
>
> The devastation of the Jewish quarter during the war, and its later (very controversial) demolition to make room for the Stadhuis/Muziektheater (City Hall/Music Theater) and Metro, architecturally marked this neighborhood like no other in the city. Today it is a hodgepodge of the old and new.

TOP ATTRACTIONS

㉝ Joods Historisch Museum *(Jewish Historical Museum)*. Four Ashkenazi synagogues (or *shuls*, as they are called in Yiddish), dating from the 17th and 18th centuries were combined with glass-and-steel constructions in 1987 to create this warm and impressive museum commemorating the four-century history of the Jewish people in Amsterdam and the Netherlands. Back in the 17th century, Ashkenazi Jews fled the pogroms in Central and Eastern Europe. They weren't exactly welcomed with open arms by the already settled Sephardic Jews (who resented the increased competition imposed by their often poorer brethren); consequently separate synagogues were built. Four of them make up this complex: the **Neie Sjoel** (New Synagogue, 1752), traces the subject of Jewish identity; the **Grote Sjoel** (Great Synagogue, 1671), presents the tenets of Judaism; the **Obbene Sjoel** (Upstairs Synagogue, 1686), is where the bookshop and café are found; and the **Dritt Sjoel** (Third Synagogue, 1700) houses a collection that includes an 18th-century Sephardic Torah Mantle, a magnificent carved wood Holy Ark dating from 1791, and the autobiographical art of the Berlin artist Charlotte Solomon (1917–43). The museum also features a separate children's museum, a resource center, and one of the city's few purely kosher cafés. Whether or not you tour the collections or regular exhibitions, check out the excellent tours of the Jewish Quarter conducted by this museum. ⊠ *Nieuwe Amstelstraat 1, Centrum* ☎ *020/531–0310* ⊕ *www. jhm.nl* 🖾 *€9* ☉ *Daily 11–5.*

㉘ Museum het Rembrandthuis *(Rembrandt House Museum)*. This is the
Fodor'sChoice house that Rembrandt bought, flush with success, for 13,000 guilders
★ (a princely sum) in 1639, and where he lived and worked until 1656 when declared bankrupt. The inside is a remarkable reconstruction job, as the contents have been assembled based on inventories made when Rembrandt was forced to sell everything, including an extravagant collection of art and antiquities (a contributing factor in his money troubles). He originally chose this house on what was then the main street of

the Jewish Quarter, to experience firsthand the faces he would use in his Old Testament religious paintings. The house interior has been restored with contemporaneous elegant furnishings and artwork in the reception rooms, a collection of rarities that match as closely as possible the descriptions in the inventory, and the main studio, occasionally used by guest artists, which is kept fully stocked with paints and canvases. But it doesn't convey much of the humanity of Rembrandt himself. When he left here, he was not only out of money, but also out of favor with the city after relationships with servant girls following the death of his wife, Saskia. The little etching studio is perhaps the most atmospheric. Littered with tools of the trade, a printing press, and a line hung with drying prints (there are demonstrations), it's easy to imagine Rembrandt finding respite here, experimenting with form and technique, away from uncomfortable schmoozing for commissions (and loans) in the grander salon. The museum owns a huge collection of etchings with 260 of the 290 he made represented, and a changing selection is on permanent display. ⊠ *Jodenbreestraat 4–6, Centrum* ☎ *020/520–0400* ⊕ *www. rembrandthuis.nl* ☜ *€8* ◷ *Daily 10–5.*

▌QUICK
BITES

On the corner of the Stopera complex by a statue of local hero Spinoza, is busy Dantzig (⊠ Zwanenburgwal 15, Centrum ☎ 020/620–9039), with incomparable views over the Amstel but very slow service, even by Amsterdam standards. Soup en Zo (⊠ Jodenbreestraat 94A, Centrum ☎ 020/422–4243) has the best soup in Amsterdam, hands down.

㉜ Muziektheater/Stadhuis *(Music Theater/Town Hall).* Universally known as the Stopera—not just from the combining of "Stadhuis" (Town Hall) and "Opera" but from the radical opposition expressed during its construction—the brick-and-marble complex, opened in 1986, has been described as a set of dentures, and there were moans that its "two for one" nature was a tad too typical of the bargain-loving Dutch. Before the first brick was in place, locals protested over the razing of historic houses in the old Jewish Quarter and around Nieuwmarkt to make way for it. Look for the moving memorial laid in stones around the building that marks the spot of a Jewish orphanage. It tells how, in 1943, after German troops arrived, three teachers voluntarily accompanied 100 children to the extermination camp of Sobibor: "None of them returned. May their memory be blessed." The interior is impressive, with 14-meter-high open foyers and stunning acoustics for its resident companies, the Netherlands Opera (DNO) and National Ballet (HNB). Backstage tours are run once a week (Saturday at noon) or by prior arrangement for groups. From September to May, singers from the Opera and Conservatory perform in the free lunchtime concerts in the Boekmanzaal in the Stopera complex.

City Hall is architecturally the more functional side with municipal offices and the wedding chamber: Dutch marriages between any combination of sexes must have a ceremony in the Town Hall. For a (rather frightening) illustration of sea-level calculation, head for the glass tubes full of water and sculptured wall panel demonstrating the N.A.P., Normal Amsterdam Peil (normal sea level). ⊠ *Waterlooplein 22 or Amstel 3,*

See the ingredients Rembrant used to mix oil paints, as well as huge collection of etchings, at Museum het Rembrandthuis.

Centrum ☎ *020/625–5455* ⊕ *www.stopera.nl* ✉ *Tours €5.00* ⊘ *Mon.– Sat. 10–6; tours Sat. at noon or by arrangement; call 020/551–8103.*

㉖ **Pintohuis** (Pinto House). Scholar and grandee Isaac de Pinto escaped the
★ Inquisition in Portugal to become a significant investor in the Dutch East Indies Company in Amsterdam. He bought this Italian Renaissance–style house in 1651. It was grandly renovated by his son, together with architect Elias Bouwman, in the 1680s. In the 1960s it was almost demolished so that the street could be widened, but activist squatters saved the building. The interior is lushly decorated, particularly the painted ceilings by 17th-century master Jacob de Wit, with more recent additions by the entrance: spot the little cherub reading a book, a reference to the building's current manifestation as a public library. ✉ *Sint Antoniebreestraat 69, Centrum* ☎ *020/624–3833* ✉ *Free* ⊘ *Mon. and Wed. 2–8, Fri. 2–5, Sat. 11–4.*

㉞ **Portugese Synagoge** *(Portuguese Synagogue).* With Jerusalem's Temple of Solomon as inspiration, Elias Bouwman and Danield Stalpaert designed this noted synagogue between 1671 and 1675 for the Sephardic Jewish community, the first Jews to settle in the Netherlands. They were descendants of Spanish and Portuguese Jews (Sepharad is Hebrew for Iberian), escaping the inquisitions or forced conversion to Catholicism in the 15th and 16th centuries. On its completion it was the largest synagogue in the world, and its spare, elegantly proportioned wood interior has remained virtually unchanged through the centuries. It is still magically illuminated by hundreds of candles in two immense candelabrum during services. The buildings around the synagogue house the world-famous Ets Haim ("Tree of Life") library, one of the oldest

DID YOU KNOW?

Built between 1603 and 1611, the magnificent Zuiderkerk was originally a Protestant church, but now serves as an information center. It was designed by master builder Hendrick de Keyser, who was also responsible for the Noorderkerk and Westerkerk. Notice that the north and south facades are decorated in the so-called Amsterdam Renaissance style, a style very characteristic for the work of de Keyser.

still-functioning Jewish libraries in the world. ☒ *Mr. Visserplein 3, Centrum* ☎ *020/624–5351* ⊕ *www. esnoga.com* 🗖*€6.50* ☽ *Apr.–Oct., Sun.–Fri. 10–4; Nov.–Mar., Sun.–Thurs. 10–4, Fri. 10–2.*

31 Waterlooplein. Amsterdam's most famous flea market was once an area bordered by the Leper and Peat canals that often took the brunt of an overflowing Amstel River and therefore housed only the poorest of Jews. In 1886 it became the daily market for the surrounding neighborhood—a necessity, since Jews were not allowed to own shops at the time. It became a meeting place whose chaos of wooden carts and general vibrancy disappeared along with the Jewish population during World War II. And yet it still pro-

XXX IS FOR AMSTERDAM

Those XXX symbols you see all over town are not a mark of the city's triple-x reputation. They're part of Amsterdam's official coat of arms—three St. Andrew's crosses, believed to represent the three dangers that have traditionally plagued the city: flood, fire, and pestilence. The coat's motto (valiant, determined, compassionate) was introduced in 1941 by Queen Wilhelmina in remembrance of the February Strike in Amsterdam—the first time in Europe non-Jewish people protested against the persecution of Jews by the Nazi regime.

vides a colorful glimpse into Amsterdam's particular brand of pragmatic sales techniques. Its stalls filled with clothes, bongs, discarded electronics, and mountains of Euro knickknacks can be a battle—although sometimes a worthwhile one—to negotiate. ☒ *Waterlooplein, Centrum* ☽ *Mon.–Sat. 9–5.*

27 ★ Zuiderkerk *(South Church).* Gorgeous enough to have inspired both Sir Christopher Wren and giant of Impressionism Claude Monet, this famous church was built between 1603 and 1611 by Hendrick de Keyser, one of the most prolific architects of Holland's Golden Age (he chose to be buried here). It was one of the earliest churches built in Amsterdam in the Renaissance style and was the first in the city to be built for the (protestant) Dutch Reformed Church. In 1944 during the hunger winter, it was a morgue. The church's hallowed floors, under which three of Rembrandt's children are buried, are now the domain of the City Planning Office and are filled with detailed models of Amsterdam's ambitious future building plans. The church tower—a soaring accumulation of columns, brackets, and balustrades—is one of the most glorious exclamation points in Amsterdam; its bells are played every Thursday and it is open for climbing from April to September or by prior arrangement. ☒ *Zuiderkerkhof 72, Centrum* ☎ *020/552–7987* ⊕ *www.zuiderkerk.amsterdam.nl* 🗖*Free* ☽ *Mon.–Fri. 9–5, Sat. 12–4.*

WORTH NOTING

29 Gassan Diamonds. By the beginning of the 18th century, Amsterdam had a virtual monopoly in the diamond industry in Europe, so when diamonds were discovered in South Africa in 1869, there was a windfall for Amsterdam's Jewish communities, a third of whom worked in the diamond trade. Built in 1879, Gassan Diamonds was once home to the Boas diamond-polishing factory, the largest in the world, where 357 diamond-polishing machines processed 8,000–10,000 carats of rough

Eco Architecture

Dutch architecture is known for its creative approach to practical problems, and right now eco architecture (bringing environmental awareness to building design) is hot. With its focus on sustainability, the renewal of the Eastern Docklands and NDSM is a perfect example of this trend. Amsterdam's newest zone, IJburg—a complex of eight islands (seven of them created from scratch) that will eventually house 45,000 people—is a work in progress, but the combination of floating homes, eco-effective houses, and planning tussles between dense housing versus the need for green spaces, has sustainability at its core. The transformation of industrial spaces to cultural places just keeps on going. In 2012, the Annie MG Schmidt complex opens in Zeeburgeiland in and on top of two former sewage treatment silos. It's cutting-edge and incredibly clever.

diamonds a week. Today, Gassan offers polishing and grading demonstrations and free one-hour tours, in 27 languages, of the building and its glittering collection of diamonds and jewelry. ⊠ *Nieuwe Uilenburgerstraat 173, Centrum* ☎ *020/622–5333* ⊕ *www.gassandiamonds.nl* ☜ *Free* ☉ *Daily 9–5.*

25 **Montelbaanstoren** *(Montelbaans Tower).* Rembrandt loved to sketch this slightly leaning redbrick tower, which was built in 1516 as part of the city's defenses. In 1606, the ubiquitous Hendrick de Keyser oversaw the building of a new tower complete with clockworks that was known as "crazy Jan" by locals, since the time was never correct and the bells pealed at odd times. The year 1611 saw the tower embark on a lean too far, and with lots of manpower and ropes it was reset on a stronger foundation. Since 1878, it has housed the City Water Office. ⊠ *Oude Schans 2, Centrum* ☎ No phone.

QUICK BITES

The best place to view the Montelbaanstoren is from the patio of the crooked Café Sluyswacht (⊠ *Jodenbreestraat 1, Centrum* ☎ *020/625–7611*) overlooking Oudeschans. But beware of the slant. You don't want to tumble into the water after a few beers.

30 **Mozes und Aäronkerk** *(Moses and Aaron Church).* Landmarking the eastern corner of the Waterlooplein flea market, this structure once had a warehouse facade to disguise its function as a clandestine Catholic church. If this rarely used church could speak, it would name-drop the great philosopher Spinoza (it was built on the location of his birth house) and Liszt (it hosted a recital of his that he considered his all-time best). Originally built in 1649, it was rebuilt in 1841 by architect T. Suys the Elder, then refurbished in 1900. The name of the church refers to the figures adorning two gable stones of the original edifice, now to be seen in the rear wall. Today it functions as an adult education center. ⊠ *Waterlooplein 205, Centrum* ☎ *020/622–1305* ☉ *Hrs vary.*

2

THE WATERFRONT

Amsterdam was built on water—it's the source of the city's wealth and cultural history (although Rotterdam has long surpassed it as the world's busiest port). Before Centraal Station was built, the center of the city was open to the sea. International shipping routes ended here, sluicing bounty into the city via the Amstel and the man-made canals that loped around. With the massive development around the station and landmark buildings going up east, west, and north across the water (North being the city's most populous but least glamorous district), a shiny new Amsterdam is being built on the waterfront.

Directly to the west of Centraal Station are the Westerlijke Eilanden (Western Islands), which housed the heavy and polluting industries of the 17th century: shipbuilders, pickling factories, and smokehouses for fish. The old warehouses give this neighborhood a special "village within the city" feel. It borders one of the city's main green areas, the Westerpark, which runs parallel with the train lines coming out of Centraal Station. In the park, the Westergasfabriek ⇨ *(see Nightlife and the Arts)* is the place to go for funky international festivals, art cinema, clubbing and cafés, conferences, music, and experimental exhibits.

The opposite direction will bring you to the Eastern Docklands, also an area that has been completely redeveloped since the 1990s. Architectural highlights of this former squatters' paradise include the swoopy-roofed (like a wave) cruise-ship Passenger Terminal Amsterdam, the Muziekgebouw Aan 't IJ (Music Building on the IJ) ⇨ *(see Nightlife and the Arts)*, Amsterdam's amazing new library, the biggest in Europe, and some startling bridges and futuristic housing projects. The waterfront

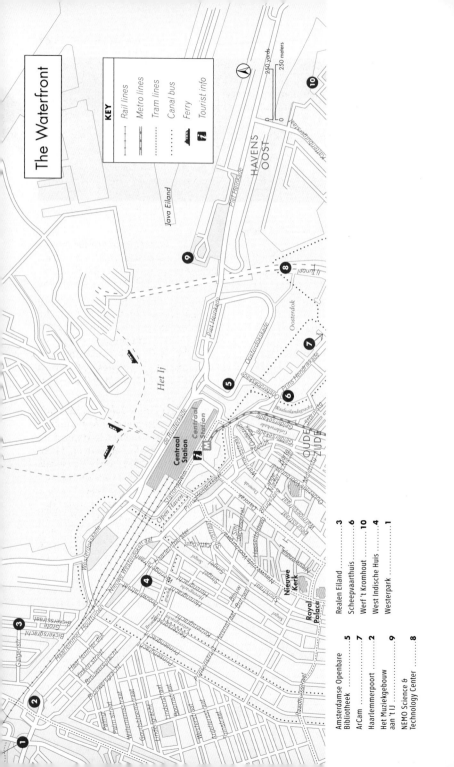

The Waterfront

KEY

- Rail lines
- Metro lines
- Tram lines
- Canal bus
- Ferry
- Tourist info

Java Eiland

HAVENS OOST

250 yards
250 meters

Het Ij

Centraal Station

IJ Tunnel

Oosterdok

OUDE ZIJDE

Nieuwe Kerk

Royal Palace

in Amsterdam North on the other side of the IJ, once a bleak industrial no-man's-land, is buzzing with new international art spaces, restaurants and clubs, and in 2011, a new architectural landmark, the EYE Film Institute Netherlands.

TRULY MOVING MUSIC

One of the most spectacular features of Amsterdam's Muziekgebouw aan 't IJ is the flexibility of its main auditorium. It has three movable walls, including an acoustic ceiling that can move up and down to allow notes to resonate from 1.5 up to 3.5 seconds at a time (a new musical record).

TOP ATTRACTIONS

❽ NEMO Science & Technology Center. Opened in 1997, this green copper-clad building designed by Renzo Piano—co-creator of the Pompidou Center in Paris—is an international architectural landmark: a ship's hull rising colossally out of the middle of the water, over the Coen Tunnel entrance to Amsterdam North. A rooftop café and summer "beach" terrace (*Boven*NEMO or above NEMO) offer a superb panorama of the area. It's worth a visit in the summer, just for the view.

There are five floors of fantastical, hands-on, high-tech fun from the giant bubbles on the ground floor to experiments in the wonder lab and interactive exhibitions like Teen Facts. Until the renovations of the Scheepvartmuseum are complete, the VOC replica ship is moored here for the passionate pirates in your party. ✉ *Oosterdok 2, Centrum* ☎ *020/531–3233* ⊕ *www.e-nemo.nl* ⊡*€12.50* ⊘ *Oct.–May, Tues.–Sun. 10–5; June–Sept., daily 10–5.*

❺ Openbare Bibliotheek Amsterdam *(Amsterdam Public Library).* Europe's biggest public library offers a multifarious collection of information to around 7,000 visitors per day. The €80 million building, designed by architect Jo Coenen, is staffed by 200 employees dressed in imaginative outfits created by fashion guru Aziz Bekkaoui. The "bieb," as locals call it, has a big theater, seminar and conference rooms, art spaces, and an extensive music library. A superb children's section is set below a terraced central lounge area. Park yourself in the comfy designer furniture and peruse a mind-boggling international magazine collection. With 1,200 desks, half of them with PCs connected to the Internet, you can study and surf in peace, for free. The seventh-floor La Place restaurant has an outside terrace with a spectacular view over the city. Amsterdam Conservatory is right next door with regular free recitals by students. ✉ *Oosterdokskade 143, Centrum* ☎ *020/523–0900* ⊕ *www. oba.nl* ⊘ *Daily 10–10.*

WORTH NOTING

❼ ARCAM. Architecture Centrum Amsterdam is dedicated to promoting modern Dutch architecture and organizes exhibitions, lectures, and tours (there's an extensive list of specialist tour companies and individuals on their Web site), and publishes a wide range of maps and guides both print and online, including ARCAM's selection of the contemporary essential for Amsterdam: 25 Buildings You Should Have Seen. Its swoopy and silver building has already become an architectural icon in

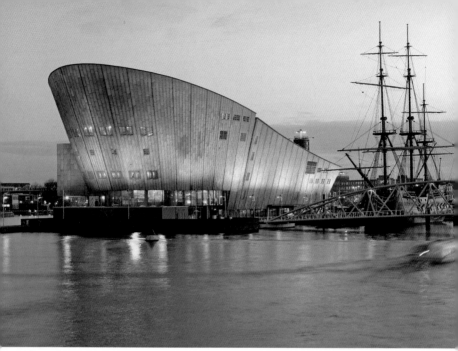

The Nemo Science Museum and a fun replica of an old VOC ship. Nemo was designed by starchitect Renzo Piano, of Centre Pompidou fame.

itself. ✉ *Prins Hendrikkade 600, Centrum* ☎ *020/620–4878* ⊕ *www.arcam.nl* ✉ *Free* ☉ *Tues.–Fri. 1–5.*

❷ Haarlemmerpoort. This Neoclassical gatehouse, rebuilt in 1840, was one of four entrances to Amsterdam until the mid-18th century. It has been variously used as a military post, train station, fire station, and a police station; in 1986 it was restored and converted into private apartments. A bit of a weird white elephant looming in a traffic crossing, it is a handy marker to find your way the Westerpark, one of the city's most hip and upcoming parks. ✉ *Haarlemmerplein 50, Jordaan.*

❾ Het Muziekgebouw aan 't IJ *(Music Building on the IJ).* Just 200 meters from Centraal Station and built on a peninsula on the IJ, this spectacular building's design (compliments of Danish architects 3XN) was based on the shape of a ship. Since opening in 2005, it has become a main concert hall for both classical and jazz fans: the black box jutting out is the legendary jazz venue, **Bimhuis**. The glass building is architecturally stunning with its ship's ramp entrance and the Zen-like simplicity of its three natural colors (concrete, black, and light maple wood). The floor-to-roof glass walls provide angular transparency and spectacular views into the building and out onto the IJ. Weather variations—clouds, rain, sunshine, and light— organically change the atmosphere inside. Its multifunctional main auditorium seats 725; a smaller auditorium seats 100 people, and foyers and extensive conference and catering facilities lure in business visitors who are not strictly here for the music. There are regular workshops for kids (ages 7+) in the educational **Klankspeel-tuin** (sound garden). Pay a lunchtime visit to chill out in café-restaurant Star Ferry and enjoy the waterfront terrace. ✉ *Piet Heinkade 1,*

Centrum ☎ *020/788–2000* ⊕ *www. muziekgebouw.nl.*

❸ **Realeneiland** (Reals Island). About a dozen blocks to the west of Centraal Station, there are three off-the-beaten-track islands built on landfill back in the 17th century. These Western Islands—known in Dutch as De Westelijke Eilanden—were constructed as a safe warehouse zone. The nautical ambience is particularly beloved by Amsterdammers, who all seem to have recreational boats, and other seafaring folk. From smallest island, Prinseneiland, follow the Galgenstraat (Gallows Street), which once offered a vista of bodies (or bits of bodies—sometimes the heads were placed elsewhere) on the town's gallows across the water. Bickerseiland is a jumble of modern housing, boats, and in the little farm, bunnies. Across the white wooden drawbridge, is Realeneiland, renowned for the little row of 17th-century merchant's houses with biblical gables on Zandhoek. "De Gouden Reael" is the name the governor general of the Dutch East Indies, Laurens Reael, gave to his house, now a waterside bar and restaurant. It wittily refers to his namesake; a golden real was a Spanish coin from the 16th century. Now a waterside café serving regional French cuisine, it's a perfect spot to raise a toast to the old days and watch boats sail along the Westerdok. ⊠ *Zandhoek 14Centrum* ✛ *follow Haarlemmerstraat/Haarlemmerdijk from Centraal Station and go under the railway tracks at Buiten Oranjestraat or at Haarlemmerplein.*

❻ **Scheepvaarthuis** *(Shipping Office).* With its extravagantly phantasmagoric zinc-roof detailing spilling over various sculpted sea horses, boat anchors, sea gods (Neptune and his four wives), dolphins, and even shoals of fish, this is one of Amsterdam's most delightful turn-of-the-20th-century structures. Built in 1912 to sport a suitably prow-shaped front, it was used as the headquarters for the major shipping firms that brought back all that booty from Java and the Spice Islands during the final Dutch colonial years. It's now a five-star hotel, the Grand Amarâth. The 20th-century master architects Piet Kramer, Johan van der May, and Michel de Klerk all contributed to the design of the building; their structure was one of the opening salvos by the fantastic Amsterdam School. After admiring all the ornamentation on the facade, amble around the sides to take in the busts of noted explorers, such as Barentz and Mercator, along with patterned brickwork and strutting iron tracery. Wander inside to check out the Seven Seas restaurant design, enjoy a drink at the classically restored bar, or book a private tour of the upper floors of the building, with its equally lavish interior. ⊠ *Prins Hendrikkade 108, Centrum* ☎ *No phone.*

🔟 **Werfmuseum 't Kromhout** *(Shipyard*
☪ *Museum Kromhout).* Started in
1757 by Kromhout, a ship's car-
penter whose name literally means
bent wood, this is one of Amsterdam's oldest functioning shipyards.
Almost 300 ships were built here
during its heyday in the late 19th
century. By the early 20th century,
Kromhout was producing the diesel
engines used by Dutch canal boats.
Boats and engines are still restored
here, so expect to shuffle your way
through wood shavings and inhale
the smells of tar, diesel, and varnish.

The mechanics tend to get particularly excited by the historical collection of 22 antique engines and will tell you all about them if given
a chance. ⊠ *Hoogte Kadijk 147, Centrum* ☎ *020/627-6777* ⊕ *www.
machinekamer.nl* ⌑ *€4.50* ☉ *Tues. 10–3, or by prior arrangements for
groups larger than 15.*

❹ **West Indische Huis** *(West Indies House).* These former headquarters of the
West India Trading Company (WIC) have major historical significance.
Although not as sovereign as the VOC, it was essentially given free rein
to trade on Africa's west coast, the Americas, and all the islands of the
West Pacific and New Guinea, and to oversee the infamous export of
70,000 slaves from West Africa to the Caribbean between 1626 and
1680. In these rooms, the decision was made to buy Manhattan for
60 guilders. Silver bullion, piled up by Piet Pieterszoon Hein (or Pieter
Pietersen Heyn), was collected here in 1628 after Piet won another of
his infamous sea battles. Now used as a center for the John Adams
Institute, by television production companies and a catering firm, you
can come into the courtyard of the building via its side entrance on
Herenmarkt to see the statue of Peter Stuyvesant. ⊠ *Herenmarkt 93–7,
Jordaan* ☎ *No phone.*

❶ **Westerpark.** Just beyond the Jordaan is one of contemporary Amster-
☪ dam's most cherished spaces. It's a park, first and foremost, with lawns,
playgrounds, water fountains, a fabulous designer paddling pool, and
a couple of tennis courts. Here you'll also find the sprawling terrain of
the city's old gas works—the Westergasfabriek. Cafés, galleries, clubs,
and a great arthouse cinema occupy the former industrial landscape
that has been lovingly detoxed, replanted, and refurbed, building by
building. And even more delightfully (and unlike the Vondelpark),
behind it lies some natural wilderness: two children's farms, a natural playground for kids, and some protected areas with nature walks
between them. ⊠ *Haarlemmerweg 8–10, JordaanAmsterdam* ⊕ *www.
westergasfabriek.nl.*

THE CANAL RINGS

Amsterdam has 165 canals, stretching for 75 km around the city with 1,500 bridges crossing them. The first were developed for defense and then transport, but in the 17th century came an original piece of town planning (and epic job-creation scheme) to deal with the need for expansion: a girdle of canals wrapping right round the city center.

The first phase of the construction of the Grachtengordel, or canal belt, began with the **Herengracht** (Gentlemen's canal) in 1612. This was followed some 50 years later with a second phase—the **Keisersgracht** (Emporer's canal) and **Prinsengracht** (Princes' canal). Developing from west to east (like a giant windshield wiper, according to historian Geert Mak), the innermost canal, the **Singel**, was widened and the main canals were intersected with radial canals like the **Brouwersgracht, Leliegracht,** and **Leidsegracht** (all of which are well worth a diversion). The grandest stretch of the grandest canal is supposedly along the Herengracht between Leidsestraat to the Amstel, which is known as the **Gouden Bocht** (golden bend). The Grachtengordel is quintessential Amsterdam. As you explore, keep in mind that when these impressive canal houses were built for the movers and shakers of the 17th-century Golden Age, home owners were taxed on their houses' width, not height. A double frontage and staircase (two adjacent lots) displayed wealth and prestige, as did the number of windows facing the canal, and ornate gables and decorative features (such as finely wrought railings). While there's considerable scrolling variation from one house to the next, creating that attractive higgledy-piggledy gabled skyline for which Amsterdam is famous, it's very harmonious, and from a historic point of view, remarkably intact. Sixteen hundred buildings in these canals have protected heritage status, and as of July 2010 the Canal Ring is officially on the UNESCO World Heritage List.

The marble-lined interiors are no less spectacular and surprisingly deep. Be sure to visit one of the canal-side museums to get a fuller

Lanskroon, a classic Amsterdam café on the Singelgracht and the Heisteegs, serves fantastic stroopwafels.

appreciation. Open Gardens Weekend (⊕ *www.opentuinendagen.nl*) in June and Open Monument Weekend (⊕ *www.openmonumentendag. nl*) in September offer additional chances to see inside properties rarely open to the public. Early morning, before the cruise boats churn up the water, can be a special time. Look out for the special Amsterdam light that turns the windows of the Keizersgracht and Herengracht lilac.

TIMING

A wander along one of these canals will provide some of the most memorable images of your trip, so allocate at least a morning or afternoon for exploring. If you don't want to go gable spotting in the rain, stick out a hand for the Stop/Go bus that trundles all the way round the Prinsengracht.

Numbers in the margin correspond to numbers on the Canal Rings map.

WESTERN CANAL RING

The section leading from the Brouwersgracht, where the grand canals start, to the Leidsestraat, includes fine views and excellent shopping opportunities, particularly south of the Rozengracht in the *negen straatjes* (nine little streets) that run between the canals. If you're planning to visit the Anne Frank House, make an early start or prebook your tickets or time slot online.

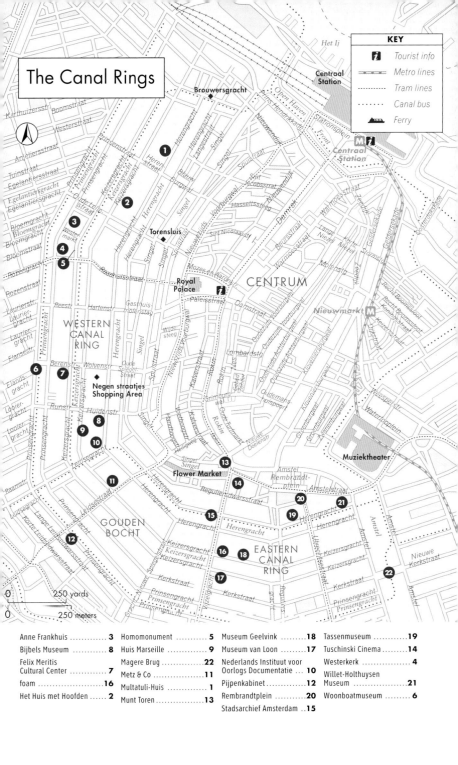

The Canal Rings

Het Ij

Centraal Station

Brouwersgracht

Open Haven

Torensluis

Royal Palace

CENTRUM

Nieuwmarkt

WESTERN CANAL RING

Negen straatjes Shopping Area

Muziektheater

Flower Market

GOUDEN BOCHT

EASTERN CANAL RING

Rembrandt-plein

Nieuwe Kerkstraat

0   250 yards

0   250 meters

Gables and Hooks

Amsterdam's famous neck gables. Keep an eye peeled for bell and step gables.

The gabled houses on the Canal Ring are Amsterdam's most picture-perfect historic feature. Starting in the 16th century, the different gable types were used to camouflage the end of sharp, pitched roofs and architectural idiosyncrasies. Gable variants include spout, step, neck, elevated neck, Dutch, bell, and cornice, and they often include splendid scrollwork and ornamentation. Styles came and went, so the type of gable can reflect how old a house is (provided they are both the same age; nowadays, sometimes the gable is saved and the house behind redeveloped). The Brouwersgracht (brewers' canal) has colorful facades harking back to Amsterdam's brewing trade with the towns of the Hanseatic League. Some gables include decorative panels that show what was being stored: grain, wood, gold, or coffee. Others have symbolic pictorial decorations and many carry the merchant family's shield. One thing all canal houses have in common is the hook in the gable, to which a pulley wheel and rope can be attached. This handy manual elevator system was developed from medieval shipping techniques; it's pretty impossible to move bulky goods up and down the precariously steep staircases found inside most Amsterdam houses. Boxes, pianos, couches or whatever are winched up using the rope and pulley, and hauled in through exceptionally wide removable windows. Keep your eyes peeled as you walk through the city and you may see a few Dutch movers in action.

TOP ATTRACTIONS

❸ **Anne Frankhuis** *(Anne Frank House).*
Fodor'sChoice   Anne Frank, one of the most
★   famous authors of the 20th century, wrote the inspiring story of a Jewish girl who died at age 15 after hiding with her family from the Nazis. In the pages of *The Diary of Anne Frank* (published posthumously in 1947 as *The Annex* by her father— the title she chose) the young Anne

> **INTERNATIONAL CELEBRITY**
>
> Anne's diary has been translated into more than 65 languages and has sold more than 30 million copies, making her the international celebrity she always dreamed of being.

recorded two increasingly fraught years living in secret in a warren of rooms at the back of this 1635 canal house. Anne Frank was born in Germany in 1929; when she was four her family moved to the Netherlands to escape growing anti-Jewish sentiment. Otto Frank operated a pectin business and decided to stay in his adopted country when the war finally reached the Netherlands in 1940. In July 1942 he took his wife and daughters, Anne and her sister, Margo, into hiding, and a week later they were joined by the Van Pels family: Auguste, Hermann, and their son, Peter. Four months later, dentist Fritz Pfeffer moved in.

The five adults and three children sought refuge in the attic of the rear annex, or *achterhuis*, of Otto's business in the center of Amsterdam. The entrance to the flat was hidden behind a hinged bookcase. Here, like many *onderduikers* ("people in hiding") throughout Amsterdam, Anne dreamed her dreams, wrote her diary, and pinned up movie-star pictures to her wall (still on view). Five trusted employees provided them with food and supplies. In her diary, Anne chronicles the day-to-day life in the house: her longing for a best friend, her crush on Peter, her frustration with her mother, her love for her father, and her annoyance with the petty dentist, who was called Dussel in her diary. In August 1944, the Franks were betrayed and the Gestapo invaded their hideaway. All the members of the annex were transported to camps. Anne and Margot died of typhoid in Bergen-Belsen a few months before the liberation. Otto Frank was the only survivor of the annex. Miep Gies, one of the friends who helped with the hiding, found Anne's diary after the raid and kept it through the war. Now, millions of children read it and its tale of humanity's struggle with fascism. ✉ *Prinsengracht 263-267, Centrum* ☎ *020/556–7105* ⊕ *www.annefrank.nl* 💶 *€8.50* ⊙ *Mar.–Sept., daily 9–9; Sept.–Mar., daily 9–7.*

BE AWARE   The line to get into the Anne Frank House is extremely long, especially in the summer. It moves (sort of) quickly, but it's best to arrive early or book tickets online to avoid the worst crowds.

❷ **Het Huis met de Hoofden** *(The House with the Heads).* The Greek dei-
★   ties of Apollo, Ceres, Mars, Minerva, Bacchus, and Diana welcome you—or rather busts of them do—to this magnificent example of Dutch Renaissance architecture, one of the three houses in Amsterdam with a side house, the forerunner of the double house. (The **Bartolotti House**, Herengracht 170–172 and De **Dolfijn** (The Dolphin), Singel 140–142 are the other spectacular examples.) This 1622 mansion is attributed

to architect Pieter de Keyser, son of the more famed Hendrick. One story attached to the house relates to a maid and a crew of burglars: as they emerged from some hiding place, she chopped off their heads one by one and then (maybe) married the seventh. In 2007 the mansion was bought by Joseph R. Ritman, owner of a world-famous collection of spirituality literature, the Hermetic Philosophy Library (open to the public at Bloemstraat 15); although this building is not open to the public yet, at some point in the future the library will be moved here. ⊠ *Keizersgracht 123, Centrum* ☎ *No phone* ⊕ *www. ritmanlibrary.nl.*

TOWERS BRIDGE

A bust of Dutch writer Multatuli holds a place of honor on the **Torensluis** *(Tower Bridge),* the oldest (and the widest) bridge in Amsterdam. It was originally built over a 17th-century sluice gate and bookended with towers. The rooms with barred windows that you see at the base of the bridge were used as a lockup for drunks and have now been turned into an art space called brug9. ⊠ *Singel between Torensteeg and Oude Leliestraat, Centrum.*

❶ Multatuli-Huis. This museum honors the beliefs and work (and continues the legacy) of Eduard Douwes Dekker (1820–87), aka Multatuli (from the Latin, meaning "I have suffered greatly"), who famously wrote *Max Havelaar, or the Coffee Auctions of the Dutch Trading Company,* a book that uncovered the evils of Dutch colonialism. The son of an Amsterdam sea captain, Dekker accompanied his father to the Dutch Indies (Indonesia) and joined the Dutch Civil Service. After years of poverty and wandering, in 1860 he wrote and published his magnum opus, denouncing and exposing the colonial landowners' narrow minds and inhumane practices. Today, Dutch intellectuals and progressive thinkers respect him mightily. ⊠ *Korsjespoortsteeg 20, Centrum* ☎ *020/638–1938* ⊕ *www.multatuli-museum.nl* ☉ *Weekends noon–5 and Tues. 10–5. Closed Sat. in July.*

❹ Westerkerk *(Western Church).* Built between 1602 and 1631 by (you ★ guessed it) Hendrick de Keyser, the Dutch Renaissance–style Westerkerk was the largest Protestant church in the world until St. Paul's Cathedral in London was built in 1675. Its 85-meter tower, the tallest in the city, is topped by a gaudy copy of the crown of the Habsburg emperor Maximilian I, who gave Amsterdam the right to use his royal insignia in 1489 in gratitude for support given to the Austro-Burgundian princes.

The church is renowned for its organ and carillon (there are regular concerts). The carillon is played every Tuesday between noon and 1 by a real person (a carillonneur) but is automated at other times with different songs tinkling out on the quarter hour, day and night (it drives some locals nuts). Anne Frank described the tunes in her diary. Rembrandt, who lived on Rozengracht 188 during his poverty-stricken last years, and his son, Titus, are buried (somewhere) here. Rembrandt's posthumous reputation inspired some very surreal television three centuries later, when a body was unearthed that was mistakenly thought to be his. While exposed to the glare of the news cameras, the skull turned to dust. The Westertoren (Westerkerk Tower) is a fun climb from April to the end of November. ⊠ *Prinsengracht 281 (corner of Westermarkt), Centrum* ☎ *020/624–7766* ⊕ *www.westerkerk.nl* ⊙ *Apr.-Oct., Mon.-Fri. 11–3; July and Aug. also open on Sat. 11–3* 🖾 *Free for interior; €6 for Westertoren.*

WORTH NOTING

8 **Bijbels Museum** *(Bible Museum).* Although this museum does indeed have a massive collection of Bibles—as well as exhibits with archaeological finds from the Mid-

> **ENGRAVED IN STONE**
>
> A line from a poem, engraved on one of the marble triangles of the Homomonument reads "Naar vriendschap zulk een mateloos verlangen" (Such an endless desire for friendship). This text is an extract from the poem "To a Young Fisherman" by Jacob Israël De Haan (1881–1924).

dle East and models of ancient temples that evoke biblical times—what probably draws more people is the building itself and its beautifully restored interior and garden. The two classical canal houses built in 1662 by Philips Vingboons were known as the Cromhout houses after their first owner, rich merchant Jacob Cromhout. (The crooked leg on the gable stone is a play on his name, which means bent wood in Dutch.) Highlights include the kitchens, garden rooms and garden, and 18th-century painted ceilings by Jacob de Wit. ⊠ *Herengracht 366–368, Centrum* ☎ *020/624–2436* ⊕ *www.bijbelsmuseum.nl* 🖾 *€8* ⊙ *Mon.-Sat. 10–5, Sun. 11–5.*

7 **Felix Meritis Cultural Center.** The recently restored home of the former Felix Meritus Society (happiness through achievement), is a typical building of the Enlightenment, and indeed its Neoclassical architecture arose in the year of the French Revolution, 1789. It housed a society dedicated to the study and promotion of economics, science, painting, music, and literature. It has an observatory and concert hall (Robert and Clara Schumann performed here twice). After the dissolution of the society in 1888, it was owned by printers, occupied by the Communist Party, and then became a venue for performing arts under the name Shaffytheater. It's now a European Centre for Arts, Culture, and Science (and that's Culture with a very big C). Readings, panels, and discussions are hosted here with the aim of promoting international cultural exchange. Drop by to pick up a program or a coffee in its café with huge windows overlooking the canal. ⊠ *Keizersgracht 324, Centrum* ☎ *020/623–2321* ⊕ *www.felixmeritis.nl.*

5 **Homomonument** *(Homosexual Monument).* This, the world's first memorial to persecuted gays and lesbians, designed by Karin Daan, was unveiled in 1987. Three huge triangles of pinkish granite—representing past, present, and future—form a larger triangle. On May 4 (Remembrance Day), there are services here commemorating the homosexual victims of World War II, when thousands were killed (the 50,000 sentenced were all forced to wear pink triangles stitched to their clothing). Flowers are laid daily for lost friends, especially on the descending triangle that forms a dock of sorts into Keizersgracht. The points of the triangles point to the Anne Frank House, the National Monument on Dam, and the COC Center, the gay-and-lesbian organization founded in 1946, discreetly called the Center of Culture and Leisure Activities. Nearby is the kiosk housing **Pink Point** (☎ *020/428–1070* ⊕ *www.pinkpoint. org*) the best source of information on gay and lesbian Amsterdam. It is open daily 10–6. ⊠ *Westermarkt, Centrum.*

⑨ Huis Marseille *(Marseille House).* This cutting-edge, contemporary photography museum is housed in six exhibition rooms of a 17th-century canal house originally owned by a rich merchant with business interests in Marseille (the warehouse at number 403 also belonged to the house). The widest possible range of genres is covered with new shows every three months. They also have around 2,000 photographic books which can be consulted in the library. ⊠ *Keizersgracht 401, Centrum* ☎ *020/531–8988* ⊕ *www.huismarseille.nl* ⊠ *€5* ⊙ *Tues.–Sun. 11–6.*

⑪ Metz & Co. When the New York Life Insurance Company opened this building in 1891, its soaring six floors brought a touch of Manhattan to Amsterdam's canals—literally, as architect J. van Looy had also designed the company's lofty skyscraper in Manhattan. By 1908, the Metz department store had converted the offices into showcases for Liberty fabrics and De Stijl teapots. The cupola on the roof was designed by Gerrit Rietveld in 1933, and on the sixth floor is a café with dazzling views, grubby windows, and surprising sandwich prices. "We are Luxury" is the byline for the store; perhaps they should change it to "We are jolly expensive, have a ban on taking photographs, and not very friendly." ⊠ *Leidsestraat 34, Centrum* ☎ *020/520–7020* ⊙ *Mon. 11–6, Tues.–Sat. 9:30–6, Sun. noon–6, café open same hrs.*

⑩ Nederlands Instituut voor Oorlogs Documentatie *(Netherlands Institute for War Documentation).* Established in 1945, this institute has collected vast archives of documents, newspapers, 100,000 photos, and 50,000 books relating to the occupation of World War II. This is where Otto Frank donated his daughter's diary. More recently, the institute has expanded its sights to take in the period between World War I to present day, with particular emphasis on the former colony of Indonesia. It also houses the Center for Holocaust and Genocide Studies. Its collections are increasingly being digitized and available online. Although the reading room is not really designed for the merely curious, you will be welcomed if you want to pursue academic or family-related research; requests must be submitted in writing. The French Renaissance–style exterior was inspired by Chateau Chenonceau in the Loire. ⊠ *Herengracht 380, Centrum* ☎ *020/523–3800* ⊕ *www. niod.nl* ⊙ *Mon. 1–5:30, Tue.–Fri. 9–5:30, closed weekends.*

⑫ Pijpenkabinet *(Pipe Cabinet).* Considering Amsterdam's rich history of tobacco trading and its population's long tradition of rolling their own "shag," there should actually be a much larger museum dedicated to this subject. Perhaps this museum could relate such local

POLITICAL PUNCH

The release of the Netherlands Institute for War Documentation's government-commissioned report on the role of a Dutch battalion (Dutchbat) in the 1995 fall of Srebrenica in the former Yugoslavia and the ensuing mass murder of 8,000 Muslim men resulted in Prime Minister Wim Kok stepping down and dissolving his Cabinet.

DID YOU KNOW?

The iconic Magere Brug captures the essence of quaint, watery Amsterdam, so it's no wonder that it appears in a number of films, including *Diamonds are Forever*. This pedestrian- and bicycle-only bridge is spectacularly lit at night with 1,200 lightbulbs, so it's the perfect destination for an after-dinner stroll.

2

facts as how urine-soaked tobacco was hailed as an aphrodisiac in the 16th century, or how "tobacco-smoke enema applicators" were used until the mid-19th century in attempts to revive those found unconscious in the canals, and how Golden Age painters employed tobacco and its smoke as a metaphor for the fleeting nature of life. But as things stand, there is only this collection of more than 20,000 pipe-related items. You might also want to check out the library or buy a pipe in the Smokiana shop. ✉ *Prinsengracht 488, Centrum* ☎ *020/421–1779* ⊕ *www.pijpenkabinet.nl* ⌸ *€5* ⊙ *Wed.–Sat. noon–6.*

QUICK BITES

Along Westermarkt's southerly side is an excellent fish stall where you can sample raw herring or smoked eel (if you're so inclined). An equally traditional Dutch way of keeping eating costs down is to pack one's belly with pancakes. There've been a few new openings, but the **Pancake Bakery** (✉ *Prinsengracht 191, Centrum* ☎ *020/625–1333*) remains one of the best-known places in Amsterdam to try them, with a menu that offers a near infinite range of topping possibilities—from the sweet to the fruity to the truly belly-gelling powers of cheese, pinapple, and bacon. **Foodism** (✉ *Oude Leliestraat 8, Centrum* ☎ *020/627–6424* ⊕ *www.foodism.nl*) is a hip place for sandwiches and smoothies. **Spanjer en Van Twist** (✉ *Leliegracht 60, Centrum* ☎ *020/639-0109)* is only five minutes from the Anne Frank House for lunch under the trees.

6 **Woonboatmuseum** *(Houseboat Museum)*. There are around 2,000 houseboats in Amsterdam (and one especially for cats—the Poezenboot [Cat Boat] asylum that floats opposite Singel 38). The converted 1914-built sailing vessel, the *Hendricka Maria*, provides a glimpse into this unique lifestyle. It almost feels as if you are visiting Grandma—there's even a special child-play zone. ✉ *Prinsengracht opposite No. 296, Centrum* ☎ *020/427–0750* ⊕ *www.houseboatmuseum.nl* ⌸ *€3.50* ⊙ *Mar.–Oct., Tues.–Sun. 11–5; Nov.–Feb., Fri.–Sun. 11–5.*

EASTERN CANAL RING AND REMBRANDTPLEIN

The Eastern end of the Canal Ring that leads to the Amstel is a bit more commercial with two busy pitches, Leidseplein and Rembrandtplein, close by. The richest merchants originally settled on the Herengracht, a section known as the Gouden Bocht (Golden Bend). The elaborate gables, richly decorated facades, colored marbles, and heavy doors create an imposing architecture that suits the bank headquarters of today as well as it did the patrons of yore.

TOP ATTRACTIONS

22 **Magere Brug** *(Skinny Bridge)* Of Amsterdam's 60-plus drawbridges, the

Fodor's Choice ★

Magere Brug is the most famous and provides gorgeous views of the Amstel and surrounding area. It was purportedly first built in 1672 by two sisters living on opposite sides of the Amstel who wanted an efficient way of sharing that grandest of Dutch traditions: the *gezellig* (socially cozy) midmorning coffee break. Walk by at night when it's spectacularly lit and often drawn up to let boats pass through. Many

CLOSE UP

Amsterdam's Hofjes—the Historic Almshouses

Claes Claeszhofje

Hidden behind innocent-looking gateways throughout the city center, most notably along the main ring of canals and in the Jordaan neighborhood, are some of Amsterdam's most charming houses. There are over 40 *hofjes* (little courtyards surrounded by almshouses), mainly dating back to the 18th century when the city's flourishing merchants established hospices for the elderly. Their philanthropy was supposed to be rewarded by a place in heaven. But be warned (and be prepared for disappointment): today's hofje residents like their peace and quiet, and often lock their entrances to keep out visitors. The most notable examples on the Grachtengordel can be viewed only on open days.

Begijnhof *(Beguine Court)*. Here, serenity reigns just feet away from the bustle of the city. The Begijnhof is the tree-filled courtyard of a residential hideaway where women lived a spiritual and philanthropic life from

1150 onwards. Documents from the 14th century mention the "Beghijn-huis" with some rules and regulations for membership. They were simple: no hens, no dogs, and no men. Free lodging was provided in return for caring for the sick and educating the poor.

No. 34 is one of two remaining wooden houses in the city following 15th-century fires that consumed three-quarters of the city. The small **Engelsekerk** (English Church) dates from 1400. Its pulpit panels were designed by a young Piet Mondriaan. After the Alteration of 1578 the church was relinquished to Protestants (and used by the Pilgrim Fathers visiting in 1607). When senior Begijn Cornelia Arents died in 1654, she said she'd rather be buried in the gutter of the Begijnhof than in the—now Protestant—church. Her wish was granted the following year when her remains were moved; look for the granite slab and plaque on the wall between the church and lawn. The replacement chapel, **Begijnhof-Kapel** (Begijn-Chapel) was designed by Philips Vingboons and approved by the city (as was the mode), provided it didn't look like a church from the outside. ⊠ *Entrances on the north side of Spui and on Gedempte Begijnensloot opposite Begijnensteeg, Centrum* 🕑 *Begijnhof-Kapel Mon. 1–6:30, Tues.–Fri. 9–6:30, weekends 9–6.*

The Begijnhof is by far the most famous hofje, but there are a few other little gems to explore that are generally open. The **Sint Andrieshofje** (⊠ *Egelantiersgracht 105–141, Jordaan*), built in 1617, is the oldest courtyard almshouse in Amsterdam.

The **Claes Claeszhofje** (⊠ *Junction of Egelantiersstraat 28–54, Eerste Egelantiersdwarsstraat 1–5, and Tuinstraat 35–49, Jordaan*) is two joined hofjes: the Zwaardvegershofje (sword makers' hofje) and the three-house hofje founded in 1616 by the Anabaptist draper Claes Claesz Anslo (note his coat of arms atop one entry). Today's tenants are artists and music students. Don't miss the **Huis met de Schrijvende Hand** ("House with the Writing Hand"), topped by a six-stepped gable.

The **Zevenkeurvorstenhofje** (⊠ *Tuinstraat 197–223*) was founded around 1645, though the houses standing today are from the 18th century, and the **Karthuizerhof** (⊠ *Karthuizersstraat 21–131, Jordaan*) was founded in 1650 and has a courtyard with two 17th-century pumps.

On the Prinsengracht, between the Prinsenstraat and the Brouwersgracht, are two hofjes very close to one another. The **Van Brienen** (Prinsengracht 85–133, closed to the public)

The Karthuizerhof and a happy occupant.

and **De Zon** (Prinsengracht 159–171, open weekdays 10–5) both have plaques telling their stories.

For a moment of peace, visit the **Suykerhoff-hofje** and take in its abundantly green courtyard. These houses opened their doors in 1670 to Protestant "daughters and widows" (as long as they behaved and exhibited "a peace-loving humor") and provided each of them with free rent, 20 tons of turf, 10 pounds of rice, a vat of butter, and some spending money each year. If only the same were done today. ⊠ *Lindengracht 149–163, Centrum.*

Seeing the city by boat is an unforgettable experience.

replacements to the original bridge have come and gone, and this, dating from 1969, is just the latest. ✉ *Between Kerkstraat and Nieuwe Kerkstraat, Centrum.*

⑰ Museum van Loon. Once home to one of Rembrandt's most successful
★ students, Ferdinand Bol, this house and its twin, No. 674 next door (home of the Kattenkabinet; a five-room museum dedicated to cats), were built in 1672 by Adriaan Dortsman and extensively remodeled in the 18th century by Abraham van Hagan and his wife, Catherina Tripp, whose names are entwined in the ornate brass balustrade on the staircase. It was occupied by the Van Loon family from 1886 to 1960. After extensive restoration to take it back to its glory days of the 18th century, it was opened as a museum in the 1970s. The elegant salons include many Van Loon portraits and possessions, including paintings known as *witjes,* illusionistic depictions of landscapes and other scenes. The symmetrical garden is a gem. Facing the rear of the house, the recently restored Grecian-style coach house holds exhibitions and in the future (hopefully) will serve teas. ✉ *Keizersgracht 672, Centrum* ☎ *020/624–5255* ⊕ *www.museumvanloon.nl* ✉ *€7* ⊙ *Wed.– Mon. 11–5. Closed Tues.*

⑮ Stadsarchief Amsterdam *(City Archives).* Established in 1914, the city's
★ archives comprise millions of maps, drawings, prints, books, photography, and film about Amsterdam; a staggering 32 km worth, the biggest in the world. But (like the Rijksmuseum), there's a manageable highlights taster with 300 of the "most attractive, unusual, valuable, and moving" items on permanent display in the Treasury, the city's former bank vaults that look like the tomb of an Egyptian pharaoh. The epic

checkerboard building, completed in 1926 and named in honor of its theosophist architect K. P. C de Bazel, is also fascinating and infused with its creator's religious beliefs. In theosophy, a building is an art form that can express a higher message using mathematical principles to achieve total harmony. Have deep thoughts over lunch in the café or browse the excellent on-site bookstore, which sells every available Amster-relevant publication. The additional exhibitions (for which there is usually a small charge) are also terrific. ✉ *Vijzelstraat 32Centrum* ☎ *020/572–0202* ⊕ *www.stadsarchief.amsterdam.nl* 🎟 *Free* ⏰ *Tue.–Sat. 10–5, Sun. 11–5. Closed Mon.*

🔞 **Tuschinski Cinema.** Although officially the architect of this "Plum Cake"—as it was described when it first opened in 1921—was H. L. De Jong, the financial and spiritual force was undoubtedly Abram Icek Tuschinski (1886–1942), a Polish Jew who after World War I decided to build a theater that was "unique." And because interior designers Pieter de Besten, Jaap Gidding, and Chris Bartels came up with a dizzying and dense mixture of Baroque, Art Nouveau, Amsterdamse School, Jugendstil, and Asian influences, it is safe to say that he achieved his goal. The frescoes of elegant women by Pieter Den Besten were only discovered in 2000 under layers of paint. It began as a variety theater welcoming such stars as Marlene Dietrich, but it soon became a cinema, and to this day watching movies from one of the extravagant private balconies remains an unforgettable experience—especially if you are in the "love seats" with champagne. Sobering note: Tuschinski died in Auschwitz. ✉ *Reguliersbreestraat 26–28, Centrum* ☎ *0900–1458* ⊕ *www.tuchinski.nl.*

🔞 **Willet-Holthuysen Museum.** Here's a rare chance to experience what it was
Fodor'sChoice like to live in a gracious mansion on the Herengracht in the 18th cen-
★ tury. In 1895, widow Sandrina Louisa Willet-Holthuysen bequeathed this house to the city, along with all of its contents. It was actually built in 1687 but has been renovated several times and is now under the management of the Amsterdam Historisch Museum. Take an hour or so to discover its interiors and artwork, including a sumptuous ballroom and *cabinet des merveilles* (rarities cabinet). Complete the Dutch luxury experience by lounging in the French-style garden in the back. ✉ *Herengracht 605, Centrum* ☎ *020/523–1822* ⊕ *www.willetholthuysen.nl* 🎟 *€7* ⏰ *Weekdays 10–5, weekends 11–5.*

WORTH NOTING

🔞 **FOAM.** Dutch photographers such as Inez van Lamsweerde, Vinoodh Matadin, Hendrik Kerstens, and Rineke Dijkstra are world renowned and they've all had shows here. This photography museum also holds regular international large-scale exhibitions from fashion (Kate Moss) to heritage, alongside smaller shows for up-and-coming artists. The shop, café (with Wi-Fi), small library, and museum are all housed in a dramatic contemporary interior. ✉ *Keizersgracht 609, Centrum* ☎ *020/551–6500* ⊕ *www.foam.nl* 🎟 *€8 plus additional exhibition charge* ⏰ *Daily 10–6, Thur. and Fri. 10–9.*

🔞 **Munt Toren** *(Mint or Coin Tower).* This tower received its name in 1672, when French troops occupied much of the surrounding Republic, and

Amsterdam was given the right to mint its own coins here for a brief two-year period. The spire was added by Hendrick de Keyser in 1620, and the weather vane on top in the shape of a gilded ox is a reference to the calves market close by: Kalverstraat. The guardhouse, which now houses a touristy Dutch porcelain shop, has a gable stone above its entrance, which portrays two men and a dog in a boat. This is a symbolic representation of the city, where warrior and merchant bonded together by loyalty—that would be the dog—are sailing toward the future. ⊠ *Muntplein, Centrum.*

18 **Museum Geelvinck.** Don't miss this canal-house museum with an unusual entrance on the Keizersgracht. Access is via the tradesmen's entrance (the old coach house) and then through the lovely garden to the rear of the house, which has its front door on the golden bend of the Herengracht. Built in 1687 for Albert Geelvinck and his much younger wife, Sara Hinlopen, it's been the home for Amsterdam's most notable families. The interiors are reconstructions though no less interesting for that. Enthusiastic curators will be only too happy to fill you in on some of the details. There are regular concerts in the garden—the Sweelinck musical collection is housed here. ⊠ *Keizersgracht 633, Centrum* ☎ *020/639–0747* ⊕ *www.museumgeelvinck.nl* ⊠ *€7* ☉ *Daily 11–5. Closed Tues. and Thurs.*

20 **Rembrandtplein** (Rembrandt Square). Smaller than the Leidseplein, this touristy square (which used to be the city's butter market) is the focus for hotels, restaurants, cafés, and nightlife venues. After recent refurbishment, the statue of the man himself in the middle of the square looks even more imposing. Café Schiller at No. 26 is an Art Deco haven from the scrum. ⊠ *One block south of the Amstel River Centrum.*

19 **Tassenmuseum** *(Handbag Museum).* Housed in a building from 1664, this unusual museum has the largest collection (some 4,000) of handbags and purses in the world plus, regular exhibitions highlighting the work of contemporary designers. There are beautiful examples going back several centuries and even a few man bags—check out the goatskin model with 18 secret pockets that could be buckled to the belt of a 16th-century merchant-about-town. And what's not to love about a leather clutch bag in the shape of a luxury liner complete with funnels (it was a freebie for first-class passengers on the maiden voyage of the Normandie) or a 19th-century wallet with embroidered love poem? All of this is the collection of one woman, Hendrijke Ivo, and it all started with a tasseled bag bought in Norwich, England. There are workshops for kids, a café overlooking a lovely garden, and (of course) a shop. ⊠ *Herengracht 573, Centrum* ☎ *020/524–6452* ⊕ *www.tassenmuseum. nl* ⊠ *€7.50* ☉ *Daily 10–5.*

THE JORDAAN AND THE LEIDSEPLEIN

The sock-shaped district to the west of the Canal belt is the Jordaan—pronounced Yore-*dahn*, the city's most singular neighborhood. Directly below it, marking the midpoint of the Grachtengordel is the bustling Leidseplein, Amsterdam's vortex for the performing arts, with street performers, music venues, theaters, and jazz bars.

The Leidseplein is the tourist center of the city and, like Rembrandt-plein, is surrounded by cheap eateries and bars, their terraces packed with visitors and shoppers set for the Leidsestraat. Cafés like Reijnders (⊠ *Leidseplein 6*), Eijlders (⊠ *Korte Leidsedwarsstraat 47*), and the Art Deco American Hotel (keep an eye out for the statue of the woodcutter in the trees nearby) are more authentic, less tacky respites.

If you walk down the alleyway to the right of the white Stadsschouw-berg theater (⊠ *Leidseplein 26*), past the Melkweg and Sugar Factory (nighttime music/theater/happening venues) and over the Leidsegracht, you have reached the southern perimeter of the Jordaan. Built to house canal-belt construction workers in the 17th century, the city's smellier industries such as tanning and brewing were also banished here. Living conditions were overcrowded and squalid (its 1895 population was 80,000; now it's a mere 14,000) and the inhabitants gained a reputation for rebelliousness and community spirit. In the 1950s, this reached mythical proportions—aided by the nationally popular local singer Johnny Jordaan and others who depicted an idealized vision of a poor but tight-knit and socially aware community in songs like Geef mij maar Amsterdam (essentially, you can keep Paris, Amsterdam is finer in every way) that are still belted out in the cafés Twee Zwaantjes and Café Nol. You can pay homage to him on the Elandsgracht by Johnny Jordaanplein opposite the Houseboat Museum, where there's a group of statues. This was one of several canals filled in for sanitary reasons in the 19th century. At the other end of the street is De Looier Indoor Antiques Market (⊠ *Elandsgracht 109*). North of the Rozengracht, the

DID YOU KNOW?

Amsterdam has 165 canals, stretching for 75 km around the city with 1,500 bridges crossing them. Sixteen hundred buildings in these canals have protected heritage status and, as of July 2010, the Canal Ring is officially on the UNESCO World Heritage List. As you explore, keep in mind that when these impressive canal houses were built for the movers and shakers of the 17th-century Golden Age.

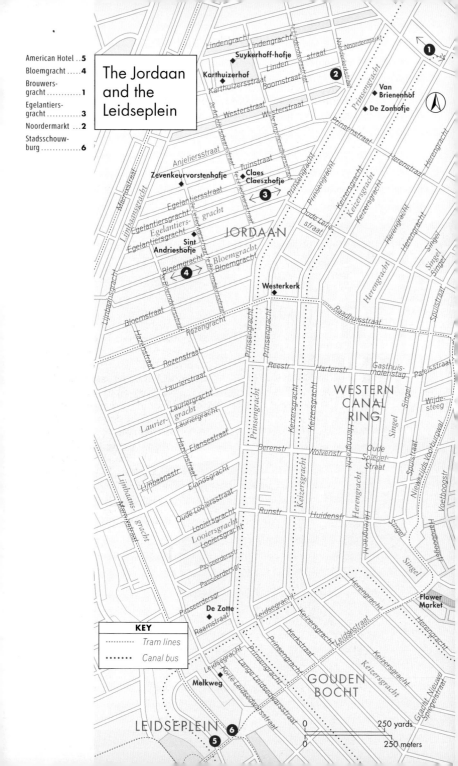

The Jordaan and the Leidseplein

Lindengracht · Lindengracht · straat

Noorderkerkstraat · Noordermarkt ❶

Suykerhoff-hofje

Karthuizerhof

Karthuizersstraat · Linden · straat

Boomstraat

◆ Van Brienenhof

◆ De Zonhofje

Westerstraat · Westerstraat

Prinsenstraat

Prinsengracht

Herengracht

Anjeliersstraat

Tuinstraat

◆ Claes Claeszhofje

Zevenkeurvorstenhofje ◆

Egelantiersstraat ❸

Egelantiersstraat

Egelantiersgracht · gracht

Egelantiersgracht · Egelantiersgracht

Prinsengracht · Prinsengracht

Keizersgracht · Keizersgracht

Herengracht · Herengracht

Singel · Singel

Sint Andrieshofje

JORDAAN

Oude Leliestraat

Bloemgracht · Bloemgracht ❹

Bloemgracht · Bloemgracht

◆ Westerkerk

Raadhuisstraat

Bloemstraat

Rozengracht

Rozenstraat

Reestr · Hartenstr

Gasthuis-molensteeg · Paleisstraat

WESTERN CANAL RING

Singel · Wijde steeg

Laurierstraat

Lauriergracht · gracht

Laurier- · Lauriergracht

Berenstr · Wolvenstr

Oude Spiegel-Straat

Nieuwezijds Voorburgwal

Elandsstraat

Lijnbaansstr.

Elandsgracht

Runstr · Huidenstr

Herengracht

Singel

Voetboogstr

Oude Looiersstraat

Looiersgracht

Looiersgracht

Passeerdersgr.

Passeerdersgracht

Herengracht

Singel

Flower Market

De Zotte

Passeerdersstr · Raamstraat

Leidsegracht

Leidsegracht · Leidsestraat

Kerkstraat

Keizersgracht · Leidsestraat

Herengracht

KEY

· · · · · · · · *Tram lines*

• • • • • • • *Canal bus*

Melkweg

Lange Leidsedwarsstraat

Korte Leidsedwarsstraat

Prinsengracht

GOUDEN BOCHT

Keizersgracht

Gracht · Nieuwe Spiegelstraat

LEIDSEPLEIN ❺ ❻

0 ___ 250 yards

0 ___ 250 meters

Jordaan becomes even more scenic. Although rough-and-tough times continued into the 1970s, it's now one of the trendiest parts of town. But in many ways, the Jordaan will always remain the Jordaan, even though its narrow alleys and leafy canals are now a wanderer's paradise lined with quirky boutiques, idiosyncratic architectural details, excellent restaurants, and galleries, particularly in the southern end.

Numbers in the text correspond to numbers in the margin and on the Jordaan and Leidseplein map.

TOP ATTRACTIONS

❹ **Bloemgracht** *(Flower Canal).* Lined with suave "burgher" houses of
★ the 17th century, this canal has been termed the "Herengracht of the Jordaan" (Gentlemen's Canal of the Jordaan). It was a center for paint and dye manufacturers, which made sense, because the Jordaan was populated with Golden Age artists: Rembrandt ran a studio here. Although modern intrusions have been made, Bloemgracht is still proudly presided over by "De Drie Hendricken," three houses set at No. 87 to 91 owned by the Hendrick De Keyser heritage organization, with their gable stones for the farmer, a city settler, and a sailor. ⊠ *Between Lijnbaansgracht and Prinsengracht, Jordaan.*

❶ **Brouwersgracht** *(Brewers' Canal).* Regularly voted Amsterdam's most
Fodor's Choice beautiful street, this wonderful canal at the northern border of the
★ Jordaan is lined by residences and former warehouses for brewers, fish processors, and tanneries who traded here in the 17th century when Amsterdam was the "warehouse of the world." Without sacrificing the ancient vibe, most of the buildings have been converted into luxury apartments. Of particular note are Nos. 204–212 and their trapezium gables. At No. 162, there are two dried fish above the door. This decoration on a metal screen was the forerunner of the gable stone denoting occupation. The canal provides long views down the grand canals that are perfect for photo-ops. The Brouwersgracht runs westward from the end of the Singel (a short walk along Prins Hendrikkade from Centraal Station) and forms a cap to the western end of the Grachtengordel. On top of the old canal mansions dotting the Brouwersgracht are symbols referring to the breweries that used this waterway to transport their goods to thirsty drinkers hundreds of years ago. ⊠ *Jordaan.*

❸ **Egelantiersgracht** *(Eglantine Canal).* Named for the flowering "eglantine" (the floral names for canals in the district are certainly at odds with the fragrance emanating from them in their early days), this is one of the loveliest canals in the area. Many of the houses along this canal and the streets around it were first occupied by Golden Age painters and artisans, including the legendary mapmaking Blaeu family. Hidden here is the **St. Andrieshofje,** famous for its Delftware entryway. Certainly not hidden (it is usually jammed with people) is the famed **Café 't Smalle,** (on the corner of the Prinsengracht). This ivy-covered *proeflokaal* (tasting house), complete with waterside terrace, was where Pieter Hoppe began his *jenever* distillery in 1780, an event of such global significance that 't Smalle is recreated in Japan's Holland Village in Nagasaki. ⊠ *Between Lijnbaansgracht and Prinsengracht, Jordaan.*

Catch a show and laugh out loud at the Boom Chicago Lounge.

QUICK BITES

The city's best apple pie can be had at **Winkel** (⊠ *Noordermarkt 43, Centrum* ☎ *020/623-0223*). For a funky setting and perhaps an inspired designer sandwich, head to **Finch** (⊠ *Noordermarkt 5, Centrum* ☎ *020/626-2461*). If you're more thirsty than hungry, try the brown café **Café Chris** (⊠ *Bloemstraat 42, Centrum* ☎ *020/624-5942*), which has been pouring beverages since 1624. Its coziness is taken to absurd lengths in its tiny men's bathroom, whose urinal position outside the door means that pranksters can easily shock you out of your reveries with a quick pull of the flusher. Be warned.

❷ Noordermarkt *(Northern Market).* In 1620, as the Jordaan expanded, city planners decided to build a church at this end of town for poorer residents. The **Noorderkerk** (Northern Church) designed by Hendrick de Keyser and completed after his death by his son Pieter, was built on egalitarian lines in the form of a Greek cross (four equal arms) with the pulpit in the middle. Until 1688 the surrounding square, Noordermarkt, was a graveyard whose residents were moved to make room for a market, and the commerce is still notable. On Mondays, there's a flea market, with a textile market on Westerstraat, and on Saturdays, there's a popular organic farmers' market with a general market along Lindengracht. There are excellent eating opportunities around the square, including a foodies' favorite, Bordewijk (⊠ *Noordermarkt*). Other restaurants on Westerstraat, including **De Buurman** (⊠ *Westerstraat 30, Centrum* ☎ *020/425–0788*) are top-notch. ⊠ *Bounded by Prinsengracht, Noorderkerkstraat, and Noordermarkt, Centrum.*

WORTH NOTING

⑤ **Eden Amsterdam American Hotel.** This landmark was designed by Willem Kromhout in 1902. He grafted Neo-Gothic turrets, Jugendstil gables, Art Deco windows, and a charming freestyle clock tower onto a proto–Amsterdam School structure. Its famed Art Deco–style Café Americain, where Mata Hari held her wedding reception, went from bohemian to being boycotted when it banned hippies in the '60s. It's the perfect place for a spot of tea. ✉ *Leidsekade 97, Jordaan* ☎ *020/556–3000* ⊕ *www.edenamsterdamamerican.com/.*

⑥ **Stadsschouwburg** *(Municipal Theater)*. After burning down and being rebuilt several more times, the current Neo-Renaissance facade that dominates Leidseplein, with its lushly Baroque horseshoe interior, was created in 1890. The nation's theater scene was somewhat staid until 1968, when, during a performance of the *Tempest*, the actors were showered with tomatoes. The nationwide protest, the "tomato campaign," showed people's discontent with the established theater's lack of social engagement. It resulted in subsidies for newer theater groups—many of which now form the old guard who regularly play here. Today, Dutch theater is dynamic, strongly physical and visual, with an often hilariously absurdist sense.

Although the majority of the programming is in Dutch, there's also a constant stream of visiting theater and dance companies. The International Theater & Film Books store downstairs next to the entrance also comes highly recommended by theater lovers. The Uitburo, where you can buy tickets for all cultural events, is also located here; pick up a free copy (in Dutch) of the going-out newspaper *Uitkrant*. ✉ *Leidseplein 26, Jordaan* ☎ *020/624–2311* ⊕ *www.ssba.nl; www.theaterandfilmbooks.com.*

QUICK BITES

Intellectuals and media types hang out at café **De Balie** (✉ *Kleine Gartmanplantsoen 10, Museum District* ☎ *020/553–5151* ⊕ *www.debalie.nl*). Americans will feel right at home at the hilarious improv café and **Boom Chicago Lounge** (✉ *Leidseplein 12, Museum District* ☎ *020/423–0101 tickets* ⊕ *www.boomchicago.nl/en*). This recently renovated upstairs space allows people to enjoy a decent dinner before seeing Boom's later evening show. In summer there is a terrace option. **Wildschut** (✉ *Roelof Hartplein 1–3, Museum District* ☎ *020/676–8220*) one of Amsterdam's first grand cafés, is an elegant respite after culture or shopping.

THE MUSEUM DISTRICT

The Museumplein, which is the heart of the Museum District in the Old South district of the city, offers a solid square mile of Western culture—from the state art collections and Golden Age treasures of the Rijksmuseum, to 19th-century artists at the Van Gogh Museum, through the 20th century and beyond at the Stedelijk Museum, to the hallowed halls of the Concertgebouw, one of the most famous concert halls in the world.

But if this cultural Valhalla isn't really your thing, the vast expanses of green on the modern Museumplein and romantic tree-lined avenues and lakes of Vondelpark are perfect places for people-watching, while the city's best upmarket fashion emporia on the PC Hooftstraat and antiques shops along Nieuwe Spiegelstraat are everything a shopaholic (or window version) could wish for.

It's always been a plush district. At the end of the 19th century, the city wanted a zone for luxury housing here but was dithering on how to develop it even as the cultural institutions were being put in place: the Rijksmuseum (1885), the Concertgebouw (1886), and the Stedelijk (1895). Eventually the decision to create an open space was agreed. In 1973, the Van Gogh Museum joined the square. The past few years have seen some well-publicized cultural chaos with delays and confusion over the redevelopment of the Rijksmuseum and Stedelijk, but finally the scaffolding is coming down and it looks like they will be worth the wait.

There are a couple of interesting diversions for the architecturally curious around the park. If you enter via the gate on the Nassaukade, look up to your right. That building with the jutting gold capsule is the work of supercool architect Rem Koolhaas in a not-so-SuperDutch moment. Roemer Visscherstraat 20–30a is a stretch of housing illustrating seven

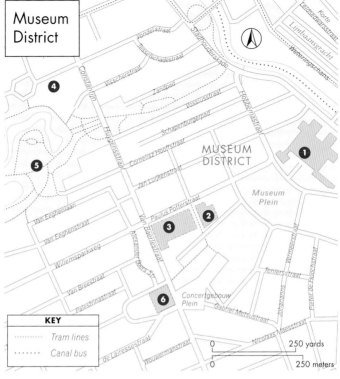

national architectural styles from German romantic to English cottage built in 1894.

TIMING

Doing all three museums is probably achievable in a morning as the both the Stedelijk and Rijksmuseum are in highlights mode until the main buildings reopen (and the Stedelijk is going to win that race), but it doesn't allow much time to linger and will depend on the queues. Visit on a Wednesday and you can sandwich in a free lunchtime concert at the Concertgebouw.

Numbers in the text correspond to numbers in the margin and on the Museum District map.

TOP ATTRACTIONS

Concertgebouw *(Concert Building).* This globally acclaimed concert hall ★ has been home to the Royal Concertgebouw Orchestra, one of the world's greatest, since 1892 and has welcomed an endless stream of top international artists. With a Viennese classicist facade and golden lyre at its peak, this sumptuous example of Neo-Renaissance style, designed by Al van Gendt, is music mecca to more than 800,000 visitors per year. There are two concert halls, and on Wednesdays, from September to June, you can attend a free lunchtime concert in one of them and take in your surroundings at the same time. Tours (generally in English) of

Even though the Rijksmuseum is being renovated, it's still possible to view masterpieces like Rembrandt's *The Night Watch.*

the building take place on Mondays from 5 to 6 and on Sundays from noon to 1 and cost €10. ⊠ *Concertgebouwplein 2–6, Museum District* ☎ *0900/671–8345 box office* ⊕ *www.concertgebouw.nl.*

QUICK BITES

For Concertgebouw-goers, a handy pre- or postconcert dining option is **Brasserie Keyzer** (⊠ *Van Baerlestraat 96, Museum District* ☎ *020/671–1866*), which can do a three-course dinner of brasserie favorites in an hour for music lovers. Other neighborhood options worth making a small detour for include **Spring** (⊠ *Willemsparkweg 177, Museum District* ☎ *020/675–4421* ⊕ *www.restaurantspring.nl*) Nip into the Neoclassical **Hollandsche Menege** (the oldest riding school in the Netherlands; ⊠ *Vondlestraat 140*) and enjoy a cup of tea in one of Amsterdam's best-kept secrets. Inspired by the famous Spanish Riding School in Vienna, and recently declared a national monument, the building's café is open to the public and overlooks the riding arena where classes are regularly held.

❹ ★ Eye Film Institute Netherlands. In December 2009, four Dutch film organizations, including the Filmmuseum, joined forces to form one sector-wide institute. In 2011 they'll move to the new building across the harbor designed by Delugan Meissl Associated Architects. Until then their home is an elegant 19th-century pavilion in the Vondelpark, where they screen a great collection of art-house classics with Wednesday-afternoon performances for kids, and the permanently packed Vertigo café with terraces overlooking the park. There are outdoor sunset performances in the summer. The library collections (⊠ *Vondelstraat 69-71*) cover the whole of cinematic history, from the earliest hand-tinted movies up to recent digital productions. ✉ *Vondelpark 3, Museum District* ☎ *020/589–1400* ⊕ *www.eyefilm.nl* 🎟 *Free* ⊙ *Library: weekdays (except Wed.) 1–5.*

① **Rijksmuseum** *(State Museum).* Designed by P. J. H. Cuypers in the late 1880s, the Rijksmuseum is a magnificent turreted building that glitters with gold leaf and is textured with sculpture—a fitting palace for a national art collection. It is home to Rembrandt's *The Night Watch*, Vermeer's *The Kitchen Maid*, and world-famous masterpieces by Steen, Ruisdael, Brouwers, Hals, Hobbema, Cuyp, Van der Helst, and their Golden Age ilk. During renovations (until 2012–13), there's a highlights exhibition in the Philips Wing where you can see all these. When the museum reopens, you can look forward to more than 150 rooms of paintings, sculpture, and objects with Western and Asian roots, dating from the 9th through the 19th century. The bulk of the collection is of 15th- to 17th-century paintings, mostly by Dutch masters, as well as drawings and prints from the 15th to the 20th century. Take your entrance ticket to Café Cobra on Museumplein (the Rijksmuseum has no catering) for a 15% discount on the menu. ■TIP➜ Don't leave the country without visiting the mini-museum at Schiphol Airport (✉ *Holland Boulevard between piers E and F behind passport control* ☎ *020/653–5036* 🎟 *Free* ⊙ Weekdays 7 AM–8 PM). ✉ *Stadhouderskade 42; entrance during renovations: Jan Luijkenstraat 1, Museum District* ☎ *020/674–7000* ⊕ *www.rijksmuseum.nl* 🎟 *€12.50* ⊙ *Daily 9–6. Library, Print Room, and Reading Room: Tues.–Sat. 10–5. ID required.*

Fodor's Choice ★

QUICK BITES
The Rijksmuseum doesn't have a café but show your entrance ticket at the **Cobra Café** (✉ **Hobbemastraat 18, Museum District** ☎ **020/470-0111** ⊕ www.cobracafe.nl) across Museumplein to get a 15% discount off anything on the menu. Don't leave before checking out the bizarre bathrooms in the basement.

③ **Stedelijk Museum of Modern Art.** The scaffolding is finally off at the Stedelijk, following a massive refurbishment of this wedding-cake Neo-Renaissance structure built in 1895. The futuristic addition by globally acclaimed local architects Benthem/Crouwel is known around town as "the bathtub" and incorporates a glass-walled restaurant. After World War II the Stedelijk rapidly collected more than 100,000 paintings, sculptures, drawings, and prints, as well as photography, graphic design, applied arts, and new media. Works by 20th-century modernists such as Chagall, Cézanne, Picasso, Monet, and Malevich live alongside the vast postwar melange of CoBrA—including Appel and Corneille; American Pop artists like Warhol, Johns, Oldenburg, and Liechtenstein; abstract Expressionists such as de Kooning and Pollock; and contemporary

KRAMER'S BRIDGE

Architectural buffs shouldn't miss the 1925 bridge crossing Singelgracht on the Leidsestraat. Its swoopy Amsterdam School style was designed by Piet Kramer (1881-1961), along with 220 other Amsterdam bridges. For more information on Amsterdam's historic bridges, visit ⊕ www.bmz. amsterdam.nl.

German Expressionists including Polke, Richter, and Baselitz. Displays of Dutch essentials like De Stijl school (including the amazing *Red Blue Chair* that Gerrit Rietveld designed in 1918 and Mondriaan's 1920 *Composition in Red, Black, Yellow, Blue, and Grey*) are complemented by large retrospectives or themed programs, featuring current hotshots on the art scene. ✉ *Paulus Potterstraat., Museum District* ☎ *020/573–2911* ⊕ *www.stedelijk.nl* 💶 *€12.50* ⊙ *Daily 10–6.*

② **Van Gogh Museum.** Amsterdam's most popular museum opened its doors

Fodor'sChoice in 1973. It's a remarkable, light-infused space, based on a design by

★ famed De Stijl architect Gerrit Rietveld, venerating the short, certainly not sweet, but highly productive career of everyone's favorite tortured 19th-century artist. First things first: Vincent was a Dutch boy, so his name is not pronounced like the "Go" in Go-Go Lounge but rather like the "Go" uttered when one is choking on a whole raw herring. The collection's roots trace directly back to brother Theo van Gogh, Vincent's artistic and financial backer. The 200 paintings and 500 drawings on display here begin in 1880, when Van Gogh was 27, and end in 1890, when he took his own life. The *Potato Eaters,* the series of *Sunflowers,* and landscapes such as *Irises* and *Wheatfield with a Reaper* are some of Van Gogh's most famous pieces, but his love affair with Japonisme and some remarkable portraits are also included. A bonus of the Van Gogh Museum is that it holds temporary exhibits of other important 19th-century artists and collections of art, graphic design, photography, and sculpture related to Van Gogh's development as a painter in its modern oval extension, which opened in 1999 and is connected to the main galleries by an underground walkway. No retail opportunity is passed up in the museum shop that occupies an ever expanding space. ✉ *Paulus Potterstraat 7, Museum District* ☎ *020/570–5200* ⊕ *www. vangoghmuseum.nl* 💶 *€14* ⊙ *Sat.–Thurs. 10–6, Fri. 10–10.*

⑤ **Vondelpark.** On sunny days, Amsterdam's "Green Lung" is the most

☺ densely populated section of the city. Vondelpark is *the* place where sun is worshiped, joints are smoked, beer is quaffed, picnics are luxuriated over, bands are grooved to, dogs are walked, balls are kicked, lanes are biked, jogged, and rollerbladed on, and bongos are bonged. By evening, the park has invariably evolved into one large outdoor café. The great thing about this park is that, as long as you stay relaxed and go with the flow, you can dress however, hang however, and do whatever. A mysterious man danced around the park for years on 1970s silver roller skates, wearing silver body paint and a silver G-string (even in winter), with shaved legs and chest, headphones, and a silver cap with propeller, and nobody batted an eyelid.

In 1865 the Vondelpark was laid out as a 25-acre "walking and riding park" for residents of the affluent neighborhood rising up around it. It soon expanded to 120 acres and was renamed after Joost van den Vondel, the "Dutch Shakespeare." Its naming was explained in the 1945 guidebook for Canadian Liberators (*Dutch on so many levels*): "We hardly ever seem to allow a great man to be great in his lifetime but we honor him copiously when he is dead. This prevents them from becoming conceited and it doesn't cost much to name a park or street after them." Landscaped in the informal English style, the park is an

The Van Gogh Museum holds temporary exhibitions in the modern oval extension, which is connected to the main galleries by an underground walkway.

irregular patchwork of copses, ponds, children's playgrounds, and fields linked by winding pathways. The park's focal point is the open-air theater, which offers free summer entertainment from Wednesday through Saturday. Kids and adults always get a kick out of the flock of parakeets—apparently the progeny of two escaped pets—that live here year-round. You can also rent Rollerblades at the **Vondeltuin Rent-a-Skate** (⊠ *Vondelpark 7, Museum District* ☎ *06/2157–5885* ⊕ *www.skatedokter.nl*). If your kids are teeners, join the Friday Night Skate crowd that takes over the city's streets in summer, meeting at the Film-museum at 8 PM. Other forms of specialized exercise to be found in the park include spontaneous tai chi and group meditation (usually dotted around the park).

Over the years a range of sculptural and architectural gems have made their appearance in the park. Picasso even donated a sculpture, *The Fish,* on the park's centenary in 1965, which stands in the middle of a field to deter football players from using it as a goalpost. The terraces of the **Blue Teahouse,** a rare beauty of functionalist Nieuw Bouw archi-tecture, built beside the lake in 1937, are packed throughout the day, starting with dog walkers in the early morning to clubbers by night. ⊠ *Stadhouderskade, Museum District.*

OFF THE
BEATEN
PATH

Amsterdamse Bos (Amsterdam Woods). The largest of Amsterdam's parks covers almost a thousand acres and is located a few miles south of the city in the suburb of Amstelveen. It incorporates 137 km (85 mi) of footpaths and 51 km (32 mi) of bicycle paths traversed by 50 bridges—many designed in the early-20th-century Amsterdam School style with characteristic redbrick and sculpted-stone detailing. The area was planted and constructed from 1934 onward, as a job creation scheme under the motto "five years' work for a thousand men" and it ended up providing jobs for 20,000 people during the Depression. There are wide recreational fields, a boating lake, the impressive Olympic Bosbaan rowing course (overlooked by the terraces of grand café De Bosbaan), and numerous playgrounds and water play areas for toddlers. A popular family attraction is an organic goat farm with a playground and lunchroom, a sunny terrace, and lots of chickens hopping about between the goats. Your kids can feed other kids—the four-legged kind—milk from a bottle, and cuddle bleating babies in the barn. The soft ice cream is made entirely of goat's milk (which does not contain lactose), and homemade goat cheese is on sale. It takes about 30 minutes by bike from the Vondelpark.

Coming out of the southern exit of the park, take a left onto the Amstelveenseweg and follow this busy road under the highway on the bicycle path until you reach the *Bezoekerscentrum* (visitor center) for the park on the right. Public transport to the Amsterdamse Bos is plentiful. For example, Buses 170 and 172 run from Leidseplein to Van Nijenrodeweg, opposite the visitor center. The Museum tram (⊕ *www. museumtramlijn.nl*) passes through on Sundays from Easter to October between 11 and 5:30; get on at Haarlemmermeer Station. There's a nice 15-minute boat trip (⊕ *www.rederij-oeverloos.nl*) that leaves from the pancake house Boerderij Meerzicht to beaches on the other side of the Nieuw Meer. You can (of course) also explore by bike; rent one at the entrance of the Amsterdamse Bos from June through August (*P020/644–5473*). Maps, suggested routes, and signposting are plentiful throughout the park. For example, follow the signs to the **Grote Vijver** (Big Lake) to hire kayaks and pedal boats from April through September (*P020/645–7831*).

Visit Bezoekerscentrum (Visitor Center) (✉ *Bosbaanweg 5, Amstelveen* ☎ *020/545–6100,* ⊕ *www. www.amsterdamsebos.nl*) to learn about natural history and the management of the woods, open daily noon–5. If you didn't pack your own lunch, the **Boerderij Meerzicht** (✉ *Koenenkade 56, Amstelveen* ☎ *020/679–2744* ⊕ *www.boerderijmeerzicht.nl*) is a traditional Dutch pancake house, with a petting zoo and playground for the kids. For the goat farm, follow the blue signs past Boerderij Meerzicht to **Geitenboerderij "De Ridammerhoeve"** (✉ *Nieuwe Meerlaan 4, Amstelveen* ☎ *020/645–5034* ⊕ *www.geitenboerderij.nl*).

2

THE PIJP

Named for its dirty narrow streets and even narrower houses, De Pijp (The Pipe) began at the end of the 19th century as a low-income neighborhood for workers with cheaply built housing to match. Today it is *the* up-and-coming bohemian part of town.

Many streets in this neighborhood are named after painters, including main thoroughfare Ferdinand Bolstraat, for Rembrandt's former pupil who escaped to the grand canals (and what is now the Museum van Loon) when he married money. A Dutch institution started on this street in 1941 when baker J. I. De Borst took the name of it for his shop (and then had a brain wave about selling food from automatic dispensers); he called it FEBO house. From the 1890s through the early 1990s, cheap rents attracted poor families, market hawkers, students, artists, and wacky radicals, causing a common comparison with Paris's Latin Quarter. From his De Pijp grotto, the writer Ferdinand Bordewijk depicted Amsterdam during World War I as a "ramshackle bordello, a wooden shoe made of rock"; Piet Mondriaan began formulating the revolutionary art of De Stijl in an attic studio on Ruysdaelkade (No. 75); Eduard Jacobs sang absurd, sharply polemical sketches of the neighborhood's pimps, prostitutes, and disenfranchised heroes that figure in the Dutch musical cabaret called *kleinkunst* (small art), with national icons like Freek de Jonge and Hans Teeuwen. The Amsterdam School diamond quarter is an interesting slice of history and the multiwindowed former Royal Asscher Diamond Company on Tolstraat 127 (note the names of surrounding streets: Saffiersstraat for sapphires, Smaragstraat for emeralds, etc.) that housed factory workers. De Pijp is also the territory of urban planner and philanthropist Samuel Sarphati who is commemorated in the park (named after him) with a statue.

The Heineken Brewery attracted the first Spanish guest workers to the neighborhood during the early 1960s. Though they no longer brew here, you can still indulge in the Heineken Experience. Later, waves of guest workers from Turkey and Morocco and citizens from the former

Shop like the Dutch at the Albert Cuypstraat Market.

colonies of Surinam and Indonesia revitalized the area around Albert Cuypstraat with (much-needed) culinary diversity. By the 1980s, De Pijp was a truly global village, with more than 126 nationalities *in situ*. Due to be completed by 2015, construction for a new underground Metro line has literally ripped through this area. That said, De Pijp remains a prime spot for cheap international eats and pub-crawling at local bars and cafés. *Numbers in the text correspond to numbers in the margin and on the Pijp map.*

TIMING

Dinner here, with an hour or so wandering before and a bit of barhopping after, is a good way to taste the vibe of the district. Or visit the market in the morning followed by lunch or a picnic.

TOP ATTRACTIONS

❷ Fodor's Choice ★ **Albert Cuypmarkt** *(Albert Cuypstraat Market)*. More than 100 years old, the Albert Cuypmarkt is one of the biggest and busiest street markets in Europe. Like the majority of street names in De Pijp, it is named after a Golden Age painter. From Tuesday to Saturday, thousands of shoppers throughout the city flock to its 268 stalls selling fruit and vegetables, fish (live lobsters and crabs), textiles, and fashion, with a decades-long waiting list for a permanent booth. Things can get dramatic—if not occasionally violent—at 9 every morning on the corner of Sweelinckstraat 1, where the lottery for that day's available temporary spaces takes place. ⊠ *Albert Cuypstraat between Ferdinand Bolstraat and Van Woustraat, De Pijp* ⊗ *Mon.–Sat. 9–6 (but often earlier if the weather is bad).*

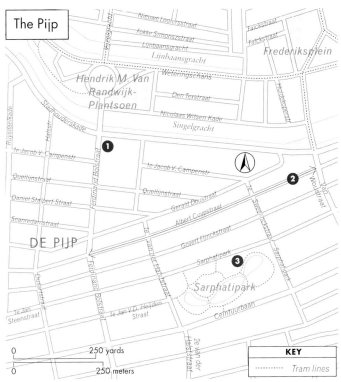

The Pijp

KEY

·········· *Tram lines*

The best multicultural snacks can be found around the Albert Cuypmarkt. If you want to keep things cheap and speedy, then try Surinamese cuisine at **Albina** (✉ *Albert Cuypstraat 69, De Pijp* ☎ *020/675–5135*). Fill up on the roti, rice, or noodle dishes. If you've got a sweet tooth, go directly to the kitschy and kid-friendly **De Taart van m'n Tante** (✉ *Ferdinand Bolstraat 10, De Pijp* ☎ *020/776–4600*), for fantastical cakes.

❶ **Heineken Experience.** Founded by Gerard Heineken in 1863, the Heineken label quickly became one of the world's most famous (and popular) beers. It's no longer brewed here, though the Heineken horse-drawn dray clip-clops across town with kegs. The original brewery has now been transformed into the "Heineken Experience," an interactive center that offers tours of the facilities. Everything from vast copper vats to beer-wagon shire horses are on view, and if you've ever wanted to know what it feels like to be brewed and bottled, the virtual reality ride Brew U will clue you in. Others may want to exercise their privilege of drinking multiple beers in a very short time. (Note: this tour is open only to visitors over the age of 18.) ✉ *Stadhouderskade 78, De Pijp* ☎ *020/523–9666* ⊕ *www.heinekenexperience.com* 💶 *€15* 🕙 *Daily 11–7.*

Fodor's Choice
★

CLOSE UP

Multicultural Holland

The face of Holland has changed dramatically since World War II. New arrivals have created a melting-pot society, and today the Netherlands is one of Europe's most ethnically diverse lands. But many don't realize the country is merely continuing a long tradition.

The first immigrants started arriving in the 17th century, during the Netherlands' Golden Age. While the gulden was pouring into Holland, the rest of Europe struggled with poverty and high unemployment. At the time, around half the people in the city were first-generation migrants. Regardless of what they thought of all these foreigners, the pragmatic Dutch tolerated them because they realized they were vital for keeping the economy moving. The country also gained a reputation as a haven for refugees, and at various times offered shelter to Portuguese and German Jews, French Huguenots, and the Pilgrim Fathers.

In the 20th century, things stepped up a gear. Funded by Marshall Aid, the Dutch economy experienced unprecedented growth in the 1950s and 1960s. Labor was needed, and migrant workers were invited. Initially they came from Italy, Greece, and Spain; then in large numbers from Morocco and Turkey. Today there are around one million Muslims in Holland—about 6% of the population. At the same time, the dismantling of the Dutch empire meant new arrivals from ex-colonies such as Surinam and Indonesia.

More recently, refugees arrived from war-torn Somalia. Then, since the country joined the European Union in 2004, a new wave has flooded in from Poland, Romania, and other points east. However, despite the nation's outwardly tolerant face, there are discontented rumblings. Many view the influx of different cultures as a threat to the traditional "Dutch" way of life. Theo van Gogh's brutal murder by a Dutch Moroccan youth for "blasphemy," caused huge shock waves. In the 2010 elections, there was a shift away from liberal parties in the Netherlands, as in England, and the rise of the PVV (Party for Freedom) and its flamboyant anti-Islam leader Geert Wilders is viewed with some trepidation.

WORTH NOTING

❸ **Sarphatipark.** This miniature Bois de Boulogne was built by and named after the noted city benefactor Samuel Sarphati (1813–66), whose statue graces the central fountain. With its paths undulating along trees, ponds, and expanses of grass, this park can be considered a big square rather than a small park but it's a perfect place to picnic on everything you picked up at the Albert Cuypmarkt. ⊠ *Bounded by Ceintuurbaan and Sarphatistraat, De Pijp.*

EAST OF THE AMSTEL

Compared with many parts of the city, there's a gracious and spacious feel to the Plantage with wide boulevards, parks, and elegant 19th-century architecture similar to the Museum District. It's a nice wander with a handful of family attractions and some excellent museums.

Its earliest roots are in the 17th century, when the area was divided into 15 parks and it was a recreational zone for the wealthy. Rare plants brought back on VOC ships were taken to the **Hortus Botanicus**, one of the oldest botanical gardens in the world, where famous botanists like Linnaeus researched. On the corner of the Linnaeusstraat (the street where Theo van Gogh was murdered), the **Tropenmuseum** provides insight into different cultures. Top draw in the area is **Artis Zoo** and its Neoclassical aquarium built in 1882, which you can also appreciate from the roadside.

Opposite the zoo is the marvelous **Verzetzmuseum** (Resistance Museum). There are other poignant reminders that from the late 19th century up to the Second World War, this was a neighborhood for wealthier Jewish families. In little Wertheim park is the **Auschwitz memorial** with its engraved message: *Nooit Meer* (Never Again). After German occupation in 1941, Jews were forbidden to assemble in public places, and the **Hollandse Schouwburg** became the Jewish theater where weddings (banned from the Town Hall) could take place. There's a film of one of the last in the exhibition upstairs. When the Germans requisitioned the theater in 1942, Jews were gathered here to be sent to their death. Between 1941 and 1944, 104,000 Jews were deported from the Netherlands; 1,169 survived.

Along the Amstel itself, the enormous **Hermitage Museum** has been a big cultural hit since it opened in 2009 with artworks direct from its base in Russia.

Cycling to village of **Ouderkerk aan de Amstel** (45 minutes away along the river) is a great bike trip. Pick up the river opposite the Stopera.

The left bank (the Hermitage side) is quieter, past rowers, fishermen, munching cows and De Zwaan windmill, with a good view over the water of the Riekermolen windmill where Rembrandt sketched. The village itself includes ancient churches, the Portuguese Jewish Cemetery where Spinoza's family is buried and the enthusiastically curated Museum Ouder-Amstel about the area. If you return down the other side, you'll pass a couple of imposing 17th-century summer houses, including the **Wester-Amstel** (Amsteldijk-Noord 55), which is open from May to October, with an outside sculpture garden and period-authentic chickens (Hollandse Blauw: delicious) pecking away on their own little island.

> **HERON ALERT**
>
> Artis Zoo apparently has one of the biggest breeding colonies of voluntarily captive rare grey herons in the country—one in three of the last surviving "wild" night herons hangs out here at feeding time. News travels fast about good grub, as a semi-tame group of Egyptian geese has now arrived, staking out their turf and steadfastly refusing to travel south in winter. After gorging themselves on Artis grub for half the year, they voluntarily shift over to the Amsterdam canals for summer pickings. So much for ancient migration patterns.

TIMING

Families happily spend all day in the zoo, but a morning may suffice to see the Jewish sites and the Verzetsmuseum with lunch by the Amstel before tackling the Hermitage.

TOP ATTACTIONS

6 **Artis** *(Amsterdam Zoo).* Short for *Natura Artis Magistra* (Nature Is the Teacher of the Arts), Artis was continental Europe's first zoo and is the world's third oldest. Built in the mid-19th century, the 37-acre park is home to a zoo, a natural-history museum and zoological research center, a planetarium with regular films (not just about space), a butterfly pavilion, a geological museum and an aquarium with 500 species of freshwater and saltwater fish, and a fun cross-section of an Amsterdam canal complete with eels and dumped bicycles. Several animal quarters (the poor lions . . .) are showing their age but Artis has redevelopment plans. It's a good family day out, and the zoo and all its museums are accessible on a single ticket. The Artis Zoo Express canal boat from Rederij Lovers combines a visit to the zoo with an (expensive) hour-long canal tour (in 15 languages) and goes from Centraal Station. ⊠ *Plantage Kerklaan 38-40, East of the Amstel* ☎ *020/523–3400* ⊕ *www.artis.nl* 🖃 *€15–18.50* ☻ *Daily Apr.–Oct. 9–6; Nov.–Mar. 9–5; ZOOmeravond (each Saturday evening in July and August) till sunset.*

1 **Hermitage Amsterdam.** Taking advantage of 300 years of historical links between Amsterdam and St. Petersburg, Professor Mikhail Piotrovsky, director of the State Hermitage Museum in St. Petersburg, and Ernst Veen, director of the Nieuwe Kerk museum in Amsterdam, chose this spot on the Amstel for a new outpost. In 2009, the final refurbishment stage of the Amstelhof was complete and there's certainly a lot of it, with huge, high white interiors and smaller side rooms connected by long unadorned corridors. The allocation for exhibition space is

Fodor's Choice
★

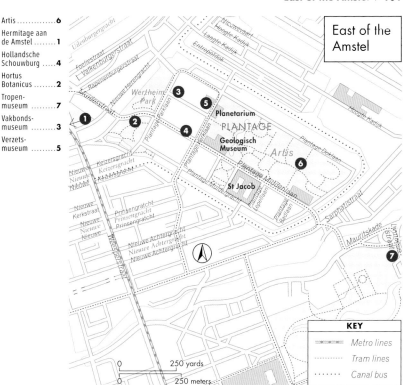

East of the Amstel

KEY
- Metro lines
- Tram lines
- Canal bus

actually much smaller than you might imagine from the outside (or the entry price), but the size of the shop and café are not. But when the material on show is of the highest quality, this matters not a bit. ⊠ *Amstel 51* ☏ *020/530–7488* ⊕ *www.hermitage.nl* ◩ *€15, I amsterdam Card €3, children under 17 free* ◷ *Daily 10–5; Wed. 10–8.*

② **Hortus Botanicus Amsterdam**. This wonderful botanical garden was origi-
★ nally laid out as a medicinal herb garden in 1638 by the Amsterdam City Council before the collection expanded to include exotic plants from the East India Company's forays into foreign lands. A total of 8,000 species is represented in the ornamental gardens and the three-climate-greenhouse. There's also a butterfly house. One of the treasures, perhaps the oldest potted plant in the world, is a 300-year-old Eastern Cape giant cycad. The orangery houses a wonderful café terrace—one of the most peaceful places in the city to enjoy a cup of coffee. In fact, Hortus harbors the leafy descendants of the first coffee plants ever introduced into Europe. A Dutch merchant stole one of the plants from Ethiopia and presented it to Hortus in 1706; they in turn sent a clipping to a botanist in France, who saw to it that further clippings reached Brazil. ⊠ *Plantage Middenlaan 2a, East of the Amstel* ☏ *020/625–9021* ⊕ *www.hortus-botanicus.nl* ◩ *€7.50* ◷ *Weekdays 9–5, weekends 10–5; Dec. and Jan. closes at 4.*

The world-class Hermitage Amsterdam.

Plancius (✉ *Plantage Kerklaan 61a, East of the Amstel* ☎ 020/330–9469 ⊕ *www.restaurantplancius.nl*) is a consistently reliable eatery opposite the zoo. It's open for breakfast, brunch, lunch, and dinner and has nice daily specials. Or check out a traditional local brown café, **Eik & Linde** (Oak & Lime) (✉ *Plantage Middenlaan 22, East of the Amstel* ☎ 020/622–5716), whose history can be traced to 1858. This old-fashioned, family-run bar has not lost its prewar charm to the prefab fittings or hyper-trendy design. In fact, the clock behind the bar runs backwards, so you can happily lose all sense of time. The owners pride themselves on reasonable pricing and a friendly atmosphere.

⑤ **Verzetsmuseum** *(Dutch Resistance Museum).* From May 14, 1940, to
★ May 5, 1945, the Netherlands was occupied by Nazi Germany. This museum, voted the best historical museum in the Netherlands, looks at the population's response: who resisted and how. All forms of resistance are covered: strikes, forging documents, hiding and escape (such as the Dutch–Paris route), armed resistance, and espionage. What is really great about the collections is that there's a rich context of everyday life told through personal documents, interviews, and sound fragments that not only communicate what occupied life really felt like but also engages visitors to consider their own behavior and choices today. In educational programs for children aged 10 and up, the concept of "Resistance" is given a positive twist, using examples from World War II to make kids aware of the importance of mutual respect, freedom, the fragility of democracy, and their own responsibility in dealing

with discrimination and persecution in their own lives. Displays also show how some of today's main Dutch newspapers, like *Het Parool* (Password) and *Vrij Nederland* (Free Netherlands), began as illegal underground newsletters. ⊠ *Plantage Kerklaan 61, East of the Amstel* ☎ *020/620–2535* ⊕ *www.verzetsmuseum.org* ⊒ *€5* ⊗ *Tues.–Fri. 10–5, Sat.–Mon. noon–5.*

WORTH NOTING

4 Hollandsche Schouwburg *(Dutch Theater).* From 1892 to 1941, this was a popular theater staging Dutch plays by luminaries such as Herman Heyermans and Esther de Boer-van Rijk and performed by artists like Louis "Little Big Man" Davids. In 1941, the Nazi occupiers made it into a Jewish-only theater, before using it as a gathering point for deportation of the city's Jews who were brought here between August 1942 and November 1943. In 1993, the Jewish Historical Museum renovated the theater, turning it into a memorial where the 6,700 family names of 104,000 Dutch Jews who were deported are displayed. Their very moving digital online memorial (⊕ *www.joodsmonument.nl*) features a colored dot for each person who was persecuted during the Nazi occupation and didn't survive the Shoah. There is also an exhibition on the Nazi occupation and an educational program showing documents, photographs, and videos. It is the large and silent courtyard that is perhaps the most effective remembrance of the 80,000 souls that began their journey to the extermination camps through this theater's doors. ⊠ *Plantage Middenlaan 24, East of the Amstel* ☎ *020/531–0340* ⊕ *www.hollandscheschouwburg.nl* ⊒ *Free* ⊗ *Daily 11–4.*

7 Tropenmuseum *(Museum of the Tropics).* The country's largest anthropological museum was first built to educate the Dutch about their colonial history in Indonesia and the West Indies, but now excels in hands-on exhibits covering all non-Western cultures. A gorgeous, sky-lighted, tiered interior is rich with wood, marble, and gilt, and not only displays endless pieces of antiquity, art, and musical instruments, but also makes these accessible through workshops and in playful, simulated villages and bazaars that you walk through, touching, smelling, hearing music, and feeling the physical experience of life in Java, the Middle East, India, Africa, and Latin America (where you'll also find the city's smallest Internet café, El Cybernetico). There's also a great patio where you can enjoy food from the globe-embracing café. At the **Tropenmuseum Junior** (⊕ *www.tropenmuseumjunior.nl*), children can participate directly in the life of another culture through fun programs involving art, dance, song, and sometimes even cooking.

EXOTIC SUSHI

Mysterious fish thefts have plagued the Artis Aquarium for years. Illegal exotic fish dealers were prime suspects, but no evidence could be found. Mastermind of the "inside jobs" turned out to be Okkie the octopus, living in a solo tank next door. Crawling out of his aquarium at night, Okkie dropped in on his fishy friends, devouring a few before sneaking back to digest his sushi feast in the peace and quiet of his own home. Okkie's tank has a new glass ceiling that should stop his late-night snacking.

Escape the hustle and bustle at the Hortus Botanicus.

Every weekend the smallest children (under six) and their parents can visit the Kartini Wing, where they can enjoy drawing, building, and folding. For children aged four and over, there are special children's routes through the museum and events on Wednesday afternoons and holidays. All children's activities are in Dutch only. ⊠ *Linnaeusstraat 2, Plantage* ☎ *020/568–8200* ⊕ *www.tropenmuseum.nl* ⧉ *€9, Tropenmuseum Junior €2 extra* ☉ *Daily 10–5.*

③ Vakbondsmuseum *(Trade Union Museum).* The history of Dutch trade unions may not seem especially scintillating, but its famed architect, H. P. Berlage, considered this building, De Burcht (The Citadel), his most successful work. Built in 1900 for the country's first modern labor collective, the Diamond Workers Union, Berlage incorporated his strong socialist principles into the essential structure. Climb the tower for a view of the neighborhood and enjoy a small display of Berlage's fine architectural blueprints while you're up there. In the various meeting rooms, note the fantastic murals by Richard and Henriette Roland Holst representing the past, present, and future of socialism, stained glass depicting the workers' battle, and the decorative details that fuse Jugendstil with Arts and Crafts stylings on ceilings, doors, and walls. The excellent collection of posters shows the graphic influence of the Soviet avant-garde on designs of the time. Currently being restored, it is due to reopen at the end of 2010. ⊠ *Henri Polaklaan 9, East of the Amstel* ☎ *020/624–1166* ⊕ *www.deburcht.org (Web site is in Dutch only)* ⧉ *€2.50* ☉ *Tues.–Fri. 11–5, Sun. 1–5.*

Where to Eat

WORD OF MOUTH

"I made reservations early for 7PM figuring we'd be tired and might only want a small bite before heading to bed. We all said that was exactly what we wanted, but when we got [to Envy] the food was so good, we ate large. We sat at a table outside—in Amsterdam, next to a canal—how could it get any better?"

—T4TX

Updated by
Steve Korver

Until a decade or two ago, it seemed that eating in Amsterdam was tinged more with the flavor of Calvinism than with any culinary influence. All too often the filling yet unenlightened fare of charred fish or meat, overboiled potatoes, and limp vegetables remained the standard. Today, happily, things have changed.

Many of the city's former industrial- and harbor-related buildings are being transformed into distinctive dining establishments. The term "New Dutch Cuisine," thanks to the emergence of young chefs who are finding their inspiration from around the globe, means exotic foamy-textured pea soup with chanterelles and pancetta; cod smothered in a sauce based on chorizo and fennel; or turbot and truffle wrapped in potato spaghetti, stewed chard, and veal sauce. International urban eating trends make it highly probable that you'll encounter sushi shacks, soup shops, noodle joints, and organic bakeries selling hearty Mediterranean breads.

Although traditionally hearty Dutch food really shines only in the winter months, there are a few imported-but-typically-Dutch culinary trips that cannot be missed: the Indonesian *rijsttafel* (rice table), where dozens of differently spiced vegetables, meats, and fish dishes are served with rice; and cheese fondue, which the Dutch appropriated from the Swiss probably because it appealed to their "one pot, many forks" sense of the democratic. And of course, one should take advantage of the ubiquitous fish stalls and stores by stopping and refueling on raw herring or some smoked delight from the sea.

PRINSEN EILAND

BICKERS EILAND

WESTERDOK EILAND

WESTERDOK

0   900 ft

0   300 meters

NOORD 5

Haarlemmer-Houttuinen

Nieuwe Westerdokstraat

De Ruijterkade

Noord Hollandsch Kanaal

Het IJ

Nassaukade

Singelgracht

Brouwersgracht

Prinsengracht

Keizersgracht

Herengracht

Westerdok

Prins Hendrikkade

Open Haven

Singel

Stationsplein

Centraal Station

THE WATERFRONT
Dishes often
inspired by
the sea

THE JORDAAN
Quality cuisine
in the most
distinctive of
neighborhoods

Centraal Station

Oosterdok

dokskade

Oosterdok

Gelderskade

Gelderskade

**WESTERN HALF
OF THE CENTRUM**
Student appeal vs.
New Dutch Cuisine

Warmoesstraat

JORDAAN

Lijnbaansgracht

Bloemgracht

Rozengracht

Egelantiersgracht

Raadhuisstraat

Spuistraat

Nieuwezijds Voorburgwal

CENTRUM

Damrak

Beursstraat

Warmoesstraat

**DE WALLEN
RED LIGHT
DISTRICT**

Nieuwmarkt

**THE RED LIGHT
DISTRICT**
From cheap
Asian spots to
the ultraposh

**WESTERN
CANAL RING**

Royal Palace

Paleisstraat

Kloveniersburgwal

Oudezijds Voorburgwal

Oudezijds Achterburgwal

NIEUWMARKT

**WESTERN
CANAL RING**
Canalside
treasures
with culinary
ambition

Berenstr. Wolvenstr.

Utrechtsegracht

Prinsengracht

Keizersgracht

Herengracht

Singel

Rokin

Rokin

Rokin

Kloveniersburgwal

**NIEUWMARKT
AND ENVIRONS**
Fancy a terrace
or a casual
café?

Marnixstraat

Nieuwe Doelenstr.

Amstel

Amstel

Muziektheater

Zwanenburgwal

Waterlooplein

Flower Market

Rembrandt-
plein

THE LEIDSEPLEIN
Late-night
eats and hidden
delights

**GOUDEN
BOCHT**

Herengracht

Keizersgracht

Prinsengracht

Vijzelgracht

**EASTERN
CANAL RING**

Amstel

Wibautstraat

**EAST OF
AMSTEL**
A relaxed
approach
to dining

Weteringschans

**EASTERN CANAL RING
AND REMBRANDTPLEIN**
Posh dining picks

Vondelpark

Stadhouderskade

Lijnbaansgracht

Singelgracht

Weteringschans

Rijksmuseum

**THE MUSEUM
DISTRICT**
Brasseries
befitting
high culture

Paulus Potterstraat

Van Gogh
Museum

Museum
Plein

Hobbemakade

Boerenwetering

Hendrik M. van
Randwijk-
Plantsoen

THE PIJP
From ethnic cheap
to ethnic chic

Stadhouderskade

WHERE TO EAT PLANNER

Eating Out Strategy

Where should we eat? With thousands of Amsterdam eateries competing for your attention, it may seem like a daunting question. But fret not—our expert writers and editors have done most of the legwork. The selections here represent the best this city has to offer. Search "Best Bets" for top recommendations by price, cuisine, and experience. Or find a review quickly in the listings, organized alphabetically within neighborhoods. Dive in, and enjoy!

In This Chapter

Hours

One thing you should be aware of is the Dutch custom of early dining; in fact, the vast majority of the city's kitchens turn in for the night at 10 PM—though many of the newer establishments are moving away from this long-held tradition. It should also be noted that many restaurants choose Monday as their day of rest. Lunches are usually served between noon and 2 PM, but many restaurants in Amsterdam are open for dinner only.

With Kids

As befitting a relaxed town, residents tend to be welcoming towards children in restaurants. In the listings, look for the ☺, which indicates a restaurant that is especially accommodating when eating out with children.

Reservations

Making reservations in advance for the more upscale restaurants is always a good idea. But with the recent economic downturn, restaurants are much more accommodating, so you can always try to walk in and wait for a table. In the listings we note only when reservations are essential or if they are not accepted.

Prices and Price Chart

A 15% service charge is automatically included on the menu prices. However, the trend is for most diners to throw in an extra euro or two on smaller bills and €5 or €10 on larger bills.

WHAT IT COSTS IN EUROS					
	¢	$	$$	$$$	$$$$
AT DINNER	under €10	€10–€15	€16–€22	€23–€30	over €30

Price per person for a median main course or equivalent combination of smaller dishes, excluding tax (6% for food and 19% for alcoholic beverages).

DID YOU KNOW?

Canal-side cafés are perfect for a midday break, when you can relax with an afternoon drink and take in Amsterdam's famous scenery. With more than 45 miles' worth of canals in the city, you are sure to find a canal and café to suit your tastes.

BEST BETS FOR AMSTERDAM DINING

With thousands of restaurants to choose from, how will you decide where to eat? Fodor's writers and editors have selected their favorite restaurants by price, cuisine, and experience in the Best Bets lists below. In the first column, Fodor's Choice designations represent the "best of the best" in every price category. You can also search by neighborhood for excellent eats—just peruse the following pages.

RESTAURANT REVIEWS

Listed alphabetically within neighborhoods. Use the coordinate (✢ 1:B2) at the end of each listing to locate a site on the corresponding map.

THE OLD CITY CENTER (HET CENTRUM)

Expect the unexpected when dining in the Centrum, where restaurant visits run the gamut from extraordinarily bad to really great. The good thing about eating here is that menu prices are just as diverse, which means that everyone's taste buds can be accommodated.

WESTERN HALF OF THE CENTER

This side of the center has lots of history, but none of the neon of the Red Light District. It's the intellectual heart of Amsterdam and a magnet for roaming hipsters, who often load up at a restaurant around Spui Square before washing it down with some nightlife in an ancient bar or the latest lounge.

$$-$$$ ✕**Brasserie De Poort.** Restored in the Old Dutch style (complete with
DUTCH polished woods and ceiling paintings), this restaurant—part of the Die Poert van Cleve hotel complex—is, in fact, officially Old Dutch. Its roots as a steak brasserie stretch back to 1870, when it awed the city as the first place with electric light. By the time you read this, De Poort will have served nearly 6 million of its acclaimed juicy slabs, served with a choice of eight accompaniments. The menu is supplemented with other options such as smoked salmon, a traditional pea soup thick enough to eat with a fork, and a variety of seafood dishes. ⊠ *Nieuwezijds Voorburgwal 176–180, Centrum* ☎ *020/622–6429* ⊕ *www.dieportvancleve.com* ☰ *AE, DC, MC, V* ✢ *1:A3.*

$-$$ ✕**Café Luxembourg.** One of the city's top grand cafés, Luxembourg has
CAFÉ a stately interior and a view of a bustling square, both of which are
Fodor's Choice maximized for people-watching. Famous for its brunch, its classic café
★ menu includes a terrific goat cheese salad, dim sum, and excellent Holtkamp *krokets* (croquettes, these with a shrimp or meat-and-potato filling). The "reading table" is democratically packed with both Dutch and international newspapers and mags. ⊠ *Spuistraat 24, Centrum* ☎ *020/620–6264* ⊕ *www.luxembourg.nl* ☰ *AE, DC, MC, V* ✢ *1:A5.*

$$-$$$ ✕**De Roode Leeuw.** Evoking a sense of timeless classicism along a strip
DUTCH that is decidedly middle-of-the-road, De Roode Leeuw has red banquettes, dark paneling, and romantic lighting. It has the city's oldest heated terrace—a good place to enjoy a selection from the impressive champagne list. You'll find poshed-up native fare served here, be it eel (caught fresh from the nearby IJsselmeer before being stewed) in a creamy herb sauce, or Zeeland mussels steamed and served with french fries and salad. Besides attracting passing tourists, the restaurant has also built up a sizable local following. ⊠ *Damrak 93, Centrum* ☎ *020/555–0666* ⊕ *www.restaurantderoodeleeuw.nl* ☰ *AE, DC, MC, V* ✢ *1:B3.*

$$$ ✕**De Silveren Spiegel.** Despite appearances, this precariously crooked
DUTCH building near the solid Round Lutheran Church is here to stay. Designed by the ubiquitous Hendrik de Keyser, it has managed to remain standing

since 1614, so it should last through your dinner of contemporary Dutch cuisine. In fact, take time to enjoy their use of famous local ingredients, such as succulent lamb from the North Sea island of Texel and honey from Amsterdam's own Vondelpark. There are also expertly prepared fish plates, such as roasted fillet of red snapper with a homemade vinaigrette. The full five-course menu will set you back €52.50. Lunch is available only for large groups. ⊠ *Kattengat 4–6, Centrum* ☎ *020/624–6589* ⊕ *www.desilverenspiegel.com* ⊟ *AE, MC, V* ⊗ *Closed Sun. No lunch* ✛ *1:B1.*

$$$–$$$$ **D′ Vijff Vlieghen.** The "Five Flies" is a rambling dining institution that
DUTCH   takes up five adjoining Golden Age houses. Yet the densely evocative Golden Age vibe—complete with bona fide Rembrandt etchings, wooden *jenever* (Dutch gin) barrels, crystal and armor collections, and an endless array of old-school bric-a-brac—came into being only in 1939. You'll find business folk clinching deals in private nooks here, but also busloads of tourists who have dibs on entire sections of the restaurant: book accordingly. The overpriced menu of new Dutch cuisine emphasizes local, fresh, and often organic ingredients in everything from wild boar to purely vegetarian dishes. Lack of choice is not an issue here: the wine list, and the flavored jenever are—like the décor—of epic proportions. ⊠ *Spuistraat 294–302, Centrum* ☎ *020/530–4060* ⊕ *www.thefiveflies. com* 🏛 *Jacket and tie* ⊟ *AE, DC, MC, V* ⊗ *No lunch* ✛ *1:A5.*

$–$$ ✕ **Haesje Claes.** Groaning with pewter tankards, stained glass, leaded-
DUTCH   glass windows, rich historic paneling, Indonesian paisley *fabriks*, and tasseled Victorian lamps, this restaurant's "Old Holland" vibe and matching menu attract lots of tourists. And why change a winning formula? The Pieter de Hooch–worthy interiors eclipse the food, although the (somewhat overpriced) dishes include an excellent pea soup and a selection of *stamppotten* (mashed dishes that combine potato with a variety of vegetables or meats). On cold winter nights, opt for the *hutspot,* a stamppot of mashed potato and carrot supplemented with steamed beef, sausage, and bacon. ⊠ *Spuistraat 273, Centrum* ☎ *020/624–9998* ⊕ *www.haesjeclaes.nl* ⊟ *AE, MC, V* ✛ *1:A4.*

$$–$$$ ✕ **Kantjil & de Tijger.** Although you can order à la carte at this large and
INDONESIAN   spacious Indonesian restaurant, the menu is based on three different *rijsttafel (*rice tables*)*, with an abundance of meat, fish, and vegetable options, all varying in flavor from coconut-milk sweet to distressingly spicy (the light local *witbier* beer is an excellent antidote). You can also choose to hit their to-go counter around the corner (⊠ *Nieuwezijds Voorburgwal 352)* for cheap noodles. ⊠ *Spuistraat 291–293, Centrum* ☎ *020/620–0994* ⊕ *www.kantjil.nl* ⊟ *AE, DC, MC, V* ⊗ *No lunch weekdays* ✛ *1:A4.*

¢–$ ✕ **Keuken van 1870.** This former soup kitchen, where sharing tables is
DUTCH   still the norm, offers the best and most economic foray into the world of traditional Dutch cooking. The kitchen serves such warming singularities as hutspot, its more free-ranging variant *stamppot* (a stew made with potatoes, greens, and chunks of cured sausage), *erwtensoep* (a sausage-fortified, extremely thick pea soup), and, naturally, a full range of meat, fish, vegetable, and potato plates. The restaurant continues to serve a daily three-course meal for a measly €9.50. Bless 'em.

Spuistraat 4, Centrum ☎ *020/620–4018* ⊕ *www.keukenvan1870.nl* ▭ *AE, MC, V* ⊗ *Closed Sun. No lunch* ✛ *1:B2.*

$$$$
ECLECTIC
✕**Supperclub**. The concept is simple but artful. Over the course of an evening, diners casually lounge on mattresses while receiving endless courses of food (and drink) marked by irreverent flavor combinations. DJs and live performances enhance the clublike, relentlessly hip vibe. Supperclub's popularity suggests that one should really go only in large groups, as it's not really an intimate setting. *⊠ Jonge Roelensteeg 21, Centrum* ☎ *020/344–6400* ⊕ *www.supperclub.nl* ⌖ *Reservations essential* ▭ *AE, DC, MC, V* ⊗ *No lunch* ✛ *1:A4.*

THE RED LIGHT DISTRICT

The city's Red Light District peddles more than just flesh and porn. It's also host to many bargain Asian restaurants and the fine delicacies of some of Amsterdam's most esteemed eateries.

¢–$
CONTINENTAL
Fodor's Choice
★
✕**Bakkerswinkel**. This genteel yet unpretentious bakery and tearoom evokes an English country kitchen, one that lovingly prepares and serves breakfasts, high tea, hearty-breaded sandwiches, soups, and divine (almost manly) slabs of quiche. The closely clustered wooden tables don't make for much privacy, but this place is a true oasis if you want to indulge in a healthful breakfast or lunch. It opens at 8 AM daily. There are several other locations: such as one complete with a garden patio in the Museum District and another at Westergasfabriek. *⊠ Warmoestraat 69, Red Light District* ☎ *020/489–8000* ⊕ *www.debakkerswinkel.nl* ▭ *No credit cards* ⊗ *Closed Mon. No dinner* ✛ *1:C3.*

$–$$
THAI
✕**Bird**. After many years of success operating the chaotic and tiny Thai snack bar across the street, Bird's proprietors opened this expansive 100-seat restaurant. Now they have the extra kitchen space to flash-fry their options from an expanded menu, and enough room to place the chunky teak furnishings they have imported from Thailand. The best tables—where you can enjoy coconut-chicken soup with lemongrass followed by fruity curry with mixed seafood—are at the rear overlooking the canal. *⊠ Zeedijk 72–74, Red Light District* ☎ *020/620–1442* ⊕ *www.thai-bird.nl* ▭ *AE, DC, MC, V* ✛ *1:C3.*

$$$–$$$$
MEDITERRANEAN
✕**Blauw aan de Wal**. In the heart of the Red Light District is a small alley that leads to this charming oasis, complete with the innocent chirping of birds. "Blue on the Quay" is set in a courtyard that once belonged to the Bethanienklooster monastery; it now offers a restful environment with multiple dining areas, each with a unique and serene view. Original wood floors and exposed-brick walls hint at the building's 1625 origins, but the extensive and inspired wine list and the open kitchen employing fresh local ingredients in its Mediterranean-influenced cuisine both have a contemporary chic. After starting with a frothy pea soup with chanterelle mushrooms and pancetta, you may want to indulge in a melt-in-the-mouth, herb-crusted lamb fillet. *⊠ Oude Zijde Achterburgwal 99, Red Light District* ☎ *020/330–2257* ⊕ *www.blauwaandewal.com* ▭ *AE, MC, V* ⊗ *Closed Sun. No lunch* ✛ *1:C3.*

$$$–$$$$
SEAFOOD
Fodor's Choice
★
✕**Bridges**. Bridges is the freshly reinvented restaurant located in the Sofitel Amsterdam hotel. You will pass a Karel Appel wall mural upon entering, before getting distracted by the inner courtyard (where you can have an aperitif and, later, dessert), and a raw bar covered with

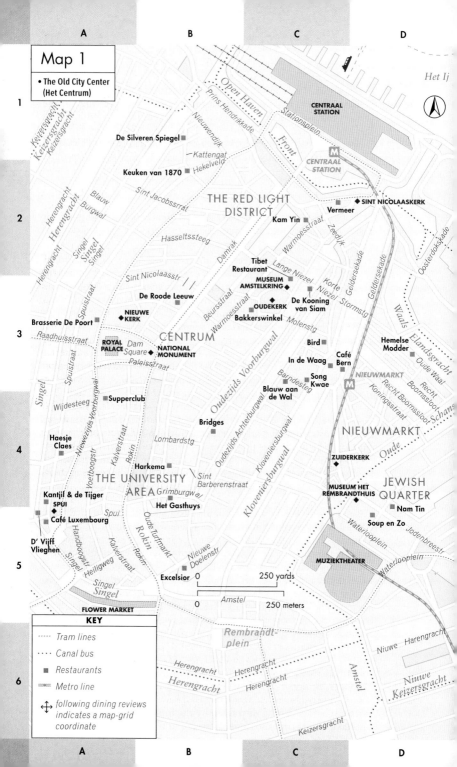

oysters, sushi, lobster, and fresh fish tartare. The kitchen produces an array of global fish dishes that use few but always fresh ingredients in hopes to showcase the natural flavors of the fish, like the monkfish with green pea risotto and asparagus tempura, and the miso-marinated cod with glass noodles and ginger. Guests can certainly put their faith in the wine choices coming out of their vinothèque. In short: Bridges is the perfect destination for a celebratory meal. ⊠ *Sofitel Amsterdam The Grand, Oudezijds Voorburgwal 197, Centrum* ☎ *020/555–3560* ⊕ *www.bridgesrestaurant.nl* ⚲ *Reservations essential* ▬ *AE, DC, MC, V* ✛ *1:B4.*

$–$$ ✕ **De Kooning van Siam**. Sitting smack in the middle of the Red Light THAI District, this Thai establishment takes delight in the fact that Brad Pitt once came to dine. It should take more from the fact that it is favored by local Thai residents. Although the ancient beams and wall panels are still visible in this old canal house, the furniture and wall decorations refreshingly dilute the sense of Old Dutchness. Sensitive to wimpier palates, the menu balances such scorchers as stir-fried beef with onion and chili peppers with milder options. ⊠ *Oudezijds Voorburgwal 42, Red Light District* ☎ *020/623–7293* ⊕ *www.dekooningvansiam.nl* ▬ *AE, DC, MC, V* ☯ *Closed Sun. No lunch* ✛ *1:C3.*

$–$$ ✕ **Harkema**. This brasserie along the city's premier theater strip has FRENCH infused a former tobacco factory with light, color, and general design savvy. The kitchen, which is open between noon and 11 PM, serves reasonably priced lunches and French classics like *croque monsieur* (French-style grilled cheese and ham sandwich), and a wall of wine bottles assures something to appeal to all tastes. ⊠ *Nes 67, Red Light District* ☎ *020/428–2222* ⊕ *www.brasserieharkema.nl* ▬ *MC, V* ✛ *1:B4.*

¢–$ ✕ **Kam Yin**. Representative of the many Surinam snack bars found ECLECTIC throughout the city, Kam Yin offers this South American country's unique fusion of Caribbean, Chinese, and Indonesian cuisines that arose from its history as a Dutch colony. Perhaps the most popular meal is the *roti,* a flat-bread pancake, which comes with lightly curried potatoes and vegetable or meat additions. If you come for lunch, try a *broodje pom,* a sandwich filled with a remarkably addictive mélange of chicken and cassava root (mmmmm, root vegetable). Basic, clean, convivial, and noisy, Kam Yin shows extra sensitivity with its speedy service, long hours (daily noon–midnight), and a doggybag option. ⊠ *Warmoesstraat 6–8, Red Light District* ☎ *020/625–3115* ▬ *No credit cards* ✛ *1:C2.*

$$$$ ✕ **Restaurant Vermeer**. With its milk-
FRENCH white walls, dramatic black-and-
Fodor's Choice white patterned floors, Delft plates,
★ fireplace hearths, and old chandeliers, this stately place does conjure up the amber canvases of the great Johannes. Its superposh vibe, however, suggests that no milkmaid will be able to afford the prices here, set

---

WORD OF MOUTH

"We also ate at Brasserie de Poort (in the Hotel Die Port van Cleve). That was our "splurge" meal and it was our best meal of the trip. I had a tomato soup with goat cheese worked into it, which was thick and creamy and absolute heaven. We both had *hutspot,* which was similar to stamppot, with potatoes, sausages and bacon, which was hearty and filling." —amyb

CLOSE UP

Indonesian Rice Tables

Holland's famed *rijsttafel,* or rice table, was the ceremonial feast of the Dutch colonists in Indonesia centuries ago. The Dutch are famously pragmatic; when originally confronted with the many dishes that came from the thousands of islands that made up their former colony of Indonesia, they simply decided to try dozens of different small portions at a time, and serve them with rice. A rice table consists of approximately 10–25 appetizer-size dishes, meant to be shared among a group of people. When you sit down and place your order, the staff will bring a number of hot plates, warmed by candles, to the table. The ritual of describing the dishes is a ceremony in itself, and one should pay heed to which dishes are described as the spiciest. (And perhaps order a tongue-soothing *witbier* to wash it all down.) Once you face the dizzying array of platters, put two spoonfuls of rice in the center of your plate and limit yourself to one small taste of everything. Otherwise, you're licked from the start. Then repeat.

The following is a guide to some of our favorite items.

STARTERS
Soto ajam: a clear chicken broth with vegetables and rice noodles.

Krupuk: crackers of dried fish or shrimp meal fried in oil.

Loempia: deep-fried rolls of bean sprouts, vegetables, and meat; basically a much larger take on the Chinese egg roll.

Saté: a skewer of bite-size morsels of *babi* (pork), *kunding* (lamb), or *ajam* (chicken), drenched in a rich peanut sauce or a sweetened, thick soy sauce.

MEAT
Babi ketjap: pork in soy sauce.

Frikadel goring: fried minced meat. A watered-down sausage version of this has become standard fare in all Dutch snack bars—it's almost as popular as *frites* (French fries).

Rendang: Sumatran spicy meat, often beef, lovingly stewed in no fewer than 11 spices.

VEGETABLES
Gado-gado: a mix of cold, cooked vegetables such as beans and cabbage, drowned in a spicy peanut sauce.

Paksoy: a leafy green that is often steamed and sprinkled with sesame oil.

Sambal boontjes: butter beans or French beans spiced with a chili paste.

Sambal goring tahu: stir-fried wafers of fermented soy beans with a sauce of *sambal* (crushed chili paste).

Sayur lodeh: vegetables cooked in a coconut cream broth, which helps take the bite out of peppery spiciness.

SEAFOOD
Ikan lada hitam: baked fish splashed with black pepper and a spiced soy sauce.

Ikan Bali: baked fish in a Bali sauce.

Oedang blado: baked shrimp in a spicy sauce.

Oedang piendang koening: grilled jumbo shrimp in a sweet-and-sour sauce and lemongrass.

Sambal goreng cumi cumi: baked squid in a spicy *sambal* (crushed chili paste) made of hot peppers.

Gado-gado, a staple of Indonesian rijsttafel.

within the 17th-century wing of the NH Barbizon Palace Hotel. The way chef Christopher Naylor combines tastes, textures, and temperatures is masterful, may it be a lettuce soup with ice cream of sour cream and a mist of eel, or an Iberico pork loin glazed with cockles. And for €100 you can get the full nine-course roller coaster of dishes. An army of waitstaff is on hand to ensure that the service is always impeccable. ⊠ *Prins Hendrikkade 59–72, Red Light District* ☎ *020/556–4885* ⊕ *www.restaurantvermeer.nl* ⊟ *AE, DC, MC, V* ⊗ *Closed Sun. No lunch Sat.* ✣ *1:C2.*

¢–$

CHINESE

✕ **Tibet Restaurant.** This place is famous for its budget prices and late-night hours (daily 1:30 PM–1:30 AM). Although you can get some authentic dishes here, like *momo* (dumplings) and various pork offerings that come either in spicy "folk-style" chunks or milder "family-style" shreds, the majority of the menu is ironically dedicated to standard Chinese Szechuan fare. ⊠ *Lange Niezel 24, Red Light District* ☎ *020/624–1137* ⊟ *AE, MC, V* ✣ *1:C2.*

NIEUWMARKT AND THE UNIVERSITY AREA

The Nieuwmarkt and square is an eclectic mix of upscale eateries at the beating heart of Nieuwmarkt, and student-friendly (read reasonably priced) hangouts that surround it. The adjoining streets are dotted with the type of venues that live up to the reputation of Amsterdam as the laid-back, chilled out European capital. Perfect places to linger over a glass of wine or a *pilsje* (a little glass of beer), or indulge in local snacks or full-blown meals.

¢–$
DUTCH
Fodor's Choice
★

✕ **Café Bern.** This dark and woody café, as evocative as a Jan Steen 17th-century interior, has been serving the same cheese fondue for decades, and for good reason: it's just about perfect. Go with a group and dunk those bread bits into that wonderfully gooey mess. Besides their famed cheese fondue, they also offer salads and some meat fondues where you can grill meats at the table. Like the Dutch, you, too, may be inspired to establish cheese fondue as your own celebratory meal of choice. ⊠ *Nieuwmarkt 9, Centrum* ☎ *020/622–0034* ☇ *Reservations essential* ═ *No credit cards* ☾ *No lunch* ✢ *1:C3.*

$$–$$$
CONTINENTAL

✕ **Hemelse Modder.** This bright, stylish, informal, and vegetarian-friendly restaurant is on one of the city's broadest canals and has a long-standing reputation for high quality at a great price. You can select à la carte or from a nicely priced three-course menu costing €29.50. Indulge in, say, a cauliflower tart with beetroot salad topped with raspberry dressing, or a Dutch grey mullet in a parsley-and-garlic marinade with fennel, rocket mash, and summer herb dressing. The inspired choices show a global sweep but invariably come to rest within the borders of France, Great Britain, and the Netherlands. But do tuck into one of the mountainous grand desserts, including the "heavenly mud" mousse of dark and white chocolate that gives the restaurant its name. ⊠ *Oude Waal 11, Centrum* ☎ *020/624–3203* ⊕ *www.hemelsemodder.nl* ═ *AE, DC, MC, V* ☾ *Closed Mon. No lunch* ✢ *1:D3.*

¢–$
DUTCH

✕ **Het Gasthuys.** Bustling and student-filled, this place near the university serves handsome portions of traditional Dutch home cooking, choice cuts of meat with simple sauces, fine fries, and piles of mixed salad. You can sit at the wood bar or take a table high up in the rafters at the back, surrounded by ancient wallpapers. In summer you can watch the passing boats from the enchanting canal-side terrace. ⊠ *Grimburgwal 7, Centrum* ☎ *020/624–8230* ⊕ *www.gasthuys.nl* ═ *No credit cards* ✢ *1:B4.*

$$–$$$
MEDITERRANEAN

✕ **In de Waag.** The lofty beamed interior of the historic Waag (weigh house) has been converted into a grand café and restaurant. Although the reading table houses computer terminals with free Internet access, a strict dinner-lighting policy of candles only—from a huge wooden candelabra, no less—helps maintain the building's medieval majesty. The menu is heartily Mediterranean, with entrées like Texel lamb with couscous and spinach, and fillet of dorade with potato mousseline. The long wooden tables make this an ideal location for larger groups, and if you happen to belong to a party of eight, you should definitely book the spooky evocative tower room. Daytime hunger pangs are also catered to from 10 AM on, when you can enjoy a sandwich, a salad, or a snack on the spacious terrace. ⊠ *Nieuwmarkt 4, Centrum* ☎ *020/422–7772* ⊕ *www.indewaag.nl* ═ *AE, DC, MC, V* ✢ *1:C3.*

$
CHINESE
☺

✕ **Nam Tin.** This massive and massively overlighted restaurant is like thousands of other Chinese restaurants in the world, in that they ignore the setting in favor of an encyclopedic Cantonese menu. As a hangover-curing bonus, they serve dim sum from noon until 5 daily and until 10 on Sunday. The restaurant is known to be kid-friendly. ✉ *Jodenbreestraat 11, Centrum* ☎ *020/428–8508* ⊕ *www.namtin.nl* ⊟ *No credit cards* ✛ *1:D4.*

¢–$ ✕ **Song Kwae.** Perhaps influenced by their Chinese competitors, this

THAI buzzing Thai joint offers speedy service and high-quality food at a budget price. Alongside the traditional red and green Thai curries and the stir-fry options, there are specialties such as green papaya salad with crab and *potek,* a searingly spicy mix of meats and fish. In the summer, the seating spills over onto the street with its views of Nieuwmarkt. ✉ *Kloveniersburgwal 14, Centrum* ☎ *020/624–2568* ⊕ *www.songkwae. nl* ⊟ *AE, DC, MC, V* ✛ *1:C3.*

¢ ✕ **Soup en Zo.** Only in the last few years, perhaps because *Seinfeld* is still

VEGETARIAN showing here, has the concept of speedy soup purveyors hit Amsterdam. "Soup Etc." leads the pack by being particularly speedy (at least between 11 and 8 on weekdays and noon and 7 on weekends), as well as health conscious. Four soups are available daily (you can even ask for a taste), served with chunky slices of whole-grain breads, and the menu also offers salads and exotic fruit juices imported from Brazil. Once you're fortified, you can rush back to searching for bargains at the Waterlooplein flea market or window-shopping for arts and antiques around its second, Museum District location. ✉ *Jodenbreestraat 94a, Centrum* ☎ *020/422–2243* ⊕ *www.soupenzo.nl* ⊟ *No credit cards* ✛ *1:D5.*

THE WATERFRONT

Amsterdam's historic harbor is getting the finishing touches on what is hoped to be an image-polishing boardwalk that will perhaps evolve into the city's premier entertainment zone. And naturally, many once purely industrial buildings have been transformed into dining hot spots.

$ ✕ **Balraj.** For almost 35 years, Bal-

INDIAN raj has been a favorite of curry connoisseurs. The décor is unremarkable—though the restaurant is impeccably clean and the plastic flowers are always fresh. The friendly fellows who serve delicious snacks, soups, and meals from their homeland, however, are a pleasure. You'll break out in the happiest of sweats when indulging in the chicken Madras, which you can wash down with sweet cardamom tea. ✉ *Haarlemmerdijk 28, The Waterfront Jordaan* ☎ *020/625–1428* ⊕ *www.balraj.nl* ⊟ *No credit cards* ⊘ *No lunch* ✛ *2:A1.*

> **SEASONAL FARE**
>
> Traditional Dutch winter fare includes such stalwarts as *zuurkool met spek en worst* (sauerkraut with bacon and sausage); *hutspot* (a hodgepodge of potato and carrots served with sausage or a meatball); *stamppot* (a hodgepodge of potato and sauerkraut served with sausage or a meatball); and *erwetensoup,* also called *snert,* a thick pea soup fortified with a variety of meats. Summer meals include the famed *asperges,* the tender, white local asparagus, and *mossellen,* or mussels from the pristine waters of Oosterschelde in Zeeland. All hearty and delicious, to say the least.

The chef poses behind the raw bar at Bridges.

$$ ✕**Bickers a/d Werf.** A true hideaway on Bickers Island, this is a place
ECLECTIC   for which the possibility of getting lost is worth it. With an all-wood
terrace, it resembles a harbor with a watery nautical view. The interior is stark, industrial, and modern. The food is tasty—think shrimp
croquettes and chips served in a paper cone and accompanied by an
excellent mayonnaise. The portions are considerable. ⊠ *Bickerswerf 2,
Bickers Island, The Waterfront, Centrum* ☎ *020/320–2951* ⊕ *www.
bickersaandewerf.nl* ▭ *MC, V* ☺ *Closed Mon. and Tues.* ✛ *2:A1.*

$$ ✕**Fifteen.** This franchise of superstar chef Jamie Oliver does exactly
ECLECTIC   the same as the London original: it trains young adults as kitchen team
players while filming them for a reality television show. Shockingly,
it's proven to be a remarkably consistent success, thanks in part to its
slightly out-of-the-way but waterfront location in the up-and-coming
Eastern Docklands neighborhood. While the kids learn under the tutelage of well-established chefs, diners indulge in such mains as roasted
leg of rose lamb with slow-cooked fennel, classic salsa verde and fresh
summer purslane, or wild mushroom crespelle with a poached free-range egg and a stem artichoke salad. ⊠ *Jollemanhof 9, The Waterfront,
Centrum* ☎ *020/509–5015* ⊕ *www.fifteen.nl* ▭ *No credit cards* ☺ *No
lunch* ✛ *2:B5.*

$–$$ ✕**Kilimanjaro.** This relaxed and friendly pan-African restaurant serves
AFRICAN   dishes from all over the continent, but focuses on the often-vegetarian
enjera pancake-based meals of Ethiopia (which you famously eat with
your hands). Have a seat on the summer patio, order either a *mongooza*
beer (served in a calabash) or a fruity cocktail, and then round off
your meal with freshly ground Ethiopian coffee served with popcorn,
before taking a lazy stroll around the harbor. ⊠ *Rapenburgerplein 6,*

The Waterfront, Centrum ☎ 020/622–3485 ▤ AE, MC, V ⊘ *Closed Mon. No lunch* ✛ 2:D4.

$$ ╳ **Odessa.** This floating restaurant—it's an old Russian merchant ship
ECLECTIC   from Ukraine—attracts hipsters and water-lovers alike. Its eclectic cuisine might include a skin-fried codfish fillet or lamb with merguez sausages served with spring vegetables and *la Ratte* potatoes. You also can get a three-course dinner for €25, as well as water views of some acclaimed local architecture. In the summer, the deck is open to diners, and on sporadic Sundays there are all-you-can-eat barbecues. Dancing begins after dark. ✉ *Veemkade 259, The Waterfront Centrum* ☎ 020/419–3011 ⊕ *www.de-odessa.nl* ▤ AE, DC, MC, V ⊘ *Closed Sun.–Tue. No lunch* ✛ 2:C6.

$–$$ ╳ **OPEN.** Just west of Central Station, this new and sleekly designed
FRENCH   glass-and-metal-outfitted restaurant atop an old 1920s railway offers
Fodor'sChoice   360-degree views of the IJ river. An open kitchen and a golden bar provide a perfect combination of seasonal French and Italian classics and
★   fine wine. Entrées, such as the steak tartare or ravioli of lamb, rosemary, and orange, can be ordered as whole or half dishes. Long hours make it a perfect stop for a late lunch or a late dinner. ✉ *Westerdoksplein 20, The Waterfront Centrum* ☎ 020/620–1010 ⊕ *www.open.nl* ✍ *Reservations essential* ▤ AE, MC, V ✛ 2:A1.

$$ ╳ **Panama.** A posh pioneer in the Eastern Docklands in the harbor's
SEAFOOD   former power station, Panama serves authentic dishes from around the world, with a special emphasis on fish. But you can stop in for a soup, a sandwich, or a salad pretty much any time of the day. Although the original 19th-century industrial architecture is still in view, the furnishings bring everything up to date. Plan to continue your evening in the attached nightspot, where the warm use of red, blue, and gold evokes a vision of an old-fashioned jazz club. ✉ *Oostelijke Handelskade 4, The Waterfront Centrum* ☎ 020/311–8686 ⊕ *www.panama.nl* ✍ *Reservations essential* ▤ AE, DC, MC, V ✛ 2:C6.

THE CANAL RINGS

If you're in Amsterdam for just one meal, head for the canals. In the midst of a storybook setting you'll find all manner of restaurants from glass-walled bistros to dining rooms that play on the city's rich merchant past. In the summer, outdoor terraces put you at the water's edge.

WESTERN CANAL RING

The intrinsically posh sector of the Grachtengordel ring and its intersecting streets is a foodie paradise. Meals here come equipped with the potential for an after-dinner romantic walk to aid digestion: the arches of the bridges are prettily lit, and their watery reflections pull at the heartstrings of even the most way-worn of travelers.

FEASTS TO REMEMBER

As you hunker down for a good Dutch meal, remember this: holiday celebrations of yesteryear were marked by the drunken gobbling of whole pheasants, just like the boisterous 17th-century depictions of feasts painted by Franz Hals, Jan Steen, and Jacob Jordaens. Dig in!

CLOSE UP

Dutch Cheese

To say that the Dutch like cheese is like saying the Italians are partial to pasta; a mere glimpse into a local supermarket will attest to this.

Shelves are piled high from floor to ceiling with cheeses of all colors, shapes, and forms: sliced, diced, grated, or in giant wheels. No matter if it's *jong* (young), *belegen* (aged) or *oud* (ancient)—the Dutch live for their cheese. In fact, they have been long known as *kaaskoppen*, or "cheese heads." It is said they received this nickname not only for their passion for this dairy product, but also from their habit during the Middle Ages of using a wooden cheese mold as protective head gear during battle. Indeed, they positively live for the stuff—and they've been producing it for more than two millennia.

Here's a rundown of the most popular Dutch cheeses:

GOUDA
Gouda is one of the best-known Dutch cheeses. It is traditionally produced in wheels, but today you can also find it in squares and blocks. A young Gouda has a creamy flavor and soft consistency; as it matures it acquires a more robust flavor and firmer texture. Gouda made with herbs is now popular in Holland, with the cumin-seed variety especially pleasing to the palate.

EDAM
Along with Gouda cheese, Edam is another popular variety in Holland. The round shape and bright red color of Edam makes it instantly recognizable to people from around the world. However, the red color means a cheese was marked for export. Locally, the Edam (as well as Gouda) usually wears a yellow or, if aged, a black coat. Whatever the color, its appearance is obtained by spraying the cheese with wax to form a protective layer. Edam is very mild, with slightly salty or nutty flavors. Calorie counters rejoice at the thought of Edam, since it is made with low-fat milk. Those in the know recommend pairing Edam with dark beer—indeed, creaminess matches creaminess. Naturally, this negates any savings of calories.

OTHER POPULAR HARD CHEESES
Other popular Dutch cheeses include *Leidse kaas* (often supplemented with cumin seeds), which, like Edam, is made with skimmed milk and rates as one of the oldest-produced cheeses in the country; *Frisian Clove,* a firm-textured cheese spiced with cloves; the hole-ridden *Maasdammer,* which is similar to Swiss Emmentaler but much more creamy; and *Boerenkaas,* a raw milk "farmers' cheese" that is indeed traditionally made on farms.

SOFT CHEESES
Yes, that famously stinky, soft cheese Limburger did originate in the Dutch and Belgian provinces of Limburg. But in the course of the 19th century it became so popular in Germany it is now predominately produced there. There are also quite a few varieties of cream cheeses, many using different herb mélanges, but most unique for visitors is the fresh cheese *Kwark* (Quark). Comparable to yogurt, it is made from skim milk, comes in many different forms, and often with fruit. It is one of the country's most popular light desserts.

A selection of cheeses at Restaurant Vermeer.

$$$–$$$$
FRENCH

✗**Christophe.** The William Katz–designed interior, which evokes this artist's acclaimed ballet scenery, remains one of the best reasons to visit Christophe. Chef Jean-Joel Bonsens's ever-evolving menu—always loaded with vegetarian options—may include entrées such as roasted lobster with soft garlic and potatoes, or sweetbreads with rosemary, asparagus, and compote of preserved lemon. You can preorder a 'boat box' in case you want to take your meal on a canal cruise. ⊠ *Lelie-gracht 46, Canal Ring* ☎ *020/625–0807* ⊕ *www.restaurantchristophe.nl* ⌂ *Reservations essential* 🏛 *Jacket and tie* ☰ *AE, DC, MC, V* ⊗ *Closed Sun. and Mon. No lunch* ✛ *3:A2.*

$–$$
CONTINENTAL

✗**Café Van Puffelen.** The ancient Van Puffelen, on a particularly mellow stretch of canal, offers both a startling array of herbed and spiced *jenevers* (Dutch gin) in its role as *aproeverij* (tasting house) and, in addition, a huge restaurant section in which to settle the belly. The menu is of the modern café variety, but it's the frequently changing specials (a three-course dinner costs € 19.50 and is served Sunday–Wednesday) that draw so many regulars. If the main dining room gets too boisterous, you can always escape to the more secluded and intimate mezzanine or, in the summer, the terrace. ⊠ *Prinsengracht 375–377, Canal Ring* ☎ *020/624–6270* ⊕ *www.goodfoodgroup.nl* ⌂ *Reservations essential* ☰ *AE, DC, MC, V* ⊗ *No lunch Mon.–Wed.* ✛ *3:A3.*

$$$
CONTINENTAL

✗**De Belhamel.** Set on the edge of the Jordaan, this restaurant is blessed with Art Nouveau detailing and wallpaper that is so darkly evocative of fin-de-siècle living it may inspire a thirst for absinthe and symbolist poetry. But the views of the Herengracht Canal and the attentive and friendly service create a romantic setting in which to settle down and enjoy the French and Italian–inspired menu. In the winter, hearty

Map 2

• The Waterfront

250 yards
250 meters

KEY

····· Tram lines
···· Canal bus
■ Restaurants
▬▬ Metro line
✛ following dining reviews indicates a map-grid coordinate

HAVENS OOST

Odessa
Panama
Fifteen
Kilimanjaro

Java Eiland

Muziekgebouw

Het Ij

Sumatrakade
Javakade
Oostelijke

Piet Heinkade

STEDELIJK MUSEUM

Oosterdokskade
Prins Hendrikkade
Oosterdok

Prins Hendrikkade

Kattenburgerstraat
Nieuwevaart
Hoogte Kadi
Laagte Kadi

CENTRAAL STATION

de Ruijterkade

Open Havert Front

Oosterdokskade

Waalseilandsgracht
Oude Waal
Recht Boomssloot
Krom Boomssloot
Recht Boomssloot
Koningsstraat
Keizerstraat

Rapenburger
Uilenburgerstraat
Nieuwe Uilenburgerstraat

Stationsplein
Prins Hendrikkade

Gelderskade
Geldersekade
's Gravelandse Veer
Korte Niezel

NIEUWMARKT

Damrak

Lange Niezel
Molensteeg
Oudezijds Voorburgwal
Oudezijds Achterburgwal

Barndesteeg
Kloveniersburgwal
Koningsstraat

Sint Antoniesbreestraat
Dijkstraat
NIEUWMARKT
OUDE ZIJDE

Singel
Martelaarsgracht
Prins Hendrikkade
Warmoesstraat
Nieuwebrugsteeg
Oudebrugsteeg

Nieuwendijk
Sint Jacobsstraat
Oude Nieuwstraat
Hasselsteeg

Brugsteeg
Oudezijds Kolk
Zeedijk

Rechtboomssloot
Jodenbreestraat
Zwanenburgwal

Nieuwe Westerdokstraat
Haarlemmer Houttuinen
Westerdoksdijk

Nieuwe Westerdokstraat
Haarlemmerstraat
Brouwersstraat
Brouwersgracht

Herengracht
Herenstraat
Keizersgracht
Prinsengracht

Spuistraat
Singel
Nieuwezijds Voorburgwal
Nieuwezijds Kolk
Nieuwendijk
Nieuwezijds Armsteeg

Blauw Burgwal

NIEUWE KERK
ROYAL PALACE
Paleisstraat

Raadhuisstraat

Nes
Rokin
Kalverstraat
Mozes-en-Aaron Str.

Nes
Lombardsteeg
Damstraat

Singel
Gasthuis-molensteeg

Wijde-steeg
Spuistraat

Bickersgracht
Grote Bickersstraat
Zeilmakerstr.
Blokmakerstr.

Bickers a/d Werf
Open
Amsterdam
Balraj

Haarlemmer dijk
Vinkenstraat

game dishes (such as venison with a red wine and shallot sauce) are featured; in summer, lighter fare is offered, and the seating spills out into the street. ✉ *Brouwersgracht 60, Canal Ring* ☎ *020/622–1095* ⊕ *www.belhamel.nl* ▭ *AE, MC, V* ✛ *3:B1.*

EVERYDAY SPECIALS

Embracing a sense of the democratic is the best advice for lunchtime: just follow the locals into a brown café or bar (also often called an *eetcafe*, eating café) to enjoy a *broodje* (sandwich) or *uitsmijter* (fried eggs with cheese and/or ham served on sliced bread). If you like the vibe, ask what they're serving for dinner. It's probably reasonably priced and based on what was cheapest and freshest at the market that morning.

$$$ ✗ **D' Theeboom**. Proprietor George
FRENCH Thurbert has been setting high stan-
Fodor's Choice dards for the city's French restau-
★ rants for decades in this formal and Art Deco–stylish institution set in a historic, canal-side, former cheese warehouse behind the Dam. The flavor of the dishes is only enhanced by the choices on the sophisticated wine list. Take a seat on the terrace on a sunny day and you'll likely settle in for a long and happy linger. ✉ *Singel 210, Canal Ring* ☎ *020/623–8420* ⊕ *www.theeboom.com* ▭ *AE, DC, MC, V* ☾ *No lunch* ✛ *3:A2.*

$$$$ ✗ **Envy**. This eatery offers a new take on dining in Amsterdam. The
MEDITERRANEAN sleek sexy furnishings are lit by low-hanging spotlights. The menu is comprised of appetizer-sized dishes (priced around €10 each) that can be shared by the whole table. Each of these dishes—including prawns and avocados with lemongrass, and ravioli filled with baby spinach— are as gorgeously presented as the waitstaff. The restaurant is perfect for foodies, as they can watch the chefs at work. ✉ *Prinsengracht 381, Canal Ring* ☎ *020/344–6407* ⊕ *www.envy.nl* ✍ *Reservations essential* ▭ *AE, DC, MC, V.* ☾ *No lunch Mon–Thurs.* ✛ *3:A3.*

$ ✗ **Goodies**. Free from all pretension, this spaghetteria is merely out to
ITALIAN serve homemade pastas, healthful salads, and tasty meat and fish dishes of the highest quality for the friendliest of prices. You will, however, be packed like sardines at the wooden tables and benches (moved onto the street during warm weather). By day, Goodies switches modes and becomes a popular café serving filling sandwiches on wedges of hearty bread, plus salads and deliciously thick fruit shakes. ✉ *Huidenstraat 9, Canal Ring* ☎ *020/625–6122* ⊕ *www.goforthegoodies.nl* ✍ *Reservations essential* ▭ *No credit cards* ✛ *3:A4.*

¢ ✗ **Lust**. "Lust" has a slightly different meaning in Dutch, and suggests
CONTEMPORARY a less aggressive desire best translated as "appetite." And if you've worked up a lunchy one while wandering the Nine Streets specialty shopping area, this is a truly satiating place for healthful club sandwiches, pastas, and salads. Be sure to visit the wacky washroom before you leave. ✉ *Runstraat 13, Canal Ring* ☎ *020/626–5791* ⊕ *www. lustamsterdam.nl* ▭ *AE, DC, MC, V* ✛ *3:A4.*

¢–$ ✗ **Pancake Bakery**. It's hard to go wrong when going out for Dutch
DUTCH pancakes in Amsterdam. But the quaint Pancake Bakery rises above the pack of similar eateries with its medieval vibe, canalside patio near the Anne Frank House, and a mammoth menu with more than 70 choices

3

of sweet and savory toppings. There are also omelettes, and a convincing take on the folk dish of *erwtensoep* (a superthick, smoked sausage-imbued pea soup). ⊠ *Prinsengracht 191, Canal Ring* ☏ *020/625–1333* ⊕ *www.pancake.nl* ⊟ *AE, MC, V* ✛ *3:A2.*

$$–$$$
MEDITERRANEAN

✕ **Pianeta Terra.** Marble-clad, intimate, and softly lighted, this restaurant has a menu that embraces the whole Mediterranean region (and that pays respect to vegetarians and organic farmers). The daily set menus are a sure bet, and may include carpaccio of swordfish with Pecorino cheese or octopus and mussels prepared in a traditionally Moroccan *tagine* (clay pot). The pasta, like the bread, is made fresh daily on the premises from organic ingredients. ⊠ *Beulingstraat 7, Canal Ring* ☏ *020/626–1912* ⊕ *www.pianetaterra.nl* ⊰ *Reservations essential* ⊟ *AE, DC, MC, V* ☉ *No lunch* ✛ *3:A4.*

¢–$
AFRICAN

✕ **Rainarai.** Here you'll find North African staples such as couscous, tagines, hummus, and baklava. You can order food to go and dig in while sitting on a canal-side bench, or squeeze into one of the restaurant's few tables. For a sit-down dining experience with cushion seating and waitstaff, head to their nomadic tent, which was recently set up in the Westergasfabriek west of De Jordaan (⊠ *Polonceaukade 40* ☏ *020/486–7109*). ⊠ *Prinsengracht 252, Canal Ring* ☏ *020/624-9791* ⊕ *www.rainarai.nl* ⊟ *No credit cards* ☉ *Closed Mon.* ✛ *3:A3.*

$$
MEDITERRANEAN

✕ **Van de Kaart.** This subcanal-level eatery with its peaceful dining room offers a savvy and stylish balancing of Mediterranean tastes. Though the menu is in continual flux, it may include shrimp sausages, octopus with a salad of couscous, basil, and black olives, or a galantine of organic chicken with shiitake mushrooms. You can also opt for one of three surprise menus (€34.50 for three courses, €44.50 for four courses, and €52.50 for the six-course tasting menu). A great wine list sells many by the glass. ⊠ *Prinsengracht 512, Canal Ring* ☏ *020/625-9232* ⊕ *www.vandekaart.com* ⊟ *AE, DC, MC, V* ☉ *Closed Sun. No lunch* ✛ *3:A5.*

$–$$
ECLECTIC

✕ **Walem.** As if ripped from the pages of *Wallpaper* magazine, this sleekly hip and trendy all-day grand café serves elegant breakfast and lunch options—as well as plenty of both cappuccino and champagne. Dinnertime is fusion time, as the chefs create salads of marinated duck and chicken, crispy greens, and buckwheat noodles, or slather a roast duck with bilberry sauce and serve it with a hodgepodge of arugula. In the summer, you can relax in the formal garden or on the canal-side terrace. Late at night, guest DJs spin hip lounge tunes for an appreciative crowd. ⊠ *Keizersgracht 449, Canal Ring* ☏ *020/625-3544* ⊕ *www.diningcity.nl/walem/* ⊟ *AE, MC, V* ✛ *3:A4.*

EASTERN CANAL RING AND REMBRANDTPLEIN

The Eastern Canal Ring and the Rembrandtplein are packed with some of the city's poshest restaurants. Main streets of culinary interest include upscale Utrechtsestraat, which takes you on an around-the-world culinary trip, and the lively Reguliersdwarsstraat, jammed with sidewalk cafés to satisfy your people-watching urge. Informally dubbed the city's "Gay Street," Reguliersdwarsstraat is as much known for its eateries as for its hip gay patrons.

$–$$
JAPANESE

✕ **An.** This long-popular Japanese eatery once offered only takeout; now you can linger over an evening meal along with some excellent plum

Riverfront restaurant, OPEN.

wine (*umeshuu*). Although the menu focuses on sushi, the kitchen also offers fantastic baked tofu (*atsuage*) and some superdelicious *gyoza*—steamed or fried dumplings filled with veggies or seafood. You may still choose to forgo dining in the oddly Mediterranean-style dining room and take your meal to a nearby bench on the Amstel or to the green expanses of Saraphatipark. ⊠ *Weteringschans 76, Canal Ring* ☎ *020/624–4672* ⊕ *www.japansrestaurantan.nl* ▭ *No credit cards* ⊙ *Closed Sun. and Mon. No lunch* ✛ *3:B6.*

$$$$ ✕ **Beddington's**. Although both the flavor and presentation of dishes here
ECLECTIC are decidedly French, many of chef Jean Beddington's creations hint at other influences: her youth spent in English country kitchens, the three years she spent mastering macrobiotic cooking in Japan, or any number of other influences she has gleaned from her culinary travels across the globe. The frequently changing menu is prepared with a feather-light touch. If you want to find out what the fuss is all about, be sure to reserve ahead. ⊠ *Utrechtsedwarsstraat 141, Canal Ring* ☎ *020/620–7393* ⊕ *www.beddington.nl* ⊲ *Reservations essential* ▭ *AE, MC, V* ⊙ *Closed Sun. and Mon. No lunch* ✛ *3:D4.*

$$$–$$$$ ✕ **Breitner**. Whether for romance or the pure enjoyment of fine con-
FRENCH temporary dining, Breitner gets high marks. With a formal interior of rich red carpeting and muted pastel colors, and a view across the Amstel River that takes in both the Muziektheater-Stadhuis (Music Theater–City Hall complex) and the grand Carre Theater, this spot serves French-inspired dishes, many of which pack a flavorful punch. The seasonal menu may include starters such as baked quail with goose liver and bacon, and entrées such as skate with Indonesian-style vegetables or smoked rib of beef with a sauce of whole-grain mustard and

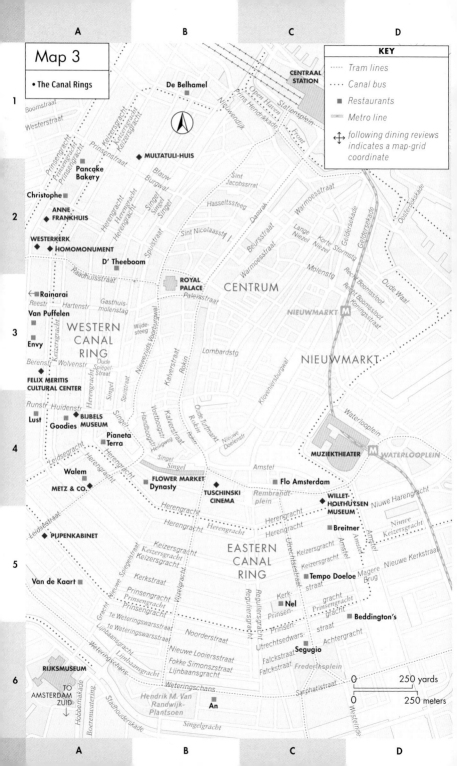

Map 3

• The Canal Rings

KEY
- ⋯⋯ Tram lines
- ⋯ Canal bus
- ■ Restaurants
- ▦ Metro line
- ↔ following dining reviews indicates a map-grid coordinate

A **B** **C** **D**

1

Boomstraat
Westerstraat
De Belhamel
CENTRAAL STATION
Open Haven Front
Prins Hendrikkade
Nieuwendijk

2

Prinsengracht
Keizersgracht
Prinsengracht
Prinsenstraat
Pancake Bakery
Christophe ■
ANNE FRANKHUIS
WESTERKERK
HOMOMONUMENT ◆
D' Theeboom
♦ MULTATULI-HUIS
Blauw Burgwal
Herengracht
Singel
Singel
Singel
Sint Nicolaasstr
Spuistraat
Sint Jacobsstraat
Hasseltssteeg
Warmoesstraat
Damrak
Lange Niezel
Korte Niezel
Beursstraat
Warmoesstraat
Stormstg
Gelderskade
Oosterdokskade
Geldersekade

3

←Rainarai
Reestr
Hartenstr
Van Puffelen
Envy
Berenstr
Wolvenstr
FELIX MERITIS CULTURAL CENTER
Raadhuisstraat
Gasthuis-molensteg
ROYAL PALACE
Paleisstraat
CENTRUM
Wijde-steeg
Nieuwezijds Voorburgwal
Oude Spiegel-straat
Spuistraat
Singel
Herengracht
WESTERN CANAL RING
Kalverstraat
Rokin
Lombardstg
Molensteg
Oude Waal
Korte Boomssloot
Lange Boomssloot
Koningsstraat
NIEUWMARKT Ⓜ
NIEUWMARKT
Kloveniersburgwal

4

Runstr
Huidenstr
Lust ■
Goodies ■
♦ BIJBELS MUSEUM
Pianeta Terra
Leidsegracht
Walem ■
METZ & CO. ■
FLOWER MARKET
Dynasty
Herengracht
Heiligeweg
Handboogstr
Voetboogstr
Singel
Singel
Kalverstraat
Rokin
Oude Turfmarkt
Nieuwe Doelenstr
Amstel
Rembrandt-plein
Flo Amsterdam ■
TUSCHINSKI CINEMA
WILLET-HOLTHUYSEN MUSEUM
Herengracht
Herengracht
Nieuwe Harengracht
Waterlooplein
MUZIEKTHEATER Ⓜ WATERLOOPLEIN

5

←Leidsestraat
♦ PIJPENKABINET
Van de Kaart ■
Nieuwe Spiegelstraat
Keizersgracht
Keizersgracht
Kerkstraat
Prinsengracht
Prinsengracht
Vijzelgracht
Herengracht
Herengracht
EASTERN CANAL RING
Breitner ■
Kerk
Prinsen-
Nel ■
Reguliersgracht
Regulierssgracht
Utrechtsedwars-
Prinsen-
straat
Tempo Doeloe ■
Amstel
Amstel
Keizersgracht
Keizersgracht
gracht
Prinsengracht
gracht
Beddington's ■
Nieuwe Keizersgracht
Nieuwe Kerkstraat
Magere Brug

6

RIJKSMUSEUM
TO AMSTERDAM ZUID ↓
Hobbemakade
Boerenwetering
Stadhouderskade
1e Weteringswarsstraat
1e Weteringswarsstraat
Weteringschans
Lijnbaansgracht
Noorderstraat
Nieuwe Looiersstraat
Fokke Simonszstraat
Lijnbaansgracht
Weteringschans
Hendrik M. Van Randwijk-Plantsoen
An ■
Singelgracht
Falckstraat
Falckstraat
Segugio ■
Frederiksplein
Sarphatistraat
Achtergracht
Utrechtsedwars-
straat
Westeinde

0 ——— 250 yards
0 ——— 250 meters

A **B** **C** **D**

marinated vegetables. Foie gras, fabulous desserts, and an innovative wine list allow you to step into the realm of pure decadence. As to be expected, the service is flawless and the patrons do their part to reflect Breitner's high standards by dressing smartly. ⊠ *Amstel 212, Canal Ring* ☎ *020/627–7879* ⊕ *www.restaurant-breitner.nl* ⌂ *Reservations essential* ▭ *AE, MC, V* ⊘ *Closed Sun., last wk of July, first wk of Aug. No lunch* ✛ *3:C5.*

$$$–$$$$
ASIAN
✕ **Dynasty**. Although its name has nothing to do with the 1980s television show of the same name, this restaurant's regular clientele (show-biz types, football heroes, dangling arm candy) does sometimes resemble a casting call for a soap opera. Although it's not required, you may want to dress the part when you come here. The interior is certainly fanciful: the Art Deco starting point blurs into an Asian frenzy of rice-paper umbrellas and golden Buddhas. In the summer, you should try for a table on the "dream terrace" set in a majestic Golden Age courtyard. Chef K. Y. Lai's menu, which is full of Cantonese, Thai, Malaysian, and Vietnamese culinary classics, is as ambitious as the décor; his drunken prawns (jumbo shrimp marinated in an intoxicating broth of Chinese herbs and Xiaoxing wine) are reliably excellent. ⊠ *Reguliersdwarsstraat 30, Canal Ring* ☎ *020/626–8400* ⊕ *www.restaurantdynasty.nl* ⌂ *Reservations essential* ▭ *AE, MC, V* ⊘ *Closed Tues. No lunch* ✛ *3:B4.*

$$$–$$$$
FRENCH
✕ **Flo Amsterdam**. Everything shines here: the copper, the mirrors, the white tablecloths and, of course, the food. Part of a popular chain, Flo serves classic French dishes to a devoted crowd. Indulge in their heavenly fish soup, head to their Fruits de Mer bar, or have your waiter prepare steak tartare at your table. (Due to local activism, they did remove foie gras from their menu). ⊠ *Amstelstraat 9, Canal Ring* ☎ *020/890–4757* ⊕ *www.floamsterdam.com* ⌂ *Reservations essential* ▭ *AE, MC, DC* ⊘ *No lunch Sat. and Sun.* ✛ *3:C4.*

$–$$
ECLECTIC
✕ **Nel**. Located in part of an ancient wooden church, Nel is graced with perhaps the most beautiful terrace in town. New owners bring a reasonably priced menu that hops the globe from pastas to burgers to gazpacho. You can always just drop by for a drink and enjoy the view and the sunshine. ⊠ *Amstelveld 12, Canal Ring* ☎ *020/626–1199* ⊕ *www.nelamstelveld.nl* ⌂ *Reservations essential* ▭ *AE, MC, V* ✛ *3:C5.*

$$$
ITALIAN
✕ **Segugio**. Two local and long-respected Italian chefs came together a few years ago to open this temple to the taste buds—and they brought some of their ancient family recipes with them. The Venetian-style stucco walls give the dining room a rustic and genuine feel. In the summer you can have aperitifs on the patio, and in the winter you can request a table by the open fire. Foodies can try the chefs' four-course menu for

PANCAKE CRAVINGS

With both sweet and savory toppings, *pannenkoeken* (pancakes) are also a mainstay on the menu of many cafés. They are a specialty at such places as the **Pancake Bakery**, the Upstairs **Pannenkoekenhuis** (⊠ *Grimburg-wal 2, Old Side* ☎ *020/626–5603*), and the **Boerderij Meerzicht** (⊠ *Koenenkade 56, Buitenveldert* ☎ *0290/679–2744*), which is an out-of-the way petting zoo and playground in the heart of Amsterdamse Bos (Amsterdam Forest).

3

€48.50. But making a choice from the main menu—perhaps a sublime risotto of the day, or a roasted rabbit hopped up with capers and olives—is usually a sure bet, too. ⊠ *Utrechtsestraat 96, Canal Ring* ☎ *020/330–1503* ⊕ *www.segugio. nl* ⌂ *Reservations essential* ⊟ *AE, DC, MC, V* ⊙ *Closed Sun. No lunch* ✛ *3:C6.*

$$$–$$$$ ✕**Tempo Doeloe.** For decades, this
INDONESIAN   has been a safe and elegant—albeit somewhat cramped—place to indulge in that spicy smorgasbord of the gods, the Indonesian rice table. Stay alert when the waitstaff points out the hotness of the dishes; otherwise you might wind up having to down several gallons of antidotal *witbier* (a sweet local wheat beer). It can get rushed here so it's best to book for a quieter weeknight. ⊠ *Utrechtsestraat 75, Canal Ring* ☎ *020/625–6718* ⊕ *www.tempodoeloerestaurant.nl* ⌂ *Reservations essential* ⊟ *AE, DC, MC, V* ⊙ *No lunch* ✛ *3:C5.*

> ## WALL-O-FOOD
>
> The ubiquitous **FEBO** snack-bar chain serves *patat* (french fries) with a stunning variety of toppings (we like the satay sauce and mayo combo), along with mysterious-looking choices of deep-fried meats and cheeses. If you don't want to wait in line, buy your food right out of the wall. It's surprisingly fresh and like all things greasy, it tastes good.

THE JORDAAN AND THE LEIDSEPLEIN

THE JORDAAN

Its maze of narrow streets lined with leaning gabled houses make the Jordaan a unique backdrop for lunch or dinner. The streets most heavily laden with eateries include Westerstraat and Lindengracht. (Don't look for a canal in the case of the latter one, as it has long been paved over.) And most recently, the painfully scenic side streets found in the area between Bloemgracht, Prinsengracht, Westerstraat, and Marnixstraat have evolved into a culinary 'Little Italy' of sorts.

$–$$ ✕**Amsterdam.** Getting here requires going west of the Jordaan, and
FRENCH   beyond the Westergasfabriek cultural complex. This spot is an industrial
☺   monument: for a century, this plant pumped water from coastal dunes. Now, under a sky-high ceiling, one can dine on French dishes—from rib-eye béarnaise and steak tartare to wonderful fish dishes like grilled tuna with ratatouille—in a bustling environment favored by families and larger groups. If it's too noisy for you, seek refuge on the peaceful terrace. ⊠ *Watertorenplein 6, Jordaan* ☎ *020/682–2666* ⊕ *www. cradam.nl* ⊟ *AE, DC, MC, V* ✛ *2:A1.*

¢–$ ✕**Burgermeester.** Indeed, they are "burger masters" here. Perhaps one
FAST FOOD   can quibble and say that their bun tends to fall apart when you take a bite, but this just attests to the juiciness of the burger. Burgermeester's healthful range of options includes beef, tuna, and lamb, to name a few, and a number of side dishes like the baked potato, corn on the cob, and a variety of salads. ⊠ *Elandsgracht 130, Jordaan* ☎ *020/423–6225* ⊕ *www.burgermeester.eu* ⊟ *No credit cards* ✛ *4:B5.*

$$–$$$ ✕**Café de Reiger.** This excellent neighborhood brown café ("brown"
DUTCH   because of its nicotine-stained nature) has a long history of being packed

with boisterous drinkers and diners. Its past is reflected in its tile tableaux and century-old fittings. The Dutch fare is of the bold meat-potato-vegetable variety, always wonderfully prepared and sometimes even with an occasional adventurous diversion, such as the sea bass tastily swimming in a sauce of fennel and spinach. But regulars usually just opt for the spare ribs. At lunchtime there is a menu of sandwiches and warm snacks. ⊠ *Nieuwe Leliestraat 34, Jordaan* ☎ *020/624–7426* ⌂ *Reservations not accepted* ▭ *No credit cards* ☽ *No lunch* ✛ *4:C3.*

$–$$
ITALIAN

✕ **Cinema Paradiso.** This former art-house cinema is now a designer eatery serving excellent starters—both the *carpaccio* and *gambas* (prawns) are heavenly. You can also choose from a wide array of simple pastas and pizzas. The restaurant doesn't take reservations, but you can linger at the bar while you wait for a table (sometimes for quite a stretch). ⊠ *Westerstraat 184–186, Jordaan* ☎ *020/623–7344* ⊕ *www. cinemaparadiso.info* ▭ *AE, MC, V* ☽ *Closed Mon. No lunch* ✛ *4:B2.*

$
VEGETARIAN

✕ **De Vliegende Schotel.** The Flying Saucer has been providing tasty and inexpensive vegetarian fare for a couple of decades now. With a relaxed vibe and a squatter's aesthetic, this is alternative Amsterdam at its best, one that you will grow to appreciate all the more if you wash your dinner down with some organic beer or wine. ⊠ *Nieuwe Leliestraat 162, Jordaan* ☎ *020/625–2041* ⊕ *www.vliegendeschotel.com* ▭ *AE, MC, V* ☽ *No lunch* ✛ *4:B3.*

$$
SPANISH
Fodor'sChoice
★

✕ **La Oliva.** Its extended name "La Oliva Pintxos y Vinos" describes what's served here: a huge selection of warm and cold *pintxos* (Northern Spanish tapas that run the range from oysters and other shellfish, to pata negra with flambéed pears) that can be paired with one of their stellar wines (many of which can be ordered by the glass). The friendly waitstaff is ready to help you find your optimum selection. Round out your meal with the chocolate mousse with marinated strawberries before walking it off in the scenic neighborhood of Jordaan. ⊠ *Egelantiersstraat 122–4, Jordaan* ☎ *020/320–4316* ⊕ *www.laoliva.nl* ▭ *MC, V* ☽ *Closed Mon.* ✛ *4:C2.*

$$
DUTCH

✕ **Moeders.** As can be expected from a place called Mothers, we're talking about Dutch home cooking here. In a café-style room alive with conversation and full of antiques and photos of mothers (to which you can contribute your own snapshot), guests are treated to simple yet inventive homegrown dishes prepared with a refined gusto even if it's just simple mashed potatoes or a steak fried in butter. They also have a daily dish special for €10. On sunny days ask for a table on their canal-side terrace. ⊠ *Rozengracht 251, Jordaan* ☎ *020/626–7957* ⊕ *www.moeders.com* ⌂ *Reservations essential* ▭ *MC, V* ☽ *No lunch Mon.–Fri.* ✛ *4:A4.*

$$
ITALIAN
Fodor'sChoice
★

✕ **Toscanini.** In the heart of Amsterdam is this true-blue Florentine trattoria, a perennial favorite with professionals and media types. The open kitchen, skylighted ceiling, wooden floors and tables,

---

WHO'S NEXT IN LINE?

Most *slagers* (butchers) and *bakkers* (bakers) supplement their incomes by preparing *broodjes* (sandwiches) of every imaginable meat and cheese topping. Traditional lines don't form, so pay attention to who was already there when you arrived.

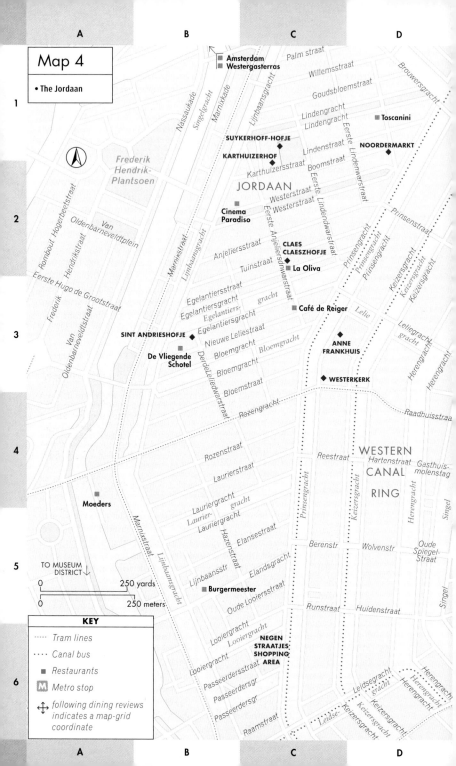

Map 4

• The Jordaan

1

2

3

4

5

6

Palm straat
Willemsstraat
Goudsbloemstraat
Lindengracht
Lindengracht

■ Toscanini

SUYKERHOFF-HOFJE ◆
KARTHUIZERHOF ◆

Lindenstraat
Boomstraat

NOORDERMARKT ◆

Karthuizersstraat

JORDAAN

Westerstraat
Westerstraat

Cinema
Paradiso ■

Anjeliersstraat

CLAES
CLAESZHOFJE ◆

Tuinstraat

■ La Oliva

Egelantiersstraat
Egelantiersgracht
Egelantiers-
gracht
Egelantiersgracht

gracht

■ Café de Reiger

Lelie

SINT ANDRIESHOFJE ◆

Nieuwe Leliestraat

Bloemgracht

ANNE
FRANKHUIS ◆

De Vliegende
Schotel ■

Bloemgracht

Bloemgracht

Bloemstraat

◆ WESTERKERK

Rozengracht

Raadhuisstraat

Rozenstraat

WESTERN

Laurierstraat

Reestraat
Hartenstraat
Gasthuis-
molenstag

CANAL

RING

Moeders ■

Lauriergracht
Laurier-
gracht
Lauriergracht

Elansestraat

Berenstr
Wolvenstr

Oude
Spiegel-
Straat

Lijnbaansstr

Elandsgracht

Burgermeester ■

Oude Looiersstraat

Runstraat
Huidenstraat

Looiergracht
Looiergracht

NEGEN
STRAATJES
SHOPPING
AREA

Looiergracht

Passeerdersstraat

Passeerdersgr

Passeerdersgr
Passeerdersgr

Raamstraat

Leidse-

Frederik
Hendrik-
Plantsoen

Rombout Hogerbeetsstraat

Van
Oldenbarneveldtplein

Frederik Hendrikstraat

Eerste Hugo de Grootstraat

Van Oldenbarneveldtstraat

Nassaukade
Singelgracht
Marnixkade

Lijnbaansgracht

Marnixstraat

Lijnbaansgracht

Marnixstraat
Lijnbaansgracht

Eerste Lindendwarsstraat
Eerste Anjeliersdwarsstraat

Eerste Lindenstraat

Prinsengracht
Prinsengracht
Prinsengracht

Prinsengracht

Keizersgracht
Keizersgracht
Keizersgracht

Prinsenstraat

Brouwersgracht

Leliegracht
gracht

Herengracht
Herengracht

Herengracht
Herengracht

Singel

Singel

Leidsegracht
gracht

Herengracht
Herengracht

Keizersgracht
Keizersgracht

DerdeLeliedwarsstraat

TO MUSEUM
DISTRICT ↓

0	250 yards
0	250 meters

KEY

---- Tram lines

···· Canal bus

■ Restaurants

Ⓜ Metro stop

✥ following dining reviews
   indicates a map-grid
   coordinate

A   B   C   D

Serrano ham stuffed with a crab and salmon mousse at Restaurant D'Theeboom.

and attentive service all work to create a sort of "country kitchen" atmosphere. The cooks pride themselves on their ability to create any regional dish, but you will undoubtedly find your favorite already listed on the extensive menu. The risottos are profound, the fish dishes sublime, the desserts decadent, and the wine list inspired. What more can one ask? ☒ *Lindengracht 75, Jordaan* ☎ *020/623–2813* ⊕ *www. toscanini.nu* ⟿ *Reservations essential* ▭ *AE, DC, MC, V* ☉ *Closed Sun. No lunch* ✢ *4:D1.*

$–$$ ✕**Westergasterras.** Located in the arts complex, Westergasfabriek, just
CAFÉ behind the Jordaan, the Western Gas Terrace restaurant overlooks park green, and a former city gas container that is now an industrial monument. With its outdoor seating blurred with its indoor seating by retractable glass walls, Westergasterras is a perfect destination—on a lazy afternoon or evening—to enjoy the sun. Their café-style dishes include soups, sandwiches, pastas, tapas, grilled entrecote, and apple pie. On weekends they have been known to start a barbecue. ☒ *Klönneplein 4–6, Westergasfabriek, Jordaan* ☎ *020/684–496* ⊕ ▭ *MC, V* ☉ *Variable hrs in winter* ✢ *4:B1.*

THE LEIDSEPLEIN

The bustling square called Leidseplein is the heart of Amsterdam's nightlife. It gets the shortest amount

FISH SNACKS

A favorite Dutch snack can be purchased at the fish stalls found on many of the city's bridges—raw herring that has been saltwater-cured in vats. This working person's "sushi" tastes best at the start of the fishing season (late May to early June). Eat it on a bun (broodje haring) or just sliced up. Afficiandos like it topped with raw onions and pickle slices.

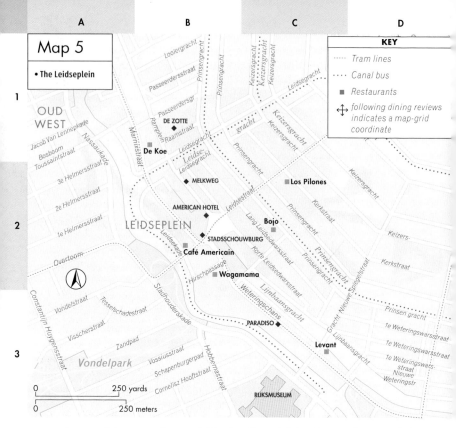

Map 5

• The Leidseplein

KEY

····· Tram lines

···· Canal bus

■ Restaurants

⬦ following dining reviews
indicates a map-grid
coordinate

of shut-eye of any neighborhood, explaining its popularity with late-night munchers. Although the eateries on the square require that you dig deep in your wallet, the surrounding streets are packed with more affordable restaurants.

¢–$ ✕ **Bojo.** There are plenty of mediocre late-night eateries around the
INDONESIAN Leidseplein, but the bamboo'd and somewhat-cramped Bojo stands out for serving huge portions of enjoyable food. You'll find everything here, from *saté* (skewered and barbecued meats) to vegetarian *gado-gado* (vegetables drowned in a spicy peanut sauce) to their one-plate rice tables where several different small dishes are brought together. Bojo is open daily until 2 AM. ⊠ *Lange Leidsedwarsstraat 49–51, Leidseplein* ☎ 020/622–7434 ⊕ *www.bojo.nl* ⊟ *AE, DC, MC* ⊗ *No lunch Mon.–Wed.* ⬦ *5:C2.*

$$–$$$ ✕ **Café Americain.** Though thousands of buildings in Amsterdam are
FRENCH designated historic monuments, few have their *interiors* landmarked as well. This one is, and for good reason: it's an Art Deco display of arched ceilings, stained glass, leaded-glass lamps, wall paintings, and a huge antique reading table. (Mata Hari had her wedding reception here.) Though the food is less notable than the décor (the menu offers everything from light snacks to full dinners), the coffee and cakes are always excellent. ⊠ *Eden Amsterdam American Hotel, Leidsekade*

97, Leidseplein ☎*020/624–5322* ⌖*Reservations not accepted* ═ *AE, DC, MC, V* ✛ *5:B2.*

$–$$
MEDITERRANEAN

✕**De Koe.** Downstairs at "The Cow," the cooks crowded into the tiny kitchen manage to pump out wonderfully prepared dishes. Despite the restaurant's name, the ever-changing menu tends to favor less beef and more fish and ostrich (made with truffle sauce). The crowd is largely local, casual, and friendly: you won't see any yuppies here. Upstairs from the café is an equally earthy and popular bar. ✉ *Marnixstraat 381, Leidseplein* ☎*020/625–4482* ⊕ *www.cafedekoe.nl* ═ *AE, DC, MC, V* ☾ *No lunch* ✛ *5:B1.*

$–$$
TURKISH
☾

✕**Levant.** Here in a simple and modern setting you can indulge in grilled meats (and the appropriate firewaters with which to wash it all down). All the while, your children will invariably be entertained by the extraordinarily warm staff. This hidden treasure comes with a canal-side terrace (from which, on your way out, you can pay your respects to the bustling kitchen staff). ✉ *Weteringschans 93, Leidseplein* ☎*020/662–5184* ⊕ *www.restaurantlevant.nl* ⌖ *Reservations essential* ═ *MC, V* ☾ *Closed Sun. No lunch* ✛ *5:C3.*

$
MEXICAN

✕**Los Pilones.** Given how far Amsterdam is from Mexico, it may take a little courage for you to try this eatery's cactus salad (even though the main ingredient is happily de-spiked), or the popular Day of the Dead dish, enchiladas with mole (pronounced *moh*-lay and featuring a spicy chocolate-chili sauce). But even if these aren't the most authentic Mexican dishes you'll ever eat, the charming young staff and casual environment here are winners. Even better, the selection of tequilas is deliciously ample (including their very own brand), and the margaritas have all the requisite bite and zest. ✉ *Kerkstraat 63, Leidseplein* ☎*020/320–4651* ⊕ *www.lospilones.com* ═ *AE, DC, MC, V* ☾ *Closed Mon. No lunch* ✛ *5:C2.*

$
JAPANESE

✕**Wagamama.** Though it may sound like an Italian restaurant run by a large-bottomed matriarch, this is actually a slick minimalist eatery recalling a Japanese noodle shop. It's fresh, fast, and fairly cheap; just fill out a menu card and hand it to one of the waitstaff. Moments later, a hearty bowl of noodles and broth supplemented with your choice of meats, fish, and vegetables will arrive. Further sustenance comes in the form of fruit and vegetable shakes. ✉ *Max Euweplein 10, Leidseplein* ☎*020/528–7778* ⊕ *www.wagamama.nl* ═ *AE, MC, V* ✛ *5:B2.*

MUSEUM DISTRICT

With such monuments to culture as the Rijksmuseum, the Van Gogh Museum, and the Concertgebouw, it's no surprise that this ultraposh area attracts the suited and booted. In keeping with the upper-crust

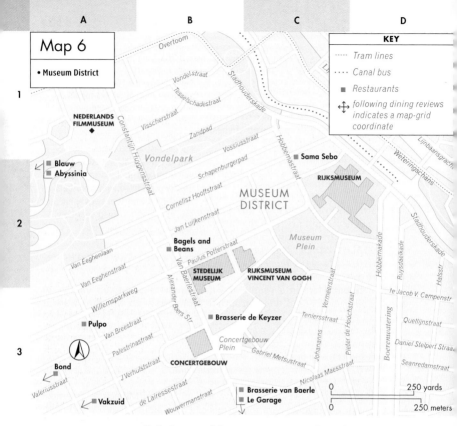

KEY

····· Tram lines

···· Canal bus

■ Restaurants

⟷ following dining reviews indicates a map-grid coordinate

Map 6

• Museum District

Overtoom

Vondelstraat

Tesselschadestraat

Stadhouderskade

Constantijn Huygenstraat

Visscherstraat

NEDERLANDS FILMMUSEUM ◆

Zandpad

Vossiusstraat

■ Blaauw
■ Abyssinia

Vondelpark

Schapenburgerpad

Cornelisz Hooftstraat

Hobbemastraat

■ Sama Sebo

RIJKSMUSEUM

MUSEUM DISTRICT

Lijnbaansgracht

Weteringschans

Jan Luijkenstraat

Van Eeghenlaan

Van Eeghenstraat

Willemsparkweg

Paulus Potterstraat

Van Baerlestraat

Alexander Boers Str

Bagels and Beans ■

STEDELIJK MUSEUM

RIJKSMUSEUM VINCENT VAN GOGH

Museum Plein

Hobbemakade

Ruysdaelkade

Stadhouderskade

Vermeerstraat

te Jacob V. Campenstr

■ Pulpo

Van Breestraat

Palestrinastraat

J Verhulststraat

■ Brasserie de Keyzer

Concertgebouw Plein

Gabriel Metsustraat

CONCERTGEBOUW

Teniersstraat

Pieter de Hoochstraat

Johannans

Quellijnstraat

Daniel Stelpert Straa

Seanredamstraat

Bond ←

de Lairessestraat

Nicolaas Maesstraat

Boerenwatering

■ Vakzuid ←

Valeriusstraat

Wouwermanstraat

■ Brasserie van Baerle
■ Le Garage

0 ———— 250 yards

0 ———— 250 meters

---

tone, you'll find some of the city's most critically acclaimed, and excruciatingly expensive, restaurants.

$ ╳ **Abyssinia.** A bit off the beaten track (but conveniently close to Von-
ETHIOPIAN   delpark), Abyssinia specializes in the eat-with-your-hands *enjera*-based meals of Ethiopia and Eritrea. Sourdough pancakes are served with a variety of spicy (and often vegetarian) dishes that have been influenced by the region's geographical position between Asia, Africa, and the Arabic world. The restaurant is filled with rattan couches, which are the perfect perch from which to drink African beer from a calabash shell or indulge in a full coffee ceremony. ⊠ *J P Heijestraat 190, Museum District* ☎ *020/683–0792* ⊕ *www.abyssinia.nl* ▭ *MC, V* ☺ *No lunch* ⟷ *6:A2.*

¢ ╳ **Bagels and Beans.** This low-key, bustling hot spot is just what the good
FAST FOOD   doctor ordered: a wealth of fresh-made bagel choices, along with fresh juices and piping-hot coffee. There are over a dozen locations, but the Museum District location wins with its remarkably pleasant and peaceful back patio. ⊠ *Van Baerlestraat 40, Museum District* ☎ *020/675–7050* ⊕ *www.bagelsbeans.nl* ▭ *AE, DC, MC, V* ☺ *No dinner* ⟷ *6:B2.*

$$$ ╳ **Blaauw.** Many believe that the best Indonesian food can only be found
INDONESIAN   in The Hague. However, Blaauw proves these critics wrong. Located a
Fodor's Choice   bit off the beaten track on the other end of Vondelpark, along the rising
★   culinary boulevard of Amstelveenseweg, the traditional batik interior

was replaced by lacquered walls and a labyrinth of nooks and crannies, so guests can still feel warm and welcome in this modern setting while sharing a rice table. Check the restaurant's Web site the next day and download a photo of yourself at your table. ✉ *Amstelveenseweg 158–160, Museum District* 🕾 *020/675–5000* ⊕ *www.restaurantblauw. nl* ⚲ *Reservations essential* ▭ *MC, V* ☉ *No lunch* ✛ *6:A2.*

$$–$$$
MEDITERRANEAN
✗**Bond**. With its golden ceiling above and lush lamps, sofas, and sounds below, Bond is as double-oh-so-'70s as it is comfortably experimental. Ditto for the dinner menu, which darts from braised rabbit, to steak grilled with heirloom mushrooms, to fish roasted with corn, wild parsnips, and oranges. Being close to the similarly gilded Concert Building, Bond can also be a great location for, say, a post-Rossini martini. Lunchtime sees things a tad more restrained, with choices running more along the lines of oysters, salads, and burgers. ✉ *Valeriusstraat 128b, Museum District* 🕾 *020/676–4647* ⊕ *www.restaurantbond.nl* ▭ *MC, V* ✛ *6:A3.*

$$$–$$$$
CONTINENTAL
✗**Brasserie de Keyzer**. In the shadow of the golden lyre that tops the Concertgebouw (Concert Building), this institution has been serving musicians and concertgoers alike for almost a century. You can come here at almost any hour for anything from a drink to a full meal. The appropriately classical, dimly lighted Old Dutch interior—comfortable as an old shoe—is paneled with dark wood and spread with Oriental rugs. Aside from such relative oddities as *ris de veau* (veal sweetbreads with orange and green-pepper sauce), the béarnaise-, tournedos-, and schnitzel-rich menu leans toward tradition, with a sole meunière being the house specialty. ✉ *Van Baerlestraat 96, Museum District* 🕾 *020/675–1866* ⊕ *www.brasseriekeyzer.nl* ▭ *AE, DC, MC, V* ✛ *6:B3.*

$$–$$$
CONTINENTAL
✗**Brasserie van Baerle**. If it's Sunday and you want to brunch on the holiest of trinities—blini, caviar, and champagne—look no further than this brasserie. The elegant modern furnishings and the professional yet personal service attracts a business crowd at lunch, as well as late-night diners still on an aesthetic roll after attending an event at the nearby Concert Building. The imaginative chef knows how to put on an inspired show with a fusion menu that includes both light and spicy Asian salads and heavier fare such as veal tartlet with sweetbreads, tongue, and winter truffles. There's outdoor dining when the weather cooperates. ✉ *Van Baerlestraat 158, Museum District* 🕾 *020/679–1532* ⊕ *www.brasserievanbaerle.nl* ⚲ *Reservations essential* ▭ *AE, DC, MC, V* ☉ *No lunch Sat.* ✛ *6:B3*

$$$–$$$$
FRENCH
✗**Le Garage**. This former garage is now a brasserie awash with red-plush seating and mirrored walls—perfect for local glitterati who like to see and be seen. This is the home of the celebrity chef Joop Braakhekke, whose busy schedule of TV appearances necessitates his leaving the kitchen in other—very capable—hands. The food is invariably excellent and uses French haute cuisine as its starting point. And yes, foie gras may be one of their favorite ingredients, but they also brew up a fine venison stew with pumpkin mash, fried mushrooms, and a sauce of mixed berries. Although champagne, fine wines, and caviar accent the essential poshness of it all, the daily, three-course power-lunch menu is quite reasonably priced at €29.50. ✉ *Ruysdaelstraat 54, Museum*

District ☎ 020/679–7176 ⊕ *www.restaurantlegarage.nl* ⊳ *Reservations essential* ⊟ *AE, DC, MC, V* ☉ *No lunch weekends* ✢ 6:B3.

$–$$
MEDITERRANEAN

✕ **Pulpo.** Friendly service, reasonable prices, and jazzy tunes make this trendy hot spot a comfortable place indeed. The main courses are simple but always top-notch—few can resist the signature squid that is featured in their fish curry with sweet potatoes, black beans, and *gremolata* (minced parsley, lemon peel, and garlic). A three-course, pre-concert, prix-fixe menu will set you back only €29. ⊠ *Willemsparkweg 87, Museum District* ☎ 020/676–0700 ⊕ *www.restaurant-pulpo.nl* ⊟ *AE, DC, MC, V* ☉ *No lunch. Closed Sun.* ✢ 6:A3.

$$$
INDONESIAN

✕ **Sama Sebo.** This busy but relaxed neighborhood restaurant acts as a good, albeit not too adventurous, "Intro to Indo" course. Since 1969, Sama Sebo has been dishing out *rijsttafel*, a feast with myriad exotically spiced small dishes, in an atmosphere characteristically enhanced by rush mats and shadow puppets. During lunch they serve simpler dishes: *bami goreng* (spicy fried noodles with vegetables or meat) and *nasi goreng* (the same, but with rice instead of noodles). At the bar, you can wait for your table while having a beer and getting to know the regulars. ⊠ *P. C. Hooftstraat 27, Museum District* ☎ 020/662–8146 ⊕ *www.samasebo.nl* ⊳ *Reservations essential* ⊟ *AE, DC, MC, V* ☉ *Closed Sun.* ✢ 6:C1.

$$–$$$
ECLECTIC

✕ **Vakzuid.** Slightly off-the-beaten-track, this sprawling bar-café-lounge-restaurant is in Section South of the still-new-looking 1928 Olympic Stadium, an architectural monument designed by one of the founders of De Stijl, Jan Wils. With its contemporary take on the functionally modern, Vakzuid fits right in. There's a huge sunny patio (accessible by water taxi) with comfortable seating under umbrellas, a solo-friendly bar specializing in coffee and designer sandwiches by day and cocktails and Asian snacks by night, a comfortable lounge area with a view over the track field, and a raised restaurant with an open kitchen serving a mix of Mediterranean and Asian cooking. ⊠ *Olympisch Stadion 35, Museum District* ☎ 020/570–8400 ⊕ *www.vakzuid.nl* ⊳ *Reservations essential* ⊟ *AE, DC, MC, V* ☉ *Closed Sat. and Sun.* ✢ 6:A3.

THE PIJP

Loud, proud, and bohemian, the Pijp is all things to all people. The original occupants of this staunchly working-class area are still around, though they are dwindling in numbers as the area becomes increasingly pricey. Today you'll see more upwardly mobile types, as well as members of the thriving Turkish and Moroccan communities. The mix is mirrored in the choice of dining options, so you can grab a roti, a bowl of *soto ayam* (Indonesian chicken soup), or a plate of seafood linguine.

$–$$
INDIAN

✕ **Balti House.** If you find yourself craving curry, the dishes at this excellent purveyor of Indian cuisine have an actual subtle variance in flavors. Some of their more addictive choices are any one of their soups or tandooris, the butter chicken, the garlic naan bread, and the homemade *kulfi* ice cream. The patio is a lovely place to sit when the sun is out. ⊠ *Albert Cuypstraat 41, The Pijp* ☎ 020/470–8917 ⊕ *www.baltihouse.nl* ⊟ *AE, MC, V* ☉ *No lunch.* ✢ 7:A2.

DID YOU KNOW?

Diners at Bazar Amsterdam can feast on North African staples likes falafel, couscous, and kebabs, morning, noon, and night, against a backdrop of tiled mosaics, colorful lights, hanging chandeliers, and an overall vibrant atmosphere.

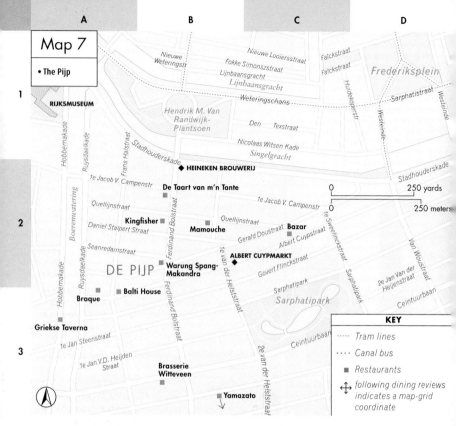

Map 7

• The Pijp

RIJKSMUSEUM

Hobbemakade
Ruysdaelkade
Frans Halstraat
Stadhouderskade
Boerenwatering
Te Jacob V. Campenstr
Quellijnstraat
Daniel Stalpert Straat
Seanredamstraat
Ruysdaelkade
Hobbemakade
Te Jan Steenstraat
Te Jan V.D. Heijden Straat

Nieuwe Weteringstr
Fokke Simonszstraat
Lijnbaansgracht
Lijnbaansgracht
Nieuwe Looiersstraat
Falckstraat
Falckstraat
Weteringschans
Hendrik M. Van Randwijk-Plantsoen
Den   Texstraat
Nicolaas Witsen Kade
Singelgracht

Frederiksplein

Huidekoperstr
Westeinde
Sarphatistraat
Westeinde
Stadhouderskade

◆ HEINEKEN BROUWERIJ

De Taart van m'n Tante

Te Jacob V. Campenstr
Quellijnstraat
Gerald Doustraat

Kingfisher

Mamouche

Bazar

Albert Cuypstraat
Te Sweelinckstraat

DE PIJP

Warung Spang-Makandra

◆ ALBERT CUYPMARKT

Govert Flinckstraat

Braque

Balti House

Ferdinand Bolstraat
Te van der Helststraat
Sarphatipark
Sarphatipark

2e Jan Van der Heijenstraat
Van Woustraat
Ceintuurbaan

Griekse Taverna

Ceintuurbaan

2e van der Helststraat
Ferdinand Bolstraat

Brasserie Witteveen

Yamazato

| 0 | | 250 yards |
| 0 | | 250 meters |

KEY	
⋯⋯	*Tram lines*
⋯⋯	*Canal bus*
■	*Restaurants*
⊹	*following dining reviews indicates a map-grid coordinate*

$ ✕**Bazar Amsterdam.** A golden-angel-capped church provides the singu-
AFRICAN lar setting for this kitsch-addled restaurant. Cheap and flavorful North
Fodor's Choice African cooking, covering the range from falafel to mixed grilled meats,
★ is served here in an environment of convivial chaos. Since it's located
alongside the country's largest outdoor market, Bazar is also the perfect
place to break for coffee (or for breakfast, lunch, or dinner for that
matter) in between rounds of market wandering. ✉ *Albert Cuypstraat
182, The Pijp* ☎ *020/675–0544* ⊕ *www.bazaramsterdam.nl* ▭ *AE, DC,
MC, V* ⊹ *7:A3.*

$$ ✕**Braque.** The recently opened Braque has Amsterdam's foodies squeal-
FRENCH ing with delight over their *confit de canard,* bouillabaisse, *vitello ton-
nato* (sliced, braised veal tenderloin topped with a cream sauce), and
entrecote steak. Braque also offers plenty of wine by the glass to help
diners find that perfect pairing without having to order a whole bottle.
Their pistachio parfait is heavenly and, at €6, a steal. ✉ *Albert Cuyp-
straat 29-31, The Pijp* ☎ *020/670–7357* ⊕ *www.caferestaurantbraque.
com* ⌨ *Reservations essential* ▭ *MC, V* ⊘ *Closed Mon. No lunch*
⊹ *7:A3.*

$$ ✕**Brasserie Witteveen.** Once upon a time this location was a legendary
CAFÉ Dutch grand café complete with Turkish carpeted tables and a dis-
☪ tinctive old-world feel. Since its reopening in 2010, the Brasserie Witteveen is now quite modern with a central bar and brasserie section,

mosaic-tiled floors, a 16-meter chesterfield, wine room, and a separate play area for children (who also have their own menu). However, it remains ultimately open and neighborly as they serve café-style dishes everyday for breakfast, lunch, and dinner. Their soups are delightful: don't miss their Dutch-style pea soup and their Zaanse mustard soup with smoked eel. ⊠ *Ceintuurbaan 256-260, The Pijp* ☎020/344-6406 ⊕ *www.brasseriewitteveen.nl* ⊟ *AE, MC, V* ✛ *7:B3.*

$$
CAFÉ
☺
✕ **De Taart van m'n Tante.** Looking like the set of a children's television program, "My Aunt's Cake" has funky tables covered with wacky and colorful pies and cakes. In fact, many of these products—which are often developed in cooperation with artists—have side careers as props in Dutch film and television productions. Quiche is the menu's only savory option. This is a perfect place to get pumped up on sugar before taking on Albert Cuyp market. ⊠ *Ferdinand Bolstraat 10, The Pijp* ☎ 020/776–4600 ⊕ *www.detaart.com* ⊟ *No credit cards* ☺ *No dinner* ✛ *7:B2.*

$–$$
GREEK
✕ **Griekse Taverna.** You won't find souvlaki or gyros here; nor will you find the activity of plate throwing as a *digestif*. But this woody and comfortable taverna does win points for its late hours (it's open until midnight) and its excellent, affordable, and fresh herbed starters, which are brought to your table en masse for you to choose from. Since these easily make a full meal, you won't have to worry about choosing one of their grilled main dishes until your inevitable next visit. ⊠ *Hobbemakade 64/65, The Pijp* ☎ 020/671–7923 ⊕ *www.degriekse taverna.nl* ⊟ *No credit cards* ☺ *No lunch* ✛ *7:A3.*

$
MEDITERRANEAN
✕ **Kingfisher.** Here you'll find a long narrow eatery frequented by a hip young crowd. The stellar kitchen pumps out sandwiches by day and an inventive and inexpensive daily special for dinner at night. Situated on a corner, it's a great spot for people-watching. ⊠ *Ferdinand Bolstraat 23, The Pijp* ☎ 020/671–2395 ⊟ *No credit cards* ✛ *7:B2.*

$$–$$$
MOROCCAN
✕ **Mamouche.** All signs of this location's past as a Hell's Angels bar have been erased; it's now a North African teahouse that takes delight in the smallest details. Romantic and posh, this spot has been a hit with locals for dishes such as couscous with saffron-baked pumpkin. Chocoholics will say a heartfelt amen when rounding off their meal with the *Hob El Habiba*, a chocolate-and-date pie. ⊠ *Quelijnstraat 104, The Pijp* ☎ 020/670–0736 ⊕ *www.restaurantmamouche.nl* ⊟ *MC, V* ☺ *No lunch* ✛ *7:B2.*

¢–$
INDONESIAN
✕ **Warung Spang-Makandra.** The Indonesian-inspired (via Surinam) food at this local favorite includes *loempias* (egg rolls of sorts). You can also try Japanese *rames*—a mini-rice-table-style smorgasbord on a plate. The dressed-down interior might remind you of a snack bar, but the staff is friendly and the food is tasty. No wonder the place is always busy. ⊠ *Gerard Doustraat 39, The Pijp* ☎ 020/670–5081 ⊕ *www.spangmakandra.nl* ⊟ *No credit cards* ✛ *7:B2.*

$$$–$$$$
JAPANESE
Fodor's Choice
★
✕ **Yamazato.** Located in the Hotel Okura Amsterdam, traditional and fresh Japanese food is sublimely presented in a modern atmosphere with a Zenlike sushi bar, semiprivate booths, a kimonoed waitstaff, and views over a fishpond. For those without expense accounts, there are more economical menu offerings, like miso and seafood soups, sushi, sashimi,

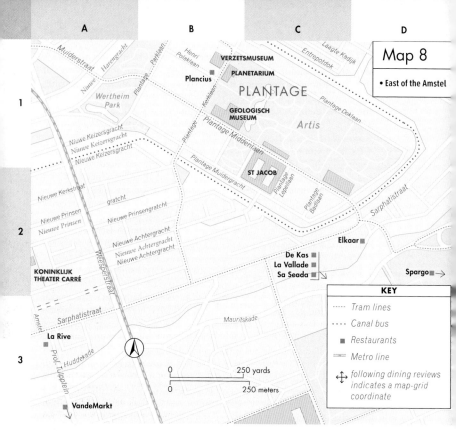

Map 8

• East of the Amstel

KEY

···· Tram lines

···· Canal bus

■ Restaurants

▦ Metro line

⬦ *following dining reviews
indicates a map-grid
coordinate*

yakitori, and grilled whole fishes and steaks. As is natural with a res-
taurant of this caliber, the wine list and the saki list are encyclopedic.
While you're here, head up to the hotel's top-floor cocktail bar, Twenty
Third Bar, for some epic views of the city. ✉ *Hotel Okura Amsterdam,
Ferdinand Bolstraat 333, The Pijp* ☏ *020/678-8351* ⊕ *www.yamazato.
nl* ⌂ *Reservations essential* ☰ *AE, MC, DC, V* ⬦ *7:B3.*

EAST OF THE AMSTEL

Head away from the historical center, east of the Amstel River, and
toward the tranquil neighborhood known as the Plantage for a truly
leisurely meal. The areas around the Hortus Botanicus and the Tropenmuseum are home to some of the nicest places for a leisurely meal.

$$$
MEDITERRANEAN
Fodor's Choice
★

✕ **De Kas.** This 1926-built municipal "greenhouse" must be the ultimate
workplace for chefs: they can begin the day picking the best and fresh-
est of homegrown produce before building an inspired Mediterranean
menu around them. For diners it's equally sumptuous, especially since
the setting includes two very un-Dutch commodities—lots of light and
a giddy sense of vertical space, thanks to the glass roof. The frequently
changing prix-fixe menu always consists of a selection of small starters,
followed by a main course and a dessert. Don't miss out on the house
cocktail: champagne with lemon basil. ✉ *Kamerlingh Onnelaan 3, East*

The serene dining room at Yamazato.

of Amstel ☎ 020/462–4562 ⊕ www.restaurantdekas.nl ⌂ Reservations essential ▭ AE, DC, MC, V ⊗ Closed Sun. No lunch Sat. ✚ 8:C2.

$$$$ ✕ **La Rive.** Located within the InterContinental Amstel Amsterdam
FRENCH Hotel—the lodging of choice for royalty, dignitaries, and rock stars—La Rive is the city's unparalleled purveyor of refined French and Mediterranean cuisines. The setting is chic, with views over the river and formal service that is solicitous but not stuffy. If you don't mind emptying your wallet, settle in for the full seven-course menu for €112 (but you might just want to settle for a two-course lunch for €49). A lobster gazpacho with Granny Smith apples and cucumber kaffir is a typical starter, and main courses reflect a marked fetish for the ultimate ingredients. For instance, a meatier choice is their Wagyu sirloin with rosemary, short rib, baby vegetables, and Barolo. You'll need to book two weeks ahead to guarantee a table. ⊠ InterContinental Amstel Amsterdam Hotel, Professor Tulpplein 1, East of Amstel ☎ 020/520–3264 ⊕ www. restaurantlarive.com ⌂ Reservations essential 🏛 Jacket and tie ▭ AE, DC, MC, V ⊗ Closed Sun. No lunch Sat. ✚ 8:A3.

$$$$ ✕ **La Vallade.** A candlelit cozy atmosphere and revered country cooking
MEDITERRANEAN inspire many to take Tram 9 to this outlying restaurant on the Ringdijk, the city's perimeter dike. Every night a new four-course menu is posted, which you can get for just €32. A lovely terrace that opens in the summer slightly increases the chances of being able to book a table. ⊠ Ringdijk 23, East of Amstel ☎ 020/665–2025 ⌂ Reservations essential ▭ No credit cards ⊗ No lunch ✚ 8:C2.

$$ ✕ **Plancius.** With its arty but calming leather-walled interior, Plancius
ECLECTIC offers a refreshing sense of space after the chaos of the Artis zoo or the cramped exhibits at the Resistance Museum. After breakfast and

lunch service, things get kicked up a notch in the evenings, when a fashionable and convivial crowd comes to hobnob. The superb menu (don't miss their blackboard daily specials) is adventurous, mixing and matching everything from Italian *panzarotti* (a folded-over pizza of sorts) to Indian lentil soup to fish steaks with teriyaki and tahini sauce. Everything is made from scratch, right down to the tapenade. ⊠ *Plantage Kerklaan 61a, East of Amstel* ☎ *020/330–9469* ⊕ *www.restaurantplancius.nl* ▭ *AE, DC, MC, V* ✛ *8:B1*.

$$–$$$ ✕ **Restaurant Elkaar.** In a white-and-red corner building, this relatively
FRENCH   new addition to the dining scene is easy to spot. Inside, the dark-wood paneling, pressed linen tablecloths, and knowledgeable waitstaff conspire to make a visit feel like a special occasion. And the food—crispy sweetbreads, pumpkin ravioli, or the *côte de boeuf* (bone-in ribeye)—do not disappoint. In summer you can dine alfresco. ⊠ *Alexanderplein 6, East of Amstel* ☎ *020/330–7559,* ⊕ *www.etenbijelkaar.nl* ▭ *AE, DC, MC, V.* ⊘ *No lunch Sat.* ✛ *8:D2.*

$–$$ ✕ **Sa Seada.** Named after a Sardinian dish, this slightly out-of-the-way
ITALIAN   eatery near Ooster Park has some of the best pizza and calzones in town (including one particularly delicious number with ricotta cheese). It also sports a great patio if things inside get a little too cozy. It's just a shame that European Union regulations no longer allow the importing of the famed Sardinian worm cheese. It's not only a crime against cheese plates everywhere, but also prevents this place from being the ultimate in authenticity. But here we can blame the EU, and not this wonderful little treasure. ⊠ *1e Oosterparkstraat 3–5, East of Amstel* ☎ *020/663–3276* ✎ *Reservations essential* ▭ *AE* ⊘ *Closed Mon. No lunch* ✛ *8:C2.*

$–$$ ✕ **Spargo.** This funky neighborhood eatery always draws a crowd
ECLECTIC   despite its slightly off-the-beaten-path location. A nicely executed menu features dishes such as lamb *tajine* (stew), roasted trout, and entrecote from the neighborhood butcher. The waitstaff, ever ready with a toothy grin, is among the most attractive and friendly in the city. In the summer you can wine and dine on the sunny terrace. ⊠ *Linnaeusstraat 37a, East of Amstel* ☎ *020/694–1140* ⊕ *www.cafespargo.nl* ▭ *AE, DC, MC, V* ✛ *8:D2.*

$$–$$$ ✕ **VandeMarkt.** "From the Market" truly defines the food here: each
MEDITERRANEAN   course of the day's three- (€39.50) or four- (€48.50) or five- (€57.50) course feast is made from the freshest ingredients found at the market that morning. As such, the vegetarian-friendly menu might include anything from a giant artichoke served with grilled seasonal mushrooms to a lobster bisque with prawn wontons to wild duck with sage sauce. (Often, dishes exhibit an Asian touch.) The setting is sleek and up-to-the-minute trendy, with simple pine floors contrasting with brightly colored walls. ⊠ *Schollenbrugstraat 8–9, East of Amstel* ☎ *020/468–6958* ⊕ *www.vandemarkt.nl* ✎ *Reservations essential* ▭ *AE, DC, MC, V* ⊘ *Closed Sun. and Mon., 3 wks in July and Aug. No lunch* ✛ *8:A3.*

Where to Stay

WORD OF MOUTH

"I very much enjoyed my stay at the Ambassade Hotel. I walked to almost every tourist and not-so-tourist location, and the hotel, while in a historic building, was in very good condition, and had all the services I needed. I felt I had chosen well."

—elaine

Updated
by Steven
McCarron

A city renowned for its canals, artistic culture, and classic 17th-century architecture, Amsterdam offers a multitude of lodging options capable of transporting any visitor back into the Golden Age.

Behind the quaint decorative facades, however, are all the modern conveniences and luxuries one could hope for. Accommodations throughout the city are egalitarian; no matter the budget, from grand hotels to family-run bed-and-breakfasts, easy access to attractions and idyllic canal views are available to all.

Naturally, there's more to any hotel stay than the panorama, which is where Amsterdam's hotels flex their muscles. Young backpackers can mingle in the city's hip hostels for as little as €20, while down-to-earth properties such as Museumzicht and Fita set exceptionally clean standards, serving customers with a smile and a personal local touch. Serene yet unexpected experiences can be found at Hotel de Filosoof and the Lloyd Hotel, which embrace Dutch philosophy and history in their unique room designs. And, of course, solid standards are taken to the next level by upmarket heavyweights such as the stately InterContinental Amstel Amsterdam and newly refurbished hotels: Park and The Grand. Although varying dramatically, they demonstrate how historic monumental buildings can be modernized and transformed into state-of-the-art facilities, providing rooms fit for royalty, business travelers, and tourists in one impressive swoop.

As the Netherlands continues to make waves at the forefront of European design, it's no surprise that the latest lodging trends are inspired by contemporary architecture firms and designers making an international impact. New hotels such as CitizenM and Hotel V have shrugged off the Golden Age facades in favor of cutting-edge interiors and furnishings, balancing budget with modern luxury. It's a trend that seems set to continue; the Marcel Wanders–designed 122-room Andaz Amsterdam, located in a former public library, is already causing a citywide stir despite not opening its doors until spring 2012.

WHERE SHOULD I STAY?

	NEIGHBORHOOD VIBE	PROS	CONS
The Old City Center (Het Centrum)	Historic monuments are in abundance, with hotels surrounded on all sides by sights, bars, restaurants, and shops.	The vibrant beating heart of the city, with all the important attractions within easy walking distance.	With its maze of narrow streets and canals, it's easy to get lost in the seedier parts of the Red Light District. Beware of pickpockets.
The Canal Rings	Independent stores line the narrow streets; Golden Age properties converted into hotels.	The many canals offer a picture-perfect postcard view at every turn. Boat companies have numerous jetties.	Local shops, cafés, and restaurants are typically overpriced, attracting more tourists than in-the-know locals.
The Jordaan	An adorable neighborhood comprised of 17th-century properties and beautiful churches.	A sense of Old Amsterdam, with its quiet narrow streets and stretches of water free of tour boats.	Original Amsterdam residents have moved away, making way for more affluent homeowners and increased prices.
The Leidseplein	The city's most central entertainment area bustles with activity from early evening to morning hours.	Bars, restaurants, theaters, concert halls, and nightclubs occupy every possible space.	Noise from bars, trams, and late-night revelers penetrates the windows of many hotels located in the thick of it.
Museum District	All of the city's top museums are found here, as well as Amsterdam's plushest shopping street.	There's enough surrounding culture to last for days, while the renowned Vondelpark is the perfect location to chill out.	Tour buses regularly block roads around the major museums.
The Pijp	A residential area where you'll get a feel for what it's like to live in the city.	Home of the famous Albert Cuypmarkt, shopping areas, local charm, and a calming respite from the central tourist traps.	Fewer famous attractions in the neighborhood means more time traveling back and forth to your hotel.
East of the Amstel	One of Amsterdam's greenest areas, with parks, the zoo, and botanical gardens all on the doorstep.	A gentle-paced neighborhood that's perfect for family outings and peaceful exploration on foot.	Deserted streets in the evening. If seeking more vibrant nightlife, you'll need a tram into the center of the city.

4

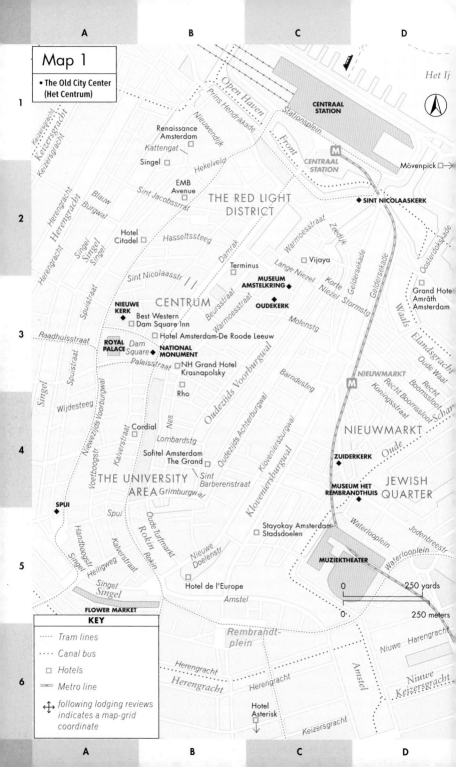

Map 1

- The Old City Center
  (Het Centrum)

Het Ij

CENTRAAL STATION

Open Haven

Prins Hendrikkade

Nieuwendijk

Stationsplein

Front

CENTRAAL STATION

Renaissance
Amsterdam

Kattengat

Hekelveld

Singel

Mövenpick

EMB
Avenue

Sint Jacobsstr

**THE RED LIGHT
DISTRICT**

SINT NICOLAASKERK

Blauw
Burgwal

Herengracht

Herengracht

Herengracht

Hotel
Citadel

Hasseltssteeg

Warmoesstraat

Zeedijk

Oosterdokskade

Singel

Singel

Sint Nicolaasstr

Damrak

Vijaya

Lange Niezel

Korte
Niezel

Geldersekade

Geldersekade

Waals

Grand Hote
Amräth
Amsterdam

Spuistraat

Terminus

**MUSEUM
AMSTELKRING**

Beursstraat

Warmoesstraat

Stormstg

Molenstg

Elandsgracht

Oude Waal

CENTRUM

**NIEUWE
KERK**

Best Western
Dam Square Inn

OUDEKERK

Recht Boomssloot

Boomssloot

Raadhuisstraat

Hotel Amsterdam-De Roode Leeuw

**ROYAL
PALACE**

Dam
Square

**NATIONAL
MONUMENT**

Paleisstraat

Oudezijds Voorburgwal

Barndesteg

NIEUWMARKT

Koningsstraat

Schar

Spuistraat

Wijdesteeg

NH Grand Hotel
Krasnapolsky

Rho

NIEUWMARKT

Oude

Singel

Nieuwezijds Voorburgwal

Cordial

Nes

Lombardstg

Oudezijds Achterburgwal

ZUIDERKERK

**JEWISH
QUARTER**

Voetboogstr

Kalverstraat

**THE UNIVERSITY
AREA**

Sofitel Amsterdam
The Grand

Sint
Barberenstraat

Grimburgwal

Kloveniersburgwal

Kloveniersburgwal

**MUSEUM HET
REMBRANDTHUIS**

Jodenbreestr

SPUI

Spui

Oude Turfmarkt

Rokin

Nieuwe
Doelenstr

Stayokay Amsterdam-
Stadsdoelen

Waterlooplein

Waterlooplein

Handboogstr

Kalverstraat

Heiligweg

Rokin

MUZIEKTHEATER

0   250 yards

Singel

Singel

Hotel de l'Europe

Amstel

0   250 meters

FLOWER MARKET

KEY

····· Tram lines

····· Canal bus

□ Hotels

▬ Metro line

⬧ following lodging reviews
  indicates a map-grid
  coordinate

Rembrandt-
plein

Niuwe Harengracht

Herengracht

Herengracht

Herengracht

Amstel

Niuwe
Keizersgracht

Hotel
Asterisk

Keizersgracht

Keizersgracht

Keizersgracht

WHERE TO STAY PLANNER

Lodging Strategy

Where should we stay? With hundreds of Amsterdam hotels, it may seem like a daunting question. But fret not—our expert writers and editors have done most of the legwork. The selections here represent the best this city has to offer—from the best budget stays to the sleekest designer hotels. Scan "Best Bets" on the following pages for top recommendations by price and experience. Or find a review quickly in the listings— search by neighborhood, then alphabetically. Happy hunting!

Smoking

Smoking is banned in public spaces within buildings in the Netherlands. As such, smoking within hotel receptions, foyers, bars, and restaurants is illegal.

In This Chapter

Facilities

Most hotels offer TV, phone, and tea and coffeemakers. Due to the temperate climate and volume of monumental buildings, air-conditioning is far from being a standard option, found more commonly in the moderately and high-priced accommodations. Internet and Wi-Fi are found in almost all hotels; however, many may charge a fee. In larger hotel chains with business suites, free high-speed Internet at computer terminals and in-room Wi-Fi are more commonly available.

Parking in Amsterdam is restricted and expensive. Few hotels have private parking garages, instead partnering with nearby facilities and offering discounted street parking or utilizing citywide valet services. Parking fees vary on average from €24 to €60 per day.

Prices and Price Chart

Hotel room prices in Amsterdam typically include a VAT (value added tax) of 6% and a city tax of 5%. The majority of hotels follow the European Plan (EP) for meals, meaning breakfast is an additional charge per day. Low budget hotels often buck this trend by offering a Continental Plan comprised of a varied hot and cold buffet. While almost all major credit cards are accepted, a 5% surcharge is not uncommon, particularly in smaller hotels. High season in Amsterdam runs from April through September.

WHAT IT COSTS IN EUROS

	¢	$	$$	$$$	$$$$
FOR TWO PEOPLE	under €75	€75–€120	€121–€165	€166–€230	over €230

Prices are for two people in a standard double room in high season, including the 6% VAT (value-added tax).

HOTEL REVIEWS

Listed alphabetically within neighborhoods. Use the coordinate (✛ 1:B2) at the end of each listing to locate a site on the corresponding map.

THE OLD CITY CENTER (HET CENTRUM)

If you want to stay in the heart of Amsterdam, head for the area surrounding Dam Square. Its bustling crowds mean you'll always have company. The adjacent Red Light District may cast a less-than-rosy glow, but this part of Amsterdam is a must-see area that remains one of the city's most historic neighborhoods.

$$–$$$ **Best Western Dam Square Inn.** Just around the corner from the Royal Palace, this hotel is a surprisingly quiet oasis because of its location on a narrow, pedestrian-only street. The Amsterdam School–style building is adorned with storybook-ornate brick-and-stone trim and a gabled roof; inside, rooms are modern and comfortable with terra-cotta and dark green furnishings. The building once housed a liquor distillery, and you can still enjoy a visit to the tasting house next door. A nice plus here is the hotel's level of service. It's no surprise that visitors return again and again. **Pros:** gorgeous building; on a meandering lane just off Dam Square. **Cons:** rooms fill up fast; reception area feels claustrophobic. ⊠ *Gravenstraat 12–16, Centrum* ☎ *020/623–3716* ⊕ *www.bestwesterndamsquareinn.com* ➔ *38 rooms, 1 suite* ⚲ *In-room: safe, Wi-Fi. In-hotel: bar, laundry service, Internet terminal, no-smoking rooms* ▤ *AE, DC, MC, V* ⦿⧍ *EP* ✛ *1:A3.*

$–$$ **Cordial Hotel.** Young international travelers are drawn to this hotel because it is easy on the budget, informal, and centrally located. Front rooms face the busy Rokin shopping street, and there's a terrace in front of the hotel for people-watching while enjoying a drink. All units are sparely outfitted with utilitarian furnishings, but are bright and clean. There's a cold breakfast buffet included in the price. **Pros:** budget-friendly stay; good location. **Cons:** basic rooms; noise from nearby construction. ⊠ *Rokin 62–64, Centrum* ☎ *020/626–4411* ⊕ *www.cordialhotel.nl* ➔ *52 rooms* ⚲ *In-room: no a/c, safe, Wi-Fi. In-hotel: bar, Wi-Fi hotspot* ▤ *AE, DC, MC, V* ⦿⧍ *CP* ✛ *1:A4.*

$$–$$$ **EMB Avenue.** This hotel occupies several historic buildings, including one that used to be a warehouse for the United East India Company. Its rooms, though small, are comfortable, and are furnished in a bright, cheerful contemporary style. Double window glazing and extra-thick walls ensure that you won't be disturbed by street noise or rambunctious neighbors. The large and varied breakfast buffet gets consistent raves. **Pros:** historic building; quiet interior despite bustling neighborhood. **Cons:** smallish rooms. ⊠ *Nieuwezijds Voorburgwal 33, Centrum* ☎ *020/530–9530* ⊕ *www.embhotels.nl* ➔ *80 rooms* ⚲ *In-room: Internet, Wi-Fi. In-hotel: bar, laundry service, Wi-Fi hotspot, no-smoking rooms* ▤ *AE, DC, MC, V* ⦿⧍ *CP* ✛ *1:B2.*

$$$$ **Grand Hotel Amrâth Amsterdam.** Perfect for anyone into Amsterdam School–style architecture and design (basically Art Nouveau, but more sober), or for anyone looking for quiet luxury without unnecessary extravagance. Originally the office for the major Dutch shipping

BEST BETS FOR AMSTERDAM LODGING

Fodor's offers a selective listing of quality lodging experiences in every price range, from the city's best budget options to its most sophisticated luxury hotel. Here, we've compiled our top recommendations by price and experience. The very best properties—in other words, those that provide a particularly remarkable experience in their price range—are designated in the listings with the Fodor's Choice logo.

Fodor'sChoice ★

Ambassade, p. 158
CitizenM, p. 178
Flying Pig Uptown Hostel, p. 171
Hotel de Filosoof, p. 172
Hotel Fita, p. 172
Hotel V, p. 168
InterContinental Amstel Amsterdam, p. 183
Lloyd Hotel, p. 183
Mövenpick, p. 154
Museumzicht, p. 175
Park Hotel Amsterdam, p. 169
Sofitel Amsterdam The Grand, p. 156

By Price

¢

Flying Pig Uptown Hotel, p. 171
Hans Brinker, p. 168
Stayokay Amsterdam-Vondelpark, p. 176

$

CitizenM, p. 178
Conscious Hotel Museum Square, p. 170
Dikker and Thijs Fenice, p. 166
Hotel de Filosoof, p. 172
Museumzicht, p. 175
Nadia, p. 165
Rembrandt, p. 184

$$

Amsterdam Wiechmann, p. 165
Hotel Fita, p. 172
Hotel V, p. 168
Mövenpick, p. 154
NH Schiller, p. 164
Piet Hein, p. 175

$$$

Ambassade, p. 158
The College Hotel, p. 170
Lloyd Hotel, p. 183

Okura Amsterdam, p. 180
Park Hotel Amsterdam, p. 169

$$$$

Dylan Amsterdam, p. 159
InterContinental Amstel Amsterdam, p. 183
Grand Hotel Amrâth Amsterdam, p. 151
Hotel Pulitzer Amsterdam, p. 160
Sofitel Amsterdam The Grand, p. 156

By Experience

BEST B&B'S

Hotel Fita, p. 172
Museumzicht, p. 175
Seven Bridges, p. 164

BEST-KEPT SECRET

Hotel de Filosoof, p. 172
Rembrandt, p. 184

BEST SERVICE

Dylan Amsterdam, p. 159
InterContinental Amstel Amsterdam, p. 183
Park Hotel, Amsterdam, p. 169
Nadia, p. 165
Sofitel Amsterdam The Grand, p. 156

BUSINESS TRAVEL

Apollo First, p. 178
Bilderberg Garden, p. 178
CitizenM, p. 178
Mövenpick, p. 154

HOTEL DINING

Mövenpick, p. 154
Sofitel Amsterdam The Grand, p. 156

KID-FRIENDLY

Eden Lancaster Hotel, p. 181
Hotel Asterisk, p. 153
Hotel Fita, p. 172
Lloyd Hotel, p. 183
Mövenpick, p. 154
Park Hotel Amsterdam, p. 169
Okura Amsterdam, p. 180

MOST ROMANTIC

The College Hotel, p. 170
Hotel V, p. 168
Lloyd Hotel, p. 183
Sofitel Amsterdam The Grand, p. 156

companies, the appropriately called "Shipping House" (*Scheepvaar-thuis*) was reopened as the Amrâth Hotel in June 2007, after a massive renovation. Fortunately, almost all the original owners' symbols, sculptures, wood paneling, and stained-glass art remain, even the furniture, wallpaper patterns, and signage. While the rooms themselves are everything you would expect, the public areas lack the grandeur often found in five-star hotels. The atmosphere may be studiously restrained, but the service is friendly, professional, and prompt. Across from the Centraal Station and around the corner from the Red Light District, the Amrâth offers well-heeled customers a genuine Amsterdam experience. **Pros:** architecturally unique; intimate; impressive wellness center. **Cons:** modest public areas; small bar; diminutive entrance. ⊠ *Prins Hendrik-kade 108, Centrum* ☎ *020/552–0000* ⊕ *www.amrathamsterdam.com* ↘ *142 rooms, 21 suites* ⚿ *In-room: safe, refrigerator (some), DVD (some), Internet, Wi-Fi. In-hotel: restaurant, room service, bar, pool, gym, spa, laundry service, Internet terminal, Wi-Fi hotspot, no-smoking rooms* ⊟ *AE, DC, MC, V* ⊚| *EP* ✛ *1:D3.*

4

$$–$$$ ⛄ **Hotel Amsterdam–De Roode Leeuw.** On the corner of Dam Square and across from the city's leading department store, De Bijenkorf, the Hotel is a cut above the rest of the competition on the Damrak. The front guest rooms, showcasing the elegant 18th-century facade, have soundproof windows that serve as a buffer to the outside world. The rooms at the back or on the "executive floor" are also safe bets. The hotel's restaurant, De Roode Leeuw, has built up a sizable following thanks to its heated terrace, Dutch haute cuisine, and encyclopedic champagne list. **Pros:** easy access to transportation; central location; excellent restaurant. **Cons:** small lobby; lackluster room furnishings. ⊠ *Damrak 93–94, Centrum* ☎ *020/555–0666* ⊕ *www.hotelamsterdam.nl* ↘ *79 rooms, 2 suites* ⚿ *In-room: safe, refrigerator, Internet. In-hotel: restaurant, laundry service, Internet terminal, Wi-Fi hotspot, no-smoking rooms* ⊟ *AE, DC, MC, V* ⊚| *EP* ✛ *1:B3.*

¢–$ ⛄ **Hotel Asterisk.** A touch of the 19th century still hovers about this
⊛   extremely friendly hotel. Some guest rooms feature decorative ceiling moldings and chandeliers. Major art museums, the Leidseplein, the Flower Market, and the Rembrandtsplein are all within walking distance of the hotel, which is on a quiet street. For children, cots and high chairs are available if you request them in advance. Only the main building has an elevator. Breakfast is included in the price only if you pay cash in advance. **Pros:** kid-friendly environment; good value for money; good deal on breakfast. **Cons:** not all rooms have private baths; Web site often outdated. ⊠ *Den Texstraat 16, Centrum* ☎ *020/626–2396* ⊕ *www.asteriskhotel.nl* ↘ *40 rooms, 7 with shared bath* ⚿ *In-room: no a/c, safe, Internet. In-hotel: some pets allowed* ⊟ *AE, MC, V* ⊚| *CP* ✛ *1:C6.*

$$–$$$ ⛄ **Hotel Citadel.** Set in a spiffy brick seven-story building, and topped with a jaunty two-story mansard roof, the Citadel is on a busy main street near the Royal Palace, Dam Square, and the Magna Plaza shopping mall. Rooms at the back of the building are quieter, but top-floor rooms at the front provide a sweeping view of gabled rooftops. All are furnished no-frills style, with modern wood furniture and patterned upholstery. **Pros:** lovely building; a stone's throw from sights

like the Anne Frank House. **Cons:** rooms devoid of charm; noise from trams. ✉ *Nieuwezijds Voorburgwal 98–100, Centrum* ☎ *020/627–3882* ⊕ *www.hotelcitadel.nl* ⤴ *38 rooms* ♿ *In-room: Wi-Fi. In-hotel: room service, bar, laundry service, parking (paid), no-smoking rooms* ▭ *AE, DC, MC, V* ⦿| *CP* ✛ *1:B2.*

$$$$ 🏨 **Hotel de l'Europe.** Owned by Freddy Heineken's daughter, Charlene de Carvalho, this quiet, gracious, and plush hotel has a history extending back to 1638 (although its delightful, storybook facade dates only to the 19th century). Overlooking the Amstel River, the Muntplein, and the Flower Market, it may be familiar to those who remember the setting of Hitchcock's *Foreign Correspondent*. The chandeliered lobby leads off to the lounge, aglow with gold-trimmed ceiling coves and blackamoor lamps—the perfect setting for high tea (served in full glory here). Guest rooms are furnished with reserved classical elegance and all modern conveniences; the hotel was refurbished in 2010, and the luxury Dutch Masters wing, comprising 23 suites, was added in the adjoining building. The restaurant's fine French food is ooh-la-la. **Pros:** statuesque building; cozy bar serving free snacks; balconies perfect for people-watching. **Cons:** cavernous yet largely unused lobby area; entrance is on a narrow busy street. ✉ *Nieuwe Doelenstraat 2–14, Centrum* ☎ *020/531–1777* ⊕ *www.leurope.nl* ⤴ *109 rooms, 23 suites* ♿ *In-room: safe, kitchen (some), refrigerator, Wi-Fi. In-hotel: restaurant, room service, bar, pool, gym, spa, bicycles, laundry service, Internet terminal, Wi-Fi hotspot, parking (paid), some pets allowed, no-smoking rooms* ▭ *AE, DC, MC, V* ✛ *1:B5.*

$$–$$$ 🏨 **Mövenpick.** A striking, reflective glass skyscraper built on an island
⏱   within the blossoming docks area, the Mövenpick stands apart from
Fodor's Choice   the city's traditional hotel scene thanks to its riverfront placement and
★   stunning views of the Amsterdam skyline and beyond. The downside of the location is the walk or short tram ride back into the city center. Fortunately culture vultures can make the most of classical and jazz concerts at the neighboring Muziekgebouw aan 't IJ complex, while in-house restaurant Silk Road ($$$) produces high-quality East-meets-West cuisine. At first sight the hotel may seem business oriented, but it's soft around the edges—welcoming families and selling its own brand of ice cream—and is within walking distance of science center NEMO. In spring and summer, some of the world's largest cruise ships regularly dock beside the hotel, wowing children and adults alike. **Pros:** upper floor suites offer the best views in town; the little-known terrace is a great waterfront spot for refreshments. **Cons:** lacks Dutch character; a deceptively strenuous walk from Centraal Station with luggage. ✉ *Piet Heinkade 11, Eastern Docklands Centrum* ☎ *020/519–1200* ⊕ *www. moevenpick-amsterdam.com* ⤴ *377 rooms, 31 suites* ♿ *In-room: safe, refrigerator, Wi-Fi. In-hotel: restaurant, room service, gym, laundry service, Internet terminal, Wi-Fi hotspot, parking (paid), no-smoking rooms* ▭ *AE, MC, V* ⦿| *CP* ✛ *1:D2.*

$$$–$$$$ 🏨 **NH Grand Hotel Krasnapolsky.** Until the Hilton came along, this hotel was Holland's biggest. As you'll see when you take a table in the Kras's soaringly beautiful *Wintertuin* (Winter Garden), Amsterdam's loveliest place for luncheon, it was also one of the best. Sitting in this masterpiece of 19th-century allure, replete with potted palms, greenhouse roof, Victorian chandeliers, and buffet tables stocked with cakes and roses, will make you feel like a countess or duke. Sadly, the rest of this 1866 landmark isn't as impressive. Unfortunately, a mishmash of revamping over the years was done with a progressively penurious attitude toward living space. Last renovated in 2003, the guest rooms—now numbering more than 468—vary greatly in size and tend toward disappointingly serviceable functionality. There are some memorable dining spots here, however; you can linger over a *jenever* cocktail at the Proeflokaal Wynand Fockink (Tasting House Wynand Fockink), enjoy French cuisine at Restaurant Reflet, or feast on Asian delights at the Shibli Bedoin restaurant. **Pros:** well situated on the Dam Square; great view of Royal Palace; near transportation. **Cons:** gargantuan size; impersonal feel. ✉ *Dam 9, Centrum* ☎ *020/554–9111* ⊕ *www.nh-hotels.com* ↘ *426 rooms, 7 suites, 35 apartments* ⌕ *In-room: safe, kitchen (some), refrigerator, Wi-Fi. In-hotel: 3 restaurants, room service, bar, gym, spa, bicycles, laundry service, Internet terminal, Wi-Fi hotspot, parking (paid), no-smoking rooms* ▭ *AE, DC, MC, V* ⍦ *EP* ✛ *1:B3.*

$$–$$$ ⌖ **Renaissance Amsterdam**. It's not every day that a 17th-century church is part of a hotel, but an underground passage connects the Renaissance with the domed Koepelkerk, an erstwhile Lutheran church that now serves as this hotel's conference center. Smack-dab in the middle of the Centrum (city center), between Dam Square and Centraal Station, this ultramodern hotel's top floors provide panoramic views of the city. Another high point is the hotel's highly popular fitness center, where you can have a complete workout or relax with a massage, steam bath, whirlpool, or sauna. The soaring lobby is basically modern, trimmed out with wood and equipped with wireless Internet access. **Pros:** a stone's throw from Centraal Station; on a charming thoroughfare. **Cons:** basic rooms; corridors resemble university residence halls. ✉ *Kattengat 1, Centrum* ☎ *020/621–2223* ⊕ *www.renaissancehotels. com* ↘ *396 rooms, 6 suites* ⌕ *In-room: safe (some), refrigerator, Internet, Wi-Fi. In-hotel: 3 restaurants, room service, bar, gym, laundry service, Internet terminal, Wi-Fi hotspot, parking (paid), no-smoking rooms* ▭ *AE, DC, MC, V* ⍦ *EP* ✛ *1:B1.*

$$ ⌖ **Rho Hotel**. Few hotels have as marvelous a lobby as this one, thanks to the building's origins as a 1910 theater. Jugendstil ornament, tile trim, and etched glass all conjure up the soigné style of the turn of the 20th century. A rich maroon color is carried out in furnishings throughout the hotel, conveying a bit of the music-hall tinkle; guest room furnishings for the most part, however, are modern and standard issue. Happily located on a quiet side street off the Dam Square, the Rho is within walking distance of theaters, nightlife, and shopping. **Pros:** gorgeous high-ceilinged lobby; near some fabulous restaurants. **Cons:** alley entrance; basic rooms. ✉ *Nes 5–23, Centrum* ☎ *020/620–7371* ⊕ *www. rhohotel.com* ↘ *167 rooms* ⌕ *In-room: safe, refrigerator, Wi-Fi. In-hotel: bar, bicycles, laundry service, Wi-Fi hotspot, parking (paid), some pets allowed, no-smoking rooms* ▭ *AE, MC, V* ⍦ *CP* ✛ *1:B3.*

$$ ⌖ **Singel Hotel**. The three renovated 17th-century canal houses that make up this property are charmingly lopsided and quirky-looking,

with cheerful, striped window canopies. The historic exterior belies the modern furnishings and comforts you'll discover within, which include an elevator and express ironing and shoeshine service. If you want a view of the Singel canal, book a front or side room. From the hotel, it's just a short stroll to the Kalvertoren and Magna Plaza shopping malls, as well as the Dam Square. **Pros:** near Amsterdam's best restaurants and bars; lovely façade; doting service. **Cons:** often noisy on weekends; not all rooms have views. ⊠ *Singel 13–17, Centrum* ☎ *020/626–3108* ⊕ *www.singelhotel.nl* ⤳ *32 rooms* ♿ *In-room: no a/c, safe, Internet, Wi-Fi. In-hotel: room service, bar, laundry service, Wi-Fi hotspot, some pets allowed, no-smoking rooms* ⊟ *AE, DC, MC, V* ⊚ *CP* ✛ *1:B2.*

$$$$
Fodor's Choice
★

Sofitel Amsterdam The Grand. For captivating elegance, nothing tops the facade of the Grand, with its Neoclassical courtyard, white sash windows, carved marble pediments, and roof topped with chimneys and gilded weather vanes. If it seems lifted from a Rembrandt painting, that's because this hotel's celebrated city-center site has a long and varied history: it was built in the 14th century as a convent, then went on to house the offices of the Amsterdam Admiralty. After being rezoned by Napoléon, it became Amsterdam's city hall from 1808 to 1988, and then finally reopened in 1992 as one of the city's most deluxe hotels, where guests like Mick Jagger and President Jacques Chirac of France have made their home-away-from-home. The guest rooms here feature traditional-luxe furniture, fine fabrics, and quiet hues, plus every manner of business mod con. The Bridges, the newly refurbished bright and spacious restaurant ($$$–$$$$), sports a Karel Appel mural and some of the most stylish French dishes in town. The glorious garden is also a great place to enjoy afternoon tea. **Pros:** beautiful courtyard; variety of dining options; good chance of spotting a celebrity. **Cons:** run-down neighborhood; rather noisy location. ⊠ *Oudezijds Voorburgwal 197, Centrum* ☎ *020/555–3111* ⊕ *www.thegrand.nl* ⤳ *125 rooms, 52 suites* ♿ *In-room: safe, refrigerator, Internet, Wi-Fi. In-hotel: 3 restaurants, room service, bar, pool, gym, spa, bicycles, laundry service, Internet terminal, Wi-Fi hotspot, parking (paid), no-smoking rooms* ⊟ *AE, DC, MC, V* ⊚ *EP* ✛ *1:B4.*

¢

Stayokay Amsterdam-Stadsdoelen. Located in a canal house at the edge of the Red Light District, this hostel is a backpacker's Ritz. Usually filled with young, friendly international travelers, it has a reputation as the most *gezellig*, or cozy, place to stay in Amsterdam. Some say if you're looking for simple accommodation at a bargain-basement price, you can't do better. The dormitories are immaculate, with breakfast and bedsheets included in the price. You can get meals and drinks at the café. Everyone congregates in the lobby to make new friends, watch TV, or use the Internet. **Pros:** cheap and cheerful; friendly vibe; near the city's best secondhand bookstores. **Cons:** dorm-style accommodations; books up fast. ⊠ *Kloveniersburgwal 97, Centrum* ☎ *020/624–6832* ⊕ *www.stayokay.com* ⤳ *10 dormitories, 178 beds* ♿ *In-room: no a/c, no phone, no TV, Wi-Fi. In-hotel: restaurant, bar, bicycles, laundry facilities, Internet terminal, Wi-Fi hotspot, no-smoking rooms* ⊟ *AE, MC, V* ⊚ *CP* ✛ *1:C5.*

Mövenpick Amsterdam

Ambassade

$–$$ ☐ **Terminus.** Eleven 18th-century town houses make up the Terminus— between the Berlage Exchange and the Oudekerk (Old Church), two famed historic sites. The views of the Old Church—Amsterdam's oldest—are wonderful, but unfortunately, its bell chimes every half hour around the clock, which means it can be heard in some rooms even through the double-glazed windows. The modern glass-paneled entrance manages not to detract from the traditional beauty of the buildings, and there's a solarium for sunny days. The guest-room interiors are elegantly modern, comfortable, and boring. The location is the greatest draw here: you're in the heart of the city, surrounded by landmarks and in the major shopping district. **Pros:** close to historic monuments; pleasant and helpful staff. **Cons:** no-frills accommodations; nearby streets attract late-night revelers. ⊠ *Beursstraat 11–19, Centrum* ☎ *020/622–0535* ⊕ *www.terminus.nl* ⤵ *105 rooms* ⚭ *In-room: no a/c, safe (some). In-hotel: bar, laundry service, Wi-Fi hotspot, some pets allowed, no-smoking rooms* ⊟ *AE, MC, V* ⫶⊚⫶*EP* ✛ *1:B2.*

$ ☐ **Vijaya.** As with many 18th-century canal-house hotels, the exterior here is eye-catching—this one has a particularly ornate gable—and the inside is modernized. Comfortably furnished rooms in front have a canal view, but the rooms at the back are quieter. The family rooms sleep five. Near Dam Square, the main shopping streets and Centraal Station, you are also just a short tram ride away from the major museums. **Pros:** authentic Amsterdam vibe; near plenty of restaurants; rooms for families. **Cons:** near Red Light District; some unsavory characters milling around. ⊠ *Oudezijds Voorburgwal 44, Centrum* ☎ *020/638–0102* ⊕ *www.hotelvijaya.com* ⤵ *30 rooms* ⚭ *In-room: no a/c, Wi-Fi. In-hotel: 2 restaurants, Internet terminal, some pets allowed, no-smoking rooms* ⊟ *AE, MC, V* ⫶⊚⫶*CP* ✛ *1:C2.*

THE CANAL RINGS

Most Grachtengordel (Canal Ring) lodgings are in older buildings with all the Golden Age trimmings. As for neighborhoods, these canal-side hotels are listed as either in the Western Canal Ring, northwest of the Golden Bend area, or the Eastern Canal Ring, to its southeast.

WESTERN CANAL RING

The Western Canal Ring is separated from its eastern counterpart by the Leidsestraat, a narrow street running from the Leidseplein in the south to the Koningsplein in the north. West of the Leidsestraat lies the Nine Streets shopping area, with roads named for the animals whose hides were used in the district's tanning industry.

$$$ ☐ **Ambassade.** Ten 17th- and 18th-century houses have been folded
Fodor's Choice   into this hotel on the Herengracht near the Spui square. Friday's book
★   market on the square might explain the Ambassade's popularity with book-world people: Doris Lessing, John Le Carré, Umberto Eco, and Salman Rushdie are regulars, and novelist Howard Norman set part of his book *The Museum Guard* here. Two lounges—one of which functions as a breakfast room—and a library are elegantly decorated with Oriental rugs, chandeliers, clocks, paintings, and antiques. The canal-side rooms are spacious, with large floor-to-ceiling windows and solid

functional furniture. The rooms at the rear are quieter but smaller and darker; attic rooms have beamed ceilings. The service is attentive and friendly. **Pros:** on a picturesque canal; hub for literati. **Cons:** slightly wayworn interiors; rooms at rear can be small and dark. ⊠ *Herengracht 341, Western Canal Ring* ☎ *020/555–0222* ⊕ *www.ambassade-hotel. nl* ↵ *52 rooms, 7 suites, 1 apartment* ⌂ *In-room: DVD (some), Internet, Wi-Fi. In-hotel: restaurant, room service, bicycles, laundry service, Internet terminal, Wi-Fi hotspot, some pets allowed, no-smoking rooms* ⊟ *AE, MC, V* ⍓ *EP* ✛ *2:A4.*

$–$$ ⌁ **Chic&Basic.** Relatively new to Amsterdam's budget hotel scene, Chic&Basic's overtly earnest title may generate the occasional guffaw, but it's a mission statement that's appealing for those in an austere mood. Clean simple designs dominate the breakfast area and foyer, with its white chairs and walls accented by bright bursts of colors. Although certainly 'chic' to a point, the 'basic' is reflected in the lack of fine details; the hanging art is bland stock photography and there's little in the way of decorative trimmings. It's also worth noting that the hotel remains in transition: half of the building has been upgraded to the contemporary style, while the other half awaits modernization, still offering vintage European-style wooden furniture and carpeting. Its central canal-facing location is a perfect balance of peaceful but near the action, with restaurants and bars only moments away. **Pros:** a design vibe for the budget conscious; great location; some rooms at the back have a small terrace. **Cons:** ongoing modernization; not all rooms have a view. ⊠ *Herengracht 13-19, Western Canal Ring* ☎ *020/522–2345* ⊕ *www.chicandbasic.com* ↵ *26 rooms* ⌂ *In-room: no a/c (some), safe (some), Internet, Wi-Fi. In-hotel: bicycles, laundry service, Internet terminal, Wi-Fi hotspot, parking (paid), no-smoking rooms.* ⊟ *AE, DC, MC, V* ⍓ *CP* ✛ *2:B1.*

$$$$ ⌁ **Dylan Amsterdam.** Known for her chic London properties, Anouska Hempel opened this Amsterdam outpost as the city's first "designer" hotel. It's located at (and incorporates a stone-arch entranceway from) the site of the historic Municipal Theater, which burned down in the 17th century. Today, the elegant rooms here are decorated with lacquered trunks, mahogany screens, modernist hardwood tables, and luxurious upholstery. One suite commands a view of the canal; many other rooms overlook a serene central courtyard. The hotel's restaurant Vinkeles ($$$–$$$$) offers an acclaimed French menu in a vogueish setting that functioned as a bakery between 1787 and 1811. **Pros:** a taste of old Amsterdam; good for celebrity spotting; updated business facilities. **Cons:** some parts of the hotel feel overdesigned; not all rooms have water views. ⊠ *Keizersgracht 384, Western Canal Ring* ☎ *020/530–2010* ⊕ *www.dylanamsterdam.com* ↵ *33 rooms, 8 suites* ⌂ *In-room: safe, Wi-Fi. In-hotel: restaurant, room service, bar, gym, spa, bicycles, laundry service, Internet terminal, Wi-Fi hotspot, parking (paid), no-smoking rooms* ⊟ *AE, DC, MC, V* ⍓ *EP* ✛ *2:A4.*

$$ ⌁ **Estheréa.** This hotel, which incorporates six 17th-century houses, has been run by the same family for three generations. The property has been modernized but still retains its historic charm; the lobby is filled with antiques and brass chandeliers, and the smallish, pastel-hued

rooms have Adamesque ceilings and doors, along with plush head-boards made from cushions and brass rods. The owners and staff are young, enthusiastic, and highly professional. Free coffee and tea are available 24 hours a day in the lounge. **Pros:** efficient and friendly staff; harmoniously decorated public areas; lovely breakfast room. **Cons:** no restaurant. ⊠ *Singel 303–309, Western Canal Ring* ☎ *020/624–5146* ⊕ *www.estherea.nl* ↙ *92 rooms* ♨ *In-room: safe, refrigerator, DVD, Wi-Fi. In-hotel: room service, bar, laundry service, Internet terminal, Wi-Fi hotspot, parking (paid), no-smoking rooms* ▭ *AE, DC, MC, V* ⊠OI*EP* ✛ *2:A3.*

$$–$$$ ⊡**Hampshire Inn Prinsengracht.** With vast town-house windows over-looking the houseboat-graced Prinsengracht Canal, these two 18th-century canal houses are a popular choice. When the weather is fine, it's delightful to breakfast in the hotel's garden, which also has its own small guesthouse, a simple affair that sleeps up to four. Front rooms have a view of the Prinsengracht; back rooms overlook the garden. A short walk takes you to the Rembrandtplein, the Flower Market, and the main shopping area by the Kalverstraat. **Pros:** great location; some rooms have garden views. **Cons:** some rooms are uncomfortably small; rooms tend to book up fast. ⊠ *Prinsengracht 1015, Western Canal Ring* ☎ *020/623–7779* ⊕ *www.prinsengrachthotel.nl* ↙ *34 rooms* ♨ *In-room: no a/c, safe, Wi-Fi. In-hotel: room service, bar, bicycles, laundry service, Internet terminal, Wi-Fi hotspot, no-smoking rooms* ▭ *AE, MC, V* ⊠OI*EP* ✛ *2:B5.*

¢–$ ⊡**Hegra.** In a 17th-century building on the Herengracht canal, this hotel embodies what the Dutch call *klein maar fijn* (small but good). Rooms are unpretentious but comfortable, and the ones in front have a canal view. Some have shared baths. The absence of amenities is offset by the cordiality of the family that runs the property, the great location (near the Anne Frank House, shopping streets, and the major art museums), and the relatively gentle price tag. **Pros:** pleasant staff; good value. **Cons:** basic furnishings; not all rooms have private bathrooms. ⊠ *Herengracht 269, Western Canal Ring* ☎ *020/623–7877* ⊕ *www.hotelhegra.nl* ↙ *11 rooms, 2 with shared bath* ♨ *In-room: no a/c, no phone, no TV, Wi-Fi. In-hotel: Internet terminal, Wi-Fi hotspot, parking (paid), no-smoking rooms* ▭ *AE, DC, MC, V* ⊠OI*CP* ✛ *2:A3.*

$$$$ ⊡**Hotel Pulitzer, Amsterdam.** A clutch of 17th- and 18th-century houses—25 in all—were combined to create this rambling hotel sprinkled with landscaped garden courtyards that are featured in the blockbuster movie *Ocean's Twelve*. It faces the Prinsengracht and the Keizersgracht canals and is just a short walk from both the Dam Square and the Jordaan. The place retains a historic quality: most guest rooms—which are surprisingly spacious compared with its labyrinth of narrow halls and steep stairs—have beam ceilings and antique styl-ings. An appropriately historical soundtrack is provided every half hour when the nearby Westerkerk chimes. Modern touches include heated bathroom floors and wireless Internet. **Pros:** friendly vibe; efficient staff; beautiful high-beam ceilings in some rooms. **Cons:** clanging of church bells; rooms vary in quality. ⊠ *Prinsengracht 315–331, Western Canal Ring* ☎ *020/523–5235* ⊕ *www.pulitzeramsterdam.com* ↙ *230 rooms,*

3 suites ☆ In-room: safe, refrigerator, Wi-Fi. In-hotel: restaurant, room service, bar, gym, bicycles, laundry service, Internet terminal, Wi-Fi hotspot, parking (paid), some pets allowed, no-smoking rooms ▤ AE, DC, MC, V ¶ EP ✛ 2:A3.

$$$$ ⊤ **Seven One Seven.** Designer Kees van der Valk savvily applied his discerning eye to the interior of this hotel. Men's suiting fabrics have been used to upholster the overstuffed armchairs and sofas, and guest rooms—each of which is named for a different composer, artist, or writer—are filled with classical antiquities, framed art, flowers, and candles. Breakfast can be served in the suites or downstairs in the Stravinsky Room, where coffee, tea, cakes, wine, and beer are available for the asking throughout the day and evening. There's also a plush library (which is the designated smoking room) and a pretty back patio. **Pros:** wonderful atmosphere; free refreshments throughout the day. **Cons:** no restaurant; staff is not big on smiles. ✉ *Prinsengracht 717, Western Canal Ring* ☎ *020/427–0717* ⊕ *www.717hotel.nl* ⤵ *8 suites ☆ In-room: refrigerator, DVD, Wi-Fi. In-hotel: room service, bicycles, laundry service, Internet terminal, Wi-Fi hotspot, no-smoking rooms* ▤ *AE, DC, MC, V* ¶ *CP* ✛ *2:A5.*

$$–$$$ ⊤ **'t Hotel.** Guests return year after year to this romantic canal-side hotel. It occupies an 18th-century house and is a national monument (which is why there is no elevator, although if you're physically restricted there is a stair lift). Rooms here are larger than those in similar historic lodgings; those in the rear are especially quiet. Room 8 on the top floor has a beautiful garden view. **Pros:** on a quiet stretch of canal; close to dining options. **Cons:** no real communal area; no restaurant. ✉ *Leliegracht 18, Western Canal Ring* ☎ *020/422–2741* ⊕ *www.thotel. nl* ⤵ *8 rooms ☆ In-room: no a/c (some), safe, refrigerator, Wi-Fi. In-hotel: Internet terminal, Wi-Fi hotspot, no-smoking rooms* ▤ *AE, MC, V* ¶ *CP* ✛ *2:A2.*

$$–$$$ ⊤ **The Toren.** The historic setting for the founding of the Free University, this canal-side hotel's two buildings date from 1638 and are overlooked by the Westerkerk *toren* (Western Church tower). Modernized in 2007, designer Wim van de Oudeweetering cultivated a romantic boutique vibe with guest rooms decked out with marble fireplaces and chandeliers (although some also offer such modern conveniences as double whirlpool bathtubs). There's also an elegant bridal suite, and a lovely garden cottage that enjoys its own sun lounge and terrace. The service often exceeds even its four-star status. **Pros:** wonderful salon; helpful staff. **Cons:** no restaurant; lobby gets busy. ✉ *Keizersgracht 164, Western Canal Ring* ☎ *020/622–6352* ⊕ *www.hoteltoren.nl* ⤵ *38 rooms, 2 suites ☆ In-room: safe, refrigerator, DVD, Wi-Fi. In-hotel: room service, bar, bicycles, laundry service, Internet terminal, Wi-Fi hotspot, some pets allowed, no-smoking rooms* ▤ *AE, DC, MC, V* ¶ *EP* ✛ *2:A2.*

EASTERN CANAL RING AND REMBRANDTPLEIN

Rembrandtplein may be a glaring tribute to neon and nightclubs, but the area east of the square offers a peaceful respite. Here you'll find kid-friendly attractions like Artis Zoo, the Hortus Botanicus, and the Tropenmuseum.

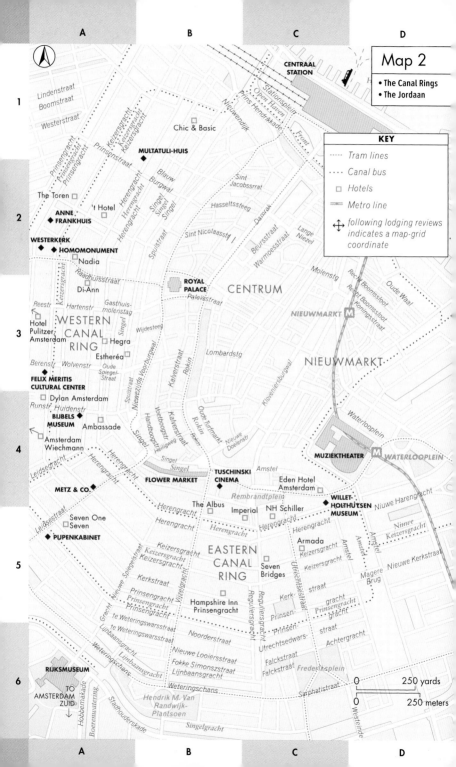

$$$–$$$$ **The Albus.** The exterior of the Albus has been graciously designed to conjure up the look of yesteryear. Inside, seven floors offer rooms of comfortable size. Even the street-side rooms, which overlook the Munt Tower and Flower Market, are remarkably quiet because of their double-paned windows. The hotel lobby and guest rooms are tastefully decorated with wicker chairs and contemporary paintings from the owners' collection. The buffet in the light and cheerful breakfast room serves Dutch specialties as well as more run-of-the-mill fare. **Pros:** Dutch specialties at breakfast; child-care facilities. **Cons:** restaurant has disappointing view; noise from ongoing construction near hotel. ⊠ *Vijzelstraat 49, Eastern Canal Ring and Rembrandtplein* ☎ *020/530–6200* ⊕ *www. albushotel.com* ↘ *74 rooms, 3 apartments* ⚙ *In-room: no a/c, safe, kitchen (some), Internet, Wi-Fi. In-hotel: restaurant, bar, laundry service, bicycles, Internet terminal, Wi-Fi hotspot, no-smoking rooms* ☰ *AE, DC, MC, V* ⊕ *2:B5.*

$–$$ **Armada Hotel.** A superb canal-side location at the corner of the Utrechtsestraat—where there's excellent shopping and dining—is the main draw here. The rooms are simple and some have shared bathrooms. The breakfast room has an aquarium, and—in 17th-century style—small Oriental carpets covering the tables. **Pros:** friendly staff; excellent location near Rembrandtplein. **Cons:** basic furnishings; some rooms don't have their own bathrooms; some carpets are worn. ⊠ *Keizersgracht 713, Eastern Canal Ring and Rembrandtplein* ☎ *020/623–2980* ↘ *26 rooms, 8 with shared bath* ⚙ *In-room: no a/c, Wi-Fi. In-hotel: bar, Wi-Fi hotspot, no-smoking rooms* ☰ *AE, DC, MC, V* ⏴◉⏵ *EP* ⊕ *2:C5.*

$$–$$$ **Eden Hotel Amsterdam.** Although it can get quite noisy when the discos empty in the wee hours, this gigantic hotel is perfectly situated for those who like the club scene and surrounding nightlife. Rooms in front have views of the Amstel River, whereas rooms elsewhere have few views but are quieter. The street appears to be down at the heels, but the inside of the hotel is clean, comfortable, and modern. There is wireless Internet access in the lobby and on the second floor. **Pros:** views of the Amstel; close to Rembrandtplein; cheerful lobby. **Cons:** on a run-down street; lots of traffic noise. ⊠ *Amstel 144, Eastern Canal Ring and Rembrandtplein* ☎ *020/530–7878* ⊕ *www.edenhotelgroup.com* ↘ *210 rooms, 8 apartments* ⚙ *In-room: safe, kitchen (some), refrigerator, Internet. In-hotel: restaurant, bar, laundry service, Wi-Fi hotspot, no-smoking rooms* ☰ *AE, DC, MC, V* ⏴◉⏵ *EP* ⊕ *2:C4.*

$–$$ **Imperial.** This Parisian-looking hotel is on a pedestrian-only street with cobblestones and a terraced square. Rooms are individually decorated, in styles ranging from sedate to cheerful to bold, to appeal to every kind of taste. There is no elevator, and although the stairs are modern (as opposed to steep traditional Dutch staircases), you must walk up at least two flights of them. **Pros:** efficient staff; close to Rembrandtplein. **Cons:** some of the rooms are lackluster; noise spills out from local bars. ⊠ *Thorbeckeplein 9, Eastern Canal Ring and Rembrandtplein* ☎ *020/622–0051* ⊕ *www.imperial-hotel.com* ⤵ *14 rooms* ♨ *In-room: no a/c, safe, Internet, Wi-Fi. In-hotel: Internet terminal, Wi-Fi hotspot, no-smoking rooms* ⊟ *MC, V* ⊘| *EP* ⊹ *2:C5.*

$$–$$$ 🛈 **NH Schiller.** Frits Schiller built this hotel in 1912 in the Art Nouveau variant known as Jugendstil. He may have been an artist of modest ability, but a huge number of his paintings, whose colors inspired the inventive furnishings of the modernized rooms, are proudly displayed throughout the hotel. His friends, bohemian painters and sculptors, came to the Schiller Café, which became a famous meeting place and is still an informal and popular bar with Amsterdammers. In the lobby lounge you can check your e-mail to the hum of the espresso machine from the Brasserie Schiller. **Pros:** friendly staff; popular bar. **Cons:** noise from nearby nightclubs; lacks the charm of a smaller property. ⊠ *Rembrandtplein 26–36, Eastern Canal Ring and Rembrandtplein* ☎ *020/554–0700* ⊕ *www.nh-hotels.com* ⤵ *92 rooms* ♨ *In-room: no a/c, refrigerator, Wi-Fi. In-hotel: restaurant, room service, bar, laundry service, Internet terminal, Wi-Fi hotspot* ⊟ *AE, DC, MC, V* ⊘| *EP* ⊹ *2:C5.*

$–$$ 🛈 **Seven Bridges.** One of the famous canal sights in Amsterdam is the lineup of seven consecutive bridges that can be seen gracing Reguliersgracht. This atmospheric little retreat, which looks over these bridges, also takes its name from them. Occupying an 18th-century house in the heart of "Golden Bend" country (yet just a few blocks from Rembrandtplein), this hotel offers uniquely stylish guest rooms, all meticulously decorated with dark woods, Oriental rugs, handcrafted and inlaid bed frames, and Art Deco tables. The proud owner scouts the antiques stores and auction houses for furnishings, and all have thorough documentation. The top-floor, beam-ceilinged rooms are the smallest and are priced accordingly; the first-floor room No. 5 is practically palatial, with its own private terrace. Nail down your reservation well in advance. **Pros:** friendly owners; breakfast delivered to your room; wonderful view. **Cons:** no public areas; next door to a coffee shop. ⊠ *Reguliersgracht 31, Eastern Canal Ring and Rembrandtplein* ☎ *020/623–1329* ⊕ *www.sevenbridgeshotel.nl* ⤵ *6 rooms* ♨ *In-room: refrigerator (some), Internet, Wi-Fi. In-hotel: Internet terminal, Wi-Fi hotspot, no-smoking rooms* ⊟ *AE, MC, V* ⊘| *CP* ⊹ *2:C5.*

THE JORDAAN AND LEIDSEPLEIN

THE JORDAAN

While wandering this most singular of neighborhoods, you may decide it's your favorite in the city. So why not stay here? The bells from the Westertoren take you back in time; sleepy little canals and narrow cobblestone streets with lopsided 17th-century houses give the area a special charm. On the surface, the neighborhood still looks very much as it did when Anne Frank lived here, although behind the weatherworn exteriors it now sports numerous fascinating boutiques and antiques shops.

$$ ⬚**Amsterdam Wiechmann.** A favorite with rock musicians—of both the punk (Sex Pistols) and country (Emmylou Harris) persuasions—the Wiechmann's main claim to fame is announced by a gold record displayed in the lobby, the pride and joy of the owner, John Boddy. There are delightful personal touches, like a teapot collection and framed Delft blue tiles, throughout the lobby and adjoining breakfast room, and fresh flowers are everywhere. The maze of hallways through the hotel's three buildings leads to guest rooms of wildly varying sizes; these are plainly decorated but enlivened by quilted bedspreads and floral drapes. Some have bedside tables covered by rugs (an old Dutch tradition). It's worth the extra money to get a room with views over the canal. **Pros:** smiling staff; spic-and span rooms; quiet location. **Cons:** rooms are quite small; no restaurant. ⊠ *Prinsengracht 328–332, Jordaan* ☎ *020/626–3321* ⊕ *www.hotelwiechmann.nl* ↘ *37 rooms, 1 suite* ♿ *In-room: no a/c, safe, Wi-Fi. In-hotel: bar, Internet terminal, Wi-Fi hotspot, some pets allowed, no-smoking rooms* ⊟ *MC, V* ⊙*CP* ✢ *2:A4.*

$ ⬚**Di-Ann.** Just a few minutes' walk from the Westertoren, Anne Frankhuis, and the Royal Palace, this friendly hotel occupies a gorgeously historic building with gable roofs, Romanesque balconies, and half-moon windows. Perched above a ground floor filled with shops, overlooking the regal Herengracht, and several blocks from the hectic Dam Square, the Di-Ann is right in the middle of all the action (perhaps too much so: delicate sleepers should opt for a room in the rear). When you enter, you need to climb a traditional narrow steep staircase, so if you have any mobility problems, this isn't the hotel for you. Some of the attractively modern guest rooms have balconies, and those in the rear overlook a garden. Other rooms have views of the Westertoren, Royal Palace, or canal. The breakfast room allures with crown moldings, a chandelier, and flowered wallpaper. **Pros:** good views; close to Dam Square. **Cons:** steep staircase; noisy location. ⊠ *Raadhuisstraat 27, Jordaan* ☎ *020/623–1137* ⊕ *www.hoteldiann.com* ↘ *42 rooms* ♿ *In-room: no a/c, safe, Wi-Fi. In-hotel: Internet terminal, Wi-Fi hotspot, no-smoking rooms* ⊟ *AE, MC, V* ⊙*CP* ✢ *2:A3.*

$ ⬚**Nadia.** The exterior of this 19th-century building is an architectural extravaganza, complete with kiosk corner turret, Art Nouveau–y portals, and redbrick trim. Inside, rooms are white, modern, and casual, and some have adorable views overlooking the canals. (Sleepers bothered by noise should opt for rooms in the rear.) The breakfast room is idyllic, bathed in a rosy orange glow and topped by a chandelier, with leafy views out the windows. The friendly staff will encourage you to help yourself to a welcome drink at the check-in minibar when you arrive. **Pros:** multilingual staff; lovely views. **Cons:** steep staircase; no-frills rooms. ⊠ *Raadhuisstraat 51, Jordaan* ☎ *020/620–1550* ⊕ *www.nadia.nl* ↘ *52 rooms* ♿ *In-room: no a/c, safe, refrigerator, Wi-Fi. In-hotel: room service, laundry service, Internet terminal, Wi-Fi hotspot, parking (paid), no-smoking rooms* ⊟ *AE, MC, V* ⊙*CP* ✢ *2:A2.*

THE LEIDSEPLEIN

It can be noisy in the city's busiest square, but then again sometimes it pays to be centrally located.

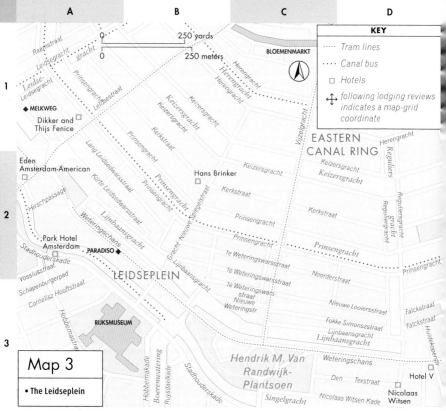

Map 3

• The Leidseplein

$-$$ 🛏 **Dikker and Thijs Fenice.** "Lavish," "classical," and "cozy" are some of the adjectives typically used to describe this hotel, which has a regal address on the Prinsengracht Canal. The hotel first opened as a shop in 1895 and has been renowned for fine dining since its founder, A. W. Dikker, entered into a partnership in 1915 with H. Thijs, who apprenticed with the famous French chef Escoffier. The busy location—happily, all the majestic sash windows are double-glazed—is convenient to the major shopping areas and one block from the Leidseplein, the nightlife center of the city. The Art Deco–style rooms are fully modernized, although they retain a regal quality with dark-wood furniture, scarlet upholstery, and gilt-edged mirrors. Room 408 has a wonderful beamed ceiling. If the temptations of the canals overpower you, you can make use of the hotel's jetty. **Pros:** water views; babysitting service; lots of dining options nearby. **Cons:** small lobby gets crowded; rooms book up fast. ⊠ *Prinsengracht 444, Leidseplein* ☎ *020/620–1212* ⊕ *www.dtfh. nl* ⬎ *42 rooms* ⌂ *In-room: no a/c (some), refrigerator, Internet, Wi-Fi. In-hotel: room service, bar, laundry service, Internet terminal, Wi-Fi hotspot, parking (paid), some pets allowed, no-smoking rooms* ▭ *AE, DC, MC, V* ⊖*EP* ⊕ *3:A1.*

$$$$ 🛏 **Eden Amsterdam-American.** Housed in one of the city's most fancifully designed buildings—one that is said to form the missing link between Art Nouveau and the Amsterdam School—the American (the name everyone

Hotel V

Park Hotel Amsterdam

knows it by) is a beloved Amsterdam landmark. Directly on Leidseplein, this 1902 castlelike structure is an agglomeration of Neo-Gothic turrets, Jugenstil gables, Art Deco stained glass, and an Arts and Crafts clock tower. Gloriously overlooking the Stadhouderskade (the reason the hotel has its own boat landing), this place is near everything—nightlife, dining, sightseeing, and shopping.

Guest rooms are sizable, bright, and furnished in a modern Art Deco style, and you have a choice between canal and bustling-square views—the latter option having the bonus of small balconies. Newlyweds might want to indulge in the Mata Hari Honeymoon Suite, which is named after the spy fatale who celebrated her own wedding here. **Pros:** alluring history; great for celebrity spotting; near canal boat dock. **Cons:** busy lobby; late check-in time. ✉ *Leidsekade 97, Leidseplein* ☎ *020/556–3000* ⊕ *www.amsterdamamerican.com* ⤴ *175 rooms, 16 suites* ⚐ *In-room: safe, refrigerator, Internet. In-hotel: restaurant, room service, bar, gym, laundry service, Internet terminal, Wi-Fi hotspot, no-smoking rooms* ⊟ *AE, DC, MC, V* ❙◎❙ *EP* ✛ *3:A2.*

¢   ⚏ **Hans Brinker.** Housed in a brick building that was a monastery about half a century ago, this hostel has rooms that are no-frills but sparkling clean, with white walls and blue floors. The dorms have bunk beds, and the private rooms have bathroom facilities. As basic as it is, it's never boring. You can boogie in the disco, drink at the bar, enjoy incredibly cheap meals (guests only) in the dining room. From 5 to 6 PM, you'll find your fellow backpackers guzzling beer in the bar during happy hour. And it's all "happening" at Leidseplein, just around the corner. **Pros:** offers lots of facilities under one roof; you'll meet people from all over the globe. **Cons:** staff can be brusque; checking in seems to take forever. ✉ *Kerkstraat 136, Leidseplein* ☎ *020/622–0687* ⊕ *www.hans-brinker. com* ⤴ *120 rooms with shared baths, 500 beds* ⚐ *In-room: no a/c, no phone, safe (some), no TV. In-hotel: restaurant, bar, Internet terminal* ⊟ *MC, V* ❙◎❙ *CP* ✛ *3:B2.*

$$–$$$
Fodor's Choice
★
⚏ **Hotel V.** This effortlessly hip hotel promises an Amsterdam experience through the eyes of a local. The staff are openly passionate about the city and keen to share tips on the latest nightspots and tastiest new eateries. Fortunately, when they haven't successfully moved you onto yet another cultural experience, the exquisitely designed interiors are a pleasure to lounge in, be it the massive leather couch in the foyer, the ornate bar, or well-finished bedrooms. Despite an almost overuse of rich dark colors, the contemporary furnishings and textiles balance perfectly to ensure the rooms and corridors feel spacious, luxurious, and welcoming. Leidseplein and the museums are just a walk away. **Pros:** quality of detail in design and furnishings; friendly staff offer an insider city perspective. **Cons:** located off the main tourist track; rooms in a secondary building accessed by an outdoor walkway. ✉ *Weteringschans 136, Leidseplein* ☎ *020/662–3233* ⊕ *www.hotelv.nl* ⤴ *48 rooms, 6*

apartments 🔥 *In-room: no a/c, safe, kitchen (some), Internet, Wi-Fi. In-hotel: bar, bicycles, laundry service, Internet terminal, Wi-Fi hotspot, parking (paid), no-smoking rooms* ☰ *AE, DC, MC, V* ⚟ *CP* ✛ *3:D3.*

$–$$ ☎ **Nicolaas Witsen**. If you're just looking for a place to hang your hat and get a quiet night's sleep, the Nicolaas Witsen is a good choice. Run by the same affable family for two generations, the redbrick-and-white-trim hotel is on a peaceful street within walking distance of the Rijksmuseum and the Heineken Experience. The standard-issue guest rooms have white walls punctuated by lots of windows, Swedish-wood furniture, and modern bathrooms. The breakfast room is cheery, and there is a family room that sleeps up to four people. **Pros:** quiet location; close to numerous dining options. **Cons:** no-frills interior; rooms on the small side. ✉ *Nicolaas Witsenstraat 4, Leidseplein* ☎ *020/626–6546* ⊕ *www. hotelnicolaaswitsen.nl* ↴ *28 rooms* 🔥 *In-room: no a/c, safe, Wi-Fi. In-hotel: bar, bicycles, laundry service, Internet terminal, Wi-Fi hotspot, parking (paid), no-smoking rooms* ☰ *AE, MC, V* ⚟ *CP* ✛ *3:D3.*

$$$–$$$$ ☎ **Park Hotel Amsterdam**. At first glance, the Park looks like everyone's
⟳ dream of a grand Netherlandish hotel: it's topped by a idyllic pepper-
Fodor's Choice pot tower, and its 18th-century building set with regal windows is mir-
★ rored charmingly in the Singel River. But though this stately Amsterdam fixture has one foot in history, the other is firmly entrenched in today, thanks to its modern-luxe décor, amenities, and Pan-Asian restaurant Momo ($$$–$$$$), which has proved a hit with locals and travelers alike. The neon lights of Leidseplein's shops, casino, and clubs are around the corner, and the sylvan glades of Amsterdam's gorgeous Vondelpark are just across the road, beckoning you to take an early morning jog. The major art museums are also within walking distance. The hotel also offers a babysitting service and children's menus. **Pros:** stylishly appointed rooms; convenient location between Leidseplein and the Vondelpark. **Cons:** no particular Dutch flavor; bureaucratic staff is slow to answer requests. ✉ *Stadhouderskade 25, Leidseplein* ☎ *020/671–1222* ⊕ *www.parkhotel.nl* ↴ *189 rooms, 21 suites* 🔥 *In-room: safe, refrigerator, DVD (some), Internet, Wi-Fi. In-hotel: restaurant, room service, bar, bicycles, laundry service, Internet terminal, Wi-Fi hotspot, parking (paid), no-smoking rooms* ☰ *AE, MC, V* ⚟ *EP* ✛ *4:C1.*

MUSEUM DISTRICT

If you've come to Amsterdam for its reputation as the city of the arts, then you should book a room in this quarter. All the city's top museums are here, the priciest shopping strip is just around the corner, and the lovely green Vondelpark is just to the west. Little wonder that this entire area has been colonized by fine hotels.

$–$$ ☎ **Aalders**. Occupying a cozy, charming town house, this busy (and completely smoke-free) hotel has reasonably sized rooms with large windows overlooking a quiet street. All rooms have shower or bath; double rooms have twin beds. Breakfast is served in a large and beautiful second-floor room. **Pros:** friendly staff; close to museums. **Cons:** rooms vary in size; some bathrooms extremely cramped. ✉ *Jan Luykenstraat 13–15, Museum District and Environs* ☎ *020/662–0116* ⊕ *www.*

hotelaalders.nl ↝ *28 rooms* ⚭ *In-room: no a/c, Wi-Fi. In-hotel: bar, bicycles, laundry service, Internet terminal, Wi-Fi hotspot, no-smoking rooms* ▭ *AE, DC, MC, V* ☉ *Closed 2 wks in mid-Dec.* ❡⃝ *CP* ✢ *4:B2.*

$ 🛈 **Atlas.** Just a block from the Vondelpark, this hotel, housed in an Art Nouveau mansion, is renowned for its personal, friendly, and generally relaxing atmosphere. The Atlas discreetly blends into its well-to-do residential area and is within easy walking distance of the museums and cozy bars and restaurants. Rooms are decorated with contemporary artwork on the walls. **Pros:** friendly staff; well-used public areas; close to the Vondelpark. **Cons:** mostly residential area; room furnishings feel randomly assembled. ⊠ *Van Eeghenstraat 64, Museum District and Environs* ☎ *020/676–6336* ⊕ *www.hotelatlas.nl* ↝ *23 rooms* ⚭ *In-room: no a/c, safe, Internet. In-hotel: room service, bicycles, laundry service, no-smoking rooms* ▭ *AE, DC, MC, V* ✢ *4:A2.*

$$–$$$ 🛈 **Bilderberg Jan Luyken.** This small, formal, and stylish town-house hotel offers a peaceful sanctuary, complete with serene garden and restrained Art Nouveau stylings. Located in a trio of quaint 19th-century five-story town houses, its exterior is outfitted with wrought-iron balconies, cute gables, and the usual ugly roof extension. The interior design is largely *Wallpaper*-modern—tripod lamps, steel ashtrays, Knoll-ish chairs. Guest rooms can be on the snug side, and service and housekeeping leave a bit to be desired. The hotel is just one block away from the Museumplein and fashionable shopping streets; perhaps this explains its popularity with musicians in town who play the nearby Concertgebouw. There's a lovely little "relaxation" room with a tanning lounge, Turkish bath, and hot tub, and the hotel's trendy bar, Wines and Bites, serves high-quality wine along with snacks and lunches. **Pros:** leafy environs; modern rooms; proximity to museums. **Cons:** slightly unwelcoming entrance; can be hard to find. ⊠ *Jan Luykenstraat 58, Museum District and Environs* ☎ *020/573–0730* ⊕ *www.bilderberg.nl* ↝ *62 rooms* ⚭ *In-room: safe, Wi-Fi. In-hotel: room service, bar, spa, bicycles, laundry service, Internet terminal, parking (paid), no-smoking rooms* ▭ *AE, DC, MC, V* ❡⃝ *EP* ✢ *4:A3.*

$$$–$$$$ 🛈 **The College Hotel.** This hotel occupies an 1895 school building, giving it a unique character. Although owned by a private company, the hotel is operated as a training ground for students of the country's top hotel management schools (which accounts for the fresh-faced staff). The building has wide grand corridors and stairwells, and the rooms have high ceilings, carpets you can sink into, and gleaming bathrooms. **Pros:** historic building; trendy bar; in-room massages. **Cons:** staff can be easily distracted; location not very convenient. ⊠ *Roelof Hartstraat 1, Museum District and Environs* ☎ *020/571–1511* ⊕ *www. thecollegehotel.com* ↝ *40 rooms* ⚭ *In-room: safe, Internet, Wi-Fi. In-hotel: restaurant, room service, bar, bicycles, laundry service, Wi-Fi hotspot, parking (paid), no-smoking rooms* ▭ *AE, DC, MC, V* ❡⃝ *EP* ✢ *4:B3.*

$–$$ 🛈 **Conscious Hotel Museum Square.** Small and refined, with a cherry-and-white facade, this hotel is within walking distance of the Concertgebouw and the major art museums, as well as a large selection of good restaurants and trendy brasseries. The Vondelpark is nearby, but you can enjoy your own little piece of private heaven in the hotel's tranquil Japanese garden. Newly refurbished, it lays claim to being the most sustainable hotel in town; even the modern room furnishings make use of organic or recycled materials. **Pros:** light and airy rooms; efficient staff. **Cons:** no particular Dutch flavor. ✉ *De Lairessestraat 7, Museum District and Environs* ☎ *020/671–9596* ⊕ *www.conscioushotels.com* ⤵ *36 rooms* ♿ *In-room: no a/c (some), safe, Wi-Fi. In-hotel: bar, laundry service, no-smoking rooms* ⊟ *AE, MC, V* ⦿ *EP* ⊹ *4:B3.*

$$–$$$ ☎ **EMB Memphis**. Classically proportioned, mansard-roofed, and ivy-covered—what more do you want from an Amsterdam hotel facade? This elegant, exceptionally spacious hotel was once the private residence of Freddy Heineken, of brewery fame. Formerly decorated in a classical style, the entire hotel is now fresh, modern, and airy, so if you want Vermeer-style interiors, this isn't the place for you. But the new design is energizing: the breakfast room is bright and welcoming, the bar-lounge is sleek, the guest rooms are modern and tranquil. As formal but not as expensive as the deluxe hotels, and embraced by a serene residential neighborhood, the Memphis is near the Concertgebouw. Extra beds are available, and children under 12 are welcome at no additional charge. The large bar has comfortable armchairs and tables and serves light meals. In summer you can make use of the small terrace, shielded from the main road. **Pros:** pleasant modern lobby and bar area; lovely rooms; equally suited to business and leisure travelers. **Cons:** rooms on the small size; location is a bit far from the sites. ✉ *De Lairessestraat 87, Museum District and Environs* ☎ *020/673–3141* ⊕ *www.memphishotel.nl* ⤵ *74 rooms* ♿ *In-room: safe (some), Internet, Wi-Fi. In-hotel: restaurant, room service, bar, bicycles, laundry service, Internet terminal, Wi-Fi hotspot, parking (paid), some pets allowed, no-smoking rooms* ⊟ *AE, DC, MC, V* ⊹ *4:A3.*

$–$$ ☎ **Europa 92**. You can't miss the Europa: it has a neon sign nearly larger than its four-story facade. Within easy walking distance of the Vondelpark and the elegant shopping street P. C. Hooftstraat, this family-run hotel has a lovely garden, which you may wish to escape to after realizing that the No. 1 tram passes the front—be sure to opt for the quieter rooms at the back, two of which contain small kitchenettes and provide a garden view. **Pros:** friendly staff; close to the Vondelpark. **Cons:** slightly run-down location; rooms can be noisy. ✉ *1e Constantijn Huygenstraat 103–107, Museum District and Environs* ☎ *020/618–8808* ⊕ *www.europa92.nl* ⤵ *47 rooms, 2 suites* ♿ *In-room: no a/c, no phone, safe, Internet, Wi-Fi. In-hotel: bar, laundry service, Wi-Fi hotspot, parking (paid), some pets allowed, no-smoking rooms,* ⊟ *AE, DC, MC, V* ⦿ *CP* ⊹ *4:A1.*

¢   ☎ **Flying Pig Uptown Hostel**. For those backpackers who like to chill out and save a load of money, the Flying Pig is the favored choice of "piggies" everywhere. The admittance policy is strict: if you're not a backpacker aged 16 to 35, you'll have to look elsewhere. The price includes not only breakfast and sheets, but also Internet, guided tours, and the use of in-line skates (so lace up and explore the park, or join the once-weekly night skate throughout the city). There's a bar claiming to serve the cheapest beer in town, and you can cook with other guests in the

Fodor'sChoice
★

kitchen. If you're traveling with an amour or don't mind sharing with a friend, the best deal is to book a queen-size bunk bed in one of the dorms. **Pros:** fun vibe; tons of activities. **Cons:** no particular Dutch flavor; can be noisy. ⊠ *Vossiusstraat 46, Museum District and Environs* ☎ *020/400–4187* ⊕ *www.flyingpig. nl* ↰ *4 rooms, 25 dormitories* ⓧ *In-room: no phone, no TV (some), Wi-Fi (some). In-hotel: bar, no-smoking rooms* ⊟ *AE, MC, V* ⦿| *CP* ✛ *4:B2.*

$-$$ ⊡ **Hestia.** On a street of extraordinary 19th-century houses, the Hestia is parallel to the Vondelpark and close to the Leidseplein. Fitted out with red brick, white trim, and a cute mansard roof, it's certainly easy on the eyes. The Hestia is family operated, with a helpful and courteous staff, and is the kind of place that reinforces the image of the Dutch as a clean and orderly people. The hotel's breakfast room has a view of the garden, and a large family room has a lovely sitting area in a bay window with stained glass that also overlooks the garden. The rooms are basic, light, and simply modern. Four of the rooms are very small, but so is their cost. **Pros:** friendly staff; close to museums. **Cons:** some rooms are on the small side; rooms book up fast. ⊠ *Roemer Visscherstraat 7, Museum District and Environs* ☎ *020/618–0801* ⊕ *www.hotel-hestia. nl* ↰ *18 rooms* ⓧ *In-room: no a/c, safe, Wi-Fi. In-hotel: room service, laundry service, Wi-Fi hotspot, some pets allowed, no-smoking rooms* ⊟ *AE, DC, MC, V* ⦿| *CP* ✛ *4:B1.*

$-$$ ⊡ **Hotel de Filosoof.** Bona-fide Amsterdam philosophers can regularly
Fodor's Choice   be found ensconced in this hotel's comfy armchairs. Monthly lectures
★   and discussion evenings are hosted here for locals, many of whom are, naturally, artists, writers, and thinkers. Even the decorator of this hotel has picked up on the philosophical motif: each of the guest rooms is decorated with a different theme. (There is an Aristotle room furnished in Greek style, with passages from the works of Greek philosophers hung on the walls, and a Goethe room adorned with Faustian texts.) Some of the rooms are a little silly—the Walden, for instance, sports some landscape daubs on the wall—but the Spinoza is a total knock-out: an homage to Golden Age style, complete with black-and-white floors, a 19th-century library lamp, and framed paintings, it is a jewel that fancier hotels in town could well take as a model. Enjoy breakfast, or merely relax, in the large garden. **Pros:** off-the-wall interior; interesting guests. **Cons:** can be hard to find; furnishings are a tad wayworn. ⊠ *Anna van den Vondelstraat 6, Museum District and Environs* ☎ *020/683–3013* ⊕ *www.hotelfilosoof.nl* ↰ *34 rooms, 4 suites* ⓧ *In-room: no a/c, Wi-Fi. In-hotel: bar, laundry service, Internet terminal, Wi-fi hotspot, no-smoking rooms* ⊟ *AE, MC, V* ⦿| *CP* ✛ *4:A1.*

$$ ⊡ **Hotel Fita.** Hans and Loes de Rapper have run this property for more
☾   than 30 years, placing an emphasis on the spic-and-span. Therefore,
Fodor's Choice   this peaceful hotel, a turn-of-the-20th-century town house, is not only
★   dustless but is off-limits to smokers. In the morning, you can enjoy

Hotel de Filosoof

Hotel de Filosoof

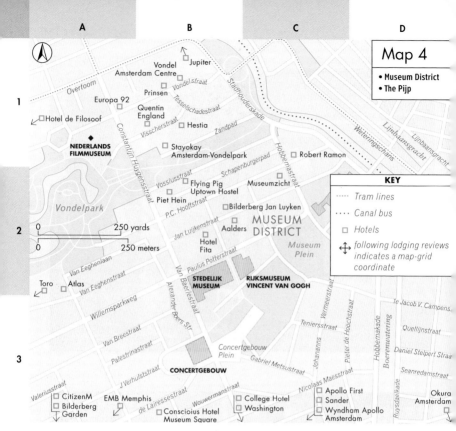

fresh-baked bread, homemade jam, and Hans's Dutch pancakes, along with freshly squeezed orange juice, at the buffet breakfast. Coffee lovers can also make use of the espresso capsule machines in their room. Another plus: you won't be charged for telephone calls within Europe and to the United States. The Rijksmuseum, Van Gogh Museum, Stedelijk Museum, and Concertgebouw are literally around the corner. **Pros:** staff with a sense of humor; free telephone calls; free laundry service. **Cons:** no real public areas; décor is on the twee side. ✉ *Jan Luykenstraat 37, Museum District and Environs* ☎ *020/679–0976* ⊕ *www.fita.nl* 🛏 *15 rooms* ⚇ *In-room: no a/c, safe, Wi-Fi. In-hotel: laundry service, Internet terminal, no-smoking rooms* 🖃 *AE, DC, MC, V* ⊘ *Closed Dec. 15–Jan. 15* ⦿ *CP* ✛ *4:B2.*

¢–$ 🔆 **Jupiter.** On a quiet residential street not far from the Vondelpark, the Jupiter hotel, though its arched doorway and windows are rimmed with neon lighting, has a plain homey interior and an elevator. You're a short walk away from the Rijksmuseum and the Concertgebouw, as well as the shops in the chic P. C. Hooftstraat. **Pros:** quiet location; close to museums; nice bathrooms. **Cons:** no particular Dutch flavor; staff could be friendlier. ✉ *2e Helmersstraat 14, Museum District and Environs* ☎ *020/618–7132* ⊕ *www.jupiterhotel.nl* 🛏 *20 rooms* ⚇ *In-room: no a/c, safe, Wi-Fi. In-hotel: some pets allowed, no-smoking rooms* 🖃 *No credit cards* ⦿ *CP* ✛ *4:B1.*

$ ⬚ **Museumzicht**. The name "Museum View" is accurate: this hotel is
Fodor'sChoice   directly across the street from the Rijksmuseum. The owner once ran
★   an antiques shop, so the house is filled with wonderful objects such as
Art Deco wardrobes, streamlined lamps, and Lloyd Loom chairs. The
breakfast room–lounge has a Murano glass chandelier and Art Deco
pottery on the chimney walls. Elsewhere hang 19th- and 20th-century
landscapes and portraits. The rooms are simple but delightful, with
pastel-striped wallpaper and little etchings. The hotel is on the top floors
of the building, and guests must climb a narrow and intimidatingly steep
stairway with their luggage to the reception desk and to the rooms—the
owners highly recommend traveling light. **Pros:** quiet location; clean
rooms; view of the Rijksmuseum. **Cons:** steep staircase; no particular
Dutch flavor. ⊠ *Jan Luykenstraat 22, Museum District and Environs*
☎ *020/671–2954* ⊕ *www.hotelmuseumzicht.com* ⤵ *14 rooms, 11 with
shared bath* ⬧ *In-room: no a/c, no phone, safe (some), Wi-Fi. In hotel:
Wi-Fi hotspot.* ▭ *AE, MC, V* ⎢◯⎢ *CP* ✛ *4:C2.*

$$–$$$ ⬚ **Piet Hein**. Salons don't come any sleeker than the ones inside this
ornate brick Vondelpark mansion. Extending into its neighboring building to add 21 new rooms in 2010, the hotel's entire décor has been
refreshed with gleaming surfaces and sharply contrasting tones; the
stark black-and-white furnishings are softened by natural wood accenting. For bursts of real color, simply look outside the windows, as front
rooms have fine views of Vondelpark (always in demand—even booking far in advance doesn't guarantee you one of these rooms). Those
in the back look out over the garden and terrace. The P. C. Hooftstraat, the Concertgebouw, and the city's major art museums are nearby.
Pros: attracts a young crowd; overlooks the Vondelpark. **Cons:** parking options outside the hotel are very limited. ⊠ *Vossiusstraat 51–53,
Museum District and Environ* ☎ *020/662–7205* ⊕ *www.hotelpiethein.
nl* ⤵ *81 rooms* ⬧ *In-room: no a/c (some), safe, Wi-Fi. In-hotel: room
service, bar, laundry service, some pets allowed, no-smoking rooms*
▭ *AE, DC, MC, V* ⎢◯⎢ *CP* ✛ *4:B2.*

$$ ⬚ **Prinsen**. P. H. H. Cuijpers, the architect of the Rijksmuseum and Cen-
traal Station, also created this adorable hotel. A chalet roof, dormers,
bay window, jigsaw trim, Neoclassical columns, and sculpted reliefs of
cats (one showing a cat chasing mice) all decorate the exterior, which
was built around 1870. The storybook feeling, however, ends as soon as
you step in the door: the interiors have all been gutted and renovated.
Many of the bedrooms are still cheery and gracious, though, and on
the ground floor, there's a bright yellow breakfast room overlooking a
lovely garden. On a quiet street next to the Vondelpark, the hotel makes
all its guests very welcome. **Pros:** fanciful facade; gay-friendly vibe; close
to the Vondelpark. **Cons:** bland interior; staff can be brusque. ⊠ *Vondel-
straat 36–38, Museum District and Environs* ☎ *020/616–2323* ⊕ *www.
prinsenhotel.nl* ⤵ *45 rooms, 1 suite* ⬧ *In-room: no a/c, safe, Wi-Fi.
In-hotel: bar, laundry service, Internet terminal, some pets allowed,
no-smoking rooms* ▭ *AE, DC, MC, V* ⎢◯⎢ *CP* ✛ *4:B1.*

$–$$ ⬚ **Quentin England**. The intimate Quentin England is one of a series
of adjoining buildings dating from 1884, each of which is built in an
architectural style of the country whose name it bears. Rooms are

simple and vary greatly in size, but are all cozy and clean. The tiny breakfast room is particularly enchanting, with flower boxes on the windowsills, dark-wood tables, and fin de siècle decorations. Behind the reception desk is a small bar and espresso machine. The hotel offers tremendous character and attention in place of space and facilities. **Pros:** friendly staff; close to museums. **Cons:** no-frills rooms; guests must pay in advance. ⊠ *Roemer Visscherstraat 30, Museum District and Environs* ☎ *020/616–6032* ⊕ *www.quentinenglandhotel.com* ⟿ *40 rooms, 3 with shared bath* ⌂ *In-room: no a/c, no phone. In-hotel: no-smoking rooms* ▭ *AE, MC, V* ⦿ *EP* ✛ *4:B1.*

$ ⌇ **RobertRamon.** Despite its location, at the foot of the exclusive P. C. Hooftstraat and south entrance to the Rijksmuseum, this hotel is anything but pretentious. It's a lively and friendly place and a good choice for those who want to enjoy the Leidseplein nightlife. The rooms boast a chic design vibe and the bathrooms are spacious. **Pros:** friendly staff; close to museums. **Cons:** rooms facing the tramlines are a bit noisy; rooms can be cramped. ⊠ *P. C. Hooftstraat 24, Museum District and Environs* ☎ *020/671–4785* ⊕ *www.robertramon.com* ⟿ *51 rooms* ⌂ *In-room: no a/c, safe, Wi-Fi. In-hotel: laundry service, Internet terminal, Wi-Fi hotspot, no-smoking rooms* ▭ *AE, MC, V* ⦿ *EP* ✛ *4:C1.*

$$ ⌇ **Sander.** The Sander offers rooms best described as traditionally Dutch: clean and comfortable. Seating areas in window bays give some rooms additional charm. The bar and breakfast room open out onto a garden. The hotel is welcoming to everyone. **Pros:** gay-friendly vibe; close to museums; inexpensive rates. **Cons:** simple furnishings; rooms book up fast. ⊠ *Jacob Obrechtstraat 69, Museum District and Environs* ☎ *020/662–7574* ⊕ *www.hotel-sander.nl* ⟿ *20 rooms* ⌂ *In-room: no a/c, safe, DVD (some), Wi-Fi. In-hotel: room service, bar, laundry service, Internet terminal, Wi-Fi hotspot, no-smoking rooms* ▭ *AE, MC, V* ⦿ *CP* ✛ *4:C3.*

¢   ⌇ **Stayokay Amsterdam-Vondelpark.** Word of mouth has made this hostel so popular that more than 75,000 backpackers stay here every year. Hidden on a small side path within the Vondelpark, the location is almost like being in a secret forest, despite being only minutes away from the hustle and bustle of the city. Put your bike in the hostel's covered shed, ogle the parrots in the trees, then do a few rounds of the park (a great place to connect with new people). Accommodations range from rooms that sleep two to dormitories for 20, and sheets are included in the price. In the spacious lounge, you can use the Internet, watch TV, play pool, or get acquainted with backpackers from around the world. Some rooms are available for those with disabilities. This is probably the cleanest hostel anywhere—your mother would definitely approve. **Pros:** quiet location in the Vondelpark; clean rooms. **Cons:** no particular Dutch flavor; harried staff. ⊠ *Zandpad 5, Museum District and Environs* ☎ *020/589–8996* ⊕ *www.stayokay.com* ⟿ *100 rooms, 536 beds* ⌂ *In-room: no a/c, no phone, no TV, Wi-Fi. In-hotel: restaurant, bar, bicycles, laundry facilities, Internet terminal, no-smoking rooms* ▭ *AE, MC, V* ⦿ *CP* ✛ *4:B1.*

$$–$$$ ⊞ **Toro.** In a prim and proper 19th-century-style villa on the southern border of the Vondelpark, this hotel offers a relaxing atmosphere. The views of the park and a small lake, and an interior tastefully furnished with antiques, oil paintings, and chandeliers provide a special homelike environment that is rare in Amsterdam. Rooms are bright and spacious, and some have balconies. Set near the area of the park far from the museum quarter and its shops, slightly outside the city center in a chic residential area, the hotel is, nevertheless, convenient to tramlines and lends itself to a lovely stroll through the park from the heart of Amsterdam. **Pros:** peaceful atmosphere; cozy interior; views of the Vondelpark. **Cons:** out-of-the-way location; staff can be hard to find. ⊠ *Koningslaan 64, Museum District and Environs* ☎ *020/673–7223* ⊕ *www.hoteltoro. nl* ⤶ *22 rooms* ♿ *In-room: safe, refrigerator, Internet. In-hotel: room service, bar, bicycles, laundry facilities, laundry service, no-smoking rooms* ═ *AE, DC, MC, V* ⊙ *CP* ✛ *4:A2.*

$$–$$$ ⊞ **Vondel Amsterdam Centre.** On a quiet street next to the Vondelpark and very close to the Leidseplein, this hotel is refined and contemporary. The lobby and bar are filled with comfortable suede sofas, light-wood furnishings, sunlight, and flowers. The similarly colored rooms and apartments, generous in size, are enhanced with flashes of crimson, and a small garden terrace makes for a verdant oasis. Suites are on the top floor and have large windows that follow the shape of the roof and give you a scenic view of the neighborhood. Throughout the hotel are paintings by Amsterdam artist Peter Keizer. The hotel, like the park, gets its name from the 17th-century poet Joost van den Vondel, and the rooms are named after his poems. A lavish breakfast buffet is available, but is not included in the rate. **Pros:** artsy vibe; lovely garden terrace with breakfast served outdoors in summer. **Cons:** staff could be friendlier; rooms book up fast. ⊠ *Vondelstraat 20, Museum District and Environs* ☎ *020/612–0120* ⊕ *www.hotelvondel.nl* ⤶ *75 rooms, 3 suites* ♿ *In-room: no a/c (some), safe, Internet, Wi-Fi. In-hotel: restaurant, room service, bar, bicycles, laundry service, Wi-Fi hotspot, no-smoking rooms* ═ *AE, DC, MC, V* ⊙ *EP* ✛ *4:B1.*

$–$$ ⊞ **Washington.** Just a stone's throw from the Museumplein, this hotel often attracts international musicians in town to perform at the nearby Concertgebouw—except perhaps those who play the cello (the steep staircase is hard to navigate with bulky baggage). Owner Johan Boelhouwer is helpful and will lend from his collection of guidebooks. The breakfast room and lounge are filled with antiques and marvelous brass chandeliers, and the hotel is meticulously polished and sparkling clean. The rooms are simply and charmingly decorated in white and pastel shades. Large windows let in a flood of light. There are also two comfortable and cozy apartments with their own kitchens; some also have living rooms, bathtubs, and pianos. **Pros:** laid-back aura; friendly staff; popular with musicians. **Cons:** no elevator; books up fast. ⊠ *Frans van Mierisstraat 10, Museum District and Environs* ☎ *020/679–7453* ⊕ *www.hotelwashington.nl* ⤶ *22 rooms, 4 with shared bath, 1 suite, 2 apartments* ♿ *In-room: no a/c, safe, Wi-Fi. In-hotel: bicycles, laundry service, Wi-Fi hotspot* ═ *AE, V, MC* ⊙ *CP* ✛ *4:B3.*

THE PIJP

Both budget and posh, homey and businesslike, accommodations come together in the more quiet residential neighborhoods of The Pijp and the high-toned Oud Zuid (Old South). They are set a mere 15-minute canal ride away from Centraal Station, but far enough removed from center-city crowds.

$$–$$$ **Apollo First.** The big neon sign here seems more suitable for a cinema, but once you're inside this family-run hotel you'll be surrounded by quiet elegance. Black walls, gold trim, overstuffed chairs, and glittering chandeliers and sconces make the lobby a modern jewel box. Upstairs, you'll want to opt for a quieter room at the back: these chambers allow you to fully savor the tranquility of the hotel's sylvan garden terrace. A few steps out the door, the chic shops of the Apollolaan start; you're also within walking distance of Museum Square. **Pros:** atmospheric interior; gorgeous garden terrace; upper-crust neighborhood. **Cons:** out-of-the-way location; expensive breakfast. ⊠ *Apollolaan 123, De Pijp and Environs* ☎ *020/577–3800* ⊕ *www.apollofirst.nl* ⤶ *40 rooms, 3 suites* ⚬ *In-room: no a/c, safe, kitchen (some), Internet, Wi-Fi. In-hotel: room service, bar, bicycles, laundry service, Internet terminal, some pets allowed, no-smoking rooms* ▭ *AE, DC, MC, V* ⍩ *EP* ✥ *4:C3.*

$$–$$$ **Bilderberg Garden.** This bulky modern hotel looms over a tree-lined street in Oud Zuid (Old South), Amsterdam's poshest neighborhood. The hotel underwent a dramatic top-to-toe face-lift in 2006, giving the whole place a bright and cheery atmosphere. Bathrooms have robes and slippers, and a trouser press in every room. The hotel is most often noted for its top restaurant, the Mangerie De Kersentuin (The Cherry Orchard). Although the property lacks any sort of historic allure, you can find plenty of that within walking distance: the Vondelpark, Concertgebouw, and the elegant shops in the Apollolaan are just short strolls away. **Pros:** refurbished rooms; excellent restaurant. **Cons:** mostly business clientele; rooms near lobby can be noisy. ⊠ *Dijsselhofplantsoen 7, De Pijp and Environs* ☎ *020/570–5600* ⊕ *www.bilderberg.nl* ⤶ *120 rooms, 2 suites* ⚬ *In-room: safe, DVD, Wi-Fi. In-hotel: restaurant, room service, bar, bicycles, laundry service, Internet terminal, Wi-Fi hotspot, parking (paid), some pets allowed, no-smoking rooms* ▭ *AE, DC, MC, V* ⍩ *EP* ✥ *4:A3.*

$–$$ **CitizenM.** Although tucked away near the financial district in the south
Fodor's Choice of Amsterdam, this up-and-coming hotel is quite trendy. No detail has
★ been overlooked, from the logo-bearing juice cartons and toiletries to the quirky signs on toilet doors. While you'll find plenty of suited business types departing each morning, a mixed array of young and older guests mingle informally at the Asian-style restaurant bar and lavish public spaces, broken down into living room–like compartments. The beds in the guest rooms are unusually large and comfortable, while all room features are controlled by a single, surprisingly straightforward, touch-screen remote control (if you reuse your room key in another branch of the chain, it remembers your climate and lighting choices). Intimacy should be considered, however, as each room's sci-fi-like glass tubes, containing the toilet and shower, leave little to the imagination. **Pros:** luxurious furnishings surpass the price tag; king-size

CitizenM

CitizenM

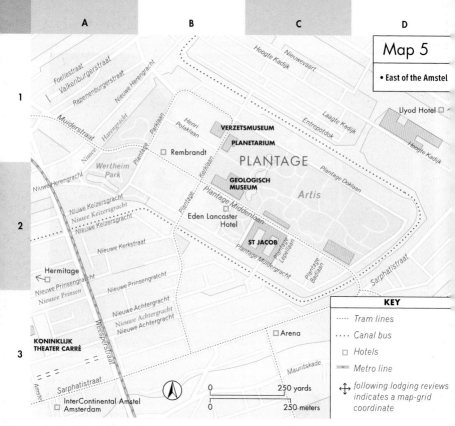

Map 5
• East of the Amstel

KEY

···· Tram lines

···· Canal bus

☐ Hotels

▭▭ Metro line

⬦ following lodging reviews
indicates a map-grid
coordinate

beds; informal vibe. **Cons:** the stacked box exterior doesn't inspire; its out-of-the-way location means you'll have to hop on a tram to get to the sights. ✉ *Prinses Irenestraat 30, De Pijp and Environs* ☎ *020/811–7090* ⊕ *www.citizenmamsterdamcity.com* ➯ *215 rooms* ⚹ *In-room: safe, Wi-Fi. In-hotel: restaurant, bar, Internet terminal, Wi-Fi hotspot, parking (paid), no-smoking rooms* ▭ *AE, MC, V* ⎪◎⎪ *EP* ⬦ *4:A3.*

$$$ 🛏 **Okura Amsterdam.** This local landmark sports the largest barometer
ⓒ in the Netherlands; every day after the sun goes down, the building forecasts the next day's weather by changing color. Inside, there's a cavernous dramatic lobby with inch-thick carpeting, guest rooms with dark-wood furniture and flat-screen TVs, and two marvelous, Michelin-starred restaurants to choose from: Yamazato ($$$$), serving Japanese food that's touted as the best in the city, and the classic French Le Ciel Bleu ($$$$). One interesting extra that's sure to help you get back on your feet if you've arrived after a long flight is the hotel's jet-lag program, which uses light therapy to help you adjust to your new surroundings. **Pros:** wonderful rooms; cozy top-floor bar; close to many dining options. **Cons:** lacks a personal touch; staff can have difficulties with simple requests. ✉ *Ferdinand Bolstraat 333, De Pijp and Environs* ☎ *020/678–7111* ⊕ *www.okura.nl* ➯ *301 rooms, 34 suites* ⚹ *In-room: safe, kitchen (some), refrigerator (some), Internet. In-hotel: 4 restaurants, room service, 2 bars, pool, gym, bicycles, laundry facilities,*

laundry service, Internet terminal, Wi-Fi hotspot, parking (paid), no-smoking rooms ⊟ *AE, DC, MC, V* ⌘*EP* ⊹ *4:D3.*

$$$$ ⛄ **Wyndham Apollo Amsterdam.** Amsterdam is often called the "Venice of the North," and five of its canals converge near the Apollo. A modernist palace framed by lovely trees, it's in the swank and suave Apollolaan district, known for its elegant shops and within easy walking distance of the Museum Quarter. Guest rooms are luxurious and modern. Downstairs, the tangerine and terra-cotta-hued La Sirene offers a French-Mediterranean menu. Few can resist feasting on fish on the restaurant's beautiful canal-side terraces (higher-priced rooms also offer great views of the canals). As *un touche finale*, the hotel even has its own private marina. **Pros:** quiet location; refurbished rooms. **Cons:** slightly out-of-the-way location; overburdened staff. ⊠ *Apollolaan 2, De Pijp and Environs* ☏ *020/673–5922* ⊕ *www.wyndhamapolloamsterdam.com* ⬎ *226 rooms, 18 suites* ⚷ *In-room: safe (some), refrigerator, Wi-Fi. In-hotel: restaurant, room service, bar, gym, laundry service, Internet terminal, Wi-Fi hotspot, parking (paid), no-smoking rooms* ⊟ *AE, DC, MC, V* ⌘*EP* ⊹ *4:C3.*

EAST OF THE AMSTEL

The small tranquil neighborhood known as the Plantage is a great choice if you want a more relaxed stay. The Hortus Botanicus, Artis Zoo, and the Tropenmuseum dominate this *Oost* (East) Amsterdam area. The Tropenmuseum backs on to the Oosterpark neighborhood, which is bordered by the Linneausstraat, Populierenweg, Amstel River, and Mauritskade. It's a mainly residential area with the exception of the busy Wibautstraat.

$–$$ ⛄ **Eden Lancaster Hotel.** The higher-priced rooms in this hotel have a view of a verdant lawn—a reminder of the hotel's location in the district known as the Plantage. The Artis Zoo is opposite the hotel, and the Tropenmuseum is within walking distance, which makes the hotel a great choice for kids. Rooms are light and cheerful, if a bit unremarkable. **Pros:** rooms designed for families; leafy neighborhood; close to zoo. **Cons:** no particular Dutch flavor; out-of-the-way location. ⊠ *Plantage Middenlaan 48, East of the Amstel* ☏ *020/535–6888* ⊕ *www.edenlancasterhotel.com* ⬎ *91 rooms* ⚷ *In-room: no a/c, safe, Internet. In-hotel: bar, laundry service, Internet terminal, Wi-Fi hotspot, parking (paid), no-smoking rooms* ⊟ *AE, DC, MC, V* ⌘*EP* ⊹ *5:B2.*

$ ⛄ **Hermitage.** Peace and quiet await you at this friendly hotel occupying an 18th-century canal house. Freshly modernized in 2009, the hotel offers a contemporary palette of high-contrast tones; effectively relaxing overall, although the busy tiling in some bathrooms is dizzying to say the least. There's a room to suit everyone, from a small attic room to a family-sized room that sleeps five. There's also a pleasant hotel garden where you can relax and forget the passing world. **Pros:** staff members are friendly; leafy location; relaxed vibe. **Cons:** out-of-the-way location; books up fast due to regular guests. ⊠ *Nieuwe Keizersgracht 16, East of the Amstel* ☏ *020/623–8259* ⊕ *www. hotelhermitageamsterdam.com* ⬎ *22 rooms* ⚷ *In-room: no a/c, no*

Lloyd Hotel

Lloyd Hotel

phone, Wi-Fi. In-hotel: Internet terminal, Wi-Fi hotspot, no-smoking rooms ⊟ *AE, MC, V* ⏻ *EP* ✛ *5:A2.*

$$–$$$ ⛪ **Hotel Arena.** This grand complex in a former 19th-century orphanage consists of the hotel, a restaurant, and a dance club (complete with frescoed walls that reflect its former function as a clandestine church). For those who like spare minimal style, the hotel is strikingly austere. The lobby is minimalist black with an impressive cast-iron staircase leading up to the rooms. The hotel uses the hottest young Dutch architects and designers in the hotel's continual evolution. Rooms—some of which are split level to form a lounge area—are furnished with modernist furniture by Gispen, Eames, and Martin Visser. **Pros:** fun vibe; stylish interior; hip bar and nightclub within the building. **Cons:** no-frills rooms; out-of-the-way location. ⊠ *'s-Gravesandestraat 51, East of the Amstel* ☎ *020/850–2400* ⊕ *www.hotelarena.nl* ⤴ *116 rooms, 7 suites* ⚴ *In-room: safe, Internet, Wi-Fi (some). In-hotel: restaurant, bar, laundry service, Internet terminal, Wi-Fi hotspot, parking (paid), no-smoking rooms* ⊟ *AE, DC, MC, V* ⏻ *EP* ✛ *5:C3.*

$$$$ ⛪ **InterContinental Amstel Amsterdam.** Elegant enough to please a queen, extroverted enough to welcome Madonna, Michael Jackson, and the Rolling Stones, this grand dowager has wowed all onlookers since it opened its doors in 1867. With its palatial facade, sash windows, and historic roof dormers this is a fairy-tale setting guaranteed to bring out your inner prince or princess. You'll feel like a visiting dignitary when entering the magnificent lobby, with its grand double staircase that demands you glide, not walk, down it. The guest rooms are the most spacious in the city (though they shrink considerably on the top floor), and the décor features Oriental rugs, brocade upholstery, Delft lamps, and a color palette of warm tones inspired by Makkum pottery. Fresh tulips are placed in all of the rooms, and the bathrooms spoil guests with showerheads the size of dinner plates. The generous staff-to-guest ratio, the top-notch food—in particular, at the lovely La Rive restaurant—the riverside terrace, the Amstel Lounge (perfect for drinks), and the endless stream of extra "little touches" (such as yacht service) will make for a truly baronial experience. **Pros:** historic building; suites large enough to do cartwheels in; the most attentive hotel staff in Amsterdam. **Cons:** the door between the pool and the changing rooms is noisy; hard to find elevator. ⊠ *Professor Tulpplein 1, East of the Amstel* ☎ *020/622–6060* ⊕ *www.amsterdam.intercontinental.com* ⤴ *55 rooms, 24 suites* ⚴ *In-room: safe (some), kitchen (some), DVD, Internet, Wi-Fi. In-hotel: 2 restaurants, room service, 2 bars, pool, gym, laundry service, Internet terminal, Wi-Fi hotspot, parking (paid), no-smoking rooms* ⊟ *AE, DC, MC, V* ⏻ *EP* ✛ *5:A3.*

$$$ ⛪ **Lloyd Hotel.** From the outside, the Art Deco–style Lloyd Hotel looks slightly severe, but its appearance fits with its history. Built in 1921 as a hotel for Eastern European immigrants, it then became a prison, and then a detention center, before finally emerging as accommodations for artists. The vast café-cum-lobby is effortlessly stylish, with colossal white walls and plenty of natural light streaming in through windows. Its rooms are quirkily and almost all uniquely designed, with unusual furniture that has been featured in many fashion magazine spreads.

Fodor's Choice
★

4

One of the funkiest lodging choices is the "rough music room," with its log cabin–style walls, bed big enough for eight, and lime-green bathroom. Most rooms have extra-large tables, grand pianos, and kitchens. **Pros:** historic building; quirky interior; rooms priced for all budgets. **Cons:** out-of-the-way location; some of the more popular rooms are difficult to reserve. ✉ *Oostelijke Handelskade 34, Eastern Docklands* ☎ *020/561–3636* ⊕ *www.lloydhotel.com* ↴ *117 rooms, 16 with shared bath, 14 suites* ⚳ *In-room: no a/c, kitchen (some), Internet, Wi-Fi. In-hotel: restaurant, room service, bar, laundry service, Internet terminal, Wi-Fi hotspot, parking (paid), no-smoking rooms* ⊟ *AE, MC, V* ⦺ *EP* ✛ *5:D1.*

$ 🏠 **Rembrandt.** Because it's close to the University of Amsterdam, Hortus Botanicus, and Tropenmuseum, the Hotel Rembrandt is often populated with academics and museum people—which explains the library of 1,800 books. The rarified air is particularly thick in the remarkable breakfast room: the 18th-century paintings and exquisitely painted woodwork on the ceiling, and the wood paneling and beams dating from 1558, were brought here in the 19th century. Most of the rooms at the back of the hotel facing the garden are quiet, though there are now double-glazed windows in front. **Pros:** great character; near museums. **Cons:** no real public areas. ✉ *Plantage Middenlaan 17, East of the Amstel* ☎ *020/627–2714* ⊕ *www.hotelrembrandt.nl* ↴ *17 rooms* ⚳ *In-room: no a/c, Wi-Fi. In-hotel: room service, laundry service, Internet terminal, Wi-Fi hotspot, parking (paid)* ⊟ *AE, MC, V* ⦺ *EP* ✛ *5:B1.*

Nightlife and the Arts

WORD OF MOUTH

"De Jaren has a lovely outside terrace. The café is very light, airy and spacious. There's a bar, a restaurant and, a very customer friendly international reading table, with daily newspapers from around the world."

—bellini

NIGHTLIFE AND THE ARTS PLANNER

Hours

Bars and cafés open during the day, normally close at 1 or 2 AM weekdays and at 2 or 3 weekends. Establishments that open around 9 PM in the evening stay open until 3 weekdays and 5 AM on weekends. Clubs stay open until 4 AM weekdays and 5 AM on weekends. Live gigs start as early as 8 or 9 PM or as late as midnight (especially the ones at Paradiso). Theater shows usually kick off earlier. Always check the official Web sites for updates or call ahead.

Where to Get Tickets

Tickets can be purchased at either the **AUB Ticketshop** ⊠ Leidseplein 26, Leidseplein ☎ 0900/0191 (Daily 9–6) ⊕ www.aub.nl ☉ Mon.–Sat. 10–7:30, Sun. noon–7:30, or at **VVV Ticketmaster** ⊠ Stationsplein 10, Centraal Station ☉ Daily 10–4, Sun. noon–4, or at theater box offices. Reserve tickets to performances at the major theaters through the AUB Web site or by calling +31 020/621–1288 from abroad. To be sure to get into a club, just arrive early (around 10 PM) and pick up tickets at the register or buy tickets early through the venue's Web site.

Late-Night Transportation

If you're heading out late, know that trams stop running at midnight. Grabbing a cab is your best option for getting home. They can sometimes be flagged down on the streets, but it's better to wait in line at a designated taxi stand; most venue employees can direct you to the closest one. Alternatively, you can use the cumbersome night buses, but the routes are difficult and time-consuming.

Where to Get Info

For the latest on what's happening, you'd do well to browse through the many fliers, pamphlets, booklets, and magazines that can be picked up at cafés such as De Balie, Café De Jaren, and Dantzig.

The Dutch-language Uitkrant can be found at its headquarters at the **Amsterdams Uitboro (AUB)** ⊠ Leidseplein 26, Leidseplein ☎ 0900/0191 (Daily 9–6) ⊕ www.aub.nl ☉ Mon.–Sat. 10–7:30, Sun. noon–7:30.

I amsterdam is the city's official site (⊕ www.iamsterdam. com) and an excellent source of information. There are several good English-language publications. Pick up the monthly Time Out Amsterdam (⊕ www.timeoutamsterdam. nl) at most tourist offices, bookshops, and newsstands. Unfold Amsterdam (⊕ www.unfoldamsterdam.nl) is a new monthly that comes in the form of a poster and focuses on the underground music scene, as does the magazine Subbacultcha! (www.subbacultcha.nl). Vice magazine (⊕ www.viceland.nl) is written in both in Dutch and English.

Updated by
Niels Carels

Amsterdam's nightlife can have you careening between smoky coffee shops, chic wine bars, mellow jazz joints, laid-back lounges, and clubs either intimate or raucous. The Dutch are extremely sociable people who enjoy going out, so don't hesitate to join the revelry. It will definitely make for a memorable trip.

5

The bona fide local flavor can perhaps best be tasted in one of the city's ubiquitous brown café-bars—called "brown" because of their woody walls and nicotine-stained ceilings. Here, both young and old, the mohawked and the merely balding, come to relax, rave, and revel in every variety of coffee and alcohol.

Thankfully, the city's club scene has been picking up after a long lull that began in the '90s, when some of the most established venues like RoXY, Mazzo, and iT closed their doors for good.

New clubs such as Trouw, Studio 80, and Club Up and Air are programming cutting-edge acts and DJs, and old standbys like Paradiso, Melkweg, and Bitterzoet still pull in big names on a weekly basis. Amsterdam is also home to several important electronic music festivals: the Amsterdam Dance Event (⊕ *www.amsterdam-dance-event.nl*) and 5 Days Off (⊕ *www.5daysoff.nl*) are the biggest.

BROWN CAFÉS

Along with French's *ennui* and Portuguese's *saudade*, a Dutch word often makes linguists' list of culturally untranslatable terms. *Gezelligheid*, however, is a positive one, referring to a state of total coziness created by warm social circumstances. People, places, and things are all contributing factors, though if you want to experience *gezelligheid* like a true Lowlander, learn this equation: drink + conversation with friends = *gezellig*! The best place for these pleasures is a traditional brown café, or *bruine kroeg*. Wood paneling, wooden floors, comfortably worn furniture, and walls and ceilings stained with eons' worth of tobacco smoke are responsible for their name—though today a little

Weather permitting, Cafe t' Smalle sets up a great canal-side seating area that overlooks a bridge—lovely!

artfully stippled paint achieves the same effect. Customarily, there is no background music, just the hum of *kletsen* (chitchat) and the housecat meowing. There will also be a beer or two, and perhaps a *jenever* (Dutch gin) as the evening wears on.

Café Chris. This venue has been pouring beverages since 1624, when it served as the local bar for builders of the Westerkerk. The cozy factor is enhanced by the smallest washrooms in town. ⊠ *Bloemstraat 42, Jordaan* ☎ *020/624–5942* ⊕ *www.cafechris.nl.*

Café Sluyswacht. Beware: the slant of this oldie-but-goodie can lead to nausea after one too many beers on the patio. A quintessential Amsterdam view of the Oudeschans, however, has been bringing relief since 1695. ⊠ *Jodenbreestraat 1, Jewish Quarter and Plantage* ☎ *020/625–7611* ⊕ *www.sluyswacht.nl.*

De Admiraal. Once the tasting house of an old family distillery, 200 years later this Jordaan spot still serves potent liqueurs, including Dutch *jenever.* ⊠ *Herengracht 319, The Canal Ring* ☎ *020/625–4334* ⊕ *www. de-ooievaar.nl.*

De Dokter. Beer and liquor are just what "the doctor," the tiniest brown bar in the country, have been ordering for centuries. ⊠ *Rozenboomsteeg 4, The Old City Center (Het Centrum)* ☎ *020/626–4427.*

De Engelse Reet. Also referred to as "The Pilsner Club," this decidedly ancient and unmistakably brown venue is like stepping back into some lost age when beer was the safest alternative to drinking water. ⊠ *Begijnensteeg 4, The Old City Center (Het Centrum)* ☎ *020/623–1777.*

CLOSE UP

A Jenever Primer

The indigenous liquor of the Netherlands is *jenever,* a potent spirit that was invented in the mid-1600s, when an alchemist in Leiden discovered a way to distill juniper berries. It was first sold as medicine, but by the late 17th century people liked it so much that they soon started drinking it for fun. Soon the English got in on the *jenever* game. They bumped up the alcohol content, smoothed over the rough-edged flavor, and called it gin.

There are two basic kinds of *jenever*—*oude* (old) and *jonge* (young). The names aren't a matter of aging, but of distilling techniques. Young *jenever* uses a newer (post-WWII) distilling technique that produces a lighter, less outspoken spirit. Old *jenever* has

a much more pronounced flavor. If you want to drink *jenever* like a true Lowlander, find yourself a *proeflokaal,* an old-fashioned "tasting house." We recommend the legendary **Wynand Fockink,** which has been hydrating Amsterdammers since 1679. Once you have made your choice from the milder *jonge* saps or the more sophisticated *oude* spirits, let the fun begin. The bartender fills a sherrylike glass until it is so precariously full that you must lean over the bar, hands behind your back, and take your first sip without touching the glass. Only then are you free to lift the glass by its dainty stem. When *jenever* is served with a beer it is called a *kopstoot,* literally meaning "headbang." This should be taken as a warning to the uninitiated.

De Prins. Like a number of cafés in the Jordaan, this mainstay is blessed with a canal-side patio. ✉ *Prinsengracht 124, Jordaan* ☎ *020/624–9382.*

De Reiger. With a distinctive Jugendstil bar and highly touted food, this joint is a favorite of beautiful people and seasoned locals alike. ✉ *Nieuwe Leliestraat 34, Jordaan* ☎ *020/624–7426.*

De Twee Zwaantjes. If you want to hear the locals sing folk music on a Saturday evening or a Sunday afternoon, stop by this classic canal-side café. ✉ *Prinsengracht 114, Jordaan* ☎ *020/625–2729* ⊕ *www.detweezwaantjes.nl.*

Nol. Only getting started at 9 each night (except Tuesday), Nol resonates with lusty-lunged native Jordaaners having the time of their lives. ✉ *Westerstraat 109, Jordaan* ☎ *020/624–5380* ⊕ *www.cafenolamsterdam.nl.*

Rooie Nelis. Despite the area's tendency toward trendiness, this café has kept its traditional Jordaan vibe. ✉ *Laurierstraat 101, Jordaan* ☎ *020/624–4167* ⊕ *www.caferooienelis.nl.*

Fodor'sChoice ★ **'t Smalle.** Set with Golden Age chandeliers, leaded-glass windows, and the patina of centuries, this charmer is one of Amsterdam's most glorious spots. The after-work crowd always jams the waterside terrace here, though you are just as well to opt for the historic interior, once home to one of the city's first *jenever* distilleries. It's not surprising to learn that a literal copy of this place was created for Nagasaki's Holland Village in Japan. ✉ *Egelantiersgracht 12, Jordaan* ☎ *020/623–9617.*

Fodor'sChoice ★ **Wynand Fockink.** This is Amsterdam's most famous—and miraculously least hyped—*proeflokaal* (tasting room). Opened in 1679, this dim-lit, blithely cramped little bar just behind the Hotel Krasnapolsky has a menu of more than 60 Dutch spirits that reads like poetry: *Bruidstranen* (bride's tears) and *Boswandeling* (a walk in the woods) are just two favorite flavors. Call ahead for a guided tour of the distillery. ✉ *Pijlsteeg 31, The Old City Center (Het Centrum)* ☎ *020/639–2695* ⊕ *www.wynand-fockink.nl* ⊙ *Daily 3–9.*

> **KOEKJE BIJ?**
>
> As frugal as the Dutch are, one act of their generosity is the *koekje bij* phenomenon: a small "cookie on the side" (or sometimes, piece of chocolate) is always served perched on the saucer of a hot beverage.

BARS, CAFÉS AND LOUNGES

Perhaps like the diners of New Jersey, brown cafés will remain an institution as much for the sake of wood-paneled nostalgia as for practical reasons: affordability and coziness. In recent years though, brown has given way to black, as Amsterdam's watering holes take on a sleeker intercontinental vibe. If a Berlin DJ hasn't popped in for the evening, a digital jukebox pulsates loungey, deep house beats. Diners go gaga over Asian-fusion menus. Frosted walls shed mood lighting onto the latest Droog furniture. And even the Jack Russell faces a threat as favorite purse pooch from hip rivals like the French bulldog.

Bar With No Name. Too popular to be incognito, this Nine Streets mainstay is now referred to by its address, the coordinates of which fall right where hiply understated intersects with charmingly pretentious. The '70s-style decor and dim-sum-y menu attract advertising types, but a housecat named Jippie keeps all the anonymity in check. ✉ *Wolvenstraat 23, The Canal Ring* ☎ *020/320–0843.*

Boom Bar. If you're a lounging American, you'll find a familiar home at this part and parcel of the same-named comedy club. The music will be comfortingly retro for most Gen Xers, and there's a terrace and an array of fruity cocktails for those on the summer backpack circuit. Boom also got permission to hold clubs nights on Friday (techno and house) and Saturday (queer-leaning dance party). ✉ *Leidseplein 12, Museum District* ☎ *020/423–0101* ⊕ *www.boomchicago.nl.*

Brasserie De Brakke Grond. As would be expected from a theater-happy neighborhood, the Nes houses some prime drinking holes. Fans of Belgian beer should stop by this café next door to the Flemish Cultural Center to select from dozens of options, consumable out on the spacious patio or within the classy restaurant. ✉ *Nes 43, The Old City Center (Het Centrum)* ☎ *020/626–0044* ⊕ *www.brasseriedebrakkegrond.nl.*

Café Cuba. The always lively Nieuwmarkt mainstay serves relatively cheap cocktails and offers a jazzy electronic sound track that inspires many of the hipster and student regulars to light up a joint in the back. ✉ *Nieuwmarkt 3, The Old City Center (Het Centrum)* ☎ *020/627–4919.*

CLOSE UP

Cheers to Dutch Beers

If you think Dutch beer begins and ends with Heineken, think again! The Netherlands has a thriving little industry of microbrews and produces some top-notch stuff. While most of the beer can be roughly broken down into three mouthwatering categories (*pils, witte bier,* and *bokbier*), *pils* (pilsner) is by far the most popular and commonly consumed. A refreshing light golden lager, it is served in smaller glasses and with more foam (two fingers' worth) than you're probably used to. In summer, Amsterdammers find refreshment in *witte bier,* a white zesty brew served with a twist of lemon. *Bokbier,* a stronger variety of *pils,* is made with warming spices. The Dutch also love Belgium brews, so you'll have no problem finding Trappist beers, Lambics, fruit beers, wheat beers, and dark brown ales.

OUR FAVORITE WATERING HOLES

Brouwerij 't IJ. Perched under a windmill on the eastern outskirts of the city is an evocative, if out of the way, microbrewery. Choose from any one of their coveted home brews (Plzen, Natte, Zatte, Struis, Columbus and IJwit; the delicious Paasij beer is made only around Easter). *Funenkade 7, East of the Amstel* *020/622–8325* *www.brouwerijhetij.nl* *Daily 3–8.*

Café Belgique. As the name suggests, this welcoming little café, located right behind Nieuwe Kerk, has an excellent selection of Belgian ales. *Gravenstraat 2, The Old City Center (Het Centrum)* *020/625–1974.*

Café Gollem. Quite popular with students and locals, the well-known brown café near Dam Square has far too many beers to try in one go. Ditto for its same-named sister in The Pijp. *Raamsteeg 4, The Old City Center*

(Het Centrum) *No phone* *www.cafegollem.nl* *Daniel Stalpertstraat 74, The Pijp* *020/676–7117.*

De Zotte. The name of this little pub off the Leidseplein translates to "really really drunk," and with around 100 Belgian beers available, it's aptly named. *Raamstraat 29, Jordaan* *020/626–8694* *www.dezotte.nl.*

Het Elfde Gebod. Right in the heart of the Red Light District, this cozy bar has five Belgian beers on tap and over 50 bottled. *Zeedijk 5, The Old City Center (Het Centrum)* *No phone* *www.hetelfdegebod.com.*

In de Wildeman. This busy, jolly brown café attracts a wide range of types and ages. There are 200 bottled brews to chose from, 17 beers on tap, and a featured beer of the month. *Kolksteeg 3, The Old City Center (Het Centrum)* *020/638–2348* *www.indewildeman.nl.*

BEST BEER STORE

Located behind Dam Square, **Bierkoning** is the best beer store in Amsterdam, and possibly even the Netherlands. They have more than 950 beers in stock and tons of glassware and other accessories. The friendly knowledgeable staff can tell you everything you ever wanted or needed to know about Belgian and Dutch beers. *Paleisstraat 125, The Old City Center (Het Centrum)* *020/625–2336* *www.bierkoning.nl.*

Café de Jaren. This light and airy multilevel café has a lovely terrace overlooking the Amstel. It's exceedingly popular with a big cross-section of the population, from students and hipster knitting circles to artists and businessmen. ⊠ *Nieuwe Doelenstraat 20, The Old City Center (Het Centrum)* ☎ *020/625–5771* ⊕ *www.cafedejaren.nl.*

Café de Koe. Hardly bovine, the "Cow's Café" is a fine place to chew the cud or graze a little, and is especially favored by local musicians and students. ⊠ *Marnixstraat 381, Leidseplein* ☎ *020/625–4482* ⊕ *www.cafedekoe.nl.*

★ **Café Luxembourg.** This favorite haunt of the famous food critic Johannes van Dam is known for its dark Art Deco interior and a glassed-in terrace that's perfect for watching people on the Spui. Those with less interest in urban sociology can entertain themselves at the communal table with an assortment of international newspapers and magazines. ⊠ *Spui 24, The Old City Center (Het Centrum)* ☎ *020/620–6264* ⊕ *www.luxembourg.nl.*

Café Schiller. Part of the same-named hotel, this place has a real sense of history thanks to a wooden fin de siècle interior that other grand cafés would sell their souls for. Still, the glory is fast fading as Rembrandtplein gets seedier and a long-patronizing media crowd finds other places to slake their thirst. ⊠ *Rembrandtplein 26, Rembrandtplein* ☎ *020/624–9846.*

★ **Café Vertigo.** Not only does the Nederlands Filmmuseum have an atmospheric cellar restaurant, great for a premovie meal or postflick refreshments, but the stunningly scenic terrace provides open-air seating for watching the chaos that is the Vondelpark. ⊠ *Vondelpark 3, Museum District* ☎ *020/612–3021* ⊕ *www.vertigo.nl.*

Fodor's Choice
★ **College Hotel.** Seeking a little New Amsterdam in Old Amsterdam? Stop by the lounge-bar of this relatively new hotel, where dark oak floors, sleek black tables, low lights, and sequestered seating arrangements evoke an old boys' club in midtown Manhattan—minus the elitism. In fact, almost all the staff are service-industry students in training. Seek the fireplace out on a chilly night, and on Sundays from June to September there's live samba. ⊠ *The College Hotel, Roelof Hartstraat 1, Museum District* ☎ *020/571–1511* ⊕ *www.steinhotels.com/college.*

Dantzig. With a view of the Amstel River, this grand café jutting out from the Stopera complex is the perfect point for a pre- or postperformance bevvy. The staff is as allegro as you'll get in this city. ⊠ *Zwanenburgwal 15, The Old City Center (Het Centrum)* ☎ *020/620–9039* ⊕ *www.dantzig.info.*

De Balie. Like Wi-Fi antennae, dark-rimmed eyeglasses peek over PowerBooks as a well-read and socially conscious crowd fills the café-bar of this center for culture and politics. It's the ideal spot to pick up local event flyers or, for that matter, a date. ⊠ *Kleine Gartmanplantsoen 10, Leidseplein* ☎ *020/553–5131* ⊕ *www.balie.nl.*

De Buurvrouw. In this small sawdusted and kitsch-strewn haven, students and alternative types don't mind yelling over the latest in loud guitars and funky beats. They also enjoy a pool tournament every now and

Wonderful canal views make Café de Jaren a great place to grab a drink.

then. ⊠ *St. Pieterspoortsteeg 29, The Old City Center (Het Centrum)* 🕾 *020/625–9654* ⊕ *www.debuurvrouw.nl.*

De Kroon. This grand café dating back to 1898 is popular for both its intimate seating arrangements and a U-shape bar surrounding old-style wooden museum cases filled with zoological specimens. In the evenings, a yuppie clientele sits pretty, high above the noisy, street-level clubs on Rembrandtplein, including the Club Escape conglomerate next door. ⊠ *Rembrandtplein 17, Rembrandtplein* 🕾 *020/625–2011* ⊕ *www. dekroon.nl.*

Finch. With a funky interior and epic views of a canal and a church square, the café attracts thirsty, artsy types. ⊠ *Noordermarkt 5, Jordaan* 🕾 *020/626–2461.*

Het Blauwe Theehuis. The Vondelpark's quietly pulsating epicenter is a blue space-ship-shaped "teahouse" with a massive, multitiered terrace attracting all manner of folks by day and a hip clubby crowd by night. On Sunday nights and summertime Fridays, DJs are on hand to provide a gentle but beat-driven sound track. ⊠ *Vondelpark 5, Museum District* 🕾 *020/662–0254* ⊕ *www.blauwetheehuis.nl.*

Kapitein Zeppos. Nestled on an easy-to-miss alley, this former cigar factory is still redolent of jazzy times past. On weekdays, neighboring University of Amsterdam scholars talk books and drink espressos. Evenings are perfect for a memorable glass of wine or a simple meal, especially with live music on some Sundays. ⊠ *Gebed Zonder End 5, The Old City Center (Het Centrum)* 🕾 *020/624–2057* ⊕ *www.zeppos.nl.*

Kingfisher. For a flavor of the neighborhood's regentrified café culture, check out this favorite corner bar that fills up most nights with parched Pijpers. ⊠ *Ferdinand Bolstraat 24, The Pijp* ☎ *020/671–2395.*

Lime. This slick minimalistic lounge sandwiched between the Red Light District and Chinatown offers a nicely unpretentious aura. ⊠ *Zeedijk 104, The Old City Center (Het Centrum)* ☎ *020/639–3020.*

Lokaal 't Loosje. An old tram warehouse where the arty and the studenty unite. The place dates back over two centuries, with tile wall hangings from 1912 adding to the authenticity of antiquity. ⊠ *Nieuwmarkt 32–34, The Old City Center (Het Centrum)* ☎ *020/627–2635.*

Lux. A fantastic 1960s look and an attractive young crowd keeps it lively at this Marnixstraat club. ⊠ *Marnixstraat 397, The Old City Center (Het Centrum)* ☎ *020/422–1412.*

The Tara. This labyrinth of an Irish bar is large enough to host live music and large-screen football (soccer) matches. Yet, there are still plenty of cozy nooks left over for a quiet meal, Wi-Fi Web surfing, or cuddling with ye olde sweetheart. ⊠ *Rokin 89, The Old City Center (Het Centrum)* ☎ *020/421–2654* ⊕ *www.thetara.com.*

Fodor's Choice **Twenty Third.** The newest addition to the Okura, already with two highly
★ acclaimed restaurants and perhaps the country's finest hotel service, is this champagne bar named after the top floor on which it perches. Besides the eagle-eye view of Amsterdam South, there are 17 different kinds of champagne and snacks (if caviar could be so categorized) from the highly touted Ciel Bleu restaurant next door. ⊠ *Hotel Okura, Ferdinand Bolstraat 333, The Pijp* ☎ *020/678–8344* ⊕ *www.okura.nl.*

Star Ferry. Whether or not you have the musical motivation to visit the Muziekgebouw aan 't IJ, the building's café is worth the hike alone. On a clear afternoon or night, stop by for a meal or a drink and take in the panoramic views of the harbor and the ever-booming docklands of Amsterdam. ⊠ *Muziekgebouw aan't IJ, Piet Heinkade 1, Eastern Docklands* ☎ *020/788–2090* ⊕ *www.starferry.nl.*

Werck. This former coach house to the Westerkerk is now a watering hole for yuppies, Jordaanites, and the loungey house DJs who serve them their smooth late-night beats. During the day, tourists from the nearby Anne Frank House bring brighter-colored clothing to the café-scape, both on the bi-level interior and outside on the spacious patio. ⊠ *Prinsengracht 277, Jordaan* ☎ *020/627–4079* ⊕ *www.werck.nl.*

Wildschut. This 1920s Amsterdam School edifice is a delightful place for coffee, Wi-Fi Web-surfing, or a pre- or postrecital stop, with the Concertgebouw just down the road. At nightfall, it's also the place to meet pin-striped-suited yuppies by the dozen. The large terrace has great views for architecture enthusiasts. ✉ *Roelof Hartplein 1–3, Museum District* ☎ *020/676–8220* ⊕ *www.goodfoodgroup.nl.*

Winkel. This corner café's eminent *appeltaart* (apple pie) beckons locals and travelers alike. The mastermind behind Saturday's organic market once owned the place, so you can bet there's living memory here of fresh food and conscious consumership. ✉ *Noordermarkt 43, Jordaan* ☎ *020/623–0223.*

COFFEE SHOPS

Coffee shops (that really sell weed) tend to be dim noxious places, with an interior decor rivaling that of your local deli. *However, below are a few of the cleaner and more sophisticated establishments in the city.* Still, the vibe is really different (almost the antithesis) to the *gezelligheid* of Amsterdam's precious brown cafés.

Abraxas. Down a small alley, just a stone's throw from the Dam, you'll come upon what would seem to be the multilevel home of a family of hip hobbits. You'll think better once you make out the poor-postured travelers smoking joints or nibbling on ganja cakes. A small satellite branch, Abraxas Too, can be found at Spuistraat 51. ✉ *Jonge Roelensteeg 12–14, The Old City Center (Het Centrum)* ☎ *020/625–5763* ⊕ *www.abraxasparadise.nl.*

Barney's. This regular Cannabis Cup–winning coffee shop brings together two stand-alone concepts: a wide variety of smokeables and all-day breakfasts of the world (served from 9:30–1 PM in the coffee shop). Barney's Brasserie also serves breakfast all day long and is located a few doors up at Haarlemmerstraat 98. ✉ *Haarlemmerstraat 105, Jordaan* ☎ *020/625–9761* ⊕ *www.barneys.biz.*

Dampkring. As much as being stoned and being starstruck seem antithetical, this coffee shop has become even more popular after its use as a set for *Ocean's Twelve* (and the tacky decision to loop movie clips above the bar). The possibility of sitting where Brad may have toked-up notwithstanding, the weed menu is exceptional and the smoothie selection remarkable. ✉ *Handboogstraat 29, The Old City Center (Het Centrum)* ☎ *020/638–0705* ⊕ *www.dedampkring.nl.*

READY, SET, TOKE!

During November, a conspicuous number of tourists with glazed-over eyes and smiles that stretch from dreadlock to dreadlock can be spotted around Amsterdam. No, Phish isn't in town—it's **Cannabis Cup**, the weeklong contest sponsored by *High Times* magazine. The premise of this event is to provide a friendly competition among the city's pot purveyors to see who has the best stuff. Winners are selected by public judges who have all-access to the pot at stake, though at the cost of a €250 judges' pass.

Okura Hotel's super-swank champagne bar, Twenty Third, is named after the floor it's located on.

De Rokerij. For over a decade, this coffee shop has managed to maintain a magical-grotto aura that, ironically enough, requires no extra indulgences to induce a state of giddy transcendence. Dim lights, Indian-inspired murals, and low-to-the-ground seating keep the vibe chill regardless of how busy the Leidseplein headquarters can get. De Rokerij's other branches may inspire smaller-scale out-of-body experiences. ⊠ *Lange Leidsedwarsstraat 41, Leidseplein* ☎ *020/622–9442* ⊕ *www.rokerij.net* ⊠ *Amstel 8, The Canal Ring* ☎ *020/620–0484* ⊠ *Singel 8, The Canal Ring* ☎ *020/422–6643* ⊠ *Elandsgracht 53, Jordaan* ☎ *020/623–0938.*

Green House. Another Cannabis Cup darling, and a not uncommon docking station for celebrities staying at the Grand Hotel up the block, this chain is renowned for quality weeds and seeds. Artful mosaics provide a trippy background, and storefront tables let patrons take in a breath of fresh air. ⊠ *Oudezijds Voorburgwal 191, The Old City Center (Het Centrum)* ☎ *020/627–1739* ⊕ *www.greenhouse.org* ⊠ *Waterlooplein 345, The Old City Center (Het Centrum)* ☎ *020/622–5499* ⊠ *Tolstraat 91* ☎ *020/673–7430.*

Kadinsky. This chain serves mellow jazz alongside scrumptious chocolate-chip cookies, providing a refreshingly understated approach to getting high. ⊠ *Rosmarijnsteeg 9, The Old City Center (Het Centrum)* ☎ *020/624–7023* ⊠ *Zoutsteeg 14, The Old City Center (Het Centrum)* ☎ *020/620–4715.*

Yo-Yo. This is a quintessential friendly neighborhood coffee shop, which—lucky for its bohemian bourgeoisie neighbors—is in the heart

Lighting Up in Amsterdam

Unless you're a regular user, checking out one of those euphemistically named venues where marijuana is sold is hard to justify from a "when in Rome" rationale. The coffee shop industry caters mostly to travelers, and the Dutch are reported to smoke less pot than most other European populations. That said, if you do decide to indulge in Amsterdam's infamous weed scene, there are a few things you should know.

THE SELECTION
Most coffee shops sell a robust selection of both weed and hash, sold anywhere from €5 to €20 per gram. Don't hesitate to describe your dream high to the dealer, and he (or, rarely, she) will try to accommodate you.

HANDLING YOUR HIGH
Be wary. Dutch-sold marijuana is potent and blows the socks off the most hard-core potheads. If cannabis is not your usual drug of choice, don't feel you have to play cool: ask questions of the staff and use caution whatever your medium—joint, bong, or brownie. If you do overindulge, try not to panic. Find a quiet place, take deep breaths, and remember that the discomfort will pass. Sometimes consuming something sweet will help to soften the high.

THE DEAL ON DEALING
Amsterdam is home to an estimated 240 coffee shops, but statistics are looking grim for those who go gaga for ganja. An April 2007 law that prohibits the side-by-side sale of marijuana and alcohol has forced proprietors to dry out their bars to retain coffee shop licenses. What's more, since July 1, 2008, Amsterdam, like many other cities, has become smoke

free. Smoking tobacco is banned from public interior spaces, including coffee shops, and is only allowed in designated smoking areas. Confusingly for visitors and locals alike, it is legal to smoke a pure joint (rolled with just weed or hash) in a coffee shop, but not in bars, restaurants, and clubs. Currently, it's acceptable to sell small amounts of marijuana via the "front door" of a coffee shop where the customer enters. However, the "back door," through which the product arrives, is linked to the illegal world of the mysterious wholesale supplier. Technically, selling marijuana is a no-no, officially prohibited, but the government has barely bothered to enforce this legislation—the buzzword here is "decriminalized." Thanks to the Dutch Opium Act of 1976, an important distinction is made between hard drugs and soft drugs—weed being soft.

STAYING LEGAL
The Netherlands currently allows up to 5 grams of marijuana and several other cannabis-laden comestibles (pot brownies, space cakes, ganja cookies) to be dispensed at a licensed venue to anyone over 18. It also condones possession of up to 30 grams by individuals, solely for personal use. While marijuana must be purchased on regulated premises, takeaway to a more discreet spot is another option. The ins and outs of the trade can get as fuzzy as a stoner's Monday morning. So, what's the Lowlands' logic to all this? Cannabis is recognized as a substance that has the potential for psychological addiction, yes, but it is not believed to create an "unacceptable risk" to the body or, for that matter, to society.

5

of the multicultural Pijp. ⊠ *2e Jan van der Heijdenstraat 79, De Pijp* ☎ *020/664–7173.*

DANCE CLUBS

If you feel the need to get up off the bar stool and shake your groove thing, Amsterdam has a few venues for just that.

Air. Opened in 2010, Air is located at the Rembrantplein, at the same spot where the once legendary club iT stood. Air aims for an intimate yet luxury vibe, with loads of dimly lit nooks and multiple bars. If you're traveling with a crowd, know that table service for up to eight people can be booked in advance. House, club, techno, and urban sounds prevail on the dance floor. ⊠ *Amstelstraat 16, The Old City Center (Het Centrum)* P*020/820–0670* ⊕ *www.air.nl.*

Akhnaton. If you're a world-music buff, think about heading to this renowned venue known for its tight and sweaty African and salsa club nights. ⊠ *Nieuwezijds Kolk 25, The Old City Center (Het Centrum)* ☎ *020/624–3396* ⊕ *www.akhnaton.nl.*

Bitterzoet. Bitterzoet changed owners in 2009 and even though the interior has been pimped out, the packed program of DJs, bands, and even theater still packs them in. The music scene here is diverse, but hip-hop, funk and soul are top dog. ⊠ *Spuistraat 2* ☎ *020/521–3001* ⊕ *www.bitterzoet.com.*

Canvas. Housed in a former newspaper building, just like its neighboring club Trouw, Canvas is located on the seventh floor and offers splendid views over the city. The restaurant and cocktail bar are satisfying, and the music is as diverse as it comes: live jazz, experimental house, hip-hop, indie, and so forth. ⊠ *Wibautstraat 150, East of Amstel* ☎ *020/71–3817* ⊕ *www.canvasopde7e.nl.*

Club Up. Up is an intimate little shoebox of a venue that shares some of their amenities with member's only artists' society De Kring. Arty house parties and banging electro nights attract a hip crowd that's sometimes sprinkled with puzzled tourists in search of a dive bar. ⊠ *Korte Leidsedwarsstraat 26–1, Leidseplein* ☎ *020/623–6985* ⊕ *www.clubup.nl.*

Club Roses. What used to be plain old Club More and then Club More Amor, recently changed names again (a nod to its location on Rozengracht, aka the Roses Canal). Latin-flavored tunes prevail with DJs playing salsa, Caribbean, and other Hispanophilic beats. ⊠ *Rozengracht 133, Jordaan* ☎ *020/624–2330* ⊕ *www.clubroses.nl.*

> ### SOWING WEEDS
>
> Those with a green thumb (who do not live in a country where growing of pot is punishable with jail time) may want to consider getting to the root of their high. Marijuana seeds can be purchased from seed shops, coffee shops, and smart shops. A 10-pack can cost somewhere between €30 and €100. Amsterdam's legendary seed shops include **Dutch Passion** (⊠ *Utrechtsestraat 26* ☎ *020/625–1100* ⊕ *www.dutch-passion.nl*) and **The Flying Dutchman** (⊠ *Oudezijds Achterburgwal 131* ☎ *020/428–4110*).

CLOSE UP

Psilocybin—uh, can you spell that?

Only two decades after the Dutch government condoned the sale of marijuana and hash under the Opium Act of 1976, another "soft drug" came onto the scene: psilocybin. More commonly known as magic mushrooms or paddos, psilocybin was legal until December 2008. The stuff was banned after some fatal accidents with visitors (even though paddo consumption was never proven). The ban still stands and smart shops can no longer sell the mushrooms, either fresh or dried. Smart shops are still allowed to sell a veritable salad of other "natural" high-producing substances—peyote, aphrodisiacal herbs and oils, and herbal XTC.

If you choose to take any of these products, use your own innate smarts: not only are many of them illegal if carried outside the Netherlands, they can produce strong—and not necessarily pleasant—judgment-impairing hallucinations. As of 2010 there's an ongoing national debate about whether to lift the ban, but so far nothing is set in stone. Do confirm local laws before you go foraging for fresh fungi.

Conscious Dreams. Hans van den Hurk is attributed for having opened this very first smart shop in 1994, as a place to promote mind-body awareness. Besides the usual suspects of "natural" drugs, you'll find a selection of "harm reduction kits" said to speed up the recovery process after a hyper-conscious weekend. Lounge beats play overhead and Internet awaits your access. ✉ *Warmoesstraat 12, The Old City Center (Het Centrum)* ☎ *020/421–7000* ⊕ *www.consciousdreams.nl.*

Inner Space. "The only legal coke alternative" and liquid drops to produce "that real MDMA feeling" are among the products sold here. So are mushroom grow kits, marijuana seeds, and some good ol' vitamin C. ✉ *Spuistraat 108, The Old City Center (Het Centrum)* ☎ *020/624–3338* ⊕ *www.innerspace.nl* ✉ *Staalstraat 5, The Old City Center (Het Centrum)* ☎ *020/320–0064.*

5

Escape. Thursdays through Sundays, this megaclub opens its doors to some 2,500 people. The great Escape is meant for those who take "dress to impress" literally and are keen to dance under laser lights as DJs spin techno and all its new-millennial derivatives. In celebration of its recent 20-year anniversary, the conglomerate, also comprising the more intimate club Escape deLux (with its own entrance on Amstel 70), has expanded with a studio of MTV-esque aspirations, an LED-ceilinged lounge, and a café. ✉ *Rembrandtplein 11–15, Rembrandtplein* ☎ *020/622–1111* ⊕ *www.escape.nl.*

Flex Bar. A favorite with the electro, techno, and acid crowd, Flex Bar has an excellent sound system and a fun attitude. Of late, management has been leaning more towards corporate rentals and private parties. Still, the lineup programming is one of the freshest in town when it's open to the public. ✉ *Pazzanistraat 1, Amsterdam West* ℗ *020/486–2123* ⊕ *www.flexbar.nl.*

Jimmy Woo's. Thursday through Sunday, this is probably the hottest club in town for the rich and the famous and their wannabes.

The urban grooves are funky and the sound system, not too shabby. ⊠ *Korte Leidsedwarsstraat 18, Leidseplein* ☎ *020/626–3150* ⊕ *www. jimmywoo.nl.*

Korsakoff. This is a dark but friendly magnet for the pierced and tattooed rockers among us who like their music industrially rough and ready (there's a bit of trance, techno, and dubstep thrown in too). And somehow, as only the complexities of Dutch culture will permit, the club feels cozy, albeit in a scruffy way. ⊠ *Lijnbaansgrach 161, Jordaan* ☎ *020/625–7854* ⊕ *www.korsakoffamsterdam.nl.*

Odeon. If you feel like some weekend dancing in a gracious old canal house, head for this 17th-century beer brewery turned 19th-century concert hall, which reopened in 2005 to provide cocktails, dining, fashion shows, and spinning from superhip DJs. Many of its rooms retain their spectacular painted and stucco ceilings. ⊠ *Singel 460, The Old City Center (Het Centrum)* ☎ *020/521–8555* ⊕ *www.odeonamsterdam.nl.*

Panama. A pioneer in the up-and-coming nightlife and culture zone of the Eastern Docklands is this nightclub with a plush and golden interior. Sadly, in 2005 it was forced to trade in its inspired lineups—which included everything from tango orchestras to circus acts—for more commercially viable house music. ⊠ *Oostelijke Handelskade 4, Eastern Docklands* ☎ *020/311–8686* ⊕ *www.panama.nl.*

The Power Zone. Amsterdam's megaclub can pack in thousands of revelers and often does, thanks to a fairly easygoing door policy (just don't come as a pack!). There is plenty of room for lounging and dancing to the latest happy house tunes. ⊠ *Daniel Goedkoopstraat 1–3,* ☎ *020/681–8866* ⊕ *www.thepowerzone.nl.*

Studio 80. With its dim lighting and clever programming, Studio 80 is unlikely to share its clientele with the neighboring clubs, who tend to attract those with a penchant for hair product. On any given night, you'll find infamous house producers that operate on the alternative side of electronic music, Israeli DJs, or unapologetic pop programs that cater to a smart young crowd. ⊠ *Rembrandtplein 17, The Canal Ring* ☎ *020/521–8333* ⊕ *www.studio-80.nl.*

Trouw. This cutting-edge club is in a former newspaper building. There are two main halls and an excellent restaurant where you can refuel. The music leans towards underground techno, dubstep, and experimental electronica, which suits the industrial décor splendidly. ⊠ *Wibaustraat 127, East of Amstel* P*020/463–7788* ⊕ *www.trouwamsterdam.nl.*

GAY, LESBIAN AND MIXED BARS

GAY

Whether or not Amsterdam is the "Gay Capital of the World," as proclaimed by some admirers of the Netherlands' long-standing acceptance of gays and their right to marry, the city undoubtedly has a *trés* gay nightlife. While every nook and cranny is fair game to experience the whole gamut of Amsterdam's sexual orientations and gender-based identities, the gay scene divides into something of a three-ring circus throughout the city center.

If you're into throbbing music and strobe lights, then the Escape club might be just the thing.

Reguliersdwarsstraat Predictable and pretty, the venues here attract mostly men in their 20s, 30s, or 40s (with the occasional sugar-daddy grandpa who still has pecs of steel). It's trendy but tactful, cruisey but only after a certain hour. This is not to say, however, that things can't get a little bit X-rated. What's more, just the thought of the Thermos Saunas *(see below)*, not too far away on Kerkstraat, has a way of steaming up the scene. Of the three districts, the one that has evolved along **Warmoestraat** is considerably the least egalitarian. One of the main streets that borders the Red Light District, it feels a little too cut off from the rest of the city. There are a few bars that do welcome all walks of life (including straight folks), but the majority of the clubs here are men-only, leather-heavy, and dungeon-prone. Your surest bet at all-encompassing *homo-gezelligheid* is **Amstel,** located right off Rembrandtplein. These coordinates make it likely you'll have to dodge some drunken Rembrandtplein tourists or their speeding taxis, but it's well worth it. Kitschy gay pubs, lively lesbian clubs, and drag bars, Amstel is a haven of pansexual hospitality.

ARC. With fusion-inspired finger food and €5 Wednesday cocktail nights, this lounge is suited for a scene from *Sex and the City*. Passé as the premise may be, it remains a magnet for fashionable gay men and pansexual hipsters. ⊠ *Reguliersdwarsstraat 44, Rembrandtplein* ☎ *020/689–7070* ⊕ *www.bararc.com.*

Club Church. This new kid on the block has three floors of play-and-dance space with changing theme nights six times a week. If you're looking to cruise this is a good bet. ⊠ *Kerkstraat 52, Leidseplein* ☎ *020/111–1111* ⊕ *www.clubchurch.nl.*

Cockring. This strictly men-only venue is almost an institution in the leather scene. It also stays open until the wee hours of the morning. ✉ *Warmoestraat 96, The Old City Center (Het Centrum)* ☎ *020/623–9604* ⊕ *www.clubcockring.com.*

Cuckoo's Nest. Back in 1984, this bar was so leather-lined it put San Francisco's Folsom Street to shame. Today it attracts a more diverse crowd, many of whom find their way to what's rumored to be one of the biggest dark rooms in Europe. (See the Web site for a concise chart of "common hanky codes.") ✉ *Nieuwezijds Kolk 6, The Old City Center (Het Centrum)* ☎ *020/627–1752* ⊕ *www.cuckoosnest.nl.*

Dirty Dick's. Let's just say that the name of this leather cruise bar has a bite that doesn't even come close to its bark. ✉ *Warmoestraat 86, The Old City Center (Het Centrum)* ☎ *020/627–8634.*

Downtown. With its sunny terrace, this café is a pleasant daytime pit stop for coffee and sandwiches. ✉ *Reguliersdwarsstraat 31, Rembrandtplein* ☎ *020/622–9958* ⊕ *www.coffeeshopdowntown.nl.*

Le Montmartre. This kitschy corner attracts a comfortably out, all-ages, all-classes crowd stopping in for a drink and perhaps a sing-along before heading out clubbing. ✉ *Halvemaansteeg 17, Rembrandtplein* ☎ *020/620–7622* ⊕ *www.cafemontmartre.nl.*

Queen's Head. You won't find Queen Beatrix here, but a mainstream crowd of well-built and fun-loving princes enjoying DJ beats and parties that pour out onto the sidewalk. ✉ *Zeedijk 20, The Old City Center (Het Centrum)* ☎ *020/420–2475* ⊕ *www.queenshead.nl.*

Soho. Varnished wood, red leather seats, and brass-framed mirrors provide the backdrop for the outrageous flirting that goes down in this English-style pub. The ever-popular happy hour makes Soho a go-to for locals as well as a magnet for visitors. ✉ *Reguliersdwarsstraat 36, Rembrandtplein* ☎ *020/422–3312* ⊕ *www.pubsoho.eu.*

Thermos Sauna. Men interested in more than just a little dip into the city's gay scene might consider taking the plunge at Amsterdam's most luxurious saunas for men, which provide ample opportunity for fraternizing in the Finnish sauna, Turkish steam bath, whirlpool, the "rest cabins," or at the bar. Experience all the amenities, including a swimming pool, rooftop terrace, restaurant, and, for the multimedia-minded, a video room and Internet service. (✉ *Raamstraat 33* ☎ *020/623–9158* ⊕ *www.thermos.nl* ☉ *Noon–8* AM.

The Web. Leather, piercing, and tattoos predominate, but meeting one's soul mate at this cruise bar is not out of the question. ⊠ *Sint Jacobstraat 6, The Old City Center (Het Centrum)* ☎ *020/623–6758* ⊕ *www.thewebamsterdam.nl.*

LESBIAN

Compared to many other coordinates on the globe, Amsterdam has had women's rights and gay rights down pat for several decades. What can still use a little more loving, however, is society's accommodation of gay women, particularly when it comes to nightlife. This sector of sex in the city still has some evolving to do, yet the scene is steadily expanding its repertoire with an increasing number of lesbian bars and nightclubs.

> ### HERE AND QUEER?
>
> For more information about gay life in Amsterdam, visit the gay-and-lesbian information kiosk Pink Point (⊕ *www.pinkpoint.org*) located at the Homomonument on the corner of Keizersgracht and Westermarkt; it's open daily from 10–6. For details on gay nightlife, consult the listings at ⊕ *www.amsterdam4gays.com.*

Flirtation. This highly successful women-only dance event for young lesbians and bi-curious girls takes over club Panama four times a year, with a bevy of female DJs, special acts, and live performances. ⊠ Oostelijke Handelskade 4, *Eastern Docklands* P020/311–8686 ⊕ *www.flirtation.nl.*

Garbo. Taking place every first Saturday of the month at Miranda Paviljoen and Brasserie de Lakey, this is a women-only dance night for lesbians and bisexuals, with a chance to have a bite to eat beforehand. It's advised to book ahead. ⊠ *Amsteldijk 223, East of Amstel* ☎ *020/644–5768* ⊕ *www.garboforwomen.nl.*

Saarein2. Amsterdam's best lesbian bar, as it's been labeled, has a cozy brown-café character in the Jordaan and a relatively new "mixed" policy. ⊠ *Elandsstraat 119, Jordaan* ☎ *020/623–4901* ⊕ *www.saarein.infol.*

Vive-la-Vie. For almost three decades pretty women have been vying for space in these petite quarters on the edge of Rembrandtplein. Today the bar is popular as ever, also being straight-friendly and open to men—so long as they behave. ⊠ *Amstelstraat 7, Rembrandtplein* ☎ *020/624–0114* ⊕ *www.vivelavie.net.*

MIXED

With a population of just 750,000 inhabiting what are essentially a series of canal-determined concentric circles, it's hard for Amsterdam residents not to bump into one another. Some confluences are less felicitous than others, but you can always count on the ones at "mixed" bars to be merry and gay. As with most mixed venues, gay men usually outnumber lesbians and straight folk.

Amstel Taveerne. Tankards and brass pots hanging from the ceiling reflect the friendly crowd of locals around the bar. Go just for the raucous sing-alongs that erupt whenever an old favorite is played. ⊠ *Amstel 54, Rembrandtplein* ☎ *020/623–4254* ⊕ *www.amsteltaveerne.nl.*

COC. Founded in 1946, this center of the Dutch Association for the Integration of Homosexuality is the oldest organization of its kind in the world and today has several chapters throughout the country. Stop by to see what's happening while you're in town. ⊠ *Rozenstraat 8, Jordaan* ☎ *020/623–4596* ⊕ *www.cocamsterdam.nl.*

De Trut. Every Sunday night since the mid-'80s, the basement of an old squat in an unmarked building has opened its doors to a rainbow of folk—particularly *potten en flikkers* (dykes and fags). The nice thing about partying here (besides the fact that it's a blast) is that all of the workers are volunteers, and all proceeds from the evening go to various gay-rights nonprofit organizations. The beer and the entrance fee are cheap, but be sure to arrive 15 minutes before the doors open at 11; the line gets long and you'll be turned away once capacity is reached. ⊠ *Bilderdijkstraat 165, Amsterdam West* ☎ *020/612–3524* ⊕ *www. trutfonds.nl.*

Getto. Every color and chromosome combination is welcome at this self-proclaimed "place for like-minded people." The menu of typical Americana fair and fun cocktails—virgin and experienced—reads as though under the influence of a John Waters script. ⊠ *Warmoesstraat 51, The Old City Center (Het Centrum)* ☎ *020/421–5151* ⊕ *www.getto.nl.*

Habibi Ana. Meaning "my sweetheart" in Arabic, Habibi Ana is a one-of-a-kind experience in Amsterdam and, quite possibly, the world over. Founded by the same-titled foundation, this bar caters to gay, bisexual, and transsexual men and women of Arab descent. ⊠ *Lange Leidsedwarsstraat 4–6, Leidseplein* ☎ *No phone* ⊕ *www.habibiana.nl.*

Lellebel. This decade-old drag-show bar is renowned for its extravagant weekend performances. Recent additions to the weekday program include karaoke, salsa, and a Wednesday night Transgender Café. ⊠ *Utrechtsestraat 4, The Canal Ring* ☎ *020/427–5139* ⊕ *www.lellebel.nl.*

Fodor's Choice
★

PRIK. Not only is this a highly popular bar-café, but its block is rather off-the-beaten-*queer*-path, which was intended by its founding gay couple as a means to be as all-inclusive as possible. The staff and clientele are as effervescent as the venue's name—*prik* means bubbles in Dutch and (among other things) refers to the prosecco on tap. They also serve great cocktails and finger food. ⊠ *Spuistraat 109, The Old City Center (Het Centrum)* ☎ *020/320–0002* ⊕ *www.prikamsterdam.nl.*

JAZZ CLUBS

Amsterdam has provided a happy home-away-from-home for jazz musicians since the early '50s, when such legends as Chet Baker and Gerry Mulligan would wind down after their official show at the Concertgebouw by jamming at one or another of the many bohemian bars around the Zeedijk. For the last quarter century, the world-statured but intimate Bimhuis has taken over duties as the city's major jazz venue with an excellent programming policy that welcomes both the legendary jazz performer and the latest avant-garde up-and-comer.

Alto. Every night hear the top picks of local ensembles and some well-respected locals in the smoky, jam-packed environment of one of

Amsterdam's oldest jazz joints. A little blues can be enjoyed here as well. ⊠ *Korte Leidsedwarsstraat 115, Leidseplein* ☎ *020/626–3249* ⊕ *www.jazz-cafe-alto.nl.*

Fodor's Choice **Bimhuis.** The best-known jazz place in town left its classic digs in 2005 ★ in favor of the brand-spanking-new—and utterly awesome—Muziekgebouw aan 't IJ. Everyone, from old legends to the latest avant-gardist, agrees: it's close to perfect. Views of the city are breathtaking and the music you'll hear inside has been known to leave listeners panting for more. ⊠ *Piet Heinkade 3, Eastern Docklands* ☎ *020/788–2150 office; 020/788–2188 box office* ⊕ *www.bimhuis.nl.*

Bourbon Street Jazz & Blues Club. Mainstream blues and jazz are served up to a largely out-of-town clientele, but it does the job—and a late one at that, open until 5 in the morning Fridays and Saturdays and 4 all other days. ⊠ *Leidsekruisstraat 6–8, Leidseplein* ☎ *020/623–3440* ⊕ *www.bourbonstreet.nl.*

Casablanca. On the edge of the Red Light District sits this neighborhood's classic club, dating back to the 1940s. For better or for worse, cracks are appearing in its jazzy foundation as the programming gets diluted with cabaret, DJ sets, and karaoke. ⊠ *Zeedijk 24–26, The Old City Center (Het Centrum)* ☎ *020/625–5685* ⊕ *www.casablanca-amsterdam.nl.*

Cotton Club. Fans of more traditional jazz should check out the legendary venue named after its original owner, the Surinamer trumpet player Teddy Cotton. Although the club's music is not usually live, its gregarious crowd is certainly lively. ⊠ *Nieuwmarkt 5, The Old City Center (Het Centrum)* ☎ *020/626–6192* ⊕ *www.cottonclubmusic.nl.*

ROCK MUSIC VENUES

Quaint yet cosmopolitan, Amsterdam has been the place where many of the world's musicians dream of one day playing. The Melkweg and Paradiso have savvily kept their fingers on the pulse of every major musical trend since the late '60s. Today both legendary venues and a whole new-millennium phalanx of other clubs manage to keep the music real. The long-clichéd unholy trinity of sex, drugs, and rock and roll may not define Amsterdam as well as it used to, but the city remains one of the defining places for musicians worldwide to indulge in dreams of excess. And this makes for a rocking dance floor.

De Nieuwe Anita. The quirky Nieuwe Anita is loved by the alternative crowd and home to screenings of cult classics, spoken word nights, live gigs organized by underground magazine *Subbacultcha!*, and much more. ⊠ *Frederik Hendrinkstraat 111, Amsterdam West* ☎ *No phone* ⊕ *www.denieuweanita.nl.*

Heineken Music Hall. The relatively new and rather-out-of-the-way concert hall with a capacity for 5,500 has a sterile but acoustic-rich environment. It's usually for touring bands that have outgrown (and most likely sold out) the Melkweg and Paradiso. ⊠ *Arena Boulevard 590, Amsterdam Southeast* ☎ *0900/300–1250* ⊕ *www.heineken-music-hall.nl.*

Check out the new Bimhuis theater on the water—perfect in every sense.

Hotel Arena Tonight. From tabernacles to turntables, yet another of Amsterdam's churches has been refurbished to accommodate the city's nightlife. Part of Hotel Arena complex, this club is popular for its hip roster of DJs and weekend programs. ✉ *'s-Gravensandestraat 51, East of the Amstel* ☎ *020/850–2420* ⊕ *www.hotelarena.nl.*

★ **Maloe Melo.** What could be nicer than a friendly hangout dive and venue for rock, blues, and roots musicians? Sometimes said characters are joined on stage by bigger musical celebrities, fresh from their gigs at more reputable venues. ✉ *Lijnbaansgracht 163, Jordaan* ☎ *020/420–4592* ⊕ *www.maloemelo.com.*

OCCII. The former squat and slightly out of the way hole-in-the-wall is just beyond the gates of the Vondelpark's western exit. Nevertheless, OCCII (pronounced "oh-chee") has stayed true to its punky vibe over the years, and also softened enough to let a little world music programming in. ✉ *Amstelveenseweg 134, Museum District* ☎ *020/671–7778* ⊕ *www.occii.org.*

OT301. This legalized squat is housed in the former film academy and offers fun, alternative nights with live bands and DJs. Also on the premises are nonprofit organic restaurant Peper and an art gallery. ✉ *Overtoom 301, Amsterdam West* ☎ *No phone* ⊕ *www.ot301.nl.*

★ **Paradiso.** This former church of a pop temple is the country's most famous concert space, intact with vaulted ceilings and stained glass. It began its days as a hippie squat allowed by the local government in hopes that it might encourage the emptying of the Vondelpark (then serving as the crash pad for a generation). To this day, Paradiso remains an epic venue for both music's legends and up-and-comers, regardless of their genre. Most concerts are followed by a club night extending into the early hours that showcases the latest dance sounds. Flexible staging arrangements also make this a favorite venue for performance artists and multimedia events. ✉ *Weteringschans 6–8, Leidseplein* ☏ *020/626–4521* ⊕ *www.paradiso.nl.*

Sugar Factory. Self-stylized as a "night theater," the Factory opened its doors across from the Melkweg in 2005 with big ambitions: taking clubbing into the 21st century and beyond. An average evening may involve DJs, as well as bands, theater, dance, spoken word, and slam poetry. ✉ *Lijnbaansgracht 238, Leidseplein* ☏ *020/626–5006* ⊕ *www.sugarfactory.nl.*

The Waterhole. A favorite with tourists, this Leidseplein landing strip usually showcases a blues and rock cover band of dubious distinction—but it remains a friendly place to trade tales of the road. ✉ *Korte Leidsedwarsstraat 49, Museum District* ☏ *020/620–8904* ⊕ *www.twaterhole.nl.*

Westergasfabriek. A potential pleasure-palace extraordinaire is in a gas factory founded in 1883 and reopened in 2003 as an arts and cultural center. The site comprises 13 monumental buildings of various sizes and shapes that play host to film and theater companies, fashion shows, corporate functions, movie shoots, art exhibitions, operas, techno parties, and assorted festivals. There are also bars, nightclubs, and restaurants. ✉ *Haarlemmerweg 8–10, Amsterdam West* ☏ *020/586–0710* ⊕ *www. westergasfabriek.nl.*

Winston. If a small-scale club is what you're after, take a hike up the Warmoesstraat. But when it comes to quality programming, size doesn't matter. Winston offers a bit of everything—from punk to DJs, from neo-Christian to the easiest of easy tunes. ✉ *Warmoesstraat 129–131, The Old City Center (Het Centrum)* ☏ *020/623–1380* ⊕ *www.winston.nl.*

MIDNIGHT MUSEUM CRAWL

For one night in early November, all the city's major museums stay open until the wee hours to host a variety of themed parties. If you only have a very short period of time to visit Amsterdam, elasticize those euros by arriving for **Museum Nacht**. At this fantastic party, you'll find activities such as tangos under Rembrandt's *Night Watch*, house beats at the Jewish Historical Museum, bossa nova in the Stedelijk, master classes on how to paint like Bob Ross, and ghost stories for kids in the Bible Museum. For annual details see ⊕ *www.n8.nl.*

THE ARTS

Although a relatively small city, Amsterdam packs a giant cultural wallop with its numerous venues—from former churches and industrial monuments to the acoustical supremacy of the Concertgebouw—and festivals that invariably highlight both homegrown and international talent. So book that ticket fast! Amsterdam's theater and music season begins in September and runs through June, when the Holland Festival of Performing Arts is held.

CABARETS

September marks the official start of the cultural season, as the greater majority of Amsterdam's performing arts do not give shows during the summer. But don't fret: June, July, and August are jam-packed with festivals (both in the city and its environs), outdoor concerts and movie screenings, and appearances by many foreign artists stopping through Amsterdam on their summer tours.

Boom Chicago. This is what happens when a bunch of zany expat Americans open their own restaurant-theater to present improvised comedy inspired by life in Amsterdam and the rest of the world. Dinner and seating begin at 6, with show time at 8:15; on weekends there are also late shows. ⊠ *Leidseplein 12, Leidseplein* ☎ *020/423–0101* ⊕ *www. boomchicago.nl* ☽ *Daily 6:00*PM.

Comedy Café Amsterdam. For some straight—and often English—stand-up, check the schedule of this club next door to the Hard Rock Café. ⊠ *Max Euweplein 43–45, Leidseplein* ☎ *020/638–3971* ⊕ *www. comedycafe.nl.*

Comedy Theater in de Nes. This fairly new, intimate venue is home to up-and-coming Dutch comedians. Inspired by American comedy clubs, it has a fully fledged bar that stays open during shows. In short, it's the Paradiso of comedy. ⊠ *NES 100, The Old City Center (Het Centrum)* P*020/422–2777* ⊕ *www.comedytheater.nl.*

De Kleine Komedie. For many years, this riverside theater has been the most vibrant venue for cabaret and comedy mainly in Dutch. ⊠ *Amstel 56–58, East of the Amstel* ☎ *020/624–0534* ⊕ *www.dekleinekomedie. nl.*

Toomler. Borrowing its name from the Yiddish word for "noisemaker," this is the podium for the Dutch stand-up group Comedytrain. The programming is often English-friendly, with regular appearances by international guests. ⊠ *Breitnerstraat 2, Amsterdam South* ☎ *020/670–7400* ⊕ *www.toomler.nl.*

FILM

Have you ever wondered how the Dutch came to speak such impeccable English? History's answer to this is that a small nation with few resources had no choice but to speak the language of the people with whom they traded. Pop culture's answer to this is much simpler: Hollywood! All films and TV are subtitled, not dubbed, so viewers are constantly exposed to English. What's more, in a nation whose last half-century would generally be characterized by political peace and social harmony, it's no wonder local folks yearn for a bit of good old-fashioned American cussing

THEO'S FILMS

Albeit posthumously, the controversial director Theo van Gogh, who was assassinated by a radical Dutch Muslim in 2002, has had a recent surge of stateside attention, with three of his movies being remade by Steve Buscemi (*Interview*), Stanley Tucci (*Blind Date*), and John Turturro (*06/05*).

and carnage. The Dutch have a big soft spot for master of unease David Lynch, and they can never get enough of Tarantino and the Coen Brothers. Conversely, a number of Dutch directors—alienated by the long lackluster local scene—have manifested their blockbuster destinies in Hollywood. Creator of *Basic Instinct* and *RoboCop*, the notorious Paul Verhoeven, is the nation's most famous export.

Cinecenter. Sleek modern decor fills the lounge of this theater opposite the Melkweg, while four screens downstairs play artier and more internationally acclaimed films. ✉ *Lijnbaansgracht 236, Leidseplein* ☎ *020/623–6615* ⊕ *www.cinecenter.nl.*

FILM FESTIVALS

If you're a film lover with a flexible schedule, plan your trip around Holland's big film events. The International Film Festival Rotterdam (⊕ *www.filmfestivalrotterdam.com*) is in late January/early February; the International Documentary Film Festival Amsterdam (⊕ *www.idfa.nl*) and the smaller budget documentary sideshow the Shadow Festival (⊕ *www.shadowfestival.nl*) are in November; the Imagine Amsterdam Fantastic Film Festival (⊕ *www.imaginefilmfestival.nl*) is in April.

De Uitkijk. Opened in 1913, this small canal-side "lookout," as its name means in Dutch, ranks as the city's oldest cinema. No longer just a one-hit wonder, the theater was spruced up in 2007 and now presents a more diverse program consisting of documentaries, kid flicks, and movies screened in cooperation with the Film Museum. ✉ *Prinsengracht 452, Leidseplein* ☎ *020/623–7460* ⊕ *www.uitkijk.nl.*

EYE, Film Instituut Nederland (Film Museum). True film buffs should definitely pay a visit to this gold mine of more than 35,000 films and a library open to the public. Not only are revival screenings culled from this collection, but there are also special programs that comprise outdoor screenings and silent films accompanied by live piano music. It's also home to one of the nicest terraces in town. ✉ *Vondelpark 3, Museum District* ☎ *020/589–1400* ⊕ *www.filmmuseum.nl.*

Filmhuis Cavia. This is one of several repertory cinemas that show a savvy blend of classics and modern world cinema, with programming that is decidedly edgy and politically alternative. ✉ *Van Hallstraat 52-I, Amsterdam West* ☎ *020/681–1419* ⊕ *www.filmhuiscavia.nl.*

Kriterion. This film house is run by students and reflects their world-embracing tastes (especially during its late shows that encourage the more cultish of movies). The adjoining café is always buzzing with chatty humanities types, but that's not to say that the long-graduated among us are unwelcome. ✉ *Roetersstraat 170, East of the Amstel* ☎ *020/623–1708* ⊕ *www.kriterion.nl.*

The Movies. A full-swing 1920s ambience sets the stage for artsy and indie flicks at this film house. The cozy restaurant, lively bar, and smiling staff could leave you wanting little more. ✉ *Haarlemmerdijk 157–165, Jordaan* ☎ *020/624–5790* ⊕ *www.themovies.nl.*

Pathé De Munt. The largest cinema in the city center has 13 screens showing the latest mainstream films. It's a typical blockbuster venue and lacks the charm of the smaller movie houses. It makes up for it by offering plenty of legroom, state-of-the-art sound systems, and huge screens. ⊠ *Vijzelstraat 15, Rembrandtplein* ☎ *0900/1458* ⊕ *www.pathe.nl.*

Rialto. Away from the maddening crowd, this little theater is noted for showing world cinema and more highbrow film classics. ⊠ *Ceinturbaan 338, The Pijp* ☎ *020/662–3488* ⊕ *www.rialtofilm.nl.*

Studio K. The Amsterdam foundation Kriterion, which has been promoting student-run business ventures since World War II, has

> **NES TIX**
>
> Amsterdam's Off Broadway–type theaters are centered along the Nes, an alley leading off the Dam. One-stop ticket shopping for the Brakke Grond, De Engelenbak, and Frascati can be done at the central ticket office (⊕ *www.indenes.nl*). You can also visit the office located at **Brakke Grond** ⊠ *Nes 45, The Old City Center (Het Centrum)* or reserve tickets by calling 020/626–6866 (Monday–Saturday, from 1 PM up until showtime).

added yet another venue to its résumé. Opened in autumn 2007, this two-screen movie house shows not only art and foreign films, but with a theater, an open stage, and a restaurant-bar, it's a multidisciplinarian's dream come true. ⊠ *Timorplein 62, East of the Amstel* ☎ *020/692–0422* ⊕ *www.studio-k.nu.*

★ **Tuschinski.** Since 1921, this eclectic Art Deco reverie has been the most dazzling—not to mention central—place for moviegoers to escape from reality. Owned by the country's main movie distributor, the theater has six screens showing the latest Hollywood blockbusters and the occasional Dutch film or art-house number. ⊠ *Reguliersbreestraat 26, Rembrandtplein* ☎ *0900/1458.*

MUSIC

Some of Amsterdam's most esteemed music venues also happen to be in the city's most beautiful structures. Enjoy a night of music in a breathtaking, and acoustically stellar, setting.

Bethanienklooster. Many of the city's churches are being used these days by music lovers and players *(see also Nieuwe Kerk, Noorder Kerk, Nicolaas Kerk, and Oude Kerk in Exploring Amsterdam).* This former monastery still provides a calm and holy setting for regular chamber music concerts. ⊠ *Barndesteeg 6B, The Old City Center (Het Centrum)* ☎ *020/625–0078* ⊕ *www.bethanienklooster.nl.*

Beurs van Berlage. The architectural landmark and progenitor of the Amsterdam School has two concert halls—including the unique glass-box "diamond in space" Amvest Zaal—with the Netherlands Philharmonic and the Netherlands Chamber Orchestra as the in-house talent. ⊠ *Damrak 213, The Old City Center (Het Centrum)* ☎ *020/521–7575* ⊕ *www.beursvanberlage.nl.*

Fodor's Choice
★ **Concertgebouw.** There are two auditoriums, large and small, under one roof at the Netherlands' premier concert hall, famous for having one of the finest sound systems the world over. With its Viennese Classicist

DID YOU KNOW?

First described as the "Prune Cake" when opened in 1921, the interior of Tuschinski is a dizzying and dense mixture of Baroque, Art Nouveau, Amsterdam School, Jugendstil, and Asian influences. It began as a variety theater welcoming such stars as Marlene Dietrich, but it soon became a cinema, and to this day watching movies from one of the extravagant private balconies remains an unforgettable experience—especially if you order champagne.

facade surmounted by a golden lyre, this building opposite the Rijks-museum draws 800,000 visitors to 800 concerts per year. In the larger of the two theaters, the **Grote Zaal,** Amsterdam's critically acclaimed **Koninklijk Concertgebouworkest** (Royal Concert Orchestra), whose recordings are in the collections of most self-respecting lovers of classical music, is often joined by international soloists. Their reputation has only grown in the last decade under the baton twirling of conductor Riccardo Chailly, who passed the honor to the highly regarded Latvian Mariss Jansons in 2004. Guest conductors read like a list from the

> **OPEN-AIR ENTERTAINMENT**
>
> Theatrical events in the Vondel-park have a long and glorious history. Nowadays, during the **Openluchttheater** season, there's a lunchtime concert and a midafternoon children's show on Wednesdays, Thursday night shows are in the bandstand, and there's theater every Friday night. Various activities take place on Saturdays, and theater events and pop concerts are held on Sunday afternoons. It's a full agenda!

musical heavens: Mstislav Rostropovich, Nikolaus Harnoncourt, and Bernard Haitink. Visiting maestros like these naturally push the prices up, but the range remains wide: expect to pay anywhere between €5 and €100. But throughout July and August, tickets for the Robeco Summer Concerts, which involve high-profile artists and orchestras, are an excellent bargain. The **Koorzaal** (the "Choir Hall"), is a smaller venue for chamber music and up-and-coming musicians, and is the usual setting for the free lunchtime concerts on Wednesdays at 12:30, that take place from September through June. ⊠ *Concertgebouwplein 2–6, Museum District* ☎ *020/671–8345* ⊕ *www.concertgebouw.nl.*

★ **Engelse Kerk.** The former Pilgrims' hangout has weekly concerts of baroque and classical music that always seeks to employ period instruments. English-language church service is on Sunday mornings at 10:30. ⊠ *Begijnhof 48, The Old City Center (Het Centrum)* ☎ *020/624–9665* ⊕ *www.ercadam.nl.*

Muziekgebouw aan 't IJ. Opened in 2005, this self-monikered "Concert hall for the 21st Century" is a huge asset to the city's arts and culture scene. What's more, it's home to legendary jazz club Bimhuis *(see above),* and the Star Ferry café has a splendid panoramic view of the IJ's harbor. ⊠ *Piet Heinkade 1* ☎ *020/788–2010* ⊕ *www.muziekgebouw.nl.*

Fodor'sChoice
★ **Muziektheater.** Seating 1,600 people to witness its international performances throughout the year, this urban coliseum is home to **De Nederlandse Opera, Het Nationale Ballet,** and the newly established **Holland Symphonia,** all of whose repertoires embrace both the classical and the 20th century. On Tuesdays from September through May, you can catch free lunchtime concerts in the Boekmanzaal from the Nederlands Kamerorkest, Opera Studio Nederland, and Holland Symfonia. Doors open at 12:15, and are first-come, first-served. ⊠ *Amstel 3/Waterlooplein 22, The Old City Center (Het Centrum)* ☎ *020/625–5455* ⊕ *www.het-muziektheater.nl.*

Dutch-Style Theater

Such internationally statured companies as **Dogtroep** (⊕ www.dogtroep. nl), **PIPS:lab** ⊕ www.pipslab.nl), and **Vis-à-Vis** (⊕ www.visavis.nl) are specialists in the typically Dutch school of spectacle theater, which is hardly bound by language and goes in search of unique locations—and other dimensions—to strut its stuff. Groups like this usually participate, along with many others of like mind from around the world, in the amazing annual **Over het IJ Festival** This festival is held every July at the abandoned shipyard-turned-postmodern-culture-center NDSM in Amsterdam North *(see above)*, gathering together dozens of dance and theater troupes dedicated to the more wild and physical aspects of the arts. ☎ 020/492–2229 ⊕ www. ijfestival.nl. If you happen to be in town for the first two, and sometimes the third, weeks of August, don't miss **Parade**, a traveling tent city that specializes in quirky performances and a social and carnivalesque ambience. ⊠ *Martin Luther Kingpark, Amsterdam South* ☎ 033/465–4555 ⊕ www. deparade.nl.

5

Orgel Park. In this newest church-turned-cultural venue, just off the Vondelpark, an international roster of professional organists and students perform thematically inspired concerts and genre-bending improvisational pieces. The organ was never so hip. ⊠ *Gerard Brandtstraat 26, Museum District* ☎ 020/515–8111 ⊕ *www.orgelpark.nl.*

★ **Vondelpark Openluchttheater.** Skaters, joggers, cyclists, and sun worshippers gather in the Vondelpark each summer to enjoy the great outdoors. Between late May and September, they're joined by the culture vultures all heading to the park's open-air program of music, dance, cabaret, and children's events. ⊠ *Vondelpark Museum District* ☎ 020/428–3360 ⊕ *www.openluchttheater.nl.*

★ **Waalse Kerk.** Founded in 1409, restored in 1647, and rebuilt in 1816, this courtyarded church is as intimate as it is elegant. Musicians from both the Netherlands and abroad give regular concerts. A mass in French is given on Sunday mornings at 11. ⊠ *Walenpleintje 159, The Old City Center (Het Centrum)* ☎ 020/623–2074 ⊕ *www.waalsekerk-amsterdam.nl.*

OPERA AND BALLET

Koninklijk Theater Carré. Although more focused on commercial and large-scale musicals, this former circus theater also schedules many acclaimed Eastern European companies performing ballet and opera classics. Tom Waits liked the scene so much that he did a two-night stand here in 2005. ⊠ *Amstel 115–25, East of the Amstel* ☎ 0900/252–5255 ⊕ *www.theatercarre.nl.*

Fodor's Choice ★ **Muziektheater.** This theater's huge and flexible stage acts as a magnet for directors with a penchant for grand-scale décor, such as Robert Wilson,

Catch any number of outstanding shows at the Muziektheater.

Willy Decker, and Peter Sellars. ⊠ *Amstel 3/Waterlooplein 22, The Old City Center (Het Centrum)* ☎ *020/625–5455* ⊕ *www.muziektheater.nl.*

Fodor's Choice
★ **Stadsschouwburg.** The red-and-gold plushness of the city theater is home to the underrated **Nationale Reisopera** (National Travelling Opera). It also regularly hosts visiting companies from all over the world. ⊠ *Leidseplein 26, Leidseplein* ☎ *020/624–2311* ⊕ *www.ssba.nl.*

DANCE AND THEATER

Although many associate the Dutch dance scene with two names—Het Nationale Ballet and Nederlands Dans Theater—there are many more innovative local companies. Certainly the Hungarian ex-pat Krisztina de Châtel, now teamed up with Itzik Galili under the umbrella of Dansgroep Amsterdam, (⊕ *wwwdansgroepamsterdam.nl*)) has turned Amsterdam into a jumping-off point for international acclaim, thanks to her physical approach that also often employs the latest technologies in the visual arts. One annual not-to-be-missed event—that mixes both local and international names of a cutting-edge nature—is the month-long Julidans (⊕ *www.julidans.nl*), which is centered around the Stadsschouwburg.

Brakke Grond. Part of the Flemish cultural center, the Brakke Grond is infamous for welcoming experimental theater and dance performances from the Netherlands' neighbor to the south. ⊠ *Nes 45, The Old City Center (Het Centrum)* ☎ *020/622–9014* ⊕ *www.brakkegrond.nl.*

De Engelenbak. This venue is best known for its "Open Bak," an open-stage event each Tuesday where virtually anything goes. It's the longest-running theater program in the Netherlands, where everybody gets their 15 minutes of potential fame; arrive at least half an hour before the show starts to get a ticket. Otherwise, the best amateur groups in the country perform between Thursday and Saturday. ⊠ *Nes 71, The Old City Center (Het Centrum)* ☏ *020/626–3644* ⊕ *www.engelenbak.nl.*

Frascati. The three stages here all create a sense of intimacy for both performers and spectators. The close-knit quality is reinforced on Frascati's regular open-stage nights, when audience members are invited to take the stage. ⊠ *Nes 63, The Old City Center (Het Centrum)* ☏ *020/751–6400* ⊕ *www.theaterfrascati.nl.*

International Theaterschool. Handily located near the Waterlooplein, this institution unites students and teachers from all over the world to share their experiences, learning and creating in the fields of dance and theater. Dance performances—some of which are announced in *Uitkrant*—vary from studio shots to evening-long events in the Philip Morris Dans Zaal theater. Also worth checking out is the international theater school festival hosted every June. ⊠ *Jodenbreestraat 3, The Old City Center (Het Centrum)* ☏ *020/527–7700* ⊕ *www.theaterschool.nl.*

Koninklijk Theater Carré. For lavish, large-scale productions, this former circus home built in the 19th century is the place to go. ⊠ *Amstel 115–125, East of the Amstel* ☏ *0900/252–5255* ⊕ *www.theatercarre.nl.*

Melkweg. The relatively small stage of this multimedia center brings together both local and international dance names to strut their stuff in a more intimate setting. ⊠ *Lijnbaansgracht 234a, Leidseplein* ☏ *020/531–8181.*

Muiderpoorttheater. Although not within the Nes zone, this theater also follows an off-Broadway path by presenting new faces of the international drama and dance scene in an intimate setting. ⊠ *2e Van Swindenstraat 26, East of the Amstel* ☏ *020/668–1313* ⊕ *www.muiderpoorttheater.nl.*

Muziektheater. This gracious and spacious hall also hosts the **Nederlands Dans Theater** (⊕ *www.ndt.nl*), which has evolved into one of the most celebrated modern dance companies in the world, under choreographers Jiri Kylian and Hans van Manen. ⊠ *Waterlooplein 22/Amstel 3, The Old City Center (Het Centrum)* ☏ *020/625–5455* ⊕ *www.muziektheater.nl.*

NDSM. What were once industrial shipyards have been reinvented as, quite possibly, the city's largest *broedsplaats*, or government-sponsored "breeding ground" for the arts, where regular theater performances and festivals take place. And with a ferry departing from behind Centraal Station, getting there has never been easier. ⊠ *TT Neveritaweg 15, Eastern Docklands* ☎ *020/330–5480* ⊕ *www.ndsm.nl.*

Stadsschouwburg. Host of the Julidans festival, this theater often has a variety of modern dance offerings. The red velvet is primarily paved for those attending Dutch theater, though there are occasional English programs. ⊠ *Leidseplein 26, Leidseplein* ☎ *020/624–2311* ⊕ *www.ssba.nl.*

Sugar Factory. The club and "night theater" opened its doors in 2005 with the agenda to infuse the witching hours with theater, dance, art, and poetry—often all in one go. ⊠ *Lijnbaansgracht 238, Leidseplein* ☎ *020/626–5006* ⊕ *www.sugarfactory.nl.*

Tropeninstituut Theater. Part of the Tropics Institute, this theater hosts international companies dedicated to non-Western dance—from classical Indian to reinvented tango. ⊠ *Linnaeusstraat 2, East of the Amstel* ☎ *020/568–8500.*

Warner en Consorten. Formed in 1993, this group embraces an interdisciplinary concept of street theater: sculpture, dance, physical acting (such as mime), and music collide and challenge the concepts of theater, urban life—and reality. The results are often Dada-istically hilarious. Public space is the starting point: streets are analyzed, crowd behavior studied, passersby observed. During the winter months, the company finds abandoned warehouses and factories for venues; in the summer, city streets are the theaters. ⊠ *Hemkade 18, Zaandam (20-min. train ride from Amsterdam's Centraal Station)* ☎ *075/631–1980* ⊕ *www. warnerenconsorten.nl.*

Westergasfabriek. The former gas-factory complex *(see Dance and Rock Clubs)* employs its singular performance spaces for a variety of shows and festivals that often embrace the more visual and more avant-garde of the entertainment spectrum. ⊠ *Haarlemmerweg 8–10, Amsterdam West* ☎ *020/586–0710* ⊕ *www.westergasfabriek.nl.*

Shopping

WORD OF MOUTH

"Diamond Factory Tour: some people hate it, we went to The Gassan and found it very educational, and they were candid and diplomatic when provoking questions (i.e. blood diamonds) were asked; no pressure to purchase."

—Shanghainese

SHOPPING PLANNER

Tax Free Shopping

Nearly all the price tags you see will already include Value Added Tax (V.A.T.), or what the Dutch call B.T.W. (*belasting over de toegevoegde waarde*). Most consumer goods and luxury items (including alcohol) are taxed 19%; basic goods and service, 6%. If you're a non–European Union (EU) resident, you can claim this back.

When spending €50 or more at a store, ask for a V.A.T. refund form to be completed on your behalf and keep your receipt. Repeat this ritual wherever you shop. Before leaving the EU, have your form stamped by an airport customs official—be ready to show your receipts and all the new, unused goods you've purchased (thus keeping them separate from checked-in luggage). Afterwards, get remunerated at a refund-service counter or mail in your request.

Global Refund is a European-wide service with more than 240,000 affiliated stores and hundreds of refund counters. Its Tax Free Check remunerates shoppers via cash, check, or credit-card adjustment. For more information see ⊕ *www.globalrefund.com* or ☎ 866/706–6090 within the United States or ☎ 800/32–111–111 within the EU.

Getting Oriented

Getting your shop on in Amsterdam won't require GPS. Just down the road from Centraal Station is **Nieuwendijk,** the city's oldest shopping street, today a pedestrians' paradise for chain-store-hopping and basics at a bargain. The Dam forms the delta of **Kalverstraat,** the city's other roaring river of international retailers and favorite Dutch franchises open seven days a week. Nearby **Leidsestraat** is a scaled-down version equipped with an escape route of canal-side cafés. Just east is the **Spiegelkwartier,** one of Europe's most fabled agglomerations of antiques shops.

Peek around the Rijksmuseum and you'll find **P. C. Hooftstraat.** The "*Pay-Say,*" as locals refer to it, is Amsterdam's own little Madison Avenue, bustling with global luxury brands and their new-moneyed fannies. For those less *loco* about their labels, head to the adjoining **Van Baerlestraat,** offering concessions to match the area's well-heeled cultural consumers. Get back to Amsterdam's more egalitarian enterprises in **The Pijp,** where shops appealing to young and old, tried and trendy, native and newcomer offset the market-frenzied Albert Cuyp*straat.* Continue farther south, through to the other side of the Vondelpark, and you'll come upon **Cornelis Schuytstraat.** Footballers' wives and fashionistas love "*De Schuyt,*" an undeniably cozy cluster of chichi clothing and shoe boutiques, sleek homeware, and fancy delis.

If price tags listed in more than one currency leave you cold, get off the tourist trek. Chic boutiques, vintage stores, and quirky gift shops dot the **Nine Streets,** a sweet li'l hair comb of a neighborhood tucked behind the right ear of the Dam. From there, head northward through the **Jordaan,** where trendy and traditional cross-fertilize to produce quintessential Amsterdam charm. Don't miss the gamut of high-end specialty stores on **Haarlemmerstraat** and **Haarlemmerdijk.** Still haven't found what you seek? Take a foray into classic Amsterdam shopping on **Utrechtsestraat.** This beloved neighborhood main street is so close to Rembrandtplein you can hear the clubs' bass lines pumping yet so civilized you would think you were invited to a private sale, eight blocks long.

PRINSEN EILAND
BICKERS EILAND
WESTERDOK EILAND

Westerdok

Haarlemmer-Houttuinen

Nieuwe Westerdokstraat

De Ruijterkade

Het IJ

NOORD 5

0 — 900 ft
0 — 300 meters

Nassaukade

Singelgracht

Lijnbaansgracht

Brouwersgracht

Prinsengracht

Keizersgracht

Herengracht

Singel

Open Haven

Prins Hendrikkade

Centraal Station

Stationsplein

Ⓜ Centraal Station

Droogbak

Warmoesstraat

JORDAAN

Egelantiersgracht

Bloemgracht

Rozengracht

Raadhuisstraat

Spuistraat

Nieuwezijds Voorburgwal

HAARLEMMERSTRAAT
Quality quirkiness

CENTRUM

Damrak

Beursstraat

DE WALLEN
RED LIGHT
DISTRICT

Nieuwmarkt Ⓜ

WESTERN
CANAL RING

Royal Palace

Paleisstraat

Warmoesstraat

NIEUWMARKT

Prinsengracht

NINE STREETS
Vogue and vintage

KALVERSTRAAT
No chains, no gains

Singel

Rokin

Kloveniersburgwal

Oudezijds Achterburgwal

Jodenbreestr.

Berenstr. Wolvenstr.

Marnixstraat

Herengracht

Rokin

Nieuwe Doelenstr.

Amstel

Muziektheater

Waterlooplein Ⓜ

Waterlooplein

LEIDSESTRAAT
Like the mall –
with canals

Flower Market

Amstel

Rembrandt-plein

Blauwbrug

GOUDEN
BOCHT

Keizersgracht

EASTERN
CANAL RING

Amstel

LEIDSEPLEIN

Weteringschans

Stadhouderskade

Prinsengracht

Vijzelgracht

UTRECHTSESTRAAT
Classy consumption

Amstel

PC
HOOFTSTRAAT
Fabled labels

Vondelpark

Rijksmuseum

Lijnbaansgracht

Weteringschans

Frederiks-plein

MUSEUM
DISTRICT

Paulus Potterstraat

Hobbemakade

Singelgracht

Boerenwetering

Hendrik M. van
Randwijk-
Plantsoen

DE PIJP

Van Gogh
Museum

Museum
Plein

Stadhouderskade

TOP DUTCH DESIGNERS

While the Benelux has several internationally renowned design schools, the ArtEZ Fashion Institute Arnhem in the province of Gelderland takes credit for graduating masters of left-field haute couture Viktor & Rolf.

(Above) Shopping on the Leidsestraat. (Top right) Ilja Visser's Ready to Fish. (Bottom right) One of the seven racks at Open Shop.

Following in their wake—and making it less stuffy and more democratic in the process—are Bas Kosters, Claes Iversen, Iris van Herpen, Daryl van Wouw, and Ilja Visser, all of whom have garnered *Idol*-level acclaim across the country for conflating their individual perspectives with ready-to-wear sensibility. Though note: the Dutch clean-lined approach has long been characterized as, at best, Calvinism dressed in Calvin Klein. Send that old generalization to Good Will. The turn of the millennium prompted another turning—of sartorial asceticism on its own shaven head. Welcome to new Dutch fashion. Decades know no boundaries, inseams and necklines cross-dress, and sociocultural references are as irreverent as they are irrelevant.

NINE STREETS PLUS ONE

The Nine Streets has a distinctly old-world feel. This cluster of quaint canal crossings between the Rozengracht and the Leidsegracht dates back to the 17th century, then inhabited by artisans whose leather trade is commemorated in the street names. Today, the neighborhood offers one-of-a-kind retail. And in fall 2009, Hazenstraat joined in, becoming the district's 10th street.

DARYL VAN WOUW

This Amsterdam fashion darling first gleaned attention as the perpetually headphoned judge on *Holland's Next Top Model* (yes, like the U.S. version but with refreshingly fewer catfights and more kilos). Today, Van Wouw's canal-side boutique is the flagship for his eternally reincarnating urbanwear. Though both guys and gals sport the signature retro hoodies, DvW's punky leggings and futuristic tunics endear him to the urbane misses. ⊠ *Prinsengracht 705A, The Canal Ring* ☏ *020/428–6374* ⊕ *www.darylvanwouw.com.*

READY TO FISH

Unlike many of her creative compatriots, Ilja Visser is less concerned with appearing edgy than outfitting women in clothes with, like the sea, their own natural ebb and flow (apropos of her surname, meaning "fisher"). After years of consistently well-received catwalk shows, this is the designer's first boutique, bringing the public a ready-to-wear collection that holds onto Visser's signature scalloped sleeves and low-inseamed trousers in nature-at-sunset palettes. Despite being housed in a 17th-century tobacco and coffee warehouse, Ready to Fish provides a timely antidote of tranquility for an overstimulated industry. ⊠ *Prinsengracht 581, The Canal Ring* ☏ *020/330–9332* ⊕ *www. www.readytofish.nl.*

YOUNG DESIGNERS UNITED

Predictable party wear got you down? Young Designers United offers many a one-off to intrigue fellow fête-makers. Since 2003, this collective has been giving 10 locally schooled, up-and-coming designers a rack to call their own (for half-year stints at a time, anyway). These couturiers produce new women's wear and accessories on a weekly basis. Working toward establishing a label or shop of their own, many take cues from customer feedback—meaning you could have a hand in shaping the next big trend. ⊠ *Keizersgracht 447, The Canal Ring* ☏ *020/626–9191* ⊕ *www.ydu.nl.*

OPEN SHOP

Seven days a week, seven designers man—or, more commonly, *wo*man—seven racks showcasing one-of-a-kind handmade clothes, shoes, and accessories. Like their young creators, each collection preaches its own distinct style of streetwear. A dashiki made of sports jersey material, feather-tasseled clogs, eco-fabric T-shirts reading "100% Halal," and psychedelic harem pants are all fair game here. So, what holds the collective together? Affordability, superaffable staff, and successfully channeling Punky Brewster's *joie de vivre.* ⊠ *Nieuwezijds Voorburgwal 291, The Old City Center (Het Centrum)* ☏ *020/528–6963* ⊕ *www.openshopamsterdam.com.*

6

Updated by Karina Hof

Famous for their business savvy and wily ways with trade, the Dutch are often called frugal. They're sticklers for even-steven (recognize the phrase "going Dutch"?) and are sometimes called, less euphemistically, cheapskates. Now, now . . .

One common explanation for this is that the nation is always preparing for a flood: waste not, want not—the waters are always nigh. Others will point to Calvinism's purse-nursing influence. Some blame socialism. Whatever postdiluvial mythology you believe, it's true: many Lowlanders monitor their bank accounts with a lip-trembling fervor other societies reserve for prayer. Yet lo and behold, they do spend money. You'll see this most glaringly in Amsterdam's youth culture, not unlike other Western young folk, who zoom around on Vespas, accessorized by Blackberry or Burberry, rushing to drop their government-subsidized allowances at cafés and clubs. On the whole, however, Dutch society shops sensibly and unsnobbishly. Trade consumer reports with locals and you'll find that many conduct thorough prepurchase research, advocate discount-rate *abonnements* ("subscriptions"), exploit the country's own little eBay known as Marktplaats.nl, and dig anything secondhand, vintage, or antique. Amsterdammers, in particular, love auctions, estate sales, and flea markets (the mother of all occurring on Queen's Day when the city becomes one gigantic sidewalk sale). So, what does all this mean for you? First, there are numerous ways to shop—find a consumption pattern best suited to your personal conspicuity. And second, because Dutch merchants are fair—and empathic—you'll, more often than not, get what you pay for.

DEPARTMENT STORES

C & A. Perched on the ever-busy Damrak, across the road from the Beurs van Berlage, this representative European chain department store is a longtime fixture on Amsterdam's shopping landscape. The budget-minded come here for clothing and accessories, and the basement caters to Generation Y. On the ground floor, there are always sales racks; if you have the patience to paw through them, you may be rewarded with some amply discounted finds. ⊠ *Beurspassage 2 or Damrak 79, The Old City Center (Het Centrum)* ☎ *0900/8010* ⊕ *www.c-en-a.nl.*

De Bijenkorf. Akin to, say, Macy's is "The Beehive," the nation's best-known department store and the swarming ground of its moneyed middle classes. Top international designer lines of clothing, shoes, and cosmetics are well stocked, along with a decent repertoire of furniture, appliances, and one of the best stationery selections in town. The in-house eateries are upscale with a ground-floor café corner that success-fully channels a retail refueling post à la Paris. ⊠ *Dam 1, The Old City Center (Het Centrum)* ☎ *0900–0919* ⊕ *www.bijenkorf.nl.*

★ **HEMA.** The *Hollandsche Eenheidsprijzen Maatschappij Amsterdam* or "De Hema" as it's called by locals, stocks not only your basic needs, but also some surprisingly hip designer items—and for the friendliest of prices. Cosmetics, vitamins, undergarments, and power tools are some of the best bargains, and the chain is cherished for its store-brand smoked sausage and birthday cakes. ⊠ *Nieuwendijk 174–176, The Old City Center (Het Centrum)* ☎ *020/623–4176* ⊕ *www.hema. nl* ⊠ *Kalvertoren, Kalverstraat 212, The Old City Center (Het Centrum)* ☎ *020/422–8988* ⊠ *Ferdinand Bolstraat 93–93A, The Pijp* ☎ *020/676–3222.*

★ **Maison de Bonneterie.** With its over-a-century-old skylighted cupola, chandeliers, and majestic staircases, this is Amsterdam's loving homage to the *grand magasin*. The prices aren't always right, but the ambience is appreciated by many types of shoppers, from fashionistas in need of a last-minute designer frock to proper ladies who dutifully match hand-bag with shoes. ⊠ *Rokin 140–142, The Old City Center (Het Centrum)* ☎ *020/531–3400* ⊕ *www.debonneterie.nl.*

Metz & Co. Landmarked by its Rietveld-designed cupola and the right to bear the royal coat of arms, this stately department store has presided over the Grachtengordel since 1908, though was first established in 1740. It carries a scrupulously edited collection of high-end interna-tional designs for him, for her, and for home. The tranquil top-floor café offers a bird's-eye view of the city and decent but pricey lunch fare. ⊠ *Leidsestraat 34–36, The Canal Ring* ☎ *020/520–7020* ⊕ *www. metzenco.nl.*

Peek & Cloppenburg. This Dam mainstay specializes in durable, middle-of-the-road clothing. The shop has recently been adding more Euro-pean lines, including attractive Italian and French knitwear and casuals. ⊠ *Dam 20, The Old City Center (Het Centrum)* ☎ *020/623–2837* ⊕ *www.peekundcloppenburg.com.*

Vroom & Dreesmann. If Dutch department store behemoth De Bijenkorf is Macy's, V & D, as it's called, is JCPenney. From ties to towels, the selections are decent, though will make neither an impression nor, when it comes to your wallet, a depression. Adjacent eatery La Place offers a relatively robust array of food, cafeteria-style, and its bakery practically spills into the department store, scenting the accessories department with a dash of sugar. ⊠ *Kalverstraat 203, The Old City Center (Het Centrum)* ☎ *0900/235–8363* ⊕ *www.vroomendreesmann.nl.*

MARKETS

Whether hunting for treasures or trash, you can unearth terrific finds, often at rock-bottom prices, at any of Amsterdam's open-air markets. They're also just the place to enjoy freshly squeezed orange juice, pickled herring on a bun, or a *stroopwaffel* (syrup-filled waffle) hot off the griddle.

Albert Cuypmarkt. This century-old market, found on Albert Cuypstraat between Ferdinand Bolstraat and Van Woustraat, is the heart of The Pijp. It's open Monday through Saturday from 9–5, rain or shine, and you're likely to hear the vendors barking out their bargain deals over the pleasant sound track of a street musician. Interspersed among the crowds, stalls sell food, clothing, fabrics, plants, and household goods from all over the world. Just about every ethnic culture is represented here by purveyors, their goods, and their buyers. Be sure to try some of the exotic nibbles, or just order the Dutchman's favorite fast food—*frites,* piping-hot French fries served with mayonnaise, ketchup, curry sauce, or peanut satay dip. ⊕ *www.albertcuypmarkt.com.*

★ **Bloemenmarkt.** Hands down, this is one of Amsterdam's must-sees. Along the Singel canal, between Koningsplein and Muntplein, the renowned Flower Market is where blooming wonders are purveyed from permanently moored barges. Besides bouquets of freshly cut flowers, you'll find plants, small trees, bulbs, seeds, and a colorful array of souvenir trinkets. The market is open Monday–Saturday 9:30–5:30, Sunday 11–5:30.

Boekenmarkt. The city has a number of book markets, though its most famous takes place every Friday on Spui Square, from 10 to 6. Under the little white tents, it's an antiquarian and used book–browsing paradise.

Dappermarkt. Its length running along the eponymous street between Mauritskade and Wijttenbachstraat, this market has, since 1910, been a consumer crossroads for what is today known as Amsterdam Oost ("East"). Like the Albert Cuypmarkt, a couple hundred stalls, set up Monday through Saturday (9–6), sell everything from discount clothing and cosmetics to flowers and food. Flavors here are, like much of the neighborhood clientele, mostly of Eastern background. Successful juxtaposition of 100% pure lamb meat donor kebabs with Indonesian *lumpia* is surely just one reason *National Geographic Traveler* has included the market in its top-10 list of markets worldwide. ⊕ *www.dappermarkt.eu.*

Lapjesmarkt. Fabric lovers will think they've taken a magic carpet to heaven when they visit the so-called rag market, which takes place on

Hawking oranges at the Monday flea market at the Noordermarkt.

Mondays from 8 to noon, adjacent to Noordermarkt. Down along Westerstraat, you'll find stalls with every possible kind of fabric—beautiful rainbow-colored Asian silks embedded with mirrors and embroidery, batiks from Indonesia, Surinam, and Africa, fabulous faux furs, lace curtains, velvet drapery materials, calicos, and vinyl coverings, all being admired and stroked by eager shoppers. Couturiers rub elbows with housewives, vendors measure out meters, and the crowds keep getting denser.

Lindenmarkt. On Saturday from 9 to 5 check out the Noordermarkt's less yuppified sister, which winds around Noorderkerk and runs down the length of Lindengracht. All the basics are here, though you'll find exceptionally tasty food stalls.

Modern Art Market. Fair weather on Sundays from March through December brings good opportunity for a rotating series of some 25 artists to sell their paintings, lithographs, textiles, and other objets d'art in the Rembrandtplein area. Organized by the Kunstkring Thorbecke Foundation (☎ 052/720–1559 ⊕ *www.modern-art-market.nl*), the market takes place on Thorbeckeplein (just off the Rembrantplein) from 10:30 to 6.

Nieuwmarkt. At the northern end of Kloverniersburgwal, the square known as Nieuwmarkt hosts a small-scale *boerenmarkt,* or farmers' market, on Monday through Saturday from 9 to 5. You'll find essential oils, fresh soaps, and other New Age needs alongside flowers, cheese, organic breads, and fresh-pressed juices. On Sundays from 9 to 5, delightful curiosa, art, and books appear when the *antiekmarkt* (antique market) throws the shrouds off its stalls.

★ **Noordermarkt.** The Noordermarkt is probably most cherished by Amsterdammers for its weekly *boerenmarkt,* the organic farmers' market held every Saturday from 9 to 6 around the perimeter of the Noorderkerk. With comestibles such as free-range meats, cruelty-free honey, homemade pestos, and vegan cakes on offer, it's an orgasm for the organic-loving. Just be prepared to open your wallet. On Mondays, from 9 to 1, the Noordermarkt shape-shifts into what is locally known as the *maandagmarkt* (Monday Market). Evocative of the Old World, it's a sprawling affair, mostly of used clothing, books, and toys, but careful collectors can find a range of good stuff, from antique silverware and pottery to wartime and advertising memorabilia.

Postzegelmarkt. Philatelists, dust off your tweezers. During good weather, you'll find the city's stamp market set up near the Spui along Nieuwezijds Voorburgwal, held on Wednesdays and Saturdays from 1 to 4. And there are some coins for you numismatists, too.

Waterlooplein. Few markets compare with Amsterdam's famous flea market that hugs the backside of the Stopera (the complex whose descriptive name derives from an ever-pragmatic blending of *stadhuis* for "city hall" and "opera," in reference to the Muziektheater *(see Nightlife and the Arts chapter).* Waterlooplein is a descendant of the haphazard pushcart trade that gave this part of the city its distinct lively character in the early part of the 20th century. It's amusing to see the old telephones, typewriters, and other arcana all haphazardly displayed—as well as the shoppers scrambling and vying with each other to reacquire such items. Professional dealers sell secondhand and vintage clothing, hats, and purses. New fashions are mostly for generic alterna-types who will enjoy a wide selection of slogan T-shirts, hippie bags, and jewelry for every type of piercing. The flea market is open Monday–Saturday 9–6.

SPECIALTY STORES

ANTIQUES AND GOLDEN AGE ART

Fodor'sChoice   **Anouk Beerents.** The Hall of Mirrors at the Palace of Versailles may
★   be evoked should you have the opportunity to visit the dazzling, sky-lighted quarters of this Jordaan atelier-cum-store. For 20 years, the ever-gracious Anouk Beerents has been buying 18th- and 19th-century antique mirrors from France and Italy, and then restoring them for local and international clients (including, for example, Ralph Lauren shops in the United States). Replete with ornate gold- or silver-gilded frames, some 400 museum-quality mirrors (some actually from the Palace of Versailles) hang upon the walls of this space, which is so large that customers are invited to park their cars inside. Visits are by appointment only and shipping can be arranged to other countries. ⊠ *Prinsengracht 467, The Canal Ring* ☎ *020/622–8598* ⊕ *www.anoukbeerents.nl.*

Bruno de Vries. An unusual collection of antique money banks is displayed at this gallery, along with Art Deco and Jugendstil lamps, as well as items from the Amsterdam School of Architecture. ⊠ *Elandsgracht 67, Jordaan* ☎ *06/2027–2947* ⊕ *www.brunodevries.com.*

Antiquing on a Budget

For more gently priced collections, you might rather opt to tiptoe past the 18th-century tulipwood armoires and explore an increasingly popular neighborhood for adventurous collectors—the Jordaan. In stark contrast to the elegant stores in the Spiegelkwartier with their beautiful displays, the tiny unprepossessing shops dotted along the Elandsgracht and connecting streets, such as the 1e Looiersdwarsstraat, offer equally wonderful treasures. Those who take the time to carefully examine the backroom shelves, nooks, and crannies of a small shop may be rewarded with a big find. Prices here are also more in keeping with a downtowner's budget for interior décor. Indeed, this is one of the best-kept secrets of New York's antiques shop dealers, who often scour the Jordaan for their imported wares. You can also enjoy happy hunting in the shops on Rozengracht and Prinsengracht, near the Westerkerk, which offer country Dutch furniture and household items; take a look at the antiques and curio shops along the side streets in that part of the city. Many of the antiques shops in the Spiegelkwartier and the Jordaan keep irregular hours and some are open by appointment, so it's wise to call first.

Christie's Amsterdam. The internationally known auction house hosts sales of art, furniture, wines, jewelry, and porcelain. Even if you leave empty-handed, the surrounding neighborhood is well worth the journey. ⊠ *Cornelis Schuytstraat 57, Amsterdam South* ☎ *020/575–5255* ⊕ *www.christies.com.*

D. I. Haaksman. Among a glittering array of 18th- and 19th-century crystal chandeliers here, you'll find just the illumination you're looking for from leading names such as Bagues and Baccarat. ⊠ *Elandsgracht 55, Jordaan* ☎ *020/625–4116* ⊕ *www.dihaaksman.nl.*

Jan Beekhuizen Kunst en Antiekhandel. For antique European pewter from the 15th through the 19th centuries, Jan Beekhuizen is the authority. His store also carries antique furniture, Delftware, metalware, and other collectible objects. ⊠ *Nieuwe Spiegelstraat 49, The Canal Ring* ☎ *020/626–3912* ⊕ *www.janbeekhuizen.nl.*

Kunst & Antiekcentrum De Looier. For a broad range of vintage and antique furniture, curios, jewelry, clothing, and household items, try this cooperative, housing more than 80 dealers, making it the largest covered art and antiques market in the Netherlands. You wouldn't be the first to get a great buy on an antique doll, a first-edition book, military memorabilia, or even a jeweled trinket here. The best days to go are Wednesday, Saturday, or Sunday, when all the vendors, including the *tafeltjesmarkt* (one-day table rentals), are present. Right after a book on *Delftsblauw* (Delft Blue porcelain) collectibles was published some years ago, a virtual army of dealers from the United States descended on De Looier market and snapped up just about every piece of Delft (if foolishly ignoring the large assortment of equally interesting and collectible Makkumware). ⊠ *Elandsgracht 109, Jordaan* ☎ *020/624–9038* ⊕ *www.looier.com.*

6

★ **Prinsheerlijk Antiek**. Spanning 1,800 square feet, this emporium sells a princely assortment of furniture, bric-a-brac, and chandeliers dating from the early 18th century, as well as unique clock cases, Swedish-style birch wood furniture, and Dutch handpainted folk pieces. Many items come from royal families and palaces, such as the spectacular sofa with griffin's arms that originally graced a Swedish castle. The shop also includes a renowned work studio, where antique furniture is upholstered and refurbished. ✉ *Prinsengracht 579, The Canal Ring* ☎ *020/638–6623* ⊕ *www.prinsheerlijkantiek.nl.*

Salomon Stodel. Museum curators and collectors do their shopping at this nearly 150-year-old rare antiques store. ✉ *Rokin 70, The Old City Center (Het Centrum)* ☎ *020/623–1692* ⊕ *www.salomonstodel.com.*

Sotheby's. Many antiques dealers buy from the fabled auctions held at the Amsterdam branch of this auction house. The Dutch are some of the savviest businesspeople in the world, but you can try to beat them to the bid. ✉ *De Boelelaan 30, Buitenveldert* ☎ *020/550–2200* ⊕ *www. sothebys.com.*

Fodor'sChoice
★
Spiegelkwartier. A William and Mary–era harpsichord? One of the printed maps that figured prominently in Vermeer's *Lutenist*? An 18th-century bed-curtain tie-up? Or a pewter nautilus cup redolent of a Golden Age still life? All these and more may be available in Amsterdam's famous array of antiques stores in the city's "Mirror Quarter," centered around Nieuwe Spiegelstraat and its continuation, Spiegelgracht. If perusing fine art is more your scene, the Quarter also houses around 20 contemporary art galleries and 10 tribal and oriental art specialists. But—with five double-sided blocks' worth of shops and galleries, from the Golden Bend of the Herengracht nearly to the Rijksmuseum—this section of town often requires a royal House of Orange budget.

Wildschut Antiquiteiten. Once you squeeze past the marvelous wooden wardrobes that fill this store, chances are you'll encounter owner Michael Wildschut at the back, restoring his latest acquisition. A tribute to European craftsmanship, the chests and armoires come mainly from northern France and are made of fine woods such as mahogany. These pieces have been restored with loving care, and can be fit with shelves or drawers as you so desire, and then shipped to your home address. ✉ *1e Looiersdwarsstraat 8B, Jordaan* ☎ *06/2187-6724* ⊕ *www. wildschut-antiek.nl.*

Willem Vredevoogd. Specializing in top names such as Lalique, Cartier, and Boucheron, Willem's is where to go for antique jewelry. ✉ *P. C. Hooftstraat 82, Museum District* ☎ *020/673–6804.*

ART: MODERN TO CONTEMPORARY

Many of the galleries that deal in modern and contemporary art are centered on the Keizersgracht and Spiegelkwartier, and others are found around the Western Canal Ring and the Jordaan. Artists have traditionally gravitated to low-rent areas. De Baarsjes, a neighborhood in Amsterdam West, is increasingly attracting small galleries that showcase exciting works of art. With a shabbiness reminiscent of the early days of New York's SoHo, it's worth a detour for adventurous art lovers. *The* tourist office Web site ⊕ *www.iamsterdam.com* is a reasonable source of information on current exhibitions. Other helpful sources are the bilingual art zine *PRESENTeert*, available at select galleries and online ⊕ *presenteert.wordpress.com*, and the Web site ⊕ *www.galeries. nl*. Opening times vary greatly, so it's a good idea to check out the listings or first call the gallery for information.

AYACS. The Amsterdam Young Artist Circuit, as this gallery is more formally known, gives new, usually academy-fresh talents a professional space in which to present their work. If you're in the market for some native art more affordable than a Mondriaan, drop in on ongoing exhibitions Fridays from 5 to 7, on weekend afternoons, or by appointment. ⊠ *Keizersgracht 166, The Canal Ring* ☎ *020/622–8579* ⊕ *www.ayacs.nl.*

Galerie De Stoker. Though mainly featuring sculptures in papier-mâché and stone, this Amsterdam West venue is also noted for its innovative ceramic fountains. The atelier behind the gallery is open to visitors. ⊠ *Witte de Withstraat 124, Amsterdam West* ☎ *020/612–3293* ⊕ *www. destoker.nl.*

Galerie Ei. Artist Judith Zwaan displays her whimsical colorful paintings and papier-mâché sculptures, influenced by Niki de Saint-Phalle and the CoBrA group, as well as the art and culture of West Africa. Other exciting new artists regularly exhibit at the small gallery. ⊠ *Admiraal de Ruijterweg 154, De Baarsjes* ☎ *020/616–3961.*

Kunsthandel M. L. De Boer. Founded in 1945, this gallery is renowned for showing contemporary figurative and abstract works by Dutch, French, and Belgian artists, as well as by Dutch and French masters from the 19th century and early 20th century. Since M. L. De Boer's death in 1991, the gallery has been kept open by his son expressly for exhibitions of modern works from the gallery's own collection. ⊠ *Keizersgracht 542, The Canal Ring* ☎ *020/623–4060* ⊕ *www.kunsthandeldeboer.com.*

Nico Koster Galerie Moderne. This gallery is a top contender in the Spiegelkwartier, showcasing art from the international CoBrA collection, with a specialization in Corneille's early works. ⊠ *Nieuwe Spiegelstraat 44, The Canal Ring* ☎ *020/776–9991* ⊕ *www.nicokoster-galeriemoderne.com.*

Peter Donkersloot Galerie. Formerly known as Galerie Hoopman, this is a top stop for contemporary art along the Spiegelkwartier. It was rechristened in 2006, when Mr. Hoopman joined forces with Peter Donkersloot. ⊠ *Spiegelgracht 14–16, The Canal Ring* ☎ *020/623–6538* ⊕ *www.peterdonkerslootgalerie.nl.*

BOOKS

ABC Treehouse. For the past decade, the American Book Center has been hosting bookshop-related events and exhibitions in their former warehouse space, just across from their new headquarters on the Spui. The Treehouse has also built a solid reputation for all kinds of Anglophonic activities, such as English-language readings, open-mike nights, and its annual Thanksgiving potluck dinner. ⊠ *Voetboogstraat 11, The Old City Center (Het Centrum)* ☎ *020/423–0967* ⊕ *www.treehouse.abc.nl.*

★ **American Book Center**. What began in the early '70s as an erotic magazine outlet has grown into reputedly the largest English-language book emporium on the continent. True to its name, the stock is strongly oriented toward American tastes and expectations, with its vast selection spread over seven stories. (Students, senior citizens, and teachers receive a 10% discount.) ⊠ *Spui 12, The Old City Center (Het Centrum)* ☎ *020/625–5537* ⊕ *www.abc.nl.*

★ **Antiquariaat Kok**. This antiquarian's heaven has, for the last 60 years, offered readers oodles of treasures on Amsterdam history. It also takes pride in housing the city's largest secondhand Dutch-language book collection and a fair share of other literature nicely shelved according to subject. ⊠ *Oude Hoogstraat 14–18, The Old City Center (Het Centrum)* ☎ *020/623–1191* ⊕ *www.nvva.nl/kok.*

Architectura en Natura. Rarely does anyone leave the shop empty-handed—not with its stock of beautiful oversized art and photography books spanning architecture, nature, landscape design, and gardening. ⊠ *Leliegracht 22, Jordaan* ☎ *020/623–6186* ⊕ *www.architectura.nl.*

Athenaeum Boekhandel. Since the late '60s, this mainstay on the Spui has been one of the Netherlands's largest independent bookshops. Celebrity authors sometimes pop in, and scholars and university students often rely on the stock for academic literature. ⊠ *Spui 14–16, The Old City Center (Het Centrum)* ☎ *020/514–1460* ⊕ *www.athenaeum.nl.*

Athenaeum Nieuwscentrum. For the city's best selection of international periodicals and newspapers, as well as a smattering of cool local zines, follow your way to the unmissable red-and-white awning on the Spui. ⊠ *Spui 14–16, The Old City Center (Het Centrum)* ☎ *020/514–1470* ⊕ *www.athenaeum.nl.*

Fodor's Choice **Boekie Woekie**. Artists love this shop and offshoot gallery for its assemblage of self-published and small-press books, catalogs, and journals
★ from around the world. If nothing else, look for the Boekie Woekie postcards created by the owners themselves, three artists from the Netherlands, Germany, and Iceland. ⊠ *Berenstraat 16, The Canal Ring* ☎ *020/639–0507* ⊕ *www.boekiewoekie.com.*

Book Exchange. Redolent of a bygone era in a rural New England town, this browse-worthy shop sells used English-language books on all subjects and many a secondhand paperback. ⊠ *Kloveniersburgwal 58, The Old City Center (Het Centrum)* ☎ *020/626–6266* ⊕ *www.bookexchange.nl.*

De Slegte. Possibly the largest bookstore in Amsterdam, this is a true haven for book hunters. Every floor stocks tomes in various languages, across all genres, and covering many subjects. The shop is known for its large nonfiction collection of popular titles at bargain prices, and upstairs floors have a humongous antiquarian book section. ⊠ *Kalverstraat 48–52, The Old City Center (Het Centrum)* ☎ *020/622–5933* ⊕ *www.deslegte.com.*

The English Bookshop. Get served tea in a cozy little shop while the staff recommend reading according to your personal tastes. Secondhand books, Dutch authors translated into English, children's books, and lots of fine literature is at your fingertips. ✉ *Lauriergracht 71, Jordaan* ☎ *020/626–4230* ⊕ *www.englishbookshop.nl.*

Evenaar Literaire Reisboekhandel. Armchair travelers and ground-stomping wayfarers visit this store for publications on travel, anthropology, and literary essays. What you need to know about foreign cultures you'll discover here. ✉ *Singel 348, The Old City Center (Het Centrum)* ☎ *020/624–6289* ⊕ *www.evenaar.net.*

Kookboek Handel. Cookbooks from all over the world, many in their original language, harmoniously share shelf space at the Kookboek Handel. ✉ *Haarlemmerdijk 133, Jordaan* ☎ *020/622–4768* ⊕ *www.kookboekhandel.com.*

Lambiek. Grawlix of praise go to Lambiek for being the oldest $%*!-ing comic bookstore on the continent. ✉ *Kerkstraat 132, The Canal Ring* ☎ *020/626–7542* ⊕ *www.lambiek.net.*

Mendo. If you're in the market for one of those luxe oversized photography books costing three figures—or just feel like flipping through one—head to Mendo. Also a home base for the same-named graphic design agency, the shop sells design books for every kind of artist, including the starving. ✉ *Berenstraat 11, The Canal Ring* ☎ *020/612–1216* ⊕ *www.mendo.nl.*

Oudemanhuis Book Market. This tiny, venerable, covered book market is snuggled in the heart of the University of Amsterdam's meandering edifices. Booksellers in this alleyway have been hawking used and antiquarian books, prints, and sheet music for more than a century. ✉ *Oudemanhuispoort, The Old City Center (Het Centrum).*

Premsela. Tempting window displays allure browsers into this specialty shop for art books. ✉ *Van Baerlestraat 78, Museum District* ☎ *020/662–4266* ⊕ *www.premsela.nl.*

Selexyz Scheltema. With five floors of books on every imaginable subject, plus an international spread of newspapers and magazines, and a Bagels & Beans café on the first floor, this is one of Amsterdam's busiest and best-stocked international bookstores. It'll come close to satisfying Americans jonesing for a Barnes & Noble fix. ✉ *Koningsplein 20, The Canal Ring* ☎ *020/523–1411* ⊕ *www.selexyz.nl.*

Waterstone's. Take refuge from Amsterdam's hectic shopping street in this four-floor edifice of English-language books, ranging from children's stories to computer manuals. There's also a huge selection of magazines from the United Kingdom. ✉ *Kalverstraat 152, The Old City Center (Het Centrum)* ☎ *020/638–3821* ⊕ *www.waterstones.com.*

CERAMICS AND CRYSTAL

Breekbaar. Here you'll find a top-brand selection of zany glassware and unique china, including a splendid menagerie of Ritzenhoff stems and saucers. The owner is a jovial, cigar-smoking gent who seems he could have been created by Lewis Carroll. ✉ *Weteringschans 209, The Canal Ring* ☎ *020/626–1260* ⊕ *www.breekbaar.com.*

De Glaswerkplaats. If you're seeking a personalized souvenir, consider stopping by this studio on the Nine Streets, where you can order custom-made designs in fused or stained glass. Classes and workshops are

Couzijn Simon/Anton Heyboer Winkel has a little something for everyone.

also held at the shop. ✉ *Berenstraat 41, The Canal Ring* ☎ *020/420–2120* ⊕ *www.glassierkunst.nl.*

Frides Laméris. For superb porcelain, glass, and tiles, all minted before 1800, visit this Spiegelkwartier venue. ✉ *Nieuwe Spiegelstraat 55, The Canal Ring* ☎ *020/626–4066* ⊕ *www.frideslameris.nl.*

Hogendoorn & Kaufman. Fancy a gift fit for a king? Well-oiled shoppers and devout collectors know there is only one address in Amsterdam that can please. This shop sells the crème de la crème, with the best designs from Baccarat, Lalique, Daum, and Swarovski in crystal, Royal Delft, Makkum, Lladró, Herend, and special designs from Fabergé, Meissen, Mats Jonasson, and others (with free worldwide shipping, too). Some items are moderately affordable, such as a Royal Delft dish with Dick Bruna's Miffy bunny, personalized with your child's name for less than €100. ✉ *Rokin 124, The Old City Center (Het Centrum)* ☎ *020/638–2736* ⊕ *www.hogendoorn-kaufman.com.*

't Winkeltje. This rummager's delight is a charming spot to search for small souvenirs. It's easy to pass the time pawing through the jumble of hotel porcelain, glass, and vintage postcards. ✉ *Prinsengracht 228, Jordaan* ☎ *020/625–1352.*

CHILDREN

Azzurro Kids. Designer togs, shoes, and accessories for babies, boys, and girls can be found here. Armani Jr., Braez, Dolce & Gabbana, and other notable labels are ready to turn your little one into a walking advertisement. ✉ *P. C. Hooftstraat 122, Museum District* ☎ *020/673–0457* ⊕ *www.azzurrofashiongroup.com.*

Couzijn Simon/Anton Heyboer Winkel. Simon's toy treasures will make your child as pop-eyed as some of the vintage dolls here. The shop, which dates back to the mid-18th century, when it first opened as a pharmacy, is crammed with wonders: a rocking horse from three centuries ago, a 4-foot-long wooden ice skate that once served as a sign, antique trains, collector teddy bears, and porcelain dolls dressed for a costume ball. In the back is a small garden and a cottage, now the atelier of Dutch painter Anton Heyboer, whose works are for sale. ⊠ *Prinsengracht 578, The Canal Ring* ☎ *020/624-7691.*

De Beestenwinkel. The delightful corner store has nothing but animal toys of every breed and in all price ranges, as well as some fine souvenir choices for the young at heart. ⊠ *Staalstraat 26, The Old City Center (Het Centrum)* ☎ *020/623-1805* ⊕ *www.beestenwinkel.nl.*

De Winkel van Nijntje. Most department stores and toy shops in the Netherlands carry the classic children's brand, but here, at one of only three shops in the country, you'll find every imaginable Nijntje product—clothes, books, night-lights, tooth-fairy boxes, car seats, and more. ⊠ *Scheldestraat 62, Amsterdam South* ☎ *020/664-8054* ⊕ *www.dewinkelvannijntje.nl.*

Gone with the Wind. Specializing in mobiles from around the world, this mecca of mirth also sells unusual handcrafted wooden flowers and toys and spring-operated jumping toys. ⊠ *Vijzelstraat 22, The Old City Center (Het Centrum)* ☎ *020/423-0230* ⊕ *www.gonewind-mobiles.com.*

Kleine Eland. If your toddler back home simply must have a dollhouse version of a four-story gabled canal house, head to this Jordaanese gem. Also available here are kiddie carts in the shape of jumbo jets and fire engines, collectible medieval-style castles, figurines, and unusual wooden rockers in the form of bears, ducks, and motorcycles. ⊠ *Elandsgracht 58, Jordaan* ☎ *020/620-9001* ⊕ *www.kleineeland.nl.*

't Schooltje. Your toddler in Armani, Versace, and Da-Da? If that's a yes, pay a visit to the Little School boutique where high-end clothing and shoes for infants to 16-year-olds are the curriculum. ⊠ *Overtoom 87, Museum District* ☎ *020/683-0444* ⊕ *www.schooltje.nl.*

CLOTHING

MEN AND WOMEN

★ **De Hoed van Tijn.** You're forgiven for thinking you've time traveled into the Roaring '20s when entering this hat shop. Dutch royalty among their clientele, De Hoed van Tijn is most sought out for its Flapper-style cloches and bespoke sinamay hairpieces. ⊠ *Nieuwe Hoogstraat 15, The Old City Center (Het Centrum)* ☎ *020/623-2759* ⊕ *www.dehoedvantijn.nl.*

★ **Destination Shop.** When Macedonia native Robert Risteski first came to Amsterdam it was for a one-month holiday. Two decades later, with an art-school degree, fashion-award laurels, and retail experience aplenty, this hipsters' hipster can be found in a one-room shop a hanger's throw from the Rijksmuseum. Kokontozai, Marjan Pejovski, And Beyond, Mundi and Ostwald Helgason are all household names. The clothes are so doted upon you might think you were in the proprietor's private wardrobe—until seeing the price tag. ⊠ *Weteringstraat 46H, The Canal Ring* ☎ *06/1920–0480* ⊕ *www.destinationshop.nl.*

Ennu. Haute couture gets Gothic à la the likes of Rick Owens, Comme des Garçons, and PRPS at this exclusive boutique. The shop's name is a blending of the Dutch words *en nu*—for "and now"—aptly intimating that once you've shopped here, what's left to live for? ⊠ *Cornelis Schuytstraat 15, Amsterdam South* ☎ *020/673–5265* ⊕ *www.ennu.nl.*

H&M. Like IKEA, this sensational Swedish chain has gone global, while offering remarkably cheap, classic, and trendy threads. H&M is the perfect sartorial answer to the Dutch's sense of democracy, and Amsterdammers swarm its various franchises in droves. ⊠ *Kalverstraat 125, The Old City Center (Het Centrum)* ☎ *0900–1988* ⊕ *www.hm.com* ⊠ *Nieuwendijk 141, The Old City Center (Het Centrum)* ☎ *0900–1988.*

> ### THE GLOBE-HOPPING BUNNY
>
> Created by Utrecht native Dick Bruna in 1955, Nijntje is to the Netherlands what Mickey Mouse is to the United States. Rarely does a Dutch child today go without at least one Bruna book or toy. The beloved storybook bunny is named after the Dutch word for "little rabbit," *konijntje,* though you may know her by her less diphthongy international handle, Miffy. Experts in cuteness, the Japanese are especially fond of Miffy as well as her diverse animal friends, whose simple lines and expressionless features are no doubt a pre-pastel-colored harbinger to Hello Kitty.

McGregor. Chunky knitwear and the odd flash of tartan are characteristic of this international chain with a distinctly Scottish air. ⊠ *P. C. Hooftstraat 114, Museum District* ☎ *020/675–3125* ⊕ *www.mcgregor-fashion.com.*

Mulberry Company. Stylish fashions and luxury goods come from across the English Channel to please those with an affinity for the foxhunting look. ⊠ *P. C. Hooftstraat 46, Museum District* ☎ *020/673–8086* ⊕ *www.mulberry.com.*

Sissy-Boy. Casual yet colorful threads are found at this unfortunately named Dutch chain, which will prove edgy to Esprit types, but dull to H&M regulars. ⊠ *Van Baerlestraat 15, Museum District* ☎ *020/671–5174* ⊕ *www.sissy-boy.nl* ⊠ *Kalverstraat 199, The Old City Center (Het Centrum)* ☎ *020/638–9305* ⊠ *Leidsestraat 15, Leidseplein* ☎ *020/623–8949.*

VINTAGE

Episode. It's grandma's attic meets the Salvation Army at this stylists' playground with branches in Antwerp, London, and Paris. The prices are right, though some items appear to have been not-so-gently worn. ⊠ *Berenstraat 1, The Canal Ring* ☎ *020/626–4679* ⊕ *www.episode.eu* ⊠ *Waterlooplein 1 The Old City Center (Het Centrum)* ☎ *020/320–3000.*

Ilovevintage.nl. The name says it all. And in 2010, this online store got some vintage digs, a canal-side building replete with sewing atelier, lounge, and photo studio. ✉ *Prinsengracht 201, The Canal Ring* ☎ *020/330–1950* ⊕ *www.ilovevintage.nl.*

Lady Day. Specializing in vintage from the '50s, '60s, and '70s, along with new retro-inspired designs, this shop is a go-to for fashion tourists and industry insiders. ✉ *Hartenstraat 9, The Canal Ring* ☎ *020/623–5820* ⊕ *www.ladydayvintage.com.*

Laura Dols. Here it's all about the nifty '50s: prom dresses, petticoats, wedding gowns, furs, hats, and olden-days linens (not for those who shun secondhand hankies). ✉ *Wolvenstraat 6 and 7,The Canal Ring* ☎ *020/624–9066* ⊕ *www.lauradols.nl.*

Zipper. The '80s are highly regarded here, though amid Wrangler corduroys and trucker hats, you'll find plenty more quality pieces from decades past. ✉ *Huidenstraat 7, The Canal Ring* ☎ *020/623–7302* ⊕ *www.zipperstore.nl* ✉ *Nieuwe Hoogstraat 8, The Old City Center (Het Centrum)* ☎ *020/627–0353.*

MENSWEAR
Fodor's Choice
★
English Hatter. This beacon to times past offers pullovers, tweed jackets, deerstalkers, and many other trappings of the English country gentleman. The cozy shop barely has room in which to turn around, but the inventory is large and the business bustling. Women can also buy hats here. ✉ *Heiligeweg 40, The Old City Center (Het Centrum)* ☎ *020/623–4781* ⊕ *www.english-hatter.nl.*

Jojo. Discounted luxury one-offs from Italy and France are sold at this haberdasher frequented by old-world gents and dandy-aspiring hipsters. ✉ *Huidenstraat 23, The Canal Ring* ☎ *020/623–3476.*

Oger. Wives accompany their corporate husbands to this Dutch purveyor of Italian custom-tailored suits, so they can ogle the shop clerks who look like moonlighting male runway models. This store takes "dressed to the nines" to a 10 in its self-proclaimed goal to "Latinize" its clients' sense of style. ✉ *P. C. Hooftstraat 75–81, Museum District* ☎ *020/676–8695* ⊕ *www.oger.nl.*

Society Shop. This mainstay among the museums sells all the classics that Dutch politicians and businessmen dig. ✉ *Van Baerlestraat 20–22, Museum District* ☎ *020/664–9281* ⊕ *www.thesocietyshop.com.*

WOMEN'S
WEAR
American Apparel. The international franchise famous for cruelty-free cotton knits and infamous for its pornographiclike marketing campaign may just as well have been called "Amsterdam Apparel." ✉ *Westerstraat 59–61, Jordaan* ☎ *020/330–2391* ⊕ *www.americanapparel.net.* ✉ *Utrechtsestraat 85, The Canal Ring* ☎ *020/624–6635.*

Buise. Women inspired by the betwixt-beach-and-bar look of LA fashion (or what paparazzi capture of it on film anyway) should sashay their ballerina flats here *tout suite.* ✉ *Cornelis Schuytstraat 12, Amsterdam South* ☎ *020/670–4904* ⊕ *www.buise.nl.*

Bodysox. A modern-day hosiery haven that sells socks, tights, nighties, and lingerie. ✉ *Leidsestraat 35, The Canal Ring* ☎ *020/422–3544.*

Concrete. Along with esoteric urban labels and vintage Levi's and Nikes, you'll find the obligatory stock of high-tops, hoodies, and plastic Japanese toys requisite for stores of this milieu. ✉ *Spuistraat 250, The Old City Center (Het Centrum)* ☎ *0900–26627383* ⊕ *www.concrete.nl.*

CLOSE UP

The Jean Scene

The recent rise of new-school haberdashers and so-called denim labs is keeping Amsterdammers big on the jean scene. And we're not just talking skinny vs. bootlegged or low-rise vs. mom, but a whole new world of custom-cut, Japanese-imported dungaree luxury that lets you select just the right metal for your rivet. Here are some shops to explore for men and women both.

290 Square Meters. ⊠ *Houtkopersdwarsstraat 3, East of the Amstel* ☎ *020/419–2525* ⊕ *www.290sqm. com.*

Acne Studio. ⊠ *Oude Spiegelstraat 8, The Canal Ring* ☎ *020/422–6845* ⊕ *www.acnestudios.com.*

Blue Blood. ⊠ *Cornelis Schuytstraat 18, Amsterdam South* ☎ *020/673–3847* ⊕ *www.bluebloodbrand.com*⊠ *PC Hooftstraat 142, Museum District* ☎ *020/676–6220.*

Denham. ⊠ *Prinsengracht 493, The Canal Ring* ☎ *020/331–5039* ⊕ *www. denhamthejeanmaker.com.*

Tenue de Nîmes. ⊠ *Elandsgracht 60, Jordaan* ☎ *020/320–4012* ⊕ *www. tenuedenimes.com.*

6

Cora Kemperman. This Dutch minichain appeals to a set of self-labeled modern women with a penchant for architectural cuts and monochrome. Think a futuristic Eileen Fisher. ⊠ *Leidsestraat 72, The Canal Ring* ☎ *020/625–1284* ⊕ *www.corakemperman.nl.*

Edgar Vos. The creations of this Dutch designer cater to women who seek garments that are classic and feminine, but never frilly. Hand-beaded and hand-embroidered details on fine silk, wool, and linen make his clothes especially attractive and spotlight the influence of his apprenticeship to Dior and Balmain. ⊠ *P. C. Hooftstraat 136, Museum District* ☎ *020/671–2748* ⊕ *www.edgarvos.nl* ⊠ *Beethovenstraat 57 Amsterdam South* ☎ *020/662–7460.*

Individuals Statement Store. The Amsterdam Fashion Institute proudly sells the creations of its third-year students just next door to the Maagdenhuuis, a university building notorious as the site of history-making student sit-ins. Print-wary and asymmetrically inclined as these aspiring new designers may be, the clothes are surprisingly wearable and small gift items affordable. ⊠ *Spui 23, The Old City Center (Het Centrum)* ☎ *020/525–8133* ⊕ *www.individualsatamfi.nl.*

★ **Kauppa.** If your Nordic track doesn't lead to Scandinavia this time, enjoy a bit of Finland in Holland. Kauppa carries the latest collections by famous textiler Marimekko—from its vibrant, crisply cut women's prêt-a-porter to party napkins emblazoned with the classic red poppy design—along with other edgy, often eco-friendly Finnish goods. ⊠ *Oude Spiegelstraat 6A, The Canal Ring,* ☎ *020/622–4848* ⊕ *www.kauppa.nl.*

Marlijn. Those who really want to make an individual fashion statement should make an appointment with couturiere Marlijn Franken. This Dutch designer has created looks for numerous celebrities, and if you're keen on having a transparent plastic suit, an iridescent,

A girl's best friend.

slashed-silk dress, or anything else outrageously luscious, she can do it. ✉ *Govert Flinckstraat 394 hs, The Pijp* ☎ *020/671–4742* ⊕ *www.marlijnamsterdam.nl.*

Pauw. It's a wonder that the shops in this chain always appear in clusters, with two or three sharing the same block, when you consider how pricey their collection is. For those who can afford it, however, Madeleine Pauw's pieces are just plain beautiful, particularly for the sophisticated and perhaps equestrian-inspired type of woman, be she a professional or society dame. ✉ *Van Baerlestraat 72 Museum District* ☎ *020/671–7322* ⊕ *www.pauw.nl* ✉ *Leidsestraat 16, Leidseplein* ☎ *020/626–5698.*

Pina. For ladies who lunch, power-lunching execs, or one and the same, this is a go-to for dress-to-impress apparel. In a neighborhood brimming with boutiques, Pina offers a well-edited selection of contemporary European designs—they pray to patron saint Patrizia Pepe here. ✉ *Keizersgracht 233, The Canal Ring* ☎ *020/320–8225* ⊕ *www.pina-amsterdam.nl.*

Rika. Swedish stylist Ulrika Lundgren's boutique with upstairs atelier may be smaller than your walk-in closet, but her designs are shipped all over the world, reaching the likes of Kate Moss—who's been spotted carrying one of her famous tote bags. Ideal for posturing to look like a rock star trying not to look like a rock star. ✉ *Oude Spiegelstraat 9, The Canal Ring* ☎ *020/330–1112* ⊕ *www.rikaint.com.*

★ **Tamago Amsterdam.** With the Rijksmuseum and a slew of uppity galleries as neighbors, this shop has some keeping up to do. And it does. Established by the tastemakers behind exclusive boutique Cobra

Mode (located in Den Bosch though lauded throughout the land), Tamago showcases the Japanese label Minä Perhonen, alongside other sartorial avant-gardists. ✉ *Spiegelgracht 13, The Canal Ring* ☎ *020/626–6054* ⊕ *www. tamagoamsterdam.nl.*

★ **Van Ravenstein.** This chic boutique is one of a handful of retail outlets in Holland for Viktor & Rolf ready-to-wear. But instead of A-bomb fashion—seldom seen outside museums and off the runway—you'll find the duo's smart, beautifully cut ready-to-wear clothing. The shop also carries top Belgian designers such as Martin Margiela, Dirk van Saenne, and Dries van Noten. On Saturdays, they open the bargain basement and the deals are outrageously well priced. ✉ *Keizersgracht 359, The Canal Ring* ☎ *020/639–0067* ⊕ *www. van-ravenstein.nl.*

> ## DIAMOND DRILL
>
> Even if you're not in the market for new rocks, a visit to a diamond factory is worth one of its free, guided tours. You'll learn all about the industry's "four Cs"—carat, color, clarity, and cut—and get to watch workers plying their trade. There's also a replica of the factory's most famous cut—the Koh-I-Noor diamond, one of the prize gems of the British crown jewels.

DIAMONDS AND JEWELRY

Diamonds are hardly ever a bargain. But compared with other cities, and thanks to Amsterdam's centuries-old ties to South Africa, they brilliantly border on that category here. The city's famous factories even allow one-stop shopping.

Amsterdam Diamond Center. Several diamond sellers are housed in this large tourist's to-do opposite the Dam. Besides diamonds, one can shop for other jewelry, watches, and silver gifts. ✉ *Rokin 1–5, The Old City Center (Het Centrum)* ☎ *020/624–5787* ⊕ *www. amsterdamdiamondcenter.nl.*

BLGK. This Nine Streets stop specializes in handmade Byzantine-inspired silver and gold jewelry. ✉ *Hartenstraat 28, The Canal Ring* ☎ *020/624–8154* ⊕ *www.blgk.com.*

★ **Bonebakker.** In business since 1792, this is one of the city's oldest and finest jewelers. Founder Adrian Bonebakker was commissioned by King Willem II to design and make the royal crown for the House of Orange. Today you'll find watches by Piaget, Corum, Chaumet, Cartier, and Jaeger-LeCoultre, and beautiful silver and gold tableware. Some of the silver designs produced here in the 1920s have been exhibited in Dutch museums, such as the Willet-Holthuysen. ✉ *Rokin 88–90, The Old City Center (Het Centrum)* ☎ *020/623–2294.*

Coster Diamonds. Kitty-corner to the Rijksmuseum, this store-disguised-as-a-museum hasn't really maintained its luster. The shabby interior décor notwithstanding, you can purchase some nice ice or other jewelry. ✉ *Paulus Potterstraat 2–8, Museum District* ☎ *020/305–5555* ⊕ *www. costerdiamonds.com.*

Galerie RA. This gallery tucked into the armpit of an ABN-AMRO bank shows wearable art by Dutch and international jewelry designers. ✉ *Vi-*

jzelstraat 80, The Old City Center (Het Centrum) ☎ 020/626–5100 ⊕ *www.galerie-ra.nl.*

Grimm Sieraden. Small but savvy, this boutique is known for unearthing the latest in jewelry by trendy young designers. ⊠ *Grimburgwal 9, The Old City Center (Het Centrum)* ☎ 020/622–0501 ⊕ *www. grimmsieraden.nl.*

Hans Appenzeller. Situated on a tiny street near the university is one of the international leaders in contemporary jewelry design. ⊠ *Grimburgwal 1, The Old City Center (Het Centrum)* ☎ 020/626–8218 ⊕ *www. appenzeller.nl.*

Premsela & Hamburger. Fine antique silver and jewelry have been purveyed here since 1823. And—how progressive!—it's open most Sundays. ⊠ *Rokin 98, The Old City Center (Het Centrum)* ☎ 020/624–9688 ⊕ *www.premsela.com.*

Schaap and Citroen. This century-old company carries top brands like Rolex, but also more moderately priced wristwatches and jewelry. ⊠ *P. C. Hooftstraat 40, Museum District)* ☎ 020/671–4714 ⊕ *www. schaapcitroen.nl.*

Tiffany & Co. Little turquoise boxes. ⊠ *PC Hooftstraat 86–88, Museum District* ☎ 020/305–0920 ⊕ *www.tiffany.com.*

FOOD AND BEVERAGES

CHEESE **De Kaaskamer.** This store stinks—of a smell testifying to its terrific selection of cheese. In addition to the usual Dutch suspects (Edam, Gouda, Old Amsterdam, and the smoked curds), this family business also sells choices from France, Greece, Italy, and Switzerland. There's also a rich assortment of accompanying cold cuts, olives, freshly made sauces, and dried fruits. ⊠ *Runstraat 7, The Canal Ring* ☎ 020/623–3483 ⊕ *www. kaaskamer.nl.*

CHOCOLATE **Arti Choc.** Chocoholics, take note, this Amsterdam South secret not only sells handmade bonbons, but will also custom-design just about anything you can imagine made from chocolate. The staff is lovely, and serves a very generous scoop of gelato, ideal to take along on a walk through the nearby Vondelpark. ⊠ *Koninginneweg 141, Amsterdam South* ☎ 020/470–9805 ⊕ *www.artichoc.nl.*

Australian Homemade. This Nijmegen-founded, now-global chain's chocolate is consumed en masse by Amsterdammers—its silver, space-age vacuum-sealed packaging finds a way onto the racks of many third-party vendors (including the local Albert Heijn grocery chain). But, no doubt, Australian's all-natural ingredients do make delectable chocolate and ice cream, as well as the best milkshake in town. ⊠ *Singel 437, The Old City Center (Het Centrum)* ☎ 020/428–7533 ⊕ *www.australianhomemade. com* ⊠ *Spui 5, The Old City Center (Het Centrum)* ☎ 020/627–4430 ⊠ *Leidsestraat 101, Leidseplein* ☎ 020/622–0897.

Chocolaterie Pompadour. After 40 years, the civilized still sit here for afternoon tea and tart. The front of the store attends to a steady stream of chocoholics—no less cultivated, just on the go. The Florentines are an éclat in their own right. ⊠ *Huidenstraat 12, The Canal Ring* ☎ 020/623–9554 ⊠ *Kerkstraat 148, The Canal Ring* ☎ 020/330–0981.

Be sure to eat as much of the cheese as possible.

★ **Patisserie Holtkamp.** From Sachertorte to sabayon, Holtkamp has mastered all the European pastry classics. However, this 120-year-old local business is just as beloved for savory Dutch specialties like the *kroket*. Their 33,000-piece weekly production of the deep-fried ragout roll has made them famous. Beware Saturday morning lines out the door. ⊠ *Vijzelgracht 15, The Canal Ring* ☎ *020/624–8757* ⊕ *www. patisserieholtkamp.nl.*

Puccini Bomboni. Seemingly dreamed up by Roald Dahl, this chocolatier sells knockout bonbons: one is usually enough to satiate the most gluttonous among us. The unusual ingredients include cognac, prune, pepper, and tamarind. ⊠ *Singel 184, The Old City Center (Het Centrum)* ☎ *020/427–8341* ⊕ *www.puccinibomboni.com* ⊠ *Staalstraat 17, The Canal Ring* ☎ *020/626–5474.*

Slagerij Yolanda en Fred de Leeuw. Restaurant-weary? Pack a picnic from *the* premier butcher in town where the black-coated staff stand ready to recommend their finest cut of brisket or stuff your made-to-order capon. ⊠ *Utrechtsestraat 92, The Canal Ring* ☎ *020/623–0235* ⊕ *www. slagerijdeleeuw.nl.*

COFFEE, TEA, AND SPIRITS

Cave Rokin. As its name suggests, this liquor store can be found in a cellar finely stocked with a range of European and New World wines, *jenevers* (Dutch gins), and *advocaats* (eggnogs made with brandy). The staff is knowledgeable and helpful. Tastings can be arranged for larger parties. ⊠ *Rokin 60, The Old City Center (Het Centrum)* ☎ *020/625–0628* ⊕ *www.caverokin.nl.*

De Bierkoning. Nearly 1,000 different types of beer can be purchased at this veritable museum of a specialty shop. The 300 beer-brand glasses on offer also make for a unique gift (and assuage long guilt-ridden pub pilferers). ⊠ *Paleisstraat 125, The Old City Center (Het Centrum)* ☎ *020/625–2336* ⊕ *www.bierkoning.nl.*

★ **Formocha.** What began as a simple hair salon on a shady Jordaan side street, 14 years later, expanded to indulge owner Amanda Yiu's other passion: tea. Fine leaves from Taiwan and Yiu's native Fujian, China, are sold by the gram in this tranquil shop with a small sipping station regularly occupied by the nation's most renowned food critic, Johannes van Dam. If you can't get farther East yourself, Formocha is a most worthy stop on the ancient spice route. ⊠ *Binnen Dommersstraat 24HS, Jordaan* ☎ *020/625–5233* ⊕ *www.formocha.nl.*

Geels & Co. Since 1880, this Warmoesstraat store has sold tea, coffee, and brewing utensils. It's a great place to find gifts like replica antique spice necklaces and traditional Dutch candy (not easy to find elsewhere). Don't miss the tiny museum upstairs with its display of antique coffee paraphernalia from around the world. ⊠ *Warmoesstraat 67, The Old City Center (Het Centrum)* ☎ *020/624–0683* ⊕ *www.geels.nl.*

Jacob Hooy & Co. Filled with teakwood canisters and jars bearing Latin inscriptions, fragrant with the perfume of seeds, flowers, and medicinal potions, this health-and-wellness store has been in operation on Nieuwmarkt since 1743. Gold-lettered wooden drawers, barrels, and bins contain not just spices and herbs, but also a daunting array of *dropjes* (hard candies and medicinal drops) and teas. ⊠ *Kloveniersburgwal 12, The Old City Center (Het Centrum)* ☎ *020/624–3041* ⊕ *www.jacobhooy.nl.*

Kaldi. This shop sells specialty coffees and teas from around the world, as well as everything related to their preparation, from brewing apparatus to accompanying biscotti. A few tables in the back let you sit and get caffeinated on the spot. ⊠ *Herengracht 300, The Canal Ring* ☎ *020/428–6854* ⊕ *www.kaldi.nl.*

GIFTS AND SOUVENIRS

Baobab. This shop's interior is like something out of Ali Baba's cave of treasures or *1,001 Nights.* You'll find a rich trove of jewelry, statuary, and all kinds of objects from such locales as India and the Middle East. ⊠ *Elandsgracht 105, Jordaan* ☎ *020/626–8398* ⊕ *www.baobab-aziatica.nl.*

★ **Brilmuseum.** A must-visit when you're strolling the Nine Streets, this boutique displays a collection of eyeglasses from antique to contemporary in a setting that evokes the atmosphere of the 17th century (the upstairs galleries actually have museum status). It's open only Wednesday through Saturday. ⊠ *Gasthuismolensteeg 7, The Canal Ring* ☎ *020/421–2414* ⊕ *www.brilmuseumamsterdam.nl.*

Cats & Things. Cat lovers return again and again to Ine van Bercum's headquarters for feline-related gifts and useful items for the kitty. Van Bercum is also a very knowledgeable cat breeder, and of course, a real cat named Annabel is on hand to welcome customers with a purr-fect greeting. ⊠ *Hazenstraat 26, Jordaan* ☎ *020/428–3028* ⊕ *www.catsandthings.nl.*

Cortina Papier. Poet or paper-pusher, you'll find a luscious array of note-books, albums, stationery, gift wrap, and 26 colors of writing ink here. And if even for five minutes, you'll forget all about the invention of the computer. ⊠ *Reestraat 22, The Canal Ring* ☎ *020/623–6676* ⊕ *www.cortinapapier.nl.*

De Condomerie. A discreet, well-informed staff promote healthful sexual practices at this condom emporium (with an equally handy online store). It's also strategically located on one of the city's bou-levards for gay nightlife. ⊠ *War-moesstraat 141, The Old City Center (Het Centrum)* ☎ *020/627–4174* ⊕ *www.condomerie.com.*

PARALLAXE

Whether you're a pro photog-rapher, amateur porn-maker, or simple collector of lenses, this place will fulfill all your filmic needs: Super 8 cameras, Polaroids, projector lamps, ad infinitum. Owner Johan Parallaxe combs flea markets, antique fairs, and estate sales looking to grow his shop and, in the process, feed his own personal obsession. ⊠ *Pieter Langendijkstraat 64, Amsterdam West* ☎ *020/412–2082* ⊕ *www. parallaxe.nl.*

6

De Witte Tanden Winkel. Anyone for champagne-flavored toothpaste? Whether concerned about dental hygiene or looking for some kind of oral novelty, consider visiting this small shop stocked with everything teeth related. The toothbrush Ferris wheel in the window is also worth a gander. ⊠ *Runstraat 5, The Canal Ring* ☎ *020/623–3443* ⊕ *www. dewittetandenwinkel.nl.*

Dom. With its black walls, Prince-pumping sound system, and cheeky-themed bath and body works, DOM feels more like the backroom of a club than a funky gift shop. Though that's not a complaint. ⊠ *Spuist-raat 281 A–C, The Old City Center (Het Centrum)* ☎ *20/428–5544* ⊕ *www.dom-ck.com.*

★ **The Fair Trade Shop.** In the market for Colombian coffee, silver jewelry, a set of salad tongs, new salsa beats, or a handcrafted photo album from India? You'll find a rainbow of such items from this shop of the same-named global organization promoting the fair compensation of prod-ucts imported from developing communities. ⊠ *Heiligewg 45, The Old City Center (Het Centrum)* ☎ *020/625–2245* ⊕ *www.fairtrade.nl.*

Heineken the City. Does a Heine really taste better when tapped at the source? At this hip satellite branch of the Heineken Experience gift store, you can order a personalized six-pack to let the folks back home decide. Souvenir apparel comes courtesy of Dutch designers commissioned to put their own artful spins on the green corporate logo. ⊠ *Amstelstraat 31, The Canal Ring* ☎ *020/530 4770* ⊕ *www.heinekenthecity.nl.*

H. J. Van de Kerkhof. Holland's leading fashion and theatrical costume designers frequent this funky archive of unusual ribbons, tassels, lace edgings, and other fashion trim available for retail customers. (The store is closed Friday through Sunday.) ⊠ *Wolvenstraat 9, The Canal Ring* ☎ *020/623–4084.*

Knuffels/De Klompenboer. Located in a former metro station, Knuffels is the upstairs venue that sells toys, including a fun-loving selection of *knuffels* (the word for hugs and, by extension, cuddle toys). Downstairs is the *klompen* shop, where you can order wooden shoes in all sizes and colors, as well as request handpainted or wood-burned designs. ✉ *Sint Anthoniesbreestraat 39–51, The Old City Center (Het Centrum)* ☎ *020/427–3862* ⊕ *www.woodenshoefactory.com.*

Nieuws. Small quirky presents can be found at this crossroads for gag gifts, kitsch, and novelty items. ✉ *Prinsengracht 297, The Canal Ring* ☎ *020/627–9540* ⊕ *www.peoplesgiftstore.com.*

The Otherist. This friendly gift shop has a perfectly edited collection of contemporary, often cheeky jewelry, stationery, toys, and homewares. The goods come from around the globe, spanning Denmark to Uruguay. ✉ *Leliegracht 6, Jordaan* ☎ *020/320–0420* ⊕ *www.otherist.com.*

★ **Skatezone.** The dike-plugging Dutch boy Hans Brinker would have loved this modern skating outlet, which stocks well over 150 models of ice skates in all styles: from those made for wintertime canal gliding to hockey skates. The shop carries top brands such as Viking, Raps, Bauer, CCM, Zandstra, Graf, with a large variety of *noren,* the most popular style of speed skates for adults, as well as traditional Dutch wooden training skates for children (the double blades make for easier balance). Skatezone is also the place to rent in-line skates manufactured by all the bigwigs in extreme sports, including Rollerblade, K2, and Powerslide. ✉ *Ceintuurbaan 57–59, The Pijp* ☎ *020/662–2822* ⊕ *www.skatezone.nl.*

Souvenir Shop Holland. Although souvenir shops can be found on every other street corner in Amsterdam, this one is distinguished by its better class of products, such as Delft cuckoo clocks and automated miniature windmills. Sure, you may find a number of these items elsewhere, but they're often displayed just across the aisle from total kitsch, risqué mementos, or drug paraphernalia. In other words, feel free to bring your grandmother to this shop. ✉ *Nieuwendijk 226, The Old City Center (Het Centrum)* ☎ *020/624–7252* ⊕ *www.souvenirshopholland.com.*

A Space Oddity. This little shop combs a big world for robots, toys, and memorabilia from TV and film classics. ✉ *Prinsengracht 204, Jordaan* ☎ *020/427–4036* ⊕ *www.spaceoddity.nl.*

Yogisha. Yoga mats, clothing, and other *om*-inspiring items. ✉ *Ceintuurbaan 378, The Pijp* ☎ *020/664–0743* ⊕ *www.yogisha.nl.*

HAIR AND BEAUTY

Ariane Inden. This salon has a full line of Dutch cosmetics and does makeovers. The upstairs parlor also offers a range of skin treatments. ✉ *Utrechtsestraat 127, The Canal Ring* ☎ *020/422–0426* ⊕ *www.arianeinden.com.*

Barrio. What happens when a couple of Amsterdam hipsters spend a year camping out of their Winnebago, on adventures from Berlin to Barcelona? They return home to open a hair salon-cum-clothing boutique, hocking the latest trends in urban art-school-wear along with matching kicks and accessories. They also give it a Spanish name, in remembrance of their community-spirited inspiration for new cuts in hair and clothes. ✉ *Voetboogstraat 20, The Old City Center (Het Centrum)* ☎ *020/663–2918* ⊕ *www.barrio.nl.*

Hairpolice. Those seeking something more—than their own head of hair, that is—frequent this small salon right off the Bloemenmarkt. They're famous for Rainbow Brite do's and the rigmarole of dread maintenance, but also offer vanity extensions and coiffure of a generally voluminous nature. ⊠ *Geelvincksteeg 10, The Canal Ring* ☎ *020/420–5841* ⊕ *www. hairpolice.nl.*

ICI Paris XL. The top brands in makeup and perfumes are sold at this Belgian chain of cosmetics. The staff is as polished and professional as the shop—the salesladies and occasional salesgents look airbrushed, which isn't necessarily a bad thing. ⊠ *P. C. Hooftstraat 132–134, Museum District* ☎ *020/675–8032* ⊕ *www.iciparisxl.nl* ⊠ *Leidsestraat 67, Leidseplein* ☎ *020/320–9751.*

Kiehl's. This global chain of herbal-friendly cosmetics, which first began as a New York City apothecary in 1851, is a perfect addition to all the nose-powdering shops along the P. C. Hooftstraat periphery. ⊠ *Hobbemastraat 4, Museum District* ☎ *020/675–0891* ⊕ *www.kiehls.com.*

Kinki Kappers. Now with branches in Germany and Spain, this hip Dutch chain whose name means "exciting" in local slang attracts a diverse clientele. Whether you seek a mainstream bob or bilevel dye job, the staff is well equipped, many with inspiring heads of their own. ⊠ *Haarlemmerdijk 17, Jordaan* ☎ *020/625-6000* ⊕ *www.kinki.nl* ⊠ *Utrechtsestraat 34, The Canal Ring* ☎ *020/625–7793* ⊠ *Overtoom 245, Amsterdam West* ☎ *020/689–4553.*

La Savonnerie. For 10 years, this sweet little shop has been hand-making its own brand of palm oil soap. There are more than 70 different scents, colorfully ranging from Aqua to Winterberry, and, best of all, bars can be custom engraved. ⊠ *Prinsengracht 294, Jordaan* ☎ *020/428–1139* ⊕ *www.savonnerie.nl.*

Lush. Enticing scents and spunky staff lure you into this modern-day beauty shop, where the handmade soaps, "bath bombs," and massage stones appear good enough to eat (if you don't mind getting a little glitter on your tongue). ⊠ *Leidsestraat 14, Leidseplein* ☎ *020/423–4315* ⊕ *www.lush.nl* ⊠ *Kalverstraat 98, The Old City Center (Het Centrum)* ☎ *020/330–6376.*

manMAN Beautycare. In case the name left you guessing, this salon is just for *him*. Whether you're metro or macho, manMAN offers massage, depilation, skin-care, and hand and foot treatments. ⊠ *Roelof Hartstraat 13HS, Amsterdam South* ☎ *020/670–7733* ⊕ *www. manmanbeautycare.nl.*

A TWOFER THAT TURNS HEADS

Pontifex Essential Oils and Incense/Doll Hospital E. Kramer. On the off chance you're looking for a potion that will promote inner peace and harmony, and you also happen to have an antique porcelain doll that needs a tune-up, you have only one place to go. On one side of this Nine Streets shop, you'll find candles, incense, and nearly 200 types of ethereal and spiritual oils. On the other side, shopkeeper Kramer carries on a 40-year-old tradition of doll repair and recapitation (there are shelves of bodyless heads to choose from). ⊠ *Reestraat 18–20, The Canal Ring* ☎ *020/626–5274.*

Check out the uber-cool collection at Droog Design store.

Rob Peetoom. The ultramodern surroundings at this hair-and-makeup salon are full of beautiful people trying to get more beautiful. ✉ *Elandsgracht 68, Jordaan* ☎ *020/528–5722* ⊕ *www.robpeetoom. nl* ✉ *De Bijenkorf, Dam 1, The Old City Center (Het Centrum)* ☎ *020/422–3902.*

★ **Skins Cosmetics.** A Sephora gone small town, this Nine Streets boutique carries an extensive selection of exclusive brands of cosmetics and hair-care products. On-site hairdressers for men and women and makeup artists will tend to your looks. ✉ *Runstraat 9, The Canal Ring* ☎ *020/528–6922* ⊕ *www.skins.nl.*

Fodor's Choice
★ **Tommy'z Toko.** Shiny-haired yuppies may be invading Amsterdam West, but salon Tommy'z Toko is keeping the wild styles of decades past alive and well. Who is the sheared genius behind it all? Tommy Hagen, a regular hairstylist at New York Fashion Week whose creations for the major glossies are inspired by heads spotted everywhere, from 1930s prison mug shots to new jack swing videos on MTV. So, what to do about your do? Call for an appointment. Prices range from €30 to €115, depending on the service and which stylist you see. For a cut by Tommy himself, men pay a mere €55 and women, €70. ✉ *Admiraal de Ruijterweg 85, Amsterdam West* ☎ *020/638–7872* ⊕ *www.tommyztoko.nl.*

HOUSEWARES

BeBob Design Interior. Collectors and galleries stock up here on hard-to-find historic designs of chairs, sofas, tables, office chairs, and lighting fixtures from top lines. ✉ *Prinsengracht 764, The Canal Ring* ☎ *020/624–5763* ⊕ *www.bebob.nl.*

CLOSE UP

Cutting-Edge Dutch Design

Ever since Gerrit Rietveld produced his "Red and Blue Chair," the Dutch have been in the international limelight, famous for graphic design, fashion (clothing, jewelry, accessories), industrial design, interior design, furniture design, advertising, and architecture. Rietveld has been followed by the likes of Bruno Ninaber van Eyben (inventor of the pendant watch and the Dutch Euro), Trude Hooykaas (architect), Frans Molenaar (fashion), Jan Jansen (shoes), Ted Noten (jewelry), KesselsKramer (advertising), and Marcel Wanders (industrial designer best known for his Knitted Chair). These and other equally acclaimed designers have works displayed in commercial galleries and modern art museums alike. Since 45,000 Dutch designers produce more than 2.5 billion euros worth of new stuff per year, you'd think somebody could tell you exactly what "Dutch Design" is. But it's too diverse to pin down, and ranges from modern, conceptual, kitsch, functional, sober, conceptual, innovative, ironic, experimental, intelligent, and alternative to everything in between.

Marcel Wanders' famous egg vase

A steady stream of new talent, graduating from one of the numerous national institutes dedicated to design, make Dutch Design a perennially hot topic that takes center stage no matter what time of year you visit. The Utrecht School for the Arts (HKU), Design Academy Eindhoven (dubbed the "School of Cool" by *TIME* magazine), the Industrial Design department at TU Delft, and the Rietveld Academy in Amsterdam are talent pools feeding into the trend mecca that the Netherlands has become. To dive deep into Dutch design, visit **Droog Design** (✉ *Staalstraat 7B, The Old City Center (Het Centrum)* ☎ *020/523-5050* ⊕ *www.droogdesign.nl*), a shop and gallery featuring young talents whose work captures the collective's *droog* ("dry") sense of humor. **The Frozen Fountain** (✉ *Prinsengracht 645, The Canal Ring* ☎ *020/622-9375* ⊕ *www.frozenfountain.nl*) pools the Benelux's most edgy of designers in home goods, furniture, and jewelry. ⇨ *See Shopping for more design stores.*

A Droog table and chair, produced and designed by Richard Hutton

Blond Amsterdam. What began as a small atelier taking personal orders for goofy-captioned caricatures on handpainted china has exploded into a mega–lifestyle brand whose now made-in-China products are sold across Dutch department stores. The two blond art-school grads behind the company have even left their mark on KLM sandwich packaging. ⊠ *Gerard Doustraat 69, Amsterdam South* ☎ *020/428–4929* ⊕ *www.blond-amsterdam.nl.*

Bloom. Five-star hotel bed sheets may be heavenly. Gossamer-like pure cotton linens imported from India by someone who combines her appreciation for fabric with helping Indian street children, well, that's nirvana. Besides beddings, Bloom sells women's and children's apparel made of equally good karmic substance. ⊠ *Prinsengracht 272, The Canal Ring* ☎ *020/320–1176* ⊕ *www.bloomprints.nl.*

Capsicum. Not your run-of-the-mill material store, this place makes fabric-holics drool with all its gorgeous weaves, prints, and colors. ⊠ *Oude Hoogstraat 1, The Old City Center (Het Centrum)* ☎ *020/623–1016* ⊕ *www.capsicum.nl.*

★ **Coco-Mat.** Since opening this Dutch flagship shop in May 2003, the Greek chain has been crowded with customers seven days a week. Troll for decadently comfortable orthopedic beds, ergonomic sofas, pretty tables, curtains, and bed and bath linens. Glass floor panels reveal the downstairs area, which is devoted to children's furnishings and adorable soft toys. ⊠ *Overtoom 89, Amsterdam South* ☎ *020/489–2927* ⊕ *www.coco-mat.nl.*

De Kasstoor. This three-floor home store began in 1892 on the very same city block where it purveys sleek contemporary furniture and household goods. Across the street are two other equally reputable Kasstoor businesses. **Wonen2000 Bed & Bad** (⊠ *Rozengracht 215–217* ☎ *020/521–8712*) sells plush linens and bathroom accessories. **Wonen2000 IDC** ⊠ *Rozengracht 219–221* ☎ *020/521–8710*) sells innovative European furniture, while also offering forth its in-house group of architects and interior designers. ⊠ *Rosengracht 202–210, Jordaan* ☎ *020/521–8112* ⊕ *www.dekasstoor.nl.*

Fodor'sChoice **Droog Design.** Besides exhibiting highlights of its collection, this design
★ collective also sells a number of its edgy, often industrial, furniture and home accessories. What began as a decidedly Dutch group now comprises designers from all over the globe, who have together cultivated an international reputation for groundbreaking interior design. ⊠ *Staalstraat 7B, The Old City Center (Het Centrum)* ☎ *020/523–5050* ⊕ *www.droogdesign.nl.*

Fodor'sChoice **Duikelman.** Kitchen supplies never had it so good, and neither did the
★ professional or amateur cooks who shop here. At the main store, just off Ferdinand Bolstraat, you'll find 10,000 of the finest quality cooking utensils and appliances. Cross the street (⊠ *Gerard Doustraat 54* ☎ *020/673–1385*), and you'll come upon cookbooks, porcelain dishes, and art school–designed tea towels; next door are ovens that take baking to a whole new level. ⊠ *Ferdinand Bolstraat 68–68a, The Pijp* ☎ *020/671–2230* ⊕ *www.duikelman.nl.*

★ **The Frozen Fountain.** This gallery-cum-store carries contemporary furniture and innovative home accessories from such top Dutch designers as Hutten, Arad, Newson, Starck, Wanders, and Jongerius. You can find custom-made scrapwood cabinets by Piet Hein Eek, as well as artistic perfume dispensers, jewelry, and carpets. The store juxtaposes minimalism with paper-cut chandeliers and rococo seats. Part of the space serves as a museum shop for the Netherlands Textile Museum, where original European fabrics are on offer. ✉ *Prinsengracht 629–645, The Canal Ring* ☎ *020/622–9375* ⊕ *www.frozenfountain.nl.*

THE TUMBLE MAN

Duikelman is named in honor of the original "Tumble Man." In the 1940s, Joop van Hal, grandfather to David Appelboom, the business's current owner, had invented a flashlight that automatically shut off when flipped over in a downward tumbling—*"duikelen"*—motion. This timely device was a crucial invention, helping to keep the Dutch army strategically obscured from enemy sight. It also began the Appelboom family's tradition of selling simple yet well-designed tools, now in more tranquil times.

HEMA. Even the Dutch equivalent of Sears has high-style household items at reasonable prices, and a cool minimalist design. ✉ *Nieuwendijk 174–176, The Old City Center (Het Centrum)* ☎ *020/623–4176* ⊕ *www.hema.nl.*

Kitsch Kitchen. This is a supermarket of wacky, tacky, plasticky housewares that greatly appeals to the Dutch's postmodern approach to interior design. Here's where Amsterdammers pick up that Virgin of Guadalupe votive candle to accompany the Alessi pepper grinder on an IKEA coffee table. ✉ *Rozengracht 8–12, Jordaan* ☎ *020/462-0051* ⊕ *www.kitschkitchen.nl.*

& klevering Zuid. You'll find yourself in a rainbow world at this quiet corner, thanks to its wide range of tints in porcelain and glass tableware, colorful household accessories, and bright table linens. Top European design brands are all here, including stainless steel cookware from Iittala, Peugeot pepper mills, lush towels and bathrobes from Van Dijck Sanger, and artistic storage boxes from Galerie Sentou. ✉ *Jacob Obrechtstraat 19a, Amsterdam South* ☎ *020/670–3623* ⊕ *www.klevering.nl.*& **klevering Centraal.** ✉ *Haarlemmerstraat 8, Jordaan* ☎ *020/422–2708.*& **klevering Stad.** ✉ *Staalstraat 11, The Old City Center (Het Centrum* ☎ *020/421–3029.*

Tike Design. If Jonathan Adler and Dalí were roommates they would order all their ottomans from here. The designer footstools range from €700 to €17,500. ✉ *Pieter Grimburgwal 15, The Old City Center (Het Centrum)* ☎ *020/428–8510* ⊕ *www.tikedesign.com.*

MUSIC

Broekmans & Van Poppel. Apropos of the neighboring Concertgebouw, this store specializes in recordings, sheet music, and accessories for classical and antiquarian music. ✉ *Van Baerlestraat 92–94, Museum District* ☎ *020/675–1653* ⊕ *www.broekmans.com.*

6

Fodor's Choice ★ **Concerto.** With a staff channeling the cast of *High Fidelity*, this bilevel, multidoored music mecca is filled with new and used records and CDs covering all imaginable genres. ✉ *Utrechtsestraat 52–60, The Canal Ring* ☎ *020/623–5228* ⊕ *www.concertomania.nl.*

★ **Rush Hour.** In the Netherlands, this is *the* premier record shop for quality house, techno, left-field vinyl releases, and international imports from Detroit to Tokyo. It's also a world-renowned mail-order outlet, an exclusive record label, and a bunch of boys who know how to throw a good party. ✉ *Spuistraat 98, The Old City Center (Het Centrum)* ☎ *020/427–4505* ⊕ *www.rushhour.nl.*

South Miami Plaza. The vast SMP has just about every music category, including the Dutch answer to country music, *smartlap*. Listening booths are available, too. ✉ *Albert Cuypstraat 116, The Pijp* ☎ *020/662–2817* ⊕ *www.southmiamaplaza.nl.*

> ### CO-OPTING THE CLOG
>
> So you love your Crocs. But you may well forget about those riddled pieces of galactic resin once you try on a pair of *klompen*. Though you'll find a fantastic selection of stylish modern offshoots, the classic wooden Dutch clog is still used by farmers, fishermen, and factory workers. Traditionally worn over a thick pair of *geitenwollen sokken* (socks made from goat's wool), *klompen* help keep toes warm while providing durable soles to stomp through wet and muddy surfaces. Some creative residents have co-opted the clog, using it as a wall-mounted flowerpot on their terraces.

SENSUAL SHOPPING

Mail & Female. Said to be the first business in Europe to present women's sex toys in a tasteful manner, two decades later, Mail & Female isn't just a mail-order catalog. Besides being a successful online portal, it's a brick-and-mortar shop commanding prime real estate far from anything red-lighted. ✉ *Nieuwe Vijzelstraat 2, The Canal Ring* ☎ *020/623–3916* ⊕ *www.mailfemale.com.*

Marlies Dekkers. This Dutch designer's name has become synonymous with undergarments that could possibly turn the Red Light District one shade darker. With shops found worldwide, Dekkers has underdressed-to-impress many a celebrity, though women—of all ages and exhibitionisms—adore her. ✉ *Cornelis Schuytstraat 13, Amsterdam South* ☎ *020/471–4146* ⊕ *www.marliesdekkers.nl* ✉ *Berenstraat 18, The Canal Ring* ☎ *020/421–1900.*

RoB Flagship Store. Serving a largely gay men's community for nearly 30 years, this self-touted "epicenter of Amsterdam leather life" sells hides, rubber, and other pliable gear to those of a dungeon-y demeanor. ✉ *Warmoesstraat 71, The Old City Center (Het Centrum)* ☎ *020/428–3000* ⊕ *www.rob.nl.*

SHOES

Antonia By Yvette. Two generations of women, each with their own doorway, under one roof and one motto: "Crazy about shoes." Yvette carries hip footwear from top European designers for men and women. Her mother next door carries slippers, clogs, Birkenstocks, and boots for

Christmas time on the Kalverstraat.

every kind of precipitation. ✉ *Gasthuismolensteeg 18, The Canal Ring* ☎ *020/320–9433* ✉ *Gasthuismolensteeg 16, The Canal Ring* ☎ *020/627–2433* ⊕ *www.antoniabyyvette.nl* ⊕ *www.depantoffelwinkel.nl.*

Dr. Adams. The good doctor sells chunkier, more adventurous styles of shoes for men and women. ✉ *P. C. Hooftstraat 90, Museum District* ☎ *020/662–3835* ⊕ *www.dradams.nl* ✉ *Leidsestraat 25, Leidseplein* ☎ *020/626–4460* ✉ *Oude Doelenstraat 5–7, The Old City Center (Het Centrum)* ☎ *020/622–3734* ✉ *Kalvertoren, Kalverstraat 212–220, The Old City Center (Het Centrum)* ☎ *020/427–2565.*

★ **Fred de La Bretoniere.** This is *the* shop to find a classic style that still lets you walk with your own unique verve. Fred de la Bretoniere has been selling men's and women's leather footwear since 1970, and it's no surprise that his shoes have been entered into the permanent collections of several Dutch design museums. ✉ *Sint Luciënsteeg 20, The Old City Center (Het Centrum)* ☎ *020/623–4152* ⊕ *www.bretoniere.nl* ✉ *Utrechtsestraat 77, The Canal Ring* ☎ *020/626–9627.*

Hester van Eeghen. Since 2000, cool, contemporary Dutch design has been available for ladies' feet—that is, after being manufactured from fine leather in Italy. And if you like Van Eeghen's shoes, walk west to her eponymous handbag boutique (✉ *Hartenstraat 37* ☎ *020/626–9212*). Geometry never before seemed so colorful or portable. ✉ *Hartenstraat 1, The Canal Ring* ☎ *020/626–9211* ⊕ *www.hestervaneeghen.com.*

Jan Jansen. Forget fairy godmothers: this is where today's urban Cinderella finds her glass slippers. Since the '60s, the Nijmegen-born artist and craftsman has made museum-worthy footwear beloved for its conceptual design, outrageous color, and uncompromised wearability.

✉ *Rokin 42, The Old City Center (Het Centrum)* ☎ *020/625–1350* ⊕ *www.janjansenshoes.com* ✉ *Roelof Hartstraat 16, Amsterdam South* ☎ *020/470–0116.*

Onitsuka Tiger. With just a few flagships stores scattered throughout the world, Amsterdam provides some uppity canal-side real estate for this hip Japanese line of Asics sneakers. There seems to be a style for every breed of tulip. ✉ *Herengracht 365, The Canal Ring* ☎ *020/528–6183* ⊕ *www.onitsukatiger.nl.*

Otten & Zn. This neighborhood cobbler will gladly recork your worn-out Birkenstocks though in the process may tempt you to a brand-new pair. Here you'll find an array of hippie-chic sandals, clogs, boots, and Wellies. ✉ *Eerste van der Helststraat 31 HS, The Pijp* ☎ *020/662–9724* ⊕ *www.ottenenzoon.hyves.nl.*

Patta. Named after the Surinamese slang for "shoes," this boutique for the urban-hip sells an exclusive selection of sneakers from all over the globe. It's where to find those limited-edition retro suede New Balances you've always wanted. Preview the current stock on the store's Web site. ✉ *Nieuwezijds Voorburgwal 142, The Old City Center (Het Centrum)* ☎ *020/528–5994* ⊕ *www.teampatta.nl.*

Shoebaloo. One might mistake the interior of this store for that of a spaceship. Some of the shoe styles are just as wild (the Day-Glo tiger-striped stilettos, for example), though many are simply high-end leather heels for vampy fashionistas. ✉ *P. C. Hooftstraat 80, Museum District* ☎ *020/671–2210* ⊕ *www.shoebaloo.nl* ✉ *Leidsestraat 10, Leidseplein* ☎ *020/330–9147* ✉ *Koningsplein 7, The Canal Ring* ☎ *020/626–7993* ✉ *Cornelis Schuytstraat 9, Amsterdam South* ☎ *020/662–5779.*

United Nude. Entering UN feels more like walking into an art gallery than a shoe shop. No wonder, the man behind this brand's flagship store—and the various models of the signature floating-heeled pump contained therein—is the same-named nephew of celebrity architect Rem Koolhaas, who designed the Prada store in New York City's SoHo. ✉ *Spuistraat 125A, East of the Amstel* ☎ *020/419–2525* ⊕ *www.unitednude.com.*

7

Day Trips from Amsterdam

WORD OF MOUTH

"Keukenhof in bloom is sheer magic! Don't miss it! The countryside around it is endless tulip bulb fields, flat as a pancake, and beautiful when in bloom.

—USNR

Updated by
Ann Maher

The Netherlands is such a manageably small country that there's practically no excuse not to explore a little further afield. Castles, seaside resorts, historic towns, and tulip fields are just outside the city, and with Amsterdam's great transport connections, very accessible.

Most historic towns and attractions are under an hour away—even the Wadden Islands can be reached in a couple of hours. Whether you are driving or cycling, the routes are well maintained and clearly signposted. Trains and regional buses are frequent and punctual with a range of passes for discount travel. The tourist board can print out a travel schedule for a specific destination which is particularly useful if you are having to switch between metro, bus, and train all on one journey.

GUIDED TOURS

Entrepreneurs in the Netherlands offer a smorgasbord of excursions for individuals and groups.

Bus tours of the Holland-in-a-hurry variety, whether half or full-day excursions, can be booked directly with the operator or via the **VVV** (⊠ *Just in front of Centraal Station, Amsterdam* ☎ *0900/400–4040* ⊕ *www.iamsterdam.com/visiting*). For more contemporary touring in summer months, **Museum De Paviljoens** (☎ *036/545–0400* ⊕ *www. depaviljoens.nl*) runs a tour of land art on Sundays in Flevoland. **Orangebike** (☎ *020/528–9990* ⊕ *www.orangebike.nl*), **Yellowbike** (☎ *020/620–6940* ⊕ *www.yellowbike.nl*), and **MacBike** (☎ *020/624–8391* ⊕ *www. macbike.nl*) (the red ones) all run a guided tour to the country and offer other self-guided options for architectural and culinary interests. **Joy Ride Bike Tours** (☎ *06/4361–1798* ⊕ *www.joyridetours.nl*) have an enthusiastic approach to private trips covering "anywhere you can ride a bike to from Amsterdam." Suggestions include longer (but leisurely) visits to villages such as Durgerdam and Oude Kerk, with a swimming stop, and the possibility of tulips (or whatever is in bloom) in the spring.

For watery options, **Wetlands Safari** (☎ *020/686–3445* ⊕ *www. wetlandssafari.nl*) runs canoe trips through a 17th-century landscape. Guided tours last five and a half hours and the €38 fee covers transport

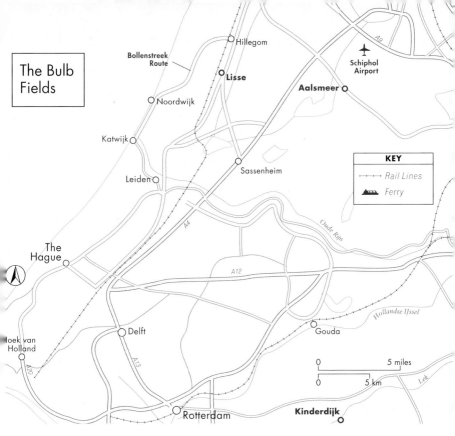

KEY

+———+	*Rail Lines*
🚢	*Ferry*

Hillegom

Bollenstreek
Route

Lisse

Schiphol
Airport

Aalsmeer

Noordwijk

Katwijk

Sassenheim

Leiden

Oude Rijn

The
Hague

A4

A12

Hollandse IJssel

Delft

Gouda

oek van
Holland

A13

A20

0	5 miles
0	5 km

Lek

Rotterdam

Kinderdijk

from Amsterdam and back, coffee, and lunch. They can also organize customized tours. Be sure to wear rain boots or old footwear.

Boat excursions from Amsterdam include **Pampus Island** (☎ *0294/262–326* ⊕ *www.pampus.nl*), with its fort, that is part of the (UNESCO heritage) Amsterdam Defence Line. It can be reached from IJburg (☎ *020/427–8888* ⊕ *www.IJburgpampus.nl.*) and Muiden. Guided or self guided tours of the island are available.

Rebus Varende Evenementen (☎ *010/218–3131* ⊕ *www.rebus-info.nl* ✉ *€13.50 and various group rates*). A three-hour trip from Rotterdam along the Lek to Kinderdijk is available from mid-April to the end of September. Boats leave from Boompjeskade where there is a ticket office, or you can buy tickets from the Rotterdam VVV. 10:45 AM and 2:15 PM departures.

THE BULB FIELDS

In the spring (late March until mid-May) the bulb fields of South Holland are transformed into a vivid series of Mondriaan paintings through the colors of millions of tulips and other flowers. The bulb fields extend from just north of Leiden to the southern limits of Haarlem, with the greatest concentration beginning at Sassenheim and ending between

DID YOU KNOW?

Keukenhof is one of the most popular attractions in Holland, having thus far clocked more than 44 million visitors in the last 60 years. Covering 32 hectares and with 100 varieties of it's 4.5 million tulips, it's the largest bulb park in the world.

Hillegom and Bennebroek. Floral HQ is the town of Lisse and the fields and glasshouses of the Keukenhof Gardens. The bulb, rather than the bloom, is the prize, and to promote growth and subdivision tulips are decapitated in the field by specialized machines designed by fanatical breeders. Timing can be volatile, but there's a general progression from croci in the middle of March, daffodils and narcissi from the end of March to the middle of April, early tulips and hyacinths from the second week of April to the end of the month, and late tulips immediately afterward. An early or late spring can shift these approximate dates by as much as two weeks.

EXCLUSIVE BLOOM

In the 17th-century floral futures market, fortunes were made and lost in a day with reckless gambling on the price of tulip bulbs. One Semper August bloom clocked in at 3,000 guilders—at that time, the cost of a decent house in Amsterdam.

Fodor's Choice **Bollenstreek Route** *(Bulb District Route)*. More popularly known as the
★ Bloemen Route (Flower Route), this series of roads meander through the bulb-growing region. It was originally designed by Dutch motoring organization ANWB, which began life as a cycling association. Look out for the small blue-and-white signs marked Bollenstreek. Driving from Amsterdam, take the A4 towards Leiden then the N207 signposted Lisse. By train, head for Haarlem and take bus 50 or bus 51, which allows you to embark and disembark along the route. Tour companies and the local VVVs (Tourist Information Offices) also organize walking and bicycle tours that usually include a visit to Keukenhof. A round-trip tour from Lisse though Hillegom, Noorderwijkerhout, Sassenheim, De Zilk and Voorhout is approximately 25 km.

Some of the towns along the Bollenstreek (particularly if you are in a car) are worth a little detour. The dunes of **Noordwijk** make it a popular seaside resort with a vast, sandy nature reserve almost as big as the bulb district itself. It is also the home of **Space Expo**, Europe's first permanent space exhibition for those with budding astronauts in the party. Part of the historic white church in **Noordwijkerhout** is made from the remains of a ship that dates from the year 1000. In **Sassenheim**, there is an imposing 13th-century ruined castle.

LISSE

27 km (17 mi) southwest of Amsterdam.

On arrival in Lisse in springtime, you will be in no doubt that this is the center of the Netherlands' biggest tourist attraction, with bumper-to-bumper tour buses and weaving cyclists overwhelming this provincial town. In the 17th century, like its neighbors Sassenheim and Hillegom, it was surrounded by country estates, of which just one remains (the rest were dug over for bulbs). The estate's former garden is the main attraction, but Kasteel Keukenhof (☎ *0252/750–690* ⊕ *www.kasteelkeukenhof.nl)* is also open to the public. If you want to include this in your visit, ring first to check opening times; you can only see inside by guided tour, for which you need a reservation. Another escape

The flower auction in Aalsmeer is put together by a cooperative of 6,000 flower farmers in the Netherlands.

from the crowds is the tower directly south of the gardens. 't Huys Dever (☎ 0252/411–430 ⊕ *www.kasteeldever.nl*) is an atmospheric 14th-century keep built by a knight and vassal of the Count of Holland.

GETTING HERE AND AROUND

By car from Amsterdam take the A4 in the direction of Schiphol and Den Hague, then take exit 4. Continue on the N207 to Lisse and follow the signs for the Keukenhof. Parking costs €6. You can buy a ticket in advance from the Web site (⊕ *www.keukenhof.nl*). Buses are available from Leiden Centraal (bus 54 aka "Keukenhof Express") or Haarlem (bus 50 or bus 51) or The Hague (bus 89). The most convenient route from central Amsterdam is from Schiphol Airport (bus 58). For bus departure times, call ☎ 0900/9292. Bicycles can be rented at a number of places including Haarlem railway station, Van Dam in Lisse outside the gardens, or you can hire a bike in Amsterdam and take it with you (the bike will also need a train ticket).

ORIENTATION

Lisse is a village with all sights close at hand, though you will want to arm yourself with a map for bicycle touring. There are few snacking opportunities out in the fields, so bear this in mind if you're cycling.

TIMING

Many visitors spend all day at Keukenhof though try not to spend any of it in a queue. Booking your ticket online or buying a combination bus/entrance ticket will save you time at the front desk.

ESSENTIALS

Bicycle Rentals Van Dam (✉ *Parkeerterrein De Keukenhof, Stationsweg 166a, Lisse* ☎ *06/1208–9858* ⊕ *www.rent-a-bikevandam.nl*)

Taxis **Taxi Direct ZH** (☎ 0172/740–909).

Visitor Information VVV Lisse
(✉ Grachtweg 53 ☎ 0252/414–262
⊕ www.vvvlisse.nl).

EXPLORING

Keukenhof. The 17-acre Keukenhof park and greenhouse complex
were founded in 1950 by Tom
van Waveren and other leading
bulb growers. It's one of the largest open-air flower exhibitions in
the world, and draws huge crowds
between the end of March and the
end of May. As many as 7 million
tulip bulbs bloom here every spring,
either in hothouses or flower beds

> ### THE FLOWER PARADE
>
> If you're visiting the Netherlands
> on the last Saturday in April, don't
> miss the annual **Bulb District
> Flower Parade**—known locally
> as the *Bloemencorso*. A series of
> extravagantly designed floats con-
> structed from millions of blooms,
> and accompanied by marching
> bands, parade along a 40-km (20-
> mi) route that extends from Noord-
> wijk and on to Sassenheim, Lisse,
> Hillegom, Bennebroek, Heemstede,
> and finally ends in Haarlem.

along the sides of a lake. In the last weeks of April (peak season) you
can catch tulips, daffodils, hyacinths, and narcissi all flowering simul-
taneously. In addition there are blooms on show in the pavilions along
with floral demonstrations and exhibitions about the history of tulips.
Leading Dutch bulb-growing exporters use it as a showcase for their latest hybrids, which unfortunately means that commercial, not creative,
forces are at play here. Some of the planting is of the rather gaudy tulip
varieties, and there's no holding back on the bulb-buying opportunities. It's a lovely—if squashed at times—wander around meandering
streams, placid pools, and paved paths. The avenues were designed by
Zocher, designer of the Vondelpark. Keukenhof's roots extend back to
the 15th century, when it was the herb farm (Keukenhof means "kitchen
courtyard") of one of Holland's richest ladies. Any sense of history has
almost been obliterated, though there is a historical garden recreating
the oldest botanical garden in the Netherlands in Leiden and at least
a nod to contemporary trends in the "Inspiration" section. Head for
the windmill for some calm and a vista over the surrounding fields, or
view the crowds from a distance with an hour-long boat tour (book this
inside the windmill). This is the Netherlands' most popular springtime
attraction, and it's easy to reach from all points of the country. Traveling independently rather than in an organized group should present no
problem—just follow the crowds. ✉ Lisse ☎ 0252/465–555 ⊕ www.
keukenhof.nl ⬚ €13.50 ⊙ Late Mar.–May, daily 8–7:30.

AALSMEER

13 km (8 mi) southwest of Amsterdam.

A small town bordered just north of Schiphol Airport, on the edge of
the Westeinder Plassen, it's no exaggeration to say this is one of the
flower capitals of the world, thanks to the auction that sells 37 million
flowers every day.

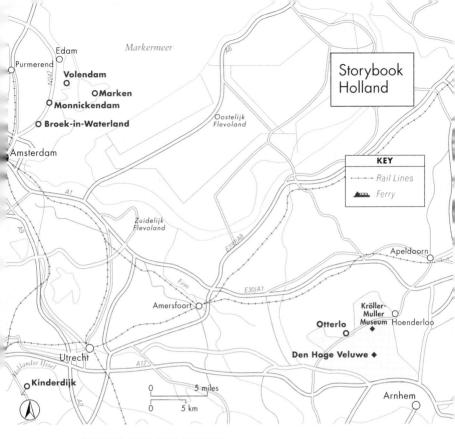

KEY

⊶ Rail Lines

🚢 Ferry

GETTING HERE AND AROUND

By car from Amsterdam from the A10 (ring) take the A4 in the direction of Den Haag, then exit 3 signposted Aalsmeer (N201). Follow signs for Bloemenveiling, and once inside the complex follow the route to the visitors' car park. For public transport, take bus 172 from Amsterdam Centraal (which also stops in Leidseplein) or bus 198 from Schiphol.

ESSENTIALS

Taxis **TCA Taxi Centraal Amsterdam** (☎ *020/677–7777*).

Visitor Information VVV Aalsmeer (Hollands Midden) (✉ *Drie Kolommenplein 1, Aalsmeer* ☎ *0297/325–374* ⊕ *www.vvvaalsmeer.nl*).

EXPLORING

Bloemenveiling FloraHolland. Five days a week from the predawn hours until midmorning, the largest flower auction in the world takes place in the biggest commercial building in the world—it's the size of 120 foot ball fields. You can watch the proceedings from the catwalk above as carts laden with flowers and plants zip about at warp speed. The buying system is what's called a Dutch auction—the price goes down, not up, on a large "clock" on the wall (though there are also Internet buyers these days). The buyers sit lecture-style with buzzers on their desks; the first to register a bid gets the bunch, and they work their way through

In the 17th and 18th centuries, Broek-in-Waterland was a popular place for merchants and seafarers from Amsterdam to live.

37 million buys daily. ✉ *Legmeerdijk 313, Aalsmeer* ☎ *0297/393–939* ⊕ *www.floraholland*.com ✉ *€5* ☉ *Weekdays 7–11*AM.

STORYBOOK HOLLAND

Much of the Netherlands is so picturesque that it's almost postcard perfect. Best of all, it's accessible. Tulips, castles, windy beaches, epic engineering feats that hold back the waters, you won't have to travel far to experience authentic landscape and sights. For the heritage-inclined, the folkloric villages of the Zuiderzee have an interesting story to tell. Volendam and Marken are sleepy little fishing ports lost in time, where boys can still be seen wearing Hans Brinker costumes and canal vistas recall ink sketches by Rembrandt.

BROEK-IN-WATERLAND

14 km (9 mi) northeast of Amsterdam. Follow route N247 and take exit S116 from the ring road.

The streets of this atmospheric Waterland village are lined with detached single-story 17th- and 18th-century houses, many painted a particular shade of gray. There are opportunities for lunch or picnics around a big lake that freezes in the winter, making it an excellent spot for watching (or participating in) a Dutch obsession: ice-skating.

GETTING HERE AND AROUND

By car from Amsterdam start on the S116, take the N247 (Nieuwe Leeuwarderweg), and follow signs to Broek-in-Waterland. There is no train station in Broek-in-Waterland, so from Amsterdam public transportation is by bus. The 110, 112, 116, 118 (Volendam/Edam), 111/115 (Marken/Monnickendam), 114 (Hoorn) all go through Amsterdam Centraal. You can buy a Waterland day ticket (Arriva) for €7.50 or a family day ticket for €12 (two adults, three children) and combine visits to several villages in this region in one day. This is a popular cycling trip suitable for enthusiastic eight-year-olds upwards. Take one of the free ferries behind Centraal Station that cross the IJ, and follow the signs.

> **BOAT RENTALS**
>
> When exploring various villages, go native and rent a canoe or a kayak from **Kano & Electro-boot Waterland** (✉ *Drs. J. van Disweg 4, Broek-in-Waterland* ☎ *020/403–3209*).

ORIENTATION

There are new and old bits, and when you cycle from Amsterdam, you need to go *through* the foot tunnel to reach the nicest part of the *dorp* (village) with the cafés and lake. At weekends in the summer, there's an entertaining ferry crossing to Holysloot.

TIMING

Broek-in-Waterland is less than a half hour by bus from Amsterdam Centraal so if you only have time for a quick trip, this is a very accessible and authentic option.

ESSENTIALS

Bicycle Rentals Wim Rijwiel-en Bromfietshandel (✉ *Laan 44, Broek-in-Waterland* ☎ *020/403–1462*).

Taxis Matthaei Taxi Nr 55 (✉ *Broek-in-Waterland* ☎ *06/4186–1824*).

EXPLORING

★ No 18th-century visitor on the Dutch leg of a grand tour would miss this picturesque, wealthy Waterland village where even the local grocer is called *Posch*. Broek-in-Waterland has a centuries-old reputation of being the cleanest town in all the Netherlands and everything is still immaculate. The village is full of pretty 17th- and 18th-century wooden houses built for merchants and farmers (83 of the houses have national historic status). Back in the day, the residents here amassed legendary fortunes. The 16th-century church is the burial place for Dutch East India Company businesswoman Neeltje Pater who left the enormous sum of 7 million guilders when she died in 1789. Today's inhabitants include media moguls and finance types. (Check out the superchic houseboats, with matching speedboats, on the dike leading into the village.) It's a charming step-back-in-time stroll around the village, where you can admire **De Kralentuinen,** the fine houses with hedges clipped into Baroque patterns and elaborate garden mosaics studded with antique blue glass beads. Hundreds of years ago, Dutch sea merchants used these beads to trade with primitive cultures for spices and other goods; the beads that were left over and brought back to Holland were used to decorate such gardens. There's an old-fashioned pancake house and a slightly funkier café for a spot of lunch or, if you prefer, bring a picnic. It's a lovely area to explore by boat, canoe, or kayak and you can rent all of them here. Potter round the **Havenrak**, the large lake which is popular with ice skaters in the winter, or go for a more extensive Waterland tour.

MONNICKENDAM

4.7 km (3 mi) north from Broek-in-Waterland, 16 km (10 mi) northeast of Amsterdam. Take Route N247.

This is a bustling little town without the full-on folkloric ex-fishing-village effect of its neighbors Marken and Volendam, but no less charming for that. Now a yachting base with an interesting mix of old and new and swanky vessels in the harbor, there are some good restaurants, a boutique hotel, and (not only tourist-kitsch) shopping opportunities. Its landmark is the Speeltoren with a carillon and (on-the-hour) galloping knights.

GETTING HERE AND AROUND

If you're driving from Amsterdam, take the S116, then the N247 (Nieuwe Leeuwarderweg), and follow signs to Monnickendam. It's a trip of 10–15 minutes. By bus it's a few minutes further from Broek-in-Waterland on the 110, 111, 114, or 116 from Amsterdam Centraal.

ORIENTATION

Get your bearings with a drink at the old weigh house, which is on the central canal, before heading for a stroll round the harbor. A recreational/camping zone (Hemmeland) with all kinds of water sports juts out into the Gouwzee.

TIMING

You can explore Monnickendam in a couple of hours or a little longer if you're looking to do some sailing or boating. In the summer months it is sometimes possible to travel to Marken on the oldest passenger ship (1887) in the Netherlands.

ESSENTIALS

Bicycle Rentals Ber Koning Tweewielers (⊠ *Noordeinde 12* ☎ *0299/651–26* ⊕ *www.berkoning.nl*).

Taxis Taxi Jado (☎ *0299/650–864* ⊕ *www.taxi-jado.com*).

EXPLORING

The historic town of Monnickendam owes its name to the monks who created a dam here in the 12th century. Granted city rights in 1355 and a prominent port by the 1660s, Monnickendam still has a large yacht harbor where swanky, spanking-new 125-foot trophy vessels (some of which are constructed here) bob alongside old Dutch sailing barges. The center of town is well preserved with narrow canals and bridges, cobbled streets, and pretty gabled houses. If you need a pit stop, take a table under the portico of the 17th-century weigh house, which is now an elegant café and restaurant. Even if you get lost as you stroll about, you won't lose track of time. Every quarter of an hour, the mellifluous bells of the Speeltoren ring out, and on the hour are accompanied by knights-on-horseback galloping round the clockwork under the watchful gaze of a female angel. The bells are part of the oldest (1597) carillon in the world and on Saturdays at 11 AM, a carillonneur climbs the ladders inside the narrow tower to give a recital. The 16th-century tower is attached to the former town hall (dating from 1764), which is now home to the **Museum De Speeltoren**, where you can view a collection of decorative blue-and-white tiles and majolica, historical artifacts, exhibits, and films on local history. You can also inquire here about walking tours—almost every building has an interesting history: one house was a hiding place for Jews during World War II. ✉ *Noordeinde 4* ☎ *0299/652–203* ⊕ *www.despeeltoren.nl/* 🎫 *€1.50.*

> ### WORD OF MOUTH
>
> "Biking in Amsterdam was AWESOME. We rented great bikes from the Marriott for 12 euros a day. The first day we went to a market then got a bike map from MacBike and took the ferry behind the train station and headed through the countryside for a 20-mile ride to Marken." —Jeff

MARKEN

8.9 km (6 mi) east of Monnickendam, 16 km (10 mi) northeast of Amsterdam. Take Route N518.

The former island of Marken was once an isolated fishing village, but today it's filled with sightseers riding over the causeway to view the characteristic green-and-white wooden houses built on piles.

GETTING HERE

From Amsterdam by car and on the S116, go through the IJ tunnel and take the N247 (Nieuwe Leeuwarderweg) and follow signs to Marken. Marken has no railway station so from Amsterdam take the 111 bus from Amsterdam Centraal. The Marken Express ferry travels between Marken and Volendam. You can board it at either harbor. It's also possible to arrange a boat tour or charter from Volendam. Visit the local VVV for further details.

ORIENTATION

This little triangular peninsula is well signposted. The lighthouse facing the sea that marks the furthest point was built in 1839.

TIMING

An hour or so may be enough in high season if you are not fond of crowds. During off-season, Marken's bleakness is impressive.

ESSENTIALS

Bicycle Rentals Fietsverhuur Marken (✉ *Marken* ☎ *06/4230–5828* ⊕ *www. dagjemarken.com*).

EXPLORING

The tidal wave that hit the Netherlands in 1916 was a defining factor in the decision to drain the Zuiderzee, but with the construction of the enclosing dam (Afsluitdijk), traditional Dutch fishing villages like Marken lost their livelihood. Heritage tourism has now taken over on this former island (a causeway to the mainland was built in 1957) that, despite the busloads of visitors, retains its charm. Many of the green-and-white gabled homes are built on timber piles, dating from when the Zuiderzee used to flood, and a maritime past is revealed in the sober Calvinist church (1904) with its hanging herring boats and lugger. There is a *klompen* (clog) maker, and *kleding* (dress) shop that includes designs dating from the 1300s, some of which are worn today. The floral chintzes are inspired by the Dutch East Indies, and the caps, in particular, are incredibly intricate. The full folkloric effect can be viewed in the films showing at the local museum.

The intimate **Marker Museum** consists of six former smokehouses (where the smoke left in a hole in the ceiling rather than a chimney) with exhibits showing the past and present life of Marken. You can see how a fisherman's family lived until about 1932. ✉ *Kerkbuurt 44–47* ☎ *0299/601–904* ⊕ *www.markermuseum.nl* 💶 *€2.50* ⏱ *Apr.–Nov. daily 10–5; Sun. noon–4.*

VOLENDAM

6.7 km (4 mi) northwest of Marken, 18 km (11½ mi) northeast of Amsterdam. Take Routes N247–N517.

Volendam once had the largest fleet of ships in the Zuiderzee and it was a star destination on the tours of American Express and Thomas Cook. In the late 19th and early 20th centuries, a colony of artists holed up at the Hotel Spaander—now a charming three-star Best Western—and left a legacy of 1,000 artworks. Tourism is more important than fishing these days, although a number of places sell smoked eel and other fishy delicacies. If you arrive at Volendam by boat (the best way to go), you will alight at the main drag full of restaurants and shops and places to have your photo taken in traditional costume. On high days and holidays, you may see the real thing as residents stroll around in traditional dress immortalized by Dutch dolls the world over. The men wear dark, baggy pantaloons fastened with silver guilders instead of buttons, striped vests, and dark jackets with caps. Women wear long, dark skirts covered with striped aprons and blouses with elaborately hand-embroidered floral panels. Their coral necklaces and famous winged lace caps complete the picture. Of course, everyone wears *klompen*.

GETTING HERE AND AROUND
Drive through the IJ tunnel on S116 and take N247 to Marken and Monnickendam. Buses 110, 112, 116, or 118 leave from Amsterdam Centraal. Once here, you'll be hard-pressed to find rental bikes.

ORIENTATION
The harbor front where the Marken Express docks is superbusy, but there are some quieter streets for wandering off the trinket-packed main drag—the *dijk* (dike). The tourist office is tucked behind here on Zeestraat next to the museum.

TIMING
After eating some smoked eel, enjoying a photo op in traditional costume, and visiting the museum, you'll probably be ready to head back in a couple of hours.

Volendam is built on a patch of reclaimed land that used to be the harbor of nearby Edam. The original spelling of the name Vollendam literally meant something like "filled dam."

ESSENTIALS

Taxis TCV Taxi Centraal Volendam (☎ 0299/323–344).

Visitor information VVV Volendam (✉ Zeestraat 37, Volendam ☎ 0299–363747 ⊕ www.vvv-volendam.nl).

EXPLORING

You can learn about Volendam's history at the **Volendams Museum**, next to the VVV, which has reconstructed rooms, such as a school filled with mannequins adorned with folkloric costumes; there's even a photograph of Josephine Baker clad in traditional garb! ✉ Zeestraat 41, Volendam ☎ 0299/369–258 ⊕ www.volendams-museum.com 🎫 €2.50 ⊙ Mar.–Dec., daily 10–5.

★ **Kaasboerderij Alida Hoeve** is a working cheese farm where you can learn how cheese is made, and purchase various cheeses. ✉ Zeddeweg 1, Volendam ☎ 0299/365–830 🎫 Free ⊙ Daily 8:30–6.

KINDERDIJK

55 km (34 mi) southwest of Amsterdam.

The camera doesn't lie when it comes to Kinderdijk, and the virtual tour on the Web site gives you a clear idea of exactly what to expect. Touristy, but unquestionably romantic.

GETTING HERE AND AROUND

It is a bit of a trek (2½ hours) from Amsterdam, and there are a number of ways to go. The most straightforward route is to head for Rotterdam Zuid on the train. From there, take the metro to Rotterdam Zuidplein, then bus 154 to Albasserdam. By car, Kinderdijk is 20 km (12½mi) from Rotterdam. Follow directions to Rotterdam, then take A15 to exit 22. There are (small) car parks by the mills. Waterbus (⊕ *www. waterbus.nl*) runs a fast ferry service from the Erasmusbrug in Rotterdam to Ridderkerk (line 1), and then you change onto another ferry (line 3) to pop across to Kinderdijk.

Ferries are every half hour and it takes about half an hour. Other tour boats are available from Rotterdam, and there is also (a pricey) water taxi or helicopter tour.

TIMING

If the weather is fine, take along a picnic and make a day of it.

EXPLORING

★ The sight of the 19 windmills at **Kinderdijk** under sail is magnificently, romantically impressive. Not surprisingly, this is one of the most visited places in the Netherlands and on the UNESCO World Heritage list. These are water-pumping mills whose job was to drain water from the Alblasserwaard polder enclosed by the rivers Noord and Lek—a function now performed by the 1950 pumping station with its humongously sized water screws, which you pass on the way to the site. The somewhat chocolate-boxy name (which means "child's dike") comes from a legend involving a baby who washed up here in a cradle after the great floods of 1421, with a cat sitting on its tummy to keep them both from tumbling out.

These windmills date back to 1740. Just 150 years ago 10,000 windmills were in operation across the country, but today only 1,000 remain. These have been saved from the wrecking ball thanks to the help of heritage organizations. The windmills are open in rotation, so there is always one interior to visit. A walk through a working windmill gives fascinating insight into how the millers and their families lived. The mills are under sail from 2 PM to 5 PM on the first Saturday in May and June, then every Saturday in July and August. Throughout the second week in September the mills are illuminated at night, really pulling out the tourist stops. You can walk around the mills area whenever you like, so it's a great way to spend a leisurely afternoon. There are a couple of cafés for snacks, but if the weather is good bring a picnic. ⊠ *Molenkade, Kinderdijk* ☎ *078/691-5179* 🗐 *Interior of mill €3.00* ⊙ *Interior Apr.–Oct., daily 9:30–5:30.*

OTTERLO/DE HOGE VELUWE

78 km (49 mi) southeast of Amsterdam, 20 km (13 mi) south of Apeldoorn, 35 km (22 mi) southeast of Amersfoort.

When German heiress Hélène Müller married Dutch industrialist Anton Kröller at the turn of the 20th century, their combined wealth and complementary tastes were destined to give pleasure to generations to come. She loved art and could afford to collect it; he bought up land

CLOSE UP

Holding the Waters at Bay

There's a good reason the Dutch countryside looks as it does, crisscrossed by canals and dikes, and dotted with more than 1,000 windmills. Those picturesque mills used to serve a vital role in keeping everyone's feet dry. About a quarter of the land, including most of the Randstad, lies below sea level, and without major human intervention, large swathes of the Netherlands would either be underwater, or uninhabitable swamp. Just think, when you land at Schiphol—the name, "ship's hole," is a clue—you should be about 20 feet below the surf.

The west coast has always been protected by high dunes, but the rest of the land had to take its chances for centuries. The first to begin the fight against the sea were early settlers who built mounds in the north of the country around 500 BC, and the battle has continued ever since. Real progress was made around AD 1200 when dikes began appearing. In the 14th century, canals were dug, and the first windmills

were built to pump the water off the land (a job now done by electric pumps). This transformed the fertile alluvial landscape, turning it into a farmer's paradise.

War on nature has waged ever since, as Holland gradually clawed back territory, by closing off the Zuiderzee inland sea in 1932 to form the Ijssel Lake, and by a century-long land reclamation program of polder building. The sea bit back with a vengeance one wintry night in 1953. On January 31 that year, a combination of exceptionally high tides and strong winds sent a storm surge pouring up the Rhine delta, killing around 2,000 and inundating 1,000 square miles of land.

Dutch engineers vowed this disaster would never be repeated. They responded by constructing an extensive network of river mouth by building the Delta Works (⇨ see Rotterdam, Chapter 8 or www.deltawerken.nl), one of the great engineering feats of the 20th century.

in Gelderland and eventually created a foundation to maintain it as a national park, building a museum to house the fruits of their expensive and discriminating taste. Today you can wander through the vast forests, heath, dunes, and moors of the Hoge Veluwe National Park, Kröller's land, and see the descendants of the wild boar and deer with which he stocked the estate. Or you can visit the world-famous museum in the middle of the park, established by Hélène and containing one of the best collections of Van Goghs in the world, as well as an excellent selection of late-19th-century and modern art. Additionally, you can visit the philanthropists' own house and hunting lodge. Children can caper about the largest sculpture garden in Europe, and the whole family can pick up one of the free bikes that are available in the park and trundle off down wooded lanes. (Note that Otterlo is only one entrance of several to the Hoge Veluwe, but it is widely considered the main gateway to the park.)

GETTING HERE AND AROUND
There are bus services from Apeldoorn and Ede/Wageningen throughout the year with bus stops in the center and by the museum. Take bus 108 (from either station) to Hoenderloo, then bus 106 to Otterlo,

which stops inside the park. From then on, you can travel by free white bicycle. By car, take the A1, A12, or A50, following signs for "Park Hoge Veluwe." There are 1,700 free white bicycles available for use inside the park, and there are versions with child seats or smaller bikes for children. Rental and cargo bikes, bikes modified for visitors with a disability, tandems, wheelchair bikes, tricycles, or electric cycles are also available but need to be booked in advance.

ORIENTATION

There are three entrances to the Park: at Otterlo (Houtkamperweg 9), Hoenderloo (Houtkamperweg 13), and at Schaarsbergen (Koningsweg 17). There are car parks by the museums, in the central area, or by the entrances to the park.

TIMING

This extensive territory with several sights is well worth a whole day.

ESSENTIALS

Bicycle Rentals (✉ *reserveringen@hogeveluwe.nl*).

Taxis Apeldoornse Taxi Service (☎ *055/533-3906*).

EXPLORING

Hoge Veluwe. Once the private property of the Kröller-Müller family, this is now the largest national park in Holland. It covers 13,300 acres of forest and grassland, moors, and sand dunes, where it is possible to stroll freely, apart from a few areas reserved for wildlife. The traditional hunting grounds of the Dutch royal family, it is populated with red deer, boar, roes, mouflons (wild sheep), and many birds; it is also filled with towering pines and hardwood trees, dotted with small villages (**Hoge Soeren,** near Apeldoorn, is particularly charming), and laced with paths for cars, bicycles, and walkers, more than 42 km (27 mi) of which are specifically designated for bicycling. Indeed, there are 1,700 white bicycles at your disposal here, free to use with the price of entrance (available at the entrances to the park, at the visitor center, De Koperen Kop restaurant, and at the Kröller-Müller museum; return them to any bike rack when you are finished).

There is a landlocked, always shifting sand dune to marvel at; the world's first museum of all things that live (or have lived) underground; plus an old hunting lodge beside a pond that provides a nice stopping place. At the heart of the park is the visitor center (**Bezoekers Centrum**), which contains exhibits on the park and an observation point for game-watching. **Jachthuis Sint Hubertus** (St. Hubert Hunting Lodge) was the private home and hunting lodge of the Kröller-Müllers, a monumental house planned in the shape of antlers, built between 1914 and 1920 by Dutch architect H. P. Berlage around the legend of St. Hubert, the patron saint of hunters. Rooms with Art Deco furniture follow in sequence from dark to light, representing Hubert's spiritual development and path of enlightenment from agnostic to saint. Free guided tours of the lodge, which is still used as a residence for visiting dignitaries, may be arranged at the park entrance only.

Inside the visitor's center is Museonder, an underground museum, offering visitors a fascinating look at life below the surface, including a

simulated earthquake. A campsite at the Hoenderloo entrance is open from April to late October (☎ *055/378–2232*), and there are four restaurants in the park: the stylish Rijzenburg, at the Schaarsbergen entrance (☎ *026/443–6733*); De Koperen Kop, a self-service restaurant in the center of the park opposite the visitor center (☎ *031/859–1289*); Café Monsieur Jacques at the Kröller-Müller Museum; and a kiosk near the Jachthuis (open only in summer). The best opportunity for game-watching is at the end of the afternoon and toward evening, and park officials advise that you stay in your car when you spot any wildlife. Special observation sites are signified by antlers on the maps provided at the entrances. ⊠ *Entrances at Hoenderloo, Otterlo, and Schaarsbergen* ☎ *0900/464–3835 at €0.20 per min* ⊕ *www.hogeveluwe.nl* 🖃 *€7.50 cars €6* ⊗ *Nov.–Mar., daily 9–6; Apr., daily 8–8; May and Aug., daily 8–9; June and July, daily 8–10; Sept., daily 9–8; Oct., daily 9–7.*

Fodor's Choice **Kröller-Müller Museum.** This ranks as the third-most-important museum
★ of art in the Netherlands, after the Rijksmuseum and the Vincent van Gogh Museum in Amsterdam. Opened in 1938, it is the repository of a remarkable private collection of late-19th-century and early-20th-century paintings, the nucleus of which are 91 paintings and 175 works on paper by Van Gogh (about 50 of which rotate on display at any given time) that, when combined with the collection in the Amsterdam museum, constitutes nearly four-fifths of his entire oeuvre. Hélène Kröller, née Müller, had a remarkable eye as well as a sixth sense about which painters created art for the ages and through her family firm, run by her husband, the means to bankroll it.

But Hélène Kröller-Müller was not myopic in her appreciation and perception. She augmented her collection of Van Goghs with works by Georges Seurat, Pable Picasso, Odile Redon, Georges Braque, and Piet Mondriaan. The museum also contains 16th- and 17th-century Dutch paintings, ceramics, Chinese and Japanese porcelains, and contemporary sculpture. The building itself, designed by Henry van de Velde, artfully brings nature into the galleries through its broad windows, glass walkways, and patios. The gardens and woods around the museum form a stunning open-air gallery, the largest in Europe with a collection of 20th-century sculptures that include works by Auguste Rodin, Richard Serra, Barbara Hepworth, Alberto Giacometti, and Jean Dubuffet. There is a gift shop and self-service restaurant on-site. ⊠ *Houtkampweg 6, in Hoge Veluwe National Park, Otterlo* ☎ *0318/591–241* ⊕ *www. kmm.nl* 🖃 *Park and museum €15* ⊗ *Park and museum Tues.–Sun. 10–5; sculpture garden closes at 4:30.*

Nederlands Tegelmuseum. See and buy is the plan at the Nederlands Tegelmuseum *(Netherlands Tile Museum)*, where Dutch tiles from as far back as the 13th century, including those old Dutch standbys, Makkum and Delft, are displayed in a former summerhouse in the village of Otterlo, not far from the Hoge Veluwe. For those with a decorative eye, the tiles for purchase in the gift shop will be irresistible. ⊠ *Eikenzoom 12, Otterlo* ☎ *0318/591–519* ⊕ *www.nederlandstegelmuseum.nl* 🖃 *€2.75* ⊗ *Tues.–Fri. 10–5, weekends 1–5.*

The Randstad

HAARLEM, THE HAGUE, DELFT, ROTTERDAM, AND UTRECHT

WORD OF MOUTH

"I love, love Delft!! It is just big enough that you can wander around (especially in late afternoon after the day-trippers leave) without fear of getting lost. I love its quaintness, its peacefulness, its picturesque canals! We are going back in October!"

—JoyC

WELCOME TO RANDSTAD

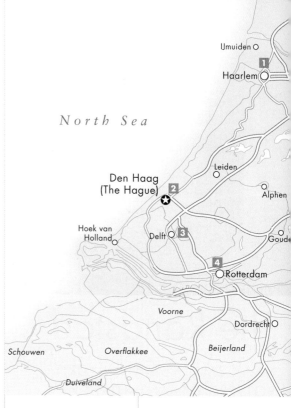

TOP REASONS TO GO

★ **Paintings, paintings, paintings:** See the old masters in Haarlem's Frans Hals Museum. Marvel at Vermeer's *Girl with a Pearl Earring* in The Hague's Mauritshuis, and visit his hometown of Delft to see where he found his muse. Or make yourself bug-eyed deciphering the graphic puzzles in The Hague's Escher in Het Paleis Museum.

★ **The views:** Climb Utrecht's Domtoren—the Netherlands' tallest church tower. Or take the elevator up Rotterdam's Euromast, the country's highest observation deck, for a bird's-eye view of Europe's busiest harbor.

★ **Old-world charm:** Wander Delft's canal-lined medieval streets—Amsterdam in miniature. And step into history in The Hague, inside the 13th-century Knights' Hall.

★ **Holland in half an hour:** Visit the miniature world of the Madurodam in The Hague, and teach kids all about the Netherlands in 30 minutes.

1 Haarlem. Just 20 minutes from Amsterdam, this city drips as much history as its illustrious neighbor. Dominated by the imposing hulk of the Great Church, many of its quiet cobbled streets have changed little since painter Frans Hals held court here.

2 The Hague. The center of Dutch government is more elegant and restrained than Amsterdam, with fewer canals but more tree-lined boulevards. The astonishing collection of masterpieces in the Mauritshuis would be reason enough to visit, but is just one in a string of fascinating museums and galleries.

GETTING ORIENTED

The towns and cities of the Randstad are all within easy reach of Amsterdam, and can be visited on day trips, for overnight stays, or incorporated into a circular tour. Rotterdam lies farthest from Amsterdam, yet is still only 73 km (45 mi) to the south, and little more than an hour away by train or car.

8

3 Delft. With long canal-lined streets and medieval houses, Delft is like a scaled-down version of Amsterdam, without the hectic pace of capital city life. It's easy to understand how Johannes Vermeer found such inspiration here.

4 Rotterdam. Rebuilt almost from scratch following the devastation of World War II, Europe's biggest port has worked hard to transform itself into a showpiece of modern architecture. By contrast, the historic area of Delfshaven—from where the Pilgrim Fathers set sail for their New England—escaped intact.

5 Utrecht. The Netherlands' highest church tower, the Domtoren, looks down majestically over twisting medieval streets, while the Oude Gracht canal offers a rare chance to stroll along a double-layered towpath.

By Tim Skelton   The towns and cities of Zuid-Holland (South Holland) and Utrecht provinces cluster around Amsterdam like filings round the end of a magnet. Each has prospered and grown independently, and today their borders virtually overlap one another to such an extent that the region is now dubbed the *Randstad* (Border City), because locals consider it one mammoth megalopolis.

A quarter of Holland's 16 million residents live within 80 km (50 mi) of the capital. Chief among these peripheral cities, The Hague is often seen as a little aloof—it *is*, after all, Holland's seat of government and home to the Dutch royal family and the International Court of Justice. Yet behind the pomp and stuffiness is a lively metropolis that is both elegant and quirky, filled with grand 17th century mansions and more than 25 public parks. The Hague's official name *'s-Gravenhage* (literally "the Count's Hedge"), harks back to the 13th century when the Count of Holland had a hunting lodge here. But to the Dutch it is always known simply as Den Haag, and that's what you'll hear on the streets.

Among the other cities of the Randstad, Rotterdam is the industrial center of the entire country, and also the world's largest port. Contrasting with the quaintness of many other Dutch towns, it is brash, forward-looking, multicultural, and home to some of Europe's most dazzling modern architecture. The imposing, futuristic skyline—being added to every year—has led to it being dubbed by some as Manhattan-on-the-Maas. That may seem a little far-fetched to anyone who has seen the real Manhattan, but skyscrapers are more plentiful here than anywhere else in the generally low-rise Netherlands.

Elsewhere, the past is more in evidence. You can pursue the ghost of Frans Hals through the Golden Age streets of Haarlem; explore the time-stained center of Utrecht; and wander through the ancient cobbled streets of Delft, which once colored the world blue. In fact, although the area is small enough to drive through in an afternoon, it would take you weeks to explore fully.

Whereas Amsterdam tends to pander to the demands of tourists, this is the beating heart of the Netherlands where the "real" people live. And it's all the more fascinating for that.

PLANNING

WHEN TO GO

This part of Holland is at its best in late spring or early autumn. High summer means too many visitors, and touring in winter often puts you at the mercy of the weather (bring your umbrella year-round). For flora lovers, mid- to late April is ideal for a trip around Haarlem, as the fields are bright with spring bulbs. Many restaurants are closed Sunday (also Monday); museums tend to close Monday.

If you're into the arts, you might prefer to schedule your trip to catch one of the area's two world-renowned festivals: the International Film Festival Rotterdam, where 300 noncommercial films are screened in late January and early February, and the Festival Oude Muziek (Festival of Early Music), where 150 concerts are held in venues across Utrecht in late August. Jazz lovers will want to time their arrival in Rotterdam to coincide with the North Sea Jazz Festival, which takes place over three days in mid-July.

GETTING AROUND

Unless you want to make a detailed exploration of the Dutch country-side, you may find it more convenient and less stressful to leave your car behind when touring the Randstad. The region is crossed by a dense network of freeways, but these are frequently clogged with commuter traffic and often grind to a halt at peak times. Avoid the jams by hopping on a train, which is the cheap, convenient, and usually reliable way to get around. *Every city in this chapter is connected to Amsterdam (and most to each other) by direct services that run at least twice each hour throughout the day.* Rotterdam, The Hague, Utrecht, and Delft have hourly train service to Amsterdam all night.

Taxis are available at the railway stations. Alternatively, to get one to collect you from your location, try one of the taxi firms recommended in this chapter or by the tourism bureau. You can't hail cabs in the street.

BY BIKE

In this flat land, a bicycle is an ideal means of getting around, and cities have safe cycle lanes on busy roads. Bikes are best rented at outlets near all major railway stations, usually called a **Rijwiel** shop or a **Fietspoint**. These shops are generally open long hours every day, and the bikes are invariably new and well maintained. Rates are €6.50–€8.40 a day, and you must show ID and pay a deposit of €50. Cheaper bikes have back-pedal brakes and no gears. Other local rental centers can be found in the regional *Gouden Gids* (Yellow Pages), under *Fietsen en Bromfietsen*.

ABOUT THE RESTAURANTS

Although this area of Holland is home to some of the country's most worldly restaurants, keep in mind that most bars also offer house specials whose prices are usually cheap enough to keep students and young people sated (keep an eye out for the *kleine kaart,* or lighter meal menu,

8

usually offered in the bar area and available throughout the day). Perennially popular dishes such as satay and pepper steak never come off the menu.

ABOUT THE HOTELS

Hotels in the Randstad range from elegant canal houses to cross-country chains with anonymous décor. Most large towns have one or more deluxe hotels that exceed all expectations. Accommodation in Rotterdam and The Hague—big convention and business cities—is at a premium, so book well in advance, although the situation is usually not as tight as it is in Amsterdam. Finding somewhere to stay in the other cities is generally less of a problem. The VVVs (tourist offices) in the region have extensive accommodation listings, and can book your reservations. Assume all rooms have air-conditioning, TV, telephones, and private bath, unless otherwise noted. Assume hotels operate on the EP meal plan (with no meals) unless stated otherwise.

WHAT IT COSTS IN EUROS				
¢	$	$$	$$$	$$$$
Restaurants	under €10	€10–€15	€15–€22	€22–€30	over €30
Hotels	under €75	€75–€120	€120–€165	€165–€230	over €230

Restaurant prices are per person for a main course only. Hotel prices are for a standard double room in high season.

SAFETY

The Netherlands is one of the safest places you'll ever visit. Still, in crowded intersections and dark alleys, it is always best to be streetwise and take double safety precautions; it may be best to keep your money in a money belt and not flaunt your expensive camera. Be especially wary of pickpockets in crowds and while riding the tram. And use common sense when going out at night. Keep to well-lighted areas and take a taxi if you are going a long distance. Although it is easy to lose yourself in a romantic 18th-century haze taking a midnight stroll along the canals, remember that muggings do very occasionally occur. Late at night, it may be best to keep to the main thoroughfares and not venture down deserted streets.

VISITOR INFORMATION

Each VVV (tourist board) across the country has information principally on its own town and region. Contact the VVV of the area you plan to travel to, and ask directly for information, as there is no one central office.

HAARLEM

A breath of fresh air just a short train ride, but a million miles, from throbbing downtown Amsterdam. Walking past the charming *hofjes* (historic almshouse courtyards), and between the redbrick gabled facades lining Haarlem's historic streets, it is easy to feel you have been transported back to the Netherlands' Golden Age of the 17th century.

This is especially true around the central market square, where the vast hulking form of Sint Bavo's (the Great Church) dominates the city skyline and evokes a bygone era. In fact, the intrusive motorized transport apart, much of Frans Hals' hometown appears unchanged for centuries. Indeed, many of the often-narrow ancient streets of the old center have remained residential and are quiet even through the middle of the day. Yet despite its many picturesque monuments and rich supply of fascinating museums, Haarlem isn't a city rooted in the past. It is home to a lively population of students—often the overspill who can't find lodgings in Amsterdam or Leiden—who bring with them a youthful vibrancy, especially at night. With hotel accommodation generally a better value and easier to come by than in nearby Amsterdam, and the city being on a compact and manageable scale, many travelers also end up staying here and using the city as a base from which to explore the surrounding region. In spring it is an easy hop from here to the Keukenhof gardens and the flower fields of the Bollenstreek Route. And with its close proximity to the dunes and the seaside resort of Zandvoort, Haarlem also attracts hordes of beach-going Amsterdammers and Germans every summer. The result is an intoxicating mix of old and new that makes the town well worth checking out.

GETTING HERE AND AROUND
20 km (12 mi) west of Amsterdam, 41 km (26 mi) north of The Hague.

Getting to Haarlem by rail is a simple matter. Around six trains make the 15-minute trip from Amsterdam's Centraal Station every hour

during the day. Seat reservations aren't permitted. Driving will take around 20–25 minutes—you'll need to head west out of Amsterdam on the N200/A200. If you have the energy, you can bike.

The center of Haarlem is compact and easy to navigate on foot, but there are plentiful buses if you need them. You can use an **OV-chipkaart** (public transport chip card)— a new electronic payment system that's been slowly rolled out nationally. These credit card–size tickets can be loaded up with credit from machines in the railway and metro stations, and are debited as you board and leave trains, trams, metros, and buses. There are information and sales points in the station. Or visit www.ov-chipkaart.nl for more information. The OV-chipkaart will eventually replace all other transport tickets, including the national *strippenkaart*, but at this writing no date for the phaseout in Haarlem had been set.

Public Transportation Information (☎ 0900/9292).

TOURS

City walking tours of Haarlem are often sold as part of a combined package by Amsterdam tour operators, and include visits to the bulb fields when these are in season (spring). City walks can also be organized by the VVV in Haarlem and cost €79.50 per guide, for up to 25 people.

TIMING

At a push, you could cover the main sights of Haarlem in half a day, but take a full day to do everything justice and to enjoy a relaxing break on the grand market square (*Grote Markt*).

ESSENTIALS

Bicycle Rentals De Wolkenfietser (✉ *Van Ostadestraat 10zw* ☎ *023/532–5577*). **Fietspoint Pieters** (✉ *Haarlem Station* ☎ *023/531–7066*).

Emergency Services National Emergency Alarm Number (☎ *112 for police, fire, and ambulance*).

Hospitals Spaarne Ziekenhuis (✉ *Spaarnepoort 1, Hoofddorp* ☎ *023/890–8900*).

Taxis Taxi Centrale (☎ *023/540–4088*).

Tourism Information VVV Haarlem (✉ *Verwulft 11,* ☎ *0900/616–1600*).

EXPLORING

Haarlem is a compact city and easy to cover on foot. From the main railway station it is about five minutes' walk south to the Grote Markt. The Frans Hals Museum is another five minutes beyond that.

TOP ATTRACTIONS

⑤ De Hallen *(The Halls)*. A branch of the Frans Hals Museum, De Hallen has an extensive collection, with the works of Dutch Impressionists and Expressionists, including sculpture, textiles, and ceramics, as well as paintings and graphics. The complex consists of two buildings—the Vleeshal and the Verweyhal House.

The **Vleeshal** (Meat Market) building is one of the most interesting cultural legacies of the Dutch Renaissance, with a fine sweep of stepped gables that seems to pierce the scudding clouds. It was built in 1602–03 by Lieven de Key, Haarlem's master builder. The ox heads that look down from the facade are reminders of the building's original function: it was the only place in Haarlem where meat could be sold, and the building was used for that sole purpose until 1840. Today it is used for exhibitions—generally works of modern and contemporary art, usually by local artists. Note the early landscape work by Piet Mondriaan, *Farms in Duivendrecht,* so different from his later De Stijl shapes.

The **Verweyhal Gallery of Modern Art** was built in 1879 as a gentlemen's club, originally named *Trou moet Blijcken* (Loyalty Must Be Proven). The building now bears the name of native Haarlem artist Kees Verwey, who died in 1995. It is used as an exhibition space for selections from the Frans Hals Museum's enormous collection of modern and contemporary art. In addition to the works of Kees Verwey, the exhibition covers such artists as Jacobus van Looy, Jan Sluijters, Leo Gestel, Herman Kruyder, and Karel Appel. Note, too, a fine collection of contemporary ceramics. ⊠ *Grote Markt 16* ☎ *023/511-5775* ⊕ *www. dehallenhaarlem.nl* ⌧*€5* ⊗ *Tues.–Sat. 11–5, Sun. noon–5.*

> ### WHICH WAY TO GO?
>
> If you arrive by train, take a good look around before you leave the railway station—it's a fabulous Art Nouveau building dating from 1908. Next, head down Jansweg (to the left of the station as you exit) for several blocks, over the Nieuwe Gracht canal and into the city center. It will take you right to the Grote Markt.

⑨ Frans Hals Museum. Named after the celebrated man himself, this not-to-be-missed museum holds a collection of amazingly virile and lively group portraits by the Golden Age painter, depicting the merrymaking civic guards and congregating regents for which he became world famous. The building itself is one of the town's smarter hofjes: an entire block of almshouses grouped around an attractive courtyard. In the 17th century this was a home for elderly men, an *oudemannenhuis*. The cottages now form a sequence of galleries for paintings, period furniture, antique silver, and ceramics. But the focal point is the collection of 17th-century paintings that includes the works of Frans Hals and other masters of the Haarlem School.

Fodor's Choice ★

Many of the works on display represent Hals at his jovial best—for instance, the *Banquet of the Officers of the Civic Guard of St. Adrian* (1624–27) or the *Banquet of the Officers of the St. George Militia* (1616), where the artist cunningly allows for the niceties of rank (captains are more prominent than sergeants, and so on down the line)

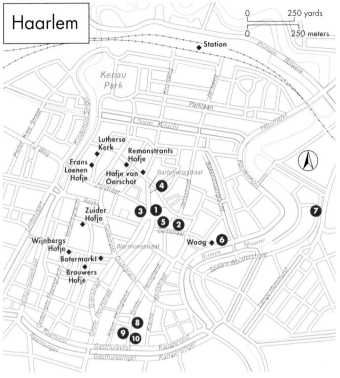

as well as emotional interaction: he was also the first painter to have people gaze and laugh at each other in these grand portraits.

As respite from nearly 250 canvases, step into the museum's courtyard—lovely, and planted with formal-garden baby hedges, of which you get only fleeting glimpses as you work your way through the galleries (most of the blinds are shut against the sunlight to protect the paintings). In one room, with curtains drawn for extra protection, is **Sara Rothè's Dolls' House**; nearby is an exquisitely crafted miniature version of a merchant's canal house. On leaving, *View of Haarlem* (1655) by Nicolaes Hals, Frans's son, bids you good-bye. ⊠ *Groot Heiligland 62* ☎ *023/511–5775* ⊕ *www.franshalsmuseum.com* 🖂 *€7.50* ⊙ *Tues.–Sat. 11–5, Sun. noon–5.*

🔟 **Gasthuis-huisjes** *(Guesthouse–little houses)*. Don't miss this series of houses with their identical step gables at the southern end of Groot Heiligland, across the street from the entrance to the Frans Hals Museum. They originally formed part of the St. Elizabeth hospital and were built in 1610.

❷ **Grote Kerk** *(Great Church)*. Late Gothic Sint Bavo's, more commonly called the Great Church, dominates the main market square. It was built in the 14th century, but severe fire damage in 1370 led to a further 150 years of rebuilding and expansion. This is the burial place

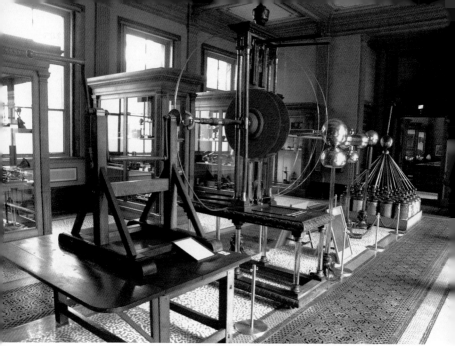
Teylers Museum is the first and oldest musuem in the Netherlands.

of Frans Hals—a lamp marks his tombstone behind the brass choir screen. Laurens Coster is buried here, too. It is rumored that he was the first European to use movable type in 1423 (sorry, Gutenberg), which he discovered while carving letters for his children; he was inspired when one of the bark letters fell into the sand and made an imprint. The church is the home of the Müller organ, on which both Handel and Mozart played. Installed in 1738, and for centuries considered the finest in the world, it has been meticulously restored to protect the sound planned by its creator, Christian Müller. Between May and October organists perform free concerts every Tuesday at 8:15 PM, and occasionally on Thursday at 3 PM. Bach fugues have never sounded so magisterial. ⊠ *Grote Markt* ☎ *023/533–2040* ⊕ *www.bavo.nl* 🎫 *€2* 🕐 *Mon.–Sat. 10–4.*

❶ **Grote Markt**. Around this great market square the whole of Dutch architecture can be traced in a chain of majestic buildings ranging from the 14th to the 19th century (with a smile and a little bravado, you can enter most of them for a quick look), but it is the imposing mass of Sint Bavo's that catches the eye and towers over everything.

QUICK
BITES

The spacious **Grand Café Brinkmann** (⊠ *Brinkmannpassage 41* ☎ *023/532–3111*), adorned with cherubic ceiling paintings, offers baguettes, pancakes, and other light snacks. Windows edged with Art Deco stained glass—which became all the shinier after refurbishing work in 2010—overlook the Grote Markt and Sint Bavo's church across the square.

6 **Teylers Museum**. Just north of the **Waag** (the Weigh House, itself now a pleasant little café)—built entirely of stone in 1598 and now a café—Teylers is the best sort of small museum. It is based on the eclectic whims of an eccentric private collector, in this case the 18th-century merchant Pieter Teyler van der Hulst. Founded in 1784, it's the country's oldest museum and has a mixture of exhibits—fossils and minerals sit alongside antique scientific instruments, such as a battery of 25 Leiden jars, dating from 1789 and used to store an electric charge. The museum itself is a grand old building with mosaic floors; its major artistic attraction is the legendary collection of drawings and prints by old masters, such

> ## HAARLEM'S HIDDEN COURTYARDS
>
> Throughout the old city center are the many historic *hofjes* (almshouse courtyards)—hidden little courtyards that make Haarlem an incredibly pleasant place to explore. Look for the Zuider Hofje, the Hofje van Loo, the Wijnbergs Hofje, and the Brouwershofje (they are all signposted). Closer to the Grote Markt are the Remonstrants Hofje, the Luthershofje, and the Frans Loenen Hofje. These secluded gardens are filled with flowers and birdsong, and offer peace and respite away from the city streets.

as Michelangelo, Rembrandt, and Raphael, based on a collection that once belonged to Queen Christina of Sweden. Much of the collection is housed in the original 18th-century museum building. ⌂ *Spaarne 16* ☎ *023/516–0960* ⊕ *www.teylersmuseum.nl* ✉ *€9* ⊗ *Tues.–Sat. 10–5, Sun. noon–5.*

WORTH NOTING

7 **Amsterdamse Poort** *(Amsterdam Gate)*. Built around 1400, this is Haarlem's only remaining city gate; remains of the city wall can be seen at its base. It's slightly to the east of the current center, just to the east of the Spaarne River.

4 **Corrie ten Boomhuis** *(Corrie ten Boom House)*. Just off the Grote Markt, and tucked into a small gabled building above a shop, this house honors a family of World War II resistance fighters who successfully hid a number of Jewish families before being captured themselves by the Germans in 1944. Most of the Ten Boom family died in the concentration camps, but Corrie survived and returned to Haarlem to tell the story in her book *The Hiding Place*. The family clock shop is preserved on the street floor, and their living quarters now contain displays, documents, photographs, and memorabilia. Visitors can also see the hiding closet, which the Gestapo never found, even though they lived six days in the house hoping to starve out anyone who might be concealed here. The upstairs living quarters are not accessible through the shop, but via the side door of No. 19, down a narrow alley beside the shop. Meeting instructions giving the time of the next guided tour are posted on the door. Note that the last tour begins 30 minutes before the posted closing times. ⌂ *Barteljorisstraat 19* ☎ *023/531–0823* ⊕ *www.corrietenboom. com* ✉ *Donations accepted* ⊗ *Apr.–Oct., Tues.–Sat. 10–4; Nov.–Mar., Tues.–Sat. 11–3.*

8

CLOSE UP

Dutch Art—Then and Now

Capture of Damietta by Haarlem Crusaders by Cornelis Claesz van Wieringen (ca. 1580–1633).

Few countries can boast of so many great artists. During the Golden Age of the 17th century, an estimated 20 million paintings were executed and every home seemed to have an oil painting tacked on the wall. Even before the arrival of Rembrandt and Vermeer, the country had a rich artistic history.

In the late 16th century, the Netherlands were divided into a Flemish south under Catholic Spanish rule, and an independent northern alliance of Dutch Protestant provinces. Before then, most painters hailed from the southern cities of Gent, Antwerp, and Brugge, and their subject matter was mostly biblical and allegorical—Jan van Eyck (1385–1441) founded the Flemish School, Hieronymus Bosch (1450–1516) crafted meticulous, macabre allegories, and Pieter Bruegel the Elder (1525–69) depicted scenes of Flemish peasant life.

In the north, a different style began surfacing. Around Haarlem, Jan Mostaert (1475–1555) and Lucas van der Leyden (1489–1553) brought a new realism into previously static paintings. In Utrecht, Gerrit van Honthorst (1590–1656) used light and shadow

to create realism never seen before on canvas.

From these disparate schools flowed the Golden Age of Dutch painting, and Hals, Rembrandt, and Vermeer all borrowed from each diverse technique. Frans Hals (1581–1666) has been called the first modern painter. A fantastically adept and naturally gifted man, he could turn out a portrait an hour. He delighted in capturing the emotions—a smile or grimace—in an early manifestation of Impressionism.

Rembrandt van Rijn (1606–69) is regarded as the most versatile artist of the 17th century. Born in Leiden, he grew rich from painting and tuition. His early works were overly ornamental, but as the years went by he dug deeper into the metaphysical essence of his subjects. When his material world collapsed around him—he was blackmailed and ruined—he somehow turned out even greater art, showing off a marvelously skilled use of light and shadow.

Jan Vermeer (1632–72), the third in this triumvirate, was a different case altogether. He produced only 35 known paintings, but their exquisite nature make him the most precious painter of his time. He brought genre art to its peak; in small canvases with overwhelming realism he painted the soft calm and everyday sameness of middle-class life.

Around the middle of the century, Baroque influences began permeating Dutch art, heralding a trend for landscapes. Artists such as Albert Cuyp and Meindert Hobbema's scenes of polder lanes, grazing cows, and windswept canals were coveted by 17th- and 18th-century collectors. Other masters were more playful in tone. Jan Steen's (1625–79) lively, satirical, and sometimes-lewd scenes are imbued with humor.

The greatest Dutch painter of the 19th century is undoubtedly Vincent van Gogh (1853–90). During his short but troubled life, he produced an array of masterworks, although he famously sold only one. He only began painting in 1881, and his first paintings often depicted dark peasant scenes. But in his last four years, spent in France, he produced endlessly colorful and arresting works. In 1890, he committed suicide after struggling with depression. To this day, his legacy continues to move art lovers everywhere.

The 20th century brought confusion to the art scene. Unsure what style to adopt, many artists reinvented themselves. Piet Mondriaan (1872–1944) is someone who evolved with his century. Early in his career he painted bucolic landscapes. Then, in 1909, at the age of 41, he began dabbling, first with Expressionism and then Cubism. He eventually developed his own style, called neo-plasticism. Using only the primary colors of yellow, red, and blue set against neutral white, gray,

and black, he created stylized studies in form and color. In 1917, together with his friend Theo van Doesberg (1883–1931), he published an arts magazine called *De Stijl* (*The Style*) as a forum for a design movement attempting to harmonize the arts through purified abstraction. Though it lasted only 15 years, the movement's effect was felt around the world.

The most vibrant movement to emerge after World War II was the experimental CoBrA (artists from Copenhagen, Brussels, and Amsterdam), cofounded by Karel Appel (1921–2006) and Constant (née Constant Nieuwenhuis, 1920–2005). With bright colors and abstract shapes, their paintings have a childlike quality. The artists involved continue to have influence in their respective countries.

Johannes Vermeer's (1632-75) most haunting work, *Girl with a Pearl Earring*, inspired Tracy Chevalier's 1999 best-selling novel as well as the 2003 film starring Scarlett Johansson.

SHOP 'TIL YOU DROP

The pedestrianized Barteljorisstraat has lots of top fashion chains, such as Vanilia, Esprit, and MEXX, as well as a number of streetwear shops for men. The top end of Kruisstraat has furniture shops, from antiques to designer, and a lot in between. Flowers can be found on Krocht, on the corner junction of Kruisstraat and Barteljorisstraat—the sumptuous displays echo the nearby tulip fields between Haarlem and the Keukenhof.

If it's art you're after, check out **Theo Swagemakers** (✉ *Stoofsteeg 6* ☎ *023/532-7761* 💶 *€4.50*), a gallery that sells artwork by Swagemakers (1898–1994) himself, as well as others. It's open Wednesday–Sunday 1–5. Other more commercial art galleries can be found along Koningstraat.

OFF THE BEATEN PATH

Zandvoort is only 9 km (5½ mi) from Haarlem and has the area's biggest and best beach around—it's a favorite of sun-starved Amsterdammers. It can get crowded but if you wander south for 10 minutes or so, you can find isolated spots among the dunes; after about 20 minutes, you come to the nude, in places gay, sunbathing beach.

8 Historisch Museum Haarlem. Located near the Frans Hals Museum, with two or three small temporary exhibitions a year, the town's history museum makes the most of its limited resources, offering insight into the history of the city and the surrounding area. Video screenings (in English), models of the city, and touch-screen computers relate stories that take you back in history. There are fascinating old prints and maps, and some apparently random exhibits, including one of the earliest printing presses, dating from the 17th century. Also on view here is an incisive exhibition on modern Dutch architecture, **ABC Architectuur Centrum Haarlem,** with plans and photographs from city projects already finished and still in the planning stages (De Bruijn's Woonhuis is particularly ingenious). ✉ *Groot Heiligland 47* ☎ *023/542-2427* ⊕ *www. historischmuseumhaarlem.nl* 💶 *€4* ☉ *Tues.–Sat. noon–5, Sun. 1–5.*

3 Stadhuis *(Town Hall).* On the market square, this 14th-century former hunting lodge belonged to the Count of Holland, who permitted it to be transformed into Haarlem's Town Hall in the 14th century. The large main **Gravenzaal** (Count's Hall) is worth a visit—if you can sneak in between bouts of confetti throwing, as there are a good number of bridal parties ascending its steps on a regular basis—to study its collection of 16th-century paintings amassed by the Count of Holland. If you wish to tour the premises, call in advance to get permission. ✉ *Grote Markt 2* ☎ *023/511–5115* 💶 *Free* ☉ *Weekdays 10–4 (when not closed for civic functions).*

WHERE TO EAT

$–$$

INDONESIAN

✕ **De Lachende Javaan.** Stepping into "The Laughing Javanese" off an old Haarlem street that hasn't changed in centuries, you are hit with a flash of color and pungent smells. You can sit upstairs at one of the window tables and look out over the sober gabled houses while eating *kambing*

City hall as seen from the Grote Markt.

saté (skewers of lamb in soy sauce) and *kipkarbonaade met sambal djeroek* (grilled chicken with a fiery Indonesian sauce), but the menu options are enormous, so you can mix and match, choosing a meal of 12 small dishes if you want. ⊠ *Frankestraat 27* ☎ *023/532–8792* ▭ *AE, DC, MC, V* ⊘ *Closed Mon. No lunch.*

$–$$
CAFÉ
✕ **Jacobus Pieck.** One of Haarlem's best *eetlokaals* (dining spots), this attracts locals with its long bar, cozy tables, and lovely sun trap of a garden. The menu offers standards but with a twist: try the Popeye Blues Salad—a wild spinach, blue cheese, and bacon number, with creamy mustard dressing for a lighter option—or, for dinner, lamb with ratatouille and rosemary jus. As you'll see, the food makes this restaurant-café very popular, so get here early or book ahead to snag a table. ⊠ *Warmoestraat 18* ☎ *023/532–6144* ⊕ *www.jacobuspieck.nl* ▭ *No credit cards* ⊘ *Closed Sun. No dinner Mon.*

$$$–$$$$
DUTCH
✕ **ml.** In a 17th-century mansion that was once a bank, this small gracious restaurant has a traditional dining room with white-painted wooden beams, brightened crisp linens, and light filtering through the mullioned windows. Ask for a table with a view of the enclosed garden (open in summer) if you've missed out on a table outside. This new restaurant has become a showpiece for chef Mark Gratema and his wife Liane's modern-Dutch creative talents. Try the monkfish with shrimp, calf's cheek, spinach, and sherry. The restaurant is convenient to both the Frans Hals and the Teylers museums. ⊠ *Kleine Houtstraat 70* ☎ *023/534–5343* ⊕ *www.restaurant-ml.nl* ⌲ *Reservations essential* ▭ *AE, MC, V* ⊘ *Closed Sun. and Mon. No lunch Tues. and Sat.*

Outdoor cafés just off the Grote Markt.

$-$$ CONTEMPORARY ★ ✕ **XO.** A very funky restaurant-bar, XO has chunky silver graphics, purple-and-gray walls, and oversize but softly lighted lamps. Throw in some fun touches—"king" chairs, complete with claw feet and red cushions; nifty recesses at the bar for extra intimacy; big stone candlesticks—and you've got an alluring setting for lunch and evening edibles. The dinner menu changes regularly but always contains mouthwatering and exquisitely presented dishes, such as cod fillet baked in a sun-dried tomato-and-truffle crust, with black pasta, spinach, and a white-wine cream sauce. For a lunchtime snack try the imaginative bread rolls stuffed with marinated salmon and horseradish cream, or a cucumber salad; a fine range of tapas is served all day. ⊠ *Grote Markt 8* ☎ *023/551–1350* w*ww.xo-haarlem.nl* ▤ *AE, MC, V.*

WHERE TO STAY

¢–$ 🏨 **Carillon.** This is an old-fashioned hotel with a friendly staff, set in the shadow of Sint Bavo's across the Grote Markt. Small rooms are spartan but fresh and comfortable, with impeccable bathrooms that include showers but not tubs. The central location and reasonable rates make it a top spot to accommodate a day of exploring and then a night out. The bar-restaurant has a nice terrace on the square. Ask for a room at the back if you want to retire early on weekends, as the front rooms are a bit noisy thanks to the neighboring bars. **Pros:** good value; friendly; great location. **Cons:** steep stairs; no elevator; front rooms can be noisy. ⊠ *Grote Markt 27,* ☎ *023/531–0591* ⊕ *www.hotelcarillon.com* 🛏 *21 rooms, 15 with bath* 🛆 *In-room: no a/c, Internet. In-hotel: restaurant, bar* ▤ *AE, DC, MC, V* ⽧ *CP.*

$$-$$$ ⛄**Golden Tulip Lion d'Or**. This modern hotel is in a pretty 18th-century building just 50 yards from the railway station and within walking distance of major downtown sights. Rooms are spacious with good lighting and upscale chain-hotel-style furnishings. The bathrooms all have tubs as well as showers. Downstairs are meeting rooms, and a reasonably priced restaurant and bar. A jogging path runs behind the hotel. **Pros:** near train station; friendly. **Cons:** far from the sights. ⊠ *Kruisweg 34–36,* ☎ *023/532–1750* ⊕ *www.goldentupliondor.nl* ⤢ *30 rooms, 4 suites* ⚲ *In-room: safe, Wi-Fi. In-hotel: restaurant, bar, parking (paid), some pets allowed* ═ *AE, DC, MC, V* ⍾ *BP.*

	ORGAN IMPROV
	Haarlem hosts an **International Organ Improvisation Competition** in even-numbered years for a week in mid-July, giving people ample opportunity to hear the renowned Müller organ in Sint Bavo's church at full throttle. Entry is free. For more information, call ☎ 020/488–0479, or visit ⊕ *www. organfestival.nl.*

$–$$ ⛄**Stempels**. From 1953 to 1992, this historic building opposite St. Bavo's was the site where all Dutch banknotes were printed. It lay abandoned for 14 years until two chefs, Martijn Franzen and Frans van Cappelle, bought the property and transformed it into an elegant hotel. Much of the original interior was saved, so the décor is a stylish blend of old and new, with chandeliers in many public areas. Sumptuous guest rooms are painted in sleek modern slates and creams. The rooms at the front have great views of the church. Bathrooms in the spacious luxury rooms have showers and tubs; others have shower only. Downstairs are meeting rooms, a bar, and a reasonably priced brasserie, plus a more upmarket restaurant (evenings only). **Pros:** great location; historic building; luxury at a reasonable price. **Cons:** lots of stairs. ⊠ *Klokhuisplein 9,* ☎ *023/512–3910* ⊕ *www.stempelsinhaarlem. nl* ⤢ *15 rooms, 2 suites* ⚲ *In-room: safe, Wi-Fi. In-hotel: 2 restaurants, bar, parking (paid)* ═ *AE, DC, MC, V* ⍾ *BP.*

NIGHTLIFE AND THE ARTS

Haarlem is more than a city of nostalgia. The **Patronaat** (⊠ *Zijlsingel 2* ☎ *023/517–5858*) is an excellent rock music venue: it's Haarlem's answer to the Melkweg in Amsterdam only without the really big bands. If you feel like bar hopping but don't want to wear a hole in your shoe, head to Lange Veerstraat or the Botermarkt square, where you'll find a lot of bars and cafés. The **Café de Linde** (⊠ *Botermarkt 21* ☎ *023/531–9688*) is a mellow place for a drink or a light meal. Located in a converted Art Deco cinema on the Grote Markt, **CaféStudio** (⊠ *Grote Markt 25* ☎ *023/531–0033*) has an exceptional range of Belgian beers. A mellow café by day, by midevening at weekends it can turn into a rowdy club (free entry) with a DJ, serious lighting, and enormous speakers to ensure the ambience is just right. **Gay Café Wilsons** (⊠ *Gedempte Raamgraacht 78* ☎ *023/532–5854* ⊗ *Thu.–Mon.*) is the in gathering place for gays in Haarlem.

THE HAGUE

It's easy to see The Hague as nothing more than Amsterdam's prissy maiden aunt—it's the Netherlands' seat of government, home to the Dutch royal family, and the International Court of Justice sits here. Most foreign embassies are located here, too.

Yet it doesn't have the honor of being the national capital, a fact that delights Amsterdammers and confounds quiz teams globally. Yet while it seems at first that the city has been handed all the serious tasks to get on with whilst Amsterdam has all the fun, those who experience the city up close will find a lively metropolis that is both elegant and quirky. Take the time to explore a little and you'll encounter more than 25 public parks, plus a maze of narrow winding streets where contemporary architecture sits comfortably and unabashed beside grand 17th-century mansions. For a time out, relax at sidewalk cafés and watch as they fill with a stream of civil servants and diplomats spilling out from the offices all around the 13th-century Ridderzaal, the centerpiece of the parliament. Visit the galleries and museums and you'll find no end of masterpieces by the likes of Rembrandt and Johannes Vermeer, or the dazzling optical conundrums of Dutch graphic artist M.C. Escher, whose logic-defying creations appear to bend the laws of physics.

If you should find yourself tiring of The Hague's grace and charm, it too has a brasher Siamese twin, in the form of neighboring Scheveningen, once a fishing port, now a tacky beach resort par excellence. Here you can lose your shirt in the city's casino—or else lose your dignity by taking a dip in the stupendously icy waters of the North Sea.

The Hague's official name is 's-Gravenhage (literally "the Count's Hedge"). It harks back to the 13th century when the Count of Holland's hunting lodge was based here, in a village then called Die Haghe. To the Dutch the city is known simply as Den Haag, and that's the name you'll always hear used on the street.

GETTING HERE AND AROUND

There are two railway stations in The Hague: one is in the central business district, the **Station Hollands Spoor** (⊠ *Stationsplein*). The other station, **Centraal Station** (⊠ *Koningin Julianaplein*), is in the residential area. Trains from Amsterdam run directly to both the Centraal and Hollands Spoor stations, but the Centraal stop is an end stop, whereas Hollands Spoor is a through destination and is used as a stop for trains to and from Amsterdam, Delft, and Rotterdam. All international and intercity trains from Brussels and Paris to Amsterdam also stop in The Hague HS (Hollands Spoor). By car from Amsterdam, take E19 via Amsterdam Schiphol Airport. To reach the city from Utrecht, take the A12. Once you're approaching the city, follow the signs for the central parking route. This is an extremely helpful ring road that covers the many inexpensive parking lots within the city center.

On buses trams and trains you can use an **OV-chipkaart** (public transport chip card)—a new electronic payment system that's slowly rolled out nationally. These credit card–size tickets can be loaded up with credit from machines in the railway stations, and are debited as you board and leave trains, trams, metros, and buses. There are information and sales points in the stations. Or visit www.ov-chipkaart.nl for more information. The OV-chipkaart will eventually replace all other transport tickets, including the national *strippenkaart*, but at this writing no date for the phaseout in The Hague had been set.

Taxis are available at railway stations, at major hotels, and at taxi stands in key locations. You can also order a taxi by phone, but they cannot be hailed in the street.

ORIENTATION

For a city that sees so much political, legal, and diplomatic action, The Hague can seem surprisingly quiet, and a pleasure to those who want to escape the crowds. It's a flat compact city, and most of the sights in the town center are within a 15-minute walk from either of the city's train stations. Tramlines 3 and 17 cover many of the sights in town, and Tram No. 10 will get you to the outlying Statenkwartier museums. Tram No. 9 goes to Madurodam. For information on specific lines, ask at the HTM offices in The Hague's stations, or at offices listed here. For information on public transport (trains, buses, trams, and ferries), call the national information line.

Contacts HTM (⊠ *Grote Marktstraat 43* ☎ *070/384-8666*). **Public Transportation Information** (☎ *0900/9292* ⊕ *www.9292ov.nl*).

TOURS

A Royal Tour that takes in the palaces and administrative buildings associated with Queen Beatrix operates April–September; the cost is €27.50 per person. The VVV also arranges a variety of tours covering everything from royalty to architecture. Or you can purchase booklets that will allow you to follow a walking tour at your own pace. The VVV does tours and has brochures for them, as well as tickets, at the VVV offices.

De Ooievaart runs boat tours around The Hague's canals. The boats depart from Bierkade and offer a peaceful and relaxing way to see the city. Trips last 1½ hours, cost €9.50, and tickets can be bought from the VVV.

Contacts **Day Trips Department, Den Haag Marketing** (☎ *070/338–5800*). **De Ooievaart** (☎ *070/445–1869* ⊕ *www.ooievaart.nl*).

TIMING

Done at a pace that will allow you to soak up The Hague's historical atmosphere, a minimal tour around the city center should take about three or four hours. If you stop to visit the main sights en route, you're looking at a very full day. At the very least, allow 30 minutes for each site you visit.

Before you start out, bear a couple of things in mind. First, as in all other Dutch cities, both walking surfaces and the weather can change at short notice; if you're going to be on your feet all day, make sure you're equipped with an umbrella and sturdy walking shoes. Second, most museums and galleries close at 5 PM, and many sites are also closed Monday, so plan accordingly.

ESSENTIALS

Bicycle rentals **Fietsverhuur Den Haag** (✉ *Noordeinde 59* ☎ *070/326–5790*). Bikes cost €10 per day to rent, with ID and a €60 deposit required.

Emergency Services **National Emergency Alarm Number** (☎ *112 for police, fire, and ambulance*).

Hospitals **Bronovo Hospital** (✉ *Bronovolaan 5* ☎ *070/312–4141*).

Pharmacies **Late-Night Pharmacy Information** (☎ *070/345–1000*).

Taxis **Taxi Centrale Den Haag** (☎ *070/390–6262*).

Tourism Information **VVV The Hague** (✉ *Hofweg 1* ☼ *Tues.–Sat. 10–5* ☎ *070/402–3336*).

EXPLORING

The Hague's center is crammed with the best the city has to offer in terms of art, history, and architecture. An exploration of a relatively small area will take you into the famed Mauritshuis Museum, through the Binnenhof, home to the famous Ridderzaal (Knights' Hall), or along the leafy Lange Voorhout, for a stroll through what in the 19th century was the place to see and be seen.

TOP ATTRACTIONS

❷ **Binnenhof and the Ridderzaal** *(Inner Court and the Knights' Hall).* The
Fodor's Choice governmental heart of the Netherlands, the Binnenhof (or Inner Court)
★ complex is in the very center of town yet tranquilly set apart from it, thanks to the charming Hofvijver (court lake). The setting creates a poetic contrast to the endlessly dull debates that go on within its walls—the basis of everyday Dutch politics. Pomp and decorum are in full fig every third Tuesday of September, when Queen Beatrix arrives at the 13th-century Ridderzaal, or Knights' Hall, in a golden coach to open the new session of Parliament.

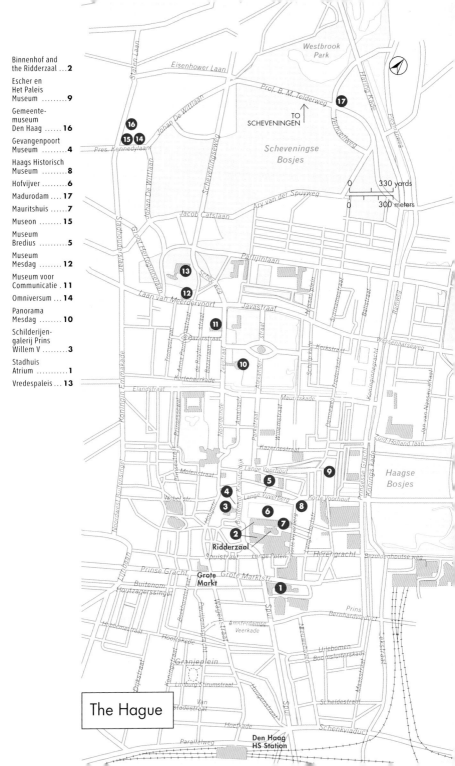

The Hague

The square in front of the Binnenhof is a great place to relax and people watch.

For many centuries the Binnenhof was the court for the Counts of Holland; it is now a complex of buildings from several eras. As you enter, the twin-turreted former castle of the Earls of Holland dominates the scene. It was originally built by Count Floris V and became a meeting hall for the Knights of the Order of the Golden Fleece (one of the most regal societies of the Middle Ages). The interior of the Great Hall simply drips with history: there are vast wooden beams, flags of the Dutch provinces, and a massive rose window bearing coats of arms. In 1900 the hall was restored to its original 13th-century glory; it is still called Knights' Hall, and you can almost feel the feasts and revelries that took place there. The room still plays a key role in Dutch legislative life.

The Binnenhof also incorporates the halls used by the First and Second Chambers of Parliament (equivalent to the U.S. Senate and House of Representatives). You can wander freely around the open outer courtyard, but entrance to the Knights' Hall and other interior rooms is by guided tour only. The vaulted reception area below the Knights' Hall contains a free exhibition detailing the political history of the Low Countries. ⊠ *Binnenhof 8a* ☎ *070/364–6144* ☐ *€6* ⊗ *Mon.–Sat. 10–4 (some areas may be closed when government meetings are taking place).*

❾ **Escher in Het Paleis Museum** *(Escher Museum).* First known as the Lange
ⓒ Voorhout Palace, this lovely building was originally the residence of
Fodor's Choice Caroline of Nassau, daughter of Prince Willem IV—in 1765 Mozart
★ performed for her here. In 2001 the palace was transformed into a museum devoted to Dutch graphic artist M. C. Escher (1892–1972), whose prints and engravings of unforgettable images—roofs becoming floors, water flowing upward, fish transforming into birds—became

world famous in the 1960s and '70s. Replete with ever-repeating Baroque pillars, Palladian portals, and parallel horizons, Maurits Cornelis Escher's visual trickery presages the "virtual reality" worlds of today. Fittingly, the museum now features an Escher Experience where you don a helmet and take a 360-degree digital trip through his unique world. Concave and convex, radical metamorphoses, and dazzling optical illusions are on view in the impressive selection of his prints (including the famed *Day*

AM I BEING WATCHED?

As you wander around the Ridderzaal, check out the carved heads by the wooden beams—the ones that seem to be looking down on you judgmentally. And indeed they are. When the hall previously served as a court, judges would tell the accused to fess up, otherwise these "eavesdroppers" would have words with the heavenly powers.

and Night and *Ascending and Descending*); distorted rooms and video cameras make children big and adults small; and there are rooms that are Escher prints blown up to the *n*th power. Don't forget to look up as you walk around—the latest addition to the museum is a series of custom-designed chandeliers by Dutch sculptor Hans van Bentem that are inspired by Escher's work. These delightfully playful creations include umbrellas, sea horses, birds, and even a giant skull and crossbones. A family ticket for €20 makes this an even more attractive museum for kids. ⊠ *Lange Voorhout 74* ☎ *070/427–7730* ⊕ *www.escherinhetpaleis.nl* ⊠ *€7.50* ☉ *Tues.–Sun. 11–5.*

QUICK BITES Down a quiet side street, off Vos in Tuinstraat and very near the Escher in Het Paleis Museum, the friendly Le Café Hathor (⊠ *Maliestraat 22* ☎ *070/346–4081*) is a great spot for a snack, a full lunch, or just a quiet drink. Wood-paneled walls and flickering candles on each table create an intimately cozy atmosphere inside, while in good weather, tables on a raft outside overlook a gently flowing canal. It's closed on Sundays.

⑯ Fodor'sChoice ★ **Gemeentemuseum Den Haag** *(Hague Municipal Museum).* Designed by H. P. Berlage (the grand Old Master of modern Dutch architecture) and completed in 1935, this is considered one of the finest examples of 20th-century museum architecture. Although its collection ranges from A to Z—Golden Age silver, Greek and Chinese pottery, historic musical instruments, and paintings by Claude Monet and Vincent van Gogh—it is best known for the world's largest collection of works by Piet Mondriaan (1872–1944), the greatest artist of the Dutch De Stijl movement. The crowning masterpiece, and widely considered one of the landmarks of modern art, is Mondriaan's *Victory Boogie Woogie*—an iconic work, begun in 1942 but left unfinished at the artist's death. The painting's signature black-and-white grid interspersed with blocks of primary color arrived only in 1998, when the Netherlands Institute for Cultural Heritage controversially paid 80 million guilders for the (then American-owned) work. Also be sure to see the dollhouse with real doll-size Delft Blue chinaware. Elsewhere, the museum's Costume Gallery contains no fewer than 55,000 items (not all are on display at one time!), providing endless inspiration for dedicated students of fashion. ⊠ *Stadhouderslaan 41* ☎ *070/338–1111* ⊕ *www.gemeentemuseum.nl* 🗐 *€10* ⊙ *Tues.–Sun. 11–5.*

❻ Hofvijver *(Court Lake).* Beside the Binnenhof, this long, rectangular reflecting pool—the venerable remains of a medieval moat—comes complete with tall fountains and a row of pink-blossomed horse-chestnut trees. Today, the lake is spectacularly surrounded by some of The Hague's most elegant historic buildings and museums.

❼ Mauritshuis. One of Europe's greatest museums, it's an incomparable feast of art in only a dozen rooms and includes 14 Rembrandts, 10 Jan Steens, and 3 Vermeers. The latter's remarkable *View of Delft* takes pride of place; its rediscovery in the late 19th century assured the artist's eternal fame. In the same room is Vermeer's (1632–75) most haunting work, *Girl with a Pearl Earring,* which inspired Tracy Chevalier's 1999 best-selling novel as well as the 2003 filmed version. For something completely different, look to Jan Steen (1626–79), who portrayed the daily life of ordinary people in the Netherlands of the 17th century. His painting *The Way You Hear It Is the Way You Sing It* is particularly telling. Don't miss local boy Paulus Potter's vast canvas *The Bull,* complete with steaming cow dung; the 7-foot-by-11-foot painting leaves nothing to be said on the subject of beef on the hoof.

As an added treat, the building itself is worthy of a 17th-century master's brush: a cream-color mansion tucked into a corner behind the Parliament complex and overlooking the Hofvijver. It was built around 1640 for one Johan Maurits, Count of Nassau-Siegen and governor-general of Dutch Brazil. The pair behind its creation, Jacob van Campen and Pieter Post, were the two most important Dutch architects of their era. ⊠ *Korte Vijverberg 8* ☎ *070/302–3456* ⊕ *www.mauritshuis.nl* 🗐 *€12* ⊙ *Tues.–Sat. 10–5, Sun. 11–5.*

❿ Panorama Mesdag. Long before TV was capable of reproducing reality, painted panoramas gave viewers the chance to immerse themselves in another world. The *Panorama Mesdag,* painted in 1880 by the renowned marine artist Hendrik Willem Mesdag and a team including his wife, Sientje Mesdag-van Houtenback, is one of the largest and finest surviving examples of the genre. The cinematic vision is a sweeping view of the sea, the dunes, and the picturesque fishing village of Scheveningen. To enhance the effect of the painting, you are first led through a narrow, dark passage, then up a spiral staircase, and out onto a "sand dune" viewing platform. To the southeast

WHO'S THAT GIRL?

Johannes Vermeer's immortal *Girl with a Pearl Earring* is one of the few paintings ever to have its own spinoff novel and movie. The enigma surrounding the work remains to this day—despite extensive investigations, historians have never been able to determine who this sphinxlike lady actually is. Some think she is Maria, the eldest of Vermeer's 11 children. The novel claims she is Vermeer's maid. Considering the complete lack of ostentatious dress and iconographic symbols, the latter could be a real possibility.

H. P. Berlage's Gemeentemuseum Den Haag is considered to be one of the finest examples of 20th-century museum architecture.

is The Hague, detailed so perfectly that old-time residents can identify particular houses. So lifelike is the 45-foot-high panorama with a 400-foot circumference that it's hard to resist the temptation to step across the guardrail onto the dune and stride down to the water's edge. ⊠ *Zeestraat 65* ☎ *070/364–4544* ⊕ *www.panorama-mesdag.nl* 🎫 *€6.50* ⊗ *Mon.–Sat. 10–5, Sun. noon–5.*

⑬ Vredespaleis *(Peace Palace).* Facing the world across a broad lawn, this
★ building houses the International Court of Justice plus a 500,000-volume law library. The court was initiated in 1899 by Czar Nicolas II of Russia, who invited 26 nations to meet in The Hague to set up a permanent world court of arbitration. The current building was constructed in 1903 with a $1.5 million gift from Scottish-American industrialist Andrew Carnegie. Built in Flemish style, its red-and-gray granite-and-brick pile has become a local landmark. Gifts from the participating nations embellish the interior and include statuary, stained-glass windows, doors, and clocks. Comparatively few litigations are heard here these days, although some still make headlines, such as the famous trial of Slobodan Milosevic. ⊠ *Carnegieplein 2* ☎ *070/302–4242* ⊕ *www. vredespaleis.nl* 🎫 *€5* ⊗ *Weekdays, guided tours only, at 10, 11, 2, 3, and 4 when court is not in session (4 pm tour is May—Sept. only). Tours must be booked in advance.*

OFF THE
BEATEN
PATH

Fodor's Choice ★ ☺ **Madurodam.** Statistically, the Dutch are the tallest people in Europe, and never must they be more aware of their size than when they visit this miniature version of their own land. Set in a sprawling "village" with pathways, tram tracks, and a railway station, every important building of the Netherlands is reproduced here, on a scale of 1:25. Many aspects of Dutch life ancient and modern are also on view: medieval knights joust in the courtyard of Gouda's magnificent Town Hall; windmills turn; the famous cheese-weighing ritual is carried out in Alkmaar; a harbor fire is extinguished; the awe-inspiring Delta Works storm surge barrier (constructed after the disastrous flooding of 1953) holds the ocean at bay; and planes land at Schiphol Airport. The world's longest miniature railway is here, too. Madurodam has two restaurants, a picnic area, a playground, and the entire exhibit is surrounded by gardens. The sunset hour is a fairy-tale experience as some 50,000 lights

> ### STREET MARKETS
>
> The main traditional street market (an organic farmers' market at that) in The Hague is generally held outside the **Grote Kerk** on Wednesday from 11 to 6. From the beginning of May until the end of October on Thursday and Sunday, there's an antiques market on **Lange Voorhout**. Wandering through the stalls on a fine day, perhaps to the accompaniment of a street musician, makes for a lovely experience. Plus there's an alfresco café for that all-important coffee and apple cake.

are turned on in the little houses. In July and August there is also an after-dark sound-and-light presentation, free to park visitors. Madurodam is in the woods that separate The Hague from the port of Scheveningen to the north. To get there take Tram No. 9 from either railway station in the city center. ⊠ *George Maduroplein 1* ☎ *070/416–2400* ⊕ *www.madurodam.nl* ⬛ *€14.50* ☉ *Sept.–mid-Mar., daily 9–6; mid-Mar.–June, daily 9–8; July and Aug., daily 9 AM–11 PM.*

WORTH NOTING

❹ **Gevangenpoort Museum** *(Prison's Gate Museum)*. This site is now a museum showcasing enough instruments of inhumanity to satisfy any criminologist. Originally a gatehouse to the local duke's castle, Gevangenpoort was converted to a prison around 1420. In 1882, it opened in its current incarnation as both a monument to its own past and a museum to apparatuses of punishment. After a slide presentation, the guided tour will take you through the torture chamber, the women's section, and the area where the rich were once imprisoned. If you're drawn to the macabre, the Gevangenpoort Museum offers a fascinating, if chilling, experience. (Note the museum was closed for major renovation work, and while it should reopen by 2011, opening times and prices could not be confirmed at this writing.) ⊠ *Buitenhof 33* ☎ *070/346–0861* ⊕ *www.gevangenpoort.nl* ⬛ *€4* ☉ *Tues.–Fri. 10–5, weekends noon–5. Guided tours only, every hr on the hr (last tour at 4).*

❽ **Haags Historisch Museum** *(Hague Historical Museum)*. One of the series of museums that encircle the Hofvijver lake, the Historical Museum is in the Sebastiaansdoelen, a magnificent Classical-Baroque mansion dating from 1636. Worthy of a visit in itself, the mansion houses collections that offer an in-depth look at The Hague's past. Treasures include Jan van Goyen's enormous 17th-century panoramic painting of the city, a collection of medieval church silver, and a dollhouse from 1910. The idyllic views out the windows over the Hofvijver lake and the greensward of the Lange Voorhout are good for the soul. ⊠ *Korte Vijverberg 7* ☎ *070/364–6940*

⊕ *www.haagshistorischmuseum.nl* ⚏ €5 ⊙ *Tues.–Fri. 10–5, weekends noon–5.*

⑮ Museon. With hands-on, interactive displays, frequent special exhibitions, and archaeological and intercultural subjects with common themes, plus children's workshops on Wednesday and Sunday afternoons (book in advance), Museon claims to be "the most fun-packed popular science museum in the Netherlands," and perhaps they're right. Permanent exhibitions center on the origins of the universe and evolution. The Museon is right next door to the Gemeentemuseum, so you can easily combine a visit to both. ⊠ *Stadhouderslaan 37* ☏ *070/338–1338* ⊕ *www.museon.nl* ⚏ *€8.50* ⊙ *Tues.–Sun. 11–5.*

⑤ Museum Bredius. Housed in an 18th-century patrician mansion, the collection of traveler and art connoisseur Abraham Bredius (1855–1946) supports the argument that the private collections are often the best. It includes works by Jan Steen, as well as nearly 200 paintings by Dutch "little masters"—whose art Bredius trumpeted. Once curator of the Mauritshuis, Bredius was the first art historian to question the authenticity of Rembrandt canvases (there were zillions of them in the 19th century), setting into motion a seismic quake that reduced the master's oeuvre to fewer than 1,000 works. The house itself, overlooking the Hofvijver, makes a fittingly elegant setting for the art. ⊠ *Lange Vijverberg 14* ☏ *070/362–0729* ⊕ *www.museumbredius.nl* ⚏ *€4.50* ⊙ *Tues.–Sun. 11–5.*

⑫ Museum Mesdag. Literally wallpapered with grand paintings and exquisite fabrics and tapestries, this oft-overlooked treasure-house is the former residence of noted 19th-century Dutch painter H. W. Mesdag. Famed for his vast *Panorama Mesdag,* he left this house as a repository for his collection of works from The Hague School, which often featured seascapes and the life of fisherfolk in nearby Scheveningen. The museum was closed for renovation at this writing, but is scheduled to reopen in the spring of 2011. ⊠ *Laan van Meerdervoort 7f* ☏ *070/364–6940* ⊕ *www.museummesdag.nl* ⚏ *€5* ⊙ *Tues.–Sun. noon–5.*

⑪ Museum voor Communicatie *(Communication Museum).* Ultramodern and with lots of space, light, and activities, the Communication Museum looks at the ways in which people have gotten in touch with one another over the years, from carrier pigeon to e-mail. Some exhibits are specifically designed for young children, allowing them to play with old telex machines or design their own cell-phone ringtones. Much of the signage is in Dutch, although English-speaking audio guides are available. ⊠ *Zeestraat 82* ☏ *070/330–7500* ⊕ *www.muscom.nl* ⚏ *€7.50* ⊙ *Weekdays 10–5, Sat. and Sun. noon–5.*

⑭ Omniversum. The IMAX theater shows a rotating program of film spectaculars, including several with nature-based and futuristic themes, on

---

BY BIKE

With plenty of cycle lanes, The Hague is as safe for cyclists as anywhere else in the Netherlands. Be wary of bikes with back-pedal brakes, which can be alarming if you're not used to them. Most railway station shops will rent you a model with handlebar brakes for a slightly higher rate.

8

Check out mini-Holland at Madurodam.

a screen six stories high. It's also one of the few Hague sights open in the evenings. ⊠ *Pres. Kennedylaan 5* ☎ *0900/666–4837* ⊕ *www. omniversum.nl* 🖳 *€9.75* ⊙ *Show times vary–check the Web site or phone to confirm.*

③ Schilderijengalerij Prins Willem V *(Prince William V Painting Gallery).* One of the last remaining Dutch art *kabinets,* this princely gallery is packed with Old Masters hung in 18th-century *touche-touche* fashion (with barely an inch between paintings). Opened in 1773 it became the Netherlands' first public museum (until then most collections were seen only by special appointment). The cream of the collection was later moved to the Mauritshuis, but many fine works remain. The long narrow room has grand Louis XVI stucco ceilings, but it nevertheless exudes an intimate homey atmosphere, as if a friend who just happened to own a collection that included works by Jan Steen and Rembrandt had asked you over to see them. The museum is scheduled to reopen in 2011 following major renovation work—check the Web site for the latest information. ⊠ *Buitenhof 35* ☎ *070/302–3456* ⊕ *www.mauritshuis. nl* 🖳 *€1.50 (free with entry to Mauritshuis)* ⊙ *Tues.–Sun. 11–4.*

① Stadhuis Atrium *(Town Hall).* Richard Meier's Neo-Modernist 1995 complex, comprising the Town Hall, Central Library, and Municipal Record Office, is an awe-inspiring creation in aluminum, glass, and white epoxy resin. Inside, take the elevator to the 11th floor (weekdays only) to get the full effect of the building's light and space. The architect's attention to mathematical relationships—every aspect of the design is based on measurements that are multiples of 17.73 inches—makes for mesmerizing effect. Meier has endeavored to show the building, both literally and metaphorically, in its best light—the quality of light in the vast central lobby belies the fact you are actually indoors. ✉ *Spui 70* ☎ *070/353–3629* ⊕ *www.atriumdenhaag.nl* 🚇 *Free* ☉ *Mon.–Wed. and Fri. 7–7, Thurs. 7 AM–9:30 PM, Sat. 9:30–5.*

WHERE TO EAT

$–$$
ECLECTIC
★

✕ **Dudok Brasserie.** These days, Dudok is *the* in place in The Hague. It's ideal for people-of-every-stripe-watching, from politicians debating over a beer, to the fashionistas toying with their salads, to pensioners tucking into an afternoon tea of cream cakes and salmon sandwiches. The vast granite-and-metal interior looks like a cross between a 1930s railway station and an ultracontemporary factory, and besides the countless small tables and roomy bar area, there's a communal central table and a packed magazine rack to keep solo diners busy. The menu combines international dishes—carpaccio of beef, steaks, and grilled chicken—with traditional Dutch fare such as mustard soup (surprisingly mild and flavorsome) and sausage with cabbage. Additional pluses include a terrace for outdoor dining and a 1 AM closing on Friday and Saturday. ✉ *Hofweg 1a* ☎ *070/890–0100* ⊕ *www.dudok.nl* ▭ *AE, DC, MC, V.*

$$–$$$
INDONESIAN
★

✕ **Garoeda.** Named after a golden eagle in Indonesian mythology, a symbol of happiness and friendship, Garoeda is something of an institution among Hagenaars, many of whom consider it the best Indonesian spot in town. Established in 1949 and spread over five floors, the restaurant is decorated with Eastern art, and filled with wicker chairs and lush plants to give it a unique "colonial" atmosphere. Waiters are dressed in traditional costume and are more than happy to advise patrons new to the Indonesian dining experience. In addition to a choice of no less than seven different rijsttafels (an exotic smorgasbord of Indonesian dishes), there is also an extensive à la carte menu, featuring some unusual finds, such as spicy mussels and crispy roasted chicken in soy sauce. ✉ *Kneuterdijk 18a* ☎ *070/346–5319* ⊕ *www.garoeda.com* ▭ *AE, DC, MC, V.*

$$$–$$$$
ECLECTIC
Fodor's Choice
★

✕ **It Rains Fishes.** Crown Prince Willem Alexander has been known to pop in here, so you know it must be good. A gleaming eggshell, ivory, and mirrored jewel box, It Rains Fishes is run by a team of international chefs, whose predominantly aquatic specialties combine Thai, Malaysian, Indonesian, and French flavors. Its name, taken from a Thai folktale of fishes jumping from the river after a heavy rainfall, finds a few echoes in the restaurant's décor, with the occasional painted fish leaping around on the ceiling and walls. Specialties include sea bass with lemon and tarragon oil, and king crab in the shell with Malay black pepper sauce. For an unorthodox but totally winning dessert, choose the Thai-basil-and-chocolate sorbet. Outdoor dining is available in good weather. ✉ *Noordeinde 123* ☎ *070/365–2598* ⊕ *www.itrainsfishes.nl* ▭ *AE, DC, MC, V* ☉ *Closed Sun. No lunch Sat.*

$$–$$$
FRENCH
★

✕ **Le Haricot Vert.** In a 17th-century building that once housed the staff of the nearby Noordeinde palace, Le Haricot Vert is a popular haunt for locals who come to enjoy good food in an intimate, candlelit atmosphere. Every possible wall surface is hung with china, sections of stained glass, pictures, and mirrors, and the overall effect is one of

8

beguiling romantic clutter. Dishes such as grilled sardines with ratatouille, and lamb fillet served with rosemary and sweet peppers, combine Dutch classics with French flair. The menu changes seasonally, so you can expect irresistible asparagus in spring and game in winter. ⊠ *Molenstraat 9a–11* ☏ *070/365-2278 www.haricotvert.nl* ⊟ *AE, MC, V* ⊘ *Closed Sun. No lunch Mon.–Wed.*

¢–$ ✕ **Lokanta.** A well-priced menu and funky colorful decorations, like floral oilcloths on the tables and gilded tissue holders, make this eatery popular with trendy young locals, who flock in to enjoy a delicious combination of Greek, Turk-

ECLECTIC
★

> ### BAR FOOD
>
> When sitting down to a glass of beer, there's little the Dutch like more than a portion of hot *bitterballen*: half a dozen or so deep-fried, breadcrumb-coated "balls," with a side of mustard for dipping. When you bite into one you'll encounter finely ground meat-based goo with negligible nutritional value. What this is exactly, no one seems to know for sure. The meat part may have once belonged to a cow, but you can bet your life it wasn't finest rump. We love them!

---

ish, and Moroccan dishes. Try the *imam beyildi* (Turkish for "the imam fainted"), the name for a dish of eggplant stuffed with a spicy meat mixture. Because Lokanta is less expensive than some other places on this central street, it fills up fast, so get there early or reserve ahead. ⊠ *Buitenhof 4* ☏ *070/392–0870* ⊟ *MC, V* ⊘ *Closed Sun. and Mon. No lunch.*

$$–$$$ ✕ **'t Goude Hooft.** Magnificently dating from 1423 but rebuilt in 1660, the oldest restaurant in The Hague has a well-preserved interior, with plenty of wooden beams, brass chandeliers, and "antique" furniture all richly redolent of the Dutch Golden Age. In warm weather, the large terrace overlooking the market square makes a pleasant spot in which to enjoy a drink and a platter of *bitterballen.* For something more substantial, try the wine-enriched beef stew. ⊠ *Dagelijkse Groenmarkt 13* ☏ *070/346–9713 www.tgoudehooft.nl* ⊟ *MC, V.*

DUTCH

WHERE TO STAY

$–$$ ▥ **Best Western Hotel Petit.** This quiet, family-style hotel, although now part of a chain, is fronted by a pretty garden, and on a quiet residential boulevard between the Peace Palace and The Hague Municipal Museum. Occupying two large houses that date from 1895, Petit is tastefully furnished in warm shades of red and gold, with the occasional period stained-glass accent. The wood-paneled bar-lounge is a nice place to relax. **Pros:** quiet; friendly. **Cons:** a little way from the center. ⊠ *Groothertoginnelaan 42* ☏ *070/346–5500* ⊕ *www.hotelpetit. nl* ⤵ *20 rooms* ⌂ *In-room: no a/c, refrigerator, Internet. In-hotel: bar, Wi-Fi, parking (paid)* ⊟ *AE, DC, MC, V* ⓞ *BP.*

$$$$ ▥ **Hotel Des Indes.** A stately grande dame of the hotel world and once a 19th-century mansion built principally for grand balls and entertainment, Des Indes has a graciousness that makes it one of the world's premier hotels. Stay here and you'll be following in the footsteps of Empress Josephine of France, Theodore Roosevelt, and the legendary

Fodor's Choice
★

ballerina Anna Pavlova (who, sorry to note, died here after contracting pneumonia on her travels). Des Indes sits on one of the city's most prestigious squares, in the heart of The Hague, surrounded by all the important buildings: the Parliament, embassies, ministries, and the best shops. The interior is a harmonious blend of Belle Epoque elements: marble fluted columns, brocaded walls, and a good deal of gilding. Luxurious and ample bedrooms have all the best facilities—there are even Jacuzzis in some of them (although not the Belle Epoque ones). The former inner courtyard is now a towering domed lounge leading to the superb formal dining room—all crystal and linen. The lounge serves high tea every day from 2 to 5 pm—it's a city institution that's as big a hit with local residents as it is with hotel guests. **Pros:** sumptuous; elegant; centrally located. **Cons:** such luxury doesn't come cheap. ⊠ *Lange Voorhout 54–56,* ☎ *070/361–2345* ⊕ *www.desindes.nl* ⤵ *79 rooms, 13 suites* ⬧ *In-room: safe, refrigerator, Wi-Fi. In-hotel: restaurant, bar, pool, gym, Wi-Fi, parking (paid)* ▭ *AE, DC, MC, V.*

$–$$$ 🛏 **Novotel Den Haag City Centre.** This Novotel is housed in what was once a cinema, and the original décor in the public areas reflected and capitalized on that fact. However, a makeover in 2010 has given the foyer a more modern and stylish appeal, so you'll need a bit of imagination to visualize its past life. The guest rooms are all decorated in shades of peach and blue, but what they perhaps lack in individual creativity they more than make up for in cleanliness and modern conveniences. And the location is ideal for shopping and sightseeing. **Pros:** central; friendly. **Cons:** not for those with an aversion to chain hotels. ⊠ *Hofweg 5–7,* ☎ *070/364–8846* ⊕ *www.accorhotels.nl* ⤵ *104 rooms, 2 suites* ⬧ *In-room: safe, refrigerator, Wi-Fi. In-hotel: restaurant, bar, parking (paid)* ▭ *AE, DC, MC, V.*

$$–$$$ 🛏 **Parkhotel Den Haag.** Situated in lovely Molenstraat, a boutique- and
★ café-busy street with a bohemian feel, the Parkhotel has been sheltering visitors since 1912. The building still exults in plenty of Art Nouveau detailing; architecture buffs won't want to miss its fabulous five-story brick-and-stone stairway, for example. Today, friendly staff plus light airy rooms with wooden floorboards and all the modern conveniences (including snazzy bathrooms) add to its charms. They were renovated in 2010. **Pros:** friendly; grand. **Cons:** expensive parking. ⊠ *Molenstraat 53,* ☎ *070/362–4371* ⊕ *www.parkhoteldenhaag.nl* ⤵ *120 rooms* ⬧ *In-room: safe, Wi-Fi. In-hotel: restaurant, bar, Wi-Fi, parking (paid)* ▭ *AE, DC, MC, V* 🍴 *BP.*

$–$$ 🛏 **Sebel.** The friendly owners of this hotel have expanded it into three buildings between the city center and the Peace Palace, one of which is a beautiful Art Nouveau house from 1882. Tidy and comfortable, the rooms are large but sparsely furnished, and have high ceilings and tall windows for lots of light and air. **Pros:** historic building; friendly staff. **Cons:** a little way from the action; fairly basic for the price. ⊠ *Prins Hendrikplein 20,* ☎ *070/345–9200* ⊕ *www.hotelsebel.nl* ⤵ *33 rooms* ⬧ *In-room: no a/c, Internet. In-hotel: bar, parking (paid)* ▭ *AE, DC, MC, V* 🍴 *BP.*

¢–$ 🛏 **Stayokay.** Stayokay is one of the leading hostel chains in Holland, and this one enjoys a location close to Hollands Spoor train station.

8

Besides the 12 double rooms, there are rooms for three to nine people each. Clean, modern, and light, the hostel is in a renovated former warehouse and has a deck on the water plus a library, Internet stations, and a pool table for when you just can't sightsee any more. **Pros:** nice canal-side deck; good value. **Cons:** like any hostel, can be noisy and you can't always choose your roommates. ⊠ *Scheepmakersstraat 27,* ☎ *070/315–7888* ⊕ *www.stayokay.com* ⤴ *49 rooms each with 3–9 beds and shared baths* ⟁ *In-room: no a/c, no phone, no TV. In-hotel: restaurant, bar, Internet terminal, parking (paid)* ⊟ *No credit cards* ⦿ *BP.*

> ### DISTINGUISHED COMPANY
>
> The Café Schlemmer's convenient location right in the heart of the city, just around the corner from the Parliament building, makes it a meeting point for some pretty high-fliers. You could find yourself rubbing shoulders with anyone from local politicians to Dutch movie stars. If you hear a gasp followed by awed chatter when someone you don't recognize walks in, it probably means they're big in Holland.

NIGHTLIFE AND THE ARTS

THE ARTS

The Hague has a thriving cultural life—look no further than the gleaming Spui theater complex for proof. The resident orchestra and ballet company are so popular that advance reservations are essential if you want to be sure of a ticket. If you do catch a show, you'll note an unusual phenomenon from the otherwise normally reserved Dutch: the compulsory standing ovation. For some mysterious reason, this response seems to be given with far greater frequency here than in other countries. For information on cultural events, call the **Haags Uitburo** (⊠ *Hofweg 1* ☎ *0900/340–3505, €0.45 per min*) or visit their Web site (⊠ *www.haagsuitburo.nl*). In addition, pick up the monthly *Den Haag Agenda*, published by the VVV tourist office, which will keep you up to date on every worthwhile event that's happening in town during your stay.

MUSIC, THEATER AND DANCE

De Appel company has a lively, experimental approach to theater and performs at its own **Appeltheater** (⊠ *Duinstraat 6* ☎ *070/350–2200* ⊕ *www.toneelgroepdeappel.nl*). Mainstream Dutch theater is presented by the national theater company **Het Nationale Toneel**, which performs at **the Royal Schouwburg** (⊠ *Korte Voorhout 3* ☎ *0900/345–6789* ⊕ *www.ks.nl*).

For an outing with children, visit **Kooman's Poppentheater** (⊠ *Frankenstraat 66* ☎ *070/355–9305* ⊕ *www.koomanspoppentheater.nl*), which performs musical shows with puppets every Wednesday and some Saturdays. Advance booking is recommended.

The **Nederlands Danstheater** (⊠ *Spuiplein 152* ☎ *070/880–0333* ⊕ *www.ldt.nl*) is the national modern dance company and makes its home at the Lucent Dance Theatre, the world's only theater built exclusively for dance performances. It has an international reputation for ground-breaking productions, which might cause a run on tickets.

The Hague's **Residentie Orkest** has an excellent worldwide reputation and performs at **Dr. Anton Philipszaal** (⊠ *Spuiplein 150* ☎ *070/880–0333* ⊕ *www.residentieorkest.nl*).

NIGHTLIFE

Though The Hague seems fairly quiet at night, don't be fooled. Behind the reserved facade are plenty of clubs and bars tucked away, often discreetly hidden down tiny backstreets. However, if you like your nightlife of the pumpingly loud variety, you'd best hop on a train to Amsterdam.

BARS

Tapperij Le Duc (⊠ *Noordeinde 137* ☎ *070/364–2394*) has a delightful old-world ambience, with lots of wood, tiles, and a magnificent fireplace.

De Paap (⊠ *Papestraat 32* ☎ *070/365–2002*) has live music most nights and a cozy welcoming aura. The beer's cheap, too. **Boterwaag** (⊠ *Grote Markt 8a* ☎ *070/365–9686* ⊕ *www.september.nl*) is a favorite—located in a 17th-century weigh house, its high, vaulted brick ceilings make this magnificent bar feel open and airy even when packed. It draws a trendy young crowd.

Paas (⊠ *Dunne Bierkade 16a* ☎ *070/360–0019*) sits beside a picturesque canal between Hollands Spoor Station and the city center. A haven for beer connoisseurs, it offers 150 brews, by far the best selection in town. Dunne Bierkade is also home to many other bars and restaurants, and has been dubbed the city's "Avenue Culinaire." **Schlemmer** (⊠ *Lange Houtstraat 17* ☎ *070/360–9000*) is a comfortable brown-style bar that is one of Den Haag's top places to see and be seen.

To enjoy an aperitif in an upmarket setting and surrounded by The Hague's bold and beautiful, a trip to **Bodega de Posthoorn** (⊠ *Lange Voorhout 39a* ☎ *070/360–4906*) is a must. You can have light meals here and the leafy terrace is particularly appealing. The friendly and relaxed **Stairs** (⊠ *Nieuwe Schoolstraat 11* ☎ *070/356–1169*) is gay-oriented, but women are welcome here, too.

MUSIC CLUBS

The latest local and international bands can be heard at **Het Paard van Troje** (⊠ *Prinsegracht 12* ☎ *070/750–3434*), where you can also dance and watch movies and multimedia shows.

SHOPPING

There is a plethora of intimate, idiosyncratic specialty boutiques to explore in The Hague, and in the larger department stores you can kid yourself that you're there only to admire the architecture—several are housed in period gems. With its historic and artistic connections, the city's art and antiques trade has naturally developed a strong reputation, and you can certainly find treasures here. Despite the Dutch reputation for thrift, haggling for antiques isn't "done." That said, you can almost always secure some kind of discount if you offer to pay in cash.

Late-night shopping in The Hague is on Thursday until 9. Increasingly in the center of town, you'll find larger stores open on Sunday. Many shops take a half day or don't open at all on Monday.

DEPARTMENT STORES

De Bijenkorf (✉ *Wagenstraat 32 [entrance on Grote Markstraat]* ☎ *0900/0919*) is Holland's premier department-store chain. It has a reputation for combining class with accessibility and is excellent for cutting-edge housewares, fashion accessories, and clothing basics. Do look, too, at the building's period detailing: the stained-glass windows, carvings, and original flooring that adorn the sweeping stairway on the left of the store.

The **Maison de Bonneterie** (✉ *Gravenstraat 2* ☎ *070/330–5300*) is The Hague's most exclusive department store—and it's got the "By Royal Appointment" labels to prove it. Built in 1913 and with an enormous central atrium, it's a glittering mixture of glass and light. On Maison de Bonneterie's four floors you'll find everything from Ralph Lauren shirts to wax candles.

SPECIALTY STORES

ANTIQUES AND FINE ART

There are so many reputable antiques and art specialists on Noordeinde and Denneweg that a trip down either street is sure to prove fruitful.

Smelik & Stokking (✉ *Noordeinde 150* ☎ *070/364–0768*) specializes in contemporary art, welcomes browsers, and has a pretty sculpture garden full of unusual pieces.

BOOKS AND PRINTS

M. Heeneman (✉ *Prinsestraat 47* ☎ *070/364–4748*) is a respected dealer who specializes in Dutch antiquarian prints, maps, and architectural renderings. Staff in this small shop are happy to advise customers, and purchases are wrapped in beautiful paper that depicts a fantasy, old Dutch town. You'll always be able to buy English-language newspapers at the city's train stations, but otherwise the centrally located **Selexys Verwijs** (✉ *De Passage 39* ☎ *070/311–4848*), one of a chain of bookstores, sells a good range of English-language magazines and books.

CLOTHING

For handmade men's shirts, visit the diplomats' favorite supplier, **FG Van den Heuvel** (✉ *Hoge Nieuwstraat 36* ☎ *070/346–0887*), in business since 1882. Both men and women can find classics with a twist in natural linens, cottons, and wools at **Hoogeweegen Rouwers** (✉ *Noordeinde 23*

WHERE TO SHOP

Denneweg, Frederikstraat, and Noordeinde are best for antiques shops, galleries, and boutiques. For quirky, one-of-a-kind gift shops, try Molenstraat and Papestraat. You'll find chain stores in the pretty, light-filled Hague Passage (Spuistraat 26), which dates from the 1880s and is the Netherlands' last remaining period mall. In the little streets behind the Passage are more fashion and home-ware boutiques. Between the Venestraat and Nieuwstraat is the charmingly named Haagsche Bluf (the name is akin to the "hot air" coming out of Washington, D.C.) pedestrian mall, featuring mainly clothing chain stores.

8

☎ *070/365–7473*). The service is as timeless as the clothes—it's the sort of place where purchases are carefully wrapped in tissue paper.

CRYSTAL, CHINA AND HOUSEWARES

Ninaber van Eyben (✉ *Hoogstraat 5* ☎ *070/365–5321*) sells the classic Dutch lifestyle look—antique-finish globes, silverware, and traditional blue-and-white china. There's plenty of room to look around without fear of breaking anything.

To see the cutting-edge side of contemporary Dutch housewares, visit **Steitner & Bloos** (✉ *Molenstraat 39* ☎ *070/360–5170*). You'll find steel bathroom accessories, geometrically shaped lights, and sofas, tables, and chairs designed along clean graphic lines.

GIFTS, SOUVENIRS AND JEWELRY

Tucked away from the crowds is **Emma Plate & Strass** (✉ *Molenstraat 22* ☎ *070/345–7027*), a tiny, very feminine store complete with white-washed walls and a wooden floor. The owner specializes in silver plate and costume jewelry, much imported from Paris and Berlin. She also stocks a small range of fabulous chandeliers, sometimes in unusual colors such as purple.

The tiny, family-run store **Loose** (✉ *Papestraat 3* ☎ *070/346–0404*) is a toy shop for grown-ups. Glass cabinets are filled with rolling pins, pots, and pans no bigger than a fingernail just perfect for dollhouse enthusiasts. Meanwhile there are also larger wooden toys, a wonderful selection of old Dutch books and albums, and, in the rear of the store, a wide range of old prints.

If you want to make your own gifts or kill some time with older kids, a good place to visit is the funky DIY-jewelry store **Jewelicious** (✉ *Prinsestraat 60* ☎ *06/3945–7829*). You can choose delicate beads—candylike glass ones, metallic baubles, or fake pearls—then join the others at the big table and string them into pretty necklaces and earrings.

Customers at **Backers & Zoon** (✉ *Noordeinde 58* ☎ *070/346–6422*) receive the sort of personal attentive service one would expect from an old-fashioned family jeweler. There's a sophisticated stock of pieces, including signet rings, diamond rings, and Fabergé-style accessories. Prices are not for the fainthearted.

Damen (✉ *Noordeinde 186* ☎ *070/360–0166*) sells exquisite handmade papers and gift wrap, as well as covered notebooks. It's a delightfully old-fashioned store that doesn't appear to have changed a great deal since it first opened in 1895.

DELFT

Fodor's Choice
★ For many travelers, few spots in Holland are as intimate and attractive as this charming little town. With time-burnished canals and cobblestone streets, Delft possesses a peaceful calm that recalls the quieter pace of the 17th-century Golden Age, back when Johannes Vermeer was counted among its citizens.

Imagine a tiny Amsterdam, but with smaller canals, narrower bridges and fewer people, and you have the essence of Old Delft. But even though the city reveres its favorite son, and folks have one foot rooted in the past, another is planted firmly in the present. In fact, today's Delft teems with hip cafés, and—being a college town—revelers can be seen piling in and out of bars almost every day of the week. It's quaint, but it's no museum piece swaddled in cotton wool to keep it safe for future generations. Nonetheless, if living it up isn't your thing, the revelry is easy to escape, and there are plenty of quiet residential corners where you could imagine Vermeer strolling the streets looking for his next subject.

If you are arriving by train in the coming years, your first impression, however, may be somewhat different. Major construction work in and around the railway station is underway. It will eventually see the train tracks moved underground, and thus the city's approaches will be greatly beautified. But that work is scheduled to last until at least 2016, and some skeptics who see the slow progress of the North-South line in Amsterdam believe it may cause disruption as far into the future as 2020. The biggest victim of all this is the Rose Windmill (*Molen de Roos*), which sits directly over the proposed underground route. For safety reasons it is closed to visitors, and the bakery that operated within has been rehoused.

Rest assured however, that once you pick your way through the chaos, the old center is—apart from a couple of sites mentioned below—largely unaffected and every bit as beautiful as it ever was.

8

GETTING HERE AND AROUND

14 km (9 mi) southeast of The Hague, 71 km (44 mi) southwest of Amsterdam.

Direct trains leave Amsterdam Central Station for Delft every half hour throughout the day—the journey time is a little under one hour. If driving, take the A10 then the A4 south from Amsterdam. The drive will take between 45 minutes and one hour, depending on traffic.

Trams also run between Delft and The Hague. On buses, trams, and trains you can use an **OV-chipkaart** (public transport chip card)—a new electronic payment system that's slowly rolled out nationally. These credit card–size tickets can be loaded up with credit from machines in the railway stations, and are debited as you board and leave trains, trams, metros, and buses. The OV-chipkaart will eventually replace all other transport tickets, including the national *strippenkaart,* but at this writing no date for the phaseout in Delft had been set.

Public Transportation Information (☎ *0900/9292*).

TOURS

The Delft City tour is a two-hour combined walking and canal boat tour, which provides the ideal way to capture the essence of the town in a nutshell if time is short. It leaves from the tourist office Sun.–Fri. at 11:30, Apr.–Sept. Tours cost €10 per person—sign up at least 30 minutes beforehand. On Saturdays during the same season, walking-only tours leave at 12:30 and cost €5.50. That ticket will also entitle you to a 10% discount on a Canal Boat tour if taken the same day. The latter cost €6 per person without the discount, and leave hourly on the hour between 11 and 5 from Koornmarkt 113.

Rondvaart Delft (✉ *Koornmarkt 113* ☎ *015/212-6385* ⊕ *www.rondvaartdelft.nl*).

TIMING

Delft is the kind of place you'll want to linger. Allow at least a day to enjoy it all, two if you take in all the museums.

ESSENTIALS

Bicycle Rentals Rijwiel Shop (✉ *Delft train station* ☎ *015/214-3033* 💳 *€6.50–€7.50 per day and a security deposit of €50 with ID* ☉ *weekdays 5:45 AM–midnight, weekends 6:30 AM–midnight*).

Emergency Services National Emergency Alarm Number (☎ *112 for police, fire, and ambulance*).

Hospitals Reinier de Graaf Gasthuis (✉ *Reinier De Graafweg 3–11* ☎ *015/260-3060*).

TaxisTaxi Central (☎ *015/285-5800*).

Visitor Information Toeristen Informatie Punt Delft (Delft Tourist Information Point) (✉ *Hippolytusbuurt 4,* ☎ *0900/515-1555*).

A Brief History of Delft

Delft has more than painterly charm—many great men lived and died here. Toward the end of the 16th century Prince William of Orange (known as William the Silent) settled in Delft to wage his war against Spanish rule. He never left: the nation's founder was assassinated in his mansion in 1584 by a spy of the Spanish Duke of Alva, and buried in the Nieuwe Kerk (New Church). Also buried here is Grotius, the humanist and father of international law. And Delft was home to Anthonie van Leeuwenhoek, who mastered the fledging invention of the microscope and was born the same year as Vermeer, 1632. Vermeer was just one of many artists who set up shop in the city—which had grown rich with the trade in butter, cloth, beer, and pottery.

Delft's history was often turbulent. In the 17th century, the canal water became tainted, forcing 180 of the 200 resident breweries to close. In 1654, the "Thunderclap," an accidental gunpowder explosion, leveled half the town and killed hundreds. But Delft rebounded thanks to riches it had amassed as the headquarters of the Dutch East India Company. The porcelains their traders brought back from the Far East proved irresistible, and in 1645 De Porceleyne Fles started making and exporting the famous blue-and-white earthenware that soon became known the world over as Delft Blue.

EXPLORING

Compact and easy to traverse despite its web of canals, Delft is best explored on foot, although water taxis are available in summer to give you an armchair ride through the heart of town. Everything you might want to see is in the old center, with the exception of the two Delft-ware factories, which are an additional 15 minutes' walk or a short taxi ride away.

TOP ATTRACTIONS

1 Bagijnhof (Bagijn courtyard). On the Oude Delft, just north of the Lambert van Meerten Museum, is a weather-beaten 13th-century Gothic gate, with ancient-looking stone relief, that leads through to a small courtyard. The city sided with the (Protestant) Dutch rebels during the Eighty Years' War, and when the (Catholic) Spanish were driven out in 1572, the city reverted to Protestantism, leaving many Catholic communities in dire straits. One group of women was permitted to stay and practice their religion, but according to a new law, their place of worship had to be very modest: a drab exterior in the Bagijnhof hides their sumptuously Baroque church.

7 Gemeenlandshuis. The pretty, tree-lined Oude Delft canal has numerous historic gabled houses along its banks and takes the honors for being the first canal in the city, and possibly the first city canal anywhere in the Netherlands. One of the finest buildings along its length, the "Common Land house," is a spectacular example of 16th-century Gothic architecture and is adorned with brightly painted shields and a coat of arms. A few yards east of here, across the canal on the corner of

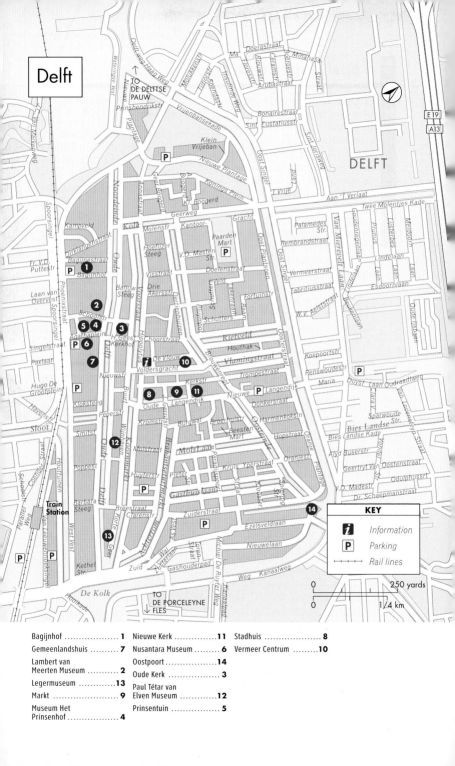

Delft

DELFT

E19
A13

KEY

i Information

P Parking

Rail lines

0 ————— 250 yards
0 ————— 1/4 km

Be sure to climb the 380-odd steps of the church tower for spectacular views of Delft and the surrounding countryside.

Hippolytusbuurt and Cameretten, is a row of *visbanken* (fish stalls), built along the canal in 1650. Fish has been sold over the counter here pretty much ever since. ✉ *Oude Delft 167.*

Kleyweg's Stads-Koffiehuis (✉ *Oude Delft 133* ☎ *015/212–4625*) looks out over the oldest and one of the most beautiful canals in Delft. Inside, you'll find a *stamtafel,* a large table laid out with newspapers and magazines, where anyone may sit and chat. There are also smaller individual tables where you can enjoy good coffee, delicious pancakes, and terrific apple pie. In fine weather, the tables on the barge moored on the canal are very popular. The café is closed Sunday.

2 ★ **Lambert van Meerten Museum.** Within the shadow of the Oude Kerk, this Renaissance-era, canal-side mansion has gloriously paneled rooms which provide a noble setting for antique tiles, tin-glazed earthenware, paintings, and an extensive collection of ebony-veneer furniture. Although much of the works on display are not the original patrician owner's (who lost a fortune when his distillery burned down and he had to auction off everything), the house and some of his collection were bought back by Van Meerten's friends. Note especially the great collection of tiles, whose subjects range from foodstuffs to warships. The gardens here are alluring, with a spherical sundial, two busts, and a stone gateway leading the eye through to the tangled woods beyond. ✉ *Oude Delft 199* ☎ *015/260–2358* ⊕ *www.lambertvanmeerten-delft. nl* 🎫 *€3.50; combined ticket to Het Prinsenhof, Nusantara, and Lambert van Meerten museums €10* ⊙ *Tues.–Sun. 11–5.*

⑨ Markt. Delft's main square is bracketed by two town landmarks, the Stadhuis (Town Hall) and the Nieuwe Kerk. Here, too, are cafés, restaurants, and souvenir shops (most selling imitation Delftware) and, on Thursday, a busy general market. Markt 52 is the site of Johannes Vermeer's house, where the 17th-century painter spent much of his youth. Not far away is a statue of Grotius, or Hugo de Groot, born in Delft in 1583 and one of Holland's most famous humanists and lawyers.

④ Museum Het Prinsenhof. A former dignitary-hosting convent of St. Agatha, the Prinsenhof Museum is celebrated as the residence of Prince William the Silent, beloved as *Vader des Vaderlands* (Father of the Nation) for his role in the Spanish Revolt and a hero whose tragic end here gave this structure the sobriquet "cradle of Dutch liberty." The complex of buildings was taken over by the government of the new Dutch Republic in 1572 and given to William of Orange for his use as a residence. On July 10, 1584, fevered by monies offered by Philip II of Spain, Bathasar Gerard, a Catholic fanatic, gained admittance to the mansion and succeeded in shooting the prince on the staircase hall, since known as Moordhal (Murder Hall). The fatal bullet holes—the *teykenen der koogelen*—are still visible in the stairwell. Today, the imposing structure is a museum, with a 15th-century chapel, a quaint courtyard, and a bevy of elegantly furnished 17th-century rooms filled with antique pottery, silver, tapestries, and House of Orange portraits, along with exhibits on Dutch history. ⊠ *Sint Agathaplein 1* ☏ *015/260–2358* ⊕ *www.prinsenhof-delft.nl* ✑ *€7.50; combined ticket to Het Prinsenhof, Nusantara, and Lambert van Meerten museums €10* ☉ *Tues.–Sat. 10–5, Sun. 1–5.*

Fodor's Choice ★ *(margin note alongside Museum Het Prinsenhof)*

⑪ Nieuwe Kerk *(New Church).* Presiding over the Markt, this Late Gothic edifice was built between 1483 and 1510. It represents more than a century's worth of Dutch craftsmanship—it's as though its founders knew it would one day be the last resting place of the man who built the nation, William the Silent, and his descendants of the House of Orange. In 1872 the noted architect P. J. H. Cuypers raised the tower to its current height. There are 22 columns surrounding the ornate black-marble-and-alabaster tomb of William of Orange, which was designed by Hendrick de Keyser and his son. The small dog you see at the prince's feet is rumored to have starved to death after refusing to eat following his owner's death. Throughout the church are paintings, stained-glass windows, and memorabilia associated with the Dutch royal family. There are other mausoleums, most notably that of lawyer-philosopher Hugo de Groot, or Grotius. In summer it is possible to climb the 380-odd steps of the church tower for an unparalleled view that stretches as far as Scheveningen to the north and Rotterdam to the south. ⊠ *Markt 2* ☏ *015/212–3025* ✑ *Combined ticket for Oude Kerk and Nieuwe Kerk €3.30, tower €3* ☉ *Apr.–Oct., Mon.–Sat. 9–6; Nov.–Jan., Weekdays 11–4, Sat. 10–5; Feb.–Mar., Mon.–Sat. 10–5.*

③ Oude Kerk *(Old Church).* At the very heart of historic Delft, the Gothic Oude Kerk, with its tower 6 feet off-kilter, is the last resting place of Vermeer. The tower seems to lean in all directions at once, but then, this is the oldest church in Delft, having been founded in 1200. Building went on until the 15th century, which accounts for the combination

Buying Delftware

It's corny, even sometimes a little tacky (miniature clogs, anyone?), but no visit to Delft would be complete without stopping at a Delft Porcelain Factory, to see plates and tulip vases being painted by hand and perhaps picking up a souvenir or two. **De Porceleyne Fles** (✉ *Royal Delftware Factory, Rotterdamseweg 196* ☎ *015/251–2030* ⊕ *www.royaldelft. com* ☞ *museum €8;* ⊙ *mid-Mar.–Oct., daily 9–5; Nov.–mid-Mar., Mon.–Sat. 9–5)* is the original and most famous home to the popular blue-and-white pottery. Regular demonstrations of molding and painting pottery are given by the artisans. These wares bear the worthy name of De Porceleyne Fles. On the bottom of each object is a triple signature: a plump vase topped by a straight line, the stylized letter "F" below it, and the word "Delft." Blue is no longer the only official color. In 1948, a rich red cracked glaze was premiered

depicting profuse flowers, graceful birds, and leaping gazelles. There is New Delft, a range of green, gold, and black hues, whose exquisite minuscule figures are drawn to resemble an old Persian tapestry; the Pynacker Delft, borrowing Japanese motifs in rich oranges and golds; and the brighter Polychrome Delft, which can strike a brilliant sunflower-yellow effect.

Another favorite place for picking up Delftware is at the pottery factories of **De Delftse Pauw** (✉ *Delftweg 133* ☎ *015/212–4920* ⊕ *www.delftpottery. com* ☞ *free tours;* ⊙ *Apr.–Oct., daily 9-4:30; Nov.–Mar., weekdays 9–4:30, weekend 11–1),* which, although not as famous as De Porceleyne Fles, produce work of equally high quality. **De Candelaer** (✉ *Kerkstraat 14* ☎ *015/213–1848)* is a smaller pottery, and its city-center location makes it a convenient stop-off for comparisons of Delftware with other pottery.

8

of architectural styles, and much of its austere interior dates from the latter part of the work. The tower, dating to 1350, started leaning in the Middle Ages, and today the tilt to the east is somewhat stabilized by the 3-foot tilt to the north. The tower, whose tilt prevents ascension by visitors, holds the largest carillon bell in the Netherlands; weighing nearly 20,000 pounds, it now is used only on state occasions. ✉ *Heilige Geestkerkhof* ☎ *015/212–3015* ☞ *Combined ticket to Oude Kerk and Nieuwe Kerk €3.50* ⊙ *Apr.–Oct., Mon.–Sat. 9–6; Nov.–Mar., Mon.–Fri. 11–4, Sat. 10–5.*

❿ **Vermeer Centrum** (Vermeer Center). Housed in the former St. Lucas Guild, where Delft's favorite son was dean for many years, the Center takes visitors on a multimedia journey through the life and work of Johannes Vermeer. Touch screens, projections, and other interactive features are interspersed with giant reproductions of the master's work, weaving a tale of 17th-century Delft and drawing you into the mind of the painter. The centerpiece is an audiovisual presentation telling the story of Delft in Vermeer's day. ✉ *Voldersgracht 21* ☎ *015/213–8588* ⊕ *www.vermeerdelft.nl* ☞ *€7* ⊙ *Daily 10–5.*

A view of the twin turrets of the Oostpoort in Delft, as seen from one of the many waterways.

WORTH NOTING

13 **Legermuseum** *(Netherlands Army Museum).* Delft's former armory makes an appropriate setting for an impressive military museum. Despite the gentle images of Dutch life, the origins of the Dutch Republic were violent. It took nothing less than the Eighty Years' War (1568–1648) to finally achieve independence from the Spanish crown. In addition to the guns, swords, and other implements of warfare, all periods of Dutch military history are explored in detail, from Roman times to the German occupation during World War II. ⊠ *Korte Geer 1* ☏ *015/215–0500* ⊕ *www.armymuseum.nl* ✉ *€7.50* ☽ *Tues.–Fri. 10–5, weekends noon–5.*

6 **Nusantara Museum.** In the same courtyard as the Prinsenhof Museum, the Nusantara has a colorful collection of ethnographic costumes and artifacts from the Dutch East Indies—most of it is ill-gotten gains from the 17th century by members of the Dutch East India Company. A large Javanese *gamelan* (percussion orchestra) takes center stage inside, and is surrounded by Indo-European batik, Hindu statuettes, shields and intricately carved spears, diamond-encrusted daggers, *wayang kulit* (shadow puppets), and a beautifully carved tomb. Other displays chart the history of the spice trade. At this writing the museum was closed for safety reasons due to its proximity to the tunneling work on the railway. Check the Web site for up-to-date information. ⊠ *Sint Agathaplein 4* ☏ *015/260–2358* ⊕ *www.nusantara-delft.nl* ✉ *€3.50; combined ticket to Het Prinsenhof, Nusantara, and Lambert van Meerten museums €10* ☽ *Tues.–Sun. 11–5.*

⓮ Oostpoort *(East Gate)*. At the southern end of the Oosteinde canal, the fairy-tale twin turrets of the Oostpoort form Delft's only remaining city gate. Dating back to 1400, with the spires added in 1514, parts of it are now a private residence, but you can still walk over the drawbridge. It is a short walk out of the center, but the effort of getting there is more than rewarded by the view.

⓬ Paul Tétar van Elven Museum. This 18th-century canal-side mansion was the former home of 19th-century painter Paul Tétar van Elven. The interior he created is charmingly redolent of Ye Olde Delft, complete with painted ceilings, antiques, and even a reproduction of an artist's atelier done up in the Old Dutch style. ⊠ *Koornmarkt 67* ☏ *015/212–4206* w*ww.museumpaultetarvanelven.nl* 🎟 *€2.50* ⊘ *Apr.–Oct., Tues.–Sun. 1–5.*

⓹ Prinsentuin *(Prince's Garden)*. Between the Prinsenhof and the Nusantara Museum is Agathaplein, a Late Gothic leafy courtyard built around 1400, which has huge chestnut trees shading an adjacent green. At the center is the Prinsentuin, a somewhat cultivated square that offers a calming respite from the city streets.

⓼ Stadhuis *(Town Hall)*. At the west end of the Markt, only the solid 13th-century tower remains from the original medieval town-hall building. The gray-stone edifice that looms over has picturesque red shutters and lavish detailing. It was designed in 1618 by Hendrick de Keyser, one of the most prolific architects of the Golden Age. Inside is a grand staircase and Council Chamber with a famous old map of Delft. You can view the Town Hall interior only by making arrangements through the Delft tourist office, which can also issue you a ticket to visit the torture chamber in Het Steen, the 13th-century tower. ⊠ *Markt 87* ⊘ *By appointment.*

> **RETAIL THE[...]**
>
> In Delft, Friday is *koop[...] ning shopping)*, the only d[...] stores are open until 9 PM (the [...] of the week everything closes a[...] PM). A large weekly market is held every Thursday from 9 to 5 on the Markt, with a flower market along the Hippolytusbuurt also on Thursday from 9 to 5. Every Saturday, there is a general market at the Brabantse Turfmarkt/Burgwal. Saturday in summer, there is a flea market on the canals in the town center and an art market at Heilige Geestkerkhof.

8

WHERE TO EAT

$–$$ ✕ **Café Vlaanderen.** Board games keep you entertained on a rainy day
CAFÉ inside the extensive café, but sunny skies will make you head for the tables set under leafy lime trees out front on the Beestenmarkt. Out back is an equally shady garden. The deluxe fish wrap makes a delicious light lunch, while evening options include a delicious tuna and swordfish brochette. ⊠ *Beestenmarkt 16* ☏ *015/213–3311* 🖃 *MC, V.*

¢ ✕ **De Nonnerie.** In the vaulted cellar of the famous Prinsenhof Museum,
FRENCH this luncheon-only tearoom has a sedate elegant atmosphere. If you can, get a table in the grassy courtyard under an umbrella, and—since you're within the House of Orange—order an Oranjeboom beer to

Vermeer: Sphinx of Delft

As one of the world's most adored artists, Johannes Vermeer (1632–75) has been the subject of blockbuster exhibitions, theater pieces, and best-selling novels (Tracy Chevalier's *Girl with a Pearl Earring*, also a sumptuous movie). He enjoys cult status, yet his reputation rests on just 35 paintings. Of course, those canvases—ordinary domestic scenes depicting figures caught in an amber light—are among the most extraordinary ever created. But Vermeer's fame is relatively recent. He died aged 42, worn out by economic woes. Only since the mid-19th century have critics rightfully revered his work. And when Proust proclaimed his *View of Delft* "the most beautiful painting in the world," audiences worldwide became enraptured.

How Vermeer painted scenes of such incomparable quietude, while living in a house filled with his 11 children, is a difficult question to answer, and little is known about his early life. We do know that his father ran an inn, and was also an art dealer, as was Johannes himself. But that doesn't seem important—the "reality" that matters is the one Vermeer captured on his canvases. The way his light traps the most transient of effects is so perfect, you almost find yourself looking around to see where the sunlight has fallen, expecting it to be dappling your own face.

wash down the fine *Delftsche Meesters palet* (three small sandwiches of pâté, salmon, and Dutch cheese) served here. Entry is via the archway from Oude Delft into the Prinsenhof Museum, down a signposted path beside the gardens. ⊠ *Sint Agathaplein* ☎ *015/212–1860* ▭ *No credit cards* ⊘ *Closed Mon. No dinner.*

¢–$
CAFÉ
✕ **De Wijnhaven.** This Delft staple has loyal regulars, drawn by the many terrace tables on a small square overlooking a narrow canal, and a mean Indonesian satay. There's a smart restaurant on the first floor, but the bar and mezzanine have plenty to offer, with lunch snacks, a reasonable menu for dinner with the latest tracks on the speakers, and great fries and salads. ⊠ *Wijnhaven 22* ☎ *015/214–1460* ▭ *MC, V.*

$$$$
FRENCH
Fodor's Choice
★
✕ **De Zwethheul.** Delft's classiest restaurant is also its best hidden: set a little outside town, it can easily be reached by cab. In a restored 18th-century building, this award-winner actually began as a humble pancake house. It's now run by top chef Mario Ridder, who took over when the former chef moved to the Parkheuvel in Rotterdam. In fine weather, you can eat on a beautiful terrace overlooking the Schie River. Specialties of the house include delights such as roasted Barbary duck with caramelized pistachio, date purée, beetroot, and balsamic sauce. ⊠ *Rotterdamseweg 480* ☎ *010/470–4166* ⊕ *www.zwethheul.nl* ⚐ *Reservations essential* ▭ *AE, DC, MC, V* ⊘ *Closed Mon. No lunch Sat.*

$$$–$$$$
FRENCH
✕ **Le Vieux Jean.** The tiny, family-run restaurant serves tasty meat-and-potatoes fare as well as good fish dishes such as *kabeljauw* (cod) with asparagus sauce. The adjoining Café de Oude Jean serves up somewhat cheaper fare. ⊠ *Heilige Geestkerkhof 3* ☎ *015/213–0433* ⚐ *Reservations essential* ▭ *AE, DC, MC, V* ⊘ *Closed Sun. and Mon.*

The picturesque red shutters of the original medieval town hall building in Delft.

$–$$
CONTEMPORARY

✕ **Stadscafé de Waag.** The ancient brick-and-stone walls of this cavernous former weigh house are adorned with hulking 17th-century balance scales. Tables on the mezzanine in the rear overlook the Wijnhaven canal, while those on the terrace in front nestle under the magnificent, looming, town clock tower. All the while, tastefully unobtrusive music creates a cool vibe for a mixed clientele. Happily, dishes such as Flemish asparagus with ham and egg, or *parelhoen* (guinea fowl) in a rich dark broth, are equal to the fabulous setting. ⊠ *Markt 11* ☎ *015/213–0393* ⊟ *AE, MC, V.*

¢–$
DUTCH

✕ **Willem van Oranje.** You might normally be wary of any large establishment on a main tourist crossroads that offers its menu in six languages, but what redeems this place, with its to-die-for view between the Town Hall and the New Church, is the wide selection of good-value Dutch pancakes. Fill up from a choice of around 50 sweet or savory (and sometimes both) flavor concoctions to suit every taste. Or if you still can't make up your mind, there are also all the usual Dutch café standards on the menu, including omelets, rolls, and salads. A more sophisticated dinner menu with heartier fish and meat favorites appears on weekend evenings. ⊠ *Markt 48a* ☎ *015/212–3059* ⊟ *MC, V.*

WHERE TO STAY

¢

⌕ **B&B Oosteinde.** This small yet friendly bed-and-breakfast is the only one of its kind in the city. Located behind the Beestenmarkt, near the fairy-tale twin towers of the city gate at Oostpoort, this welcoming house makes you feel like one of the family. Larger rooms can sleep three or four. A minimum stay of two nights is required. There are sinks in the rooms, but bathroom facilities are shared. **Pros:** friendly; good value. **Cons:** shared bathrooms. ⊠ *Oosteinde 156* 🏠🏠 *015/213–4238* ⊕ *www.bb-oosteinde.nl* ⤴ *3 rooms without bath* ♿ *In-room: no a/c. In-hotel: Wi-Fi, some pets allowed* ⊟ *No credit cards* 🍴 *BP.*

$$–$$$ 🚇 **Best Western Museumhotels Delft.** Spread through a complex of three buildings and a warren of corridors, this sprawling hotel is opposite the Oude Kerk and adjacent to the Prinsenhof Museum. Several period touches amid the chain-hotel stylings have helped this spot retain its historic charm, although this has been achieved without sacrificing any creature comforts. At this writing the hotel reception has moved temporarily around the corner to Oude Delft 189, due to nearby construction work, but it will revert to its original address when this is completed. **Pros:** good location; some rooms have canal views. **Cons:** part of a chain; parking difficult. ⊠ *Phoenixstraat 50a* 🏠 *015/215–3070* ⊕ *www. museumhotels.nl* ⤴ *66 rooms* ♿ *In-room: no a/c (some), safe, refrigerator. In hotel: bar, Wi-Fi* ⊟ *AE, DC, MC, V.*

$$ 🚇 **Bridges House.** The history of this hotel goes back to Jan Steen—one of the great painters of The Hague School—who lived and painted here. His contemporaries didn't recognize his talent, so he opened an inn and operated a brewery to supplement his income. The current owner has re-created a patrician's house in a tasteful refurbishment. Antiques grace each spacious room, all adorned with extra-long beds with custom-made Pullman mattresses. The bathrooms are fitted with enormous showerheads for a wake-up blast, and all have tubs. The breakfast room overlooks the canal. For longer stays, consider one of the apartments. **Pros:** location; canal views. **Cons:** parking is difficult. ⊠ *Oude Delft 74* 🏠 *015/212–4036* ⊕ *www.bridges-house.nl* ⤴ *10 rooms, 2 studio apartments* ♿ *In-room: no a/c, Internet* ⊟ *MC, V* 🍴 *BP.*

$$ 🚇 **Johannes Vermeer.** It's surprising that no one else thought of it before,
★   but this is the first Delft hotel to pay homage to the town's most famous local son. The buildings of this former cigar factory were completely modernized and turned into a sumptuous hotel in 2000. You'll be spoiled for choice of old-master views: rooms at the front overlook a canal, while rooms at the back have a sweeping city view that takes in three churches. In tasteful greens and yellows, the décor is unobtrusive, and the staff are pleasantly friendly. The garden behind the hotel is a mellow place to have a drink. The restaurant is open only for groups (advance arrangements essential). It's too bad, because its walls are adorned with painted copies of the entire works of Vermeer, with his *Girl with a Pearl Earring* inevitably taking center stage. **Pros:** historic building; canal views in some rooms. **Cons:** parking is difficult ⊠ *Molslaan 18–22* 🏠 *015/212–6466* ⊕ *www.hotelvermeer.nl* ⤴ *25 rooms, 5 suites* ♿ *In-room: Wi-Fi* ⊟ *AE, DC, MC, V* 🍴 *BP.*

$–$$ 🚇 **Leeuwenbrug.** Facing one of Delft's quieter waterways, this tradi-
Fodor's Choice   tional and well-maintained hotel has an Old Dutch–style canal-side
★   lounge, an ideal spot to sip a drink and rest up aching feet after a hard day's touring and shopping. The rooms are large, airy, and tastefully contemporary in décor; those in the annex are particularly appealing. Rooms at the front have canal views. The staff are very friendly and helpful, and often go out of their way to make guests feel welcome.

Pros: friendly; central; canal views in some rooms. Cons: some bathrooms a little old. ⊠ *Koornmarkt 16* 🕾 *015/214–7741* ⊕ *www.leeuwenbrug.nl* ↻ *36 rooms* ♿ *In-room: no a/c, Wi-Fi. In-hotel: bar* ═ *AE, MC, V* ⏐◯⏐ *BP.*

¢–$ 🚻 **Soul Inn.** In a quiet residential neighborhood 10 minutes' walk from the train station and the old center, the large '70s logo above the door of this 19th-century town house barely hints at the eclectic nature of this soul-inspired B&B. Each of the rooms is individually bedecked with a chaotic mixture of chintz and glitz that harks back to a time when big Afro hair was the only way to go, and color coordination had yet to be invented. It's bright, it's unique, and it's fun. The suites are also equipped with kitchen facilities. **Pros:** quirky, quiet location. **Cons:** outside the historic center. ⊠ *Willemstraat 55* 🕾 *015/215–7246* ⊕ *www.soulinn.nl* ↻ *10 rooms, 2 suites* ♿ *In-room: no a/c, kitchen (some)* ═ *MC, V* ⏐◯⏐ *BP.*

> ## PARTY TOWN
>
> From February until December, there are annual festivals throughout Delft. Highlights include the De Koninck Blues Festival in mid-February; canal-side concerts from the end of June through July and August; a week of chamber music during late August; the African Festival in early August; the Delft Jazz and Blues Festival at the end of August; a waiters' race in the Beestenmarkt in early September; and the City of Lights in mid-December. For more details, log on to (⊕ *www.delft.com*) or contact the **Delft Tourist Information Point** (⊠ *Hippolytusbuurt 4* 🕾 *0900/515-1555*).

NIGHTLIFE

8

Delft is home to one of the country's most important technical universities, and the large student population ensures the bars are always lively at night. Two good places to find a profusion of watering holes are the Markt and the Beestenmarkt. The latter is a peaceful little square where the discerning drinkers go on summery evenings to sit out under the leafy lime trees. The most humming nightspot—in fact, the only club (nearly all others are students only)—in Delft is **Speakers** (⊠ *Burgwal 45–49* 🕾 *015/212–4446* ⊕ *www.speakers.nl*). Each night there is something different going on. Stand-up comedy, in English as well as Dutch, is usually on Wednesday, with concerts on Thursday; Friday night sees theme night (1970s, for instance); Saturday hosts the techno-beat crowd; and Sunday offers salsa parties. Open regular hours are a restaurant, bar, and sidewalk café.

With its idyllic location on Delft's nicest square, **Café Vlaanderen** (⊠ *Beestenmarkt 16* 🕾 *015/213-3311*) is not only a good place to eat, it's also a fine place to chill out with a cold one. For beer lovers looking to be pleasantly bewildered by a choice of around 200 different Belgian beers, **Locus Publicus** (⊠ *Brabantse Turfmarkt 67* 🕾 *015/213–4632*) is the place to go.

ROTTERDAM

Rotterdam looks to the future like almost nowhere else. The decision to leave the past behind wasn't made entirely through choice however—the old town disappeared over-night on May 14, 1940, when Nazi bombs devastated an area greater than one square mile, sweeping away more than 36,000 buildings in just a few torrid hours.

Since then, a new landscape of concrete, steel, and glass has risen like a phoenix from the ashes, and today this world port is home to some of the 21st century's most architecturally important creations. The city skyline—especially in the areas around the station and by the Maas on the Kop van Zuid development—is constantly changing, and as each year passes it lives up more and more to its billing as "Manhattan-on-the-Maas." Many of the new buildings are commissioned from top-drawer contemporary architects including Rem Koolhaas and Sir Norman Foster, meaning they each have a striking identity.

That isn't to say the city is all glass and steel however. Areas such as historic Delfshaven—from where the pilgrim fathers set sail for the New World aboard the *Speedwell* in 1620—escaped the worst effects of the war, and still retain their old character and charm. And in between old and new, the large and leafy *Het Park* (simply "The Park") has a maze of paths weaving between small lakes and ponds to provide cool shade in summer and a welcome break from the urban sprawl at any time of year. As if that wasn't enough reason to visit, Rotterdam also boasts some of the country's best museums and top shopping opportunities.

Thanks to its location on the deltas of the Rhine and Maas rivers, Rotterdam has become the world's largest seaport. Through its harbors and the enormous Europoort pass more tons of shipping than through all of France combined. The rapid expansion of the port in the postwar years created a huge demand for labor, bringing waves of migrants from Italy, Spain, Greece, Turkey, Morocco, Cape Verde, and the Netherlands

Antilles, turning Rotterdam into one of the most ethnically diverse cities in Europe.

ORIENTATION

The city divides itself naturally into a number of main sectors. The **Central** area, south and east of the main railway station, is focused on the pedestrianized zone around the Lijnbaan and Van Oldenbarnevelt-

straat. This is where the city goes out to shop—all the major department stores and many exclusive bou-tiques are located here. Along the river are three old harbors, **Delfshaven, Oude Haven,** and **Leuvehaven,** although there is little similarity between them. Charming Delfshaven is so narrow it looks like a canal, and is lined with gabled houses dating back centuries, creating a classic Dutch scene. The Oude Haven, by contrast, is surrounded by modern build-ings, some of which, like the Blaak Rail Station and Kijk-Kubus, are among Rotterdam's most iconic buildings. To the south of the river, across the Erasmus Bridge, the **Kop van Zuid** and **Entrepot** districts are where famous architects such as Sir Norman Foster and Renzo Piano have been given free rein to design housing projects, theaters, and pub-lic buildings to complete the area's transformation into a modern and luxurious commercial and residential district. **Museumpark** is the cul-tural heart of the city, and home to four museums and bordered by a Sculpture Terrace.

GETTING HERE AND AROUND

Direct trains leave Amsterdam Centraal Station for Rotterdam as often as six times an hour throughout the day, and hourly through the night—the journey time is around one hour. If driving, take the A10, A4, and A13 freeways south from Amsterdam. The drive will take about one hour, depending on traffic.

Because the different areas of Rotterdam are fairly spread out, to get between them you may want to make use of the efficient public trans-port network (taxis are expensive). Buses and trams fan out across the city above ground, while four underground Metro (subway) lines—one north-south, three east-west—offer an even faster way of getting about. All intersect at Beurs station in the city center for easy transfers. A fifth overground Metro line runs from Hofplein (east of the main train station) to The Hague, but this is of less interest to visitors as the main line trains are a much faster means of making this journey. To use the network you'll need an **OV-chipkaart** (public transport chip card)—a new electronic payment system that has replaced the *strippen-kaart* and is now the only valid ticketing system used in the city. These credit card–size tickets can be loaded up with credit from machines in the railway and metro stations, and are debited as you board and leave trains, trams, metros, and buses. There are information and sales points in the Beurs and Centraal Station metro stations, as well as in the main bus station. Or visit the Web site (*www.ov-chipkaart.nl*) for more information.

Taxis are available at railway stations, major hotels, and at taxi stands in key locations. You can also order one by phone, but they cannot be hailed in the street. Expect to pay at least €40 for a 30-minute journey between Rotterdam and Delft.

Public Transportation Information (☎ *0900/9292*).

TOURS

The Nieuwe Maas River has flowed through Rotterdam for 700 years, dividing the city in two, and acting as the city's lifeline. A continual procession of some 30,000 oceangoing ships and some 130,000 river barges passes annually through Rotterdam to and from the North Sea. A top option for visitors to see the city's waterfront is to take a 75-minute boat tour (€9.50) with the very popular **Spido boat tours** (✉ *Willemsplein 85* ☎ *010/275–9988*). They also offer a range of other excursions lasting from just over an hour to a full day, while a variety of water taxis and water buses also operates in the Waterstad (the docks and harbors along the banks of the river). For those with an interest in Rotterdam's recent history, pick up a map from the tourist office called "Along the Fire Boundary." It has details of three self-guided walking routes that trace the edge of the area destroyed by the bombing of May 14, 1940, with detailed historical notes.

TIMING

With a day you can cover pretty much all of Rotterdam's sights. But don't forget to factor in extra time for shopping.

ESSENTIALS

Bicycle Rentals Fietspoint Rotterdam CS (✉ *Conradstraat 18, by Rotterdam Central Station* ☎ *010/412–6220*).

Emergency Services National Emergency Alarm Number (☎ *112 for police, fire, and ambulance*).

Hospitals Erasmus MC (✉ *s-Gravendijkwal 230* ☎ *010/704–0704*).

Taxis Rotterdamse Taxi Centrale (☎ *010/462–6060*).

Tourism Information VVV Rotterdam (✉ *Coolsingel 5,* ☎ *0900/361–8860*).

EXPLORING

TOP ATTRACTIONS

❶⑨ Delfshaven. The last remaining nook of old Rotterdam is both an open-air museum with rows of gabled houses lining the historic waterfront, and an area full of trendy galleries, cafés, and restaurants. Walk along the Voorhaven, Achterhaven, and neighboring Piet Heynplein and marvel at the many historic buildings; most of the port area has been reconstructed to appear just as it was when originally built. For historic sights in the environs, check out the working mill of **Korenmolen de Distilleerketel** (open Wednesday and Saturday only), the fascinating **Museum de Dubbelde Palmboom** on Rotterdam city history, and the **Oudekerk/Pilgrimvaders Kerk.** Tram No. 4 connects Delfshaven with the rest of the city, as does the nearby Delfshaven metro station. ✉ *Achterhaven and Voorhaven, Delfshaven.*

A great ship from the Netherlands' era of nautical supremacy.

⑰ Euromast. For a bird's-eye view of the contrast between Delfshaven and the majority of the city, as well as a spectacular panorama of city and harbor, visit the 600-foot-high Euromast. Designed by Maaskant in 1960, it was the Netherland's tallest building for many years; when a new medical facility was built for the Erasmus University, an additional 25 feet were added to the tower in six days, restoring it to its premier position. On a clear day, you can just about see the coast. The tower not only offers great vistas, but also packs in a number of other attractions. The main observation deck is at 315 feet, but the **Euroscoop** is a rotating panoramic elevator that will carry you another 300 feet from there to the top of the mast. For the thrill seekers among us, on weekends from May to September you can skip the elevator and rappel down from the observation deck, or shoot down the rope slide in about 10 seconds on Europe's fastest "zip wire" (make reservations via the Web at ⊕ *www.abseilen.nl*). There's also a restaurant at the top. You can even stay up the tower overnight in one of two special suites, but be warned the prices are as high as the experience. Down below, the park at the base of the Euromast is where many Rotterdammers spend time when the weather is good. ⊠ *Parkhaven 20, Delfshaven* ☎ *010/436–4811* ⊕ *www.euromast.com* 🖃 *€8.90, rappel or rope slide €45* ⊗ *Apr.–Sept., daily 9:30 AM–11 PM; Oct.–Mar., daily 10 AM–11 PM.*

⑬ Kunsthal. This "art house" sits at one end of the visitor-friendly museum quarter and hosts major temporary exhibitions. There is no permanent collection, other than the massive, multistory boxlike center itself, designed by architect-prophet Rem Koolhaas. Opinions about the building are sharply divided: some say the design bridging the gap

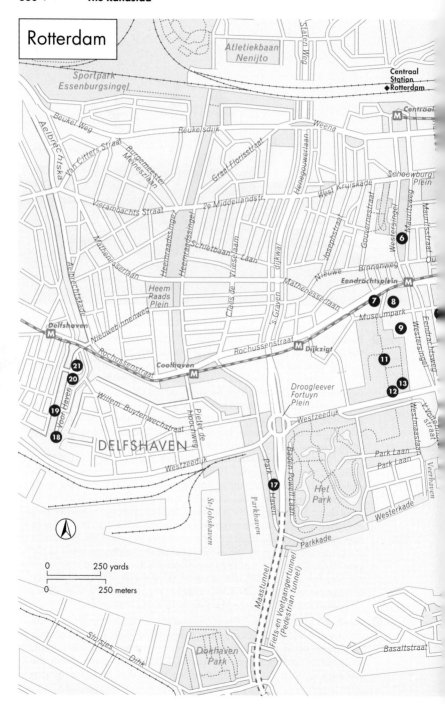

Rotterdam

Atletiekbaan
Nenijto

Staten Weg

Centraal
Station
◆ Rotterdam

M Centraal

Sportpark
Essenburgsingel

Beukel Weg

Weena

Beukelsdijk

Schouwburg
Plein

Aelbrechtska

Van Citters Straat

Burgemeester
Melnesziaan

Graaf Florisstraat

West Kruiskade

Mauritsweg

Mauritsstraat

Ou

Vierambachts Straat

2e Middellandstr.

Josephstraat

Gouvernestraat

Westersingel

6

Mathenesserlaan

Heemraadssingel

Heemraadssingel

Schietbaan Laan

Claes de Vrieselaan

's-Graven dijkwal

Nieuwe   Binnenweg

Eendrachtsplein M

Heem
Raads
Plein

Mathenesserlaan

Museumpark

7 **8**

9

Aelbrechtskade

Nieuwe Binnenweg

Delfshaven M

Rochussenstraat

Rochussenstraat

Dijkzigt M

11

Westersingel

Eendrachtsweg

Westmaasstraat

Westersingel

21

Coolhaven M

13

20

12

19

Willem Buytenwechstraat

Droogleever
Fortuyn
Plein

'sGravendijkwalGravendijkwal straat

Veerhaven

18

Pieter de Hoochweg

Westzeedijk

Park Laan

Park Laan

DELFSHAVEN

Westzeedijk

Park

Het
Park

Westerkade

St-Jobshaven

Parkhaven

17

Haven

Parkkade

Maastunnel

Fiets-en Voetgangertunnel
(Pedestrian tunnel)

0   250 yards

0   250 meters

Stuitjes   Dijk

Dokhaven
Park

Basaltstraat

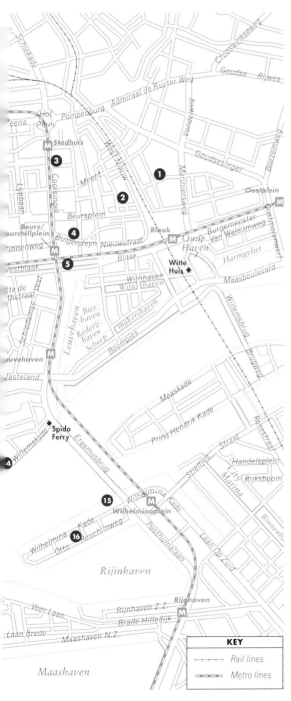

8

between the Museumpark and the dike is a clever spatial creation; others consider it an ugly mix of facades (part glass, part brick, and part corrugated iron) that has led to rusted iron, stained concrete, and cracks in the central walkway. The biggest complaint is the lack of elevator, compounded by the hazards of the central ramp, whose steep angle makes this a potential ski slope for wheelchair use. Fortunately, the eclectic exhibitions, usually three or four at any one time, are always fascinating, regardless of the setting. ⊠ *Westzeedijk 341, Museumpark* ☎ *010/440–0301* ⊕ *www.kunsthal.nl* 🖃 *€10* ⊙ *Tues.–Sat. 10–5, Sun. 11–5.*

⑤ **Maritiem Museum Rotterdam**. A sea lover's delight, the Maritime Museum
☾ is Rotterdam's noted nautical collection. Appropriately perched at the
Fodor's Choice head of the Leuvehaven harbor, it was founded by Prince Hendrik in
★ 1874. Set against the background of modern and historical maritime objects, the seafaring ways of old Rotterdammers make more sense. Star attraction of the ground floor is a large model of the Europoort, which shows how the Rotterdam area has developed over the centuries into the major seaport of today. The upper floors are mainly given over to rotating exhibitions on seafaring themes. Children have half a floor dedicated to them, called "Professor Plons" (Professor Plunge), where museum staff are on hand to help with looking through a real periscope, donning a hard hat and taking to the driving seat of a scaled-down crane, and engaging in many other activities dealing with the themes of water and ships. Kids will also love the museum's prize exhibit, the warship *De Buffel*, moored in the harbor outside, dating back to 1868. The ship has been perfectly restored and is fitted out sumptuously, as can be seen in the mahogany-deck captain's cabin. ⊠ *Leuvehaven 1, Witte de With* ☎ *010/413–2680* ⊕ *www.maritiemmuseum.nl* 🖃 *€5* ⊙ *July and Aug., Mon.–Sat. 10–5, Sun. 11–5; Sept.–June, Tues.–Sat. 10–5, Sun. 11–5.*

⑨ **Museum Boijmans van Beuningen**. Rotterdam's finest shrine to art, with
Fodor's Choice treasures ranging from Pieter Bruegel the Elder's 16th-century *Tower of*
★ *Babel* to Mondriaan's extraordinary *Composition in Yellow and Blue*, this museum ranks among the greatest art galleries in Europe. The top attraction here is the collection of old masters, which covers West European art from the 14th to the 19th century. In particular 15th- to 17th-century Dutch and Flemish art are well represented, including painters such as Van Eyck, Rubens, Hieronymous Bosch, and Rembrandt. The modern art section runs the gamut from Monet to Warhol and beyond, picking up Kandinsky, Magritte, and Dalí in between. In the Decorative Art and Design collection, both precious ornamental objects and everyday utensils dating from medieval times are displayed. In the museum café, note the fantastic collection of chairs, each by a different designer. Nearby, more artworks embellish the museum gardens. ⊠ *Museumpark 18–20, Museumpark* ☎ *010/441–9400* ⊕ *www. boijmans.nl* 🖃 *€9* ⊙ *Tues.–Sun. 11–5.*

⑳ **Museum de Dubbelde Palmboom** *(Double Palm Tree Museum)*. Devoted to the history of Rotterdam and its role as an international nexus, this museum traces the city's history from prehistoric times to the current day. The focus is on how exotic wares imported by the East India Company affected the city. The building itself is redolent of history: not only do its heavy beams and brick floors waft you back to yesteryear, but there even seems to be a faint smell of grains, recalling its many years spent as a warehouse. Ask for the informative guide in English, as all labeling is in Dutch. The first floor has some fascinating archaeological finds: one of the spouted ancient jugs has been traced to a town near Cologne, providing proof of trading contacts with the region, as traveling merchants were apparently very active in trading ceramics. ⊠ *Voorhaven 12, Delfshaven* ☎ *010/476–1533* ⊕ *www.hmr.rotterdam. nl* ⌨ *€5, ticket also valid for a same-day visit to the Schielandshuis* ⊙ *Tues.–Sun. 11–5.*

⓬ Natuurmuseum *(Natural History Museum).* Located in a historic villa-like structure together with an enormous glass wing (echoing the hip Kunsthal next door), the Natural History Museum lures its visitors with glimpses of the exhibits within, including skeletons of creatures you'll be hard put to identify. As soon as you enter the foyer, you are face to face with a mounted scary-hairy gorilla. It doesn't stop there: in one room the skeleton of a giraffe stretches as far up as you can crane your own neck. Continue on to be met by a tiger and arching elephant tusks. There is an "ironic" re-creation of a trophy hunter's display, with turtles mounted on a wall, arranged according to size. In another area, a dinner table is set, with the skulls of a human, a cow, an anteater, a lion, a zebra, and a pig as guests. Before each of them is a plate laden with their respective dining preferences. Children, meanwhile, are drawn to the 40-foot-long skeleton of a sperm whale. ⊠ *Westzeedijk 345, Museumpark* ☎ *010/436–4222* ⊕ *www.nmr.nl* ⌨ *€5* ⊙ *Tues.–Sat. 10–5, Sun. 11–5.*

➐ Nederlands Architectuurinstituut. Fittingly, for a city of exciting modern architecture, Rotterdam is the home of the **NAi,** or the Netherlands Architecture Institute. The striking glass-and-metal building—designed by Rotterdam local Joe Conen in 1993—hosts temporary displays on architecture and interior design in seven exhibition spaces, giving a holistic interpretation of the history and development of architecture, especially the urban design and spatial planning of Rotterdam. Outside, the gallery under the archive section is illuminated at night. ⊠ *Museumpark 25, Museumpark* ☎ *010/440–1200* ⊕ *www.nai.nl* ⌨ *€8* ⊙ *Tues.–Sat. 10–5, Sun. 11–5.*

㉑ Oudekerk/Pilgrimvaders Kerk *(Pilgrim Fathers' Church).* On July 22, 1620, 16 men, 11 women, and 19 children sailed from Delfshaven on the *Speedwell.* Their final destination was America, where they helped found the Plymouth Colony in Massachusetts, New England. Puritan Protestants fleeing England for religious freedom usually went to Amsterdam, but this group, which arrived in 1608, decided to live in Leiden, then 10 years later opted to travel on to the New World by leaving from Rotterdam. On July 20, 1620, they left Leiden by boat, and via Delft they reached Delfshaven, where they spent their last night in Holland. After a sermon from their vicar, John Robinson, in what has since become this church, they boarded the *Speedwell,* sailing to Southampton, England, then left on the *Mayflower* on September 5, reaching Cape Cod 60 days later.

8

The church was built in 1417 as the Chapel of Sint Anthonius, then extended and restyled in the Late Gothic period. However, in 1761 the ceilings were raised, and the current style dates back to this Regency revamp, when an ornate wooden clock tower was also added. Next to the choir is a vestry from 1819, where you can find a memorial plaque to the Pilgrim Fathers on the wall. The bell tower has a tiny balcony. The church is now owned by the Trust for Old Dutch Churches. ⊠ *Aelbrechtskolk 20, Delfshaven* ☎ *010/477–4156* ⊙ *Fri.–Sat. noon–4.*

④ Schielandshuis (*Schieland House*). Staunchly defending its position ★ against the high-rise Robeco Tower and the giant Hollandse Banke Unie surrounding it, this palatial 17th-century mansion is almost engulfed by the modern city. Happily, it holds its own as a part of Rotterdam's historical museum (the other half is the Dubbelde Palmboom in Delfshaven). Built between 1662 and 1665 in Dutch Neoclassical style by the Schieland family, it burned down in 1864, but the facade survived, and the interior was carefully restored. Another renovation in 2010 has given it a new shine. Inside are Baroque- and Rococo-style rooms reconstructed from houses in the area, clothing from the 18th century to the present day, and the famous collection of maps, the Atlas von Stolk. Because of the frailty of the paper, only a tiny selection of vintage maps is on display at any one time, usually under a specific theme. The museum's café is in a lovely garden. ⊠ *Korte Hoogstraat 31, Centrum* ☎ *010/217–6767* ⊕ *www.hmr.rotterdam.nl* ⊠ *€5, ticket also valid for a same-day visit to the Dubbelde Palmboom Museum* ⊙ *Tues.–Fri. 10–5, weekends 11–5.*

⑭ Wereld Museum. On a corner of rustic Veerhaven, surrounded by old sailing boats moored alongside modern yachts, this museum is devoted to non-Western cultures, many of which have had a sizable influence on Rotterdam. The permanent collection features more than 2,000 art objects from Asia, the Americas, Africa, and Oceania. Most of the exhibition space, however, is given over to changing themed exhibitions—usually two each year. At this writing it was devoted to displays covering the Inca civilizations of Andean South America. ⊠ *Willemskade 25, Scheepvaartkwartier* ☎ *010/270–7172* ⊕ *www.wereldmuseum.nl* ⊠ *exhibitions €12; permanent collection free entry* ⊙ *Tues.–Sun. 10–8.*

OFF THE BEATEN PATH

Fodor'sChoice ★ ☺ If you want to see the dike to end all dikes, drive South along the coast to see the Delta works and visit **Waterland Neeltje Jans.** This impressive museum offers a firsthand tour of the most important achievement of Dutch hydraulic engineering—the Delta Works, a massive dam and flood barrier that closed up the sea arms in response to the flood disaster of 1953. There are also exhibits documenting the 2,000-year history of the Dutch people's struggle with the sea. Films and slide shows, working scale models, and displays of materials give a comprehensive overview of dikes, dams, and underwater supports. The visit includes a boat trip in good weather. There is also a water playground with all kinds of interesting aquatic-based contraptions, a storm surge barrier one can stand on, a new futuristic-style whale pavilion, and even a hurricane simulator. Some attractions are closed in winter. ⊠ *Eiland Neeltje Jans, Vrouwenpolder* ☎ *0111/655–655* ⊕ *www.neeltjejans.nl* ⊠ *Jan.–Mar. €15; Apr.–Jun. and Sept.–Dec. €19;*

Museum Boijmans van Beuningen in Rotterdam.

8

Jul.–Aug. €21 ⊗ *Mar.–Dec., daily 10–5:30; Jan.–Mar., Wed., Sat. and Sun. 10–5:30.*

WORTH NOTING

⑧ Chabot Museum. This museum displays the private art collection of leading Dutch Expressionist painter and sculptor Henk Chabot, who was active between the two world wars, depicting peasants, market gardeners, and, later, refugees and prisoners. ✉ *Museumpark 11, Museumpark* ☏ *010/436–3713* ⊕ *www.chabotmuseum.nl* 🎫 *€6.50* ⊗ *Tues.–Fri. 11–4:30, Sat. 11–5, Sun. noon–5.*

⑱ Korenmolen de Distilleerketel. Set in the historic district of Delfshaven, this mill is the only working flour mill in the city. Formerly employed to grind malt to make *jenever,* the dusty-hair miller now mills grain for specific bakeries in the city, which means it is closed most of the week. ✉ *Voorhaven 210, Delfshaven* ☏ *010/477–9181* 🎫 *€2* ⊗ *Wed. 1–5 and Sat. 10–4.*

⑪ Museumpark. A project masterminded by Rem Koolhaas's Office for Metropolitan Architecture (OMA) in collaboration with French architect Yves Brunier, this modern urban garden is made up of different zones, extending from the Museum Boijmans van Beuningen to the Kunsthal. The idea is that each section is screened off from the last and creates a different impression—but each block of the garden isn't as radically different as this theory builds it up to be. The one part you should linger over is just before the bridge, where there is a memorial to city engineer G. J. de Jongh. Various artists had a hand in this, with Henk Chabot responsible for the inscription on the wall and Jaap Gidding designing the beautiful mosaic at the base of the monument, which represents Rotterdam and its surroundings at the end of the 1920s. Sculptor R. Bolle designed the bronze railings, with harbor and street scenes from the period when De Jongh was working in Rotterdam. ⊠ *Museumpark to the north, Westersingel to the east, Westzeedijk to the south, and bounded by a canal on the west side, Museumpark.*

❶ Nationaal Oonderwijsmuseum *(National Education Museum).* In a 1920s classroom you can take a seat at an old desk and try your hand at writing with an ink-dip pen or using chalk on a slate, making for a charming journey back to the good old days. ⊠ *Nieuwemarkt 1a, Meent* ☎ *010/217–0370* ⊕ *www.onderwijsmuseum.nl* 🎟 €4 ☉ *Tues.–Sun. 10–5.*

⑯ Nederlands Fotomuseum. Although Holland's Photography Museum doesn't have any permanent exhibits, the changing exhibitions are well worth looking at, and there is an extensive library open during the week for reference. The museum is housed in the **Las Palmas** building in the Kop van Zuid neighborhood. ⊠ *Wilhelminakade 332, Kop van Zuid* ☎ *010/203–0405* ⊕ *www.nederlandsfotomuseum.nl* 🎟 €7 ☉ *Tues.–Fri. 10–5, weekends 11–5.*

❻ Sculpture Terrace. Set along the Westersingel, this outdoor venue exhibits sculptures of the past 100 years, dotting the grassy bank of the canal and creating a sculpture garden. Highlights here include Rodin's headless *L'homme qui marche* (Walking Man), Henri Laurens's *La Grande Musicienne* (The Great Musician), and Umberto Mastroianni's *Gli Amanti* (The Lovers), a fascinating jumble of triangular-shape points. ⊠ *Museumpark.*

❷ Sint Laurenskerk. Built between 1449 and 1525, this church is juxtaposed against its modern surroundings. Of the three organs contained inside, the main organ ranks as one of Europe's largest. Hendrick de Keyser's statue of Erasmus in the square was buried in the gardens of the Museum Boijmans van Beuningen during the war and miraculously survived. ⊠ *Grotekerkplein 27, Sint Laurenskwartier* ☎ *010/413–1494* ⊕ *www.laurenskerkrotterdam.nl* ☉ *Tues.–Sat. 10–4.*

❸ Stadhuis *(City Hall).* At the top of the Coolsingel, this elegant 1920s building is the hallowed seat of the mayor of Rotterdam and is open for guided tours on weekdays. A bronze bust of the architect, Henri Evans, is in the central hall. With the neighboring post-office building, the two early-1920s buildings are the sole survivors of their era. ⊠ *Coolsingel 40, Centrum* ☎ *14010 (toll-free).*

❿ TENT Centrum Beeldende Kunst. The Rotterdam Center for Visual Arts is usually simply called TENT, an apt acronym for showcasing modern art by local artists of the last decade. Shows range from edgy, current-event type of stuff to tranquil designs for city gardens. The ground floor is devoted to up-and-coming artists, and the upper floor exhibits established artists' work. Artists also have a workplace to experiment with new projects. All exhibitions are temporary, lasting a maximum of three months, so call ahead to find out about the current show. Every first and third Thursday of the month there is an exciting free evening program. ⊠ *Witte de Withstraat 50, Witte de With* ☎ *010/413–5498* ⊕ *www.tentplaza.nl* 🎟 €4 ☉ *Tues.–Sun. 11–6.*

⑮ **Toren op Zuid**. An office complex by celebrated modern architect Renzo Piano, this structure houses the head offices of KPN Telecom. Its eye-catching billboard facade glitters with 1,000-odd green lamps flashing on and off, creating images provided by the city of Rotterdam, in addition to images provided by KPN and an art academy. The facade fronting the Erasmus Bridge leans forward by 6 degrees, which is the same as the angle of the bridge's pylon. It is also said that Piano could have been making a humorous reference to his homeland, as the Tower of Pisa leans at the same angle. ⊠ *Wilhelminakade 123, Kop van Zuid.*

WHERE TO EAT

Use the coordinate (✚ A4) at the end of each listing to locate a site on the Where to Eat and Stay in Rotterdam map.

$–$$$
CHINESE
✕**Asian Glories**. Reputed to be the city's best Cantonese restaurant, Asian Glories serves lunches, dinners, and Sunday brunches in a tasteful modern Asian interior or outdoors on its terrace. It's hard to choose what is most delicious; their dim sum, fresh oysters, mussels in black bean sauce, and Peking Duck consistently get raves from fussy eaters. Leave room for an exotic dessert such as ice cream with rice and red bean sauce. ⊠ *Leeuwenstraat 15, Centrum* ☎ *010/411–7107* ⊟ *AE, DC, MC, V* ⊙ *Closed Wed.* ✚ *D2.*

$$
VEGETARIAN
✕**Bla Bla**. Just around the corner from the historic heart of Delfshaven, this restaurant is always lively and frequently crowded. There is always a choice of three or four main vegetarian dishes, inspired by cuisines from around the world, and the menu changes often. Make sure you're having dinner on the early side to get the freshest ingredients—and a seat. ⊠ *Piet Heynsplein 35, Delfshaven* ☎ *010/477–4448* ⊕ *www.bla-bla.nl* ⊟ *V* ⊙ *Closed Mon. No lunch* ✚ *A4.*

$$$–$$$$
ITALIAN
✕**Brancatelli**. Around the windblown environs of the Erasmus Bridge you can find several eateries specializing in Mediterranean cuisine, Brancatelli being the best. "Kitsch" is the word that springs to mind when you spot the large glass animals on every table; add a preprogrammed player piano, and you are going to either laugh or cringe. If you feel a smile tickling, then the (very) pink table settings won't be too much, either. The friendly staff really play on being Italian, making, as they say, "a nice evening" of it, especially for groups. A typical four- or five-course menu is usually fish based. Even if the price pushes up your expectations, the presentation and sheer quality of the dishes justify the cost. ⊠ *Boompjes 264, Centrum* ☎ *010/411–4151* ⊕ *www.brancatelli.nl* 🍴 *Reservations essential* ⊟ *AE, DC, MC, V* ⊙ *No lunch weekends* ✚ *D4.*

¢–$$
CAFÉ
✕**Café Dudok**. Lofty ceilings, a cavernous former warehouse, long reading tables stacked with international magazines and papers—little wonder this place attracts an artsy crowd. At its most mellow, this spot is perfect for a lazy afternoon treat of delicious homemade pastries, but you can come here for breakfast, lunch, high tea, dinner, or even a snack after midnight. They also offer a small selection for vegetarians. The brasserie, on a mezzanine above the open kitchen at the back, looks out over the Rotte River. Since it's terribly crowded at times, you should get

8

here unfashionably early to avoid disappointment—there's nowhere else like it in Rotterdam. ✉ *Meent 88, Centrum* ☎ *010/433–3102* ⊕ *www. dudok.nl* ▭ *AE, DC, MC, V* ⊹ *D2.*

$–$$
CONTEMPORARY

✕ **Café Floor**. Adjacent to the Stadsschouwburg (Municipal Theater), Café Floor doesn't look too inviting from the outside, but the interior is modern, light, and airy; the staff are friendly; and the kitchen produces excellent food. Try the lamb brochette, so tender the meat practically dissolves on your tongue. There's also a good selection of tapas available. The delicious passion-fruit cheesecake comes from Café Dudok's kitchen. The beautiful garden at the back, and accompanying birdsong from the local fauna, make this a restful stop. This place is very popular with local and international regulars, so be prepared to be patient if you go late-ish on a Saturday. ✉ *Schouwburgplein 28, Centrum* ☎ *010/404–5288* ⊕ *www.cafefloor.nl* ▭ *AE, MC, V* ⊹ *C2.*

$$$–$$$$
ECLECTIC

✕ **De Engel**. The international kitchen of this former town house has created a loyal following, who flock here for excellent food, a sash-window view over the Westersingel, and an intimate setting (tables are very close together). The very friendly staff are more than helpful with their recommendations, as are your next-table neighbors. For a special taste treat, try the truffle soup, or the skate wing with garlic sauce. While there is a menu, daily changing seasonal specialties are always available, and often the best choice. The house recommends you simply let the chef "surprise" you, and rest assured you won't be disappointed. ✉ *Eendrachtsweg 19, Centrum* ☎ *010/413–8256* ⊕ *www. hermandenblijker.nl* ⌲ *Reservations essential* ▭ *AE, MC, V* ☾ *Closed Sun. No lunch Sat.* ⊹ *C3.*

¢–$$
INDONESIAN

✕ **Dewi Sri**. This restaurant has rijsttafel (rice table) to dream about, with creative takes on traditional Indonesian dishes. Rice table is like Indonesian smorgasbord with samplings from the menu. Choose from a multitude of tantalizing options from Indonesian, Javanese, and Sumatran menus. Some diners may find the mock wood carvings a little heavy, given the subtle flavors of the food being served. The large restaurant upstairs could feel quite empty midweek, but the staff are incredibly polite, appearing discreetly at your table just as soon as you feel the need to ask for something. All in all, this probably has the best Indonesian food in Rotterdam, so don't let the décor faze you. If you can't find space in the Dewi Sri, it shares its premises with the adjacent Warisan restaurant, which serves similarly priced and equally mouthwatering Thai food. ✉ *Westerkade 20, Scheepvaartkwartier* ☎ *010/436–0263* ⊕ *www.dewisri.nl* ▭ *AE, DC, MC, V* ☾ *No lunch weekends* ⊹ *B5.*

$$$
DUTCH

✕ **Kip**. Dark wooden floors, unobtrusive lighting, and a big fireplace make Kip's traditional interior warm and cozy. As befits the restaurant's name (which means chicken), the chicken breast (from a special Dutch breed called *Hollandse blauwhoender*) with truffles is the most popular dish, but the kitchen offers a whole lot more. There's always a daily-changing fish option, such as cod with saffron-and-fennel sauce, and plenty of meatier fare, such as veal in wild mushroom sauce. The menu must work, because this spot is always packed. In summer, a leafy garden at the back provides welcome respite from the bustle of the big city. ✉ *Van Vollenhovenstraat 25, Scheepvaartkwartier* ☎ *010/436–9923*

⊕ *www.kip-rotterdam.nl* ⬧ *Reservations essential* ▭*AE, DC, MC, V* ⊗ *No lunch* ✛ *C4.*

¢–$$ ✕ **La Place.** On the top floors of the V&D department store, La Place is
DUTCH a large self-serve café that offers everything from simple rolls to grilled
meats at reasonable prices. The salad bar is a pretty good lunch option.
The roof transforms into a sunny terrace in summer. On the ground
floor La Place Express offers a lunch option for those in a hurry: a
tempting variety of reasonably priced sandwiches, but it's takeout only
as there are no tables. ⊠ *Hoogstraat 185, Centrum* ☎ *0900/235–8363*
▭ *No credit cards* ⊗ *Closed Sun.* ✛ *D2.*

$–$$$ ✕ **Loos.** In the grand style of Rotterdam's cafés, Loos has a range of
FRENCH international magazines and newspapers on its reading racks, and in a
fun gesture, six clocks with different time zones decorate one wall. You
enter and see what looks like a forest of tables, but this trompe l'oeil
effect is largely caused by a wall-size mirror. As for the food, some dishes
are excellent, including such delights as roasted-pepper-and-smoked-
apple soup with aniseed cream, monkfish with truffle-butter sauce,
and steak with Armagnac-soaked raisins and a duck-liver-and-truffle
sauce. If you want to eat less luxuriously, try the bar menu. ⊠ *West-
plein 1, Scheepvaartkwartier* ☎ *010/411–7723* ⊕ *www.loos-rotterdam.
nl* ▭ *AE, MC, V* ⊗ *No lunch weekends (restaurant)* ✛ *C4.*

$$$$ ✕ **Parkheuvel.** Overlooking the Maas, this posh restaurant is run by chef-
ECLECTIC owner Erik van Loo, who moved from Delft's Zwethheul to take the
Fodor's Choice reins following the retirement of former chef-guru Cees Helder. It is said
★ to be popular among the harbor barons, who can oversee their dockside
territory from the bay windows of this tastefully modern, semicircular
building. Tables are covered with cream-color linens, and wood-frame
chairs are elegantly upholstered. The service here is as effortlessly attentive as you would expect from one of Holland's top five restaurants.
Luxuries such as truffles are added to the freshest ingredients, with the
day's menu dictated by the availability of the best produce at that morning's markets. Kudos and salaams are offered up by diners to many of
the chef's specialties, including the ravioli of black Bresse chicken with
pan-fried langoustines. ⊠ *Heuvellaan 21, Centrum* ☎ *010/436–0530*
⊕ *www.parkheuvel.nl* ⬧ *Reservations essential* ▭ *AE, DC, MC, V*
⊗ *Closed Sun. No lunch Sat.* ✛ *B5.*

$ ✕ **Rotown.** This arts center venue is more celebrated for its funky bar
CAFÉ than for its restaurant proper. A buzz fills the dining area, a spillover
from the crowd up front. The menu is quite extensive, although the service can be a bit hit-or-miss. But if you like a stylish, party-hearty atmosphere (bands often play at the bar), this could be worth it. ⊠ *Nieuwe
Binnenweg 17–19, Centrum* ☎ *010/436–2669* ⊕ *www.rotown.nl* ▭ *AE,
DC, MC, V* ⊗ *Dinner only* ✛ *B3.*

$$$ ✕ **Zeezout.** On an elegant riverfront terrace, around the corner from
SEAFOOD the venerable Veerhaven moored with old sailing ships, the charming
"Sea Salt" restaurant mirrors the freshness of its sea-based menu in
crisp linen tablecloths and its spotlessly clean, open kitchen, where
watching the staff work whets your appetite. A large fish mosaic
on the wall looks out across the river to the floodlighted Erasmus
Bridge; a window awning adds to the romance of the view. Try the

8

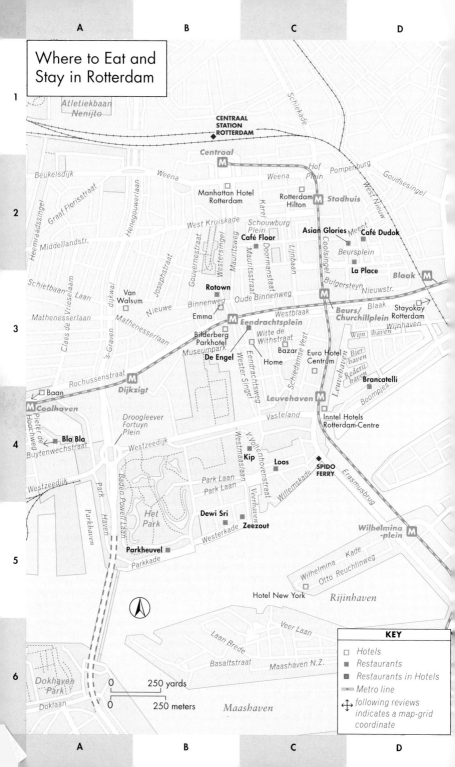

Where to Eat and
Stay in Rotterdam

**CENTRAAL
STATION
ROTTERDAM**

Atletiekbaan
Nenijto

Schiekade

Centraal Ⓜ

Beukelsdijk

Weena

Weena

Hof
Plein

Pompenburg

Goudsesingel

West Nieuw

Manhattan Hotel
Rotterdam

Rotterdam
Hilton

Stadhuis Ⓜ

Graaf Florisstraat

Heemraadssingel

West Kruiskade

Schouwburg
Plein

Asian Glories

Meent

Café Dudok

Middellandstr.

Josephstraat

Westersingel

Mauritsweg

Café Floor

Doormanstraat

Karel

Lijnbaan

Coolsingel

Beursplein

La Place

Blaak Ⓜ

Schietbaan

Laan

Claes de Vrieselaan

dijkwal

Nieuwe

Mathenesserlaan

Mathenesserlaan

Van
Walsum

Rotown

Binnenweg

Emma

Oude Binnenweg

Westblaak

Bulgersteyn

Nieuwstr.

**Beurs/
Churchillplein**

Blaak

Stayokay
Rotterdam

Wijnhaven

Ⓜ

Rochussenstraat

Dijkzigt Ⓜ

Bilderberg
Parkhotel
Museumpark

De Engel

Eendrachtsplein Ⓜ

Witte de
Withstraat

Home

Bazar

Wester Singel

Eendrachtsweg

Schiedamse Vest

Euro Hotel
Centrum

Wijn
haven

Bier
haven

Leuvehaven

Rederij
haven

Brancatelli

Coolhaven Ⓜ

Pieter de
Hoochweg

Baan Ⓜ

Buytenwechstraat

Bla Bla

Droogleever
Fortuyn
Plein

Westzeedijk

Leuvehaven Ⓜ

Vasteland

Boompjes

Inntel Hotels
Rotterdam-Centre

Westzeedijk

Baden-Powell Laan

Park
Haven

Westmaaslaan

V.Vollenhovenstraat

Park Laan

Park Laan

Kip

Loos

◆ SPIDO
FERRY

Het
Park

Veerhaven

Willemskade

Wilhelmina
-plein Ⓜ

Erasmusbrug

Dewi Sri

Westerkade

Zeezout

Parkheuvel

Parkkade

Hotel New York

Wilhelmina
Kade

Otto Reuchlinweg

Rijnhaven

⌖

Dokhaven
Park

Doklaan

| 0 | 250 yards |
| 0 | 250 meters |

Laan Brede

Basaltstraat

Veer Laan

Maashaven N.Z.

Maashaven

KEY

□ Hotels
■ Restaurants
■ Restaurants in Hotels
Ⓜ Metro line
↔ following reviews
indicates a map-grid
coordinate

turbot accompanied by shrimp, aubergine cream, and *rösti* (potato pancakes). ✉ *Westerkade 11b, Scheepvaartkwartier* ☎ *010/436–5049* ⊕ *www.restaurantzeezout.nl* ⚓ *Reservations essential* ▭ *AE, DC, MC, V* ⊘ *Closed Sun. and Mon.* ✛ *C5.*

WHERE TO STAY

Use the coordinate (✛ A4) at the end of each listing to locate a site on the Where to Eat and Stay in Rotterdam map.

$ ▦ **Baan.** This is a comfortable family-run hotel overlooking Coolhaven's harbor and only five minutes from the waterside at Delfshaven. The bright rooms have tasteful furnishings and accessories in blue and yellow pastel shades. **Pros:** family style; friendly. **Cons:** basic; a little away from the sights. ✉ *Rochussenstraat 345, Centrum* ☎ *010/477–0555* ⊕ *www.hotelbaan.nl* ⤵ *14 rooms* ⚐ *In-room: no a/c* ▭ *AE, MC, V* ᵔⵔᵔ *CP* ✛ *A4.*

$ ▦ **Bazar.** The well-traveled owner has created havens from his wanderings, with hot, deep colors evoking Turkey and Morocco throughout the individually styled rooms on the second floor, and motifs conjuring up Africa and South America on the third and fourth floors respectively. Although there is an elevator, it goes only to the third floor. The restaurant of the same name on the ground floor has, needless to say, a very international menu, and all the meat used is halal. The location on the young, busy Witte de Withstraat draws a nicely "in" crowd to both hotel and restaurant. **Pros:** top-floor rooms have balconies. **Cons:** elevator stops short of these. ✉ *Witte de Withstraat 16, Witte de With* ☎ *010/206–5151* ⊕ *www.hotelbazar.nl* ⤵ *27 rooms* ⚐ *In-room: no a/c, Internet. In-hotel: restaurant, some pets allowed* ▭ *AE, DC, MC, V* ᵔⵔᵔ *CP* ✛ *C3.*

$$–$$$ ▦ **Bilderberg Parkhotel.** Although this hotel welcomes you with a townhouse facade dramatically yoked to a metallic skyscraper, the interior bears few reminders of its 80-year history. Rooms have been renovated in uncluttered modern styles, while those at the back overlook a quiet garden. The Bilderberg also offers a wide spectrum of top-brass services. The Restaurant 70 serves an interesting fusion of nouveau global and traditional cuisine in the classical surroundings of the old wing of the hotel, and has a garden terrace open in summer. Just a few minutes' walk from the Museum Boijmans van Beuningen, this spot is centrally located. Another plus is the staff, which offers the sort of apparently effortless, unobtrusive attention to your every need that makes a stay here very pleasant. **Pros:** convenient for museums. **Cons:** rooms lack character. ✉ *Westersingel 70, Centrum* ☎ *010/436–3611 or 0800/024 5245* ⊕ *www.bilderberg.nl* ⤵ *189 rooms* ⚐ *In-room: no a/c (some), refrigerator, Wi-Fi. In-hotel: restaurant, bar, gym, laundry service, Wi-Fi, some pets allowed* ▭ *AE, DC, MC, V* ✛ *B3.*

$ ▦ **Emma.** At this hotel on social, busy Nieuwe Binnenweg, plenty of shops and nightspots are conveniently close; the nearest sidewalk café is right opposite the hotel. This is the third generation of the Orsini family seeing to the comfort of the hotel's guests. Furnishings are modern, and there is an elevator. Staffed by a friendly and approachable

8

The Stayokay Rotterdam is housed in a few of Rotterdam's most iconic and eye-catching buildings: the Piet Blom–designed "cube houses."

team, this place offers special rates for groups and those staying longer. **Pros:** central; friendly; good value. **Cons:** on noisy junction. ☒ *Nieuwe Binnenweg 6, Centrum* ☎ *010/436–5533* ⊕ *www.hotelemma.nl* ↘ *24 rooms* ⚭ *In-room: no a/c, safe, refrigerator, Internet. In-hotel: bar, parking (paid), some pets allowed* ▭ *AE, DC, MC, V* †◯† *CP* ✦ *B3.*

$ ⊞ **Euro Hotel Centrum.** Despite the businesslike, anonymous name, this is a welcoming and comfortable modern hotel with lots of flowers and plants, so the overall feeling is spruce and well cared for. They have family rooms, in case you're traveling with children. This place is particularly handy for Museumpark and strolls along the Westersingel. Enjoy the buffet breakfast before setting out. **Pros:** friendly; quiet. **Cons:** situated on a drab street. ☒ *Baan 14–20, Centrum* ☎ *010/214–1922* ⊕ *www.eurohotelcentrum.nl* ↘ *53 rooms, 2 suites* ⚭ *In-room: no a/c, Wi-Fi. In-hotel: bar, Wi-Fi* ▭ *AE, MC, V* †◯† *CP* ✦ *C3.*

¢ ⊞ **Home.** On the liveliest street in town, five minutes from the Museumpark, this hotel is right in the middle of Rotterdam's best dining, shopping, and nightlife. When you're back at the hotel, incredibly helpful staff are on hand for recommendations and assistance, making this a pad you'll really want to come back to. The rate drops the longer you stay, by as much as 50% if you stay more than 30 days—and plenty of people do, as en-suite kitchenettes and sitting areas in each room make this a popular choice for longer stays. **Pros:** good for long stays. **Cons:** basic facilities. ☒ *Witte de Withstraat 38, Witte de With* ☎ *010/411–2121* ⊕ *www.homehotel.nl* ↘ *80 rooms* ⚭ *In-room: no a/c, no phone, kitchen* ▭ *AE, MC, V* ✦ *C3.*

$$–$$$ ⊞ **Hotel New York.** Rotterdam is very much a commercial harbor city, with hotels aimed primarily at the business trade; the Hotel New York,

a converted shipping office from the first part of the 20th century, is a particularly atmospheric exception. The twin towers rising over the water of the Nieuwe Maas, across from the city center, were known to Rotterdammers for decades as the headquarters of the Holland-America Line, before being renovated and opened as a hotel. Rooms are individually decorated, with high ceilings contrasting with the modern décor, so it's not just the view that boosts the price. The enormous restaurant (which seats 400) somehow maintains an intimate café atmosphere, although those in the know delight in the afternoon tea served here but don't stay for dinner. Other amenities include an oyster bar, tea salon, and water taxi connecting the Kop van Zuid with the city center (€2.90 per person, one-way). **Pros:** great riverside location; historic building. **Cons:** away from main sights. ⊠ *Koninginnenhoofd 1, Kop van Zuid* ☎ *010/439–0500* ⊕ *www.hotelnewyork.nl* ⤵ *71 rooms, 1 penthouse apartment* 🛏 *In-room: Wi-Fi. In-hotel: restaurant, room service* ▭ *AE, DC, MC, V* ✛ *C5.*

$–$$ 🚇 **Inntel Hotels Rotterdam-Centre.** The majority of the rooms in this modern high-rise, built at the opening to the Leuvehaven inner harbor, have water views. All guest rooms are simply but tastefully decorated, wearing a designer-look edge. The conservatory-style breakfast room overlooks a terrace for true relaxation. The staff are incredibly friendly and make all efforts to make your stay pleasant. The health club on the top floor of the old building includes a pool and a sauna. **Pros:** friendly; central. **Cons:** not for those who shun big hotels. ⊠ *Leuvehaven 80, Centrum* ☎ *010/413–4139* ⊕ *www.inntelhotelsrotterdamcentre.com* ⤵ *239 rooms, 24 suites* 🛏 *In-room: safe, refrigerator, Wi-Fi. In-hotel: restaurant, pool, gym, Wi-Fi* ▭ *AE, DC, MC, V* ✛ *C4.*

$$$$ 🚇 **Manhattan Hotel Rotterdam.** The only five-star hotel in the city is on
Fodor'sChoice the first 14 floors of the Millennium tower, smack opposite Centraal
★ Station. Although this is primarily a business hotel, the slick-yet-friendly service of this landmark draws celebrity guests, such as pop and rock stars Robbie Williams and Kylie Minogue. With regal purple corridors, lined with copies of masterpieces from Vermeer to Van Gogh, and bright spacious rooms—each fitted out with a luxuriously huge bed, topped with a 10-layer mattress and sumptuous snowy-white linen—it's hard not to feel like a member of the glitterati yourself. All the lavish bathrooms have tubs and the all rooms have CD players. The panorama across town makes the extra rates for rooms from the fourth floor up more than worthwhile, with many looking out over the Erasmus Bridge and the skyline (both dramatically floodlighted after dark). Executive rooms on the upper floors also have free access to the 10th floor Executive Lounge. **Pros:** sky-high luxury. **Cons:** sky-high prices. ⊠ *Weena 686, Centrum* ☎ *010/430–2222* ⊕ *www.manhattanhotelrotterdam. com* ⤵ *224 rooms, 7 suites* 🛏 *In-room: safe, refrigerator, Wi-Fi. In-hotel: restaurant, 2 bars, gym, laundry service, Wi-Fi* ▭ *AE, DC, MC, V* ✛ *B2.*

$$$–$$$$ 🚇 **Rotterdam Hilton.** During the International Film Festival at the end of January, this hotel often hosts some of the notable participants, thanks in part to its top facilities, a number of suites, meeting rooms, and luxury appointments and amenities. A major plus is its location,

8

right in the middle of downtown. Since it tends to appeal to visitors who want a name they can rely on, it can get filled with tour groups. **Pros:** centrally located. **Cons:** lacks character. ⊠ *Weena 10, Centrum* ☎ *010/710–8000* ⊕ *www.rotterdam.hilton.com* ⤴ *246 rooms, 8 suites* ⚏ *In-room: safe, refrigerator, Wi-Fi. In-hotel: bar, gym, laundry service, Wi-Fi, some pets allowed* ⊟ *AE, DC, MC, V* ✣ *C2.*

¢–$ 🏠 **Stayokay Rotterdam.** If you're running on a budget, this modern hostel right in the middle of the city is just the ticket. Moreover, since relocating in 2009, it now occupies several of Rotterdam's most iconic and eye-catching buildings: the Piet Blom–designed "cube houses" built in 1984 between Blaak train and metro station and the Oude Haven. The latter is home to several good waterside bars. The entrance is up a level from the street, accessed via steps or a ramp. It's hard to figure out how they find space for 250 beds inside these oddly shaped structures with few obvious vertical walls, but they do. Dorms are shared with three to eight beds, but each has its own en-suite bathroom. If you book way in advance, you might be lucky and get one of the five double rooms, best for extra privacy. Unusually for a hostel, it is even air-conditioned. **Pros:** great location; good value; unusual building. **Cons:** like other hostels, you can't always choose your roommates. ⊠ *Overblaak 85–87, Centrum* ☎ *010/436–5763* ⊕ *www.stayokay.com* ⤴ *5 rooms for 2 people, 44 dorm rooms* ⚏ *In-room: kitchen (some), no TV. In-hotel: bar, laundry facilities, Internet terminal* ⊟ *MC, V* ⦶ *CP* ✣ *D3.*

$ 🏠 **Van Walsum.** On a residential boulevard within walking distance of the Museum Boijmans van Beuningen and major attractions, the Van Walsum is near the Euromast. The friendly and gregarious owner proudly restores and reequips his rooms, floor by floor, on a continuously rotating basis, with the always-modern décor of each floor determined by that year's best buys in furniture, carpeting, and bathroom tiles. There is a bar-lounge and a small restaurant that has a summer garden extension. The "comfort" rooms are worth the little extra cost for the additional facilities, including refrigerators, tea/coffee-making equipment, and air-conditioning. **Pros:** friendly. **Cons:** standard rooms a little basic. ⊠ *Mathenesserlaan 199–201, Centrum* ☎ *010/436–3275* ⊕ *www.hotelvanwalsum.nl* ⤴ *28 rooms* ⚏ *In-room: no a/c (some), refrigerator (some), Wi-Fi. In-hotel: restaurant, bar, Internet terminal, Wi-Fi, parking (paid)* ⊟ *AE, DC, MC, V* ⦶ *CP* ✣ *A3.*

NIGHTLIFE AND THE ARTS

THE ARTS

Rotterdam's arts calendar extends throughout the year. You can book tickets and find out what's going on around town through the local tourist information office, the VVV. **VVV Rotterdam Info** (⊠ *Coolsingel 195–197, Centrum* ☎ *0900/403–4065* ⊕ *www.rotterdam.info*).

DANCE   Rotterdam's resident modern dance company, **Scapino Ballet,** has the reputation of being one of the most formidably talented troupes in the country. **It performs at Rotterdamse Schouwburg** (⊠ *Schouwburgplein 25, Centrum* ☎ *010/411–8110* ⊕ *www.scapinoballet.nl*).

FILM   Partly because of the annual avant-garde **International Film Festival Rotterdam,** held in late January–early February, there is a lot of general interest in film in this city—as a result, you have many screens to choose from. The **Pathé** (✉ *Schouwburgplein 101, Centrum* ☎ *0900/1458*) is the place to head for blockbusters. The **Theater Lantaren/Venster** (✉ *Gouvernestraat 133, Centrum* ☎ *010/277–2266*) has an interesting program that shows art films in addition to hosting small-scale dance and theater performances. There's an open-air cinema at the Museumpark in September.

MUSIC   Rotterdam's renowned concert orchestra is the excellent **Rotterdam Philharmonic Orchestra,** which performs at **the large concert hall De Doelen** (✉ *Schouwburgplein 50, Centrum* ☎ *010/217–1717* ⊕ *www.dedoelen. nl*). Attracting 400,000 visitors a year, the orchestra is known for its adventurous range of music—this troupe plays not just Beethoven but has also tackled the score from the film *Jurassic Park.*

THEATER   The leading theater company of Rotterdam is **RO Theatergroup,** which performs at its own theater, **RO Theater** (✉ *William Boothlaan 8, Meent* ☎ *010/404–6888* ⊕ *www.rotheater.nl*) ; **the RO Theatergroup's subsidiary venue is the Rotterdamse Schouwburg** (✉ *Schouwburgplein 25, Centrum* ☎ *010/411–8110*). The majority of RO Theater's productions are in Dutch, as are, unfortunately, Onafhankelijk Toneel's, the city's other leader in the field. The **Nieuwe Luxor Theater** (✉ *Posthumalaan 1, Kop van Zuid* ☎ *010/496–0000* ⊕ *www.luxortheater.nl*) has 1,500 seats, and was specifically designed to cater to major stage musicals and other popular events. The theater, one of the Netherlands' largest, was designed by Australian architect Peter Wilson and has a marvelous view of Rotterdam's harbor and skyline. Performances are often in English.

Rotterdam's cultural climate facilitates the staging of productions from many semiprofessional groups, such as Turkish folk dance, classical Indian dance, and capoeira Brazilian martial art troupes. The **Theater Zuidplein** (✉ *Zuidplein 60–64, Charlois* ☎ *010/203–0203* ⊕ *www.theaterzuidplein.nl*) is particularly known for its multicultural program.

NIGHTLIFE

To get your bearings and find your way around the party scene, look out for glossy party fliers in cafés, record stores, and clothes shops selling clubbing gear. The best nights tend to be Thursday to Saturday, 11 PM to 5 AM. Most venues have a clubbing floor, with DJs working the crowd, and more ambient rooms for smoking or just plain relaxing. From hard-core techno—which has been popular here since the early '90s—to early-hour chill-out cafés, there is a wide gamut of nighttime entertainment. West Kruiskade (also known as Chinatown) is the place to go if you want lively bars and music from around the world. Nieuwe Binnenweg and Witte de Withstraat have many busy late-night cafés and clubs. Oude Haven is particularly popular with students, and the Schouwburgplein is favored by visitors to the nearby theaters and cinemas. Stadshuisplein has a number of tacky discos and bars.

8

CAFÉS   **Breakaway** (✉ *Karel Doormanstraat 1, near Centraal Station, Centrum* ☎ *010/233–0922*) is busy, with a young international crowd, and the nearest you'll get to a Dutch take on an American bar. **Café Rotterdam** (✉ *Wilhelminakade 699, Kop van Zuid* ☎ *010/290–8442*) is on the Wilhelminakade in the up-and-coming Kop van Zuid district, between the architectural designs of Sir Norman Foster, Rem Koolhaas, and Renzo Piano. This former shipping terminal is now a massive meeting center, with a large café and fantastic view of the white Erasmus Bridge. **Cambrinus** (✉ *Blaak 4, Blaak* ☎ *010/414–6702*) is a cozy café opposite Blaak station, directly below the Stayokay hostel and with a terrace on the Oude Haven. This is a popular mecca for beer lovers, with a dizzying 150 to choose from. **Locus Publicus** (✉ *Oostzeedijk 364, Blaak* ☎ *010/433–1761*) is another favorite with Belgian beer enthusiasts, with a menu that tops 200 varieties. Best of all, this one-room brown café a few minutes' walk east from Blaak station has an open log fire in winter.

De Schouw (✉ *Witte de Withstraat 80, Witte de With* ☎ *010/412–4253*), an erstwhile brown café and former journalists' haunt, is now a trendy brown bar with a mix of artists and students.

CLUBS   In a former pedestrian tunnel, the **Catwalk** (✉ *Weena-Zuid 33, Centrum* ☎ *No phone*) opens late and music really kicks off into the early hours with changing guest and house DJs from Thursday to Saturday (cover charge varies). The long, narrow **Club Vibes** (✉ *Westersingel 50a, Museumpark* ☎ *010/436–1655*) has a friendly staff who chat at the bar with early punters—this is another place you shouldn't arrive at before 1:30 AM. Music is mostly 1970s and 1980s, with some more mainstream 1990s nights. Three floors and one of the best live music lineups make **WATT** (✉ *West Kruiskade 26–28, Centrum* ☎ *010/217–9199* ⊕ *www.nighttown.nl* 💶 *€12–€20, €1.80 membership fee required*) *the* place to be in Rotterdam. If you can't get tickets for the big-band nights, make sure you catch the after-event party, definitely not to be missed. Music ranges from hip-hop to drum and bass, funk, techno, and pop. **Rotown** (✉ *Nieuwe Binnenweg 19, Museumpark* ☎ *010/436–2669*), a high-style restaurant, has new-talent bands playing on Saturday night.

GAY AND   Very much part of the late-night scene, **Gay Palace** (✉ *Schiedamsesingel 139, Centrum* ☎ *010/414–1486*) attracts crowds of young gay and lesbian Rotterdammers to its large dance floor on Saturday and some Friday nights.

LESBIAN BARS

JAZZ   For three days in mid-July, jazz lovers from around the world descend on Rotterdam for the **North Sea Jazz Festival** (☎ *015/214–8393* ⊕ *www.northseajazz.com*), which fills the Ahoy' arts complex with music. Around 180 artists perform on 15 different stages in what is one of Europe's largest and most popular celebrations of jazz.

Dizzy (✉ *'s-Gravendijkwal 127, 's-Gravendijkwal* ☎ *010/477–3014* ⊕ *www.dizzy.nl*) is *the* jazz café if you appreciate live performances. A big terrace out back hosts both Dutch and international musicians every Tuesday and Sunday. The café also serves good, reasonably priced food. Come early if you want a seat. Concerts and jamming sessions are free.

Erasmus bridge on Meuse river in Rotterdam as seen at night.

POP AND ROCK For mega-events, choose between the 13,500-seater **Ahoy'**, which holds pop concerts and large-scale operas, and **De Kuip**, Rotterdam's major football stadium, which boasts of its Bob Dylan, Rolling Stones, and U2 concerts. Tickets for both venues often sell out quickly, but De Kuip has a better sound system. **Ahoy'** (⊠ *Ahoyweg 10, Zuidplein* ☎ *010/293–3300* ⊕ *www.ahoy.nl*) hosts major pop concerts for big names such as Lady Gaga, Green Day, and Neil Young, but also hosts classical philharmonic orchestras, top jazz musicians, and top performance companies like Cirque du Soleil. Despite being able to seat more than 51,000 people, concerts at **De Kuip/Feyenoord Stadion** (⊠ *Van Zandvlietplein 1, Kop van Zuid* ☎ *010/492–9455*) usually sell out.

SHOPPING

Rotterdam is the number-one shopping city in South Holland. Its famous Lijnbaan and Beurstraverse shopping centers, as well as the surrounding areas, offer a dazzling variety of shops and department stores. Here you'll find all the biggest chains in Holland, such as Mango, MEXX, Morgan, Invito, and Sacha. The archways and fountains of the Beurstraverse—at the bottom of the Coolsingel—make this newer, pedestrianized area more pleasing to walk around. It is now one of the most expensive places to rent shop space, and has a nickname: *Koopgoot*, which can mean "shopping channel" (if you like it) or "shopping gutter" (if you don't). The Bijenkorf department store has an entrance here on the lower-street level. Van Oldenbarneveldtstraat and Nieuwe Binnenweg are the places to be if you want something different. There is a huge variety of alternative fashion to be found here.

DEPARTMENT STORES

De Bijenkorf (✉ *Coolsingel 105, Centrum* ☎ *0900/0919*) is a favorite department store, designed by Marcel Breuer (the great Bauhaus architect) with an exterior that looks like its name, a beehive. The best department store in Rotterdam, it covers four floors. There's a good range of clothing and shoes from both designers and the store's own label, plus a selection of cosmetics and perfume on the ground floor, with a Chill Out department on the same floor geared toward street- and club-wear; here, on some Saturdays a DJ keeps it mellow, and you can even get a haircut at in-store Kinki Kappers. De Bijenkorf is well-known for its excellent household-goods line, ranging from lights and furniture to sumptuous fabrics and rugs. Check out the second-floor restaurant with its view out over the Coolsingel and Naum Gabo's sculpture *Constructie*. **V&D** (✉ *Hoogstraat 185, Centrum* ☎ *0900/235–8363*) is great for household goods, stationery, and other everyday necessities. Rest your tired tootsies and admire the city view from the rooftop café, La Place, where you can indulge in a wide selection of snacks and full meals.

SHOPPING DISTRICTS AND STREETS

Exclusive shops and boutiques can be found in the Entrepotgebied, Delfshaven, Witte de Withstraat, Nieuwe and Oude Binnenweg, and Van Oldenbarneveldtstraat. West Kruiskade and its vicinity offer a wide assortment of multicultural products in the many Chinese, Surinamese, Mediterranean, and Arabic shops. The shops in the city center are open every Sunday afternoon, and there is late-night shopping—until 9—every Friday.

SPECIALTY STORES

There are numerous specialty stores all across town, and depending on what you are looking for, you should be able to find it somewhere. If in doubt, ask a fellow shopper or the tourist office.

ANTIQUES Look along the **Voorhaven** and its continuation **Aelbrechtskolk,** in Delfshaven, for the best antiques. On Sunday head to the **Schiedamsdijk,** where you can expect to find a market that specializes in antiques and old books, open noon–5.

ART GALLERIES Many galleries provide the opportunity both to look at art and buy it. These can be found along the Westersingel and in the Museumpark area, but the top galleries are on Witte de Withstraat, also lined with numerous cafés, making it an ideal street to spend some time window-shopping.

MAMA (✉ *Witte de Withstraat 29–31* ☎ *010/233–2022* ⊕ *www.showroommama.nl*) encourages the collaboration of emerging experimental artists. If you're looking for new, exciting, and innovative art with high standards, you'll find it here. Some of the work may shock; some might make you laugh out loud in delight; but all of it is art-critic-worthy. Consider film- and video-based art by the Dutch Galleon of Mayhem or the inflatable sculptures by a group of "artoonists," including a giant rabbit by Florentijn Hofman. The gallery is open Wednesday–Sunday 1–6.

BOOKS **Selexyz Donner** (⊠ *Lijnbaan 150, Centrum* ☎ *010/413–2070*) is the biggest bookstore in Rotterdam. Its 10 floors include an excellent range of English-language books, which are distributed throughout the shop under specific headings.

DESIGN **Dille & Kamille** (⊠ *Korte Hoogstraat 22, Centrum* ☎ *010/411–3338*) is a fantastic store for anyone interested in cooking. From herbs to sturdy wooden spoons to recipe books, this is a browser's heaven. It is one of the few shops in the Netherlands that still carries traditional Dutch household items, such as a huge water kettle to make tea for 25, a nutmeg mill, or a *zeepklopper*, a device that holds a bar of soap and can whip up bubbles—a forerunner to liquid dish-washing detergent. In the **Entrepot Harbor design district,** alongside the city marina at Kop van Zuid, are several interior-design stores. More like a museum of modern art and home furnishings than a mere gallery, the **Galerie ECCE** (⊠ *Witte de Withstraat 17a–19a, Witte de With* ☎ *010/413–9770* ⊕ *www.galerie-ecce.nl*) has an exclusive collection of ultramodern furniture, lamps, and glassware from Dutch and European designers and offers a custom-design service. You'll find a variety of smaller unique design items, suitable for gifts, such as coasters and wall sconces. The gallery has a new exhibition of paintings and sculpture every two months, and also specializes in the production of trompe l'oeil wall paintings.

FASHION For fashion suggestions, start with **Sister Moon** (⊠ *Nieuwe Binnenweg 89b, Centrum* ☎ *010/436–1508*), which has a small collection of exclusive hip clothing for men and women in the party scene; part of the boutique is devoted to trendy secondhand togs. Graffiti artists favor **Urban Unit** (⊠ *Nieuwe Binnenweg 63b, Centrum* ☎ *010/436–3825*), loving the look of the men's sneakers and street wear on sale (while stocking up on spray cans and other graffiti supplies). On Van Oldenbarneveldtstraat the prices rise as the stores get more label based. **Van Dijk** (⊠ *Van Oldenbarneveldtstraat 105, Centrum* ☎ *010/411–2644*) stocks Costume National and Helmut Lang, and the owner, Wendela, has two of her own design labels. You can find trendy shoes, bags, and accessories here and have plenty of room to try on clothes in the *paskamers* (fitting rooms).

Where there's fashion, there's music: keep in mind that Holland's largest concentration of international music stores can be found on the Nieuwe Binnenweg, ranging from techno to ambient, rock to Latin and African.

STREET MARKETS

The expansive **Binnenrotteplein,** between Sint Laurenskerk and Blaak railway station, is home to one of the largest street markets in the country, every Tuesday and Saturday from 9 to 5 and Friday from noon to 5. Among the 520 stalls you can find a flea market, book market, household items, used goods, food, fish, clothes, and flowers. From April to December, a fun shopping market with 200 stands is held on Sunday from noon to 5. There are often special attractions for children, and you can chill out on the terrace.

8

UTRECHT

Birthplace of the 16th-century pope Adrian VI (the only Dutch one), Utrecht has been a powerful bishopric since the 7th century and is still a major religious center.

First settled by Romans, Utrecht achieved its first glory in the 16th century, when the religious power of the town was made manifest in the building of four churches at points of an enormous imaginary cross, with the **Dom** (cathedral) in the center. It was in Utrecht that the Dutch Republic was established in 1579 with the signing of the Union of Utrecht. In addition to being home to Holland's largest university, the city has so many curiosities—high-gabled houses, fascinating water gates, hip shops, artsy cafés, and winding canals—that the traveler can almost forgive the city for being one of the busiest and most modern in Holland. Happily, the central core remains redolent with history, particularly along the Oudegracht (Old Canal), which winds through the central shopping district (to the east of the train station shopping complex). This particularly picturesque canal is unusual in the Netherlands in that the towpath is on two levels. In summer in the central area, the tables of many cafés and restaurants spill out across the street on both upper and lower levels (the latter being pedestrian only) and on both sides. Stake out a table as it all fills up quickly.

While this is a city with a third of a million inhabitants, it feels somewhat smaller. The center is relatively compact, and easy to navigate on foot (notwithstanding the fact that the twisting streets can cause you to lose your bearings even if you do have a good map). In fact, with narrow streets, many of them reserved for pedestrians, walking is the recommended way to go.

GETTING HERE AND AROUND

58 km (36 mi) northeast of Rotterdam, 40 km (25 mi) southeast of Amsterdam.

Utrecht forms the central hub of the national rail network, and tracks fan out from here in all directions. You can get a direct train from here to pretty much anywhere in the country. Around five an hour make the 25-minute trip between Amsterdam and Utrecht throughout the day. If driving, the A2 southeast from Amsterdam will get you to Utrecht in around 30 minutes, but the trip can take much longer at peak times.

On buses, trams, and trains you can use an OV-chipkaart (public transport chip card)—a new electronic payment system that's slowly rolled out nationally. These credit card–size tickets can be loaded up with credit from machines in the railway stations, and are debited as you board and leave trains, trams, metros, and buses. There are information and sales points in the stations. Or visit www.ov-chipkaart.nl for more information. The OV-chipkaart will eventually replace all other transport tickets, including the national *strippenkaart*, but at this writing no date for the phaseout in Utrecht had been set.

Public Transportation Information (☎ 0900/9292).

TOURS

For an unusual self-guided tour of Utrecht's watery highways, rent a water bike from **Canal Bike** (✉ *Oudegracht, opposite City Hall* ☎ *030/231–1527*), and cool off on the canals. Rates are reasonable and vary according to how long you keep the bike.

You can also opt for one of the many guided tours operated by the **RonDom**, a one-stop cultural and historical information center for the museum quarter, where you can buy tickets for almost everything as well as book a guided tour or a barge trip.

RonDom (✉ *Domplein 9, Utrecht* ☎ *030/236–0010* ⊕ *www.rondom.nl*).

TIMING

You could cover the essence of Utrecht in an afternoon, but allow a full day to visit all the museums. Railway buffs could spend that long in the National Railway Museum alone.

ESSENTIALS

Bicycle Rentals Rijwiel Shop (✉ *By the north end of track 19, Centraal Station, Utrecht* ☎ *030/231–1159* 💶 *€6.50–€7.50 with ID and a €50 deposit.*

Emergency Services National Emergency Alarm Number (☎ *112 for police, fire, and ambulance*).

Hospitals Universitair Medisch Centrum Utrecht (✉ *Heidelberglaan 100* ☎ *088/755–5555*).

TaxisUtrecht Taxi Company (UTC) (☎ *030/230–0400*).

Tourism Information VVV Utrecht (✉ *Domplein 9* ☎ *0900/128–8732*).

EXPLORING

If you arrive by train, you might be forgiven for thinking Utrecht is one enormous covered shopping mall, since the station is incorporated into the warren of 200-plus shops that is the Hoog Catharijne. You could get lost here for a day, but if you follow signs for *Centrum* (town center) and keep walking with determination, you will eventually come out in the historic center. The soaring tower of Domtoren, or "the cathedral that is missing," on the skyline will direct you to the center of the action.

8

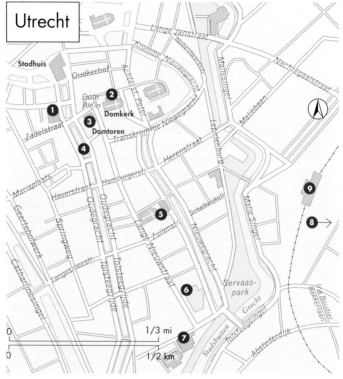

Most of the main sights are in a fairly compact area and reachable on foot within a few minutes of the Domtoren.

TOP ATTRACTIONS

7 Centraal Museum. This vast and eclectic collection ranges from a 10th-century boat to a Viktor and Rolf A-Bomb coat, and from Golden Age paintings to minimalist home furnishings. What you see depends on the theme of the current temporary exhibitions, but of the permanent displays, don't miss the **Utrecht Boat,** the complete 1,000-year-old wooden hull of a ship, excavated from a nearby riverbed in 1930, which has survived remarkably intact. The museum also has a collection of Golden Age art and artists from the Utrecht school. Across the square, modern-art lovers will make a beeline for the **Gerrit Rietveld Wing,** focused on the most famous of all De Stijl architects and designers. There is a reconstruction of his studio and lots of original Rietveld furniture. ⊠ *Nicolaaskerkhof 10* ☎ *030/236–2362* ⊕ *www.centraalmuseum.nl* ⊡ *€9* ⊙ *Tues.–Sun. 11–5.*

2 Domkerk. Holding its own against the imposing Domtoren across the square, this grand Gothic cathedral was built during the 13th and 14th centuries and designed in the style of Tournai Cathedral in Belgium. It has five chapels radiating around the ambulatory of the chancel, as well as a number of funerary monuments, including that of a

14th-century bishop. The entire space between the tower and the Domkerk was originally occupied by the nave of the huge cathedral, which was destroyed in a freak tornado in 1674 and not rebuilt. Many other buildings were damaged, and the exhibition inside Domkerk shows interesting before-and-after sketches. Today only the chancel and tower remain, separated by an open space, now a sunny square edged by a road. Behind the chancel is the **Pandhof,** a 15th-century cloister with a formal herb garden with medicinal herbs, replanted in the 1960s. If you're lucky you'll come upon classical musicians, making the most of the wondrous acoustics. A free concert is held every Saturday at 3:30. ⊠ *Achter de Dom 1* ☎ *030/231–0403* ⊕ *www.domkerk.nl* ✉ *Free, donations accepted* ⊙ *May–Sept., weekdays 10–5, Sat. 10–3:30, Sun. 2–4; Oct.–Apr., weekdays 11–4, Sat. 10–3:30, Sun. 2–4.*

> **INFORMATION**
>
> Make your way to the central Domplein, where you'll find the one-stop cultural and historical information center for the historic quarter. Inexplicably named **RonDom**, this is where you can buy tickets for almost everything, as well as book a guided tour or barge trip. There is an excellent range and display of free leaflets, to which you should help yourself. ⊠ *Domplein 9* ☎ *030/236–0010* ⊕ *www.domtoren.nl* ⊙ *Weekdays 10–6, Sat. 10–5, Sun. noon–5.*

❸ **Domtoren** *(Cathedral tower).* Soaring lancet windows add to the impression of majestic height of the famous tower of "the cathedral that is missing," the 14th-century Domtoren. The sole remnant of an enormous house of worship that was destroyed by a storm late in the 17th century (the outline of its nave can still be seen in the paving squares of the Domplein), it is more than 367 feet high. Not only is it the highest tower in the country, but its more than 50 bells make it the largest musical instrument in Holland. The tower is so big that city buses drive through an arch in its base. You can climb the tower, but make sure you feel up to the 465 steps. The panoramic view is worth the pain, though, for it stretches 40 km (25 mi) to Amsterdam on a clear day. Buy tickets in the RonDom office across the street. Tours leave hourly on the hour, Apr.–Sept. From Oct.–Mar. they leave hourly on weekends, but only every two hours through the week. ⊠ *Domplein* ☎ *030/236–0010* ✉ *€8* ⊙ *Tues.–Sat. 11–5, Sun.–Mon. noon–5; view by tour only; last tour at 4.*

❶ **Nationaal Museum van Speelklok tot Pierement** *(National Musical Box and Street Organ Museum).* This supercharming and tuneful museum is housed in an old church, and has a large collection of automated musical instruments from the 15th to the 19th century. You can wander around by yourself, but it's far more rewarding to wait for a tour (also in English), for only on these are the dazzling automata put into play. The highlight for everyone, young and old, is the tiny music box in the form of an ancient furry rabbit, which pops up out of a fading cabbage and beats time to the music with its ears. Fittingly for Holland, the development of the barrel organ—still the bane of shoppers on many busy streets—is charted from the Renaissance onward. Away from the main collection, the children's Music Factory has displays of historical instruments hardy enough for three-year-olds to try—they

8

DID YOU KNOW?

The catherdal that used to be attached to the soaring 14th-century Domtoren in Utrecht was destroyed by a storm in the late 17th century. Check out the cobblestones around the Domplein—you can still see the outline where the nave used to be.

can go at it on percussion instruments, bicycle bells, and harps. There are also interactive stands where children can shout into voice distorters, or watch themselves on a TV screen as they sing. ⊠ *Steenweg 6* ☎ *030/231–2789* ⊕ *www.museumspeelklok.nl* 🎫*€9* ☉ *Tues.–Sun. 10–5; guided tours every hr.*

❹ Oudegracht. Utrecht's long, central, sunken canal—which suffers a confusing name change at several points en route through the city—is unique in Holland, for its esplanade has upper and lower levels, with shops and galleries opening onto street level, and restaurants and cafés on the walkway just above the water (sinking water levels centuries ago led to the excavation of a lower story).

❽ Rietveld-Schröderhuis. This house exemplifies several key principles of the De Stijl movement that affected not only art but also modern architecture, furniture design, and even typography in the early part of the 20th century. The house was designed for the Schröder family by Gerrit Rietveld, one of the leading architects of De Stijl, who has many objects on view in Utrecht's Centraal Museum. The open plan, the direct communion with nature from every room, and the use of neutral white or gray on large surfaces—with primary colors to identify linear details— are typical De Stijl characteristics. Rietveld is best known outside Holland for his "Red-Blue-Yellow" chair design. Tours must be reserved in advance. Meet at the Centraal Museum 30 minutes before the scheduled tour time, and a shuttle bus takes you to the house, which is about a mile east of the city center. ⊠ *Prins Hendriklaan 50* ☎ *030/236–2310* ⊕ *www.centraalmuseum.nl* 🎫*€16 (includes guided tour and entry to Centraal Museum)* ☉ *By appointment only; tours Thu.–Sun. at 11, 12, 1, and 2.*

❾ Spoorwegmuseum *(Railway Museum).* Beyond the converted 19th-century station that serves as the entrance to this excellent museum is a vast exhibition space in the style of a rail yard. In addition to dozens of locomotives, three large sheds, called *werelden* (worlds), take you on a tour of rail history. In World 1, dealing with the birth of the railways, you follow an audio tour (available in English) through an early-19th-century English coal mine. World 2 stages a theater production based on the Orient Express. In World 3, you sit in carriages and ride the rails, while all around you the bright lights, sounds, and billowing steam evoke the Golden Age of train travel. Outside, kids can ride the *Jumbo Express* on an adventure trip past lakes and through tunnels and water jets. The museum is an easy walk from the city center. Alternatively, trains run between here and Utrecht Centraal Station eight times daily for €2 round-trip. ⊠ *Maliebaanstation* ☎ *030/230–6206* ⊕ *www. spoorwegmuseum.nl* 🎫*€14.50* ☉ *Tues.–Sun. 10–5; daily 10–5 during school vacations.*

WORTH NOTING

❺ Museum Catharijneconvent *(Convent of St. Catherine Museum).* Just a few blocks south of the Dom, this former convent houses a vast collection of religious history and sacred art. There are magnificent altarpieces, ecclesiastical vestments, beautifully illustrated manuscripts, sculptures, and paintings—including works by Rembrandt and Frans Hals. Note the

8

painting of a silvery-bearded God, by Pieter de Grebber (1640), holding what appears to be a crystal ball, inviting Jesus to sit at his right hand, in a cherub-bedecked chair. Temporary exhibitions here are first-rate. Cross the first-story walkway to get a great view of the cloister gardens. ⊠ *Lange Nieuwestraat 38* ☎ *030/231–3835* ⊕ *www. catharijneconvent.nl* 🎫 *€11.50* ⊙ *Tues.–Fri. 10–5, weekends 11–5.*

6 **Universiteits Museum.** The University Museum deals with both the history of Utrecht University and the fields of science. The first thing to grab your attention is the building itself: architects visit specially to look at Koen van Velsen's square building and his garden "boxes." A glassed-in corridor runs the length of the building, giving an immense feeling of space. One collection, bought by William I and donated to the museum, verges on the ghoulish: skulls, anatomical models, and preserved "things" in jars; medical ethics would prevent these exhibits from being preserved now, most notably the embryos, which only increases their fascination for youngsters. On the third floor, kids can have a field day. In the Youth Lab children put on mini–lab coats to do experiments and play with optical illusions (with assistants patrolling the floor to provide guidance and assistance on Wednesday, Saturday, and Sunday afternoons). A former orangery is now a garden-fronted café. ⊠ *Lange Nieuwestraat 106* ☎ *030/253-8008* ⊕ *www.museum.uu.nl* 🎫 *€7* ⊙ *Daily 11–5.*

> ### ART YOU CAN WEAR
>
> Utrecht is fiercely proud of Holland's own *enfants terribles* of the catwalk Viktor and Rolf, whose clothes hover between visual art and couture, taking a subtle yet witty stand against traditional design. Their provocative and innovative work has elevated them to such prominence that they are seen as the visionaries of haute couture's future, not just by the city of Utrecht, but by the whole fashion world.

WHERE TO EAT

$–$$
CAFÉ
✕ **Café le Journal.** This spot has the widest terrace and so catches the most sun (when there is sun to be had) of the cafés along Winkenburgstraat and Neude. Large trees soften the view across the square, so this is a prime place for lazy weekend afternoons. Inside, floor-to-ceiling framed magazine covers reflect the general news theme. The long communal table inside is stocked with newspapers, including a few English-language titles. The menu is excellent and wide-ranging. Although the café is relatively big, there is no feeling of being processed when you come here, thanks to the charming staff. Even when it is busy, you can linger over a *koffie verkerd* (café au lait) as long as you want. ⊠ *Neude 32* ☎ *030/236–4839* ▭ *No credit cards.*

$$
MEDITERRANEAN
✕ **De Artisjok.** This gracious old canal-house restaurant overlooking the fashionable New Canal has been spruced up and given a bright new lick of paint in colors that reflect the Mediterranean cuisine. The daily changing menu offers tempting selections that may include things like sole with squid tempura, or rack of lamb with celeriac purée and a honey-and-thyme sauce. ⊠ *Nieuwegracht 33* ☎ *030/231–7494* 🖉 *Reservations essential* ▭ *AE, DC, MC, V* ⊙ *No lunch.*

Many of the key principles that defined the De Stijl movement can be found at the Rietveld-Schröderhuis.

$-$$ ✗ **De Zakkendrager.** As you walk down the narrow alleyway to this gem,
CAFÉ it's easy to be misled by its unassuming exterior. Students, concertgo-
Fodor's Choice ers from the nearby Vredenburg Music Center, and fashionable young
★ locals come here for generous portions of grilled meats, excellent salads,
and an unusually large vegetarian range. The atmosphere is even better—the restaurant is cozy, friendly, and informal. The rear half opens
out into a breezy conservatory with panoramic views through glass
walls and ceiling panels. In the walled garden at the back, a 180-year-
old beech tree towers over everything. The green décor inside echoes
the foliage, creating an oasis of calm away from the bustle of the city.
⊠ *Zakkendragerssteeg 26* ☎ *030/231–7578* ▭ *AE, DC, MC, V.*

$-$$ ✗ **Eetcafé de Poort.** This place is on Ledig Erf, one of Utrecht's small
CAFÉ squares, which becomes a hive of energy and is filled with huge shade
umbrellas when the sun comes out. This café's tables spill over the
bridge, so you can sit overlooking canal-side gardens. On the far side
of the plaza, black-and-white squares are painted onto the pavement,
carrying out a popular chess theme from the surrounding cafés. The
spareribs here are a perennial favorite. ⊠ *Tolsteegbarriere 2* ☎ *030/231–
4572* ▭ *No credit cards.*

$$-$$$ ✗ **Polman's Huis.** This grand café of the old school is a Utrecht institution.
FRENCH Its spacious Jugendstil–Art Deco interior is authentic. Other reasons
to find your way here are the relaxing atmosphere and range of meal
choices, from a simple quiche to a steamed fish dinner—from a kitchen
with Mediterranean influences. ⊠ *Keistraat 2* ☎ *030/231–3368* ▭ *MC,
V* ⊗ *Closed Sun.*

$-$$ ✗ **Winkel van Sinkel.** This Neoclassical *paleis* (palace) started out in
CAFÉ the 18th century as Holland's first department store, before becoming
★

Enjoying the cafés on the Oudegracht in Utrecht.

Utrecht's foremost social hot spot. Fronted with columns and cast-iron statues of women, it conjures up images of Grecian luxe and abundance. The enormous statues were produced in England in the mid-19th century and shipped over, but they were too heavy for the crane that unloaded them, which collapsed, thereby earning the ladies the nickname "the fallen women." You can dine either on the terrace overlooking the canal or in the high-ceilinged Grote Zaal. The menu is designed to satisfy all tastes, with tempting selections such as paella, rib-eye steaks, or, for vegetarians, a delicious spring vegetable ravioli. Simpler meals such as rolls and salads are served at lunch. Try not to be in a hurry however, as service is not always that prompt. If you fancy eating after-hours, the Nachtrestaurant serves tapas until late, and a nightclub kicks in late every weekend. Monthly events include salsa and Latino nights. Check out the Web site for more details. ⊠ *Oudegracht 158; Nachtrestaurant entry via Aan de Werf* ☎ *030/230–3030* ⊕ *www.dewinkelvansinkel.nl* ▭ *No credit cards*.

WHERE TO STAY

Utrecht hotel rooms are much in demand, since the city is a business and college center. Always book as far in advance as you can. The tourism bureau (⇨ *listed above*) can help with bookings.

$–$$ 🏨 **Court Hotel**. This brand-new hotel in the Museum District occupies the Utrecht's former High Court building, which had lain empty between 2000 and 2008. The rooms are tastefully decorated in purple, gray, and white, with good-size comfortable beds and chic modern bathrooms. The on-site Brasserie has a terrace on a leafy square. There's also a more upmarket restaurant. Superior rooms are larger, and being at the back away from the street is also quieter. **Pros:** friendly; good central location. **Cons:** no room service. ✉ *Korte Nieuwstraat 14* ☎ *030/233–0033* ⊕ *www.courthotel.nl* ⤵ *27 rooms* ⚬ *In-room: refrigerator, Wi-Fi. In-hotel: restaurant, bar, Wi-Fi* ▭ *AE, MC, V.*

$$$$ 🏨 **Grand Hotel Karel V.** This former military hospital and restored 11th-century convent has been transformed into Utrecht's most luxurious hotel. The Garden Wing is a separate building surrounded by extensive gardens but lacks the historic aura of the main building, where Napoléon's brother Louis once resided. Canopied guest bedrooms are comfortably large, if the terra-cotta and gold furnishings are a bit overdone. Accent pieces are very new and yet not modern, and enormously heavy curtains are roped back to reveal almost floor-to-ceiling sash windows. Rooms in the newer Roman Wing, which opened in 2008, are more modern in style, slightly larger, and no less luxurious. The sumptuous dining room glitters with opulent metallic murals, and designer-oversize vases—a regal setting for the excellent fare. A lighter-eating alternative is served in the gardens or courtyard, if the weather is fine. **Pros:** quiet; luxurious. **Cons:** expensive. ✉ *Geertebolwerk 1* ☎ *030/233–7461* ⊕ *www.karelv.nl* ⤵ *111 rooms, 10 suites* ⚬ *In-room: refrigerator, Internet. In-hotel: restaurant, bar, pool, gym, Wi-Fi, parking (paid), some pets allowed* ▭ *AE, DC, MC, V.*

$ 🏨 **Hotel Oorsprongpark.** A convivial family hotel, this is just off one of the main transit routes to the city center. The rooms are tight and simple in furnishings and décor, but they're very clean and tidy. Those at the back have canal views. **Pros:** friendly; quiet location. **Cons:** outside of city center; basic rooms; small bathrooms. ✉ *F. C. Dondersstraat 12* ☎ *030/271–6303* ⊕ *www.oorsprongpark.nl* ⤵ *34 rooms, 4 studios* ⚬ *In-room: no a/c, Wi-Fi. In-hotel: some pets allowed* ▭ *AE, DC, MC, V* �‖ *CP.*

$–$$$ 🏨 **NH Centre Utrecht Hotel.** In the shadow of Sint Janskerk and opposite
★ a leafy square, this very friendly, modern hotel in a 19th-century jacket offers pretty and well-kept rooms at excellent prices. The attractive exterior of the 1870 building has Art Nouveau leanings, while the interior is very 21st century. Rooms are airy and stylishly understated, with floral-theme paintings on the walls. Some bathrooms have tubs. In the center of town, the hotel is ideally situated within easy walking distance of the canals, as well as plenty of shopping and dining choices. **Pros:** friendly; good central location. **Cons:** public areas less grand than the rooms. ✉ *Janskerkhof 10* ☎ *030/231–3169* ⊕ *www.nh-hotels.com* ⤵ *47 rooms* ⚬ *In-room: safe, refrigerator, Wi-Fi. In-hotel: restaurant, bar, Wi-Fi* ▭ *AE, MC, V.*

$–$$ 🏨 **Sandton Malie Hotel.** Located on a tree-lined avenue behind a stylish 19th-century facade, this classically designed hotel is both modern and attractive. Guest rooms are brightly decorated, though simply furnished. The breakfast room overlooks a pretty garden, which guests have access to in fine weather, and the bar-lounge doubles as a small art gallery. **Pros:** quiet location; some rooms have balconies. **Cons:** outside of city center. ✉ *Maliestraat 2* ☎ *030/231–6424* ⊕ *www.maliehotel.nl* ⤵ *45 rooms* ⚬ *In-room: Wi-Fi. In-hotel: bar, Internet terminal, parking (paid)* ▭ *AE, MC, V* �‖ *CP.*

8

¢ 🔲 **Stayokay Hostel Bunnik.** Backpackers and travelers on a budget can find a bargain bunk in shared dorms just outside Utrecht, only 10 minutes from town by bus. The hostel enjoys a peaceful wooded location on the banks of the Kromme Rijn river. **Pros:** good value; quiet location. **Cons:** a bus ride from town; could be noisy in a shared dorm. ⊠ *Rhijnauwenselaan 14, Bunnik* ☎ *030/656–1277* ⊕ *www.stayokay. com* ⤳ *23 dorm rooms of 2, 3, 4, 5, 6, 7, 8, or 12 beds* ⚷ *In-room: no a/c, no phone, no TV. In-hotel: restaurant, bar, Internet terminal* ⊟ *AE, V* ⦿| *CP.*

NIGHTLIFE AND THE ARTS

THE ARTS In Utrecht you can find dance on the programs of **Stadsschouwburg** (⊠ *Lucas Bolwerk 24* ☎ *030/230–2023* ⊕ *www.stadsschouwburg-utrecht.nl*), which has a major performance hall as well as the Blauwe Zaal (Blue Room) for small productions. The annual **Spring Dance** festival brings international performers to town in April, with the biggest events usually on the big squares in the center of town, the Neude.

The **Vredenburg Muziek Centrum** (⊠ *Vredenburgpassage 77* ☎ *030/231–4544* ⊕ *www.vredenburg.nl*) is the biggest venue in Utrecht for classical and pop concerts. Closed for renovation until 2012, concerts are currently being staged at two alternative sites: **Vredenburg Leidsche Rijn** (⊠ *J.C. Verthorenpad 100*) and at **Vredenburg Leeuwenbergh** (⊠ *Servaasbolwerk 1a*).

Utrecht's **Festival Oude Muziek** (☎ *030/232–9010* ⊕ *www.oudemuziek. nl*), or Festival of Early Music, in late summer each year is immensely popular, and sells out rapidly. Check the Web site for locations and events.

A full program of concerts is performed in many of Utrecht's fine churches. The best are usually heard in the **Dom** (☎ *030/231–0403*).

The 10-day annual late-September **Nederlands Film Festival** (☎ *030/230–3800* ⊕ *www.filmfestival.nl*) is a seriously taken review of the past year of Dutch productions held in Winkel van Sinkel café and most of the town's cinemas. Many international movies, often in English, are given their Dutch premieres here, and at the gala event the "Golden Calves"—the Dutch Oscars—are dished out to the year's best. More than 100,000 visitors attend the many screenings. Tickets can be bought online, by phone, or in person from the temporary pavilion that appears on the Neude Square at festival time. Most tickets cost €8–10.

NIGHTLIFE Utrecht's students strike a lively note at cafés around the center, more during the week than on weekends. Larger cafés such as the **Winkel van Sinkel** and **Oudaen** are gathering spots for all ages.

Nachtwinkel (⊠ *Oudegracht 158 a/d werf* ☎ *030/230–3030*) hosts Winkel van Sinkel's weekend serious fun nights, packing both floors with frenetic clubbers. **Polman's Huis** attracts a lively crowd of students and young professionals.

Some questionable fashion decisions or perhaps just the Elf Fantasy Fair at Kasteel de Haar.

SIDE TRIP TO KASTEEL DE HAAR

10 km (6 mi) northwest of Utrecht.

Fodor's Choice
★

The spectacular **Kasteel de Haar** is not only the largest castle in the Netherlands, but also the most sumptuously furnished. Thanks to the fortuitous way the Barons van Zuylen had of marrying Rothschilds, their family home grew into a Neo-Gothic extravaganza replete with moat, fairy-tale spires, and machicolated towers. The castle was founded back in 1165, but several renovations and many millions later, the family expanded the house under the eye of P. J. H. Cuypers, designer of Amsterdam's Centraal Station and Rijksmuseum in 1892. Inside the castle are acres of tapestries, medieval iron chandeliers, and the requisite ancestral portraits snootily studying you as you wander through chivalric halls so opulent and vast they could be opera sets.

At de Haar, be sure to explore the magnificent gardens and park, dotted with romantic paths, fanciful statues, and little bridges. As was the wont of aristo owners in the 19th century, entire villages were relocated to expand their estate parks, and in this case, Haarzuilens was reconstructed a mile from the castle. Designed in 1898 around a village square, all its cottages have red-and-white doors and shutters, reflecting the armorial colors of the Van Zuylen family. Every year in September, the village fair is kicked off by the current baron to the accompaniment of a fireworks display. As for the castle itself, you can view its grand interiors only via one of the guided tours (no kids under five), which leave on the hour and are led only in Dutch. No matter, the objects of beauty on display can be understood in any language. Once you explore this enchanted domain, you'll easily understand why Marie-Hélène van Zuylen, who grew up here, went on to become Baroness Guy de Rothschild, the late-20th-century's "Queen of Paris," famous for her grand houses and costume balls. Directions for car travelers are given on the castle Web site. For public transport, take Bus No. 127 from Utrecht Centraal Station, direction Breukelen/Kockengen, until the Brink stop in Haarzuilens, a 15-minute walk from the castle. You can also train it to Vleuten and then take a taxi. ⊠ *Kasteellaan 1, near Haarzuilens* ☎ *030/677–8515* ⊕ *www.kasteeldehaar.nl* ☜ *€8, grounds only €3, parking €3* ☉ *Grounds daily 9–5; castle Tues.–Fri. 11–4, weekends noon–4. Hrs vary slightly through the year; call to confirm.*

Side Trips to Belgium

BRUSSELS, BRUGGE, AND GENT

WORD OF MOUTH

"Just got back from Brugge! Ah—a lovely place and a must see. If you can, try and land there on a Wednesday. That's when they have their market in the center and it is really amazing."

— DaniGirlTravels

WELCOME TO BELGIUM

TOP REASONS TO GO

★ **Charming history:** Stroll the narrow cobbled streets of Brugge, about as perfectly preserved as any medieval city in Europe. Enjoy it most after dark when the buildings are floodlighted—you'll feel like you've stepped into a fairy-tale world.

★ **Quirky capital:** It may be the "Capital of Europe," but *Brusseleers* prefer to do things the "Belgian" way. Where else, but in the city of Jacques Brel, could the most enduring emblem be a small statue of a urinating boy?

★ **Brews with views:** Belgium is one of the greatest brewing nations on earth, with more than 100 breweries churning out a bewildering variety of beer. Sip in the absolute splendor of the city squares.

★ **Chocolate dreams:** Belgium's reputation as a world capital of chocolate is both well deserved and irresistible. It's difficult to recommend just one shop; simply close your eyes and follow your nose.

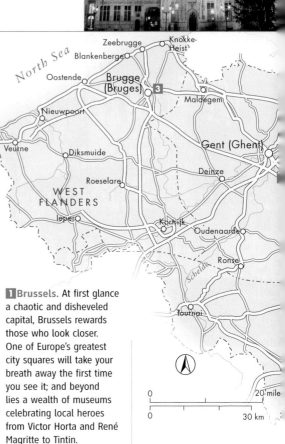

1 Brussels. At first glance a chaotic and disheveled capital, Brussels rewards those who look closer. One of Europe's greatest city squares will take your breath away the first time you see it; and beyond lies a wealth of museums celebrating local heroes from Victor Horta and René Magritte to Tintin.

2 Gent. Gent's historical center is surrounded by a real city, which gives it a lived-in real-world feel, but the spectacular medieval riverside buildings of the Graslei can easily hold their own alongside any in Brugge. And the cathedral houses one of the greatest pieces of religious art ever created: the Van Eyck brothers' *Adoration of the Mystic Lamb.*

3 Brugge. Brugge is the kind of city for which jigsaw puzzles and chocolate boxes were invented, with each impossibly gorgeous view somehow prettier and more photogenic than the last. Open up that box of chocolates and you'll find holy relics, great monuments, important medieval artworks, and, yes, chocolates.

GETTING ORIENTED

An expanding network of high-speed trains puts Brussels, Brugge, and Gent within commuting distance of many European cities. An extensive regional rail network makes it easy to hop around Belgium; the country is also covered by a large network of four-lane highways. It's an easy drive from Amsterdam, Düsseldorf, and Paris. Belgian Railways sends two trains each hour to Brugge from Brussels (60 minutes) via Gent (25 minutes from Brugge). The trains all pass through Brussels's three main stations, but Gare du Midi/Brussel Zuid is the largest and has the clearest signage and directions. It's also the terminus for the Eurostar service connecting London and Paris, as well as the Thalys network that links Amsterdam, Brussels, Cologne, and Paris. You can also travel to Brugge and Gent from Amsterdam through Antwerp station, where there are three trains an hour to Gent, one of which continues on to Brugge.

9

Updated by
Tim Skelton

Belgium has attractions out of proportion to its diminutive size. From medieval cities and abbeys where the monks run their own breweries to forested hills and famous World War I and II battlegrounds for contemplation and remembrance. It's a little country that packs a big punch. Here we'll highlight three of the country's brightest stars: Brussels, Gent, and Brugge.

Brussels's vibrant, cosmopolitan atmosphere and multicultural beat make it much more than simply the administrative hub of Europe. The city was home to a number of greats, including Victor Horta, Jacques Brel, René Magritte, Georges Remi (better known as Hergé, creator of Tintin), and a whole host of other famous people you thought were French. It brims with museums that celebrate its famous sons and daughters. But for all its world-class restaurants, architecture, and art, the city keeps a relatively low profile; that means that you'll still have plenty of breathing room to relish its landmarks, cobbled streets, and beautiful parks.

With around a million inhabitants, Brussels is arguably the only place in Belgium that really deserves the title of city in the truest global sense. And it has the grand boulevards and palaces one would expect to fine in a European capital.

Brugge and Gent are both beautiful ancient towns whose heritage has been well preserved through the ages. On a more manageable scale than the larger capital, you'll find quaint cobbled streets, medieval monuments, and even more great dining options. Their beauty is no secret though, so you're unlikely to be visiting alone. Gent, and particularly Brugge, can get exceedingly crowded during the summer months, but even then there are quieter corners and it is fairly easy to give the masses the slip. The weather may be fickle in the quieter, colder seasons, but the crowds are a lot thinner; it's then that you can feel the rhythm of life as it was many centuries ago.

PLANNING

GETTING HERE AND AROUND
PUBLIC TRANSPORTATION
In Brussels, the metro, trams, and buses operate as part of the same system and are run by the city's transport authority, STIB/MIVB (Société des Transports Intercommunaux de Bruxelles/Maatschappij voor het Intercommunaal Vervoer te Brussel). You can buy the tickets in metro stations, trains, and in some shops. ■ TIP→ A single "Jump" ticket, which can be used among all three systems in an hour-long time frame, costs €1.70 (or €2 if you buy your ticket on board a tram or bus). The best buy is a 10-trip ticket, which costs €12.30.

Information **STIB/MIVB** (☎ 070/232-000 ⊕ www.stib.be).

The De Lijn bus company provides bus, tram, and trolley service throughout Flanders. In Brugge most buses run every few minutes (less often on Sundays). Several bus lines take you from the station to the city center. In Gent, De Lijn has several trams, and dozens of bus lines. There are stops all over town, and most buses and trams run every 10 to 15 minutes. Note however that the transport system in Gent will be severely disrupted until 2012 due to major construction work in the city center—see the Gent introduction for more information. You can buy a ticket (€1.20) or a day pass (€5) at the bus terminal in Gent or Brugge. You can also pay on board, but the fares rise to €2 and €6 respectively. There are night buses on Friday and Saturday.

If you arrive in Gent by train, take tram 1 for the city center. The fare costs €1.20. You can also buy a pass for a day's worth of tram travel for €5. Buy tickets at the machines in the tram terminus—a tunnel below the rail tracks at the west end of Gent Sint-Pieters train station—they take coins and small bills. You can also buy a ticket from the driver, but as with the buses you will pay more (€2 and €6 respectively).

TRAIN TRAVEL
Brussels is one of the hubs for the Belgian National Railways (SNCB/ NMBS). Passenger trains are clean and efficient. Domestic trains use the capital's three stations: Gare du Midi, Gare Centrale, and Gare du Nord. National service is extensive and frequent. For example, four to five trains an hour link Antwerp with Brussels; the trip takes about 45 minutes.

Thalys high-speed trains to Paris, Bordeaux, Avignon, Marseille, Liège, Cologne, Aachen, Amsterdam, Rotterdam, and The Hague leave from the Gare du Midi. It takes under an hour and a half to get to Paris, and trains leave every half hour between 6 AM and 7 PM. The trip to Amsterdam takes 1 hour and 53 minutes. You can also make the journey to Amsterdam on normal hourly InterCity trains. These take an hour longer, but the advantage is they are cheaper and do not require advance reservations.

ABOUT THE RESTAURANTS
Belgium's better restaurants are on a par with the most renowned in the world. Prices are similar to those in France and Great Britain—and often cheaper. The Belgian emphasis on high-quality food filters down

to more casual options as well, from main-square cafés to the street vendors you'll find in towns large and small. The restaurants we list in this book are the cream of the crop in each price category.

ABOUT THE HOTELS

Belgium offers a range of options, from the major international hotel chains and small, modern local hotels to family-run restored inns and historic houses. Prices in metropolitan areas are significantly higher than those in outlying towns and the countryside.

WHAT IT COSTS IN EUROS					
	¢	$	$$	$$$	$$$$
Restaurants	under €10	€10–€15	€15–€22	€22–€30	over €30
Hotels	under €75	€75–€120	€120–€165	€165–€230	over €230

Restaurant prices are per person for a main course; hotel prices are for a standard double room in high season.

TIMING

Travelers can cover the main sights of Brussels in a weekend. To add on the Flemish splendor of Gent and Brugge, it's best to allow at least a day for each city.

VISITOR INFORMATION

The Brussels tourist information center in the Hôtel de Ville is open daily 9–6 (except Sunday 9–2 in winter). Gent's tourist bureau is open daily 9:30–6:30 in summer; 9:30–4:30 in winter. Tours with the guide association Gidsenbond van Genten can be booked here. Another good resource for Gent is an online "urban dissection kit" (⊕ *www.use-it. be*). This site (with English translations) is geared for students and other finger-on-the-pulse travelers. Brugge's visitor information bureau is open daily year-round, though it closes for lunch breaks on weekends. In addition to its guides and services, it has a set of lockers where you can store your bags; buy a locker token at the desk. A small branch office, also with lockers, is in the train station.

BRUSSELS

Brussels started life as a village toward the end of the 10th century. It was ruled over by various kings of Flanders through the ages, most notably Charles V, Archduke of the Habsburgs and Holy Roman Emperor. The city grew gradually around its increasingly magnificent Grand'Place, but it really began to flourish following Belgian independence in 830. By the end of the 19th century it had established itself as one of the liveliest cities in Europe.

In 1958 it was chosen for its central location and political neutrality to be the European Economic Community's new headquarters, an honor which was a precursor to its current hosting of many of the European Union's administrative and political arms. As a by-product of Europe's increasing integration, more and more international businesses have invaded the city, all wanting to be close to the hub of power. The result is a clash of old and new: swaths of steel-and-glass office buildings set only a few steps from cobblestoned streets.

But this contradiction has always been part of the city's strength—and charm. Here, it seems, architectural harmony has never been a major influence on building design. A step-gabled medieval town house may sit right beside something made of brick from the 1950s, and the only thing separating that from an anonymous concrete structure might be a swirling Art Nouveau creation designed by Victor Horta. This architectural randomness is so synonymous with the city that it's even been termed "Brusselization" by some.

In terms of population, diversity is now the capital's greatest strength; one-third of the city's million-strong population are non-Belgians. You're just as likely to hear Arabic or Swedish spoken on the streets as French or Flemish.

9

With such a mishmash of ideas and images, Brussels can seem a little slapdash at first glance. And while the city might not appeal to everyone at first, it's definitely a place that's worth getting to know better. And to know the city is to love it.

GETTING HERE AND AROUND

204 km (122 mi) south of Amsterdam.

If you are traveling by car from Amsterdam, take the A1/E19 motorway. Once you reach the E40, follow the signs to the city. The trip takes around 2½ hours.

Brussels is connected to Amsterdam by the high-speed Thalys train network, which requires advance reservations. One train an hour leaves Amsterdam for Brussels, and the journey takes just under two hours. A normal InterCity train also leaves once an hour from Amsterdam Centraal, traveling via Schiphol Airport, and takes just over 2½ hours. The advantage of the slower train is that reservations are not required. The easiest way to ensure a cab is to call Taxis Verts. You can also catch a taxi at stands around town; stands are indicated with yellow signs. All officially registered taxis have a yellow-and-blue sign on their roofs. A cab ride within the city center costs between €6 and €12. Tips are included in the fare.

ORIENTATION

While Brussels technically includes 19 communes, or suburbs, most sights, hotels, and restaurants are clustered in the center. Locals simply call this the *centre*, but the tours here distinguish a Lower Town and Upper Town. The Lower Town is physically lower, including the area around the Grand'Place and the Bourse. A steep slope leads to the Upper Town, around rue de la Régence, place Royale, and the Sablon squares. If you're arriving at Gare Centrale, a new underground passageway links the lower concourse level directly with the Marché aux Herbes in the Lower Town, close to the Grand'Place.

Detailed maps of the Brussels public transportation network are available in most metro stations and at the Tourist Information Brussels in the Grand'Place. ■ TIP➔ Get a map free with a Brussels Card (also available at the tourist office), which allows you free public transport and free admission at more than 30 museums, plus other discounts. Cards cost €24, €34, and €40 for one, two, and three days respectively. Before deciding on a card, know that most museums are closed Mondays.

BANKS AND EXCHANGE SERVICES

Currency exchange offices are clustered around the Grand'Place, while the major banks, Fortis and ING, have branches around the city. Branch hours are usually weekdays 9 AM to 1 PM and 2 PM to 4:30 PM. There are 24-hour ATMs, called Bancontact or Mister Cash and marked with blue-and-yellow signs, all around Brussels, though not as many as in most European cities. This is why long lines often sprout from downtown ATMs on weekend nights. Frustratingly, ATMs are often out of order and can be totally out of cash by Sunday evenings.

TOURS

If time is limited, several open-top bus companies run hop-on, hop-off tours covering all the main sights for €18.

IF YOU ONLY HAVE 1 DAY

Head for the Grand'Place to drink in the gilded splendor of its medieval buildings. Wander the narrow cobbled lanes surrounding the square and visit the graceful, arcaded Galeries St-Hubert, an elegant 19th-century shopping gallery. Head down rue de l'Etuve to see the Manneken Pis, the statue of the little boy who according to legend saved Brussels by urinating to extinguish a fire. Walk to the place du Grand Sablon to window-shop at its many fine antiques stores and galleries. If it's a weekend, enjoy the outdoor antiques market. Have lunch in one of the cafés lining the perimeter, and don't forget to buy chocolates at one of the top chocolatiers on the square. Then cross over rue de la Régence to see the place du Petit Sablon before walking down the street to the Musée d'Art Moderne and the Musée d'Art Ancien to view collections ranging from the Surrealism of Belgian artist René Magritte to the delicately wrought details of Pieter Bruegel the Elder's *The Fall of Icarus.* Pick out a restaurant on the fashionable rue Antoine Dansaert for dinner. Finally, return to the Grand'Place to cap off the evening with a drink at one of the cafés to see the shimmer of the golden facades under the glow of lights.

TIMING

Brussels is small enough that you can get a superficial impression of it from a car window in a single day. For a more substantial appreciation, however, you need one day for the historic city heart, another for the uptown squares and museums, and additional days for museums outside the center and excursions to the periphery.

ESSENTIALS

Emergency Services **Pan-European Emergency Number** (☎ *112*). **Police** (☎ *101*) **24-Hour English-Speaking Info and Crisis Line** (☎ *02/648–4014*).

Taxis **Taxis Verts** (☎ *02/349–4949*).

Train Stations **Gare Centrale** (✉ *carrefour de l'Europe 2, Upper Town* ☎ *02/528–2828*). **Gare du Midi** (✉ *av. Fonsny, Lower Town* ☎ *02/528–2828*). **Gare du Nord** (✉ *rue du Progres 76, St-Josse* ☎ *02/528–2828*).

Visitor Information **Brussels** (*TIB*✉ *Hôtel de Ville, Grand'Place, Lower Town* ☎ *02/513–8940* ⊕ *www.brusselsinternational.be*).

9

EXPLORING THE LOWER TOWN

TOP ATTRACTIONS

❹ **Centre Belge de la Bande Dessinée** (*Belgian Center for Comic-Strip Art*).
☺ It fell to the land of Tintin, a cherished cartoon character, to create the
Fodor's Choice world's first museum dedicated to the ninth art—comic strips. Despite
★ its primary appeal to children, comic-strip art has been taken seriously in Belgium for decades, and in the Belgian Comic Strip Center it is wedded to another strongly Belgian art form: Art Nouveau. Based in an elegant 1903 Victor Horta–designed building, the museum is long on the history of the genre but sadly short on kid-friendly interaction and

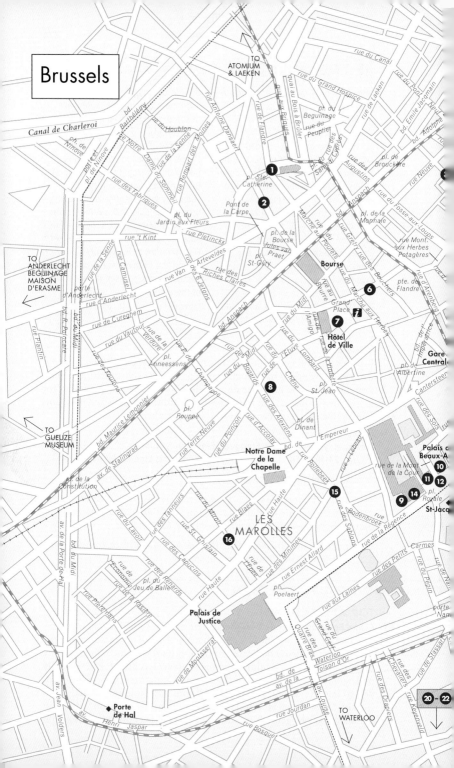

Brussels

Canal de Charleroi

TO
ATOMIUM
& LAEKEN

TO ANDERLECHT
BEGUINAGE
MAISON D'ERASME

TO GUEUZE
MUSEUM

rue du Canal

pl. du
Beguinage

quai au Bois à Brûler

rue du Grand Hospice

rue du Pont

rue de Laeken

bd. Emile Jacqmain

rue Neuve

rue du Peuplier

pl. de
Brouckère

rue Neuve

bd. Antoine Dansaert

rue de Flandre

quai aux Briques

quai aux Briques

pl. Ste.
Catherine

1

2

Pont de
la Carpe

pl. du
Jardin aux Fleurs

rue Pietinckx

rue 't Kint

rue de la Senne

rue Van
Artevelde

rue des
Riches Claires

pl. de la
Bourse

Jules van
Praet

rue St-Géry

pl. de la
Monnaie

pl. de la
fosse-aux-Loups

rue Mont
aux Herbes
Potagères

Bourse

6

pte. de
Flandre

Grand
Place

7 **i**

**Hôtel
de Ville**

rue de la
Bourse

rue au
Beurre

pl. de
l'Amigo

rue de
l'Etuve

Gare
Central

pl. de
l'Albertine

rue du Midi

rue des Alexiens

rue des Chêne

pl.
St. Jean

8

pl. de
Dinant

Empereur

rue d'Accolay

pl. de
l'Albertine

Canterstee

rue des Sols

**Palais c
Beaux-A**

10

11 **12**

rue de la Mont
de la Cour

pl.
Royale

9 **14**

St-Jacq

Notre Dame
de la Chapelle

bd. de

pl. de la
Constitution

15

rue de la Régence

Carmes

rue du Pépin

**LES
MAROLLES**

16

rue des Tanneurs

rue des Capucins

rue Haute

pl. du
Jeu de Balle

rue des Renards

pl.
Poelaert

rue aux Laines

rue des Petits

porte
Nam

**Palais de
Justice**

Waterloo
Toison d'Or

**Porte
de Hal**

rue Jourdan

av. Louise

TO
WATERLOO

20 - 22

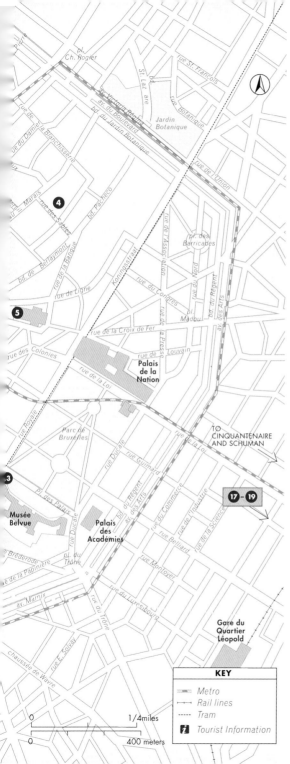

9

KEY

Metro

Rail lines

Tram

Tourist Information

Grand'Place in Brussels in undoubtedly one of the most impressive squares in Europe.

anglophone-friendly information. Tintin, the cowlicked adventurer created in 1929 by the late, great Brussels native Hergé, became a worldwide favorite cartoon character. But many other artists have followed in Hergé's footsteps, some of them even more innovative. The collection includes more than 400 original plates by Hergé and his Belgian successors and 25,000 cartoon works; those not exhibited can be viewed in the archive. There are also good temporary exhibitions from time to time, a large comic-strip shop, a library, and a lovely Art Nouveau brasserie. Most information is in French. If you enjoy this, keep an eye out for the comic-strip murals dotted on walls around the city. ⊠ *rue des Sables 20, Lower Town* ☎ *02/219–1980* ⊕ *www.comicscenter.net* ⊠ *€7.50* ⊗ *Tues.–Sun. 10–6.*

❼ **Grand'Place.** This jewel box of a square is arguably Europe's most ornate and most theatrical. It's a vital part of the city—everyone passes through at some point. At night the burnished facades of the guild houses and their gilded statuary look especially dramatic: from April to September, the square is floodlighted after sundown with waves of changing colors, accompanied by music. Try to be here for the *Ommegang*, a magnificent historical pageant re-creating Emperor Charles V's reception in the city in 1549 (the first Tuesday and Thursday in July). You'll find here a flower market, frequent jazz and classical concerts, and in December, under the majestic Christmas tree, a life-size crèche with sheep grazing around it. The Gothic **Hôtel de Ville**, which dates from the early 15th century, dominates the Grand'Place. It's nearly 300 years older than the surrounding guild houses, as it survived the devastating fires of 1695. The left wing was begun in 1402 but was soon found to be too small.

Fodor's Choice
★

Charles the Bold laid the first stone for the extension in 1444, and it was completed four years later. The extension left the slender belfry off center; it has now been fully restored. The belfry is topped by a bronze statue of St. Michael crushing the devil beneath his feet, and is a beautiful and useful landmark for navigating Brussels's winding streets. Over the gateway are statues of the prophets, female figures representing lofty virtues, and effigies of long-gone dukes and duchesses. Inside the building are a number of excellent Brussels and Mechelen tapestries, some of them in the Gothic Hall, where recitals and chamber-music concerts are frequently held. Locals still get married in the town hall, so keep an eye out for brides stepping gingerly over the cobbles on summer mornings. ⊠ *Grand'Place, Lower Town* ☎ *02/548–0447* 🎟 *€3* ⊙ *Guided tours available in English, call for times or ask at the tourist office in the right wing of the building.* On the same side of the Grand'Place as the Hôtel de Ville, the **Maison de la Brasserie** was once the brewers' guild. The building, also known as l'Arbre d'Or (the Golden Tree), now houses a modest brewery museum, appropriate enough in a country that still brews 400 different beers. There are audio guides in English. The entrance ticket entitles you to a free beer at the end of your visit. ⊠ *Grand'Place 10, Lower Town* ☎ *02/511–4987* 🎟 *€6* ⊙ *Daily 10–5.*

❽ Manneken Pis (*little man urinating*). This cocky emblem of Brussels has drawn sightseers for centuries—but after all the hype, you may be underwhelmed by the minuscule statue of the peeing boy, an image that launched a thousand tchotchkes. The first mention of the Manneken dates from 1377, and he's said to symbolize what Belgians think of the authorities, especially those of occupying forces. The present version was commissioned from sculptor Jerome Duquesnoy in 1619. It is a copy; the original was seized by French soldiers in 1747. In restitution, King Louis XV of France was the first to present *Manneken Pis* with a gold-embroidered suit. The statue now has 517 other costumes for ceremonial occasions, an ever-increasing collection whose recent benefactors include John Malkovich and Dennis Hopper, and his own personal dresser. On one or two days of the year, he spouts wine or beer, rather than water. A female version set up by an enterprising restaurateur, the *Jeanneke Pis*, can be found off the rue des Bouchers. ⊠ *rue de l'Etuve at rue du Chêne, Lower Town.*

WORTH NOTING

QUICK
BITES

A la Mort Subite (⊠ *rue Montagne-aux-Herbes-Potagères 7, Lower Town* ☎ *02/513–1318*) is a Brussels institution named after a card game called Sudden Death. This 1920s café with its high ceilings, wooden tables, and mirrored walls brews its own traditional Brussels beers, Lambik, Gueuze, and Faro, and is a favorite of beer lovers from all over the world. The sour potent beer may be an acquired taste, but, like singer Jacques Brel, who came here often, you'll find it hard to resist the bar's gruff charm.

❸ Place des Martyrs. This square holds a monument to the 445 patriots who died in the brief but successful 1830 war of independence against the Dutch. The square itself is a Neoclassical architectural ensemble built in 1795 in the cool style favored by the Austrian Habsburgs. ⊠ *rue du Persil, Lower Town.*

❶ Place Ste-Catherine. If you find the Grand'Place overrun by tourists, come to this square, a favorite of locals. It's a working market every weekday from 7 to 5, where people come to shop for necessities and banter with fishmongers. There's a stall where you can down a few oysters, accompanied by a glass of ice-cold muscadet. In the evening the action moves to the old **Vismet** (fish market), which branches off from the Eglise de Ste-Catherine. A canal used to run through here; it's now reduced to a couple of elongated ponds, but both sides are lined with seafood restaurants, some excellent, many overpriced. In good weather, there's outdoor waterside dining. ⊠ *Intersection of rue Ste-Catherine, rue du Vieux Marché aux Grains, rue de Flandre, quai aux Briques, quai au Bois à Bruler, pl. du Samedi, rue Plateau, and rue Melsens, Lower Town.*

❻ Quartier de l'Îlôt Sacré (*small sacred island neighborhood*). Flimflam art-★ ists and jewelry vendors mingle with the crowds in the narrow rue des Bouchers and even narrower petite rue des Bouchers. While many streets in central Brussels were widened as part of the preparations for the 1958 World's Fair, these tiny routes escaped being demolished after locals complained. The area was given special protection in 1959 and there are strict rules governing what changes can be made to its historic buildings. As long as you watch out for pickpockets, it's all good-natured fun in the liveliest area in Brussels, where restaurants and cafés stand cheek by jowl, their tables spilling out onto the sidewalks. One local street person makes a specialty of picking up a heaped plate and emptying it into his bag. The waiters laugh and bring another plate. The restaurants make strenuous efforts to pull you in with huge displays of seafood and game. The quality, alas, is a different matter, and there have been arrests in recent years for large-scale credit-card fraud in these restaurants. *(For some outstanding exceptions, see Where to Eat, below.)* ⊕ *www.ilotsacre.be.*

❷ Rue Antoine Dansaert. This is the flagship street of Brussels's fashionable quarter, which extends south past St-Géry and Ste-Catherine. Avant-garde boutiques sell Belgian-designed men's and women's fashions along with more familiar designer labels. There are also inexpensive restaurants, cozy bars and cafés, edgy galleries, and stylish furniture shops.

EXPLORING THE UPPER TOWN

TOP ATTRACTIONS

❶❻ Les Marolles. If the Grand'Place stands for old money, the Marolles neighborhood stands for old—and current—poverty. This was home to the workers who produced the luxury goods for which Brussels was famous. There may not be many left who still speak the old Brussels dialect, mixing French and Flemish with a bit of Spanish thrown in, but the area still has raffish charm, although gentrification is in progress. The Marolles has welcomed many waves of immigrants, the most recent from Spain, North Africa, and Turkey. Many come to the daily **Vieux Marché** (flea market) at the place du Jeu de Balle (7–1),

If you've had enough *patat frite,* then head over to the Rue des Bouchers for cuisines from around the world.

where old clothes are sold along with every kind of bric-a-brac, plain junk, and the occasional gem. For more browsing, hit the smattering of antiques shops on rue Haute and rue Blaes. This area can be sketchy at night, so you may want to leave by sunset, particularly if you're alone, though groups can enjoy some fun bars and restaurants. ⊠ *Bordered by blvd. du Midi, blvd. de Waterloo heading southwest from Palais de Justice, and imaginary line running west from blvd. Maurice Lemonnier, Upper Town.*

❿ **Musée des Instruments de Musique (MIM).** If you've ever been curious to know what a gamelan or Tibetan temple bell sounds like, here's your chance. In addition to seeing the more than 1,500 instruments on display, you can listen to them via infrared headphones, and you can hear musical extracts from almost every instrument as you stand in front of it. The more than 200 extracts range from ancient Greek tunes to mid-20th-century pieces. Paintings and ancient vases depicting the instruments being played throughout history enhance the experience. The four-story museum features a complete 17th-century orchestra, a precious 1619 spinet-harpsichord (only two such instruments exist), an armonica, a rare Chedeville bagpipe, and about 100 Indian instruments given to King Leopold II by the rajah Sourindro Mohun Tagore. Head to the rooftop café for fantastic views of the city, and call for information about occasional free concerts. ⊠ *rue Montagne de la Cour 2, Upper Town* ☎ *02/545–0130* ⊕ *www.mim.be* ✉ *€5* ☉ *Tues.–Fri. 9:30– 4:45, weekends 10–4:45.*

Fodor's Choice
★

⑪ **Musée Magritte.** The third museum in a triumvirate, this is the new kid on
Fodor's Choice the block. After years sharing display space with his contemporaries in
★ the neighboring Musée d'Art Moderne, Brussels's own surrealist genius
René Magritte (1898–1967) was finally handed the honor of his own
museum in 2009. It was clearly long overdue as it pulled in half a million visitors within the first year. You can reach it through an underground passage from the Musée d'Art Ancien, or enter via the separate
entrance on place Royale where it is housed. Note: you must buy tickets first at the central desk in the Musée d'Art Ancien. An elevator on
level two whisks you up to level three, where the collection starts. The
exhibition traces Magritte's life and work chronically, expanding key
moments through letters, sculptures, films, and of course, a great many
fine canvases. There are around 200 paintings on display, including such
masterpieces as the haunting *The Empire of Light* and *The Domain of
Arnheim.* ⊠ *Entrance at pl. Royale 1; buy tickets at rue de la Régence
3, Upper Town* ☎ *02/508–3211* ⊕ *www.musee-magritte-museum.be*
🎫 *€8, combo ticket for three museums €13* ☉ *Tues.–Sun. 10–5.*

⑮ **Place du Grand Sablon.** "Sand Square" is where the people of Brussels
★ come to see and be seen. Once, as the name implies, it was nothing
more than a sandy hill. Today, it is an elegant square, surrounded by
numerous restaurants, cafés, and antiques shops, some in intriguing
alleys and arcades. Every weekend morning a lively antiques market of
more than 100 stalls takes over the upper end of the square. It isn't for
bargain hunters, however. For a little tranquility, pop into the beautiful Notre Dame du Sablon church or across the street to the lovely
little Place du Petit Sablon garden. ⊠ *Intersection of rue de Rollebeek,
rue Lebeau, rue de la Paille, rue Ste-Anne, rue Boedenbroeck, rue des
Sablons, petite rue des Minimes, rue des Minimes, and rue Joseph Stevens, Upper Town.*

⑫ **Place Royale.** There's a strong dash of Vienna in this white, symmetrical
★ square; it was built in the Neoclassical style by Austrian overlords.
Elegantly proportioned, it is the centerpiece of the Upper Town, which
became the center of power during the 18th century. The equestrian
statue in its center, representing Godefroid de Bouillon, Belgian crusader and King of Jerusalem, is a romantic afterthought. The buildings
are being restored one by one, leaving the facades intact. Place Royale
was built on the ruins of the palace of the Dukes of Brabant, which
had burned down. The site has been excavated, and it is possible to see
the underground digs and the main hall, Aula Magna, where Charles
V was crowned Holy Roman Emperor in 1519 and where, 37 years
later, he abdicated to retire to a monastery. The church on the square,
St-Jacques-sur-Coudenberg, was originally designed to look like a Greek
temple. After the French Revolution reached Belgium, it briefly served
as a "Temple of Reason." The Art Nouveau building on the northwest
corner is the former Old England department store, now home of the
Musée des Instruments de Musique.

WORTH NOTING

⑤ **Cathédrale St-Michel et Ste-Gudule.** The twin Gothic towers and outstanding stained-glass windows of the city's cathedral look down over the
city. One namesake, Saint Michael, is recognized as the patron saint

of Brussels, but mention Saint Gudule and most people will draw a blank. Very little is known about this daughter of a 7th-century Carolingian nobleman, but her relics have been preserved here for the past 1,000 years. Construction of the cathedral began in 1226 and continued through the 15th century; chapels were added in the 16th and 17th centuries. The remains of an 11th-century Romanesque church that was on the site can be glimpsed through glass apertures set into the floor. These, as well as the crypt and treasure rooms, can be visited for a nominal fee. Among the windows in the cathedral designed by various artists, those by Bernard van Orley, a 16th-century court painter, are the most spectacular. The window of *The Last Judgment*, at the bottom of the nave, is illuminated from within in the evening. All royal weddings and christenings take place here. ⊠ *Parvis Ste-Gudule, Upper Town* ☎ *02/217–8345* ⊕ *www.cathedralestmichel.be* ⊠ *free* ⊗ *May–Sept., weekdays daily 7–6, weekends 8:30–6; Oct.–Apr., weekdays 8:30–7, weekends 8:30–6.*

⑬ Coudenberg. Under the Place Royale lie the remains of the massive *Palais* de Charles V, first constructed in the 11th century, and upgraded over hundreds of years in line with the power and prestige of Brussels's successive rulers. Destroyed by a great fire in 1731, the palace was never reconstructed. Parts of the palace, and one or two of the streets that surrounded it, have been excavated and the underground site is a fascinating glimpse into Brussels's past. You can see the remains of palace rooms and walk up the steep cobbled rue Isabelle, once the busiest street in the city. Access is through the Musée BELvue, which focuses on Belgium history and its royal family. ⊠ *pl. Palais 7, Upper Town* ☎ *070/220–492* ⊕ *www.coudenberg.com* ⊠ *€5, combined with the Musée BELvue €8* ⊗ *Weekdays 10–5; Weekends 10–6.*

⑭ Musée d'Art Ancien. In the first of three interconnected art museums, the Ancient Art Museum pays special attention to the so-called Flemish Primitives of the 15th century, who revolutionized the art of painting with oil. The Spanish and the Austrians pilfered some of the finest works, but there's plenty left by the likes of Memling, Petrus Christus, Rogier van der Weyden, and Hieronymus Bosch. The collection of works by Pieter Bruegel the Elder is outstanding; it includes *The Fall of Icarus*, in which the figure of the mythological hero disappearing in the sea is but one detail of a scene in which people continue to go about their business. Bruegel the Younger's wonderful *Fight between Carnival and Lent* is also here. There are English-language brochures and guided tours available, as well as an excellent brasserie. ⊠ *rue de la Régence 3, Upper Town* ☎ *02/508–3211* ⊕ *www.fine-arts-museum.be* ⊠ *€8, combo ticket for three museums €13* ⊗ *Tues.–Sun. 10–5.*

⑨ Musée d'Art Moderne. Rather like New York's Guggenheim Museum in reverse, the Modern Art Museum burrows underground, circling downward eight floors. You reach it by an underground passage from the Musée d'Art Ancien. The collection is strong on Belgian and French art of the past 100 years, including such Belgian artists as the Expressionist James Ensor and the Surrealists Paul Delvaux and René Magritte, as well as Pierre Alechinsky and sculptor Pol Bury. Highlights include Delvaux's *Pygmalion* and Ensor's *Skeletons Fighting for a Smoked*

9

Take a leisurely stroll though Brussels Park near the Place Royal.

Herring. Notable works by non-Belgian artists include Francis Bacon's *The Pope with Owls.* There are English-language explanatory brochures and guided tours available. ✉ *rue de la Régence 3, Upper Town* ☎ *02/508–3211* ⊕ *www.fine-arts-museum.be* 💶 *€8, combo ticket for three museums €13* ⊗ *Tues.–Sun. 10–5.*

> **DID YOU KNOW?**
>
> The amazingly prolific Adolphe Sax is honored at the Musée des Instruments de Musique. The Belgian inventor was best known for the saxophone but dreamed up dozens of wind instruments. Ever hear of the saxhorn or the saxtromba?

EXPLORING CINQUANTENAIRE AND SCHUMAN

Often known as the European Union (EU) quarter, this area combines the behemoth buildings of the government institutions, the lovely Parc du Cinquantenaire, and many of the city's best museums and sights. The area lies to the east of the city center. To get here, take Metro Line 1A or 1B to Schuman or Merode. If you are driving, simply follow the signs pointing toward the "European institutions."

The **European Union project** brought jobs and investments to the city, but in the process entire neighborhoods were razed to make room for unbendingly modern, steel-and-glass buildings, and as more countries join the EU, more massive complexes are being built. What remains of the old blocks has seen an influx of ethnic restaurants catering to the tastes of lower-level Eurocrats; the grandees eat in splendid isolation in their own dining rooms. The landmark, star-shape **Berlaymont** (✉ *rue* *de la Loi 200*) is the home of the European Commission, the executive arm of the EU. The **European Council of Ministers** (✉ *rue de la Loi 175*) groups representatives of the EU national governments and occupies the pink-marble Justus Lipsius building. The **European Parliament building** (✉ *rue Wiertz 43*), known for its rounded glass summit, looms behind the Gare du Quartier Leopold. ✉ *Place Schuman and Place du Luxembourg, Etterbeek.*

⑰ Koninklijk Museum voor Midden Afrika/Musée Royal de l'Afrique Centrale. Stellar holdings, contemporary concerns, and a history of the jaundiced colonial mind-set make for a fascinating mix at the Royal Museum of Central Africa. Part of King Leopold II's legacy to Belgium, it holds an incredible collection of 250,000 objects, including masks, sculpture, paintings, and zoological specimens. There's also a wealth of memorabilia from the central African explorations commissioned by Leopold, most notably by Henry Morton Stanley (of "Doctor Livingston, I presume?" fame), whose archive is kept here. Some sections of the museum, such as the entrance hall, are virtually time capsules from the early 20th century, while others have been updated. The attached research center has a "Living Science" exhibition open to the public, focusing on its studies of African flora and fauna. While many parts of the museum's collection are invaluable from a scholarly point of view, they came at an incalculable cost, rooted in Leopold's brutal colonial rule. The museum has been undergoing a period of soul-searching, and is in the process of updating its exhibitions to more accurately reflect the horrific nature of Belgium's time in the Congo. Renovations began in 2010, the museum's 100th anniversary, and are due to last several years, which means some sections may be closed off. There's descriptive information available in English throughout. Save some time for a walk through the museum's beautifully landscaped park. To get here from place Montgomery, take tram 44 to Tervuren. ✉ *Leuvensesteenweg 13, Tervuren* ☎ *02/769–5211* ⊕ *www.africamuseum.be* 🎫 *€4* ⊙ *Tues.–Fri. 10–5, weekends 10–6.*

QUICK BITES The Maison Antoine (✉ *pl. Jourdan, Etterbeek*) frites stand sells the best fries in the capital, accompanied by a dizzying range of sauces. This is a great place to try Belgium's famous snack (the country's secret is frying the potatoes twice in beef tallow) and most of the bars that line the square will let you sit down and order a beer to go with your paper cone of frites. Closed Sundays.

⑱ Musée des Sciences Naturelles. The highlights of the Natural Sciences Museum are the skeletons of 14 iguanodons found in 1878 in the coal mines of Bernissart—these are believed to be about 120 million years old. It has a fine collection of 50,000 stones and 30,000 minerals, and there are also displays on mammals, insects, and tropical shells, as well as a whale gallery. ✉ *rue Vautier 29, Etterbeek* ☎ *02/627–4238* ⊕ *www. sciencesnaturelles.be* 🎫 *€7, free 1st Wed. of every month 1–5* ⊙ *Tues.– Fri. 9:30–4:45, weekends 10–6.*

⑲ Musées Royaux d'Art et de l'Histoire. For a chronologically and culturally ★ wide-ranging collection of artworks, hit the sprawling Royal Museums of Art and History in the lovely Parc du Cinquantenaire, which is worth a visit in itself. The vast numbers of antiquities and ethnographic treasures come from all over the world; the Egyptian and Byzantine sections are particularly fine. Don't miss the colossal Easter Island statue. There's also a strong focus on home turf, with significant displays on Belgian archaeology and the immense and intricate tapestries for which Brussels once was famous. There's some information in English, and guided tours are available. Take a break from the dizzying collection of exhibits in the pleasant café. ⊠ *Parc du Cinquantenaire 10, Etterbeek* ☎ *02/741–7211* ⊕ *www.kmkg-mrah.be* 🖾*€5, free 1st Wed. of every month 1–5* ☉ *Tues.–Fri. 9:30–5, weekends 10–5.*

EXPLORING IXELLES

Lying just south of the city center, Ixelles includes the city's most upmarket shopping district and the vibrant beat of Brussels's African quarter, the Matonge. A favored haunt of artists and writers, it's now home to the bourgeois and bohemian alike. Its Art Nouveau homes give the area a lot of the charm that the city center has lost through overdevelopment. To get here, take Metro Line 2 to Porte de Namur or Louise. If you're driving, take the Louise exit from the Ring Road.

㉚ **Musée d'Architecture.** If Ixelles's Art Nouveau houses have made you ○ hungry for information about Brussels's architectural past, present, and future, head to the Architecture Museum. Set in a former Masonic Lodge, the knowledgeable staff and displays of documents, drawings, and photographs provide a wealth of information. The museum mounts particularly good temporary exhibitions from time to time, such as one examining the depiction of animals in architecture. ⊠ *rue de l'Ermitage 86, Ixelles* ☎ *02/649–8665* ⊕ *www.aam.be* 🖾*€4* ☉ *Tues.–Sat. 10–6.*

㉛ **Musée des Enfants.** At this museum for two- to 12-year-olds, the purpose ○ may be educational—learning to handle objects and emotions—but the results are fun. Kids get to plunge their arms into sticky goo, dress up in eccentric costumes, walk through a hall of mirrors, crawl through tunnels, and take photographs with an oversize camera. English-language guide booklets are available. To reach the museum by public transit, take tram 93 or 94 to the Buyl stop. ⊠ *rue du Bourgmestre 15, Ixelles* ☎ *02/640–0107* ⊕ *www.museedesenfants.be* 🖾*€6.85* ☉ *Sept.–July, Wed. and weekends 2:30–5.*

QUICK BITES   **Café Belga** (⊠ *pl. Eugène Flagey 18, Ixelles* ☎ *02/640–3508*), in an ocean-liner-like Art Deco building, is a favorite among Brussels's beautiful people. Sip a cocktail or mint tea at the zinc bar or sit outside and gaze at the swans on the Ixelles ponds.

㉜ **Musée Horta.** The house where Victor Horta (1861–1947), the creator **Fodor's Choice** of Art Nouveau, lived and worked until 1919 is the best place to see his ★ mesmerizing interiors and furniture. Horta's genius lay in his ability to create a sense of opulence, light, and spaciousness where little light or space existed. Inspired by the direction of the turn-of-the-20th-century British Arts and Crafts movement, he amplified such designs into an entire architectural scheme. He shaped iron and steel into fluid, organic curves; structural elements were revealed. The facade of his home and studio, built between 1898 and 1901 (with extensions a few years later), looks somewhat narrow, but once you reach the interior stairway you'll be struck by the impression of airiness. A glazed skylight filters light down the curling banisters, lamps hang like tendrils from the ceilings, and mirrored skylights evoke giant butterflies with multicolor wings of glass and steel. Like Frank Lloyd Wright after him, Horta had a hand in every aspect of his design, from the door hinges to the wall treatments. You can reach the house by tram 91 or 92, getting off at the Ma Campagne stop. Note that you're not allowed to take photos. There's very little information in English, but you can buy books, postcards, and posters in the well-equipped shop. For more examples of how Horta and his colleagues transformed the face of Brussels in little more than 10 years, ride down avenue Louise to Vleurgat and walk along rue Vilain XIIII to the area surrounding the ponds of Ixelles. ⊠ *rue Américaine 25, Ixelles* ☎ *02/543–0490* ⊕ *www.hortamuseum.be* 🖃 €7 ⊗ *Tues.–Sun. 2–5:30.*

WHERE TO EAT

Use the coordinate (⊹ E3) at the end of each listing to locate a site on the Where to Eat and Stay in Brussels map.

LOWER TOWN

$$–$$$$
BELGIAN
✕ **Aux Armes de Bruxelles**. A reliable choice among the many tourist traps of the Ilôt Sacré, this kid-friendly restaurant attracts a largely local clientele with its slightly tarnished middle-class elegance and Belgian classics: turbot *waterzooi* (stew), a variety of steaks, and mussels prepared every conceivable way. The place is cheerful and light, and service is friendly if frequently overstretched. ⊠ *rue des Bouchers 13, Lower Town* ☎ *02/511–5550* ⊕ *www.auxarmesdebruxelles.be* 🖃 *AE, DC, MC, V* ⊹ *E3.*

$–$$$
BELGIAN
✕ **Chez Léon**. More than a century old, this cheerful restaurant has expanded over the years into a row of eight old houses, while its franchises can now be found across Belgium and even in France. It's a reliable choice on the restaurant-lined rue des Bouchers—just don't expect to see any locals eating here. Heaped plates of mussels and other Belgian specialties, such as *anguilles en vert* (eels in an herb sauce) and fish soup, are continually served. ⊠ *rue des Bouchers 18, Lower Town* ☎ *02/511–1415* ⊕ *www.chezleon.be* 🖃 *AE, DC, MC, V* ⊹ *E3.*

$$$$
FRENCH
Fodor's Choice
★
✕ **Comme Chez Soi**. Pierre Wynants, the perfectionist owner-chef of what many consider the best restaurant in the country, has decorated his bistro-size restaurant in Art Nouveau style. The superb cuisine, excellent wines, and attentive service complement the warm décor. Wynants is ceaselessly inventive, and earlier creations are quickly relegated to the back page of the menu. One all-time favorite, fillet of sole with a white wine mousseline and shrimp, is, however, always available. Book weeks in advance to be sure of a table. ⊠ *pl. Rouppe 23, Lower Town* ☎ *02/512–2921* ⊕ *www.commechezsoi.be* 🖎 *Reservations essential* 🎩 *Jacket and tie* 🖃 *AE, DC, MC, V* ⊗ *Closed Sun., Mon., mid-July–mid-Aug, and Dec. 25–Jan. 10. No lunch Wed.* ⊹ *C4.*

9

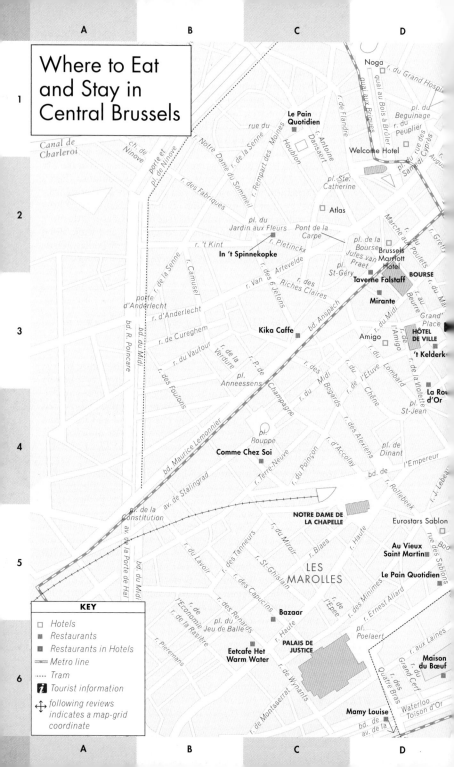

Where to Eat and Stay in Central Brussels

KEY

- ☐ Hotels
- ■ Restaurants
- ■ Restaurants in Hotels
- ▦▦ Metro line
- ···· Tram
- 🛈 Tourist information
- ↔ following reviews indicates a map-grid coordinate

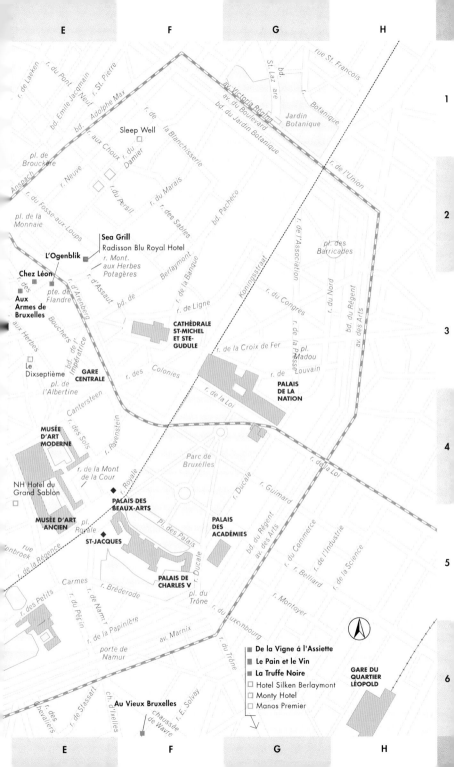

$$–$$$
BELGIAN
Fodor'sChoice
★

✕ **In 't Spinnekopke.** True Brussels cooking flourishes in this charming restaurant. The low ceilings and benches around the walls remain from its days as a coach inn during the 18th century. Choose from among 100 artisanal beers, then tuck into dishes made with the tipple, such as *lapin à gueuze* (rabbit stewed in fruit beer). Go with an appetite, as portions are huge. The knowledgeable waiters will recommend the best beers to go with your food. ✉ *pl. du Jardin aux Fleurs 1, Lower Town* ☎ *02/511–8695* ⊕ *www.spinnekopke.be* ⊟ *AE, DC, MC, V* ⊗ *Closed Sun. No lunch Sat.* ✛ *C2.*

$–$$
CONTEMPORARY

✕ **Kika Caffe.** This retro-style eatery is a great place for supper. It's a symphony in brown, with wallpaper copied from a Pedro Almodóvar film and formica-topped tables. The food is Mediterranean fusion, served in hearty portions. ✉ *blvd. Anspach 177, Lower Town* ☎ *02/513–3832* ⊟ *No credit cards.* ⊗ *Closed Sun. No lunch* ✛ *C3.*

$$–$$$
BELGIAN
Fodor'sChoice
★

✕ **La Roue d'Or.** Bright orange-and-yellow murals pay humorous homage to Surrealist René Magritte in this excellent Art Nouveau brasserie. Bowler-hatted gentlemen ascend serenely to the ceiling, a blue sky inhabited by tropical birds. The good cuisine includes traditional Belgian fare—a generous fish waterzooi and homemade frites—as well as such staples of the French brasserie repertory as lamb's tongue vinaigrette with shallots, veal kidneys with tarragon and watercress cream, and foie gras. Menus in English are on hand. ✉ *rue des Chapeliers 26, Lower Town* ☎ *02/514–2554* ⊟ *AE, DC, MC, V* ⊗ *Closed mid-July–mid-Aug.* ✛ *D3.*

¢–$
BELGIAN

✕ **Le Pain Quotidien.** These bakeries are a popular brunch spot on weekend mornings. They have spread like wildfire all over Europe (and even to New York and Los Angeles) with the same satisfying formula: hearty homemade soups, open-face sandwiches on farm-style bread, and bowls of café au lait, served at a communal table from 7:30 AM to 7 PM. ✉ *rue Antoine Dansaert 16, Lower Town* ☎ *02/502–2361* ✉ *rue des Sablons 11, Upper Town* ☎ *02/513–5154* ⊕ *www.lepainquotidien.be* ⌓ *Reservations not accepted* ⊟ *No credit cards* ✛ *C1, D5.*

$$$–$$$$
FRENCH
★

✕ **L'Ogenblik.** This split-level restaurant, on a side alley off the Galeries St-Hubert, has all the trappings of an old-time bistro: green-shaded lamps over marble-top tables, sawdust on the floor, and laid-back waiters. There's nothing casual about the French-style cuisine, however: wild duck with apples and pepper, mille-feuille of lobster and salmon with a coulis of langoustines, and saddle of lamb with spring vegetables and potato gratin. The selection of Beaujolais is particularly good. ✉ *Galerie des Princes 1, Lower Town* ☎ *02/511–6151* ⊕ *www.ogenblik.be* ⊟ *AE, DC, MC, V* ⊗ *Closed Sun.* ✛ *E3.*

¢–$$
ITALIAN

✕ **Mirante.** Don't be put off by the kitsch décor; this busy and popular Italian restaurant serves the best pizzas in town, alongside specialties from Puglia. Try the Fiorentina, a spinach pizza with a raw egg yolk in its center. ✉ *Plattesteen 13, Lower Town* ☎ *02/511–1580* ⊟ *AE, DC, MC, V* ✛ *D3.*

$$$–$$$$
SEAFOOD

✕ **Sea Grill.** Dashing superstar chef Yves Mattagne presides over the kitchen of arguably the best seafood place in town. Gastronomes rub shoulders here with tycoons and aristocrats, as they tuck into king crab from the Barents Sea, Dublin Bay prawns, Brittany lobster pressed

The only thing missing in this picture is the mayonnaise.

table-side, and line-caught sea bass crusted with sea salt. Inevitably, because of its hotel location, the restaurant feels rather corporate, but it's spacious and elegant, and service is impeccable. ✉ *Radisson Blu Royal Hotel, 47 rue du Fossé-aux-Loups, Lower Town* ☎ *02/217–9225* ⊕ *www.seagrill.be* ▭ *AE, DC, MC, V* ☯ *Closed weekends* ✛ *E3.*

¢–$$ ✕ **Taverne Falstaff.** Students, pensioners, and everyone in-between flock
BELGIAN to this century-old huge tavern with an Art Nouveau terrace and leg-
★ endarily grumpy waiters. While the menu devotes itself to straightfor-
ward Belgian cuisine throughout the day and into the night, Cuban
music and cocktails take over after 11 PM. (The kitchen is open until
5 AM on weekends.) The same group owns the next-door Montecristo
Café, which is another loud, popular, late-night spot with Latin flavor.
✉ *rue Henri Maus 19, Lower Town* ☎ *02/511–8789* ⊕ *www.lefalstaff.
be* ▭ *AE, DC, MC, V* ✛ *D2.*

$–$$$ ✕ **'t Kelderke.** Head down into this 17th-century vaulted cellar restau-
BELGIAN rant (watch out for the low door frame) for traditional Belgian cuisine
served at plain wooden tables. Mussels are the house specialty, but the
stoemp et saucisses (mashed potatoes and sausages) are equally tasty. It's
a popular place with locals, as it's open from noon to 2 AM. There are no
reservations, so turn up early to be sure to snag a table. ✉ *Grand'Place
15, Lower Town* ☎ *02/513–7344* ▭ *AE, DC, MC, V* ✛ *D3.*

UPPER TOWN

$$–$$$ ✕ **Au Vieux Saint Martin.** Even when neighboring restaurants on Grand
BELGIAN Sablon are empty, this one is full. A rack of glossy magazines is a
★ thoughtful touch for lone diners, and you're equally welcome whether
you order a cup of coffee or a full meal. The short menu emphasizes

Brussels specialties, and portions are substantial. The owner, a wine importer, serves unusually good wine for the price, by the glass or bottle. ✉ *Grand Sablon 38, Upper Town* ☎ *02/512–6476* ✍ *Reservations not accepted* ▭ *MC, V* ⊘ *Closed Mon.* ✛ *D5.*

$–$$
ECLECTIC
✕ **Bazaar.** The building along a side street in the Marolles may once have been a convent, but it now exudes a seductive allure. Candles burn in its cavernous dining room, where Moroccan lamps and sofas create intimacy in a bric-a-brac setting. It's young and fashionable; there's a disco on the lower floor on weekends. The eclectic menu includes such choices as couscous with spicy *merguez* sausages. Later in the evening, it becomes a lively bar. ✉ *rue des Capucins 63, Upper Town* ☎ *02/511–2600* ⊕ *www.bazaarresto.be* ▭ *AE, DC, MC, V* ⊘ *Closed Sun. and Mon. No lunch* ✛ *C5.*

¢–$
BELGIAN
✕ **Eetcafe Het Warm Water.** Just above the place de Jeu de Balle in the heart of the Marolles, this café is a local institution known for its set brunches. These are rib-sticking meals, with muesli, yogurt, eggs, croissants, and some combination of cheese and ham. It's a staunchly Flemish place; the staff doesn't appreciate orders in French (English is preferable). When the neighborhood had no running water, this is where residents would come to get hot water—hence the name. Before wandering down the street to the *Vieux Marché* (flea market), get a snack of tasty bread and cheese or an omelet here, washed down with a bowl of *lait russe* (milky coffee). ✉ *rue des Renards 25, Upper Town* ☎ *02/213–9159* ✍ *Reservations not accepted* ▭ *No credit cards* ✛ *C6.*

$$$$
FRENCH
★
✕ **Maison du Boeuf.** Red-meat lovers are drawn to chef Michel Thueurel's exceptional beef rib steak roasted in salt, the house specialty. There are other tempting traditional French and Belgian choices, too, mostly beef but with a couple of other choices (coq au vin, for example) as well. Upscale in every way, with gliding waiters, heavy silver cutlery, and linen tablecloths, the eatery is a favorite of politicians and high society. ✉ *Hilton Hotel, blvd. de Waterloo 38, Upper Town* ☎ *02/504–1111* ✍ *Reservations essential* 🎩 *Jacket and tie* ▭ *AE, DC, MC, V* ⊘ *Closed Sun. No lunch Sat.* ✛ *D6.*

IN AND AROUND IXELLES

$–$$
FRENCH
★
✕ **Au Vieux Bruxelles.** Open since 1882, this Brussels institution is a fun lively place to have dinner and a firm local favorite. The cuisine is decidedly Belgian, with *anguilles au vert* (eels in a green sauce) and hearty carbonnades on the menu, and best accompanied by a good beer. Naturally, everything is served with frites, and be sure to ask for the tasty homemade mayonnaise. If you're feeling too full to tackle a whole dessert, you can order a half portion. ✉ *rue St-Boniface 35, Ixelles* ☎ *02/503–3111* ▭ *AE, DC, MC, V* ⊘ *Closed Mon. No lunch except Sun.* ✛ *F6.*

$$–$$$
FRENCH
★
✕ **De la Vigne à l'Assiette.** When you take into account the high quality of the food and the wine list of this no-frills bistro off avenue Louise, the combination proves to be an exceptionally good value. The modern French cuisine of chef Eddy Dandrimont is embellished with such exotic flourishes as star anise sauce, and crisp angel-hair pasta atop grilled salmon. The excellent wine list refrains from the usual hefty markup.

⊠ *rue de la Longue Haie, Ixelles* ☎ *02/647–6803* ⊟ *AE, DC, MC, V* ⊙ *Closed Sun. and Mon. No lunch Sat.* ⊹ *G6.*

$$$$
ITALIAN
✕ **La Truffe Noire.** Luigi Ciciriello's "Black Truffle" attracts a sophisticated clientele with its modern design, well-spaced tables, and cuisine that draws on classic Italian and modern French cooking. Carpaccio is prepared at the table and served with long strips of truffle and Parmesan. Entrées may include Vendé pigeon with truffles and steamed John Dory with truffles and leeks. In summer you can eat in the garden. ⊠ *blvd. de la Cambre 12, Ixelles* ☎ *02/640–4422* ⊕ *www.truffenoire. com* ⚑ *Reservations essential* 🎩 *Jacket and tie* ⊟ *AE, DC, MC, V* ⊙ *Closed Sun. No lunch Sat.* ⊹ *G6.*

$$$
FRENCH
★
✕ **Le Pain et le Vin.** The plainspoken name, "Bread and Wine," signals an equally pared-down aesthetic in this excellent restaurant. It's co-owned by acclaimed sommelier Eric Boschman; hence, the cellar is impressively deep, and wines can be ordered by the glass to accompany different courses. The food takes the minimalist route with choices such as risotto with asparagus and tuna steak. The large garden is a plus in fine weather. ⊠ *Chaussée d'Alsemberg 812A, Uccle* ☎ *02/332–3774* ⊟ *AE, MC, V* ⊙ *Closed Sun. and Mon. No lunch Sat.* ⊹ *G6.*

$–$$$
FRENCH
✕ **Mamy Louise.** This is one of several good quality lunch spots on the pedestrianized rue Jean Stas, just off avenue Louise. With Hamptons-style décor and outdoor tables in warm weather, the varied menu includes Belgian staples like *boudin* (blood sausage), as well as quiches and salads. It's also a great place to grab a morning or afternoon coffee and a slice of delicious cake. ⊠ *rue Jean Stas 12, Ixelles* ☎ *02/534–2502* ⊟ *AE, MC, V.* ⊙ *Closed Sun.* ⊹ *D6.*

WHERE TO STAY

Use the coordinate (⊹ E3) at the end of each listing to locate a site on the Where to Eat and Stay in Brussels map.

9

LOWER TOWN

$$$$
🛏 **Amigo.** A block from the Grand'Place, the Amigo pairs contemporary design with antiques and plush wall hangings. Rooms are decorated in green, red, or blue, with silk curtains, leather headboards, and a mix of modern furniture and antiques. Works by Belgian artists hang on the walls, while Tintin pictures and figurines cheer up the mosaic-tiled bathrooms. If you'd like a view over the surrounding rooftops, ask for a room on one of the higher floors (these also have a higher rate). The Presidential Suite is the sort of place real presidents stay in, but mere mortals will have to hand over a four-figure sum (and more) per night for the pleasure. **Pros:** understated luxury; polished service; central location. **Cons:** some bathrooms are small; nearby streets can be noisy. ⊠ *rue d'Amigo 1–3, Lower Town* ☎ *02/547–4747* ⊕ *www. roccofortehotels.com* ⟿ *174 rooms, 19 suites* ⌂ *In-room: safe, refrigerator, Internet. In-hotel: restaurant, room service, bar, gym, Wi-Fi, parking (paid)* ⊟ *AE, DC, MC, V* ⊹ *D3.*

$–$$$
🛏 **Atlas.** This hotel offers unpretentious comfort and a convenient location in a building dating from the 18th century. The small rooms have cream-and-yellow walls, gray carpets, and blue-and-white furniture.

Suites, on two floors, each have a kitchenette in the lounge area. Buffet breakfasts are served in the blue-and-white basement with abstract art and the exposed brick of an ancient city wall. **Pros:** good value; convenient location. **Cons:** no-frills rooms; standard décor. ⊠ *rue du Vieux Marché aux Grains 30, Lower Town* ☎ *02/502–6006* ⊕ *www.atlas-hotel.be* ↩ *83 rooms, 5 suites* ⚐ *In-room: refrigerator, Wi-Fi. In-hotel: parking (paid)* ⊟ *AE, DC, MC, V* ⍾ *BP* ✦ *C2.*

$$$$ 🖫 **Brussels Marriott Hotel.** This branch of the Marriott chain opposite the stock exchange has a striking cream-marble lobby, and each floor has a different theme for its guest rooms. Guest rooms are done in universal corporate-travel style: cherrywood furniture, green- or yellow-striped wallpaper, and marble bathrooms. Quieter ones face an internal courtyard; those on upper floors have city views. Nearly half of the rooms are especially geared toward business travelers, with ergonomic desk chairs and no-glare lamps. **Pros:** easy access to the city center; soundproofed rooms. **Cons:** bland décor; slightly chilly staff. ⊠ *rue A. Orts 1–7, Lower Town* ☎ *02/516–9090* ⊕ *www.marriott.com* ↩ *202 rooms, 16 suites* ⚐ *In-room: safe, refrigerator, Internet. In-hotel: restaurant, bar, gym, Wi-Fi, parking (paid)* ⊟ *AE, DC, MC, V* ⍾ *BP* ✦ *D2.*

$–$$$ 🖫 **Eurostars Sablon.** On a quiet street between the Sablon and the Grand'Place, this hotel offers spacious and attractive rooms, some with canopy beds. Suites arranged in duplex style favor comfort over corporate entertainment, with a spiral staircase leading up to a tiny landing, and a modern classic-style bedroom in cherrywood and cream. **Pros:** near two of the city's prettiest squares; service with a smile. **Cons:** some rooms are a bit dark. ⊠ *rue de la Paille 2–8, Lower Town* ☎ *02/513–6040* ⊕ *www.eurostarshotels.com* ↩ *28 rooms, 4 suites* ⚐ *In-room: safe, refrigerator, Wi-Fi. In-hotel: bar, gym, parking (paid)* ⊟ *AE, DC, MC, V* ⍾ *CP* ✦ *D5.*

$$$ 🖫 **Le Dixseptième.** Here you can stay in what was once the residence of
Fodor's Choice the Spanish ambassador. The stylishly restored 17th-century building
★ lies between the Grand'Place and the Gare Centrale. Rooms surround a lovely interior courtyard, and suites are up a splendid Louis XVI staircase. Named after Belgian artists, rooms have whitewashed walls, plain floorboards, exposed beams, and suede sofas. Suites have decorative fireplaces and the honeymoon suite is particularly romantic. Some rooms have wooden beamed ceilings, and/or terraces with views across to the Grand'Place. **Pros:** romantic setting; gorgeous rooms. **Cons:** no on-site parking. ⊠ *rue de la Madeleine 25, Lower Town* ☎ *02/517–1717* ⊕ *www.ledixseptieme.be* ↩ *22 rooms, 2 suites* ⚐ *In-room: safe, kitchen (some), refrigerator, Wi-Fi. In-hotel: bar, Wi-Fi* ⊟ *AE, DC, MC, V* ✦ *E3.*

$ 🖫 **Noga.** The hotel's Web site promises a "cosy, cosy, very cosy" spot, and indeed it is. Opened in 1958, the well-maintained Noga is packed with mementos of the Jazz Age, from table lamps to black-and-white photographs of the period. There are rooms on four floors for two, three, or four people—larger rooms have sofas great for socializing. You can rent a bike, borrow a book from the library, or even order a picnic lunch to take sightseeing with you. The hotel is in the popular Béguinage quarter, near the Ste-Catherine fish market. **Pros:** trendy spot; great service; superfriendly staff. **Cons:** bathrooms lack tubs; hotel fills up quickly. ⌂ *rue du Béguinage 38, Lower Town* ☏ *02/218–6763* ⊕ *www. nogahotel.com* ⤲ *19 rooms* ⟨In-room: safe, refrigerator, Wi-Fi. In-hotel: bar, bicycles, parking (paid)* ═ *AE, DC, MC, V* ✲◐ *BP* ✛ *D1.*

¢ 🖳 **Sleep Well.** This youth hostel is bright, well run, and conveniently located for transportation links. The basic rooms sleep from one to eight people with shared bathrooms, and you have to pay extra for sheets. The more upscale rooms in the Star section have private bathrooms, and pretty striped bedspreads (sheets are included in the price). There's a comic-strip mural in the lobby, a TV room, Internet center, and lively bar with karaoke. **Pros:** clean rooms; great security; a great place to meet fellow travelers. **Cons:** extra cost for Internet access; can be noisy at night; some rooms have shared bathrooms. ⌂ *rue du Damier 23, Lower Town* ☏ *02/218–5050* ⊕ *www.sleepwell.be* ⤲ *82 rooms* ⟨In-room: no a/c, no phone, no TV. In-hotel: restaurant, bar, bicycles, Internet terminal* ═ *MC, V* ✲◐ *CP* ✛ *F1.*

$$ 🖳 **Welcome Hotel.** Among the many charms of the smallest hotel in Brussels are the incredibly friendly young owners, Michel and Sophie Smeesters. The rooms, divided into economy, business, and first class, are as comfortable as those in far more expensive establishments. Each is strikingly decorated to evoke a certain place; the Bali and China rooms are particularly lovely, with their masks and dragon motifs. The owners are constantly working on new upgrades and improvements, making this place more welcoming all the time. The Belgium room for families was opened in 2010, and deluxe rooms have whirlpool baths. Airport transfers are also offered. **Pros:** fantastic décor; lovely staff. **Cons:** rooms fill up quickly. ⌂ *rue du Peuplier 5, Lower Town* ☏ *02/219–9546* ⊕ *www.hotelwelcomehotel.com* ⤲ *14 rooms, 3 suites* ⟨In-room: safe, Wi-Fi. In-hotel: Wi-Fi, parking (paid)* ═ *AE, DC, MC, V* ✛ *D1.*

Fodor's Choice
★

UPPER TOWN

$–$$ 🖳 **NH Hotel du Grand Sablon.** Part of the Sablon square's lineup of antiques shops, cafés, and chocolate makers, this offers discreet luxury behind an elegant white facade. The reception area is set within a hushed row of private art galleries, and there's a pretty interior cobbled courtyard. Rooms are tastefully decorated in red or green. Some bathrooms have only showers, but the plush suites have whirlpool baths. Ask for a room at the back, as the square outside is often clogged with traffic and the weekend antiques market gets going at 6 AM. **Pros:** lovely older building; shady courtyard. **Cons:** front rooms can be noisy. ⌂ *rue Bodenbroeck 2–4, Upper Town* ☏ *02/518–1100* ⊕ *www.nh-hotels.be* ⤲ *193 rooms, 6 suites* ⟨In-room: refrigerator, Wi-Fi. In-hotel: restaurant, bar, Wi-Fi, parking (paid)* ═ *AE, DC, MC, V* ✲◐ *BP* ✛ *E4.*

$$–$$$$ 🖳 **Radisson Blu Royal Hotel.** Near the northern end of the Galeries St-Hubert shopping arcade, this hotel has an Art Deco facade and is decorated in a variety of styles, including "Maritime" rooms with blue-and-yellow walls and wood floors. The greenery-filled atrium incorporates a 10-foot-high section of the 12th-century city wall and serves excellent Scandinavian-style open sandwiches. **Pros:** great extras like self-filling minibars and trouser presses; near super shopping;

9

eye-popping décor. **Cons:** location is sketchy at night; staff can be scarce during the day. ☒ *rue du Fossé-aux-Loups 47, Upper Town* ☏ *02/219–2828* ⊕ *www. radissonblu.com* ⇱ *257 rooms, 24 suites* ☖ *In-room: safe, refrigerator, Wi-Fi. In-hotel: 2 restaurants, bar, gym, parking (paid)* ▭ *AE, DC, MC, V* ⦿| *BP* ✣ *E2.*

CINQUANTENAIRE AND SCHUMAN

$–$$$ ⚏ **Hotel Silken Berlaymont.** Contemporary photography inspires the Berlaymont's signature look. Each room is decorated with works of a different photographer, and the navy, black, and dark-wood furnishings are sober and smart. Attention to perspective and style are evident in the chrome, black marble, and spotlights around the hotel. Eight rooms have showers only. The green mosaic-tiled sauna, hammam, spa, and fitness center are inviting. There's a good café on-site. **Pros:** smartly turned-out hotel; pleasantly busy atmosphere; great perks for business travelers. **Cons:** often overrun with groups; not the place for a romantic getaway. ☒ *blvd. Charlemagne 11–19, Etterbeek* ☏ *02/231–0909* ⊟ *02/230–3371* ⊕ *www. hoteles-silken.com* ⇱ *214 rooms, 2 suites* ☖ *In-room: safe, refrigerator, Wi-Fi. In-hotel: restaurant, bar, gym, spa, parking (paid)* ▭ *AE, DC, MC, V* ✣ *G6.*

$–$$ ⚏ **Monty Hotel.** A stay here is like an overnight in a contemporary design
★ showroom—with breakfast in the morning. The first thing that will strike you is the full-size red fiberglass cow grazing on the decking in front as you approach. Inside, guest rooms have ingenious lighting, like winged lightbulbs by Ingo Maurer, Mario Bellini "Cuboglass" televisions, and gray-tiled bathrooms with Philippe Starck fittings. The comfortable lounge with its tomato-red walls is peppered with equally modern-classic furniture. Unlike some boutique hotels, the Monty doesn't tip over into chilly attitude; its warmth is demonstrated at breakfast, served at a friendly communal table. The hotel is out of town, but just a few steps from the Georges Henri underground tram stop, close to Montgomery. **Pros:** great design; delicious breakfasts; lively atmosphere. **Cons:** a little off the beaten track; few parking spaces. ☒ *blvd. Brand Whitlock 101, Laeken* ☏ *02/734–5636* ⊕ *www.monty-hotel.be* ⇱ *18 rooms* ☖ *In-room: no a/c, Wi-Fi. In-hotel: bar, parking (paid)* ▭ *AE, DC, MC, V* ⦿| *BP* ✣ *G6.*

SOUTH OF CENTER

$$$$ ⚏ **Manos Premier.** This upscale hotel has expansive terraces, a rose-filled garden populated by waterfowl and songbirds, and a good restaurant, Kolya. The well-appointed rooms have Louis XV and Louis XVI antiques and inviting bedspreads in green, cream, and pink. The sauna has a decadent Moroccan flavor with tiling and arched doorways. **Pros:** handsome hotel; lovely garden. **Cons:** doesn't quite live up to its high price; a few shabby carpets and corners. ✉ *Chaussée de Charleroi 100–106, St-Gilles* ☎ *02/537–9682* ⊕ *www.manospremier.com* ⤶ *55 rooms, 15 suites* ⑂ *In-room: safe, Internet. In-hotel: restaurant, bar, gym, spa, Wi-Fi* ▭ *AE, DC, MC, V* ⑂ *CP* ⑂ *G6.*

NIGHTLIFE AND THE ARTS

Although the presence of both French and Flemish drives a wedge or two through the capital's cultural landscape, it also delivers some advantages. Both Flemish- and French-language authorities inject funds into the arts scene; one notable combined effort is the annual Kunsten-FESTIVALdesArts (www.kfda.be), a contemporary arts festival held in May. A glance at the "What's On" section of weekly English-language newsmagazine the *Bulletin* reveals the breadth of the offerings in all categories of cultural life. Tickets for major events can be purchased by calling **FNAC Ticket Line** (☎ *0900/00600* ⊕ *www.fnac.be*).

THE ARTS

CLASSICAL MUSIC
The principal venue for classical music concerts is the Horta-designed **Palais des Beaux-Arts** (✉ *rue Ravenstein 23, Upper Town* ☎ *02/507–8200* ⊕ *www.bozar.be*). The complex, which also houses an art gallery and a theater, was the first multipurpose arts complex in Europe when it opened in 1928. Its Henry Le Boeuf concert hall has world-class acoustics.

NIGHTLIFE

There's a café on virtually every street corner, most serving all kinds of alcoholic drinks. Although the Belgian brewing industry is declining as the giant Inbev firm (the brewers of Stella Artois) muscles smaller companies out of the market, Belgians still consume copious quantities of beer, some of it with a 10% alcohol content and more. Most bars here have artisanal beers along with the major-brand usual suspects. The place St-Géry, rue St-Boniface, and the Grand'Place area draw the most buzz.

HIPSTER BARS
The stylish, Art Deco **Archiduc** (✉ *rue Antoine Dansaert 6, Lower Town* ☎ *02/512–0652*) attracts a thirtyish, fashionable crowd; it gets smoky up on the balcony. The sidewalk outside **Au Soleil** (✉ *rue du Marché-au-Charbon 86, Lower Town* ☎ *02/513–3430*) teems with the hip and would-be hip, enjoying relaxed trip-hop sounds and very competitive prices. Another favorite with the arty crowd is Flemish bar **Monk** (✉ *rue Ste-Catherine 42, Lower Town* ☎ *02/503–0880*), which used to be a schoolhouse.

JAZZ CLUBS
After World War II, Belgium was at the forefront of Europe's modern jazz movement: of the great postwar players, harmonica maestro Toots Thielemans and vibes player Sadi are still very much alive and perform in Brussels. Other top Belgian jazz draws include guitarist Philip Catherine, pianist Jef Neve, and the experimental ethno-jazz trio Aka Moon. **The Music Village** (✉ *rue des Pierres 50, Lower Town* ☎ *02/513–1345*) hosts a plethora of international jazz musicians. **Sounds** (✉ *rue de la Tulipe 28, Ixelles* ☎ *02/512–9250*) dishes up contemporary jazz along with good food.

9

One of the many shops in Brussels where you can get your high-end chocolate fix.

TRADITIONAL BARS Beer is one of Brussels's biggest tourist draws, and the city has a few traditional-style bars where you can sample everything from the sour delights of local Lambic to the six Trappist treasures, brewed by monks in Achel, Orval, Chimay, Rochefort, Westmalle, and Westvleteren and revered the world over. One of the best is **Bier Circus** (⊠ *rue de l'Enseignement 57, North city center* ☎ 02/218–0034), which has a huge list of brews on its menu, including some excellent organic beers. With its wooden décor and friendly staff, this is a great place to start learning about Belgian beer, and there's good food, too. The convivial **Chez Moeder Lambic** (⊠ *rue de Savoie 68, St-Gilles* ☎ 02/539–1419) claims to stock 300 Belgian beers and a quite a few foreign ones, as well as comic books to read while you sip.

GAY BARS

The city's small but lively gay quarter can be found around rue des Pierres, rue du Marché au Charbon, and rue St Géry in the Lower Town. Keep an eye out for rainbow flags in the windows. **Tels Quels** (⊠ *rue du Marché-aux-Charbon 81, Lower Town* ☎ 02/512–4587) is not only a bar, but also a resource for up-to-date information about the capital's gay scene and the publisher of a monthly magazine. **Chez Maman** (⊠ *rue des Grands Carmes 7, Lower Town* ☎ 02/502–8696), a disco with a fun drag show, is presided over by Maman herself.

SHOPPING

For generations, Brussels has been the place to indulge a taste for some of the finer things in life: chocolate, beer, lace, and lead crystal. Brussels is also heaven for comic-book collectors, and there are lots of offbeat shops to tempt magpies. While the city may not be bursting with bargains, there are inexpensive items to be found in the markets. Value-added tax (TVA) inflates prices, but visitors from outside the EU can obtain refunds. Sales take place in January and July.

SHOPPING DISTRICTS

The stylish, upper-crust shopping area for clothing and accessories spans the upper end of **avenue Louise; avenue de la Toison d'Or,** which branches off at a right angle; **boulevard de Waterloo,** on the other side of the street; **Galerie Louise,** which links the two avenues; and **Galerie de la Toison d'Or,** another gallery two blocks away. The **City 2** mall on place Rogier and the pedestrian mall, **rue Neuve,** are fun and inexpensive shopping areas (but not recommended for women alone after dark).

There are galleries scattered across Brussels, but low rents have made **boulevard Barthélemy** the "in" place for avant-garde art. On the **place du Grand Sablon** and adjoining streets and alleys you'll find antiques dealers and smart art galleries.

The **Galeries St-Hubert** is a rather stately shopping arcade lined with posh shops selling men's and women's clothing, books, and objets d'art. In the trendy **rue Antoine Dansaert** and **place du Nouveau Marché aux Grains,** near the Bourse, are a number of boutiques carrying fashions by young designers and interior design and art shops. Avenue Louise and its surrounding streets in Ixelles have a number of chic boutiques offering clothes new and vintage, jewelry, antiques, and housewares.

STREET MARKETS

Bruxellois with an eye for fresh farm produce and low prices do most of their food shopping at the animated open-air markets in almost every commune. Among the best are those in **Boitsfort** in front of the Maison Communal on Sunday morning; on **place du Châtelain,** Wednesday afternoon; and on **place Ste-Catherine,** all day, every day except Sunday. In addition to fruits, vegetables, meat, and fish, most markets include traders with specialized products, such as cheese or wild mushrooms. The most exotic market is the Sunday morning **Marché du Midi,** where the large North African community gathers to buy and sell foods, spices, and plants, transforming the area next to the railway station into a vast bazaar. You can also join the thousands of shoppers in the meat and produce market in **Anderlecht's,** housed in a 19th-century former abattoir every Friday, Saturday, and Sunday 7–2.

9

GENT

Gent's old town has been almost totally restored, and it now has the largest pedestrian area in Flanders. Take care as you walk along cobblestone streets—it can be tricky if you wear high-heeled shoes or open sandals. But the views and the sights are well worth the effort of maneuvering over difficult terrain—the Graslei is as pretty a street as any in Europe.

The gray-stone city center looks like a puzzle piece, surrounded as it is by the river Leie, its tributaries, and canals. Although many people live and work in this area, most reside nearby. One of the nicest neighborhoods to explore is the Gravensteen (also known as Patershol) area, once the residential quarter for the textile workers from the Gravensteen. Its layout is medieval but its spirit is modern—the streets are now crammed with chic cafés and restaurants. It's fast become the in place to live for well-off young couples. Gent has also carved a niche for itself as the unofficial capital of Belgian beer. Those in the know say that it has a better concentration of excellent beer bars than anywhere else in the country.

At this writing, however, there was one fly in the ointment for any upcoming trip to Gent: a large renovation project is underway and slated to continue through 2012. A large stretch, from Korenmarkt to Sint-Baafskathedraal, has become one big construction site. The cathedral, Belfort, and other sites in the affected area are still open, but the work may spoil some of your holiday pictures. Happily, both the Graslei and Gravensteen areas are unaffected. Another side effect of note is that public transport through the center has been severely disrupted. If getting around on foot is a problem, call a taxi.

While this is a bit of an inconvenience, keep in mind that once the work is complete, the center of Gent will look even more spectacular than it did before.

GETTING HERE AND AROUND

210 km (130 mi) south of Amsterdam.

To reach Gent by car, take the A4 motorway to Antwerp, and then follow the E17. The journey takes around two hours. By train, take a Thalys high-speed train to Brussels's Gare de Midi/Brussel Zuid station, then change to a Belgian Railways (SNCB/NMBS) train bound for Gent. There are two an

hour, and the trip from Brussels takes 35 minutes. Gent St-Pieters station is a little distance from the city center, so hop on a tram or take a taxi when you arrive. Tram 1 heads from the station to the center, but due to the construction work mentioned above it is currently terminating some 500 yards short of the action. If walking the final stretch is a problem for you, take a cab.

TOURS

To make the most of Gent's sights, get hold of a Gent Museum Card, which for €20 gives free entrance to the city's museums. Valid for 3 days, it is available from the tourist office and participating venues.

Another great way to see the city is from its rivers. Numerous companies run 30-minute trips, all costing €6 and leaving from landing stages clustered at the north end of Graslei and by the Groentenmarkt.

TIMING

You could cover the main sights of Gent in a half a day if pushed for time, but allow at least a day to unwind a bit and perhaps take a boat tour.

ESSENTIALS

Bicycle rentals Biker (✉ *Steendam 16* ☎ *09/224–2903*), open daily.

Emergency Services Ambulance (☎ *100*). **Duty doctors** (☎ *09/236–5000*). **Night pharmacies** (☎ *0900/10500*). **Police** (☎ *101*).

Taxis Taxi Gent (☎ *09/333–3333*).

Visitor Information Gent (✉ *Botermarkt 17A, under the Belfry* ☎ *09/266–5660* ⊕ *www.visitgent.be*).

EXPLORING

TOP ATTRACTIONS

❻ Belfort. Begun in 1314, the 300-foot belfry tower symbolizes the power of the guilds and used to serve as Gent's watchtower. Since 1377, the structure has been crowned with a gilded copper weather vane shaped into a dragon, the city's symbol of freedom. (The current stone spire was added in 1913.) Inside the Belfort, documents listing the privileges of the city (known as its *secreets*) were once kept behind triple-locked doors and guarded by lookouts who toured the battlements hourly to prove they weren't sleeping. When danger approached, bells were rung—until

The magnificent Graslei.

Charles V had them removed. Now a 53-bell carillon, claimed by experts to be one of the best in the world, is set on the top floor. One of the original bells, the Triumphanta, cast in 1660 and badly cracked in 1914, rests in a garden at the foot of the tower. The largest original bell, Klokke Roeland, is still sung about in Gent's anthem of the same name. The view from the tower is one of the city's highlights. Note that you need a guide to visit the carillon; guides are available afternoons between May and September. ⊠ *St-Baafsplein, Torenrij* ☎ *09/375–3161* 💶 *€5, guided tour €3* ⊙ *Mid-Mar.–mid-Nov., daily 10–6.*

③ **Graslei.** This magnificent row of guild houses in the original port area
Fodor's Choice is best seen from across the river Leie on the **Korenlei** (Corn Quay).
★ The guild house of the **Metselaars** (Masons) is a copy of a house from 1527; the original, which stands near the Sint-Niklaaskerk, has also been restored. The **Eerste Korenmetershuis** (the first Grain Measurers' House), representing the grain weigher's guild, is next. It stands next to the oldest house of the group, the brooding, Romanesque **Koorn-stapelhuis** (Granary), which was built in the 12th century and served its original purpose for 600 years; this was where the grain claimed by the tax collectors was stored. It stands side by side with the narrow Renaissance **Tolhuis** (Toll House), where taxes were levied on grain shipments. No. 11 is the **Tweede Korenmetershuis** (Grain Measurers' House), a late Baroque building from 1698. The **Vrije Schippers** (Free Bargemen), at No. 14, is a late Gothic building from 1531, when the guild dominated inland shipping. Almost opposite this, across the water at No. 7 Korenlei, is the **Huis der Onvrije Schippers** (Unfree Bargemen), built in 1740 and decorated with a gilded boat. The free bargemen had

Gent
(Ghent, Gand)

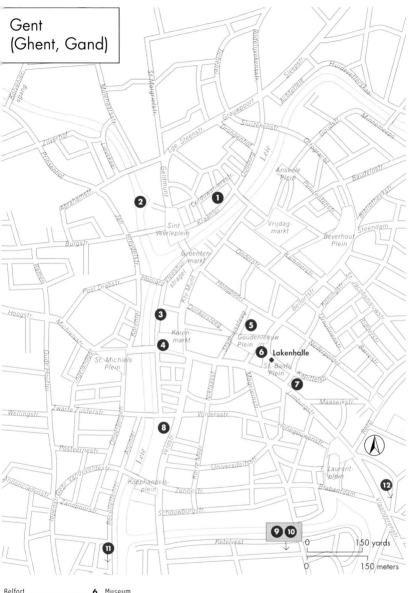

9

right of passage along the canals inside the city; the unfree had to unload their cargoes outside the city, and transfer them to the boats of the guild of free bargemen. Every night the Graslei and the other historic monuments are illuminated from sunset to midnight. ⊠ *Graslei, Gravensteen/Patershol.*

❷ **Gravensteen.** Surrounded by a moat, the Castle of the Counts of Flanders resembles an enormous battleship steaming down the sedate Lieve Canal. From its windswept battlements there's a splendid view over the rooftops of old Gent. There has been a fortress on this site for centuries. The Gravensteen, modeled after a Syrian crusader castle, was built in 1180 by the Count of Flanders on top of an existing fortress, and has been rebuilt several times since then—most recently in the 19th century to reflect what the Victorians thought a medieval castle should look like. Above the entrance is an opening in the shape of a cross, which symbolizes the count's participation in the Crusades, resulting in his death in the Holy Land.

Today's brooding castle has little in common with the original fortress, built by Baldwin of the Iron Arm to discourage marauding Norsemen. Its purpose, too, changed from protection to oppression as the conflict deepened between feudal lords and unruly townspeople. Rulers entertained and feasted here throughout the Middle Ages, and the Council of Flanders, the highest court in the land, met in chambers here for more than 500 years. At various times the castle has also been used as a mint, a prison, and a cotton mill. It was here, too, that the country's first spinning mule was installed after being spirited away from England; soon the castle's chambers echoed with the clattering of looms, and Gent became a textile center to rival Manchester. ⊠ *Sint-Veerleplein, Gravensteen/Patershol* ☎ 09/225–9306 ⊡ €8 ☉ *Apr.–Sept., daily 9–6; Oct.–Mar., daily 9–5.*

❼ **Sint-Baafskathedraal.** St. Bavo's Cathedral, begun in the austere 13th century but finished in the 16th century in the ornate Brabantine Gothic style, dramatically rises from a low, unimposing entryway. It contains one of the greatest treasures in Christendom: *De aanbidding van het Lam Gods* (The Adoration of the Mystic Lamb). Painted by brothers Jan and Hubert van Eyck, this altarpiece is one of the most beautiful and influential paintings of the Middle Ages. One of its lower panels was stolen in 1934 and was never recovered, giving rise to numerous conspiracy theories and inspiring Albert Camus' novel, *The Fall.* The cathedral's ornate pulpit, made of white Italian marble and black Danish oak, was carved in the 18th century by the sculptor Laurent Delvaux. Angels, cherubs, massive trees, flowing robes, and tresses combine to create a masterwork. A Rubens masterpiece, *Saint Bavo's*

Fodor's Choice
★

IF YOU ONLY HAVE 1 DAY

Arrive in Gent as early as possible and begin your tour with a classic view of the city's three towers from St. Michael's bridge. Divide the rest of your day between the guild houses of the Graslei district, the Gothic cathedral, and the Gravensteen, the ancient castle of the counts of Flanders. After a dinner in the lively Patershol area, take a walk around the illuminated historic district.

Entry into the Monastery, hangs in one of the chapels. Other treasures include a baroque-style organ built in 1623 and a crypt crammed with tapestries, church paraphernalia, and 15th- and 16th-century frescoes. There are no visits during services. ✉ *St-Baafsplein, Torenrij* 🎫 *Cathedral free, Mystic Lamb, €4* ☎ *09/269–2065* ⏱ *Cathedral: Apr.–Oct., Mon.–Sat. 8:30–6, Sun. 9:30–6; Nov.–Mar., daily 8:30–5. Chapel: Apr.–Oct., Mon.–Sat. 9:30–4:45, Sun. 1–4:30; Nov.–Mar., Mon.–Sat. 10:30–4, Sun. 1–4.*

> ### BOATING
>
> Boating is popular along the river and canals and a fantastic way to see the city and surrounding area. As an alternative to a boat tour, rent a self-sail motorboat from the **Minerva Boat Company** (☎ *03/233-7917* ⊕ *www. minervaboten.be*). Boats take four to five people and no special license is required. The embarkation and landing stage is at Coupure, on the corner of Lindenlei.

WORTH NOTING

9 **De Wereld van Kina (Kind en Natuur).** This natural-history museum shares an ancient abbey with the Kunsthal Sint-Pieters Abdij *(see below).* Here you'll find "school subjects" on geology, the evolution of life, human biology and reproduction, and a diorama room of indigenous birds. There's an Internet station and a sound-and-light show about Gent and Emperor Charles V, featuring a large-scale model of 17th-century Gent. ✉ *Sint-Pietersplein 14, Sint-Pietersplein* ☎ *09/244–7373* ⊕ *www. dewereldvankina.be* 🎫 *€2.50* ⏱ *Weekdays 9–5 and Sun. 2–5:30.*

1 **Het Huis van Alijn.** The Folklore Museum, the Kraanlei waterfront, and the ancient Patershol district behind it form an enchanting ensemble. The museum comprises several settings, including 18 medieval almshouses surrounding a garden, reconstructed to offer an idea of life here 100 years ago. You'll also find a Gent version of Williamsburg, Virginia, with a grocer's shop, tavern, weaver's workshop, and washroom. The chemist's shop features 17th- to 19th-century pharmacy items, and the pipe-and-tobacco collection has a large selection of snuff, pouches, and tools. The visitors' route takes you from the houses to the chapel and out through the crypt. Children are often drawn to the giant pageant figures, board games, and frequent shows in the beamed-and-brick puppet theater. The star is "Pierke," the traditional Gent puppet. There are some English-language brochures available. ✉ *Kraanlei 65, Gravensteen/Patershol* ☎ *09/269–2350* ⊕ *www.huisvanalijn.be* 🎫 *Museum €5* ⏱ *Tues.–Sat. 10–5, Sun. 11–5.*

QUICK BITES

Poesjkine (✉ *Jan Breydelstraat 12, Gravensteen/Patershol* ☎ *09/224–2919*) is a popular spot for a caffeine fix—or a simple, sinful indulgence. Locals in the know recommend the cream and chocolate desserts. It's closed Tuesday and Wednesday and the first week of August.

12 **Klein Begijnhof.** Founded in 1234 by Countess Joanna of Constantinople, the Small Beguinage (a convent of Beguine nuns), is the best preserved of Gent's three beguinages. Protected by a wall and portal, the surrounding petite homes with individual yards were built in the 17th and 18th centuries, but are organized in medieval style. Each house has a statue of a saint and a spacious lawn; a few are still occupied by genuine Beguines leading the life stipulated by their founder 750 years ago. You can walk quietly through the main building and peek into the stone chapel—the houses, however, are private. Although entry is free, a

---

BIKING

For cycling routes, pick up a bicycle map from the tourism office; it's in Flemish but easily deciphered.

---

gate closes to keep out nonresidents from 10 PM to 6:30 AM. ⊠ *Lange Violettestraat 77–273, Klein Begijnhof.*

QUICK BITES

Drop by **Het Groot Vleeshuis** (⊠ *Groentenmarkt 7, Gravensteen/Patershol* ☎ *09/223-2324*) (Great Meat Hall) for coffee or lunch and a spot of toothsome shopping. The wood-beamed hall dates from the early 15th century and was used as a covered meat market. It's an impressive blend of ancient and modern; the metal-and-glass restaurant has been cleverly constructed without affecting the old hall itself. Both shop and restaurant focus on East Flemish specialties such as Ganda ham, local mustard, and O'de Flandres *jenever*. The hall is open from Tuesday to Sunday 10 to 6.

⑩ Kunsthal Sint-Pieters Abdij. There has been an abbey on this site since the 7th century, and during the Middle Ages it was one of the richest and most important Flemish abbeys. Most of the Baroque buildings you see today were built in the 17th century, however, and now house the St. Peter's Abbey Arts Center. You can walk around the abbey, the ruined gardens, and the cellars, where there is an exhibition about the checkered history of the abbey and its monks. ⊠ *Sint-Pietersplein* ☎ *09/243–9730* ⊕ *www.gent.be/spa* 🎟 *€8* ☉ *Tues.–Sun. and public holidays 10–6.*

❽ Museum Arnold Vander Haeghen. Three of Gent's favorite locals are honored in this 18th-century former governor's home. Nobel prize–winning playwright and poet Maurice Maeterlinck (1862–1949) kept a library in this elegant Neoclassical building, which still contains his personal objects, letters, and documents. A cabinet showcases work by the artist Stuyvaert, who illustrated Maeterlinck's publications, and the painter Doudelet. Look for the 18th-century silk wall decorations in the Chinese salon. There's no descriptive information in English. ⊠ *Veldstraat 82* ☎ *09/269–8460* 🎟 *Free* ☉ *Weekdays 10–noon and 2–5.*

⑪ Museum voor Schone Kunsten. Built in 1902 at the edge of Citadelpark, the Neoclassical Museum of Fine Arts is one of Belgium's best. The museum's holdings span the Middle Ages to the early 20th century, including works by Rubens, Gericault, Corot, Ensor, and Magritte. Its collection of Flemish Primitives is particularly noteworthy, with two paintings by Hieronymus Bosch, Saint Jerome, and The Bearing of the Cross. It also has a fine collection of sculpture and French painting. The temporary exhibitions are usually exceptional. ⊠ *Ferdinand Scribedreef 1, Citadelpark* ☎ *09/240–0700* ⊕ *www.mskgent.be* 🎟 *€5* ☉ *Tues.–Sun. 10–6.*

DID YOU KNOW?

The Gravensteen in Gent was built in 1180 by count Philip of Alsace. It was modeled after the crusaders' castles that the count has seen during the second crusade. In 1885 the city purchased the castle and completely renovated it. Today the structure is in good enough shape to climb around on, and the museum inside has a few well-worn torture devices and a guillotine.

④ Sint-Niklaaskerk. St. Nicholas's Church was built in the 11th century in Romanesque style, but was destroyed a century later after two disastrous fires; it was later rebuilt by prosperous merchants. The tower, one of the many soaring landmarks of this city's famed skyline, dates from about 1300 and was the first belfry in Gent. During the French Revolution the church was used as a stable, and its treasures were ransacked. The most recent restorations were completed in 2000, renewing Belgian's best example of Scheldt-Gothic once again. ⊠ *Cataloniestraat, Torenrij* ☎ *09/234–2869* 🖃 *Free* ☉ *Mon. 2–5, Tues.–Sun. 10–5.*

⑤ Stadhuis. The Town Hall is an early example of what raising taxes can do to a city. In 1516, Antwerp's Domien de Waghemakere and Mechelen's Rombout Keldermans, two prominent architects, were called in to build a town hall that would put all others to shame. However, before the building could be completed, Emperor Charles V imposed new taxes that drained the city's resources. The architecture thus reflects the changing fortunes of Gent: the side built in 1518–60 and facing Hoogpoort is in Flamboyant Gothic style; when work resumed in 1580, during the short-lived Protestant Republic, the Botermarkt side was completed in a stricter and more economical Renaissance style; and later additions include Baroque and rococo features. The tower on the corner of Hoogpoort and Botermarkt has a balcony specifically built for making announcements and proclamations; lacelike tracery embellishes the exterior. This civic landmark is not usually open to the public, but you can arrange a tour through the Gidsenbond van Genten *(see Tours in Gent Essentials)* or see it on a guided tour offered through the city's tourist office. Look for the glorious Gothic staircase, the throne room, and the spectacularly decorated halls—the Pacificatiezaal hall is where the Pacification Treaty of Gent between Catholics and Protestants was signed. ⊠ *botermarkt 1, Torenrij* ☎ *09/266–5222* 🖃 *€4* ☉ *Guided visits only, May–Oct., Mon.–Thurs. at 2:30.*

WHERE TO EAT

$
VEGETARIAN

✕ **Avalon.** Head to this lunch spot near the Gravensteen for delicious, organic vegetarian meals—or, if you're peckish, soup or a snack. The menu features pasta, stews, and quiches. In good weather, try for a table on the terrace. Be sure to get here early, though—it's open only until 2 PM. ⊠ *Geldmunt 32, Gravensteen/Patershol* ☎ *09/224–3724* ⊕ *www.restaurantavalon.be* ▤ *AE, MC, V* ☉ *Closed Sun. No dinner.*

$$–$$$$
BELGIAN
Fodor's Choice
★

✕ **Belga Queen.** A magnificent restaurant in a magnificent location. The former corn warehouse bordering the Leie has been redesigned by the chef himself, Antoine Pinto. The large terrace leads to the ground floor's impressive bar, high tables, and cozy leather seats. The menu has daily fresh suggestions, and a three-course lunch is €15. Evening choices include modern twists on Belgian classics, such as local favorite *Gents* waterzooi prepared with *Mechelse koekoek* (a particularly tasty local breed of chicken). ⊠ *Graslei 10, De Kuip* ☎ *09/280–0100* ⊕ *www.belgaqueen.be* ⌂ *Reservations essential* ▤ *AE, DC, MC, V.*

$–$$
BELGIAN

✕ **Brasserie Keizershof.** When you're looking for a change from the familiar waterzooi but are still in the mood for comfort food, try this inexpensive tavern. Light meals and snacks are available all day—toasted sandwiches, spaghetti—but bring an appetite, because portions are huge. There's always a daily special, often the kind of food you would expect on a typical Flemish table. It can get quite busy, especially at noon, since the restaurant's size makes it a favorite of tour groups. ⊠ *Vrijdagmarkt 47, Vrijdagmarkt* ☎ *09/223–4446* ⊕ *www.keizershof. net* ⊟ *MC, V* ⊘ *Closed Sun. and Mon.*

$$
ECLECTIC
✕ **De 3 Biggetjes.** The name means "the three little pigs," and you'll definitely be tempted to wolf down the wonderful food at this tiny, step-gabled building set on the cobbled Zeugsteeg, or Sow Lane. Even if you huff and puff a bit to get there, the cooking makes the trip worthwhile. The menu combines Belgian, Vietnamese, and French influences. Seafood dishes are a highlight; chef Ly Chi Cuong relies on the daily market for turbot, sole, and the like, while other ingredients are flown in from all over the world, even the Seychelles. The set menus are a very good value. ⊠ *Zeugsteeg 7, Gravensteen/Patershol* ☎ *09/224–4648* ⌂ *Reservations essential* ⊟ *MC, V* ⊘ *Closed Wed. and Sun. No lunch Sat.*

¢–$
BELGIAN
✕ **Hot Club Reserva.** This quiet little café bistro is situated unassumingly on busy Jan Breydelstraat, so people tend to pass by without noticing. The good-value menu draws on international influences, with specialties ranging from pastas to beef bourguignonne. The room at the back has tables with river views, or head down the steps to the lowest level, where there's a small waterside terrace open in fine weather. There's live music some nights. ⊠ *Jan Breydelstraat 32–34, Gravensteen/Patershol* ☎ *0498/54–11–17* ⊟ *No credit cards.*

$$$–$$$$
BELGIAN
Fodor's Choice
★
✕ **Jan van den Bon.** With room for 30, this distinguished restaurant is a local favorite for French and classic Belgian dishes, particularly seafood and seasonal specialties. White asparagus, for instance, is cooked and sauced to perfection. Sip your aperitif on the terrace overlooking the garden, which supplies the herbs used in the kitchen. ⊠ *Koning Leopold II Laan 43, Citadelpark* ☎ *09/221–9085* ⊕ *www.janvandenbon.be* ⌂ *Reservations essential* 🍴 *Jacket and tie* ⊟ *AE, DC, MC, V* ⊘ *Closed Sun. No lunch Sat.*

$$–$$$
CONTEMPORARY
✕ **Pakhuis.** At peak times, this enormously popular brasserie in an old warehouse off the Korenmarkt crackles with energy. A giant Greek statue makes an incongruous counterpoint to the marble-top tables, parquet floors, and long oak bar. Locals rave about the seafood and the oyster bar; there's also more robust fare such as ham knuckle with sharp Gent mustard. You can choose the "market menu," based on what the chef picked up at the market that morning. ⊠ *Schuurkenstraat 4, Torenrij* ☎ *09/223–5555* ⊕ *www.pakhuis.be* ⊟ *AE, DC, MC, V* ⊘ *Closed Sun.*

9

WHERE TO STAY

$
🏠 **Astoria.** That this brick building with large shuttered windows was once a home won't surprise you once you see the bright rooms, breezily comfortable with cane chairs and tables, colorful bedspreads, and large wooden wardrobes. Public areas are done in warm colors, with wall sconces and accents of polished wood. The hotel is in a clean but somewhat bland residential area near train and tram stations.

Pros: good location for catching an early train; a rare example of free parking. **Cons:** the rumble of trains can keep you awake; far from the center. ✉ *Achilles Musschestraat 39, behind St-Pieters station,* ☎ *09/222–8413* ⊕ *www.astoria.be* ⇆ *25 rooms* ⚐ *In-room: no a/c, DVD, Wi-Fi. In-hotel: parking (free and paid)* ⊟ *AE, DC, MC, V.*

$$ 🚤 **The Boatel.** Get a different perspective on Gent by staying aboard this 1953 riverboat docked on the Leie since Portus Ganda opened. The rebuilt vessel shows off sections of the original woodwork. Cabins are large and bright, particularly the two master bedrooms above the sea line. The wood floor of the sunny breakfast room can double as the evening gathering spot or even a small meeting room. Free parking is available on the road nearby. Even though it is tightly roped to the shore, remember that boats tend to rock a bit. **Pros:** a taste of canal life; roomy cabins won't make you claustrophobic. **Cons:** reception not open 24 hours; a walk from the center. ✉ *Voorhoutkaai 44, Portus Ganda* ☎ *09/267–1030* ⊕ *www.theboatel.com* ⇆ *5 rooms* ⚐ *In-room: no a/c* ⊟ *MC, V.*

¢   🚤 **De Draeke Youth Hostel.** With its location on the edge of the Lieve canal, near the Gravensteen, this hostel makes a terrific base for city explorations. Each room that sleeps between two and five people has its own bathroom. You must pay an extra €3 per person if you're not a youth-hostel member. **Pros:** inexpensive rates; close to the action; safe. **Cons:** the reception is often unstaffed. ✉ *Sint-Widostraat 11, Prinsenhof* ☎ *09/233–7050* ⊕ *www.vjh.be* ⇆ *27 rooms* ⚐ *In-room: no a/c, no phone, no TV. In-hotel: restaurant, bar, Internet terminal* ⊟ *MC, V* ⧖ *BP.*

$ 🚤 **Erasmus.** From the flagstone and wood-beam library-lounge to the
★   stone mantels in the individually decorated bedrooms, every inch of this noble 16th-century town house has been scrubbed, polished, and decked with period ornaments. Even the tiny garden has been carefully manicured. The couple that runs this distinctive hotel near the Korenlei takes care of everything from answering the bellpull at night to serving a delicious breakfast in the parlor. **Pros:** a huge amount of charm; extremely friendly owners; professional staff. **Cons:** lacks some modern conveniences; it's a hassle to arrive late or leave early. ✉ *Poel 25, Torenrij* ☎ *09/224–2195* ⊕ *www.erasmushotel.be* ⇆ *11 rooms* ⚐ *In-room: no a/c, refrigerator. In-hotel: bar* ⊟ *AE, MC, V* ⧖ *Closed mid-Dec.–mid-Jan.*

$$ 🚤 **Gravensteen.** Steps from its namesake, this handsome 19th-century mansion exudes atmosphere—at least, from most angles. The public areas are ornate with carved stucco, a marble staircase, and a cupola. Hallways wind to small rooms with a more modern look; some have castle or canal views. Note that some rooms are in a newer, less

attractive building at the back and that bathrooms are small, some with showers only. **Pros:** atmospheric building; great views from some rooms. **Cons:** on noisy street. ⊠ *Jan Breydelstraat 35, Gravensteen/Patershol* ☎ *09/225–1150* ⊕ *www.gravensteen.be* ⤵ *49 rooms* ⇘ *In-room: no a/c (some), refrigerator, Wi-Fi. In-hotel: bar, gym, Wi-Fi, parking (paid)* ⊟ *AE, DC, MC, V.*

$ 🛏 **Ibis Gent Centrum Kathedraal.** Location is this hotel's trump card: it's close to the cathedral. As in most branches of this no-frills chain, rooms have cookie-cutter modern décor and requisite amenities. This Ibis has a dependable level of service and comfort, but lacks local character. Triples are available. There's another branch, Ibis Gent Centrum Opera, close to the Flemish Opera building; some of its rooms are a tad cheaper. **Pros:** a great value chain hotel; efficient service. **Cons:** no-frills focus; small rooms. ⊠ *Limburgstraat 2, Torenrij* ☎ *09/233–0000* ⊕ *www.ibishotel.com* ⤵ *120 rooms* ⇘ *In-room: Wi-Fi. In-hotel: restaurant, bar, parking (paid)* ⊟ *AE, DC, MC, V* ⍾| *BP.*

¢–$$$ 🛏 **Monasterium PoortAckere.** A complex comprising a former abbey, convent, and béguinage now provides a serene place to stay in a central neighborhood. Some sections date back to the 13th century; most of the buildings, though, are 19th-century Gothic Revival. There are large comfortable rooms in the Monasterium, the former convent; in the adjacent convent former cells have been transformed into small, single guest rooms with a washbasin (cold water only) and shared showers and toilets. You can take breakfast in the chapter house and have a buffet dinner in the church (available only to groups of 12 or more). **Pros:** unique style; breakfasts are outstanding. **Cons:** a lot of stairs to climb (though there are two elevators); a maze of corridors. ⊠ *Oude Houtlei 56, Torenrij* ☎ *09/269–2210* ⊕ *www.monasterium.be* ⤵ *60 rooms, 47 with bath* ⇘ *In-room: no a/c, Wi-Fi. In-hotel: restaurant, bar, bicycles, Internet terminal, Wi-Fi, parking (paid)* ⊟ *AE, DC, MC, V* ⍾| *BP.*

$–$$ 🛏 **NH Gent–Belfort.** In the heart of the old city, this grand hotel mirrors the elegance of the well-known international chain. Warmed with sandy beige colors, it sticks to a business-friendly look. Spacious rooms are well equipped; some are bi-level, with a second TV. Great weekend deals are available if you book in advance. **Pros:** comfortable rooms; cozy bar; prime location for exploring the city. **Cons:** part of a chain, albeit a good one. ⊠ *Hoogpoort 63, Torenrij,* ☎ *09/233–3331* ⊕ *www.nh-hotels.com* ⤵ *171 rooms, 3 suites* ⇘ *In-room: safe, refrigerator, Wi-Fi. In-hotel: restaurant, bar, gym, Wi-Fi, parking (paid)* ⊟ *AE, DC, MC, V.*

9

NIGHTLIFE AND THE ARTS

Check the "What's On" and "Other Towns" sections of the *Bulletin* to find schedules of the latest art shows and cultural events. You can find issues of the *Bulletin* in local newsstands and bookstores.

THE ARTS

CONCERTS   **De Handelsbeurs** (⊠ *Kouter 29, Kouter* ☎ *09/265–9160* ⊕ *www.handelsbeurs.be*) is a concert hall for all kinds of music, from jazz to folk to world to classical. **De Vlaamse Opera** (⊠ *Schouwburgstraat 3, Kouter* ☎ *09/268–1011* ⊕ *www.vlaamseopera.be*) shares its name—and

Stacks of freshly baked bread.

many opera productions—with a sister company in Antwerp; if you go, note the splendid ceiling and chandelier. Head for the **Kunstencentrum Vooruit** (✉ *Sint-Pietersnieuwstraat 23, Het Zuid* ☎ *09/267–2828* ⊕ *www.vooruit.be*) for top-quality dance, theater, and jazz programs; the venue also hosts rock and contemporary classical concerts. Grab a drink or quick meal in the cafeteria of this former cultural center of the Socialist Party.

NIGHTLIFE

As in most Belgian towns, nightlife in Gent centers around grazing and drinking and talking with friends through the wee hours. The student population generates a much busier, more varied nightlife than you'll find in Brugge or other towns in Flanders. The area around Oude Beestenmarkt and Vlasmarkt, near Portus Ganda, is mainly where young people gather for dancing and partying.

The **Town Crier** (☎ *09/222–6743* ⊕ *www.towncriers.be*), who spends his days walking the streets making announcements and tolling his bell, can also take you on a pub crawl. You'll need a reservation, though.

There are special dance nights, several gay bars, and lots of gay and lesbian organizations providing help and advice. The tourist office even provides a gay and lesbian city map. You can get more information at **Casa Rosa** (✉ *Kammerstraat 22, Het Zuid* ☎ *09/269–2812* ⊕ *www. casarosa.be*).

BARS **De Dulle Griet** (✉ *Vrijdagmarkt 50, Vrijdagmarkt* ☎ *09/224–2455*) is a quintessential Gent pub. It has more than 250 kinds of drinks but specializes in the 1.2-liter *Kwak* beer, complete with a collector's stein and stand—ask for a "Max." If you brave this beer, though, you must leave one of your shoes as a deposit when you order. The pub is open from noon until 1 or 2 AM, apart from Sunday evening when it closes early. To taste a potent Belgian specialty, head to **'t Dreupelkot** (⊠ *Groentenmarkt 12, Gravensteen/Patershol* ☎ *09/224–2120*), which produces its own jenever in a multitude of different flavors, including vanilla and chocolate. Virtually next door to the Dreupelkot, **Het Waterhuis Aan De Bierkant** (⊠ *Groentenmarkt 9, Gravensteen/Patershol* ☎ *09/225–0680*) is another great beer bar, with a small waterside terrace that fills up quickly in fine weather.

JAZZ CLUBS   The busy late-night jazz café **Het Damberd** (⊠ *Korenmarkt 19, Gravensteen/Patershol* ☎ *09/329–5337*) occupies one of the most historic pubs in Gent. Jazz musicians from all over the world play here. **Lazy River Jazz Café** (⊠ *Stadhuissteeg 5, Torenrij* ☎ *09/230–4139*) is a friendly intimate place beloved by locals and the older crowd. There are concerts as well as dance nights at **Muziekcafé Charlatan** (⊠ *Vlasmarkt 6, near Portus Ganda* ☎ *09/224–2457*). It's open every day from 4 PM; music starts up at 10 or 11. Their lineup covers alt-rock, funk, and lots of DJ nights.

SHOPPING

Langemunt and **Veldstraat** are the major shopping streets, while the smart fashion boutiques cluster along **Voldersstraat.** Gent also has several exclusive shopping galleries where fancy boutiques are surrounded by upscale cafés and restaurants; try the **Bourdon Arcade** (Gouden Leeuwplein) and **Braempoort**, between Brabantdam and Vlaanderenstraat.

MARKETS

The largest market is the attractive and historic **Vrijdagmarkt**, held Friday 7–1 and Saturday 1–6. This is where leaders have rallied the people of Gent from the Middle Ages to the present day. The huge square is dominated by a turret that was part of the tanner's guild house, and the statue in the middle is of Jacob van Artevelde, who led a rebellion from here in 1338, defending the neutrality of the city and Flanders during the Hundred Years' War. You can take home a supply of *Gentse mokken,* syrup-saturated biscuits available from any pastry shop, or famously strong Gent mustard. On Sunday mornings, also visit the **flower market** on the Kouter, where there is often a brass band playing, and sample oysters and a glass of champagne at **De Blauwe Kiosk,** a booth on the edge of the market at the corner of Kouter and Vogelmarkt.

9

BRUGGE

Wandering through the tangled streets and enjoying the narrow canals, handsome squares, and charming old gabled houses is a pleasure, but the secret got out many years ago—the city has been a powerful magnet for international tourists since the 19th century.

Indeed, tourism has long been the principal industry here, and preservation orders and bylaws ensure very strictly that the center looks much as it did in medieval days (how the modern—and modern-looking—Concertgebouw Brugge concert venue on 't Zand got planning permission is still a matter of heated debate).

Brugge's undeniable charm has made it an awful lot of friends, and turned it into an exceedingly popular weekend escape, full as it is of romantic suites and secluded hideaways.

Brugge's historic center is encircled by a ring road that loosely follows the line of the city's medieval ramparts. In fact, the ancient gates—Smedenpoort, Ezelpoort, Kruispoort, and Gentpoort—still stand along this road. Most of Brugge's sights lie inside the center, which can easily be explored on foot. Inside the ring road, the medieval city center is compact, like a small island amid the winding waterways, and every twist and turn will likely lead you to yet more unexpected pleasures. The town center is technically divided up into parishes or *kwartiers* around the local churches: Sint-Gillis, Sint-Anna, Sint-Magdalena, Onze-Lieve-Vrouwekerk, Sint-Salvators, and Sint-Jacobs. In practice, however, the center is so small that locals never use these parish names.

There are hundreds of restaurants, ranging from taverns offering a quick snack to stylish establishments serving multicourse Flemish or international (mostly French) delicacies. The seafood is great here, as it should be, since the coast is fairly nearby; and meals cooked with local Belgian beers are a treat as well. While in the Markt, snack like a Belgian on *friet met* (fries with mayonnaise). Brugge has also firmly established itself in the chocolate business. You can't walk down any street without tripping over a store these days—there are around 50 of them in town, probably the highest concentration anywhere in the world. Some are chain outlets of famous names, others are true artisanal workshops where the goodies are made on-site. They have their own guild now, and there's even a chocolate museum devoted to the history of cocoa and its final product.

Note: Although it is often called Bruges, its French name, in many guidebooks and by many English-speaking people, the city's official name is indeed Brugge (*bruhg-guh*). Use its proper Flemish title in front of the locals and you'll definitely win friends and score kudos.

GETTING HERE AND AROUND
204 km (122 mi) south of Amsterdam.

To reach Brugge by car from Amsterdam, take the A4 motorway to Antwerp, follow the E17 and then the E40, taking the Brugge exit. The journey takes around 2½ hours. Access for cars and coaches into Brugge's center is severely restricted. The historic streets are narrow and often one-way. There are huge parking lots at the railway station and near the exits from the ring road, plus underground parking at 't Zand. For those brave enough to face tackling the center's tricky one-way system, there is also underground parking at the Biekorf (behind the public library), Zilverpand, and Pandreitje, as well as parking at the Begijnhof. By train, take a Thalys high-speed train to Brussels's Gare de Midi/Brussel Zuid station and then change to a Belgian Railways (SNCB/NMBS) train for Brugge. There are two an hour, and the trip takes an hour.

TOURS
Brugge-based Quasimundo Bike Tours organizes three bike tours of Brugge and the surrounding countryside, as does Pink Bear Tours. The tourist office can help you make arrangements.

The Reien (the waterways threading through the center of Brugge) make for lovely sightseeing routes. Motor launches depart from several jetties spaced along the Dijver and Katelijnestraat and by the Vismarkt as soon as they are reasonably full (every 15 minutes or so) daily March–November and depending on the weather in December and February. The trips take just over a half hour and cost €6.

For a personalized walking tour, the tourist office can set you up with a private English-speaking guide for a minimum cost of around €50 for two hours.

TIMING
A full day at least is needed to enjoy most of what Brugge has to offer. Allow two or three days to see it all at a leisurely pace.

ESSENTIALS
Bicycle rentals **Bruges Bike Rental** (Niklaas Desparsstraat 17, B8000 ☎ *050/40–61–62* ⊙ *Daily 10–10*). **Quasimundo Bike Tours** (☎ *050/33–07–75*, ⊕ *www.quasimundo.com*). **Pink Bear Tours** (☎ *050/61–66–86*).

Emergency Services **Ambulance** (☎ *100*). **Duty doctors** (☎ *050/36–40–10*). **Night pharmacies** (☎ *050/40–61–62*). **Police** (☎ *101*).

The Groeningemuseum is a smallish museum with a great big collection.

Visitor Information In&Uit Brugge (✉ *'t Zand 34*, ☎ *050/44–46–46* ⊕ *www. brugge.be*) **Brugge** (✉ *Burg 11* ☎ *050/44–46–46* ⊕ *www.brugge.be*).

EXPLORING

TOP ATTRACTIONS

⑪ Begijnhof. This 13th-century béguinage is a pretty and serene cluster of small whitewashed houses, a pigeon tower, and a church surrounding a pleasant green at the edge of a canal. The Begijnhof was founded in 1245 by Margaret, Countess of Constantinople, to bring together the Beguines—girls and widows from all social backgrounds who devoted themselves to charitable work but who were not bound by religious vows. Led by a superintendent known as the Grand Mistress, the congregation flourished for 600 years. The last of the Beguines died about 50 years ago; today the site is occupied by the Benedictine nuns, who still wear the Beguine habit. You may join them, discreetly, for vespers in their small church of St. Elizabeth. Although most of the present-day houses are from the 16th and 17th centuries, they have maintained the architectural style of the houses that preceded them. One house has been set aside as a small museum. Visitors are asked to respect the silence. The horse-and-carriage rides around the town have a 10-minute stop outside the béguinage—long enough for a quick look round. ✉ *Oude Begijnhof, off Wijngaardstraat* ☎ *050/33–00–11* 🎟 *Free, house visit €2* ⊙ *Begijnhof daily 6:30–6:30; house Mon.–Sat. 10–5, Sun. 2:30–5.*

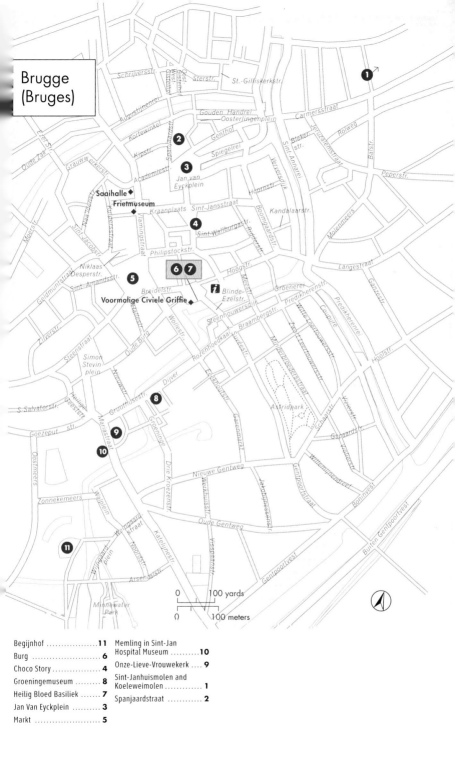

Brugge
(Bruges)

IF YOU ONLY HAVE 1 DAY

Get to Brugge as early as possible. Must-see spots are the Begijnhof near Minnewater and the great buildings around Burg and Markt squares. Soak up the artwork, including the Groeninge and Memling museums, and Michelangelo's sculpture in the Onze-Lieve-Vrouwekerk. You might take an afternoon canal ride—or, after dinner, when crowds have thinned, you can wander alongside the water. Bear in mind that Brugge is one of Europe's top tourist destinations, and has prices to match. If you plan to see a lot, get hold of a **Brugge City Card** (⊕ *www.bruggecitycard.be*), which gives free entry to 24 museums and a host of other discounts. At this writing they cost €33 or €38 for two or three days respectively, and can be ordered online, obtained from the tourist office or from participating sights. They plan on raising the price soon but by how much is still undecided.

❻ **Burg.** A popular daytime meeting place and an enchanting, floodlighted
Fodor's Choice scene after dark, the Burg is flanked by striking civic buildings. Named
★ for the fortress built by Baldwin of the Iron Arm, the Burg was also the
former site of the 10th-century Carolingian Cathedral of St. Donaas,
which was destroyed by French Republicans in 1799. You can wander
through the handsome, 18th-century law court, the Oude Gerechtshof,
the Voormalige Civiele Griffie with its 15th-century front gable, the
Stadhuis, and the Heilig Bloed Basiliek *(see below)*. The Burg is not all
historic splendor, though—in sharp contrast to these buildings stands a
modern construction by Japanese artist Toyo Ito, added in 2002. Public
opinion is sharply divided over Ito's pavilion; you'll either love it or hate
it. ⊠ *Hoogstraat and Breidelstraat.*

❽ **Groeningemuseum.** The tremendous holdings of this gallery give you
Fodor's Choice the makings for a crash course in the Flemish Primitives and their
★ successors. Petrus Christus, Hugo Van der Goes, Hieronymus Bosch,
Rogier van der Weyden, Gerard David, Pieter Bruegel (both Elder and
Younger), Pieter Pourbus—all are represented here. Here you can see
Jan van Eyck's wonderfully realistic *Madonna with Canon Van der
Paele,* in which van Eyck achieved texture and depth through multiple
layers of oil and varnish. The painter's attention to detail is all-
embracing; the canon's pouchy flesh and the nets of wrinkles around
his eyes are as carefully depicted as the crimson folds of the Madonna's
robe or her waving golden hair. There's also one of Hans Memling's
greatest works, the *Moreel Triptych.* The namesake family is portrayed
on the side panels, all with preternaturally blank expressions. As if
this weren't enough, the museum also encompasses a strong display
of 15th- to 21st-century Dutch and Belgian works, sweeping through
to Surrealist and contemporary art. The Groeninge is set back from
the street in a pocket-size park behind a medieval gate. It isn't a huge
museum; nonetheless, its riches warrant a full morning or afternoon.
An audio guide is available in English. ⊠ *Dijver 12* ☎ *050/44–87–11*
💳 *€8* ⏱ *Tues.–Sun. 9:30–5.*

Horse-drawn carriage is a timeless way to explore in Burg square.

9

QUICK BITES

At the Halve Maan (✉ *Walplein 26* ☎ *050/33–26–97*) you can sit in a pleasant courtyard and enjoy a snack with a soft drink or a beer. We recommend the latter as this is a working brewery—the only one in Brugge—producing the Brugse Zot brands that you'll see in many bars around town. If you want to tour the brewery, a 45-minute tour (hourly 11–4) costs €5.50 and includes a glass of their blond beer in its unfiltered form.

❼ Heilig Bloed Basiliek. The Basilica of the Holy Blood manages to include both the austere and the ornate under one roof—not to mention one of Europe's most precious relics. The 12th-century Lower Chapel retains a stern, Romanesque character. Look for the poignant, 14th-century Pietà and the carved statue of Christ in the crypt. From this sober space, an elaborate, external Gothic stairway leads to the stunningly lavish Upper Chapel, which was twice destroyed—by Protestant iconoclasts in the 16th century and by French Republicans in the 18th—but both times rebuilt. (Note that the Upper Chapel is closed to visitors during Eucharistic Mass on Sunday 11 to noon.) The original stained-glass windows were replaced in 1845, and then again after an explosion in 1967, when they were restored by the Brugge painter De Loddere. The basilica's namesake treasure is a vial thought to contain a few drops of the blood of Christ, brought from Jerusalem to Brugge in 1149 by Derick of Alsace when he returned from the Second Crusade. It is exposed here every Friday in the Lower Chapel 8:30 to 10 and in the Upper Chapel 10 to 11 and 3 to 4, and on other apparently random occasions for veneration: queue up to place your right hand on the vial and take a moment for quiet reflection. On Ascension Day, it becomes the centerpiece of the magnificent *De Heilig Bloedprocessie* (Procession of the Holy Blood), a major medieval-style pageant in which it is carried through the streets of Brugge. The small **museum** next to the basilica contains the 17th-century reliquary. ⌧ *Burg* ⌂ *No phone* ⊕ *www.holyblood.org* ⌸ *Museum: €1.50* ☯ *Mar.–Sept., Thurs.–Tues. 9:30–noon and 2–6; Oct.–Mar., daily 10–noon and 2–4.*

❺ **Markt.** Used as a marketplace since 958, this square is still one of the
Fodor's Choice liveliest places in Brugge. In the center stands a memorial to the city's
★ medieval heroes, Jan Breydel and Pieter De Coninck, who led the commoners of Flanders to their short-lived victory over the aristocrats of France. On the east side of the Markt stand the provincial government house and the post office, an excellent pastiche of Burgundian Gothic. Old guild houses line the west and north sides of the square, their step-gabled facades overlooking the cafés spilling out onto the sidewalk. These buildings aren't always as old as they seem, though—often they're 19th-century reconstructions. The medieval **Belfort** (Belfry) on the south side of the Markt, however, is the genuine article. The tower dates to the 13th century, its crowning octagonal lantern to the 15th century. Altogether, it rises to a height of 270 feet, commanding the city and the surrounding countryside with more presence than grace. The valuables of Brugge were once kept in the second-floor treasury; now the Belfort's riches are in its remarkable 47-bell carillon, which rings even truer thanks to the new bells it was given in 2010. (Impressing Belgians with a carillon is no mean feat, as Belgium has some of the best in the world.) If you haven't walked enough, you can climb 366 winding steps to the clock mechanism, and from the carillon enjoy a gorgeous panoramic view. Back down in the square, you may be tempted by the **horse-drawn carriages** that congregate here; a half-hour ride for up to five people, with a short stop at the Begijnhof, costs €36 plus "something for the horse." ⌧ *Intersection of Steenstraat, St-Amandstraat, Vlamingstraat, Philipstockstraat, Breidelstraat, and Wollestraat* ⌂ *050/44–87–11* ⌸ *Belfort €8* ☯ *Belfort daily 9:30–5.*

❿ **Memling in Sint-Jan Hospitaalmuseum.** This collection contains six main works (and plenty of minor ones, as well) that are of breathtaking quality and among the greatest—and certainly the most spiritual—of the Flemish Primitive school. Hans Memling (1440–94) was born in Germany, but spent the greater part of his life in Brugge. In *The Altarpiece of St. John the Baptist and St. John the Evangelist,* two leading personages of the Burgundian court are believed to be portrayed: Mary of Burgundy (buried in the Onze-Lieve-Vrouwekerk) as St. Catherine, and Margaret of York as St. Barbara. The "paintings within the painting" give details of the lives of the two saints. The miniature paintings that adorn the St. Ursula Shrine are likewise marvels of detail and poignancy; Memling's work gives recognizable iconographic details about cities, such as Brugge, Cologne, Basel, and Rome. The Memling Museum is housed in **Oud Sint-Janshospitaal,** one of the oldest surviving medieval hospitals in Europe. It was founded in the 12th century and remained in use until the early 20th century. Furniture, paintings, and hospital-related items are attractively displayed; the 13th-century middle ward, the oldest of three, was built in Romanesque style. Other fascinating

18th-century paintings show patients arriving by sedan chair and being fed and ministered to by sisters and clerics. Some of the actual sedan chairs that were used are also on display. There is a short guide to the museum in English, and the audio guide is in English, too. ⊠ *Marias-traat 38* ☎ *050/44–87–11* ⊠ *€8* ☺ *Tues.–Sun. 9:30–5.*

WORTH NOTING

❹ **Choco-Story**. This new museum may deviate from the historical quaint-ness found everywhere else in Brugge, but it makes for a diverting bookend if you've been trawling the delightful chocolate shops in town. This collection traces the history of the cocoa bean, from its origins in the Americas to its popularity in Europe. There are also chocolate-making demonstrations, and a chance to taste. If you're still hungering for food-based educational displays, Choco-Story's nearby sister, the Frietmuseum (French fry museum) at ⊠ *Vlamingstraat 33* will tell you everything you need to know about the history of the potato, and why french fries should really be called Belgian fries. It has the same open-ing times and entry charge. ⊠ *Wijzakstraat 2* ☎ *050/61–22–37* ⊕ *www. choco-story.be* ⊠ *€6* ☺ *Daily 10–5.*

❸ **Jan van Eyckplein**. This colorful yet low-key square lies at the center of Hanseatic Brugge, marked with a statue of the famed 15th-century painter. It includes the old **Tolhuis** (Customs House), built in 1477, where vehicles on their way to market had to stop while tolls were levied on goods brought from nearby ports. The building is now an information office for the province of West Flanders. The **Poortersloge,** a late-Gothic building with a slender spire, was owned by the guild of porters and used as a meeting place for the burghers. Currently, it's used to store historic documents but is occasionally open for exhibitions. The bear occupying one niche represents the legendary creature speared by Baldwin of the Iron Arm that later became the symbol of the city. ⊠ *Intersection of Academiestraat, Spiegelrei, and Spanjaardstraat.*

❾ **Onze-Lieve-Vrouwekerk**. The towering spire of the plain Gothic Church of Our Lady, begun about 1220, rivals the Belfry as Brugge's symbol. It is 381 feet high, the tallest brick construction in the world. While brick can be built high, it cannot be sculpted like stone; hence the tower's somewhat severe look. Look for the small *Madonna and Child* statue, an early work by Michelangelo. The great sculptor sold it to a merchant from Brugge when the original client failed to pay. It was stolen by Napoléon, and during World War II by Nazi leader Hermann Göring; now the white-marble figure sits in a black-marble niche behind an altar at the end of the south aisle. The choir museum contains many 13th- and 14th-century polychrome tombs, as well as two mausoleums: that of Mary of Burgundy, who died in 1482 at the age of 25 after a fall from her horse; and that of her father, Charles the Bold, killed in 1477 while laying siege to Nancy in France. Mary was as well loved in Brugge as her husband, Maximilian of Austria, was loathed. Her finely chis-eled effigy captures her beauty. ⊠ *Dijver and Mariastraat* ☎ *No phone* ⊠ *Church free; choir museum €2* ☺ *Tues.–Fri. 9:30–5, Sat. 9:30–4:45, Sun. 1:30–5.*

9

CLOSE UP

Mussels and More

The backbone of Flanders food is the local produce that's served fresh and presented simply—you won't find painted plates or veggies sculpted beyond recognition. Naturally, this is seafood country, with fresh fish shipped in daily to Brugge; the coastal towns serve authentic North Sea delicacies at terrace restaurants whipped by sand and salt air. Even in landlocked Gent, some 50 km (30 mi) from the coast, locals snack on whelks and *winkles* (sea snails) as if they were popcorn. Flemings are mad about *mosselen* (mussels)—try them steamed, curried, or bathed in a white-wine broth accented with celery, onions, and parsley. Main courses are inevitably accompanied by a mountain of *frieten* (french fries), fried twice, making them especially crisp and delicious. For death by fries, buy them piping hot and salty from a stall, as the Belgians do, and dip them in the big dollop of accompanying mayo.

Paling (eels) are one of the region's specialties. The flesh is firm, fatty, and sweet, and served in long cross-sections with a removable backbone. *Paling in t'groen* is eel served in a green herb sauce, a heady mix of sorrel, tarragon, sage, mint, and parsley. Sole and turbot are also popular main courses, served broiled, poached with a light mousseline sauce, or grilled with a rich béarnaise or mustard sauce. Herring is eaten *maatjes* (raw) in the spring. To sound like a local, try these tongue twisters when you order: *oostduinkerkse paardevissersoep* (fish soup) and *dronken rog op Nieuwpoortse wijze* (ray).

When the Flemish aren't eating their fish straight or in a blanket of golden sauce, they consume it in the region's most famous dish, *waterzooi* (a thick broth rich with cream and vegetables). The citizens of Gent have a chicken version, as well as *Gentse hutsepot* (a casserole with carrots, onions, potatoes, and meat). For a hearty dish, look for *vlaamse stoverij* (beef or pork stew with onions, braised in beer). *Paardenvlees* (horse meat), with its sweet flavor and beefy texture, is considered a delicacy.

If you visit Flanders in springtime, look for memorably delicious vegetables, such as the tender white *asperge* (asparagus), served either in mousseline sauce or with a garnish of chopped hard-boiled egg and melted butter. These pale stalks are sweeter than the familiar green ones and are called "white gold" because the Flemings snap them up as fast as they arrive during their short season. In March and April, seek out the rare, expensive *jets de houblon* (delicate shoots of the hops plant).

A cheese course is often served before—or in place of—dessert, and there are hundreds of delicious local choices, many runny and pungent. Chocolate and whipped cream are favorite dessert ingredients, and homemade ice cream turns up on all kinds of menus in warm months. Local pastries include *Gentse mokken* (hard sugar cookies), *lierse vlaaikens* (plum tarts), and *speculoos* (sugary ginger cookies), all of which are often accompanied by coffee. Warm pancakes and Belgian *waffelen* (waffles) topped with fruit or syrup are available everywhere from sidewalk stalls to fancy restaurants. The famous crisp waffles, which have a vanilla flavor, are formed in cast-iron molds with presweetened dough.

Months ending in "-ber" (September to December) are supposed to be the best season for mussels.

1 **Sint-Janshuismolen and Koeleweimolen.** The outer ramparts of the medieval city of Brugge used to be dotted with windmills; now four remain along the ring road. Of these, two can be visited and are still used to grind flour: the St-Janshuismolen (1770) and the Koeleweimolen (1765). The wooden steps leading up to them are quite steep and not for the fainthearted. The last tickets are issued 30 minutes prior to closing. ✉ *Kruisvest, Sint-Anna* ☎ *050/44-87-11* 💶 *€2* 🕑 *Sint-Janshuismolen: May–Sept., Tues.–Sun. 9:30–12:30 and 1:30–5. Koeleweimolen: June–Sept., daily 9:30–12:30 and 1:30–5.*

2 **Spanjaardstraat.** The street leads up to the quay where goods from Spain were unloaded. The house at No. 9 was where St. Ignatius of Loyola stayed when he came to Flanders on holidays from his studies in Paris. Directly ahead are the three arches of the **Augustijnenbrug.** Dating from 1391, it's the oldest bridge in Brugge. On the other side of the canal, **Augustijnenrei** is one of the loveliest quays.

WHERE TO EAT

$–$$$ ⨯**Beethoven.** Chef Chantal Mortier built up a substantial local following BELGIAN over the years; she now serves them at her intimate Flemish restaurant off the Markt, with her husband at the front of the house. In winter a fire warms up the dining room and the menu offers comforting favorites like steak (fillet, tournedos, or rib eye) with frieten. In summer the street-front tables become a prime spot for people-watching. The menu lightens up accordingly, with salads such as goat cheese and honey or shrimp and smoked salmon. Though reservations aren't mandatory, they're highly recommended. ⊠ *Sint-Amandstraat 6* ☎ *050/33–50–06* ⊟ *MC, V* ☺ *Closed Tues. and Wed.*

$$$–$$$$ ✕**Chez Olivier**. Set above a quiet canal, with white swans gliding below,
FRENCH this French charmer is purely romantic. Chef Olivier Foucad uses impeccably fresh ingredients for "light food," such as scallops in ginger and herbs, duck in rosemary honey, and lightly marbled Charolais beef. Lunches are a bargain and the staff is flexible—if you want one main course or two starters instead of the full prix fixe menu, just ask. For the best views, request a window seat next to the water. ⊠ *Meestraat 9* ☎ *050/33–36–59* ⊕ *www.chezolivier.be* ⊟ *AE, MC, V* ☺ *Closed Thurs. and Sun. No lunch Sat.*

$$$$ ✕**De Karmeliet**. This stately, 18th-century house with a graceful English
FRENCH garden is a world-renowned culinary landmark. Owner-chef Geert Van
Fodor's Choice Hecke's inventive kitchen changes the menu every two months; you
★ might be offered goose liver with truffled potatoes or cod carpaccio with asparagus. The waitstaff perfectly choreographs each course with a cool professionalism in keeping with the restaurant's formal ambience. The wine cave plumbs the best of international vintages. ⊠ *Langestraat 19* ☎ *050/33–82–59* ⊕ *www.dekarmeliet.be* ⌂ *Reservations essential* ⚏ *Jacket required* ⊟ *AE, DC, MC, V* ☺ *Closed Sun. and Mon.*

$$–$$$ ✕**De Torre**. For traditional Belgian food at honest prices, this is the
BELGIAN place. From noon until 10 PM, Flemish stew, tomato with shrimp, mussels, or fillet of sole are served as they are in many Flemish homes. The 18th-century house is decorated in Art Deco style, and the sunny terrace has a lovely view of the Reien. ⊠ *Langestraat 8* ☎ *050/34–29–46* ⊕ *www.de-torre.com* ⊟ *MC, V* ☺ *Closed Mon. Apr.–Sept.; Mon. and Tues. Oct.–Mar.*

$$$$ ✕**De Visscherie**. To find this popular seafood restaurant overlooking the
SEAFOOD Vismarkt, look for the modern sculpture of a fisherman and the large
★ fish hanging from its balcony. Business at the busy outdoor terrace has been going strong for more than 25 years. Try one of the turbot variations, monkfish with Ganda ham and melon, or the langoustines with mozzarella, herbs, and sun-dried tomatoes. If you can't decide, order the restaurant's signature dish: waterzooi with saffron. ⊠ *Vismarkt 8* ☎ *050/33–02–12* ⊕ *www.visscherie.be* ⊟ *AE, MC, V* ☺ *Closed Tues.*

$$$–$$$$ ✕**Le Mystique**. The Hotel Heritage, long established as a romantic hide-
FRENCH away close to the Markt square, now offers a romantic place to dine, too. The elegant dining room dates from 1869; its high ceilings, chandeliers, and linen tablecloths create a refined atmosphere, perfect for quiet conversation. French Chef Jérôme Papin creates exquisite modern French cuisine using the freshest seasonal ingredients. There are some permanent à la carte choices, but the popular option is to let the chef decide for you and go for the monthly menu, available in four, five, or six courses, each one with a carefully matched wine. ⊠ *Niklaas Desparsstraat 11* ☎ *050/44–44–44* ⊟ *AE, DC, MC, V* ☺ *Closed Sun. and Mon.*

$ ✕**Lotus**. The neat dining room, with its lines of flower-topped tables, fills
VEGETARIAN up quickly at this popular vegetarian café. The menu changes weekly but always has small and large plates; you might try a four-cheese quiche, a basil and beetroot salad, or curried veggies. Whatever the combination,

it's delicious and well presented. Don't miss the desserts; the lemon pie is particularly good. ⊠ *Wapenmakersstraat 5* ☏ *050/33–10–78* ⊟ *No credit cards* ⊘ *Closed Sun. and last 2 wks in July. No dinner.*

$$$–$$$$
CONTINENTAL
✕ **Spinola.** This canal-house restaurant by the Jan van Eyck statue is a real charmer. From an intimate main dining room, an iron staircase leads to the upper tables; the open kitchen is in back. Here, chef-owners Sam and Vicky Storme cook up rich Burgundian cuisine: fresh game, goose liver, shellfish, and pigeon with truffles. Dinner by candlelight is the ultimate extravagance, with a choice of some 300 wines. ⊠ *Spinolarei 1* ☏ *050/34–17–85* ⊕ *www.spinola.be* ⊟ *DC, MC, V* ⊘ *Closed Sun and Mon.*

WHERE TO STAY

Brugge is a popular weekend escape, full as it is of romantic suites and secluded hideaways. You'll find old-fashioned accents at most hotels in the "City of Swans." The tourist office can help you make reservations for lodgings in Brugge and the surrounding countryside.

$–$$
☷ **Bryghia.** This restored German-Austrian trade center is a handsome 15th-century landmark. Outside, the brick walls are lined with paned windows and flower boxes; inside, the hotel is warmed by pastel floral fabrics and beech cabinets. Bedrooms are simple yet comfortable, and the public rooms include small sitting areas and a beamed, slate-floor breakfast salon. **Pros:** efficient service; excellent buffet breakfast. **Cons:** a fair way from the main sights. ⊠ *Oosterlingenplein 4,* ☏ *050/33–80–59* ⊕ *www.bryghiahotel.be* ↪ *18 rooms* ⚭ *In-room: safe, refrigerator. In-hotel: bar, parking (paid)* ⊟ *AE, DC, V* †⚭| *BP.*

¢
☷ **De Pauw.** From the brick exterior covered with climbing roses to the fresh flowers and doilies in the breakfast parlor, this is a welcoming little inn, set in a square opposite Sint-Gillis church. Rooms have names rather than numbers to give them a homier feel, and needlepoint cushions and old framed prints add to the warmth. Breakfast, which includes cold cuts, cheese, and six kinds of bread, is served on pretty china. **Pros:** good value; cozy atmosphere. **Cons:** tiny bathrooms; very steep stairs. ⊠ *Sint-Gilliskerkhof 8* ☏ *050/33–71–18* ⊕ *www.hoteldepauw.be* ↪ *8 rooms* ⚭ *In-hotel: parking (free)* ⊟ *MC, V* †⚭| *BP.*

$$$–$$$$
★
☷ **De Tuileriëen.** Patrician tastes suffuse this 15th-century mansion. The décor is genteel, with reproduction antique furniture, Venetian glass windows, and weathered marble complemented by mixed-print fabrics and wall coverings in celadon, slate, and cream. Rooms are romantic, with marble-accented bathrooms, although those with canal views receive some traffic noise; courtyard rooms are quieter. The firelit bar is filled with cozy tartan wing chairs, and the neo-Baroque breakfast salon features a coffered ceiling. When the weather holds, breakfast is served on the terrace. **Pros:** turndown service includes chocolates; well-equipped spa. **Cons:** Wi-Fi signal patchy in some rooms. ⊠ *Dijver 7* ☏ *050/34–36–91* ⊕ *www.hoteltuilerieen.com* ↪ *22 rooms, 23 suites* ⚭ *In-room: safe, refrigerator, Wi-Fi. In-hotel: bar, pool, spa, bicycles, laundry service, parking (paid)* ⊟ *AE, DC, MC, V* †⚭| *BP.*

9

You'll find no shortage of eating and drinking establishments on the Markt.

$–$$
★
Egmond. Play lord of the manor at this refurbished 18th-century house near the Begijnhof. Public rooms have hearths and chimneypieces, beamed ceilings, and dark-wood moldings. Breakfast is served in an oak-beam hall with a Delft-tile fireplace. Each room has a special period feature or two, and all are airy, with garden views. You can stroll the perimeter of the Minnewater park; the hotel is only 10 minutes' walk from the bustle of central Brugge. **Pros:** nonsmoking hotel; pretty garden. **Cons:** rooms book up quickly. ⌧ *Minnewater 15* ☎ *050/34–14–45* ⊕ *www.egmond.be* ⤶ *8 rooms* ⌂ *In-room: safe, Wi-Fi. In-hotel: parking (paid)* ▤ *MC, V* ¶◯¶ *BP.*

¢–$
☺
Fevery. This child-friendly hotel is part of a comfortable family home in a quiet corner of Brugge. There's enough clutter to make you feel like you never left your own house, and even a baby monitor so parents can relax with a drink downstairs after putting a child to bed. Rooms are small and basic, but provide anything a modest traveler needs. Families of four should ask for the double room for €125. **Pros:** family-friendly atmosphere; owner knows the best local attractions; good value. **Cons:** rooms quite basic. ⌧ *Collaert Mansionstraat 3* ☎ *050/33–12–69* ⊕ *www.hotelfevery.be* ⤶ *10 rooms* ⌂ *In-room: Wi-Fi. In-hotel: bar, parking (free)* ▤ *MC, V* ¶◯¶ *BP.*

$$–$$$$
Fodor's Choice
★
Hotel Heritage. Once a private mansion, this 19th-century building has been converted into a lovely hotel. Guest rooms are in keeping with the building's heritage—elegant, with chandeliers, reproduction antique furniture, and warm fabrics in reds and golds. And it's well located, just a few minutes' walk from the Markt. There's a sauna and a fitness room in the vaulted cellar, and a small sun deck on the top floor. During the day the breakfast room transforms into La Mystique restaurant.

Pros: helpful staff; grand building; great location. **Cons:** some rooms are quite small. ☒ *Niklaas Desparsstraat 11* ☎ *050/44–44–44* ⊕ *www. hotel-heritage.be* ⤳ *20 rooms, 4 suites* ☖ *In-room: safe, refrigerator, DVD, Wi-Fi. In-hotel: restaurant, bar, gym, Wi-Fi, parking (paid)* ▭ *AE, DC, MC, V* ⓣⓞⓘ *BP.*

$$–$$$$ ⌂ **Martin's Relais Oud Huis Amsterdam**. Five noble, 17th-century houses
★ in the elegant Hanseatic district combine the grace of another era with the polish of a modern, first-class property. Parts of this town house date to the 1300s, and the owners have preserved such antique details as tooled Cordoba leather wallpaper, rough-hewn rafters, and Delft tiles. Rooms with canal views overlook the busy street; back rooms with red rooftop views are quieter. **Pros:** great 17th-century exteriors; eye-popping antiques; pleasant bar. **Cons:** some rooms can be noisy. ☒ *Genthof 4a* ☎ *050/34–18–10* ⊕ *www.martins-hotels.be* ⤳ *44 rooms* ☖ *In-room: safe, refrigerator, Wi-Fi. In-hotel: bar, parking (paid)* ▭ *AE, DC, MC, V* ⓣⓞⓘ *BP.*

$$$–$$$$ ⌂ **Relais Bourgondisch Cruyce**. This truly magnificent hotel is situated
Fodor's Choice in one of the most romantic corners of Brugge. Some rooms overlook
★ the Reien, and all of them, whether with classic or modern furnishings, live up to the highest expectations. Bathrooms are large and well equipped; all rooms have a large flat-screen TV. **Pros:** a fairy-tale setting; great views of the water; lovely décor throughout. **Cons:** limited parking (reserve in advance). ☒ *Wollestraat 41* ☎ *050/33–79–26* ⊕ *www. relaisbourgondischcruyce.be* ⤳ *16 rooms* ☖ *In-hotel: restaurant* ▭ *AE, MC, V.*

$$$–$$$$ ⌂ **Walburg**. One of Brugge's grandest 19th-century town houses is now a hotel, only a few blocks from the Burg. It was built by Isidoor Alderwerelt, the same architect who finished the Palais de Justice in Brussels, and most of its original features were kept when the house was renovated in 1997. The lovely rooms, tastefully decorated in different color schemes with antique furniture and marble bathrooms, are a generous 750 square feet. Classical music welcomes you in the marble lobby and you can easily imagine Viennese-style balls taking place in the dining room. **Pros:** exceptionally large rooms; speedy room service; excellent breakfasts. **Cons:** limited parking. ☒ *Boomgaardstraat 13–15* ☎ *050/34–94–14* ⊕ *www.hotelwalburg.be* ⤳ *18 rooms, 1 suite* ☖ *In-room: safe, refrigerator, Wi-Fi. In-hotel: restaurant, bar* ▭ *AE, DC, MC, V* ⊘ *Closed Jan.* ⓣⓞⓘ *BP.*

NIGHTLIFE AND THE ARTS

The West Flanders Cultural Service hosts a helpful Web site, **www. tinck.be,** that lists upcoming arts events, museum exhibits, concerts, and the like.

THE ARTS
The monthly *Agenda Brugge*, available in English, gives details of all events in the city; you can get a copy at the tourist office. Listings for events and movie screenings are also published in the local Flemish newspaper *Exit*, available at bookstores and in the public library. Movies are invariably screened in their original language with Flemish

subtitles, and there are plenty of English-language films on the local screens. The **Concertgebouw Brugge** (⊠ *'t Zand 34* ☏ *050/47–69–99* ⊕), stages music, dance, and theater events with both national and international acts.

NIGHTLIFE

Brugge is not the liveliest city at night, but there are a handful of good hangouts.

Pubs, mostly catering to an under-30 clientele, are clustered around the Eiermarkt, at the back of the Markt. Arguably the most famous of the lot, **Brugs Beertje** (⊠ *Kemelstraat 5* ☏ *050/33–96–16*), stocks around 300 different beers. There are also several bars attracting a younger crowd at 't Zand, such as **Ma Rica Rokk** (⊠ *'t Zand 6–8* ☏ *050/33–24–34*), where dance beats pound all through the night. The **Cactus Club** (⊠ *Magdalen-astraat 27* ☏ *050/33–20–14*) is the original Brugge venue for pop, rock, folk, and blues acts. It also hosts some comedy nights, occasionally in English. A somewhat older crowd gathers in **De Stoepa** (⊠ *Oostmeers 124* ☏ *050/33–04–54*), a pub and restaurant with a slight Eastern touch in its setting as well as on its menu. Here you can enjoy couscous, beef teriyaki, and several spicy dishes. There are many gay-friendly bars in Brugge. For an update on the best hangouts for gays, visit the Gaybruges Web site (⊕ *www.j-h.be/gaybruges*).

SHOPPING

Most shops in Brugge are open Monday to Saturday 9 or 10 AM to 6; some souvenir shops are also open on Sunday. Although there are a couple of tacky tourist stores, Brugge has many trendy boutiques and shops, especially along Nordzandstraat, as well as Steenstraat and Vlamingstraat, both of which branch off from the Markt. Ter Steeghere mall, which links the Burg with Wollestraat, deftly integrates a modern development into the historic center. The largest and most pleasant mall is the Zilverpand off Zilverstraat, where 30-odd shops cluster in Flemish gable houses around two courtyards fringed with sidewalk cafés.

MARKETS

The Markt is the setting for the weekly **Woensdag Markt** (Wednesday Market), with vegetables, fruit, flowers, specialty cheeses, and hams. (Occasionally, if there is a major event taking place on the Markt, the market moves to the Burg.) Brugge's biggest market is the **Zaterdag Markt** (Saturday Market) on 't Zand, selling all kinds of cheeses, hams, and cooked meats, as well as some clothing and household items. The **Vismarkt** (Fish Market) is held, appropriately, on the Vismarkt, daily except Sunday and Monday. All three markets are morning events, from 8 to approximately 12:30. On weekends from March 15 through November 15 there's a **flea market** open throughout the day along the Dijver.

Travel Smart Amsterdam and the Netherlands

WORD OF MOUTH

"Just returned from Netherlands, Germany, France. American credit card accepted almost everywhere except in machines. Tourist shops and fast food shops sometimes require purchases of a certain amount before accepting cards—perhaps 5–10 euro."

—crckwc1

GETTING HERE AND AROUND

With a history as venerable as Holland's, it's no surprise many of the country's *straten*, or streets take their name from its famous sons and daughters. In Amsterdam, for one example, Hugo de Grootstraat honors Delft's noted lawyer-philosopher (*straat* is "street"). In addition, you get all the variations: Hugo de Grootkade (*kade* is a street running parallel to a canal), Hugo de Grootplein (*plein* is "square"), ad infinitum. In Amsterdam, there's even an Eerste, Tweede, and Derde (first, second, and third) Hugo de Grootstraat. Of course, kings and queens feature too: Wilhelminastraat is named after Queen Wilhelmina, the grandmother of the current queen, Beatrix.

Other geographical terms to keep in mind are a *dwarsstraat*, which runs perpendicular to another street or canal, such as Leidsestraat and Leidsedwarsstraat. A *straatje* is a small street; a *weg* is a road; a *gracht* a canal; a *steeg* a very small street; a *laan* is a lane or avenue. *Baan* is another name for a road, not quite a highway, but busier than an average street. Note that in the Netherlands, the house number always comes after the street name on addresses.

The Dutch also have an infinite range of names for bodies of water, from *gracht* to *singel* to *kanaal* (all meaning "canal"). The difference between a singel and a gracht is hard to define, even for a Dutch person. In fact, the names can be doubly confusing because sometimes there is *no* water at all—many grachten have been filled in by developers to make room for houses, roads, and so on. Near harbor areas you'll notice *havens* (harbors), named after the goods that ships used to bring in, like in Rotterdam, *Wijnhaven* (Wine Harbor) and *Vishaven* (Fish Harbor).

Amsterdam streets radiate outward from Centraal Station; in general, street numbers go up as you move away from the station. Don't let common address abbreviations confuse you. BG stands for *Begane Grond* (ground floor); SOUT for *Souterrain* (basement); HS for *Huis* (a ground-floor apartment or main entry). Common geographical abbreviations include *str.* for *straat* (street); *gr.* for *gracht* (canal); and *pl.* for *plein* (square). For example: Leidsestr., or Koningspl.

Addresses in Belgium are segregated by language throughout the country; they hew to the official language of each destination. The only place where the street names are in both French and Flemish is the officially bilingual capital, Brussels. Addresses are written with the street name first, followed by the number. Some common terms include: for street, *straat* in Flemish and *rue* in French; for square, *plein* or *place*. *Laan* or *avenue* means avenue as do *dreef* or *drève*. *Grote markt* or *grand place* indicates a market square, usually the historic center of town.

▌ AIR TRAVEL

The least expensive airfares to the Netherlands originate from the United Kingdom and other European countries, are priced for round-trip travel, and must usually be purchased in advance online. Airlines generally allow you to change your return date for a fee; most low-fare tickets, however, are nonrefundable.

EasyJet has low fares to Amsterdam flying in from Belfast, Edinburgh, Geneva, Glasgow, Liverpool, London (Gatwick and Luton), and Nice. Transavia flies to Amsterdam and Rotterdam from Barcelona, Nice, and numerous other cities. Ryanair flies to the southern Dutch city of Eindhoven from London, Stansted, and a dozen other cities around Europe. BMIBaby flies to Amsterdam from its hub in Nottingham (East Midlands Airport).

Consolidators and Low-Cost Airlines
Transavia (☏ *0900/0737 in the Netherlands* ⊕ *www.transavia.com*). **BMIBaby** (⊕ *www.*

omibaby.com). **EasyJet** (⊕ *www.easyjet.com*). Ryanair (⊕ *www.ryanair.com*).

Air Pass Info Discover Europe Airpass
☏ 800/788–0555 ⊕ *www.flybmi-canada.* com). **FlightPass** (*EuropebyAir* ☏ 888/321– 4737 ⊕ *www.europebyair.com*). **oneworld Visit Europe pass** (⊕ *www.oneworld.com*). **SkyTeam Europe Pass** (⊕ *www.skyteam.* com). **Star Alliance Europe Airpass** (⊕ *www.* staralliance.com).

Flying time to Amsterdam is 7 hours from New York, 8 hours from Chicago, 10½ hours from Los Angeles, 9 hours from Dallas, 6½ hours from Montreal, 9½ hours from Vancouver, and 20 hours from Sydney.

Always ask your carrier about its check-in policy. Plan to arrive at the airport about two hours before your scheduled departure time—and don't forget your passport. If you are flying within Europe, check with the airline to find out whether food is served on the flight. If you have dietary concerns, request special meals when booking. Low-cost airlines don't provide a complimentary in-flight service, but snacks and drinks can be purchased on board. For help picking the most comfortable seats, check out SeatGuru.com, which has information about specific seat configurations for different types of aircraft.

Smoking is prohibited on flights to or from Amsterdam. You are not required to reconfirm flights, but you should confirm the departure time by telephone if you made your reservation considerably in advance, as flight schedules are subject to change without notice.

Airlines and Airports Airline and Airport Links.com (⊕ *www.airlineandairportlinks.com*) has links to many of the world's airlines and airports.

Airline Security Issues Transportation Security Administration (⊕ *www.tsa.gov*) has answers for almost every question that might come up.

A 2004 European Union (EU) regulation standardized the rights of passengers to compensation in the event of flight cancellations or long delays. The law covers all passengers departing from an airport within the EU, and all passengers traveling into the EU on an EU carrier, unless they received assistance in the country of departure. Full details are available from the airlines, and are posted prominently in all EU airports.

AIRPORTS

Located 17 km (11 mi) southeast of Amsterdam, **Schiphol** (pronounced "Shh-kip-hole") is the main passenger airport for Holland. With the annual number of passengers using Schiphol exceeding 45 million, it is ranked among the world's top five best-connected airports. Several hotels, a service to aid passengers with disabilities, parking lots, and a main office of the Netherlands tourist board (in Schiphol Plaza and known as "HTi"—Holland Tourist Information) can all prove most useful. The comprehensive Schiphol telephone service, charged at €0.40 per minute, provides information about flight arrivals and departures as well as all transport and parking facilities.

Rotterdam is the biggest of the regional airport options and provides daily service to many European cities; another regional airport is **Eindhoven.** An increasing number of international charter flights and some budget carriers choose these airports, as benefits include shorter check-in times and ample parking. However, there are no rail links that connect such regional airports with their respective nearby cities, so passengers must resort to taking buses or taxis.

The major international airport serving Belgium is **Brussels Airport** at Zaventem, 14 km (9 mi) northeast of Brussels. It's sometimes called Zaventem for short. Brussels Airport has nonstop flights from the United States and Canada. It also has a wide range of amenities such as airport hotels, rental car agencies, travel agencies, and communications centers where you can either connect to the Internet via your own laptop or log on with a complimentary PC. Budget carrier Ryanair uses the smaller Brussels South Charleroi Airport, 46 km (29 mi) south of Brussels, as a hub. Though farther out of the city, it's connected to Brussels by a regular bus service.

Airport Information Holland Amsterdam Schiphol Airport (✉ *17 km [11 mi] southwest of Amsterdam* ☎ *0900/0141 [€0.40 per min]* ⊕ *www.schiphol.nl*). **Rotterdam The Hague Airport** (✉ *17 km [11 mi] northwest of Rotterdam* ☎ *010/446–3444* ⊕ *www.rotterdam-airport.nl*). **Eindhoven Airport** (✉ *8 km [5 mi] west of Eindhoven* ☎ *0900/9505 [€1.30 per call]* ⊕ *www.eindhovenairport.nl*).

Airport Information Belgium Brussels Airport (☎ *0900/70–000 [€0.45 per min]* ⊕ *www.brusselsairport.be*). **Brussels South Charleroi Airport** (☎ *071/25–12–11* ⊕ *www.charleroi-airport.com*).

GROUND TRANSPORTATION

The Schiphol Rail Link operates between the airport and the city 24 hours a day, with service to Amsterdam Centraal Station (usually abbreviated to Amsterdam CS), and to stations in the south of the city. From 6:30 AM to 12:30 AM, there are up to eight trains each hour to Centraal; at other times, there is one train every hour. The trip takes about 15–20 minutes and costs €3.70. Schiphol Station is beneath Schiphol Plaza. From Centraal Station, Trams 1 and 2 go to Leidseplein and the Museum Quarter. Keep in mind that Schiphol Station is one of Holland's busiest—make sure you catch the shuttle to Amsterdam and not a train heading to The Hague! As always, when arriving at Amsterdam's Centraal Station, keep an eye out for pickpockets. You may wish to hop aboard a tram or bus to get to your hotel, so go to one of the **Gemeentevervoerbedrijf (GVB) Amsterdam Municipal Transport** booths found in front of the Centraal Station. Here you can find directions, fare information, and schedules.

Connexxion Schiphol Hotel Shuttle operates a shuttle bus service between Amsterdam Schiphol Airport and all of the city's major hotels. The trip takes about a half hour and costs €15 one-way, or €24.50 return. Hours for this shuttle bus are 6:30 AM to 9 PM, every half hour.

Finally, there is a taxi stand directly in front of the arrival hall at Amsterdam Schiphol Airport. A service charge is included, but small additional tips are not unwelcome. New laws determine that taxi fares are now fixed from Schiphol to Amsterdam; depending on the neighborhood, a trip will cost around €40 or more. A new service that might be convenient for budget travelers who count every euro is the Schiphol Travel Taxi. The taxi needs to be booked at least 24 hours in advance and rides are shared, so the trip will take a bit longer as the taxi stops to pick up and drop off passengers. Make bookings via the Schiphol Web site. A shared taxi ride costs around €21.

Contacts

Connexxion Schiphol Hotel Shuttle (☎ *038/339–4741* ⊕ *www.schipholhotelshuttle.nl*). **Schiphol Rail Link** (☎ *0900/9292 [€0.70 per min]* ⊕ *www.9292ov.nl*). **Schiphol Travel Taxi** (⊕ *www.schiphol.nl*).

FLIGHTS

When flying internationally to the Netherlands, you usually choose between a domestic carrier, the national flag carrier of the country, and a foreign carrier from a third country. You may, for example, choose to fly KLM Royal Dutch Airlines to the Netherlands for the basic reason that, as the national flag carrier, it has the greatest number of nonstop flights. Domestic carriers offer connections to smaller destinations. Third-party carriers may have a price advantage.

KLM and its global alliance partner Delta Air Lines—together with their regional partner airlines—fly from Amsterdam's Schiphol Airport to more than 400 destinations in more than 80 countries worldwide. Nearly 100 of those are European destinations, with three to four daily flights to most airports and up to 17 flights a day to London alone. Delta now handles all reservations and ticket office activities on behalf of KLM in the United States and Canada, with KLM's biggest North American hubs in Detroit and Minneapolis, and Memphis, New York, and Washington, D.C., among its gateways. KLM's direct flights connect Amsterdam to Atlanta, Los Angeles, and Miami, and numerous others. Including connections via KLM's hubs, the airline flies to more than 120 destinations in the United States from Amsterdam. In Canada, KLM serves Montreal, Toronto, and Vancouver. For more information, contact the airline at one of the reservation numbers below. For further information about schedules and special fare promotions, go to KLM's Web site.

Other international carriers include American Airlines, Continental Airlines, United Airlines, and US Airways. Dutch charter airline Martinair has direct flights to Amsterdam from Orlando and Miami. None of these carriers makes a transatlantic flight to any of the Netherlands' regional airports. If your carrier offers Rotterdam as a final destination, for example, you fly into Amsterdam, then transfer. KLM Cityhopper offers flights connecting Amsterdam with the smaller regional airports. Transavia Airlines flies from Amsterdam and Rotterdam to a number of European destinations, and many other carriers link European capitals with Amsterdam. EasyJet has budget flights to Amsterdam from several European destinations; Ryanair offers a similar service out of Eindhoven Airport. Check online or with your travel agent for details.

SN Brussels Airlines is Belgium's foremost carrier, with routes to the United States, Africa, and all over Europe. Low-cost carrier Ryanair operates an ever-expanding network of routes out of its hub at Brussels South Charleroi Airport. This can be a very economical way of getting around

Europe, and you'll get the best deals if you book well ahead.

Airline Contacts American Airlines (☏ 800/433–7300, 02/711–9969 in Belgium for service in Flemish, 02/711–9977 for service in French, 207/365–0777 in U.K. within London, 8457/789–789 outside London ⊕ www. aa.com). **British Airways** (☏ 800/247–9297 in U.S., 0870/850–9850 in U.K., 02/717–3217 in Belgium, 020/346–9559 in the Netherlands ⊕ www.britishairways.com). **Continental Airlines** (☏ 800/523–3273 for U.S. and Mexico reservations, 800/231–0856 for international reservations, 02/643–3939 in Belgium, 0845/607–6760 in U.K., 020/346–9381 in Holland ⊕ www.continental.com). **Delta Airlines** (☏ 800/221–1212 for U.S. reservations, 800/241–4141 for international reservations, 02/711–9799 in Belgium, 0800/414–767 in U.K., 020/201–3536 in Holland ⊕ www. delta.com). **KLM Royal Dutch Airlines** (☏ 070/222–747 in Belgium, 300/303–747 in Australia, 020/474–7747 in the Netherlands, 09/309–1792 in New Zealand, 0870/507–4074 in U.K. ☏ 800/447–4747 for Northwest/KLM sales office in U.S. and Canada ⊕ www.klm. com). **SN Brussels Airlines** (☏ 516/622–2248 in U.S., 0870/735–2345 in U.K., 070/351–111 in Belgium ⊕ www.flysn.com). **United Airlines** (☏ 800/864–8331 for U.S. reservations, 800/538–2929 for international reservations, 02/713–3600 in Belgium, 020/201–3708 in Holland ⊕ www.united.com).

▌ BOAT TRAVEL

International ferries link Holland with the United Kingdom. There are two daily Stena line crossings between the **Hoek van Holland** (Corner of Holland, an industrial shipping area west of Rotterdam) and Harwich, on the car ferry, taking approximately six and a half hours. The overnight crossing takes about seven hours. These are the only ferry crossings that can be booked at the international travel window in large railway stations. There is one P&O Ferries overnight crossing between the Europoort in Rotterdam and Hull, which takes about 12 hours, and one DFDS Seaways overnight crossing from Newcastle to IJmuiden, in Amsterdam, taking 15 hours.

An extensive domestic ferry system serves Holland. DFDS Seaways is a leading carrier. Ferries run from several locations, linking the Mainland to the Frisian Islands. Ferries also cross the IJsselmeer.

Hire your own boat or take a guided city canal tour of Amsterdam, Leiden, or Delft; alternatively, take a harbor tour to **check out Rotterdam's extensive Europoort,** the world's biggest harbor, and the flood barrier. There are pedestrian ferries behind Amsterdam's Centraal Station across the IJ. *For more specific information about guided tours, see individual regional chapters.*

In Belgium, Transeuropa Ferries has services between Ramsgate and Oostende, with up to five daily round-trips. Crossings take around four hours. P&O Ferries operates overnight ferry services once daily from Hull to Zeebrugge. Schedules and fares fluctuate between low (winter) and high (summer) season. Travel agencies in the United Kingdom and in Belgium sell tickets and provide exact fares and schedules. Five-day excursion fares are significantly less expensive than last-minute bookings. These must be booked at least seven days in advance.

From the U.K. to Holland or Belgium
DFDS Seaways (✉ *Sluisplein 33, IJmuiden* ☎ *0255/546–666* 🖷 *0255/546–655* ⊕ *www.dfdsseaways.com).* **P&O Ferries** (*In Holland* ✉ *Beneluxhaven, Havennummer 5805, Rotterdam/Europoort* ☎ *020/200–8333* ⊕ *www.poferries.com.* **Stena Line** (*In Holland* ✉ *Hoek van Holland Terminal, Stationsweg 10, Hoek van Holland* ☎ *0174/315–800, 0900/8123 booking [€0.10 per min]* 🖷 *0174/389–389* ⊕ *www.stenaline.nl*).

Boat and Ferry Information within Holland
DFDS Seaways (✉ *Sluisplein 33, IJ muiden* ☎ *0255/546–666* 🖷 *0255/546–655* ⊕ *www.dfdsseaways.com*).

▎BUS TRAVEL

The bus and tram systems within Holland provide excellent transport links within cities. Frequent bus services are available in all towns and cities; trams run in Amsterdam, The Hague, between Delft and The Hague, and in Rotterdam. Amsterdam and Rotterdam also have subways, referred to as the metro. Amsterdam's metro system has four lines, running southeast, northwest and southwest; Rotterdam's metro system has five lines (three east to west, one north to south, and one connecting to The Hague), which extend into the suburbs and cross in the city center for easy transfers.

Several large companies provide bus and tram services across the country, including Connexxion, BBA, and Arriva. GVB provides additional services in Amsterdam; HTM in The Hague; GVU in Utrecht; and RET in Rotterdam. There are maps of each city's network in most shelters. Buses are clean and easy to use, and bus lanes (shared only with taxis) remain uncongested, ensuring that you travel more swiftly than other traffic in rush hour.

To get around by bus, tram, or metro in Amsterdam and Rotterdam, you'll need an *OV-chipkaart* (public transport chip card)—a new electronic payment system, which you hold up to a detector each time you board and leave any bus or tram. Bought preloaded from metro, train and bus stations, from some magazine kiosks, or from drivers, these credit card–sized tickets can be topped up with credit from machines in the stations and are debited according to the distance traveled. Visit the Web site www.ov-chipkaart.nl or call the help desk ☎ *0900/500–6010* for more information.

The OV-chipkaart can also be used in other cities in the Netherlands, and on trains (note that the check-in/check-out detectors for the trains are clearly marked and in the railway stations, not on board). For now, in places other than Amsterdam and Rotterdam, the new chip card system operates in parallel with the old paper strippenkaart system (below). Eventually the latter will be phased out everywhere, as will paper train tickets, but the process is a very slow one and the end still years away.

For cities where the strippenkaart (a ticket containing 15 or 45 "strips") is still valid—at this writing, including The Hague, Haarlem, Delft, and Utrecht—each city is divided into zones, and the fare you pay depends on the number of zones you travel through. Each journey you make costs one strip plus the number of zones you travel through. A small city is one zone (two strips), but to travel across The Hague takes you through four (five strips) zones. These zones are displayed on transport maps. When you get on a bus, you show the driver your strippenkaart and simply say where your final destination is, or the number of zones you plan to travel through, and let him or her stamp the strips. You can also buy tickets for individual journeys from the driver, although this works out to be more expensive.

In some trams you have to stamp your ticket yourself in the small yellow machines found near the doors. Count the number of strips you need (note that most tourists will be traveling within a one-zone area and therefore the tickets they buy directly from the driver only contain two or three strips), fold your ticket at the bottom of the last strip required, and stamp the final strip in the machine. A stamp on a strip uses that strip, and the strips above it. Two or more people can travel on the same strippenkaart, but the appropriate number of units must be stamped for each person. The stamp indicates the zone where the journey started, and the time, and remains valid for one hour, so you can travel within the zones you have stamped until the hour is up.

Teams of ticket inspectors occasionally make spot checks. This doesn't happen often, but if you are checked and you don't have a stamped strippenkaart or your OV-chipkaart hasn't been checked in, you face a fine.

Belgium has an extensive network of reasonably priced urban and intercity buses. STIB/MIVB (Société des Transports Intercommunaux de Bruxelles/Maatschappij voor het Intercommunaal Vervoer te Brussel) covers service around Brussels and to other towns in the region. De Lijn runs buses in Flanders, including Antwerp, Brugge, and Gent. Fares and schedules are available at the STIB and De Lijn sales offices or at local travel agencies. Buy tickets from the bus driver as you board.

Bus Information for the Netherlands and Belgium Information on all public transportation, including schedules, fares for **trains, buses, trams, and ferries** in the Netherlands (☎ 0900/9292 [€0.70 per min] ⊕ www.9292ov. nl). **De Lijn** (☎ 070/220–200 [€0.30 per min] ⊕ www.delijn.be). **STIB/MIVB** (☎ 0900/10–310 ⊕ www.stib.be).

▌ CAR TRAVEL

A network of well-maintained highways and other roads covers the Netherlands, making car travel convenient, although traffic is exceptionally heavy around the bigger cities, especially on the roads in the Randstad, and those approaching the North Sea beaches on summer weekends. There are no tolls on roads or highways. Major European highways leading into Amsterdam from the borders are E19 from western Belgium; E25 from eastern Belgium; and E22, E30, and E35 from Germany. Follow the signs for *Centrum* to reach the center of the city. At rush hour, traffic is dense but not so dense as to become stationary.

In Canada Canadian Automobile Association (*CAA;* ☎ 613/247–0117).

In the U.S. American Automobile Association (☎ 800/564–6222).

RENTAL CARS

The major car-rental firms have convenient booths at Schiphol and all the region's airports, but the airports charge rental companies a fee that is passed on to customers, so you'll get a better deal at downtown locations. Consider also whether you want to get off a transatlantic flight and into an unfamiliar car in an unfamiliar city. You must be at least 21 years old to rent cars from most agencies. Some agencies require renters to be 25. You can drive in the Netherlands and Belgium with a valid U.S. driver's license.

Most major American rental-car companies have offices or affiliates in the Netherlands, but the rates are generally better if you make an advance reservation from abroad rather than from within Holland. Rates vary from company to company; daily rates start at approximately €30 for a one-day rental, €60 for a three-day rental, and €150 for a week. This may not include collision insurance or airport fee. Tax is included and weekly rates often include unlimited mileage. Most cars in Europe are stick shift. An automatic transmission will cost a little extra. Rental cars are European brands and range from economy, such as a Ford Ka, to luxury, such as a Mercedes. They will always be in good condition. It is also possible to rent minivans.

Autoverhuur (car rental) in Holland is best for exploring the center, north, or east of the country, but is to be avoided in the heavily urbanized northwest, known as the Randstad, where the public transport infrastructure is excellent. Signage on country roads is usually pretty good, but be prepared to patiently trail behind cyclists blithely riding two abreast (which is illegal), even when the road is not wide enough for you to pass.

GASOLINE

Many of the gas stations in the Netherlands (especially those on the high-traffic motorways) are open 24 hours. Those that aren't open 24 hours generally open early in the morning, around 6 or 7 AM, and close late at night, around 10 or 11 PM. Unleaded regular costs about €1.45 per liter, and major credit cards are widely accepted. If you pay with cash and need a receipt, ask for a *bon*.

Gas stations are also plentiful throughout Belgium. Major credit cards are widely accepted. If you pay with cash and need a receipt, ask for a *reçu* (French) or *ontvangstbewijs* (Flemish). Unleaded regular costs around €1.42 per liter—slightly less than in the Netherlands. Gas stations are usually self-service. Unless you have a debit card from a Belgian bank, you must pay an attendant. On Sundays and late at night, some stations may be unmanned and use a prepayment system, so look for a gas station on a major highway, which should be open around the clock.

PARKING

Parking space is at a premium in Amsterdam as in most towns, especially in the Centrum (historic town center), which has narrow, one-way streets and large areas given over to pedestrians. Most neighborhoods are metered from 9 AM to 7 PM, so it is a good idea (if not the only option) to leave your car only in designated parking areas. *Parkeren* (parking lots) are indicated by a white P in a blue square. Illegally parked cars in Amsterdam get clamped by the **Dienst Parkeerbeheer** (Parking Authority) and, after 24 hours, if you haven't paid for the clamp to be removed, towed. You'll be towed immediately in some areas of the city. If you get clamped, a sticker on the windshield indicates where you should go to pay the fine (which can be more than €100).

ROAD CONDITIONS

Holland has an excellent road network, but there is a great deal of traffic using it every day, as you might expect from a country with a high population density. In cities, you will usually be driving on narrow one-way streets and sharing the road with other cars, buses, trams, and bicyclists, so remain alert at all times. When driving on smaller roads in cities, you must yield to traffic coming from the right. Traffic lights are located before intersections, rather than after intersections as in the United States. Traffic circles re very popular and come in all sizes. Driving outside of cities is very easy; roads re very smooth and clearly marked with signs. Traffic during peak hours (7 AM–9 AM and 4 PM–7 PM) is constantly plagued with *files* (traffic jams), especially in the western part of the country. If you are going to drive here, you must be assertive. Drivers are very aggressive; they tailgate and change lanes at very high speeds. All road signs use the international driving symbols. Electronic message boards are used on some freeways to warn of traffic jams and to slow traffic down to 90, 70, or 50 kph.

A network of well-maintained, well-lighted highways (*snelweg* in Flemish, *autoroute* in French) and other roads also covers Belgium, making car travel convenient. There are no tolls. Under good conditions, you should be able to travel on highways at an average of about 120 kph (75 mph), but congestion around Brussels and Antwerp can slow things considerably. If you are traveling in Belgium outside of Brussels, be prepared for signs to change language with alarming frequency. *Uitrit* is Flemish for exit; the French is *sortie*. City driving in Belgium is challenging because of chronic double parking and lack of street-side parking. Beware of trams in some cities, and of slick cobblestone streets in rainy weather.

ROADSIDE EMERGENCIES

If you haven't joined a motoring organization, the **ANWB** (Royal Dutch Touring Club) offers 24-hour road assistance in the Netherlands. If you aren't a member, you can call the ANWB after breaking down, but you must pay a €150 on-the-spot membership charge. Emergency crews may not accept credit cards or checks when they pick you up. If your automobile association is affiliated with the **Alliance International du Tourisme** (AIT), and you have proof of membership, you are entitled to free help. To call for assistance push the help button on any yellow ANWB phone located every km (½ mi) on highways, and a dispatch

operator immediately figures out where you are. Alternatively, ring their 24-hour emergency line or their information number for details about their road rescue service.

If you break down on the highway in Belgium, look for emergency telephones located at regular intervals. The emergency telephones are connected to an emergency control room that can send a tow truck. It is also possible to take out emergency automobile insurance that covers all of your expenses in case of a breakdown on the road.

Contacts in Amsterdam and Holland ANWB **(Royal Dutch Touring Club)** (☎ *088/269–2888 emergency number, 088/269–2222 office number* ⊕ *www.anwb.nl*).

Contacts in Belgium Europ Assistance (☎ *02/533-7575*). **Touring Secours** (☎ *070/344-777* ⊕ *www.touring.be*).

RULES OF THE ROAD

Driving is on the right in the Netherlands and Belgium, and regulations are largely as in the United States. Speed limits are 120 kph (75 mph) on superhighways and 50 kph (30 mph) on urban roads. Some cities also have 30 kph (20 mph) zones around schools. In the Netherlands the limit on standard rural highways is 80 kph (50 mph), or 100 kph (62 mph) if the traffic in each direction is separated by a central barrier. In Belgium the limit is 90 kph (55 mph) on all rural highways.

For safe driving, go with the flow, stay in the slow lane unless you want to pass, and make way for faster cars wanting to pass you. In cities and towns, approach crossings with care; local drivers may exercise the principle of priority for traffic from the right with some abandon. Although the majority of cyclists observe the stoplights and general road signs, many expect you, even as a driver, to give way. The latest ruling states that unless otherwise marked, all traffic coming from the right has priority, even bicycles. The driver and front-seat passenger are required to wear seat belts, and other passengers are required to wear available seat belts.

Using a handheld mobile phone is illegal while driving, but you are allowed to drive while using a headset or earpiece. Turning right on a red light is not permitted. Fines for driving after drinking are heavy, including the suspension of license and the additional possibility of six months' imprisonment.

Fog can be a danger on highways in late fall and winter. In such cases, it is obligatory to use your fog lights.

Also be aware that on some Belgian highways, drivers (truck drivers are especially bad) don't always use their indicators and can pull out to change lane at high speed without warning—stay alert to this.

▌PUBLIC TRANSPORTATION IN AMSTERDAM

METRO

Amsterdam has a full-fledged subway system, called the metro, but travelers will usually find trams and buses more convenient for getting around, as most metro stops are geared for city residents traveling to the outer suburbs. However, the Amsterdam metro can get you from point A to point C in a quantum leap—for instance, from Centraal Station (at the northern harbor edge of the city) to Amstel Station (a train station at the southeastern area of the city, with connections to many buses and trams)—much faster than a tram, which makes many stops along the way. You'll need an OV-chipkaart, used the same way as for other public transport.

Four metro lines, including the express tram (*sneltram*), serve Amsterdam and the surrounding suburbs. A fifth, the much-vaunted Nord-Zuid metro line, is still some years away after lengthy delays—and is the cause of all the heavy construction work you may see around Amsterdam Centraal railway station. Although many stops on the existing metro lines will not be of use to the tourist, several can prove

handy. Nieuwmarkt lets you off near the Red Light District and is near the famous sights of the Oude Zijde area. Waterlooplein is near the eastern edge of the Oude Zijde, stopping at the square where the Stadhuis-Muziektheater is located, and offers access to sights of the Jewish Quarter and the Plantage; a walk several blocks to the south leads you to the Eastern Canal Ring and its many historic houses. Wibautstraat is not too far from the Amstel River and provides access to the southern sectors of the city, including De Pijp. Amstel Station is a train station near the Amstel River in the southeastern area of the city, with connections to many buses and trams. Amsterdam Zuid/WTC (South/World Trade Center) is at the southern edge of Amsterdam Zuid (South) and rarely used by any tourists. VU (Vrije Universiteit) is in the suburb of Buitenveldert. It's possible to transfer from the metro to trains at several shared stops, either by crossing the platform or merely going outside to an adjacent train station. Line 50 (Ringlijn) travels from Isolaterweg in the northeastern part of the city to Gein, a southeastern suburb. Lines 51, 53, and 54 all start at Centraal Station and follow the same routes until they head into the suburbs. They ride as a subway from Centraal Station to Amstel Station, then whiz along the rest of the routes above ground, parting ways at Spaklerweg. The No. 51 passes through Buitenveldert, stopping at the VU (Vrij Universiteit) and continuing south into Amstelveen. The 53 passes Diemen and ends up southeast in Gaasperplas. The 54 also travels southeast and shares the rest of its route with the 50, passing through Holendrecht and ending at Gein.

TRAMS AND BUSES

Many tram and bus routes start from the hub at Centraal Station. A large bus depot is on the Marnixstraat, across from the main police station, and there's another one at Harlemmermeer station in the Overtoomseveld neighborhood of western Amsterdam. Trams and buses run from

.bout 6 AM to midnight daily. The tram routes, with a network of 130 km (80 mi) of track, make this characteristic form of transport more useful than the bus for most tourists. Night owls can make use of the hourly night-bus services, with double frequency on Friday and Saturday night, but routes are restricted.

Between stops, trams brake only when absolutely necessary, so listen for warning bells if you are walking or cycling near tramlines. Taxis use tramlines, but other cars are allowed to venture onto them only when turning right. The newer fleets of buses are cleaner, and therefore nicer to use, and bus lanes (shared only with taxis) remain uncongested, ensuring that you travel more swiftly than the rest of the traffic in rush hour. If the bus is very crowded, you may have to stand, so hold on to a handrail, as the buses can travel quite fast; to **avoid rush hour,** don't travel between 7:30 and 9 in the morning or between 4 and 6 in the afternoon. As with all urban systems of transportation, keep an eye out for pickpockets.

There are 16 tramlines servicing the city. Trams 1, 2, 4, 5, 9, 13, 16, 17, 24, and 25 all start and end their routes at Centraal Station. The most frequently used trams by visitors are the 1, 2, and 5, which stop at the big central Dam Square and, along with 6, 7, and 10, also stop at Leidseplein square. The numbers 2, 3, 5, and 12 will get you to Museumplein and the Museum District. Trams 5, 16, 24, and 25 travel through Amsterdam's chic Zuid district. The No. 4 tram stops at the RAI convention center and the No. 5 will take you to Station South/World Trade Center. The remaining lines pass through East and West Amsterdam and take you farther outside the center city Centrum to areas generally more off-the-beaten-track for tourists.

More than 30 GVB buses cover all the city's neighborhoods and are a good way to get closer to specific addresses. The Conexxion bus company operates about 50 different buses that will take you from Amsterdam to all areas of Holland. Most of these depart from Centraal Station. Buses 110 to 117 travel to the "folkloric" area of North Holland, just to the north of the city, where favorite tourist destinations include Volendam, Marken, Edam, Hoorn, and Broek in Waterland.

FERRIES

Four GVB ferry lines leave from Centraal Station, but not all are of interest to tourists. The Buiksloterwegveer leaves from Pier 7 behind Centraal Station every eight to 15 minutes, day and night. The ferry transports pedestrians, cyclists, and motorcyclists across the IJ channel to North Amsterdam. There is no fee for the service. North Amsterdam may prove to be less interesting than the refreshing trip, which takes about five minutes.

TICKETS

Besides the OV-chip*kaart* system, covered above, in Amsterdam you can also buy 24, 48, 72, and 96-hour travel-anywhere tickets (€7 for one day; €11.50 for two days; €15.50 for three days; €19.50 for four days), which cover all urban bus and streetcar routes. You can also buy chip cards from the driver that are valid for one hour of unlimited travel. Fares are often reduced for children ages four to 11 and for people who are 65 years or older.

The All Amsterdam Transport Pass costs €28 and entitles you to a day of unlimited travel on tram, bus, metro, and Canal Bus plus coupons worth about €150 for major attractions, snacks, etc. This pass can be purchased at the GVB ticket office in front of Centraal Station and at the main Canal Bus office at Prins Hendrikkade. The electronic *I amsterdam Card (⇨ Day Tours and Guides)*, provides free or discounted admission to many top attractions, plus a free canal round-trip, and free use of public transport. These can be bought online or from tourist offices in Amsterdam, and cost €38, 48, or 58 for 1, 2 or 3 days, respectively.

Contacts **GVB** (✉ *Prins Hendrikkade 108–114, Centrum* ☎ *0900/9292* ⊕ *www.gvb.nl*).

▮ TAXI IN AMSTERDAM

Vacant taxis on the move through the streets are often on call to their dispatcher. Occasionally, if you get lucky, they'll stop for you if you hail them, but officially the regular practice is to wait by a taxi stand or phone them. Taxi stands are at the major squares and in front of the large hotels. You can also call Taxicentrale, the main dispatching office. A 5-km (3-mi) ride will cost about €20. A new initiative in the city is the *Wieler Taxi* (bike taxi), which resembles a larger version of a child's pedal car and isn't very practical in the rain.

Taxicentrale Amsterdam (☎ *020/677–7777*). **Wielertaxi** (☎ *06/2824–7550*).

▮ TRAIN TRAVEL

Dutch trains are modern and the quickest way to travel between city centers. Services are relatively frequent, with a minimum of two departures per hour for each route, and often more. Although many Dutch people complain about delays, the trains usually run roughly on time. Most staff speak English. Reserving a seat is not possible.

Intercity trains can come double-decker; they only stop at major stations. *Sneltreins* (express trains) also have two decks but take in more stops, so they are a little slower. *Stoptreins* (local trains) are the slowest. Smoking is not permitted on trains, and only permitted in designated zones in stations.

On the train you have the choice of first or second class. First-class travel costs 50% more, and on local trains gives you a slightly larger seat in a compartment that is less likely to be full. At peak travel times, first-class train travel is worth the difference.

Train tickets for travel within the country can be purchased at the last minute. Normal tickets are either *enkele reis* (one-way) or *retour* (round-trip). Round-trip tickets cost approximately 75% of two single tickets. They are valid only on the day you buy them, unless you ask specifically for a ticket with a different date. You can get on and off at will at stops in between your destinations until midnight. You can also use the OV-chipkaart covered above, but remember to check in on the platform before you board, and to check out when you leave the train.

You cannot buy domestic train tickets in the Netherlands with credit cards or traveler's checks. If you don't have euros, bureau de change GWK has a branch at Amsterdam Centraal Station and all major stations throughout the country. You can also buy tickets at the yellow touch-screen ticket machines in every railway station. These machines accept debit cards with a four-digit PIN code, but not credit cards. Fares are slightly lower than if you visit a manned ticket desk. Note that you can't buy tickets aboard the trains, and you risk a hefty fine if you board and travel without one.

Train fares in Holland are lower than in most other European countries, but you can save money by looking into rail passes—there is a host of special saver tickets that make train travel even cheaper. Be aware, however, that if you don't plan to cover many miles, then you may as well buy individual tickets; a *dagkaart* (unlimited travel pass for one day) costs €45.40 second class, €77.20 first class, but it is almost impossible to rack up enough miles to make it worthwhile. If you're spending a long time in Holland and plan to do a lot of traveling, inquire about the *voordeelurenkaart* (discount hours card), available for all ages. It costs €49 and entitles the holder to a 40% discount on all first- and second-class tickets, when traveling after 9 AM, or at any time on weekends and in July and August. You need a residential address to apply for this ard, as well as ID. The card proper will ake between four and six weeks to be processed and arrive on your doorstep, out you are issued a valid card for the interim time.

If you are visiting in July and August, and are traveling with one other person, check out the Zomertoer, which allows first-class unlimited travel for one day (€45).

Train is also the easiest mode of transportation within Belgium. Belgian National Railways (SNCB/NMBS) maintains an extensive network of prompt and frequent services. Intercity trains have rapid connections between the major towns and cities, while local and regional trains also stop at all smaller towns and villages in between. There are several connections every hour between the Brussels Airport and Brussels, from early morning until late evening. Tickets can be paid for using currency or a major credit card. Smoking is prohibited on all trains in Belgium.

Intercity trains link Amsterdam and Brussels in around three hours. Thalys high-speed trains link Brussels (in 1½ hours) and Amsterdam (3½ hours) with Paris. Eurostar operates high-speed passenger trains between stations in London and Brussels (Midi) in two hours. Check the Web sites for latest fares and schedules. Advance seat reservations are obligatory. Travel on both Thalys and Eurostar trains is available in first or second class. First-class seats are slightly more spacious, and first-class passengers are served complimentary beverages and a light meal.

Holland and Belgium are two of 21 countries in which you can use a Eurailpass, providing unlimited first-class travel in all 21 countries. If you plan to travel extensively, get a standard pass. Train travel is available for any 10 or 15 days within a two-month period, or for 15 or 21 consecutive days, or for one, two, or three months. Tickets are valid in first class. Those aged 25 and under can get a second-class pass at a reduced rate. Two people traveling together receive a 15%

discount; children aged 4–11 receive a 50% discount, and children under 4 travel for free. Detailed prices and options and other information can be found on their Web site. Whichever pass you choose, remember to buy it before you leave for Europe. You can buy the passes in Holland but at a *15% hike-up* compared with buying at home.

Short of flying, taking the Channel Tunnel is the fastest way to cross the English Channel: 35 minutes from Folkestone to Calais, 60 minutes from motorway to motorway, or two hours and 15 minutes from London's St. Pancras Station to Paris's Gare du Nord. The Belgian border is just a short drive northeast of Calais. High-speed Eurostar trains use the same tunnels to connect London's St. Pancras Station directly with Midi Station in Brussels in around two hours.

Eurostar (⊕ www.eurostar.com). **NS–Nederlandse Spoorwegen/Dutch Railways** (⊕ www.ns.nl). **SNCB/NMBS** (⊕ www.b-rail.be). **Thalys** (⊕ www.thalys.com).

Information and Passes **Eurail** (⊕ www. eurail.com). **Rail Europe** (✉ 44 S. Broadway, No. 11, White Plains, NY ☎ 800/622–8600 in U.S., 800/361–7245 in Canada ⊕ www. raileurope.com/us).

Train Information Holland-wide **Public Transport Information** (☎ 0900/9292 at €0.70 per min.), including schedules and fares. For lost and found (☎ 0900/321–2100 at €0.80 per min.) on train lines and in stations, ask for a form at the nearest station. **Nederlandse Spoorwegen** (*Dutch Rail* ☎ 0900/202–1163 calls cost 10¢ per minute) customer service.

Channel Tunnel Car Transport **Eurotunnel** (☎ 08443/35–3535 in the U.K., 070/223–210 in Belgium, 0810–63–03–04 in France ⊕ www. eurotunnel.com).

Channel Tunnel Passenger Service **Eurostar** (⊕ www.eurostar.co.uk). **Rail Europe** (☎ 800/622–8600 in the U.S. ⊕ www. raileurope.com).

ESSENTIALS

■ ACCOMMODATIONS

Both the Netherlands and Belgium offer a range of options, from the major international hotel chains and small, modern local hotels to family-run restored inns and historic houses. Accommodations in Amsterdam are at a particular premium at any time of year, so you should book well in advance. Should you arrive without a hotel room, head for one of the city's four VVV (Netherlands Board of Tourism) offices, which have a same-day hotel booking service and can help you find a room. A small fee is charged for this service.

The hotel situation elsewhere in the Netherlands and in Belgium is less tight outside of the summer months, but hotels in larger cities often fill with business customers during the week. Most hotels that do cater to business travelers sometimes grant substantial weekend rebates. These discounted rates are often available during the week, as well as in July and August, when business travelers are thin on the ground. Wherever you go, you will have a wider choice if you plan ahead.

■ TIP→ Assume that hotels operate on the European Plan (**EP**, no meals) unless we specify that they use the Breakfast Plan (**BP**, with full breakfast), Continental Plan (**CP**, Continental breakfast), Full American Plan (**FAP**, all meals), Modified American Plan (**MAP**, breakfast and dinner) or are all-inclusive (**AI**, all meals and most activities).

APARTMENT AND HOUSE RENTALS

In Amsterdam, **City Mundo** has an excellent network, and whatever your requirements, this creative city specialist directory will try to hook you up to your ideal spot, whether that's a windmill or a houseboat. The price drops the longer you stay, up to the maximum of 21 nights, with a minimum of two nights. Book online, at the group's Web site, where visuals and

descriptions are constantly updated as new facilities come in.

It's also worth contacting **Holiday Link,** an agency that provides contacts and addresses for home-exchange holidays and house-sitting during holiday periods, bed-and-breakfasts, rentals of private houses in Holland, and budget accommodations. The company is part of **HomeLink International,** the worldwide vacation organization in more than 50 countries, so it knows what's what.

The VVVs (tourist information offices) in each region you plan to visit all have extensive accommodations listings. They can book reservations for you, according to your specific requirements. Call the number below for the local office in the area you plan to visit.

In Belgium, apartment rentals and *gîtes* (farmhouse rentals) are easy to find in popular vacation areas. Rentals from private individuals are usually for a one- or two-week minimum. Sheets and towels are not provided. You can also rent vacation villas within the Dutch and Belgian vacation parks. These self-contained parks, in rural or seaside settings, consist of residences and facilities such as swimming pools, hiking and bicycling trails, restaurants, and activities for children. There is usually a one-week minimum, although it is often possible to rent for shorter periods during the winter months. **Center Parcs** has eight such locations in the Netherlands and two in Belgium.

Local Agents in the Netherlands **Center Parcs** (⌂ Admiraliteitskade 40, 3063ED Rotterdam ☎ 010/498–9754, 0900/660–6600 [€0.50 per min] ⊕ www.centerparcs.com). **City Mundo** (✉ Schinkelkade 30, 1075VJ Amsterdam ☎ 020/470–5705 ⊕ amsterdam. citymundo.com). **Landal Green Parks** (⌂ Box 175, 2260AD Leidschendam ☎ 070/300–3506 ⊕ www.landalgreenparks.com). **VVV tourist offices** (☎ 0900/400–4040 [€0.40 per min]).

ocal Agents in Belgium Gîtes de Wal-
onie (✉ *av. Prince de Liège 1, Namur*
☎ *081/31–18–00* 🖷 *081/31–02–00* ⊕ *www.*
itesdewallonie.net). **Vacation Villas** (⊕ *www.*
acationvillas.net).

BED-AND-BREAKFASTS

A pleasant alternative to getting accommodations in a hotel is to stay at a
B&B. You'll find a large choice scattered
throughout the Netherlands. The best
way to track down B&Bs in Amsterdam
is either through creative city accommodations specialist City Mundo or Holiday
Link, both of which deal with private
houses and longer stays. Prices vary
widely from €20 to €40 per person.

B&B accommodations are less common in
Belgium; the ones you do find usually need
to be reserved in advance and, although
clean, are very simple, often without private bathrooms. Listings are available at
local tourist information centers, but you
must make your own reservations directly
with the proprietor. *Taxistop*, a company
that promotes inexpensive lodging and
travel deals, sells a B&B guide to Belgium
and makes reservations.

Reservation Services in the Netherlands
Bed & Breakfast Holland (☎ *020/615-7527*
⊕ *www.bbholland.com*). **Bed and Breakfast**
Service Nederland (✉ *Hallenstraat 12a,*
Bladel ☎ *0497/330-300* 🖷 *0497/330-811*
⊕ *www.bedandbreakfast.nl*). **City Mundo**
(✉ *Schinkelkade 30, Amsterdam* ☎ *020/470–*
5705 ⊕ *amsterdam.citymundo.com*).

Reservation Services in Belgium Tax-
istop (✉ *Rue Thérésienne 7a/c, Brussels*
☎ *070/222-292* ⊕ *www.taxistop.be*).

HOME EXCHANGES

With a direct home exchange you stay in
someone else's home while they stay in
yours. Some outfits also deal with vacation homes, so you're not actually staying
in someone's full-time residence, just their
vacant weekend place.

Exchange Clubs Home Exchange.com
(☎ *800/877-8723* ⊕ *www.homeexchange.*
com) ; $9.95 per month for a 1-year online

membership listing. **HomeLink International**
(☎ *800/638-3841* ⊕ *www.homelink.org*) ;
$115 yearly. **Intervac U.S.** (☎ *800/756-4663*
⊕ *www.intervacus.com*) ; $99.99 yearly.

HOSTELS

Many hostels are affiliated with Hostelling
International (HI), an umbrella group of
hostel associations with some 4,500 member properties in more than 70 countries.
Other hostels are completely independent
and may be nothing more than a really
cheap hotel.

Membership in any HI association, open
to travelers of all ages, allows you to stay
in HI-affiliated hostels at member rates.
One-year membership is about $28 for
adults; hostels charge about $10–$30 per
night. Members have priority if the hostel
is full; they're also eligible for discounts
around the world, even on rail and bus
travel in some countries.

The Dutch national hostel association,
Nederlandse Jeugdherberg Centrale
(NJHC), better known as Stayokay, and
the Belgian Auberges de Jeunesse and
Vlaamse Jeugdherbergen associations are
all affiliated with HI. NJHC has an excellent Web site with visuals and information
about the many hostels in Holland.

Amsterdam is world famous for two
beloved hostels: the Flying Pig Palace and
the Stayokay Hostel in Vondelpark, open
to travelers of all ages. Hostels elsewhere
in the Netherlands and in Belgium are also
well organized and clean. Rooms with one
to 10 beds are available, and hostels are

suitable for family stays. Many are near train stations.

Organization in Holland Stayokay (Nederlandse Jeugdherberg Centrale) (✆ 020/551-3155 ⊕ www.stayokay.com).

Belgian Organizations Auberges de Jeunesse de la Belgique Francophone (✉ Rue de la Sablonnière 28, Brussels ✆ 02/219-5676 🖷 02/219-1451 ⊕ www.laj.be). Vlaamse Jeugdherbergen (✉ Van Stralenstraat 40, Antwerp ✆ 03/232-7218 🖷 03/231-8126 ⊕ www.vjh.be).

Information Hostelling International—USA (✆ 301/495-1240 ⊕ www.hiusa.org).

HOTELS

In line with the international system, Dutch and Belgian hotels are awarded stars (one to five) by the Benelux Hotel Classification System, an independent agency that inspects properties based on their facilities and services. Those with three or more stars feature en suite bathrooms where a shower is standard, whereas a tub is a four-star standard. Rooms in lodgings listed in this guide have a shower unless otherwise indicated.

One Dutch peculiarity to watch out for is having twin beds pushed together instead of having one double. If you want a double bed (or *tweepersoonsbed*), you may have to pay more. Keep in mind that the star ratings are general indications and that a charming three-star might make for a better stay than a more expensive four-star. During low season, usually November to March (excluding Christmas and the New Year) when a hotel is not full, it is sometimes possible to negotiate a discounted rate, if one is not already offered. Prices in Amsterdam are higher over the peak summer period, while those in less touristed cities may actually fall at this time when the core business trade tails off. Room rates for deluxe and four-star rooms are on a par with those in other European cities, so in these categories, ask for one of the better rooms, since less desirable rooms—and there occasionally

are some—don't measure up to what you are paying for. Most cheaper hotels quote room rates including breakfast, while for those at the top end it usually costs extra. When you book a room and are in any doubt, specifically ask whether the rate includes breakfast.

Check out your hotel's location, and ask your hotelier about availability of a room with a view, if you're not worried about the extra expense: hotels in the historic center with a pretty canal view are highly sought after. Always ask if there is an elevator (called a "lift") or whether guests need to climb any stairs. Even if you are fairly fit, you may find traditional Dutch staircases in older buildings intimidating and difficult to negotiate. Keep that in mind if you're planning on making reservations in a listed monument, such as a historic canal-side town house. The alternative is to request a ground-floor room. In older hotels, the quality of the rooms may vary; if you don't like the room you're given, request another. This applies to noise, too. Front rooms may be larger or have a view, but they may also have a lot of street noise—so if you're a light sleeper, request a quiet room when making reservations. Remember to specify whether you care to have a bath or shower, since many bathrooms do not have tubs. It is always a good idea to have your reservation, dates, and rate confirmed by fax.

Taking meals at a hotel's restaurant sometimes provides you with a discount. Some restaurants, especially country inns in Belgium, require that guests take half board (*demi-pension* in French, *half-pension* in Flemish), at least lunch or dinner, at the hotel. Full pension (*pension complet* in French, *volledig pension* in Flemish) entitles guests to both lunch and dinner. Guests taking either half or full board also receive breakfast. If you take a *pension*, you pay per person, regardless of the number of rooms.

Many hotels in Amsterdam appear to be permanently full, and throughout the year conventions can fill up business hotels in

Brussels, so book as far in advance as you can to be sure of getting what you want.

Aside from going directly to the hotels or booking a travel-and-hotel package with your travel agent, there are several ways of making reservations. The VVV (Netherlands Board of Tourism) offers a room reservation service; branches of the VVV can be found in Schiphol Airport, Amsterdam Centraal Station, and at Leidseplein. Contact the VVV's office, or go to their Web site (⇨ *Web Sites*). Hotel reservations made via the I amsterdam Web site are free; those made in person or by phone/fax incur a €15 booking fee. Among the reservations services in Belgium are Belgian Tourist Reservations, a free service for booking hotel rooms, and Toerisme Stad Antwerpen, which makes hotel and B&B reservations in Antwerp. Hotels in both countries will sometimes ask you to confirm your reservation by fax or e-mail. If you are having an extended stay, the property may request a deposit either in the local currency or billed to your credit card.

Reservation Services in Amsterdam

VVV Amsterdam Hotel Reservations
(☎ *020/201-8800* ⊕ *www.iamsterdam.com*).
VVV Netherlands Board of Tourism Switchboard (☎ *0900/400-4040 calls cost €0.40 per minute*).

Reservations Services in Belgium **Belgian Tourist Reservations (Brussels and Wallonia)** (*BTR*,✉ *Blvd. Anspach 111, Brussels* ☎ *02/513-7484*).

Belgian Tourist Reservations (Flanders) (✉ *Rue de Marché aux Herbes 61, Brussels* ☎ *02/504-0390* ⊕ *www.visitantflanders.com*).

▌COMMUNICATIONS

INTERNET
If you're traveling with a laptop, take a spare battery and an electrical-plug adapter with you, as new batteries and replacement adapters are expensive. Many hotels are equipped with jacks for computers with Internet connections, and

most also have Wi-Fi hotspots. Some offer this service to hotel guests for free; others may charge up to €15 per hour for access. You will also find cybercafés in all major cities.

Contacts Cybercafes (⊕ *www.cybercafes. com*) lists more than 4,000 Internet cafés worldwide.

PHONES
The country code for the Netherlands is 31. The area code for Amsterdam is 020. To call an Amsterdam number within Amsterdam, you don't need the city code: just dial the seven-digit number. To call Amsterdam from elsewhere in the Netherlands, dial 020 at the start of the number. In addition to the standard city codes, there are three other prefixes used: public information numbers starting with 0800 are free phone numbers, but be aware that information lines with the prefix 0900 are charged at premium rates (35¢ a minute and more). 06 numbers indicate mobile (cell) phones. Mobile signal strength is good throughout the country.

The area codes for other Dutch cities are: Delft, 015; Rotterdam, 010; Utrecht, 030; Haarlem, 023; The Hague, 070.

When dialing a Dutch number from abroad, drop the initial zero from the local area code, so someone calling from New York, for example, to Amsterdam would dial 011 + 31 + 20 + the seven-digit phone number. When dialing from the Netherlands overseas, the country code is 00–1 for the United States and Canada, 00–61 for Australia, and 00–44 for the United Kingdom. All mobile and landline phones in Holland are 10 digits long (although some help lines and information centers have fewer digits).

Since hotels tend to overcharge for international calls, it is best to use a public phone. When making a call, listen for the dial tone (a low-pitched hum), insert a credit card, then dial the number. Since the increase in cellular phones, the number of phone cells, or phone booths, is decreasing. At every railway station there

LOCAL DO'S AND TABOOS

CUSTOMS OF THE COUNTRY

The Dutch are generally warm and welcoming. Most are multilingual and proud of it. They are also open and direct when it comes to speaking their mind, and are not afraid of making personal remarks. This can sometimes come across as a bit abrupt, or even rude, but there is certainly no offense intended.

GREETINGS

When greeting people, you should shake their hand and say your name if you have not already done so. It is usual to greet family and close friends of the opposite sex with a three-cheek kiss. Common phrases are: *goede dag* (good day), *graag* (please), and *dank U wel* (thank you).

SIGHTSEEING

When visiting a Catholic or Protestant church service, you should not wear shorts. When visiting a mosque, women should wear long sleeves and pants or a knee-length skirt, and a scarf on their heads.

OUT ON THE TOWN

If you are visiting a Dutch person's home, bring a bouquet of flowers or a bottle of wine as a gift. It is polite to arrive about 10 minutes late, to allow your host time for last-minute preparations. Don't be surprised if you arrive for dinner and are offered coffee before any alcoholic aperitifs appear. During the meal, keep both hands above the table.

DOING BUSINESS

Arrive on time for business appointments. Shake hands, and use family names rather than first names. The pace of business meetings is more relaxed than in the United States, so don't rush into business too promptly; instead spend a few minutes chatting about weather or travel. If you have met your associate's family previously, ask about them before beginning business. If you are in a meeting with several Dutch people, expect negotiations to drag on. In Dutch business

it is important that everyone has a chance to air their views, even if it means discussing trivial points ad nauseam. It is a very fair system, but can also be long-winded and frustrating if you are used to quick decision-making.

Breakfast meetings are not popular in Holland, as most businesspeople take a light breakfast at home. Business lunches are far more popular. Don't be surprised if your Dutch colleagues drink milk with their lunch.

LANGUAGE

Try to learn a little of the local language. You need not strive for fluency; even just mastering a few basic words and terms is bound to make chatting with the locals more rewarding.

There are two official Dutch languages: Dutch, used widely across the country, and Friese, used only in the north. In Amsterdam, and in all other cities and towns, English is widely spoken. State schools teach English to pupils as young as eight. Not only is it the country's strong second language, but the general public is very happy to help English-speaking visitors, to the extent that even if you ask in Dutch they answer cheerfully in English. Signs and notices often have duplicated information in English, if not more languages. Even in more remote villages you can usually find someone who speaks at least a little English.

Belgium has three official languages: Flemish, French, and German (spoken by a small minority). There are four language regions: Flanders (Flemish), Brussels (bilingual), Wallonia (French), and the scant eastern sections (German). Each region is fiercely defensive of its own tongue, and linguistic hostilities exist to this day. Fortunately, most Belgians are capable and more than willing to speak English.

re still plenty of pay phones, either in the ticket hall or on the platforms.

The country code for Belgium is 32. Two- or three-digit area codes always begin with zero; the zero is dropped when calling from abroad. The city code for Brussels is 02; for Gent, 09; and for Brugge, 050. Toll-free numbers begin with 0800. Premium rate calls begin with 0900. For English-language telephone assistance, dial 1405. For international calls, dial 00, followed by the country code, followed by the area code and telephone number. All calls within the country must include the regional telephone code.

To ask directory assistance for telephone numbers outside the Netherlands, dial 0900/8418 (calls are charged at €1.15 per call). For numbers within the Netherlands, dial 0900/8008 (calls are charged at €1.15 per call).

To reach an operator, dial 0800/0410. To make a collect call, or dial toll-free to a number outside the Netherlands, dial 0800/0101.

CALLING OUTSIDE

The country code for the United States is 1.

Access Codes in Holland **AT&T Direct** (☎ *0800/022–9111*). **MCI WorldPhone** (☎ *0800/023–5103*).

Access Codes in Belgium **AT&T Direct** (☎ *0800/100–10*). **MCI WorldPhone** (☎ *0800/100–12 in Belgium*).

CALLING CARDS

Telephone cards are no longer used in public phone booths in the Netherlands. They accept credit cards instead, or local chip cards (only available with Dutch bank passes).

MOBILE PHONES

British standard cell phones work in the Netherlands and Belgium, but American and Canadian standard (nonsatellite) cell phones may not. If you have a multiband phone (some countries use different frequencies than what's used in the United States) and your service provider uses the world-standard GSM network (as do T-Mobile, Cingular, and Verizon), you may be able to use your phone abroad. Roaming fees can be steep, however: 99¢ a minute is considered reasonable. And overseas you normally pay the toll charges for incoming calls. It's almost always cheaper to send a text message than to make a call, since text messages have a low set fee. If you'd like to rent a cell phone while traveling, reserve one at least four days before your trip, as most companies will ship it to you before you travel. CellularAbroad rents cell phones packaged with prepaid SIM cards that give you a local cell phone number and calling rates. Planetfone rents GSM phones, which can be used in more than 100 countries. If you just want to make local calls, your best bet may be to consider buying a new SIM card (note that your provider may have to unlock your phone for you to use a different SIM card) and a prepaid service plan in the destination. You'll then have a local number and can make local calls at local rates. If your trip is extensive, you could also simply buy a new cell phone in your destination, as the initial cost will be offset over time.

■ TIP➔ If you travel internationally frequently, save one of your old mobile phones or buy a cheap one on the Internet; ask your cell phone company to unlock it for you, and take it with you as a travel phone, buying a new SIM card with pay-as-you-go service in each destination.

Contacts **Cellular Abroad** (☎ *800/287–5072* ⊕ *www.cellularabroad.com*) rents and sells GSM phones and sells SIM cards that work in many countries. **Mobal** (☎ *888/888–9162* ⊕ *www.mobalrental.com*) rents mobiles and sells GSM phones (starting at $49) that will operate in 140 countries. Per-call rates vary throughout the world. **Planet Fone** (☎ *888/988–4777* ⊕ *www.planetfone.com*) rents cell phones, but the per-minute rates are expensive. **rent2connect** (☎ *32/2/652–1414* ⊕ *www.locaphone.be*).

▌EATING OUT

MEALS AND MEALTIMES

Traditional Dutch cuisine is very simple and filling. A typical Dutch *ontbijt* (breakfast) consists of *brood* (bread), *kaas* (cheese), *hard gekookte ei* (hard-boiled eggs), ham, yogurt, jams, and fruit.

Lunch is usually a *boterham* (sandwich) or a *broodje* (soft roll or a baguette). Salads and warm dishes are also popular for lunch. One specialty is an *uitsmijter*: two pieces of bread with three fried eggs, ham, and cheese, garnished with pickles and onions. *Pannenkoeken* (pancakes) are a favorite lunch treat topped with ham and cheese or fruit and a thick *stroop* (syrup).

A popular afternoon snack is *frites* (french fries); try them with curry ketchup and onions, called *frites speciaal,* with a *kroket* (a fried, breaded meat roll) on the side. Another snack is whole *haring* (herring) served with raw onions. Stay away from *frikandel,* a long hot dog that can contain anything.

Diner (dinner) usually consists of three courses: an appetizer, main course, and dessert, and many restaurants have special prix-fixe deals. Beverages are always charged separately. Dutch specialties include *erwtensoep* (a thick pea soup with sausage), *zalm* (salmon), *gerookte paling* (smoked eel), *hutspot* (beef stew), *aardappel au gratin* (potato au gratin), and *lamsvlees* (lamb). Steamed North Sea mussels are almost as popular in Holland as they are in Belgium. In general, the standard of the once-dull Dutch cuisine is improving steadily. Chefs have in recent years become more adventurous, and you will find many other more exciting choices (usually French-influenced) on menus than were seen a decade ago.

An oft-seen dessert is *Dame Blanche,* meaning White Lady, made of vanilla ice cream with hot dark chocolate and whipped cream. Holland is famous for its cheeses, including Gouda, Edam, and Limburger. Indonesian cuisine is also very popular here, and a favorite lunch or dinner is *rijsttafel,* which literally means "rice table" and refers to a prix-fixe meal that includes a feast of 10–20 small spicy dishes.

Restaurants open for lunch starting at 11 AM, while restaurants opening for dinner will accept guests as early as 5 or 6 PM, closing at 11. Most restaurants are closed Monday.

Specialities you may encounter in Belgium that are not found in the Netherlands include *waterzooi,* a creamy stew made with chicken, rabbit, or fish, and *carbonnade,* a beef stew cooked in beer. *Paling in 't groen* (Flemish) or *anguilles au vert* (French) is steamed eel with a green herb sauce. Belgian endive (*chicons* in French, *witloof* in Flemish) is usually cooked with ham, braised, and topped with a cheese gratin. Complete your meal with *frites* or *frieten* (french fries), which Belgians proudly claim to have been invented not in France but in Belgium. Belgian fries are fried twice—usually in animal fat, so they don't always meet vegetarian standards. Waffles here are a dessert, not a breakfast food.

PAYING

Major credit cards are accepted in most restaurants. Visa and MasterCard are the most widely used; smaller establishments may not accept American Express or Diners Club. Some bars and cafés won't accept credit cards, though most will. Don't rely on traveler's checks for paying restaurant bills.

Tipping 15% to 20% of the cost of a meal is not common practice in the Netherlands or in Belgium. Instead, it is customary to round off the total to a convenient figure, to reward good service. If paying with a credit card, pay the exact amount of the bill with your card, and leave a few euros in cash on the table for the waiting staff.

RESERVATIONS AND DRESS

Regardless of where you are, it's a good idea to make a reservation if you can. We only mention them specifically when reservations are essential (there's no other way you'll ever get a table) or when they are not accepted. For popular restaurants, book as far ahead as you can (often 30 days), and reconfirm as soon as you arrive. Large parties should always call ahead to check the reservations policy.) We mention dress only when men are required to wear a jacket or a jacket and tie.

The Dutch and Belgians favor relatively casual dress when dining out; men in open-neck shirts are far more common than a dining room full of suits. Jackets and ties are a rarity, except in the very top establishments. If in any doubt, check ahead with the restaurant in question.

WINES, BEER AND SPIRITS

When you just ask for a "beer" in the Netherlands, you will get a small (200 milliliters) glass of draft lager beer with 5% alcohol content, known as *pils*. There are a number of national breweries that turn out similar fare—in Amsterdam it will usually be Heineken, but you may also encounter Amstel, Oranjeboom, Grolsch, Bavaria, or a number of smaller outfits. The argument for serving beer in small glasses is that you can drink it before it gets warm, and that you can also drink more of them. Many bars will also serve you a pint (500 milliliters) if you ask them. There are a number of smaller artisanal breweries that attempt different beer styles with ever-improving results— look out for the La Trappe, De Prael, Jopen and 't IJ names in particular. While the Dutch are catching up, the Belgians remain the acknowledged world beer experts. That country produces around 800 types of beer, and you will find several standards in most Dutch cafés, including white (wheat) beer, Westmalle (a Trappist brew, which comes in brown and strong blond "triple" versions), kriek (a fruit-flavored beer), and Duvel, a very strong blond beer. All the major cities also have a few specialist beer cafés, for real connoisseurs, with beer lists stretching into the hundreds. In Amsterdam, the In De Wildeman café is one of the best

places to head on that score. To discover Amsterdam's true beer culture in more depth, check out Around Amsterdam in 80 Beers (www.booksaboutbeer.com), by Fodor's writer Tim Skelton. Keep in mind that many Dutch and Belgian beers have a high alcohol content; 8%–9% alcohol per volume is not unusual.

Be sure to try locally produced *genièvre* or *jenever*, a strong, ginlike spirit taken neat. Sometimes its edge is taken off with sweeter fruit flavors like apple, lemon, and red currant. In some bars, bartenders fill the small glass to the brim, so that only surface tension keeps it from overflowing. Faced with such a delicate balance, you have to lean over and take the first sip from the bar, rather than pick up the glass.

▌ ELECTRICITY

The electrical current in the Netherlands and Belgium is 220 volts, 50 cycles alternating current (AC); wall outlets take Continental-type plugs, with two round prongs.

Consider making a small investment in a universal adapter, which has several types of plugs in one lightweight, compact unit. Most laptops and mobile phone chargers are dual voltage (i.e., they operate equally well on 110 and 220 volts), so require only an adapter. These days the same is true of small appliances such as hair dryers. Always check labels and manufacturer instructions to be sure. Don't use 110-volt outlets marked FOR SHAVERS ONLY for high-wattage appliances such as hair dryers.

Contacts Walkabout Travel Gear (⊕ *www. walkabouttravelgear.com*) has a good coverage of electricity under "adapters."

▌ EMERGENCIES

Police, ambulance, and fire (☎ *112 Europe-wide toll-free 24-hour switchboard for emergencies*). The 24-hour help-line service **Afdeling Inlichtingen Apotheken** (☎ *020/694– 8709*) (*apotheken* means "pharmacy") can direct you to your nearest open pharmacy; there is a rotating schedule to cover evenings, nights, and weekends—details are also posted at your local *apotheken*, and in the city newspapers. The **Centrale Doktersdienst** (*Central Doctor Services* ☎ 020/592-3434) offers a 24-hour English-speaking help line providing advice about medical symptoms. In the case of minor accidents, phone **directory inquiries** (☎ 0900/8008) to get the number for the outpatients' department at your nearest *ziekenhuis* (hospital). **TBB** (☎ 020/570-9595 or 0900/821-2230) is a 24-hour dental service that refers callers to a dentist (or *tandarts*). Operators can also give details of pharmacies open outside normal hours.

For less urgent police matters, call the **central number** (☎ 0900/8844). Amsterdam's **police headquarters** is at the crossing Marnixstraat/Elandsgracht and can be reached with Tramline 3, 7, 12, or 17. For car breakdowns and other car-related emergencies, call the big automobile agency in the Netherlands, the ANWB (⇨ *Car Travel, Emergency Services*).

Note that all numbers quoted above with the code 020 are for Amsterdam and surrounding area only.

Contacts in Amsterdam and the Netherlands Medical emergencies, police, fire, accidents, ambulance (☎ 112).

Contacts in Belgium Police (☎ 112 or 101). Medical emergencies, fire, accidents, ambulance (☎ 112 or 100).

Hospitals in Amsterdam For emergency treatment, the **AMC** and **Sint Lucas Andreas** hospitals have first-aid departments. The largest, most modern hospital serving Amsterdam and surroundings is the **AMC (Academisch Medisch Centrum)** (✉ *Meibergdreef 9, Amsterdam Zuidoost* ☎ 020/566-9111). It's outside the city proper, in the Holendrecht area. The **Sint Lucas Andreas Ziekenhuis** (✉ *Jan Tooropstraat 164, Amsterdam* ☎ 020/510-8911) is in the western part of the city, in Geuzenveld. **Slotervaart Ziekenhuis** (✉ *Louwesweg 6, Amsterdam* ☎ 020/512-9333) is in the southwestern part of the city. The **VU Medisch**

Centrum (✉ *De Boelelaan 1117, Amsterdam* ☎ 020/444-4444) is a university teaching hospital in the Buitenveldert area.

∎ HEALTH

SHOTS AND MEDICATIONS

Standards of health in Belgium and the Netherlands are generally very good. You won't need any immunizations and you are unlikely to get sick. Older visitors, however, may wish to consider immunization against influenza if traveling over the winter months. If you do fall ill, you've picked the right place, as Belgian healthcare is generally acknowledged as the best in the world, and the Netherlands isn't far behind.

SPECIFIC ISSUES IN AMSTERDAM, THE NETHERLANDS AND BELGIUM

While you are traveling in the Netherlands, the Centers for Disease Control and Prevention (CDC) in Atlanta recommends that you observe health precautions similar to those that would apply while traveling in the United States. The main Dutch health bureau is the GGD, which stands for Gemeentelijke Gezondheidsdienst (Communal Medical Health Service). English-speaking medical help is easy to find. Most doctors have a good English vocabulary and are familiar with English medical terms. *Drogists* (drugstores) sell toiletries and nonprescription drugs *(see also Emergencies)*. For prescription drugs go to an *apotheek* (pharmacy).

Health Warnings National Centers for Disease Control & Prevention (*CDC;* ☎ 800/232-4636 international travelers' health line ⊕ www.cdc.gov/travel). World Health Organization (*WHO;* ⊕ www.who.int).

OVER-THE-COUNTER REMEDIES

You will find most standard over-the-counter medications, such as aspirin and acetaminophen, in the *drogisterij* (drugstore). You will have difficulty finding antihistamines and cold medications, like Sudafed, without a prescription.

Medical Care in Holland For inquiries about medical care, contact the national health service agency: **GGD Nederland** (✉ *Nieuwe Achtergracht 100* ☎ *020/555–5911* ⊕ *www. ggd.nl*).

■ HOURS OF OPERATION

Banks are open weekdays 9:30 to 4 or 5, with some extending their business hours to coordinate with late-night shopping. Some banks are closed Monday mornings.

The main post office is open weekdays 9 to 6, Saturday 10 to 1:30. In every post office you'll also find the Postbank, a money-changing facility, which has the same opening hours.

Apotheken (pharmacies) are open weekdays from 8 or 9 to 5:30 or 6. There are always pharmacies on call during the weekend. The after-hours emergency pharmacy telephone number is ☎ 020/694–8709. Operators always speak English.

Most shops are open from 1 to 6 on Monday, 9 to 6 Tuesday through Saturday. Hairdressers are generally closed Sunday and sometimes Monday. If you really need a haircut on those days, try a salon at one of the larger hotels. Thursday or Friday (Thursday in Amsterdam) is a designated late-night shopping night—*Koopavond* (buying evenings)—with stores staying open until 9. *Markten* (markets) selling fruit, flowers, and other wares run from 10 to 4 or sometimes 5. Small *nachtwinkels* (late-night shops) selling food, wine, and toiletries, are open from afternoon to midnight or later. Supermarkets are open weekdays until 8 or 10 PM, Saturday until 6 or 8 PM, with most open on Sundays either from 11 to 7 or 4 to 10 PM.

Opening hours are similar in Belgium.

HOLIDAYS

In Holland, *nationale feestdagen* (national holidays) are New Year's Day (January 1); Easter Sunday and Monday; Koninginnedag (Queen's Day, April 30); Remembrance Day (May 4); Liberation Day (May 5); Ascension Day; Whitsunday (Pentecost) and Monday; and Christmas (December 25 and 26). During these holidays, banks and schools are closed; many shops, restaurants, and museums are closed as well. Some businesses close early for May 4, Remembrance Day. Throughout the Netherlands, there is a two-minute silent pause from 8–8:02 PM, and even traffic stops. Take note and please respect this custom. Although May 5 is technically a holiday, most establishments remain open and the country functions as normal. *For information on these and other holidays, see also "On the Calendar" in the front of this book.*

In Belgium, all government and post offices, banks, and most shops are closed on Belgium's national day, July 21. Businesses are also closed on Easter Monday, Labor Day (May 1), the Ascension, Pentecost, the Assumption (August 15), All Saints' Day (November 1), Armistice Day (November 11), Christmas Day, and New Year's Day. If a holiday falls on a weekend, offices close the preceding Friday or following Monday.

■ MONEY

The price tags in Amsterdam are considered reasonable in comparison with those in main cities in neighboring countries, although with the strength of the euro versus the dollar, they may feel expensive to North American visitors. Good value for the money can still be had in many places, and as a tourist in this Anglophile country you are a lot less likely to get ripped off in the Netherlands than in countries where English is less widely embraced.

Here are some sample prices: admission to the Rijksmuseum is €12.50; the cheapest seats at the Stadsschouwburg theater run €15 for plays, €20 for opera; €6.50–€9.50 for a ticket at a movie theater (depending on time of show). Going to a nightclub might set you back €5–€20. A daily English-language newspaper is €3–€5. A taxi ride (1⅓ km, or ¾ mi) costs about €8. An inexpensive hotel room for two, including breakfast, is about €60–€110, an inexpensive dinner is €20–€35 for two, and a half-liter carafe of house wine is €10. A simple sandwich item on the menu runs about €3, a cup of coffee €1.50. A Coke is €2, and a half-liter of beer is €4.

Prices throughout this guide are given for adults. Substantially reduced fees are almost always available for children, students, and senior citizens.

■ TIP➔ Banks never have every foreign currency on hand, and it may take as long as a week to order. If you're planning to exchange funds before leaving home, don't wait until the last minute.

ATMS AND BANKS

Your own bank will probably charge a fee for using ATMs abroad; the foreign bank you use may also charge a fee. Nevertheless, you'll usually get a better rate of exchange at an ATM than you will at a currency-exchange office or even when changing money in a bank. And extracting funds as you need them is a safer option than carrying around a large amount of cash.

■ TIP➔ PINs with more than four digits are not recognized at ATMs in many countries. If yours has five or more, remember to change it before you leave.

The Dutch word for ATM is *Geldautomaat*. They are widespread, and accessible 24 hours a day, seven days per week. The majority of machines work with Maestro, Cirrus, and Plus.

CREDIT CARDS

Throughout this guide, the following abbreviations are used: **AE**, American Express; **DC**, Diners Club; **MC**, Master-Card; and **V**, Visa.

It's a good idea to inform your credit-card company before you travel, especially if you're going abroad and don't travel internationally very often. Otherwise, the credit-card company might put a hold on your card owing to unusual activity—not a good thing halfway through your trip.

Record all your credit-card numbers— as well as the phone numbers to call if your cards are lost or stolen—in a safe place, so you're prepared should something go wrong. Both MasterCard and Visa have general numbers you can call (collect if you're abroad) if your card is lost, but you're better off calling the number of your issuing bank, since Master-Card and Visa usually just transfer you to your bank; your bank's number is usually printed on your card.

If you plan to use your credit card for cash advances, you'll need to apply for a PIN at least two weeks before your trip. Although it's usually cheaper (and safer) to use a credit card abroad for large purchases (so you can cancel payments or be reimbursed if there's a problem), note that some credit-card companies *and* the banks that issue them add substantial percentages to all foreign transactions, whether they're in a foreign currency or not. Check on these fees before leaving home, so there won't be any surprises when you get the bill.

■ TIP➔ Before you charge something, ask the merchant whether or not he or she plans to do a dynamic currency conversion (DCC). In such a transaction the credit-card *processor* (shop, restaurant, or hotel, not Visa or MasterCard) converts the currency and charges you in dollars. In most cases you'll pay the merchant a 3% fee for this service in addition to any credit-card company and issuing-bank foreign-transaction surcharges.

Dynamic currency conversion programs are becoming increasingly widespread. Merchants who participate in them are supposed to ask whether you want to be charged in dollars or the local currency, but they don't always do so. And even if they do offer you a choice, they may well avoid mentioning the additional surcharges. The good news is that you *do* have a choice. And if this practice really gets your goat, you can avoid it entirely thanks to American Express; with its cards, DCC simply isn't an option.

Major credit cards are accepted in most hotels, gas stations, restaurants, cafés, and shops. Be aware, however, that you cannot use credit cards to purchase train tickets in the Netherlands.

Reporting Lost Cards **American Express** (☎ 800/528–4800 in the U.S., 336/393–1111 collect from abroad ⊕ www.americanexpress. com). **Diners Club** (☎ 800/234–6377 in the U.S., 303/799–1504 collect from abroad ⊕ www.dinersclub.com). **MasterCard** (☎ 800/627–8372 in the U.S., 636/722–7111 collect from abroad ⊕ www.mastercard.com). **Visa** (☎ 800/847–2911 in the U.S., 410/581–9994 collect from abroad ⊕ www.visa.com).

Reporting Lost Cards in Amsterdam and the Netherlands: **American Express** (☎ 020/504–8666). **Diners Club** (☎ 020/654–5511). **MasterCard** (☎ 0800/022–5821). **Visa** (☎ 0800/022–3110).

Reporting Lost Cards in Belgium: **American Express** (☎ 02/676–2121). **Diners Club** (☎ 02/626–5004). **MasterCard** (☎ 01/800–307–7309). **Visa** (☎ 0800/022–3110).

CURRENCY AND EXCHANGE

The single euro is the official currency of the Netherlands and Belgium. At press time, 1 euro = 1.29 US$. Shop around for the best exchange rates (and also check the rates before leaving home).

There are eight coins—1 and 2 euros, plus 1, 2, 5, 10, 20, and 50 cents. Bills are 5, 10, 20, 50, 100, 200, and 500 euro notes. Note that because of counterfeiting concerns, few shops and restaurants will accept notes higher in value than 50 euro. If you do find yourself with higher denominations, change them in a bank. The Dutch also consider the 1 and 2-cent coins to be an irritation, and many shops round prices up or down to the nearest 5 cents.

These days, the easiest way to get euros is through an ATM, called a *geldautomaat* in the Netherlands. You can find them in airports, train stations, and throughout the cities. ATM rates are excellent because they are based on wholesale rates offered only by major banks. At exchange booths always confirm the rate with the teller before exchanging money—you won't do as well at exchange booths in airports, or in hotels, restaurants, or stores. To avoid lines at airport exchange booths, get some euros before you leave home.

GWK Travelex is a nationwide financial organization specializing in foreign currencies, where travelers can exchange cash and traveler's checks, receive cash against major credit cards, and receive Western Union money transfers. Many of the same services are available at banks.

■TIP→ Even if a currency-exchange booth has a sign promising no commission, rest assured that there's some kind of huge, hidden fee. (Oh . . . that's right. The sign didn't say no *fee*.) And as for rates, you're almost always better off getting foreign currency at an ATM or exchanging money at a bank.

Exchange Services in Amsterdam **GWK Travelex (bureau de change)** (☎ 0900/0566) branches are in or near railway stations throughout the country. The offices at **Amsterdam Schiphol Airport** (☎ 0900/0566) are open 24 hours a day, seven days a week. You can find a **GWK** branch in the hall at **Centraal Station** (☎ 0900/0566).

❚ PACKING

When coming to the Netherlands or Belgium, be flexible: pack an umbrella (or two—the topography results in a blustery wind, which makes short work of a lightweight frame); bring a raincoat, with a thick liner in winter; and always have a sweater or jacket handy. For daytime wear and casual evenings, turtlenecks and thicker shirts are ideal for winter, under a sweater. Unpredictable summer weather means that a long-sleeved cotton shirt and jacket could be perfect one day, whereas the next, a T-shirt or vest top is as much as you can wear, making it hard to pack lightly. Bring a little something for all eventualities and you shouldn't get stuck.

Essentially, laid-back is the norm. Stylewise, anything goes. Men aren't required to wear ties or jackets anywhere, except in some smarter hotels and exclusive restaurants; jeans are very popular and worn to the office. Cobblestone streets make walking in high heels perilous—you don't want a wrenched ankle—and white sneakers are a dead giveaway that you are an American tourist; a better choice is a pair of dark-color, comfortable walking shoes.

Women wear skirts more frequently than do women in the United States, especially those over 35. Men only need include a jacket and tie if you're planning to visit one of the upper-echelon restaurants.

PASSPORTS

All U.S., Canadian, and U.K. citizens, even infants, need only a valid passport to enter the Netherlands or Belgium for stays of up to 90 days.

It's a good idea to always carry your passport with you, even if think you don't need one, for example if traveling between the Netherlands and other countries within the European Schengen agreement (which includes Belgium, France, and Germany, but not the United Kingdom). You are required to carry valid ID at all times in both the Netherlands and Belgium, and although it's very unlikely that you'll be asked for it, it's better to be safe than risk a fine.

■TIP→ Before your trip, make two copies of your passport's data page (one for someone at home and another for you to carry separately). Or scan the page and e-mail it to someone at home and/or yourself.

RESTROOMS

Restrooms (*toiletten* or WC in Dutch) in restaurants, bars, and other public places in the Netherlands are generally very clean, and most are free, although you may have to pay a few cents to an attendant in some cafés.

In Belgium, paying an attendant is more common, so carry some small change with you if you get caught short. A few older cafés and bars here may only have one unisex restroom. Women shouldn't be surprised to find a urinal, possibly in use, beside the washbasin in such establishments.

Find a Loo The Bathroom Diaries (⊕ www.thebathroomdiaries.com) is flush with unsanitized info on restrooms the world over—each one located, reviewed, and rated.

SAFETY

Amsterdam is unlike any other modern metropolis: although it has had certain problems with crime, and with abuse of legalized prostitution and soft drugs, the serious crime rate is exceptionally low, so having your bike stolen is the worst thing most likely to happen to you. Still, in crowded intersections and dark alleys, it is always best to be streetwise and take double safety precautions; it may be best to keep your money in a money belt and not flaunt your expensive camera. Be especially wary of pickpockets in crowds and while riding the tram. And use common sense when going out at night. Keep to well-lighted areas and take a taxi if you are going a long distance. Although it is easy to lose yourself in a romantic 18th-century haze taking a midnight stroll along the canals in Amsterdam, remember that muggings do very occasionally occur. Late at night, it may be best to keep to the main thoroughfares and not venture down deserted streets.

In Belgium, in popular tourist areas, beware of restaurant personnel beckoning tourists on the street and luring prospective diners with a complimentary glass of champagne. At the end of the meal, the "compliments" are reflected in the tab. Avoid highway rest stops and sparsely populated metro stations late at night. Although they aren't likely to assault, tramps and derelicts tend to make train stations unsavory at night.

■TIP➡ Distribute your cash, credit cards, IDs, and other valuables between a deep front pocket, an inside jacket or vest pocket, and a hidden money pouch. Don't reach for the money pouch once you're in public.

▌ TAXES

Hotels in Holland always include the service charge, and the 6% VAT (BTW in Dutch), in the room rate. Tourist tax is never included and is a few euros extra. If in doubt, inquire when booking. In restaurants you pay a 5% service charge, 6% VAT on food items, and 19% VAT on all beverages, all of which are included in the quoted menu prices. VAT is 19% on clothes and luxury goods, 6% on basic goods. On consumer goods, it is always included in the amount on the price tag, so you can't actually see what percentage you're paying.

All hotels in Belgium charge a 6% Value-Added Tax (TVA), included in the room rate; in Brussels, there is also a 9% city tax. Belgian VAT ranges from 6% on food and clothing to 33% on luxury goods. Restaurants are in between; 21% is included in quoted prices.

When making a purchase, ask for a VAT refund form and find out whether the merchant gives refunds—not all stores do, nor are they required to. Have the form stamped like any customs form by customs officials when you leave the country or, if you're visiting several EU countries, when you leave the EU. After you're through passport control, take the form to a refund-service counter for an on-the-spot refund (which is usually the quickest and easiest option), or mail it to the address on the form (or the envelope with it) after you arrive home. You receive the total refund stated on the form, but the processing time can be long, especially if you request a credit-card adjustment.

Global Refund is a Europe-wide service with 225,000 affiliated stores and more than 700 refund counters at major airports and border crossings. Its refund form, called a Tax Free Check, is the most common across the European Continent. The service issues refunds in the form of cash, check, or credit-card adjustment.

VAT Refunds Global Refund (☎ 800/566-9828 ⊕ www.globalrefund.com).

▌ TIME

The Netherlands and Belgium are on Central European Time (CET), one hour ahead of Greenwich Mean Time (GMT). Daylight saving time begins on the last Sunday in March, when clocks are set forward one hour; on the last Sunday in October, clocks are set back one hour. Both countries operate on a 24-hour clock, so AM hours are listed as in the United States and Britain, but PM hours continue through the cycle (1 PM is 13:00, 2 PM is 14:00, etc.). When it's 3 PM in Amsterdam, it is 2 PM in London, 9 AM in New York City, and 6 AM in Los Angeles. A telephone call will get you the **speaking clock** (☎ 0900/8002) in Dutch.

▌ TIPPING

In Dutch restaurants, a service charge of about 5% is often included in menu prices. Round the bill up to a convenient figure, or leave a few euros extra, if you've really enjoyed the meal and you got good service, and leave the tip as change rather than putting it on your credit card. If you're not satisfied, don't leave anything. Though a service charge is also included in hotel, taxi, bar, and café bills, the Dutch mostly round up the change to the nearest two euros for large bills and to the nearest euro for smaller ones. Consider tipping in bars only if you were served at a table. Restroom attendants and cloakroom attendants usually have fixed charges that are clearly displayed and do not require tipping.

In Belgium, a tip (*service compris* or *service inclusief*) may be included in restaurant and hotel bills; if it is, you'll see a clear indication on the bill. If service is not included, people often round up a bit when paying, but it isn't offensive to pay the exact amount. Taxi drivers also appreciate a rounding up of the bill, but again, paying the exact amount is perfectly acceptable. Railway porters expect €1 per item. For bellhops and doormen at both hotels and nightspots, a few euros is adequate. Bartenders are tipped only for notably good service; again, rounding off is sufficient.

■ TOURS

BICYCLE TOURS

From April through October, guided 1½- to 3-hour bike trips through the central area of Amsterdam are available through Yellow Bike. Let's Go tours (contact the VVV or visit the Web site for further details) takes you out of the city center by train before introducing you to the safer cycling of the surrounding countryside. Its tours include Edam and Volendam, Naarden and Muiden, and, in season, a Tulip Tour.

Let's Go (⌧ *Tours start from VVV Netherlands Board of Tourism, Centraal Station, Centrum* ☎ *No phone* ⊕ *www.letsgo-amsterdam.com*). **Yellow Bike** (⌧ *Nieuwezijds Kolk 29, Centrum* ☎ *020/620–6940* ⊕ *www.yellowbike.nl*).

BOAT TOURS

The quickest, easiest, and (frankly) most delightful way to get your bearings in Amsterdam is to take a canal-boat cruise. Trips last from 1 to 1½ hours and cover the harbor as well as the main canal district; there is a taped or live commentary available in four languages. Excursion boats leave from *rondvaart* (excursion) piers in various locations in the city every 15 minutes from March to October, and every 30 minutes in winter. Departures are frequent from Prins Hendrikkade near the Centraal Station, along the Damrak, and along the Rokin (near Muntplein), at Leidseplein, and Stadhouderskade (near the Rijksmuseum). For a tour lasting about an hour, the cost is around €12.50, but the student guides expect a small tip

for their multilingual commentary. A free trip is included in the I amsterdam card (see above). For a truly romantic view of Amsterdam, opt for one of the special dinner and candlelight cruises offered by some companies, notably Holland International. A candlelight dinner cruise costs upward of €30. Trips for all boat tours can also be booked through the tourist office.

Operators of canal cruises include Holland International, Gray Line Amsterdam, Rederij Lovers, Rederij P. Kooij, Rederij Noord/Zuid, and Rederij Plas.

A popular option for exploring the city's canals, and some of the attractions that lie along them, is to hop on board one of Canal Company's Canal Buses (actually ferrylike passenger boats). Canal Buses, which leave from Centraal Station and travel along the canals by three different routes, allow you to disembark at points of interest along the way. Stops along the Green Line include the Anne Frank House, Rembrandtplein, and Rembrandt's House; the Red Line stops at the Rijksmuseum, City Hall, and the Westerkerk; and the Blue Line stops at the Tropenmuseum, NEMO, and the Scheepvaartmuseum. A Canal Bus Day Pass, which costs €22, is valid from the time you buy it until noon the following day; you can hop on and off the boats as many times as you like within that time. Buying a day pass also gets you reduced entry rates at some museums along the routes.

The Canal Bike *Waterfiets* is a pedal-powered boat that seats up to four. You can tour the Grachtengordel ring of canals at your own pace. For one or two people, the hourly fee is €8 per person, and for three to four people, it costs €8 per person, per hour. Rental hours are between 10 and 6:30 daily. There are five landing stages throughout the city, with two of the most popular ones across from the Rijksmuseum and across from the Westerkerk.

Fees and Schedules Amsterdam Canal Cruises (⌧ *Nicolaas Witsenkade 1a, opposite* the Heineken Brewery, De Pijp ☎ 020/626–5636 ⊕ www.amsterdamcanalcruises.nl). **Canal Bus** (✉ Weteringschans 26–1, Leidseplein ☎ 020/623–9886 ⊕ www.canal.nl). **Gray Line Amsterdam** (✉ Damrak 4, Dam ☎ 020/623–4208 ⊕ www.graylineamsterdam.com). **Holland International** (✉ Prins Hendrikkade, opposite Centraal Station, Centrum ☎ 020/625–3035 ⊕ www.hir.nl). **Museumboot Rederij Lovers** (✉ Prins Hendrikkade, opposite Centraal Station, Centrum ☎ 020/530–1092 ⊕ www.lovers.nl). **Rederij P. Kooij** (✉ Rokin, near Spui, Centrum ☎ 020/623–3810 ⊕ www.rederijkooij.nl). **Rederij Plas** (✉ Damrak, quays 1–3, Dam ☎ 020/624–5406 ⊕ www.rederijplas.nl).

BUS TOURS

Afternoon bus tours of Amsterdam operate daily. Itineraries vary, and prices range from €12 to €43. A 2½-hour city tour that includes a drive through the suburbs is offered by Key Tours. However, it must be said that this city of narrow alleys and canals is not best appreciated from the window of a coach. Also, a number of visitors feel unhappy that part of some tours involves a visit to a diamond factory, where they feel pressured into listening to a sales pitch. The same bus companies operate scenic trips to attractions outside the city.

Fees and Schedules **Key Tours** (✉ Paulus Potterstraat 8, Museum District ☎ 020/305–5333 ⊕ www.keytours.nl). **Lindbergh Excursions** (✉ Damrak 26, Dam ☎ 020/622–2766 ⊕ www.lindbergh.nl).

SPECIAL-INTEREST TOURS
ART AND ARCHITECTURE

From quaint to grandiose, Golden Age to Modernism, art and architecture in the Netherlands has never been anything less than visionary.

Contacts **Academic Arrangements Abroad** (✉ 1040 Ave. of the Americas, New York, NY ☎ 212/514–8921 or 800/221–1944 📠 212/344–7493 ⊕ www.arrangementsabroad.com).

BEER

One of Belgium's biggest draws is the extraordinary range of diverse beers it produces. It's reason enough to visit for many people.

Contacts **Beer Trips.com** (✉ Box 7892, Missoula, MT 59807 ☎ 406/531–9109 📠 419/791–9425 ⊕ www.beertrips.com).

WALKING TOURS

The Netherlands Tourist Board (VVV) maintains lists of personal guides and guided walking and cycling tours for groups in and around Amsterdam and can advise you on making arrangements. You can also contact Guidor, Nederlandse Gidsen Organisatie (Dutch Guides Organization). Typical costs range from €150 for a half day to €250 for a full day. The tourist office also sells brochures outlining easy-to-follow self-guided theme tours through the central part of the city. Among them are "A Journey of Discovery Through Maritime Amsterdam," "A Walk Through the Jordaan," "Jewish Amsterdam," and "Rembrandt and Amsterdam."

Walking tours focusing on art and architecture are organized by Stichting Arttra and Architectour. For walking tours of the Jewish Quarter, contact Joods Historisch Museum. Yellow Bike Tours organizes two-hour walking tours of the Jordaan and the Red Light District.

Probably the best deal in town is Mee in Mokum, which offers walking tours led by retired longtime residents. For a mere €5, you are given an entertaining three-hour educational tour of the inner city or the Jordaan, focusing on architecture and surprising facts. These tours are also popular with Amsterdammers who wish to discover new things about their city. The admission fee entitles you to reduced fees to a choice of museums and a reduction in the price of a pancake at a nearby restaurant. Tours are held daily and start promptly at 11 AM. You must reserve at least a day in advance. Tours are limited to eight people; private arrangements can also be made for other times of the day.

Fees and Schedules Architectour (✉ *Touwslagerstraat 13* ☎ *020/625–9123*). **Arttra Cultureel Orgburo** (✉ *Tweede Boomdwarsstraat 4* ☎ *020/625–9303* ⊕ *www.arttra.com*). **Guidor, Nederlandse Gidsen Organisatie** (✉ *Wildenborch 6* ☎ *020/624–6072* ⊕ *www.guidor.nl*). **Joods Historisch Museum** (✉ *Nieuwe Amstelstraat 1, Postbus 16737, Plantage* ☎ *020/531–0310* 🖷 *020/531–0311* ⊕ *www.jhm.nl*). **Mee in Mokum** (✉ *Tours start from Museumcafé Mokum, Kalverstraat 92, Dam* ☎ *020/625–1390 call between 1 and 4*). **Yellow Bike** (✉ *Nieuwezijds Kolk 29, Centrum* ☎ *020/620–6940* ⊕ *www.yellowbike.nl*).

❚ VISITOR INFORMATION

AMSTERDAM AND BEYOND

The VVV (Netherlands Board of Tourism) has several offices around Amsterdam. The office in Centraal Station is open Tues.–Sat. 10–6:15; the one on Stationsplein, opposite Centraal Station, is open daily 7–7; on Leidseplein, Mon.–Sat. 10–7:30, Sun. 12–7; and at Schiphol Airport, daily 7 AM–10 PM. Hours at all offices except Schiphol may vary slightly with the seasons. Each VVV within Holland has information principally on its own region.

Every town in Belgium has an official tourist office with key visitor's information, maps, and calendars of events. The helpful staff is usually trilingual (English, French, and Flemish). The offices might close for an hour at lunchtime, but during the high season they might stay open past 6. Offices in the main destinations are open on weekends as well as weekdays.

Amsterdam and the Netherlands Tourist Information VVV—Netherlands Board of Tourism (⊕ *www.iamsterdam. com* or *us.holland.com*✉ *Spoor 2b/Platform 2b, Centraal Station, Centrum* ✉ *Stationsplein 10, Centraal Station* ✉ *Leidseplein 26 Leidseplein* ✉ *Schiphol Airport, Badhoevedorp* ☎ *020/201–8880* ✉ *Hofweg 1, The Hague* ☎ *0900/340–3505 regional specialists*

✉ *Coolsingel 195-197, Rotterdam* ☎ *010/271–0120 regional specialists*).

Belgian National Tourist Office Belgian Office of Tourism (✉ *Rue Marché aux Herbes 61–63, Brussels* ☎ *02/504–0390*). **In the U.S.** (✉ *220 E. 42nd St., Suite 3402, New York, NY* ☎ *212/758–8130*).

ONLINE TRAVEL TOOLS

Amsterdam and the Netherlands For a guide to what's happening in Holland, the official site for the Netherlands Board of Tourism is ⊕ *us.holland.com*. The official Amsterdam site is ⊕ *www.iamsterdam. com*. More information is found at ⊕ *www. visitamsterdam.nl*. Other general sites are ⊕ *www.amsterdamhotspots.nl and* ⊕ *www. amsterdam.info*. ⊕ *www.channels.nl* is a Web site that guides you through the city with the help of many colorful photographs. The American Society of Travel Agents is at ⊕ *www.asta. org*. For rail information and schedules, go to ⊕ *www.ns.nl*. For airport information, go to ⊕ *www.schiphol.nl*. For flight information and reservations on KLM/Northwest, the national carrier, go to ⊕ *www.klm.com*; check out the low tariffs to other European destinations on ⊕ *www.easyjet.com*, ⊕ *www.ryanair.com*, and, for budget travelers, ⊕ *www.airfair.nl*.

INDEX

PHOTO CREDITS

1, Amanda Hall / age fotostock. 2, Keith Erskine / Alamy. Chapter 1: Experience Amsterdam and the Netherlands: 8-9, JacobH/istockphoto. 10 (top), aniad/shutterstock. 10 (bottom), Lucas Hirschegger/wikipedia.org. 11 (left), diego cervo/iStockphoto. 11 (right), Kevin Gessner/Flickr. 12, Bjorn Svensson / age fotostock. 13, Will Salter / age fotostock. 14, PjotrP/Flickr. 15 (left), Amsterdam Tourism & Convention Board. 15 (right),jhorrocks/istockphoto. 16 (top left), Meg Zimbeck/Flickr. 16 (bottom left), suvodeb/Suvodeb Banerjee. 16 (right), Andresr/shutterstock. 17 (top left), William Allum/shutterstock. 17 (bottom left), ROOS ALDERSHOFF FOTOGRAFIE/State Hermitage Museum St Petersburg. 17 (right), Amsterdam Tourism & Convention Board. 18 (left), Jarno Gonzalez Zarraonandia/shutterstock. 18 (top center), Rob Bouwman/shutterstock. 18 (top right), Rex Roof/Flickr. 18 (bottom right), jan kranendonk/shutterstock. 19 (left), Peng Chau/Flickr. 19 (top center), jan kranendonk/shutterstock. 19 (bottom center), Christopher Walker/shutterstock. 19 (right), David Ewing / age fotostock. 22, Henkje/shutterstock. 23 and 24, jan kranendonk/shutterstock. 25 (left), Nikonaft/shutterstock. 25 (right), Xtuv Photography. 26, Amsterdam Tourism & Convention Board. 27 (left), lillisphotography/iStockphoto. 27 (right), jan kranendonk/shutterstock. Chapter 2: Exploring Amsterdam: 29, Michael Zegers / age fotostock. 30, lillisphotography/iStockphoto. 31 (top), Ricardo De Mattos/iStockphoto. 31 (bottom), Yvwv/wikipedia.org. 32, April Gertler. 35, Martin Moos / age fotostock. 36, mattmangum/wikipedia.org. 40, Bob Turner / age fotostock. 45, PATRICK FORGET / age fotostock. 48, Ingolf Pompe / age fotostock. 55, Jochen Tack / age fotostock. 56, McPHOTO / age fotostock. 59, Postman81/wikipedia.org. 62, Richard Wareham / age fotostock. 65, Eric Gevaert/shutterstock. 66, Atlantide S.N.C. / age fotostock. 68, Sergio Pitamitz / age fotostock. 69, Dina Litovsky. 74, Ingolf Pompe / age fotostock. 76 and 77, Alexei Profokiev. 78, Javier Larrea / age fotostock. 81, April Gertler. 82-83, Ingolf Pompe / age fotostock. 86, Will Salter / age fotostock. 88, Amsterdam Tourism & Convention Board. 90, RABOUAN Jean-Baptiste / age fotostock. 93, Atlantide S.N.C./age fotostock. 95, Kevin Gessner/Flickr. 96, Ingolf Pompe / age fotostock. 99, Kevin Gessner/Flickr. 102, ROOS ALDERSHOFF FOTOGRAFIE/State Hermitage Museum St Petersburg. 104, PATRICK FORGET / age fotostock. Chapter 3: Where to Eat: 105, Javier Larrea / age fotostock. 106, Suzette Pauwels/Flickr. 109, Sabine Lubenow / age fotostock. 117, boo_licious/Flickr. 120, Willem+Marijke Defijn+Vernimmen. 123, serge ligtenberg. 127, Café-restaurant OPEN. 133, Restaurant D'Theeboom. 139, MAISANT Ludovic / age fotostock. 143, Hotel Okura Amsterdam. Chapter 4: Where to Stay: 145, Merten Snijders / age fotostock. 146, rob ter bekke | fotografie. 149, Will Salter / age fotostock. 157 (top), Mövenpick Hotels & Resorts. 157 (bottom), bestbib&tucker/Flickr. 167 (top), Hotel V. 167 (bottom), rob ter bekke | fotografie. 173 (top and bottom), Sandton Hotel de Filosoof en Malie Hotel. 179 (top and bottom), citizenM Hotels. 182 (top and bottom), Allard van der Hoek. Chapter 5: Nightlife and the Arts. 185, Ingolf Pompe / age fotostock. 187, John Shapiro/Khmer Arts Academy. 188, Amsterdam Tourism & Convention Board. 193, Alper Çuğun/Flickr. 196, Hotel Okura Amsterdam. 201, Ingolf Pompe / age fotostock. 206, Jeroen van der Goorbergh/Flickr. 211, sergio pitamitz / age fotostock. 214, Ton Koene / age fotostock. Chapter 6: Shopping: 217, Caroline Penn / age fotostock. 220, Ingolf Pompe / age fotostock. 221 (top), alljan moehamad. 221 (bottom), THOMAS ZUM VORDE SIVE VORDING. 222, Spiegelkwartier. 225, Ingolf Pompe / age fotostock. 228, Anouk Beerents. 233, FORGET Patrick/SAGAPHOTO.COM / Alamy. 238, Sergio Pitamitz / Alamy. 241, Meg Zimbeck/Flickr. 246, Jordanhill School D&T Dept/Flickr. 247 (top), Lourens Smak / Alamy. 247 (bottom), Hans van der Mars. 251, Michael Zegers / age fotostock. Chapter 7: Day Trips from Amsterdam: 253, Rene van der Meer / age fotostock. 254, Bas Lammers/

Flickr. 256-57, Chris Warren / age fotostock. 259, Ton Koene / age fotostock. 262, Jeremy Burgin/ Flickr. 267, FAN / age fotostock. 270-71, Jose Fuste Raga / age fotostock. 273, Chris Mellor / age fotostock. Chapter 8: The Randstad: 275, Atlantide S.N.C. / age fotostock. 276, Gastev/Mirko Tobias Schaefer/Flickr. 277 (top), Styve Reineck/Shutterstock. 277 (bottom), Worldpics/Shutterstock. 278, lynnlin/ Shutterstock. 281, wikipedia.org. 282, CMB / age fotostock. 286, Joost J. Bakker IJmuiden/Flickr. 288-89, Public Domain. 291, P. Narayan / age fotostock. 292, Ian Murray / age fotostock. 294, Rob Hogeslag/Flickr. 298, Javier Larrea / age fotostock. 301, Pixel Addict/Toni/Flickr. 304, Javier Larrea / age fotostock. 310, Jochen Tack / age fotostock. 313, W. de Jonge/wikipedia.org. 317, Michele Falzone / age fotostock. 320, Wilmar / age fotostock. 323, Mark Sunderland / age fotostock. 326, MAISANT Ludovic / age fotostock. 329, Ingolf Pompe / age fotostock. 335, Michael Zegers / age fotostock. 342, Javier Larrea / age fotostock. 347, Ljupco Smokovski/Shutterstock. 350, Worldpics/Shutterstock. 354, MAISANT Ludovic / age fotostock. 357, Carol Ann Wiley / age fotostock. 358, MAISANT Ludovic / age fotostock. 361, Jochem Wijnands / age fotostock. Chapter 9: Side Trips to Belgium: 363, San Rostro / age fotostock. 364, Rich B-S/Richard Barrett-Small/ Flickr. 365 (top), wikipedia.org. 365 (bottom), jennyt/Shutterstock. 366, Christopher Walker/Shutterstock. 369, 50u15pec7a70r/Shutterstock. 374, Ana del Castillo/Shutterstock. 377, Tupungato/Shutterstock. 380 and 387, DEGAS Jean-Pierre / age fotostock. 394, Enrique Pons / age fotostock. 396, bluecrayola/Shutterstock. 398, Javier Larrea / age fotostock. 403, ARCO / J Moreno / age fotostock. 408, Rufenach / age fotostock. 410, Wolfgang Staudt/Flickr. 412, OSOMEDIA / age fotostock. 415, Javier Larrea / age fotostock. 419, PICTURE CONTACT BV / age fotostock. 422, Fújur/Ricardo Samaniego/Flickr.

NOTES

ABOUT OUR WRITERS

Niels Carels is an Amsterdam-based novelist, scenarist, journalist, magazine editor, film critic, wine columnist, restaurant reviewer, and copywriter. In other words, he writes for a living. During his rare moments of free time he enjoys collecting sneakers and books. In the not-so-distant future he's keen to take over the World. This year Niels updated the Nightlife and the Arts chapter.

When Karina Hof left her native New Amsterdam in 2003, she thought it would be just for a year. Two master's degrees, two half-marathons, and too many boxes of hagelslag later, she's still covering the Lowlands. Her "Saturday shopping with . . " column in *Time Out Amsterdam* has let her trail Dutch celebrities on their spending sprees. This year Karina updated the Experience chapter and helped out with the Shopping.

After years of travel subsidized by carpentry and B-movie acting, writer Steve Korver came to Amsterdam in 1992. He has worked as a columnist, copywriter, editor, and contributor to publications like *The New York Times, Guardian, Time Out, McSweeney's Quarterly, Condé Nast Traveler*, and *The Globe & Mail*, as well as acting as editor-in-chief of the cultural paper *Amsterdam Weekly*. Steve updated the Where to Eat chapter.

Steven McCarron left his native Glasgow eight years ago, first settling in Rotterdam, before eventually devoting all his time to Amsterdam. As a freelance writer and editor, he knows the Amsterdam cultural scene inside and out, spending five years at the newspaper *Amsterdam Weekly*, contributing to city Web site I amsterdam, and eventually becoming music editor at *Time Out Amsterdam*. He now fronts a free publication in the city called *Unfold Amsterdam*, which is designed to inspire readers to get out and enjoy all the city has to offer. For this edition, Steven tried out beds around town to update the Where to Stay chapter.

Ann Maher first encountered herring while working as an editor for a Dutch media group in London. Eight years ago she returned to Amsterdam permanently with her opera-singer husband and son, and works as a writer, researcher, and editor on guidebooks, magazines, and cultural portals. For this edition, she updated the Exploring and Day Trips chapters. When Ann is not researching (or eating herring), she cooks and plays backgammon.

After 18 years in the Netherlands, and thoroughly addicted to uitsmijters and pannekoeken (pancakes), British-born Tim Skelton now considers himself a true Eindhovenaar. When not repairing his rusty Dutch bicycle, he writes magazine features on a range of subjects from travel to environmental issues, and is the author of *Around Amsterdam in 80 Beers*, the essential guide for any beer lover visiting the capital. He has also written a guidebook to Luxembourg for Bradt Travel Guides. For this edition he updated the Randstad and Side Trips to Belgium chapters.